NORTHLAND

AUCKLAND

Auckland

THE CENTRAL
NORTH ISLAND

WELLINGTON
AND
THE SOUTH

Wellington

WELLINGTON AND THE SOUTH
Pages 150–183

MARLBOROUGH AND NELSON
Pages 194–215

**CANTERBURY AND THE
WEST COAST**
Pages 216–251

OTAGO AND SOUTHLAND
Pages 252–289

0 kilometres   100

0 miles   100

EYEWITNESS *TRAVEL GUIDES*

NEW ZEALAND

D0167856

EYEWITNESS *TRAVEL GUIDES*

NEW ZEALAND

DORLING KINDERSLEY
LONDON • NEW YORK • DELHI • SYDNEY
PARIS • MUNICH • JOHANNESBURG
www.dk.com

A DORLING KINDERSLEY BOOK

www.dk.com

Produced by Editions Didier Millet, Kuala Lumpur

EDITORIAL DIRECTOR Timothy Auger
PROJECT MANAGER Noor Azlina Yunus
EDITORS Dianne Buerger, Zuraidah Omar
DESIGNERS Theivanai Nadaraju, Yong Yoke Lian

CONTRIBUTORS
Helen Corrigan, Roef Hopman, Gerard Hutching,
Rebecca Macfie, Geoff Mercer, Simon Noble, Peter Smith,
Michael Ward, Mark Wright

PHOTOGRAPHERS
Peter Bush, Gerald Lopez, Lloyd Park,
Ron Redfern

ILLUSTRATORS
Yeap Kok Chien, Tan Hong Yew, Denis Chai Kah Yune

MAPS
ERA-Maptec Ltd, Dublin, Ireland

Reproduced by Colourscan, Singapore
Printed and bound in Italy by Graphicom

First published in Great Britain in 2001
by Dorling Kindersley Limited
9 Henrietta Street, London WC2E 8PS

A CIP CATALOGUE RECORD IS AVAILABLE FROM THE BRITISH LIBRARY.

ISBN 0 7513 0889 7

**The information in every
Eyewitness Travel Guide is checked annually.**
Every effort has been made to ensure that this book is as up-to-
date as possible at the time of going to press. Some details,
however, such as telephone numbers, opening hours, prices,
gallery hanging arrangements and travel information are liable to
change. The publishers cannot accept responsibility for any
consequences arising from the use of this book.
We value the views and suggestions of our readers very highly.
Please write to: Senior Publishing Manager, Eyewitness Travel
Guides, Dorling Kindersley, 9 Henrietta Street, London WC2E 8PS.

◁ **Sheep and cattle grazing, Mount Hutt**

CONTENTS

**Tamatekapua Maori meeting
house, Rotorua**

INTRODUCING
NEW ZEALAND

**Pohutukawa in bloom at
Oriental Bay, Wellington**

Punting on the Avon River, Christchurch

Club rugby match on the
North Island's East Cape

Whitebait and salad

Olveston House,
Dunedin

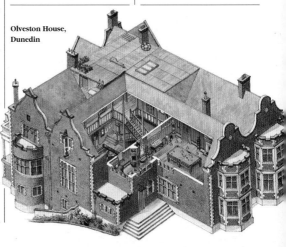

HOW TO USE THIS GUIDE

THIS GUIDE helps you to get the most from your visit to New Zealand. *Introducing New Zealand* maps the country and sets it in its historical and cultural context. The seven area chapters in *New Zealand Area by Area* describe the main sights, with photographs, illustrations and maps. Features cover topics relating specifically to the North and South islands as well as subjects of regional interest. Restaurant and hotel recommendations can be found in *Travellers' Needs*. The *Survival Guide* has practical tips on everything from making a telephone call to transport.

NEW ZEALAND AREA BY AREA

New Zealand has been divided into seven main sightseeing areas, coded with a coloured thumb tab for quick reference. A map illustrating how the two main islands have been divided can be found on the inside front cover of this guide. The sights listed within the individual areas are plotted and numbered on a *Pictorial Map*.

1 Introduction
The landscape, history and character of each region is described here, showing how the area has developed over the years and what it has to offer the visitor today.

A locator map shows the region in relation to the other areas of New Zealand.

Each area of New Zealand can be identified quickly by its colour coding.

2 Pictorial Map
This gives an illustrated overview of the whole area. All the sights covered in the chapter are numbered and there are useful tips on getting around by car and public transport.

3 Detailed Information
All the important towns and other places of interest are described individually. They are listed in order, following the numbering on the Pictorial *Map. Within each entry there is detailed information about the important buildings and other major sights.*

Features and story boxes highlight special or unique features of an area or sight.

4 Major Towns
*All the important towns are described individually.
Within each entry there is further detailed information
on interesting buildings and other sites. The* Town Map
shows the location of the main sights.

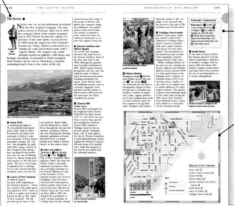

A Visitors' Checklist gives you the practical details to plan your visit, including transport information, the address of the tourist office and festivals.

The Town Map shows all major and minor roads. The key sights are plotted, along with train and bus stations, parking areas and tourist information offices.

5 Street-by-Street Map
*Towns or districts of
special interest to the visitor
are given a bird's-eye view in
detailed 3D with photographs
and descriptions of the most
important sights.*

A suggested route for a walk covers the most interesting streets in the area.

Dunedin Railway Station

Opening hours, the telephone number and transport details for the sight are given in the Visitors' Checklist.

6 The Top Sights
*These are given two or
more pages. Historic buildings
are dissected to reveal their
interiors; national parks
have maps showing facilities
and trails; museums have
colour-coded floorplans.
Photographs highlight the
most interesting features.*

Stars indicate sights that visitors should not miss.

INTRODUCING
NEW ZEALAND

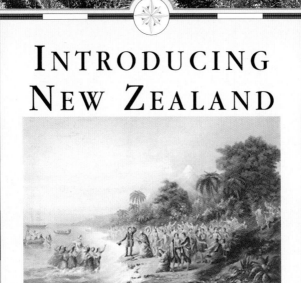

Putting New Zealand on The Map: The North Island

N EW ZEALAND LIES in the South Pacific Ocean, 1,600 km (990 miles) to the east of Australia, 10,000 km (6,210 miles) from San Francisco and a similar distance from Tokyo. Comprising two large islands and a number of smaller ones, its total land area is 270,530 sq km (104,420 sq miles), making it comparable in size to Japan or the British Isles. The main North and South islands are separated by Cook Strait, 20 km (12 miles) wide at its narrowest point. Two-thirds of the country's 3.8 million people live in the North Island, just over one million of those in Auckland, the country's largest city and the world's most populous Polynesian centre. New Zealand's capital is Wellington, at the southernmost tip of the North Island.

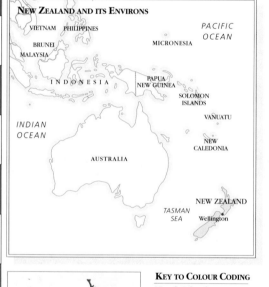

NEW ZEALAND AND ITS ENVIRONS

VIETNAM   PHILIPPINES

PACIFIC OCEAN

BRUNEI
MALAYSIA

MICRONESIA

I N D O N E S I A

PAPUA NEW GUINEA

SOLOMON ISLANDS

INDIAN OCEAN

VANUATU

NEW CALEDONIA

AUSTRALIA

TASMAN SEA

NEW ZEALAND

Wellington

KEY TO COLOUR CODING

North Island

- Northland
- Auckland
- Central North Island
- Wellington and the South

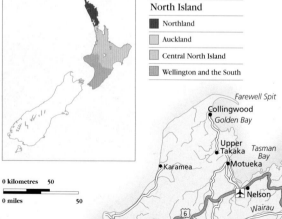

0 kilometres   50

0 miles   50

Cape Reinga

North Cape

Kaitaia

Kaikohe

Opononi

Dargaville

Tasman Sea

North Taranaki Bight

New Plymouth

Cape Egmont

Hawera

South Taranaki Bight

Wang

Farewell Spit

Collingwood

Golden Bay

Upper Takaka

Tasman Bay

Marlborough Sounds

Kapiti Island

Karamea

Motueka

Paraparaumu

Nelson

WELLINGTON

Lo
Hu

Wairau

Blenheim

Wa

Murchison

Awatere

Cape Pallise

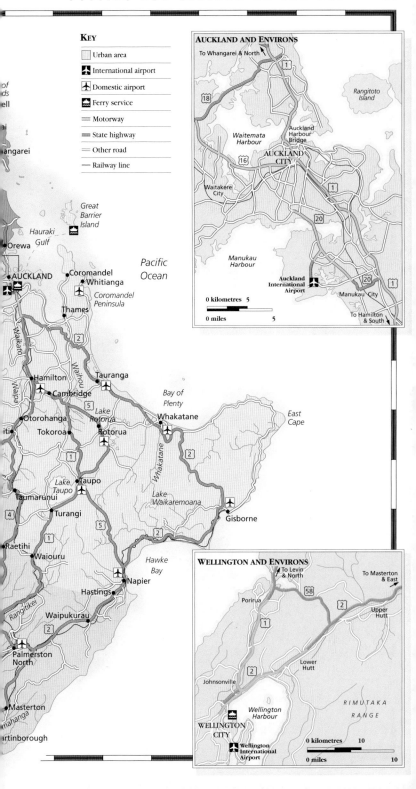

KEY

- Urban area
- ✈ International airport
- ✈ Domestic airport
- ⛴ Ferry service
- ═ Motorway
- ═ State highway
- ═ Other road
- — Railway line

AUCKLAND AND ENVIRONS

To Whangarei & North

1

18

Rangitoto Island

Waitemata Harbour

Auckland Harbour Bridge

16

AUCKLAND CITY

Waitakere City

20

1

Manukau Harbour

Auckland International Airport

Manukau City

20

1

0 kilometres 5

0 miles 5

To Hamilton & South

of ds ell

ai

angarei

Great Barrier Island

Hauraki Gulf

Orewa

Pacific Ocean

AUCKLAND

Coromandel

Whitianga

Coromandel Peninsula

Thames

Waikato

Waihou

Hamilton

Cambridge

5

Lake Rotorua

Tauranga

Bay of Plenty

Whakatane

East Cape

Maipa

iti

Otorohanga

Tokoroa

Rotorua

Whakatane

Lake Waikaremoana

1

Taumarunui

Lake Taupo

Taupo

2

Turangi

5

4

Raetihi

1

Waiouru

2

Gisborne

Hawke Bay

Rangitikei

Waipukurau

Napier

Hastings

2

Palmerston North

Masterton

mahanga

rtinborough

WELLINGTON AND ENVIRONS

To Levin & North

Porirua

58

2

To Masterton & East

Upper Hutt

1

Lower Hutt

2

Johnsonville

RIMUTAKA RANGE

Wellington Harbour

WELLINGTON CITY

Wellington International Airport

0 kilometres 10

0 miles 10

PUTTING NEW ZEALAND ON THE MAP: THE SOUTH ISLAND

THE SOUTH ISLAND, 150,440 sq km (58,070 sq miles) in area, is slightly larger than the North Island. The Southern Alps mountain chain runs almost the length of the island, with 223 named peaks higher than 2,300 m (7,550 ft). The eastern side of the alps is dry and largely non-forested, while the west coast has high rainfall and magnificent forests, lakes, mountains and glaciers. Christchurch, the largest city in the South Island, with 330,000 inhabitants, has good international travel links. To the south, Dunedin is an important university town. Stewart Island, south of Invercargill, is New Zealand's third largest island.

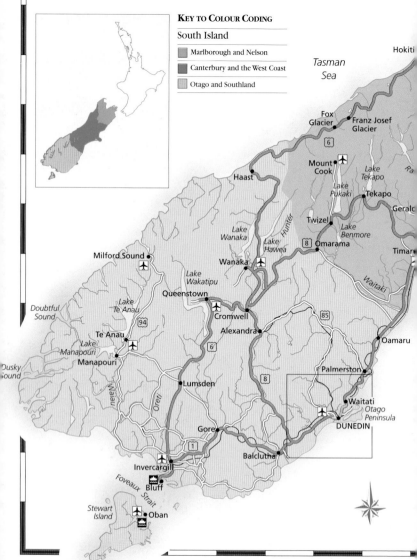

KEY TO COLOUR CODING

South Island

- Marlborough and Nelson
- Canterbury and the West Coast
- Otago and Southland

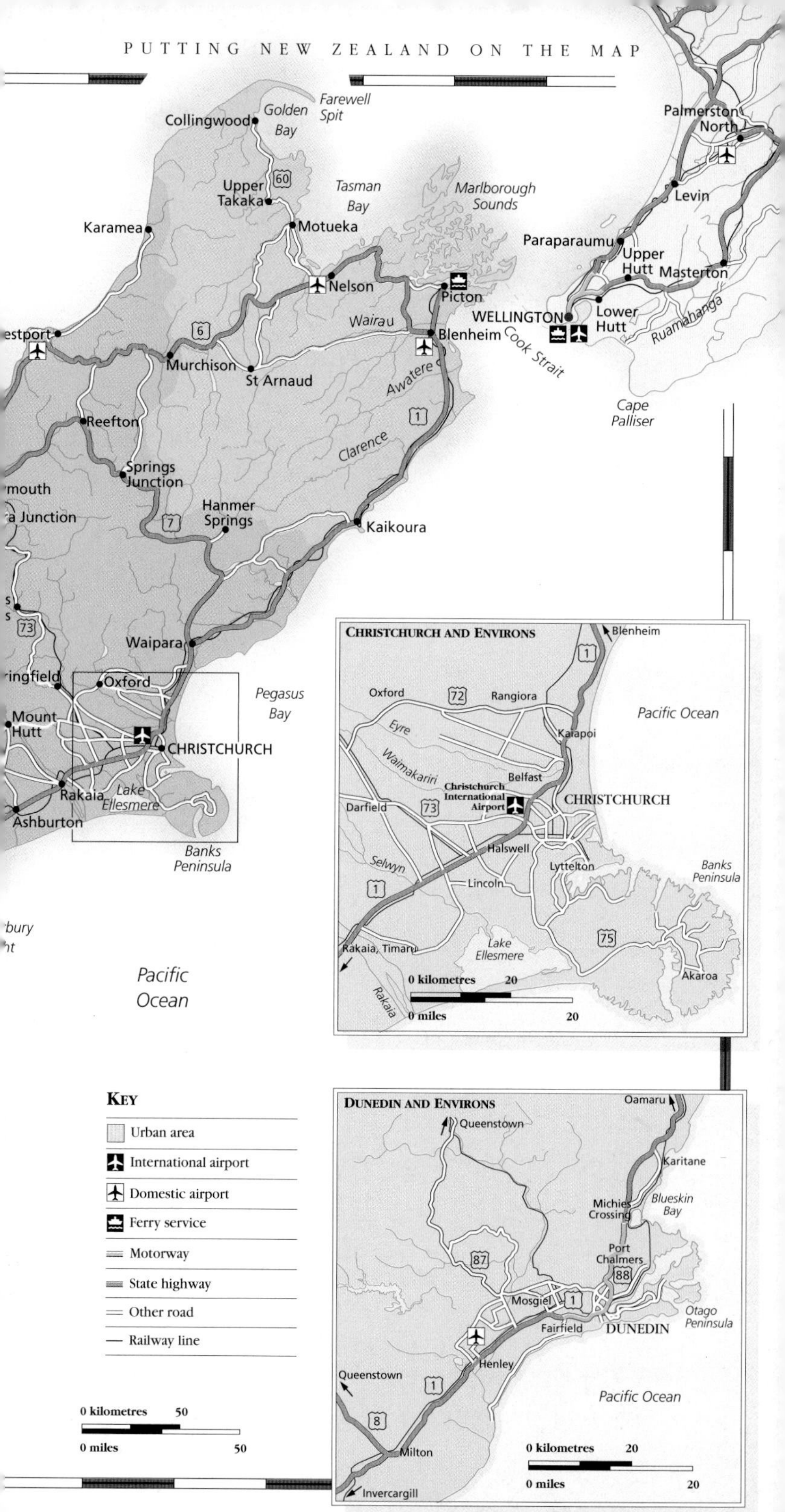

Collingwood
Golden Bay
Farewell Spit
Palmerston North
Upper Takaka
Tasman Bay
Marlborough Sounds
Levin
Karamea
Motueka
Paraparaumu
Upper Hutt
Masterton
Nelson
Picton
WELLINGTON
estport
Wairau
Blenheim
Lower Hutt
Murchison
St Arnaud
Cook Strait
Ruamahanga
Reefton
Awatere
Cape Palliser
Springs Junction
Clarence
mouth
Hanmer Springs
a Junction
Kaikoura
Waipara
73
ingfield
Oxford
Pegasus Bay
Mount Hutt
CHRISTCHURCH
Rakaia
Lake Ellesmere
Ashburton
Banks Peninsula
bury
ht

Pacific Ocean

CHRISTCHURCH AND ENVIRONS

Blenheim
1
Oxford
72
Rangiora
Pacific Ocean
Eyre
Kaiapoi
Waimakariri
Belfast
Christchurch International Airport
CHRISTCHURCH
Darfield
73
Halswell
Lyttelton
Banks Peninsula
Lincoln
1
Rakaia, Timaru
Lake Ellesmere
75
Rakaia
Akaroa

0 kilometres 20
0 miles 20

KEY

| Urban area |
| International airport |
| Domestic airport |
| Ferry service |
| Motorway |
| State highway |
| Other road |
| Railway line |

DUNEDIN AND ENVIRONS

Oamaru
Queenstown
Karitane
Blueskin Bay
Michies Crossing
87
Port Chalmers
88
Mosgiel
1
Fairfield
DUNEDIN
Otago Peninsula
Henley
Queenstown
1
8
Pacific Ocean
Milton
Invercargill

0 kilometres 50
0 miles 50

0 kilometres 20
0 miles 20

A PORTRAIT OF
NEW ZEALAND

·····················

N EW ZEALAND IS *one of the most isolated countries in the world. The Maoris, the first arrivals, called it Aotearoa, "the land of the long white cloud", the first indication to these canoe voyagers of the presence of the islands being the cloud lying above them. New Zealand's island location much affects its climate, its history and its contemporary character.*

Spanning latitudes 34 degrees and 47 degrees South, the islands of New Zealand are in the path of "the roaring forties", the winds that circle this lower part of the globe, and are separated from the nearest landmass, Australia, by 1,600 km (990 miles) of the Tasman Sea. On the International Date Line, opposite the Greenwich Meridian of zero degree, New Zealand claims to be the first country to see the sun rise.

The climate ranges from temperate to subtropical. The maritime setting creates regular rainfall and abundant vegetation. There is extensive bird and fish life but other than two bat species, the only land mammals are those introduced by early Maoris and Europeans. Comparatively a recent settlement, with a population under four million, New Zealand retains a clean, natural and untouched environment.

The snow-covered Southern Alps and glacial-formed lakes and fiords provide spectacular scenery, and there is extensive volcanic and thermal activity on the North Island central plateau. The country's coastline provides both sheltered bays and

Kiwi, a New Zealand icon

The silver fern, one of New Zealand's symbols

◁ **Aerial view of the snow-capped Southern Alps**

The coastline as seen from Tunnel Beach, south of Dunedin

harbours and superb beaches. New Zealand's tourism industry focuses largely upon this natural environment, the urban aspect being much less significant in comparison.

SETTLEMENT

Captain James Cook's circum-navigation and charting of the main islands in 1769 paved the way for the sealing and whaling industry. The unruly conditions, the concerns of missionaries over friction with the Maoris and the threat of

Captain James Cook

annexation by the French prompted the British, in 1840, to declare New Zealand a colony. At Waitangi in the Bay of Islands, a treaty was signed between the British Crown, represented by a Royal Navy party, and a number of Maori chiefs. Although the Treaty of Waitangi provided for protection of the Maoris and their natural resources, alienation of Maori land occurred well into the 20th century. Maori leaders pressed for justice and organized land marches. In 1975, the treaty was reconsidered, the Treaty of Waitangi Act passed by parliament and the Waitangi Tribunal set up to consider Maori land claims.

Planned settlement after the 1840s was mainly by English and Scottish enterprises, and today the character of cities such as Christchurch and Dunedin still reflects those origins. Auckland, the commercial centre, was and remains more cosmopolitan in make-up. Wellington's early establishment as the nation's capital contributes to its political character.

Early settlers had turned to the land, felling extensive forests both for a timber trade and for farmlands. The

Maori leader Dame Whina Cooper setting out for a land march in October 1975

independent spirit of New Zealanders can be said to derive from working-class settlers, determined to escape an oppressive English class structure. The taming of the land promoted pride in physical prowess, whether in extraordinary representation in two World Wars or in rugby, the national sport.

SOCIETY

Although an independent and democratic state, New Zealand is still a dominion of Great Britain. New Zealand's parliament, based on the Statutes of Westminster, pays allegiance to the British sovereign through its governor-general. Proposals that New Zealand become a republic have significant support in the country.

New Zealanders take pride in their history of social reform. The first in the world to give women the vote in 1893, New Zealand had established compulsory, free schooling by 1877, and by 1938 a free health system, universal superannuation and a liberal social welfare structure. The country declared its non-nuclear stance in 1986, which resulted in non-alignment of its armed forces with those of the USA and Britain.

Although the Waitangi Tribunal has enabled substantial compensation for Maoris whose land was wrongfully

The Beehive, part of the Parliament Buildings in Wellington, which houses the Ministers' offices

taken, the issues involved continue to inflame Maori–European relations. Encouragement of the immigration of Pacific Islanders by the governments of the 1960s seeking to obtain a labour force has further complicated the race issue, and today an influx of Asian immigrants has created some tensions.

Nevertheless, visitors comment on the friendliness and welcoming attitudes of New Zealanders, which may stem from a small population living, by world standards, in good quality

Arts Centre weekend market in Christchurch

The New Zealand All Blacks before playing South Africa in Dunedin in 1999

housing, in small cities that are not yet suffering from congestion or widespread crime, and with easy access to a superb natural environment. There is also a curiosity about the outside world and New Zealanders travel abroad extensively, gaining what is popularly known as "the great OE" or the overseas experience.

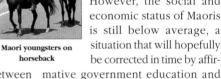

Maori youngsters on horseback

Although there is today evidence of a widening gap between rich and poor, New Zealand remains, on the whole, an egalitarian society. There are some social distinctions based upon wealth, occupation and race, but there is no class system in New Zealand based on birth and inheritance. Enterprise and energy can secure good employment and quality

of life. Almost 85 per cent of the population is urban, with 75 per cent resident in the North Island. After near decimation, the Maori population is steadily increasing and now makes up 16 per cent of the country's total. However, the social and economic status of Maoris is still below average, a situation that will hopefully be corrected in time by affirmative government education and employment policies.

WORK AND THE ECONOMY

Although agriculture is the major industry, with meat, dairy and timber products predominating, a need to compete in the world markets has required diversification. A pioneer in agricultural research, New Zealand is a leader in animal and crop technology. Its wines, particularly whites, are now internationally recognized and its quality foodstuffs are exported to markets in Asia, Europe and America. An important industry is tourism. Facilities, accommodation, restaurants and cafés now cater for all tastes.

Sheep droving on a state highway

Being a small nation that has to transport its exports long distances to foreign markets, New Zealand is vulnerable to the international economy. It does not possess substantial mineral resources, although it has been able to utilize its own natural gas and oil. It also has no large manufacturing industry. However, signs of an export market in information technology, electronics and shipbuilding are encouraging.

Outdoor dining at Mapua, Nelson

The recession in the 1980s prompted a move from welfare state to "user pays" policies, with privatization of state-owned enterprises. The major political parties are Labour (centre left) and National (centre right), with minor parties influencing the balance of power in coalitions that are formed.

Teacher and students studying in a park

SPORT AND CULTURE

New Zealand is a sporting paradise. The successful defence of the America's Cup in 2000 attracted one of the world's largest gatherings of mega-yachts. Horse racing is widespread and popular and New Zealand bloodstock is sought after worldwide. A diverse range of international entertainers, musicians, artists and dance companies make frequent visits to the country. Festivals of Pacific Island and Maori culture coincide with a resurgence of Maori art and artists. New Zealanders can claim some notable firsts. Lord Rutherford from Brightwater was the first to split the atom and Sir Edmund Hillary, with Sherpa Tenzing, was the first to reach the summit of Mount Everest. Others of international reputation are author Katherine Mansfield, international opera diva Dame Kiri Te Kanawa and space scientist Sir William Pickering.

New Zealand is today a vibrant, hospitable, multicultural nation that has forged a unique identity derived from its Maori heritage.

Street buskers providing entertainment in Auckland

New Zealand's Landscape

NEW ZEALAND is an old land with a young
landscape: some of the rocks that underlie
the country are, at 600 million years old, relatively
ancient. However, the landforms that have been
created from them are very young. The Southern
Alps, for example, began to emerge only three million
years ago and volcanic explosions and earthquakes
continue to create new forms. The overriding feature
of the landscape is its diversity: mountains, lakes,
rivers, beaches, hills, plains, volcanoes, rainforests
and fiords are all contained in a relatively small area.

Mount Ruapehu, *like other
New Zealand cone volcanoes,
erupts frequently. It sits astride
one of the world's major
volcanic centres* (see pp62–3).

The foothills of the Southern Alps, the Great
Divide between the west and east coasts, shelter
the Canterbury Plains from prevailing winds.

New Zealand's coastline *is 18,200
km (11,300 miles) long. About 80 per
cent is exposed to open sea while 20 per
cent borders sheltered waters. The coasts
harbour marine life and are popular
playgrounds for water sports.*

TECTONIC PLATE FORMATION

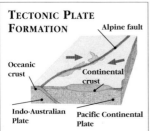

Alpine fault

Oceanic crust

Continental crust

Indo-Australian Plate

Pacific Continental Plate

For the last 20 –25 million years,
New Zealand has been lying
astride two of the world's 15
moving "plates". In the North
Island, the Pacific Continental
Plate pushes under the Indo-
Australian Plate, forming
volcanoes in between. In the
South Island, the Indo-Australian
Plate pushes under the Pacific
one, forming an alpine fault line.

SOUTH CANTERBURY AND SOUTHERN ALPS

Large-scale farming has transformed previously
forested plains into a landscape of grasslands
bisected by rivers and dotted with livestock. The
distant Southern Alps bear testimony to the powerful
geological forces which have been shaping the
country for the last 600 million years.

Tussock grasslands *cover about 10 per cent
of New Zealand's land area. Much of this area
was covered in forest or scrubland before the
early Maoris burned it while hunting for moa.*

The Bay of Islands comprises 144 offshore islands, all within 50 km (30 miles) of the coast. During glacial periods, when sea levels were lower, the islands were connected to the mainland.

Braided rivers *(see p189)* transport rock and shingle from the Southern Alps to create fertile farmlands.

Sheep, farmed for both wool and meat, thrive on South Canterbury's hill country and rolling downs.

The fiords of southwest New Zealand, carved out over millions of years by successive Ice Ages – the last 10,000 years ago – are among the most spectacular in the world (see pp278–9). The coastline of the fiords extends 1,000 km (620 miles). Doubtful Sound, at 420 m (1,380 ft) is the deepest of the fiords, while Dusky Sound, which stretches 40 km (25 miles) inland, is the longest.

THE GONDWANALAND CONNECTION

Until about 80 million years ago, New Zealand formed part of the great super continent, Gondwanaland, which comprised present-day Antarctica, Australia, India, Africa and South America. Once New Zealand floated off into isolation, many of its plants and animals evolved into forms which were never seen on other landmasses.

180 million years ago, New Zealand occupied a corner of Gondwanaland, one of the world's two massive continents; the other is called Laurasia.

135 million years ago, Gondwanaland began to split apart into the present-day continents. At this time, New Zealand was still attached to Australia.

Today, the Tasman Sea separates New Zealand and Australia, and the continents continue to drift apart. New Zealand is moving northwards towards the equator at the rate of about 30 mm (1.2 inches) a year.

Flora and Fauna

Blue penguin

New Zealand has been a land apart for 80 million years, with the result that it is home to a collection of plants and animals found nowhere else in the world. It has only two land mammals (both bats), although seals, whales and dolphins abound around the coasts. Flightless birds, a diversity of lizards, giant snails, primitive frogs and plants that are as old as the dinosaurs combine to make New Zealand unique. Despite the impact of humans on flora and fauna over the last 1,000 years, much remains to fascinate the visitor.

The tuatara is the sole remaining species of an order of reptiles which evolved about 220 million years ago. The best place to see a tuatara is at the tuatarium in Invercargill (see p284).

KAURI FORESTS
Northland's forests are dominated by massive, straight-trunked kauri trees interspersed with a mix of plants. So valuable was the timber for boat building, housing and carving that the forests have been severely reduced since the 1790s.

Kiwis are largely concentrated in the warm Northland forests where they use their long beaks to dig for food.

Giant wetas, flightless "crickets" as large as a person's hand, are harmless inhabitants of kauri forests.

The silver fern or ponga, widely adopted as a national symbol, takes its name from the silvery underside of the fronds.

SHRUBLANDS
Shrublands consist of short, scrubby plants. They are home to many species of animals and are nurseries for mature forest. Widespread throughout the country, shrublands are often areas that were once logged and are now regenerating.

The green gecko lives on the outer branches of shrubs and is a daytime hunter. It bears live young in contrast to other species which lay eggs.

Kowhai, sometimes described as New Zealand's national flower, has striking drooping yellow blooms in spring.

Manuka is a key pollen and nectar plant for bees.

BIRDS OF NEW ZEALAND

New Zealand is famed for its unusual birds. Evolving without significant predators, such as rats, cats or dogs, to menace them, they lost any reason to fly. Some not only became flightless, but also developed into some of the largest birds ever to have lived. When the Maoris arrived, they discovered the huge moa, which stood more than 2 m (7 ft) tall. As a result of being hunted, the moa became extinct several hundred years ago. Today, a few of New Zealand's ancient bird species remain, among them the kiwi, kakapo, takahe, black robin and kea, and enormous efforts are being made to ensure their survival.

The kakapo is a large, flightless, nocturnal parrot.

Kokakos are poor fliers but are noted for their singing abilities.

ALPINE LANDSCAPE
New Zealand's alpine region begins at about 1,300 m (4,270 ft) above sea level in the North Island but drops to 900 m (2,950 ft) in the South Island. Intense cold, heat, dryness and wind combine to produce tussock and shrubs adapted to cope with the climate.

AROUND THE COAST
Rocky shores, sandy beaches and muddy estuaries provide a diversity of habitats for coastal flora and fauna. Many native plants thrive in the salty environment, thanks to adaptations such as tough leaves which retain moisture in dry conditons.

Keas are South Island mountain parrots. They have a reputation for playfulness and intelligence.

The royal albatross breeds at Taiaroa Head on the Otago Peninsula (see p264) upon returning from its winter feeding grounds.

The vegetable sheep plant is a mass of thousands of small, separate plants which together resemble the wool of a sheep.

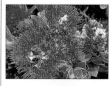
The pohutukawa's crimson flowers along the coasts of the North Island herald the arrival of Christmas.

Alpine plants climb above the competition to be noticed by pollinating alpine insects.

New Zealand fur seals are commonly seen lolling on rocks around the coasts.

New Zealand's National Parks and Reserves

Jewelled geckos

FROM THE SNOW-CAPPED volcanoes of Tongariro National Park to the sheer cliffs of Fiordland, New Zealand's national parks contain an awe-inspiring range of scenery, beautiful walking tracks, and numerous plants and animals found nowhere else in the world. The 13 national parks cover 29,000 sq km (11,200 sq miles) or about 8 per cent of the country's land surface. There are also 20 conservation parks, 3,500 reserves and 14 marine reserves in New Zealand. The Department of Conservation, which administers all these areas, safeguards a total of 30 per cent of New Zealand's land area.

Abel Tasman National Park's *golden sand beaches fringe bush-clad cliffs. Inland, deep caves and underground rivers are a feature of the limestone landscape (see pp212–13).*

Mount Cook National Park *contains the highest mountain in Australasia, Mount Cook, known as Aoraki or "cloud piercer" by the Ngai Tahu tribe, as well as New Zealand's longest glacier (see pp250–51).*

Paparoa National Park's *limestone landscape gives this area its special flavour. Along the coast, constant pounding by the Tasman Sea has sculpted the limestone into the Pancake Rocks and blowholes (see p234).*

Fiordland National Park *is a vast, remote wilderness, with snow-capped mountains, fiords, glacial valleys and lakes, waterfalls, islands and dense temperate forest (see pp278–9).*

0 kilometres   100

0 miles   100

Abel Tasm
National P.

Kahurang
National Pa

NEL

Nelson Lak
National P

Paparoa
National
Park

Westland
National Park

Arthur's Pass
National Park

CHRISTCHUR

Banks
Peninsula

Mount Aspiring
National Park

Mount Cook
National Park

QUEENSTOWN

Fiordland
National Park

Otago
Peninsula

INVERCARGILL   DUNEDIN

Foveaux Strait

Stewart Island

KEY

	National parks
	Conservation parks
	Reserves
	Marine reserves

Waipoua Forest in Northland *has the finest examples of kauri trees in the country (see p109). Kauris are among the world's largest trees. The warmer climate in this region encourages their growth.*

The Miranda Shorebird Centre, *on the west coast of the Firth of Thames, is a magnet for thousands of migratory wading birds from both home and abroad, attracted to its broad intertidal flats (see p120).*

The Crater Lake of Mount Ruapehu *in Tongariro National Park, a geological witch's cauldron, explodes periodically before settling into a semi-dormant state (see pp62–3,140–41).*

Mount Taranaki/Egmont, *the volcanic centrepiece of Egmont National Park, forms a dramatic backdrop to the nearby city of New Plymouth. It has been dormant since it last erupted in 1755 (see pp180–81).*

Architecture in New Zealand

EARTHQUAKE RISK IN New Zealand has limited the height and structure of buildings, giving towns and cities a somewhat uniform appearance, while abundant space has led to urban sprawl. Interspersed with the country's ubiquitous wooden houses are gracious historic homes and buildings, well-preserved Maori meeting houses and impressive public and commercial buildings. The latter range from early European-style structures built in stone to modern glass and concrete towers. Contemporary architecture is an eclectic mix of "New Zealand" and imported styles.

Glass and concrete towers in Auckland

Maori Meeting Houses

Communal meeting houses and storehouses have single gable roofs supported on posts sunk in the ground, and are elaborately carved. The porch bargeboards symbolize the arms of the ancestors, the ridgepole the tribal backbone, and the rafters the ribs of family lineage. Many older houses have been restored and new ones built of modern materials *(see p129)*.

The figures on wall and roof posts represent ancestors and chieftains

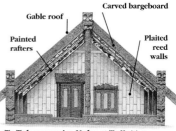

Carved bargeboard

Gable roof

Painted rafters

Plaited reed walls

Te Tokanganui-a-Nobo at Te Kuiti, a well-preserved meeting house built in 1872.

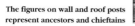

Homesteads

From the mid-1900s, wealthy sheep or cattle farmers and rich merchants demonstrated their affluence with substantial, architect-designed mansions to which they added rooms as they prospered. Stylistically varied, most mansions reflect a Victorian flavour, and some are romantically nostalgic and grandiose. The interiors are usually richly panelled, with elaborately carved stair rails, balusters, moulded ceilings and cornices *(see p263)*.

High central turret

Ornate corner turret

Wooden fretwork

Kauri timber walls

Alberton, a two-storey residence built for farmer Allen Kerr in 1862, and later extended, now lies within Auckland city.

Public Buildings

Otago University (1878) in Dunedin, built in Gothic style after Scotland's Glasgow University (1870).

By the 1860s, the construction of public buildings reinforced links with "home", reflecting, for example, the Gothic Revival style in Britain. Sometimes timber was substituted for the customary stone. The emphasis is on verticality and repeated ornamentation.

Clock tower

Local grey stonework

Lighter stone facings

Arched windows

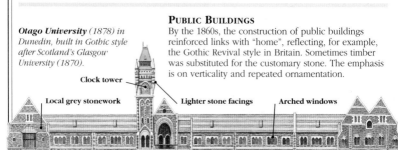

BAY VILLAS

By the 1900s, bay-fronted villas were the standard domestic house, with often a street at a time being built to a stock design. Usually constructed of timber weatherboard with corrugated iron or clay tile roofs, they ranged from single bay villas decorated with crude sawn fretwork to more sophisticated and elaborate multistorey homes for the affluent (see p159).

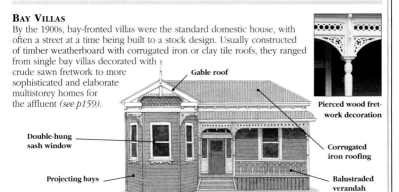

Gable roof

Pierced wood fret-
work decoration

Double-hung
sash window

Corrugated
iron roofing

Projecting bays

Balustraded
verandah

COMMERCIAL BUILDINGS

As New Zealand prospered in the early 1900s, more permanent commercial buildings replaced temporary shops and warehouses. A wide range of styles, including Classical Renaissance and Edwardian Baroque, demonstrated the substance and affluence of successful commercial enterprise. Although façades are often splendid, with Roman columns, the structure behind uses more modern techniques of steel framing and reinforced concrete. As such techniques allowed varied exterior treatment, there is little consistency of style in city buildings.

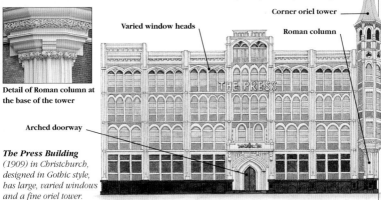

Corner oriel tower

Varied window heads

Roman column

Detail of Roman column at
the base of the tower

Arched doorway

The Press Building
(1909) in Christchurch,
designed in Gothic style,
has large, varied windows
and a fine oriel tower.

CONTEMPORARY NEW ZEALAND ARCHITECTURE

Although contemporary New Zealand architecture reflects international stylistic diversity, many architects are endeavouring to respond to the natural environment and to utilize ingredients from both Maori and European heritages.

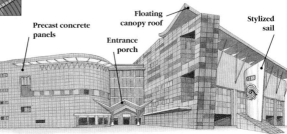

Abstract art design on
the exterior glazing

The Museum of
New Zealand Te
Papa Tongarewa,
opened in 1998,
incorporates
elements of the gable
forms of Maori
meeting houses.

Precast concrete
panels

Floating
canopy roof

Entrance
porch

Stylized
sail

Maori Culture and Art

Greenstone pendant

MAORIS HAVE DEVELOPED a complex culture derived from their Pacific Island inheritance. Climatic and seasonal conditions that differed from their former home, and a more extensive land area, permitted independent tribal development and variations in language, customs and art forms. Forests enabled them to build large canoes for transport and warfare, as well as meeting houses. Maoris excel in wood, bone and stone carving, and in plaiting and weaving. Oratory, chant, song and dance are the means of passing on ancestral knowledge, and form an essential dimension of the rituals of challenge, welcome and farewell.

Moko *(tattoo) involves incising lines into the skin and colouring them with pigment. The tradition survives and today, a number of young Maoris proudly wear* moko.

CARVING

The plentiful supply of large, straight-grained and durable timbers, and a variety of hard stones and obsidian that could be shaped into tools, enabled the early Maoris to continue the Pacific tradition of carving. Today, an increasing awareness of Maori heritage has brought about a rebirth of traditional crafts. At the New Zealand Maori Arts and Crafts Institute in Rotorua, students learn to carve wood, bone and greenstone into exquisite and intricate pendants, combs and ceremonial objects *(see p136).*

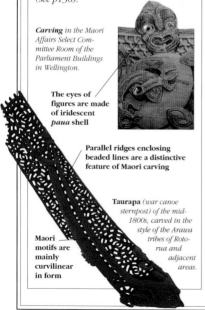

Carving *in the Maori Affairs Select Committee Room of the Parliament Buildings in Wellington.*

The eyes of figures are made of iridescent *paua* shell

Parallel ridges enclosing beaded lines are a distinctive feature of Maori carving

Taurapa *(war canoe sternpost) of the mid-1800s, carved in the style of the Arawa tribes of Rotorua and adjacent areas.*

Maori motifs are mainly curvilinear in form

SONG AND DANCE

Singing and dancing are an important feature of Maori life. They are performed on various occasions by both men and women. The *poi* dance, with its graceful movements is, however, restricted to women.

The haka *is a war dance performed by men. Eyes and tongues protrude in a gesture of defiance.*

Plaiting and weaving, *using swamp flax, reeds or bird feathers, are women's arts. This 1880s kete whakairo, or decorated bag, was woven from flax.*

Cloaks and capes *are a feature of traditional Maori dress and are made of various materials, including flax, feathers and dogskin. This engraving by Sydney Parkinson (1745–71) depicts a cloaked warrior.*

Poi balls *are stuffed with reeds and covered with woven flax fibre.*

Songs are performed with the whole being; the body, hands, legs, arms and facial expressions all play their part.

Early Maori weapons *were made of wood, stone and bone. Close hand-to-hand fighting was the main characteristic of Maori warfare. This wahaika, or short wooden hand club, from the early 1800s, is an example of a weapon used for striking.*

Skirts consist of strips of flax hanging from a belt. The green leaves are scraped and dried so that they curl into tubes.

CONTEMPORARY MAORI ARTIST

Very much a part of the remarkable renaissance in contemporary Maori art, artist Cliff Whiting celebrates his ancestral inheritance in this interpretation of the legend of creation. Using a mixture of traditional and modern materials and processes, he depicts Tane Mahuta, God of the Forests, pushing apart Ranginui, his Sky Father, and Papatuanuku, his Earth Mother, to let light enter the world.

Mural by Cliff Whiting (1974), depicting the separation of Ranginui and Papatuanuku

New Zealand Artists and Writers

FROM THE TIME of first contact, botanists, navigators, surveyors and amateur painters recorded aspects of New Zealand's flora and fauna, the Maori people and early settlements. There were also many reports, diaries and commentaries in the British press which provided interesting descriptions and accounts of the new land, such as Lady Barker's *Station Life in New Zealand* (1870). The poetry, novels and paintings of the late 19th century were very much in the European tradition, but by the 1900s distinctive national elements began to emerge in writing and art.

Lithograph of tuis (1888) by J G Kuelemans

Painting of a Maori chief by Charles Goldie

ARTISTS

THE PIONEER climate in New Zealand was not sympathetic to the arts. "Working class" settlers, struggling to survive in a strange and hostile land, had little knowledge of the arts. For the wealthy, the arts were largely a diversion for gentlewomen. Works of any substance were mainly by artists visiting New Zealand, such as Italian Girolamo Pieri Nerli and Dutchman Petrus van der Velden, who both had a romantic European view of the untamed land.

A few New Zealanders sought training in European academies, such as Charles Frederick Goldie, who in his portraits of the Maoris, romanticized them as a sad and dying race. By the

1900s, art schools and art societies had become established in New Zealand but many artists, conscious of the Impressionist movement and other developments in Europe, escaped to that more exciting milieu. Frances Hodgkins left in 1901, and although some claim her as an eminent New Zealand artist, she achieved her reputation working in Britain and France.

In the 1920s, British-trained artists, such as Robert Field and Roland Hipkins, who taught at Dunedin's art school, brought to their students the "radical" ideas of the modern movement which were well established in Europe. Expressionist, Cubist and abstract influences began to appear in the works of John Weeks, Rhona Haszard and Christopher

Perkins, and by the 1940s a number of artists saw in modernism an opportunity to explore the "national" character of the land and its people. Much of the work of Eric Lee-Johnson, Sir Tosswill Woolaston, Russell Clark and William Sutton seeks to define the substance or spirit of the land rather than give it superficial description.

In 1954 – late by world standards – the Auckland City Art Gallery presented New Zealand's first show of abstract paintings, "Object and Image", which caused a public outcry. However, artists such as Louise Henderson, Colin McCahon, Don Peebles and Rudy Gopas began to exhibit in the dealer galleries, now a feature of the larger cities.

Sculpture lagged behind painting, although Len Lye began his kinetic works as early as 1950. He moved to New York, but New Zealand is fortunate to have a substantial collection of his work at the Govett-Brewster Gallery in New Plymouth *(see p178)*. By the 1960s, significant modern works were commissioned for public places from Jim Allen, Greer Twiss, Marte Szirmay, Terry Stringer, Neil Dawson and Paul Dibble.

Since the 1970s, there has been a substantial increase in the number of full-time professional artists, including outstanding Maori artists such as Ralph Hotere, Para Matchett, Fred Graham and Shona Rapira Davies.

Dry September **(1949), oil on canvas by William Sutton**

Nga Morehu (The Survivors; 1988), a sculpture in mixed media by Shona Rapira Davies

WRITERS

NEW ZEALAND writing began to attract attention by the 1860s, but most of it was published in Britain as New Zealand lacked publishing houses. *Erewhon* (1872) by Samuel Butler is based upon his life in the high country of the South Island. *A History of New Zealand Birds* (1873) by Sir Walter Buller is still highly regarded for its careful documentation and illustrations. William Pember Reeves' *The Long White Cloud*, a romanticized version of New Zealand history, was published in 1898.

Jane Mander's *The Story of a New Zealand River* (1920) attracted some international attention for its depiction of colonial life. *Bliss*, Katherine Mansfield's first collection of short stories, marked the advent of New Zealand writing of originality and substance. Born in Wellington, Mansfield was sent to London to further her education. Although she returned briefly to New Zealand, she spent most of the rest of her life in France and England. Though produced abroad, her work, which reveals her sharp observation of human behaviour, is based upon her memories of a New Zealand childhood. Mansfield died in 1923 at the age of 34.

Katherine Mansfield

By the 1930s, there emerged a conscious determination by novelists and poets to shape a New Zealand style, using local idioms, references to the raw landscape, and characterization of its settler inhabitants. Time spent overseas in the armed forces during World War II also gave them a new perspective of their homeland and added more pungency to their writing. Typical is poet Allen Curnow's *Landfall in Unknown Seas*, a powerful evocation of the visitor confronted by an alien but compelling land.

By the 1950s, Denis Glover, Robin Hyde, Frank Sargeson and Ruth Dallas, among others, ushered in a period of substantial productivity. Novelists such as John Mulgan, Dan Davin, Roderick Finlayson, and poet James K Baxter also cast a sharply critical eye upon what they saw as a conforming and conventional society that concealed disturbing undercurrents.

Historian and poet Keith Sinclair, in his *A History of New Zealand* (1961), was one of the first to question prevailing versions of New Zealand history, which promoted colonial supremacy over "native" primitivism and biased interpretations of land settlement and the subsequent land wars. Dick Scott's research in *Ask that Mountain* (1975) revealed to New Zealanders a truer account of early settlement and relations with the Maoris. Today, writers such as Maurice Shadbolt, Fiona Kidman, C K Stead, Maurice Gee, Janet Frame and Fleur Adcock demonstrate a new maturity in their commentary upon racial and social issues.

A number of Maori novelists and poets are a voice for their people, among them Witi Ihimaera, Patricia Grace and Hone Tuwhare. In 1985, Keri Hulme, of Maori and Pakeha descent, won the prestigious British Booker Prize with *The Bone People*. Maori writer Alan Duff's *Once Were Warriors*, later made into a film of the same name, is a powerful exposure of the turbulence within the Maori people. Sylvia Ashton-Warner's novel *Spinster*, on provincial attitudes in a rural community, was made into a film in the US, as was Ian Cross's *God Boy*, an insight into adolescence and religion.

THE BONE PEOPLE

KERI HULME

Cover of *The Bone People*, a novel by Keri Hulme

James K Baxter

Farming and Horticulture

Cow on rural letter box

DESPITE BEING SO urbanized (85 per cent of New Zealanders live in cities or large towns), the country still depends heavily on its agricultural economy. Farming industries utilize more than 62 per cent of the total land area of 165,000 sq km (63,700 sq miles) and produce more than half of all export earnings. Traditionally, pastoral farming has centred on sheep and cattle but other types of livestock, such as deer, goats, pigs and poultry, are gaining in importance. Pine trees cloak hills too steep to support livestock, while horticulture and other crops now dominate fertile coastal and inland areas.

Kiwifruit, grown primarily in the Bay of Plenty (see p127)*, is successfully marketed in more than 50 countries. New Zealand supplies about a quarter of world production.*

Apples and pears, New Zealand's main pip fruits, are grown mostly in Hawke's Bay and Marlborough/Nelson. About 18 million cartons are exported annually.

Plastic sheeting protects rows of delicate berry fruits from frost.

Lines of trees between orchards serve as windbreaks.

Kiwifruit grow on vines supported by wooden trellises.

Peaches and other stone fruit, such as apricots, nectarines, plums and cherries, are concentrated in Hawke's Bay and Central Otago.

HORTICULTURE

Although pastoral farming is the major land use in New Zealand, large areas are now planted in crops. The mild, sunny climate and fertile soils of the coastal regions of the Bay of Plenty, Gisborne, Hawke's Bay, Nelson and Otago have created a stunning mosaic of orchards producing a variety of traditional pip and stone fruit as well as citrus, berry and subtropical varieties.

PASTORAL AGRICULTURE

New Zealand's 47 million sheep and 9 million cattle are bred for their meat, wool, dairy produce and hides. Beef cattle predominate in Northland, dairying in Waikato, Taranaki and Manawatu, and sheep farming in the rest of the country. Deer, goats and other livestock are scattered throughout both islands.

The Romney is the most common sheep in New Zealand and is bred for both meat and wool production.

The black and white Holstein-Friesian is the most common dairy cow, yielding more milk than other breeds.

CEREAL AND OTHER CROPS

Fields of traditional cereal crops cover much of the flatter areas in the South Island, especially in Canterbury and Southland. Here, wheat and oats are grown for home consumption and for milling, and barley and oats for the manufacture of stock feed; barley is also grown for malting at New Zealand breweries. Large-scale vegetable production has made inroads into fertile coastal regions in both the North and South islands, while new and distinct plant varieties, such as sunflowers, lavender and garlic, add colour and variety to the country's agricultural landscape.

Sunflowers, grown for their seeds, near Palmerston North

Wheat and garlic in Marlborough

Sorting and packaging is done in packhouses.

Citrus trees are planted in long, straight lines.

Other fruits, such as the citrus grapefruit and subtropical varieties like avocados, tamarillos, persimmons and pepinos (in addition to kiwifruit), are grown in small orchards in the warmer parts of New Zealand – Northland, Auckland and the Bay of Plenty — while berry fruits such as raspberries thrive in the cooler South Island.

Grapefruit

Avocados

Pepinos

Persimmon

Tamarillos

Raspberries

Grapes are grown mainly for the domestic market and for wine production (see pp34–5). Marlborough, Gisborne and Hawke's Bay are the major grape producing areas.

Deer *are bred on some 5,000 farms. Venison fetches premium prices worldwide, while deer velvet is popular in Asia.*

Goats *are farmed both domestically and commercially for their milk, meat and mohair as well as for weed control.*

Ostriches *(as shown here) and emus are among the new livestock breeds gaining in popularity.*

The Wines of New Zealand

Corbans Longridge labels

ALTHOUGH GRAPES were first planted in New Zealand as early as the 1830s, it was not until the 1980s when wine makers decided to concentrate on white wines, such as Sauvignon Blanc and Chardonnay, that the country's reputation as an excellent wine producer began. The number of wineries has since grown to almost 300, and export wine sales in 1999 reached 16.6 million litres (3.65 million gallons). In less than 20 years, the nation's wine makers have gone from producing wine of average quality to some of the best in the world. Wine drinking has also become popular in New Zealand. Many vineyards have restaurants, offer wine tastings and tours, and sell wine at the cellar door.

A visit to a vineyard *for wine tasting or a meal is a popular weekend leisure activity.*

JAMES BUSBY

Appointed by the British Government as Resident or government representative to New Zealand in 1833, James Busby (1800–71) became the country's first recorded wine maker. He had earlier studied wine making in France and had also helped to establish a wine industry in the Hunter Valley in Australia. French explorer Dumont D'Urville confirmed the promise of viticulture in the country when he heaped praise on Busby's white wine, which he sampled during an 1840 visit to the Bay of Islands.

Marlborough *is New Zealand's largest wine-growing region* (see pp204–205). *The wide, flat Wairau Valley, dry, sunny climate and slow ripening conditions combine to produce the country's finest Sauvignon Blanc.*

French settlers planted vines on Canterbury's picturesque Banks Peninsula as early as 1840 *(see pp228–9)*. Waipara, north of Christchurch *(see pp230–31)*, has become a more important wine-producing area.

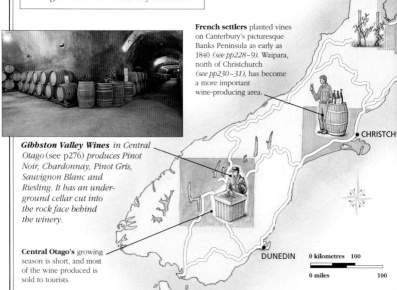

Gibbston Valley Wines *in Central Otago* (see p276) *produces Pinot Noir, Chardonnay, Pinot Gris, Sauvignon Blanc and Riesling. It has an underground cellar cut into the rock face behind the winery.*

Central Otago's growing season is short, and most of the wine produced is sold to tourists.

● CHRISTCH

● DUNEDIN

0 kilometres   100

0 miles   100

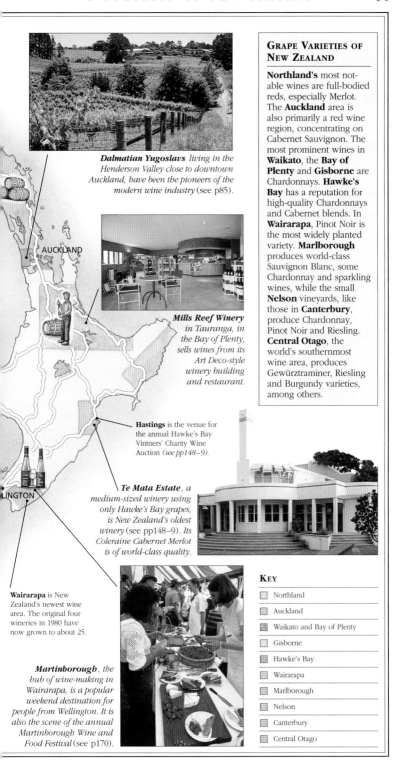

Dalmatian Yugoslavs living in the Henderson Valley close to downtown Auckland, have been the pioneers of the modern wine industry (see p85).

AUCKLAND

Mills Reef Winery in Tauranga, in the Bay of Plenty, sells wines from its Art Deco-style winery building and restaurant.

Hastings is the venue for the annual Hawke's Bay Vintners' Charity Wine Auction *(see pp148–9).*

Te Mata Estate, a medium-sized winery using only Hawke's Bay grapes, is New Zealand's oldest winery (see pp148–9). Its Coleraine Cabernet Merlot is of world-class quality.

Wairarapa is New Zealand's newest wine area. The original four wineries in 1980 have now grown to about 25.

Martinborough, the hub of wine-making in Wairarapa, is a popular weekend destination for people from Wellington. It is also the scene of the annual Martinborough Wine and Food Festival (see p170).

LINGTON

GRAPE VARIETIES OF NEW ZEALAND

Northland's most notable wines are full-bodied reds, especially Merlot. The **Auckland** area is also primarily a red wine region, concentrating on Cabernet Sauvignon. The most prominent wines in **Waikato**, the **Bay of Plenty** and **Gisborne** are Chardonnays. **Hawke's Bay** has a reputation for high-quality Chardonnays and Cabernet blends. In **Wairarapa**, Pinot Noir is the most widely planted variety. **Marlborough** produces world-class Sauvignon Blanc, some Chardonnay and sparkling wines, while the small **Nelson** vineyards, like those in **Canterbury**, produce Chardonnay, Pinot Noir and Riesling. **Central Otago**, the world's southernmost wine area, produces Gewürztraminer, Riesling and Burgundy varieties, among others.

KEY

☐	Northland
☐	Auckland
☐	Waikato and Bay of Plenty
☐	Gisborne
☐	Hawke's Bay
☐	Wairarapa
☐	Marlborough
☐	Nelson
☐	Canterbury
☐	Central Otago

New Zealand's Sporting Year

SPORT HAS ALWAYS BEEN an important part of New
Zealand cultural life. Maoris were fond of running
races, wrestling, surfing and canoe competitions,
although nothing was formalized. Freed of class
distinctions, European settlers found, when they
arrived in New Zealand, that they could enjoy
pastimes that had been denied them in Britain.
The national passion for an active recreational life
has contributed to New Zealanders
carving out an international
reputation for their sporting
prowess, producing numerous
world-class champions out of
all proportion to the size of
the country's population.

*The Lake Taupo Inter-
national Trout Fishing
Contest attracts worldwide
participation to this Mecca
of trout fishing.*

The Wellington Cup,
*like most of horse racing's
premier events, is held
during the summer months.*

**The New Zealand
Winter Cup** at Addington,
Christchurch, is one of the
important harness races on
the racing calendar.

January	February	March	April	May	June

**The Auckland Anniversary
Regatta**, in which more than
600 yachts take part, is one of
the largest yachting events in
the world.

**The First Light
Triathlon** in
Gisborne is a
popular event to
welcome in the
dawn of each
New Year.

The Provincial Trophy is cricket's premier event in New
Zealand. After rugby, cricket is the country's most popular
sport and attracts large numbers of spectators.

KEY TO SEASONS

▬▬	Cricket
▬▬	Golf
▬▬	Horse racing
▬▬	Lawn bowls
▬▬	Netball
▬▬	Rugby
▬▬	Skiing
▬▬	Surf life-saving

**The International Dragon Boat Champion-
ships** *take place on Wellington's Lambton Harbour.*

The Southern Traverse, a race for teams of three to five people, varies its course each year. Apart from cycling, competitors have to use kayaks and rafts to cross lakes and rivers.

The National Provincial Championship, rugby's top domestic prize, is the climax of the rugby season.

The New Zealand Open Golf Championship, held at a different golf course each year, attracts a world-class field.

August	September	October	November	December

The World Heli-Challenge, at Wanaka, is just one of the many adventure sports events in New Zealand.

The New Zealand Car Rally attracts overseas competitors to race over some of the country's most difficult roads.

BLACK MAGIC

No sport has had such an effect on New Zealand life as rugby union. Imported from England in the 1870s, the sport was taken up with alacrity by New Zealanders, especially Maoris and, recently, Polynesian Islanders. The standard bearers for rugby are the famous All Blacks, a name synonymous with the sport. In 1888, the Native team from New Zealand toured Britain, its uniform black with a silver fern on the chest. Known as the Blacks, they were the precursor to the first All Black team which conquered British teams in 1905.

Black attire was later adopted by other New Zealand sporting teams for international events. The national cricket team is dubbed the Black Caps and the basketball team, the Tall Blacks.

All Black Jonah Lomu

NEW ZEALAND THROUGH THE YEAR

Arts Festival poster

NEW ZEALAND'S seasons are opposite to those in the northern hemisphere. Spring arrives in September and summer comes in December, autumn is from March to May and the winter months are June, July and August. The South Island's temperatures are slightly lower than those in the North Island. Rain falls heaviest in winter in most areas, with the summer months relatively dry. Visitors need to be prepared for sudden weather changes, a feature of the maritime climate. The country's latitudinal position opens it to prevailing winds coming from west to east, ranging from gentle breezes to raging gales.

SPRING

WITH THE ONSET of finer weather, the rugby posts come down from the playing fields and cricketers start to practise their strokes. Blossom and food festivals, garden and fashion shows begin, and the horse racing season swings into gear.

SEPTEMBER

Hastings Blossom Festival *(second week)*. The country's largest fruit-growing district ushers in a new season. Highlights include concerts and a blossom parade.
Crater to Lake Challenge *(mid-Sep)*, Taupo. Multi-sport event featuring snow skiing, cycling, kayaking, water-skiing and running from the slopes of Mount Ruapehu to Taupo.

Cattle on parade at Showtime Canterbury

New Zealand Wearable Art Awards *(late Sep)*, Nelson. A choreographed evening in which art designs are worn rather than hung on a wall *(see p211)*.

OCTOBER

Rotorua Trout Festival *(early Oct)*. The annual trout fishing tournament is combined with a festival to open the trout season.
Dunedin Rhododendron Festival *(late Oct)*. Displays of rhododendrons set the Dunedin Botanic Garden and other gardens ablaze with colour in spring.
Taranaki Rhododendron Festival *(last week)*. More than 100 gardens are on view *(see p178)*.

NOVEMBER

Showtime Canterbury, Christchurch. Features the region's main Agricultural & Pastoral Show, horse races, concerts and a diverse range of events.
Southern Traverse *(mid-Nov)*, Nelson. An adventure race through some of the toughest terrain in the South Island, finishing in Nelson.
Toast Martinborough *(mid-Nov)*, Wairarapa. Showcases the best wine and food of the region, with entertainment by local artists.
Ellerslie Flower Show *(last week)*, Auckland. The largest floral exhibition in the southern hemisphere, now located permanently at the Auckland Regional Botanic Gardens.

Modelling designs in the New Zealand Wearable Art Awards

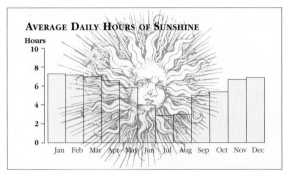

AVERAGE DAILY HOURS OF SUNSHINE

Hours

Jan Feb Mar Apr May Jun Jul Aug Sep Oct Nov Dec

Sunshine Chart
The chart gives figures for Wellington, but these are similar to other main centres. Nelson and Blenheim in the South Island, and Tauranga, Napier and Gisborne in the North Island, enjoy more sunshine hours than any other places. The least sunny region is the southern part of the South Island.

SUMMER

ALTHOUGH MANY New Zealanders head off for their annual visit to the beach, lake or high country during the summer school break, shops no longer "shut down" apart from Christmas and New Year's days. Cities and towns have become increasingly lively places during the holiday season.

Maoris performing at the Waitangi Day celebrations

DECEMBER

Kepler Challenge *(early Dec)*, Te Anau. An annual endurance run that follows the Kepler Track *(see p281)*, over mountain tops, swamps and river valleys, through magnificent scenery.
Festival of Lights *(late Dec)*, New Plymouth. Special festive lighting in Pukekura Park and city streets. There are music and dance performances in the park each evening *(see p179)*.

JANUARY

First Light Triathlon *(first week)*, Gisborne. A triathlon event to welcome in the dawn of each New Year.
Instant Kiwi World Buskers Festival *(mid-Jan)*, Christchurch. A week of street entertainment by world-class performers.
Auckland Anniversary Regatta *(late Jan)*. Up to 600 yachts take part in one of the world's largest one-day regattas on Waitemata Harbour *(see p71)*.

New Zealand Fishing Challenge *(third week)*, Tutukaka. Anglers establish new catch records each time in the largest game fishing contest in the country.
New Zealand Paragliding Nationals *(last week)*, Wanaka. Pilots from around the world fly cross-country to a designated goal.

Anniversary Day Regatta in Auckland

FEBRUARY

Waitangi Day *(6 Feb)*, Waitangi National Trust. Commemorates the signing of the Treaty of Waitangi *(see pp102–103)*.
International Dragon Boat Championships *(Chinese New Year)*, Wellington. Crews race for top honours on Lambton Harbour.
Bay of Islands International Billfish Tournament *(early Feb)*. Competitors vie for the biggest catches in coastal waters.
Aotearoa Traditional Maori Performing Arts Festival *(early Feb, even years)*, Waikato. Festival of Maori culture and art by New Zealand's best groups.
Wine Marlborough *(second Sat)*, Blenheim. Wines and food under marquees in a vineyard setting *(see p206)*.
Garden City Festival of Flowers *(third week)*, Christchurch. Prestigious festival celebrates the beauty of flowers.

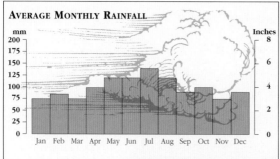

AVERAGE MONTHLY RAINFALL

mm | Inches
200 | 8
175 |
150 | 6
125 |
100 | 4
75 |
50 | 2
25 |
0 | 0
Jan Feb Mar Apr May Jun Jul Aug Sep Oct Nov Dec

Rainfall Chart
Rainfall is not evenly distributed throughout New Zealand. The west coast of the North Island and South Island is wetter than the east coast. More rain falls in winter and spring than in summer and autumn, in most areas. The figures given here are only for Wellington.

AUTUMN

AUTUMN OFTEN BRINGS the most settled weather of the year, a time of mild, calm days still warm enough for most summer activities. This is harvest season, a good time to experience wine and food festivals. Tramping, fishing and hunting are also popular autumnal pursuits.

MARCH

New Zealand International Festival of the Arts *(early Mar, even years)*, Wellington. The most prestigious event in the country's cultural calendar, this festival features some of the world's best talents *(see pp154–5)*.
Golden Shears *(first week)*, Masterton. The world's top shearers are in action at this popular event *(see p171)*.
Pasifika Festival *(first week)*, Auckland. Pacific Islanders display their art and culture *(see p91)*.
Wildfoods Festival *(mid-Mar)*, Hokitika. Possum stew and huhu grub are some of the delicacies on the menu.

The New Zealand Hot Air Balloon Fiesta in Hamilton

Round the Bays Run *(end-Mar)*, Auckland. One of the world's largest fun runs with 60,000 people taking part.
Ngaruawahia Regatta *(late Mar)*, Ngaruawahia. Maori canoes compete on the Waikato River in the hometown of the Maori Queen *(see p114)*.

APRIL

Bluff Oyster & Seafood Festival *(mid-Apr)*. Features an array of seafood, fine wine and entertainment.
Royal Easter Show *(second week)*, Auckland. Livestock competitions, art and craft awards, wine awards and the largest equestrian show in the country.
Waiheke Island Jazz Festival *(third week)*. New Zealand and over-seas musicians play at this resort island.

New Zealand Hot Air Balloon Fiesta *(mid-Apr)*, Hamilton. More than 30 balloons drift over the city and surrounding areas. *(see p116)*.
Lake Taupo International Trout Fishing Contest *(third week)*. Fishermen vie at one of the finest trout fishing locations in the world *(see p139)*.
Warbirds Over Wanaka *(Easter weekend, even years)*. Classic vintage and veteran warplanes take to the skies in this world-class event *(see p268)*.
Rotorua Marathon *(end April)*. New Zealand's oldest and most popular marathon attracts up to 5,000 runners.

MAY

Rotorua Tagged Trout Competition *(May)*. Rotorua's premier fishing competition has a $50,000 trout waiting to be hooked.

Visitors at a food stall at the Hokitika Wildfoods Festival

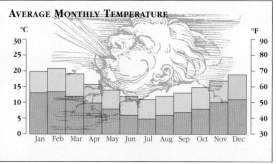

AVERAGE MONTHLY TEMPERATURE

| °C | | | | | | | | | | | | °F |

Jan Feb Mar Apr May Jun Jul Aug Sep Oct Nov Dec

Temperature Chart
The chart gives the average maximum and minimum temperatures for the city of Wellington. The North Island has mild winters and humid summers. The South Island experiences the country's hottest summer temperatures, but in winter these can plunge to below freezing point.

WINTER

O FTEN THE MOST spectacular time of the year to visit, winter also brings reduced rates on airfares, accommodation and activities. On the scenic west coast, rainfall is at its lowest and whales at Kaikoura can virtually be guaranteed to put in an appearance.

JUNE

National Agricultural Fieldays *(mid-Jun)*, Mystery Creek, Hamilton. One of the world's largest agricultural events showcases the best of New Zealand's products, with emphasis on innovative technology *(see p116)*.

JULY

Rally of New Zealand *(mid-Jul)*, Greater Auckland.

Spectators at the Rally of New Zealand in Auckland

Part of the Asia Pacific Car Rally Championships, in which drivers battle it out on the back country roads.
Queenstown Winter Festival *(third week)*. One of the highlights of the Queenstown calendar, with spectacular night skiing and firework displays.
World Heli-Challenge *(late Jul)*, Wanaka. International snowboarders and skiers take part in three days of heliskiing events.

Christchurch Arts Festival *(last week, odd years)*. A mid-winter festival of music, theatre, dance, film and the visual arts.

AUGUST

Bay of Islands Jazz and Blues Festival *(mid-Aug)*, Northland. One of the most popular events on the jazz calendar. More than 50 bands from New Zealand and overseas take part.

PUBLIC HOLIDAYS

New Year's Day (1 Jan)
Waitangi Day (6 Feb)
Good Friday (varies)
Easter Monday (varies)
Anzac Day (25 April)
Queen's Birthday (second Mon in Jun)
Labour Day (23 Oct)
Christmas Day (25 Dec)
Boxing Day (26 Dec)

Clydesdale horses and wagon at the National Agricultural Fieldays, Mystery Creek, Hamilton

THE HISTORY OF NEW ZEALAND

T HE LAST OF THE WORLD'S *significant landmasses to be colonized by people, New Zealand is a nation of immigrants. Maoris settled in the country less than 1,000 years ago, while Europeans first arrived just 350 years ago. Together, these two peoples have forged a unique identity out of their common experiences that reflects their Pacific environment.*

The date the first Maoris arrived in New Zealand is shrouded in mystery. According to legend, the first explorer to discover New Zealand was the Polynesian Kupe, around AD 950. He then returned to his ancestral homeland, Hawaiki. Four centuries later, a fleet of canoes set sail for New Zealand, guided by Kupe's directions on how to find land.

Coat of Arms of New Zealand

Basing their findings on radiocarbon dating of Maori middens, archaeologists believe that the first settlement was around AD 1300. Some scientists, however, believe that Maoris arrived as long ago as 2,000 years, but these early settlers did not survive for long. Nonetheless, the rats that they brought with them went on to devastate the native bird, lizard and frog populations.

Regardless of when they did arrive, Maoris are known to have brought a number of plants and animals with them. The mainly vegetarian *kiore*, the Polynesian rat, was considered a delicacy when fattened up on berries. Also known to have survived the journey was the native dog, the *kuri*. Root vegetables Maoris brought with them were the yam, *kumara* and *taro*. The *kumara* grew more successfully in the colder climate than the other two, and proved important in the development of Maori culture, enabling permanent settlement.

ABEL TASMAN

Since Greek times, there had been talk of a Terra Australis, or "great southern continent", to counterbalance the lands of the northern hemisphere. Such a landmass was necessary, it was argued, to offset the weight of the continents in the north and to balance the Earth on its axis. The mathematician Pythagoras speculated about the existence of such a land, but it was not until almost 2,000 years later that 17th-century Dutch explorers finally sighted Australia.

In 1642, the Dutch East India Company, a trading firm anxious to explore prospects for commerce beyond the East Indies, sent Abel Tasman south from Java in Indonesia.

TIMELINE

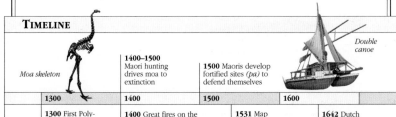

Moa skeleton

Double canoe

1400–1500 Maori hunting drives moa to extinction

1500 Maoris develop fortified sites *(pa)* to defend themselves

1300	1400	1500	1600
1300 First Polynesian inhabitants arrive from Cook and Society islands	**1400** Great fires on the South Island east coast destroy swathes of forest	**1531** Map drawn with Terra Australis on it	**1642** Dutch explorer Abel Tasman sights New Zealand

◁ **Detail from *The Signing of the Treaty of Waitangi* by Marcus King (1939)**

Maori Exploration and Voyage

IT IS STILL DEBATABLE whether Polynesians, ancestors of the Maoris, made planned voyages to New Zealand or simply drifted there by chance. However, Polynesians were skilled navigators who sailed long distances between the islands in the Pacific in large craft. Driven out of an island by starvation or intertribal warfare, some groups would have deliberately sailed to a far-off land, especially if they had been given directions by someone like Kupe who had been there *(see p43)*. With their vessels laden with plants and small animals, they would have been guided by traditional navigation clues, such as migrating birds and cloud formations.

Stern of canoe

Kupe's Anchor Stone
A 1912 photograph of a Maori elder standing beside what may be Kupe's anchor stone.

Canoe Prow
The prows of Maori waka *(canoes), carved in intricate patterns, had forward-thrusting heads to improve the canoes' performance.*

Fishing Net
Fish, a valuable part of the Maoris' food supply, were caught using a variety of nets. This wood engraving (1840) by Joel Pollack is of a landing net.

POLYNESIAN SETTLEMENT
Archaeological discoveries indicate that Polynesians came from Southeast Asia to the eastern Pacific islands, settling the lands from Hawaii to Easter Island. About 1,000 years ago, expeditions from the islands of central Polynesia reached New Zealand where they established coastal tribal settlements.

CHINA
TAIWAN
PHILIPPINES
MALAYSIA
NEW GUIN
INDONESIA
AUSTRALIA

Kuri
Maoris brought the kuri *(dog) with them on their migrations. It became extinct soon after European settlement.*

Single Canoe
The single canoe was used as a coastal vessel. It had decking made of long rods. Thwarts, lashed from one top edge to the other, served as seats.

PERIODS OF SETTLEMENT	
———	30,000 years ago
———	3,000 years ago
———	1,500–2,000 years ago
———	1,000 years ago
———	500 years ago

Double Canoes
The largest of these craft, depicted here by William Hodges, artist on Cook's 1773 voyage, were capable of carrying up to 200 people in it.

***Taro* Plant**
Few plants taken from Polynesia survived the voyage to New Zealand. Taro grew, but because it was not productive, it became a luxury food.

PACIFIC OCEAN

HAWAII

NORTH AMERICA

SOLOMON ISLANDS

SAMOA

FIJI

TONGA

TAHITI

COOK ISLANDS

EASTER ISLAND

NEW CALEDONIA

NEW ZEALAND

Kiore
The kiore *or rat was introduced from Polynesia. It was a source of food for the early Maoris.*

0 kilometres 1,000

0 miles   1,000

Canoe Regatta
Maoris today celebrate their heritage of exploration and voyage in the annual Ngaruawahia Regatta, held on the Waikato River (see p114).

Legend of Maui
An ink drawing (1907) by Wilhelm Dittmer depicts the legend of Maui, who created New Zealand by fishing the North Island out of the ocean.

Abel Tasman's ships, the *Heemskerck* and *Zeehaen*

After sailing past Tasmania, Tasman reached a point off present-day Hokitika on 13 December 1642, noting "a large high elevated land". He and the crews of the *Heemskerck* and *Zeehaen* had sighted the Southern Alps. Tasman wanted to land, but the rolling swell off the coastline convinced him to head north, where he found a relatively calm anchorage in what is now called Golden Bay. However, hostile Maoris rammed a sloop from the *Zeehaen*, and clubbed four of the Dutch sailors to death. The Dutch subsequently named the location Murderers' Bay. Tasman immediately set sail north and left New Zealand waters on 6 January 1643 without further investigation.

Abel Tasman

CAPTAIN JAMES COOK

There was a lull in European exploration of the New Zealand region for more than 100 years. No good commercial reason encouraged any visits; indeed, the reputation of the hostile Maoris discouraged them. Then, in 1769, Englishman Captain James Cook set sail on a scientific expedition of discovery to the South Pacific, to observe the transit of the sun by the planet Venus. After having observed the rare phenomenon at Tahiti, Cook sailed south until he sighted the east coast of New Zealand, on 9 October 1769.

Cook's ship, the *Endeavour*, was well equipped for its voyage, with botanists and artists on board. Besides documenting new scientific finds, Cook's mission was to assess the potential of the country as a colony. A master mariner, Cook expertly mapped the coastline and the scientists on board made hundreds of discoveries. On this first of three visits to New Zealand, he claimed the country for England. Coincidentally, a French expedition led by explorer Jean de Surville sailed within a few kilometres of Cook at the end of 1769, but neither was aware of the other's presence.

Following Cook, Europeans trickled rather than flooded into New Zealand, working as whalers, sealers and timber traders. Seeking short-term profits, few became permanent immigrants, and as soon as the resource they sought disappeared, so did they. By the early 1800s it had become uneconomic to send sealing gangs to New Zealand because most of the easy prey had been taken; whale numbers, too, plummeted.

THE TREATY OF WAITANGI

The impact of these visitors on the traditional Maori way of life was enormous. Maoris were exposed to a disastrous suite of diseases, such as measles and smallpox, and their warlike instincts were satisfied with the purchase of guns. During the 1820s, at least 20,000 Maoris were killed in intertribal "musket wars", which

TIMELINE

1791 First whaling ship sails into Doubtless Bay, Northland

1814 Samuel Marsden sets up first Anglican mission in the Bay of Islands

1821 Musket wars begin between Maori tribes

1831 Whaling stations established around Cook Strait

1833 James Busby appointed British Resident

1750	1800	1820	1830	1840

1769 Captain Cook makes first of three visits to New Zealand

1815 First Pakeha child born in New Zealand

1835 Declaration of Independence signed by 34 northern chiefs

1840 British sovereignty proclaimed. Treaty of Waitangi signed by 50 chiefs

HMS *Endeavour*

Maori chief

The Treaty House at Waitangi

changed the political face of Maori New Zealand as tribes invaded neighbouring territories, sometimes taking them permanently.

Another major influence for change was Christianity. Anglican missionary Samuel Marsden established New

Zealand's first mission station in the Bay of Islands in 1814, and although progress was slow in converting Maoris to Christianity, the faith had a significant foothold by 1840.

By then Maoris numbered about 115,000 and European settlers 2,000. While some Maoris benefitted by trading with the Europeans and growing crops for them, there was concern about increasing lawlessness, the buying up of land by Europeans and the intertribal warfare. Leading chiefs asked Queen Victoria to provide a framework of law and order. Britain, worried that the French or Americans might lay claim to New Zealand, agreed, and in 1840 drew up the Treaty of Waitangi. The Maori translation gave the chiefs a different understanding of the meaning of the treaty, and this was to have its consequences.

THE NEW ZEALAND WARS

Unlike Australia, where many of the first immigrants were convicts, New Zealand settlers came from the working and middle classes. The New Zealand Company was set up in 1837 to transplant a cross-section of English society in the Antipodes. Planned settlements were established at Wellington, Wanganui, Nelson, New Plymouth, Christchurch and Dunedin.

Following the signing of the Treaty of Waitangi, Maori–Pakeha relations were relatively harmonious for some years. If there were conflicts, they were generally over land, and isolated skirmishes occurred until 1860, the year the New Zealand Wars began. The critical point was at Waitara, Taranaki. The cause was a land sale between the government and a minor chief of the Te Ati Awa tribe who did not have the tribe's permission

---

TREATY OF WAITANGI

The Treaty of Waitangi is New Zealand's founding document, an agreement between the British Government and Maoris that is today the centrepiece of the country's race relations. At the time of signing, most, if not all, of the 50 Maori chiefs who put their names to the Treaty would not have understood the implications of what they were doing.

In return for giving Queen Victoria the right to buy land, Maoris were granted all the rights and privileges of British subjects. A clause also gave them

"full exclusive and undisturbed possession of their Lands and Estates Forests Fisheries and other properties". But misunderstanding arose because there were two different versions (Maori and English) which carried different meanings. Controversy over the Treaty continues to this day.

Signatures on the Treaty

---

to sell, a prerequisite for communal property under Maori custom. When the tribe refused to accept the bogus deal, the government retaliated by marching troops onto the land and seizing it by force.

In response, most central North Island tribes backed the Te Ati Awa, intensifying the rebellion. At the height of hostilities in the mid-1860s, British forces had increased to more than 20,000, against about 5,000 Maori warriors. On the British side were significant numbers of Maoris who were either opportunists or had a score to settle with an enemy tribe.

United, Maoris would have easily been a match for the invaders. Even divided, they came close to persuading many settlers to flee the colony. In 1868, two chiefs, Titikowarau in the west and Te Kooti in the east, won a series of significant battles, but internal squabbles saw them lose the support of the wider Maori population. By 1869, the New Zealand Wars came to a halt as Maori opposition fell away. Land sales escalated, many of them under duress. The wars resulted in the government confiscating 12,000 sq km (4,630 sq miles) of land. Some

Passengers from the Cressy Landing at Port Lyttelton by William Fox (1851)

was given to "friendly" Maori tribes, while some was handed to Pakeha settlers. It was a legacy that came back to haunt the country more than a century later, as Maoris pursued their legitimate grievances through the Waitangi Tribunal.

ECONOMIC EXPANSION

The 1861 discovery of gold in Otago, and subsequent finds on the West Coast, set the South Island on its industrial feet. Up until then, the North Island had been outstripping the South economically and in population terms; it was not until 1896 that the North Island reasserted itself.

The late 19th century saw a time of great economic expansion, thanks to large-scale government borrowing. The rail network was established, telegraph lines were installed and emigrants were assisted to the country. During the 1870s, the population doubled. Good export prices from wool (which proved to be the mainstay of the economy for the next 100 years) underpinned the frenzy of economic activity. Technological advances also played their part. The first shipload of frozen meat for Britain sailed from

Te Heubeu's Old Pa of Waitabanui at Lake Taupo by George F Angas (1847)

Otago in 1882; this technology was also vital later in shipping butter.

New Zealand soon gained a reputation for social innovation. In 1893, the Liberal Government granted the vote to women, and in 1898 it introduced a means-tested old-age pension, both of which were the first in the world.

THE WAR YEARS

As New Zealand's population reached the one million mark in 1907, the country's status as a colony of Great Britain changed to that of the Dominion of New Zealand. In 1917, the title of governor (the representative of the Queen) became that of governor-general.

World War I poster

The Liberal Party, with its progressive tax policies, old-age pensions, votes for women and breaking up of large land holdings, was hailed domestically and externally for making New Zealand "the birthplace of the 20th century". Its hold on power lasted until 1912, by which time it had lost touch with the public. The political parties it spawned, Labour and National, nevertheless continue to dominate the political scene in the country today.

World War I was a defining moment for the fledgling nation. In 1915, New Zealanders and Australians combined to form the Australian and New Zealand Army Corps (ANZAC). Ordered by the British to attack well-armed and better-placed Turkish defenders on the Gallipoli Peninsula, thousands were killed in eight months of action. The 25th of April (Anzac Day) has since been set aside to remember the soldiers' sacrifice, and is often viewed as the country's national day. For a small country, New Zealand suffered enormously during the war. Out of a total of 110,000 troops, 16,697 died and 41,262 were wounded – a massive casualty rate. Today, the war, and in particular Gallipoli, are seen as the crucible in which the country's national character was forged.

The period between the wars was one of mixed fortunes for New Zealand. While the 1920s were initially

New Zealand Expeditionary Force on the Hutt Road near Petone, Wellington, 1914

1915	1920	1930	1935	1938
1915 New Zealand troops suffer heavy losses in the Gallipoli campaign against Turkey	**1920** First Anzac Day commemoration **1933** Elizabeth McCombs first woman MP	*Elizabeth McCombs*	**1936** New Zealand pilot Jean Batten flies from England to Australia in world record time	
1914 New Zealand enters World War I on the Allied side	**1918** End of World War I	**1935** First Labour Government elected	**1936** 40-hour week introduced	

Factory workers

Relief camp for unemployed workers at Akatarawa, Hutt Valley, in the 1930s

positive, the world's economic woes engulfed the country, and by 1932 it was in the depths of the Depression. The first Labour Government, elected in 1935, spent its way out of the Depression. New Zealand gained further accolades as the social laboratory of the world with its income-related health scheme and extended pension programme.

In 1939, for the second time in the century, New Zealand found itself embroiled in a European war. Prime Minister Michael Joseph Savage was in no doubt where the country's loyalty lay: "Where Britain goes we

go, where she stands we stand." New Zealand soldiers served in Crete, the Middle East and Italy, even though the most serious threat to the country came from Japan. Towards the end of the war, troops were increasingly deployed in the Pacific and links were forged with the US. American soldiers spent time in New Zealand during the war and many took New Zealand wives back home with them. In 1951, military ties between the US, Australia and New Zealand were formalized with the signing of the ANZUS military pact.

MOVING AWAY FROM BRITAIN
After the war, while New Zealand looked to the US for its military security, its economy still remained firmly wedded to Britain. As Britain's "South Pacific farm", New Zealand had traditionally enjoyed easy access to UK's markets. As late as 1960, for example, 55 per cent of its exports landed there. But the boom times came to an end once "the old country" joined the European Union (EU) in 1973 and its priorities shifted to the continent.

Within 20 years of joining the EU, Britain took only 6 per cent of New Zealand's exports. New markets were found, and Asia became important. Hong Kong, China, Japan, Taiwan and South Korea are now among the top ten countries with which New Zealand trades.

Mirroring countries in the West, New Zealand went through great social changes during the 1960s, as baby-boomers reached adulthood and challenged conservative society. The

Interior of a Wellington clothing factory in the 1940s

TIMELINE

Sir Edmund Hillary

Carving at Waitangi Marae

1939 New Zealand fights in World War II on Allied side

1953 Sir Edmund Hillary climbs Mount Everest with Sherpa Tenzing

1961 Capital punishment abolished

1965 Combat force sent to Vietnam

1973 Frigate sent to French Polynesia to protest French nuclear testing

1940	1950	1955	1960	1970

1947 Statute of Westminster adopted by Parliament

1948 Protest against exclusion of Maoris from All Black rugby tour to South Africa

1975 Waitangi Tribunal established to investigate Maori land claims following confiscations and compensate where justified

decision to support the US with a token force in the Vietnam War was vigorously opposed, and in 1972 conscription was dropped by the new Labour Government. A year later, the government sent a frigate to French Polynesia to protest against nuclear weapons testing there.

In the mid-1970s, as imported oil price hikes affected the population, New Zealanders returned to the conservative politics of the National Party under the combative Robert Muldoon. Finally, weary of his interventionist economic policies, the electorate voted in a socially leftist but economically rightist Labour Government in 1984, headed by David Lange.

For the next six years, the country experienced a whirlwind of change as Labour floated the exchange rate, deregulated industries, removed tariffs, sold off state assets and made thousands of civil servants redundant in a quest for greater efficiency. At the same time, foreign relations were in an upheaval: New Zealand had always maintained a strong anti-nuclear weapons policy, and in 1985 the US was told that nuclear-armed or powered warships were no longer welcome in New Zealand ports. The

The *Rainbow Warrior*, sunk in Auckland Harbour in 1985

Americans suspended ANZUS, and in that same year, French saboteurs sank the Greenpeace vessel, the *Rainbow Warrior*, in Auckland.

The National Government, which came to power in 1990 led by Jim Bolger (succeeded in 1997 by Jenny Shipley), continued with economic reforms, albeit at a slower pace. However, many New Zealanders, disillusioned over a succession of unresponsive administrations, voted in a Mixed Member Proportional electoral system based on the German model. The system was first tested in 1997, which resulted in a vastly more representative parliament than before, and the emergence of the country's first elected woman prime minister, Helen Clark of the Labour Party, in 1999.

New Zealand society today has changed significantly, from a period when an overwhelming majority of the population was Pakeha to a point where Auckland is now the largest Polynesian city in the world, and an increasing number of Asians have become citizens. With its increasingly diverse cultures, New Zealand is carving out a confident and independent identity as a Pacific nation in the international community.

Representatives of the Ngai Tahu tribe and the government signing the Deed of Settlement in 1997

1980	1985	1990	1995	1997	2000
1981 First Maori language kindergarten opens **1981** Country divided by South African rugby tour with widespread protests	**1987** New Zealand wins inaugural Rugby World Cup **1987** Maori becomes official language		**1995** Team New Zealand wins America's Cup	*America's Cup yacht*	**2000** Successful defence of America's Cup
1984 Lange Government takes power	**1990** Dame Catherine Tizard first woman governor-general		**1997** First MMP Parliament elected **1997** Jenny Shipley first woman prime minister	**1997** Government compensation to Ngai Tahu tribe for land confiscations	
1985 *Rainbow Warrior* sunk	**1990** National forms government	*Jenny Shipley*			

NEW ZEALAND AREA BY AREA

MAORI KING

New Zealand at a Glance

Tucked away in the southwest corner of the Pacific Ocean, New Zealand is one of the most isolated and least populated countries in the world. It is also a land of contrasts: between the subtropical north and the cool south; the wet west and the drier east; the volcanoes of the central North Island and the mountains of the South Island. Powerful geological forces have created a landscape that is dominated by mountains, hills, lakes and rivers. These, in turn, have allowed New Zealand to become a paradise for nature lovers and outdoor enthusiasts. Sheep and cattle farming still cover large areas of the country, but more and more the accent is on diversity. The more populated north is the centre of Maori and Polynesian culture.

One of the many vineyards in Marlborough *(see pp204–205)*

The Pancake Rocks and blowholes at Punakaiki in Paparoa National Park *(see p234)*

Christ Church Cathedral in the heart of Christchurch *(see p220)*

Lake Wakatipu from the Remarkables *(see p274)*

0 kilometres   100

0 miles   100

MARLBO...
AN...
NEL...
(see pp1...)

CANTERBURY
AND THE
WEST COAST
(see pp216–251)

Christchurch

OTAGO
AND
SOUTHLAND
(see pp252–289)   Dunedin

Larnach Castle, a century-ol... stone mansion *(see p264)*

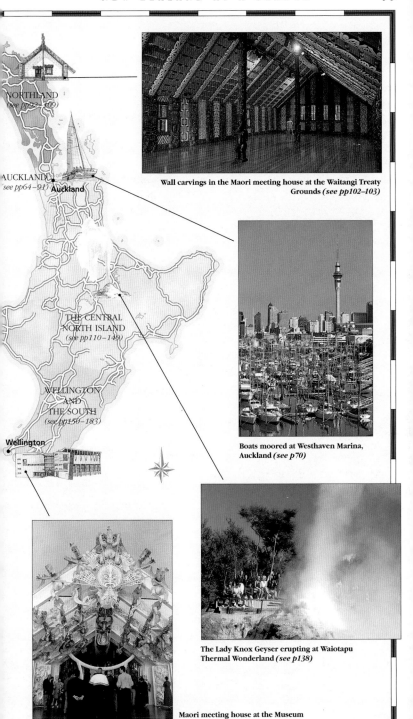

Auckland

Wall carvings in the Maori meeting house at the Waitangi Treaty
Grounds *(see pp102–103)*

Wellington

Boats moored at Westhaven Marina,
Auckland *(see p70)*

The Lady Knox Geyser erupting at Waiotapu
Thermal Wonderland *(see p138)*

Maori meeting house at the Museum
of New Zealand Te Papa Tongarewa
(see pp164–5)

THE NORTH ISLAND

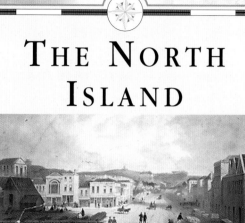

Introducing the North Island

BLESSED WITH A VARIED LANDSCAPE, the North Island also offers a range of climates, from the "winterless" north to the snow-bound mountains of the Central Plateau and the blustery winds of the south. From the tip of Northland down to Taranaki on the west and Hawke's Bay on the east, the sea lends a distinct character to each coast. Although best known for its geothermal wonders around Rotorua and the Volcanic Plateau, the North Island is also a fertile land of lush dairy pastures, highly productive orchards and rolling sheep country. The country's largest city, Auckland, and its capital, Wellington, are both located in the North Island.

Bay of Islands marlin

NORTHLAND
(see pp92–109)

The Bay of Islands *(see pp100–101) is one of New Zealand's most beautiful and historic areas. The warm, sparkling, aquamarine waters, year-round sunshine, sandy beaches and quiet coves make the area a paradise for deep-sea fishing, underwater diving, swimming and sailing.*

Mount Taranaki/Egmont *(see pp180–81), a dormant, snow-capped volcanic peak, is the centrepiece of the agriculturally rich Taranaki region and the dominant feature of Egmont National Park.*

Climber on Mount Taranaki/Egmont

The Parliament buildings *in Wellington (see p156) are interesting for their varied architectural styles. The circular, copper-domed "Beehive", which houses Cabinet offices, is in complete contrast to the square marble Parliament Buildings, home to the House of Representatives.*

The "Beehive"

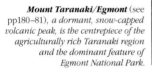

Sky Tower (see p73) is Auckland city's most dominant landmark. From its observation decks, visitors can enjoy 360-degree views of the city centre, its sprawling suburbs, harbours, and the Hauraki Gulf islands.

LOCATOR MAP

0 kilometres   50

0 miles   50

Sky Tower
CKLAND
pp64–91)

The Bath House in Rotorua (see p132), an elegant Tudor-style building situated in the English-style Government Gardens, is the town's most frequently photographed building. Originally constructed as a thermal bath house in 1908, it is now home to the excellent Rotorua Museum of Art and History.

Rotorua Museum exhibit

THE CENTRAL
NORTH ISLAND
(see pp110–149)

Rothmans Building

Napier's Art Deco buildings (see pp144–5), such as the Rothmans Building, were constructed following a devastating earthquake in 1931.

WELLINGTON
AND
THE SOUTH
(see pp150–183)

Martinborough (see p170) is the hub of wine growing in Wairarapa, and its wineries have gained a reputation as producers of red wines. A good way to experience the areas' wineries is to join one of the many vineyard tours that leave from Wellington.

Martinborough vineyard

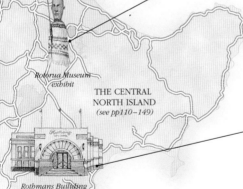

Historic Northland

Samuel Marsden

Between 700 and 1,000 years ago, the first Polynesian voyagers are believed to have come ashore on the northern coasts of the North Island. Northland is also sometimes referred to as "the cradle" of modern New Zealand. It was at Rangihoua in Northland that Samuel Marsden, the first missionary, set up an Anglican mission in 1814; at Waitangi that the Treaty of Waitangi was signed in 1840 *(see pp46–7)*; and at Russell that the nation's first capital was established in 1840 before shifting south. Here, too, were sown the first seeds of Maori rebellion against the British.

Kemp House
This Kerikeri Mission House, completed in 1822, is the oldest building in New Zealand. The house is associated with the Kemp family who lived in it for 142 years (see p104).

Waipoa Bay, Moturoa Island
Captain Cook (in 1769) and French explorer Marion du Fresne (in 1772) took water on board here. Du Fresne buried in the sand a bottle with a document claiming New Zealand for France.

Kauri trees are symbolic of Northland but much of the forest is now gone. Logging was at its height from 1870 to 1910.

Logging on the Hokianga
Charles Heaphy's painting *View of the Kahu-Kahu, Hokianga River* (1839) depicts the logging industry on the Hokianga River. The giant kauri trees made ideal ships' spars as well as timber for new settlements.

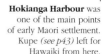

Hokianga Harbour was one of the main points of early Maori settlement. Kupe *(see p43)* left for Hawaiki from here.

Russell, Bay of Islands
This whaling and sealing town was dubbed the "Hell-hole of the Pacific" in the lawless days of the early 1800s (see p100).

Hongi Hika
After Maori chief Hongi Hika met King George IV during a trip to England in 1820, he returned home determined to become king of New Zealand. In the 1820s, he led his Northland tribe, the Ngapuhi, in many conquests of other tribes.

Kauri Gum
Gum from kauri trees, used in paints and polishes, was an important export product from Northland until World War II.

Pohutukawa
The pohutukawa has an important place in Maori mythology. Maoris believe that the spirits of the dead descend down the roots of a pohutukawa tree at Cape Reinga on their way to the homeland on Hawaiki.

Kauri logs being towed to a waiting ship.

Warrior Chieftains
Hone Heke is shown here with his wife, Harriet, and another chieftain, Kawiti. Unhappy with the Treaty of Waitangi, he was one of the first chieftains to rebel against the British.

Pa Site at Ruapekapeka
This pa (fortification) site was one of the most complex ever built. In 1846, British troops stormed it on a Sunday morning, catching the Maoris inside by surprise. They did not expect the British to fight on a day traditionally given to rest and prayer.

Volcanic Heartland

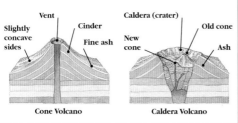

FROM WHITE ISLAND in the northeast of the North Island to Mount Ruapehu in the centre lies the Taupo Volcanic Zone, which also includes Rotorua's geothermal wonders. Here, where the Pacific "ring of fire" begins, the clash of the Pacific Continental Plate and the Indo-Australian Plate has created the conditions for one of the most active volcanic regions in the world *(see p20)*.

Skier on Mount Ruapehu

Beneath the Taupo Volcanic Zone, great slabs of crust are thrust down into the earth's mantle where they melt to form rhyolite magma. Every few thousand years, this magma reaches the surface, resulting in events like the Lake Taupo eruption of AD 186, when pumice was punched 50 km (30 miles) up into the air.

Mount Ruapehu
The North Island's tallest mountain is permanently snow-capped and cloaked by eight glaciers. Eruptions in 1995–6 emptied the crater of its lake and closed the mountain to skiers.

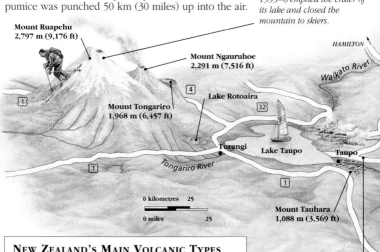

Mount Ruapehu
2,797 m (9,176 ft)

Mount Ngauruhoe
2,291 m (7,516 ft)

HAMILTON

Waikato River

Lake Rotoaira

Mount Tongariro
1,968 m (6,457 ft)

Turangi   Lake Taupo   Taupo

Tongariro River

0 kilometres   25

0 miles   25

Mount Tauhara
1,088 m (3,569 ft)

NEW ZEALAND'S MAIN VOLCANIC TYPES

There are three major types of volcano in New Zealand: volcanic fields, such as Auckland, where each eruption builds a single small volcano at a different place; cone volcanoes, where a succession of eruptions occur close to a vent to form a large cone, which is the volcano itself; and caldera volcanoes, where eruptions are often so large that the ground surface collapses into the hole left behind. The Taupo Volcanic Zone contains three frequently active cone volcanoes (Ruapehu, Ngauruhoe and White Island) and the two most productive caldera in the world (Taupo and Tarawera). Mount Ngauruhoe is the vent for the adjacent Mount Tongariro.

Vent

Slightly concave sides

Cinder

Fine ash

Caldera (crater)

New cone

Old cone

Ash

Cone Volcano

Caldera Volcano

Wairakei Geothermal Power Station
Almost 60 bores tap a vast underground water system, naturally heated by very hot rocks, to produce commercial quantities of steam.

LOCATOR MAP

Pohutu Geyser
One of only 12 geysers in New Zealand, Pohutu Geyser thunders to a height of more than 30 m (98 ft) (see pp136–7).

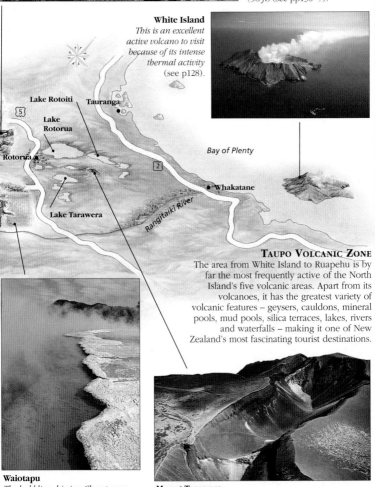

White Island
This is an excellent active volcano to visit because of its intense thermal activity (see p128).

Lake Rotoiti   **Tauranga**

Lake Rotorua

Rotorua

Lake Tarawera

Rangitaiki River

Bay of Plenty

Whakatane

TAUPO VOLCANIC ZONE
The area from White Island to Ruapehu is by far the most frequently active of the North Island's five volcanic areas. Apart from its volcanoes, it has the greatest variety of volcanic features – geysers, cauldons, mineral pools, mud pools, silica terraces, lakes, rivers and waterfalls – making it one of New Zealand's most fascinating tourist destinations.

Waiotapu
The bubbling, hissing Champagne Pool, with its beautiful ochre-coloured petrified edge, is one of the many colourful attractions at Waiotapu (see p138).

Mount Tarawera
In a volcanic explosion in 1886, a 6-km (4-mile) long, 250-m (820-ft) deep chasm was formed and the nearby Pink and White Terraces were buried (see p135).

AUCKLAND

E VERY THIRD NEW ZEALANDER *lives in the Auckland region, and the city, with its 1.06 million inhabitants, continues to expand faster than any other part of the country. Its population has increased by 13 per cent since 1991, almost double the national rate. Auckland is the place to enjoy city life, but quiet beaches and bush tracks are within an hour's drive of the central business district.*

Maoris had settled in the Auckland area as early as 1350. Tribal wars and epidemics brought about the destruction of their settlements, and the area was almost deserted when European settlers arrived in 1840. Because of its central position, good harbour and fine soil, the site was chosen as New Zealand's capital, to replace Russell in the north, after the signing of the Treaty of Waitangi in 1840 *(see pp46–7)*. However, in 1865 the capital moved south to Wellington.

Although Auckland was initially not a prosperous settlement, a gold rush in the region and increased agricultural production in the later part of the 19th century helped to develop it into what it is today – the largest and fastest growing city in New Zealand. The city has become more vibrant since the mid-1990s, due to the trend among many Aucklanders to trade in the traditional suburban villa for an inner-city apartment. Places such as Vulcan Lane, Viaduct Basin, Parnell and Ponsonby have become gathering points with cafés, bistros and up-market restaurants. The retail trade and performing arts have reaped the benefits of this migration.

Auckland is also attractive to New Zealand's Pacific Island neighbours and it now has the largest Polynesian population in the world. With Europeans, Maoris, Polynesians and Asians complementing one another, the city's cultural diversity gives it a very cosmopolitan atmosphere. This is reflected in the variety of ethnic shops and restaurants, and can be observed at the local markets, such as those in Otara and Avondale.

Surfing at Piha, on the coast west of Auckland

◁ **Sky Tower viewed from Waitemata Harbour, Auckland**

Exploring Auckland

ALTHOUGH THE AUCKLAND REGION is spread over more than 1,000 sq km (390 sq miles), many of its inner-city attractions are clustered near the waterfront and around the city's oldest parks. Panoramic views of the city, harbour and outer islands can be enjoyed from a number of extinct volcanic peaks, such as One Tree Hill *(see p82)*, and from the observation decks and revolving restaurant of Sky Tower, the city's most distinctive landmark *(see p73)*. Queen Street, long known as Auckland's "golden mile", is a major entertainment and shopping area, complemented by Parnell and Newmarket on the fringes of the city. Water is an important part of Auckland's magic, and no visit to the city is complete without a trip to Rangitoto or one of the other islands in the Hauraki Gulf *(see pp86–7)*.

Yachts moored at Westhaven Marina, Auckland *(see p70)*

HAMER STREET
JELLICOE STREE
MADDEN STREET
BEAUMONT STREET
PAKENHAM STREET
HALSEY STREET
DALDY STREET
GAUNT STREET
FANSHAWE
VICTORIA PARK
NORTHERN MOTORWAY
VICTORIA STREE
DRAKE STREET
SALE STREET
COOK STRE
UNION STREET
WELLINGTON STREET
BERESFORD ST
HEPBURN STREET
HOWE STREET
WESTERN PARK
PONSONBY ROAD
HOPETOUN STREET
KARANGAHAPE ROA
EDINBURGH
GUNDRY ST
NEWTON ROAD
0 metres 500
0 yards 500

SIGHTS AT A GLANCE

Aotea Square and Aotea Centre 10
Auckland Art Gallery 15
Auckland Domain and Winter Gardens 16
Auckland Harbour Bridge 2
Auckland Town Hall 11
Auckland War Memorial Museum 17
Ferry Building 6
Harrah's Sky City 9
New Zealand National Maritime Museum 5
Old Arts Building and Clock Tower 14
Old Customhouse 8
Old Government House 13
Queen Elizabeth II Square 7
Sky Tower 12
Viaduct Basin 4
Waitemata Harbour 1
Westhaven Marina 3

SEE ALSO

- ***Where to Stay*** pp296–8
- ***Where to Eat*** pp316–18

KEY

- Auckland Street-by-Street, *see pp68–9*
- ⛴ Ferry terminal
- ✈ To Auckland International Airport
- 🚆 Train station
- 🚌 Coach station
- ℹ Tourist information
- [P] Parking
- Park
- ✚ Hospital
- ← One-way street

GETTING AROUND

Auckland's·city centre is compact and most places of interest are within walking distance. Alternatively, visitors can take the Auckland Explorer Bus, which leaves the Ferry Building every 30 minutes from 9am and stops at 14 tourist destinations. The tour includes taped commentary in various languages. For drivers, good motorways and internal roads link the northern, southern and western suburbs, which are also serviced by buses. Regular ferry services take visitors to the islands in the Hauraki Gulf.

Rollerblading along Tamaki Drive *(see p80)*

Street-by-Street: The Waterfront

Maritime Museum sign

Excellent shops, historic buildings, top restaurants and bars, a superb view – Auckland's waterfront has something for everyone. Yet only a few years ago, this area was of little interest to residents and visitors, and the inner city, traditionally reserved for offices, was almost deserted after dark. That trend has been reversed and downtown Auckland is now a hive of activity. New and planned apartments, some on the water's edge and others in garden environments, along with numerous trendy bars and restaurants, have made the waterfront a prime living and entertainment area.

Old Customhouse
Formerly part of the city's financial district, this 1889 building houses a duty-free store (see pp71, 88).

Queen Elizabeth II Square
The international food stalls lining the square make it a popular eating and meeting place (see p71). Another food court is at the nearby Downtown Shopping Centre.

CUSTOMS STREET EAST

QUAY STREET

LOWER ALBERT ST

QUAY STREET

QUEEN'S WHARF

★ Ferry Building
At the Ferry Building, visitors can buy tickets for ferries and harbour cruises or dine at its popular ground-floor restaurant (see p71).

Princes Wharf, the departure point for overseas cruises, also attracts visitors to its restaurants and bars.

Key

— — — Suggested route

WAITEMATA HARBOUR

Boat Services
A variety of harbour cruises and ferry services to Devonport and the Hauraki Gulf islands operate from the back of the Ferry Building.

| 0 metres | 100 |
| 0 yards | 100 |

AMERICA'S CUP

Viaduct Basin was the home base for the yachts that participated in the 1999–2000 America's Cup. New Zealand successfully defended the cup it took off the Young America (USA) team led by Dennis Connor in 1995. In addition to Team New Zealand, there were 11 challenging syndicates from the United States, Australia, Asia and Europe. Their budgets varied from NZ$1 million (Young Australia) to NZ$120 million (Italy's Prada Team). The history of the cup goes back to the 1870s, but the intense emotion surrounding the challenge still remains.

New Zealand's *Black Magic* defeating its Italian challenger in the America's Cup 2000 final

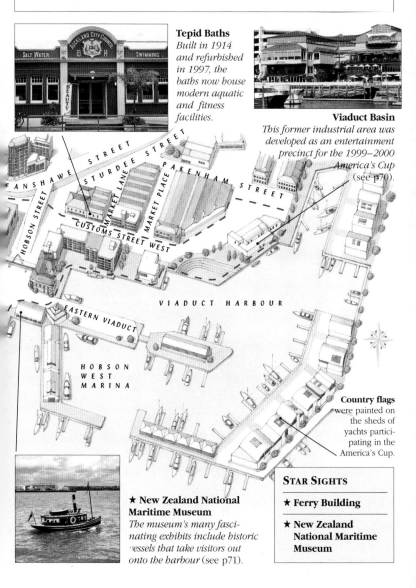

Tepid Baths
Built in 1914 and refurbished in 1997, the baths now house modern aquatic and fitness facilities.

Viaduct Basin
This former industrial area was developed as an entertainment precinct for the 1999–2000 America's Cup (see p70).

STREET
STURDEE STREET
MARKET LANE
MARKET PLACE
PAKENHAM STREET
FANSHAWE
HOBSON STREET
CUSTOMS STREET WEST

VIADUCT HARBOUR

EASTERN VIADUCT

HOBSON WEST MARINA

Country flags were painted on the sheds of yachts participating in the America's Cup.

★ **New Zealand National Maritime Museum**
The museum's many fascinating exhibits include historic vessels that take visitors out onto the harbour (see p71).

STAR SIGHTS

★ **Ferry Building**

★ **New Zealand National Maritime Museum**

A forest of masts at Westhaven Marina, viewed from the Auckland Harbour Bridge

Waitemata Harbour ❶

THIS SPARKLING harbour, with the green volcanic cone of Rangitoto Island in the background, is one of Auckland's most cherished sights. Not only does the harbour add to the city's scenic beauty, it also forms a natural barrier between the central business district and the populous North Shore. Ferries and cruise boats, as well as commercial ships, cross the harbour daily.

Auckland Harbour Bridge ❷

State Hwy 1.

IN THE LATE 19th century, ferries began taking passengers across the water from Auckland City to the north. In 1959, the Auckland

Harbour Bridge was built and ten years later, the 43-m (141-ft) high steel bridge was widened, increasing the number of lanes from four to eight. Peak hour traffic across the 1,020-m (3,350-ft) bridge is slow. Concrete barriers marking the traffic lanes are shifted twice daily by a custom-built machine to accommodate the morning flow into the city and the late afternoon return to the northern suburbs. An electronic traffic light system at both ends of the bridge clearly indicates which lanes are accessible to traffic. Despite the traffic jams, the Harbour Bridge offers some of the best views in the city.

The bridge does not only link two large areas of Auckland; State Highway 1 is also the main arterial route for northbound traffic. Southbound travellers driving across the bridge will notice a forest of masts on their left.

Westhaven Marina ❸

Westhaven Drive.

WESTHAVEN MARINA reflects Aucklanders' passion for yachting. Operating for more than 70 years, it is one of the largest marinas in the southern hemisphere, accommodating 1,950 vessels. Among the facilities are Pier Z (the home of several major charter boat companies), launching ramps for trailer craft and a mast gantry. The premises of prominent yacht clubs are on the northern side of the marina.

Viaduct Basin ❹

Cnr Halsey St and Viaduct Harbour.

LARGELY A LEGACY from the 1999–2000 America's Cup, the Viaduct Basin's up-market apartments, shops and restaurants overlook its mooring facilities. The basin is part of an extensive redevelopment of Auckland's waterfront, following the trend in cities such as Sydney, London and San Francisco. One of the best places to enjoy the precinct's vibrant atmosphere is Kermadec, a fish restaurant with a strong Pacific theme (see p318). The Loaded Hog is another popular meeting place for locals and visitors.

Café at Viaduct Basin

New Zealand National Maritime Museum **5**

Cnr Quay & Hobson sts. **(** *(09) 373 0800.* **○** *daily.* **●** *25 Dec.* 🎟️ **♿** 🚻 🍴 🛍️ 📷 **w** *www.saltysam.com.*

BOATS HAVE PLAYED a pivotal role in New Zealand's history, from those of the early Polynesian navigators who steered their canoes towards the country *(see pp44–5)*, to the whalers who made Russell *(see p100)* the centre of the whaling industry in the 1840s, and the thousands of immigrants who arrived in the 20th century. These aspects of the country's maritime past are highlighted in the museum. In Maori, the museum is called Te Huiteananui-a-Tangaroa, "the legendary house belonging to Tangaroa", god of the sea.

Even those with a limited interest in boats will enjoy the innovative exhibition galleries. One room is fitted out as a ship's interior, complete with a gently swaying floor and appropriate creaking noises. Several of the historic vessels berthed outside the museum take visitors for harbour trips.

Shore whaling exhibit at the National Maritime Museum

Ferry Building **6**

Quay St. 🚢 **○** *daily.* 🍴 🛍️

THIS 1912 Edwardian baroque building is the focal point for commuter ferries. A ten-minute ferry ride to Devonport leaves here, as do boats to Waiheke Island *(see p86)*. Designed by Alex Wiseman, the building is

The Ferry Building, a gateway to the harbour

made of sandstone and brick, with a base of Coromandel granite. Not just a transport centre, it is also known for Cin Cin on Quay *(see p318)*, a brasserie overlooking the harbour where well-heeled Aucklanders meet to dine.

Queen Elizabeth II Square **7**

Queen St.

THIS SQUARE, featuring a Japanese wind tree sculpture, links Queen Street to the waterfront. In summer, the square is a favourite place for buskers, tourists and inner-city office workers. Foodstalls sell ethnic snacks, and the City Council occasionally organizes special events.

Old Customhouse **8**

Cnr Albert & Customs sts. **(** *0800 388 937.* **○** *daily.* 🛍️

THE OLD Customhouse replaces a building that was burned down in the 1880s. Designed by Thomas Mahoney, the 1889 French Renaissance-style building is said to have been modelled on the present Selfridge's store in Oxford Street, London. It features intricate plasterwork and kauri joinery.

The building formerly housed the Customs Department, Audit Inspector, Sheep Inspector and Native Land Court. It is now home to the city's largest duty-free shop *(see p88)*.

CITY OF SAILS

Auckland is purported to have the greatest number of pleasure boats per capita of any city in the world. The city's temperate climate also means that, on average, these are used more intensively than boats in Europe or on the east coast of America. Yachting has been a popular pastime in Auckland since the 1870s, when the first sailing regattas were held on Waitemata Harbour. Safe harbours and the nearby scenic islands make sailing attractive to overseas visitors as well. Charter company charges depend on the size of the yacht, the time of the year and whether a skipper is hired. The highlight of the nautical year is the Auckland Anniversary Regatta *(see p39).*

Yacht racing on Waitemata Harbour

Casino in Harrah's Sky City

Harrah's Sky City **❾**

Cnr Victoria & Federal sts. **☎** *0800 759 2489.* ◯ *daily.* ♿ **🍴** ☐ ▣

PUNTERS REGULARLY win luxury cars at Harrah's Sky City, New Zealand's biggest casino. On level two, there are over 1,000 slot machines that dispense prizes of more than NZ$250,000. Traditional casino games, such as Caribbean stud poker, craps, blackjack, baccarat and roulette, are available on the same floor. Chinese favourites include *tai sai*, played with three dice in a clear glass dome, and *pai gow*, played with 32 domino pieces. There are 12 gaming tables and two gaming machines in the Members Club, open to guests by invitation only. For those with no experience or for gamblers who want to brush up on their skills, the casino provides free lessons.

Entertainment at Sky City is not limited to gaming. The complex is best known for the Sky Tower, the country's tallest structure *(see p73)*. There is also a hotel with 306 rooms and 38 suites. Its central location and rooms with good harbour views make it popular with visitors. In addition, there are four restaurants and five bars. The menu at Tamarind, the signature restaurant, places strong emphasis on local food, such as Nelson oysters, Waikanae crab and Waikato beef eye fillet. The complex also has conference facilities and a 700-seat auditorium-style theatre for staging local and international events.

Aotea Square and Aotea Centre **❿**

Queen St. **☎** *(09) 979 2333.*

IN THE LATE 1980s, several New Zealand souvenir shops stocked a postcard that was entirely black except for a small heading, "Night Life in New Zealand". Things have since changed. Built in 1990, the Aotea Centre, was designed by New Zealand architect Ewen Wainscott and is a hub of vibrant nightlife. On

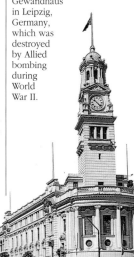

Sculpture at Aotea Square

its opening night, the centre featured New Zealand-born Dame Kiri Te Kanawa, the world-renowned opera singer. It is a venue for dance, opera, classical music, theatre and shows. It is also used for festivals, such as the World of Music Arts and Dance and the WOMAD Pacific.

Aotea Square, in front of the centre, is popular with skateboarders. The wooden *waharoa* (gateway) at its entrance was created by Maori artist Selwyn Muru. The square is flanked on one side by the Force Entertainment Centre, which includes a 460-seat Imax (widescreen) Cinema *(see p91)*, a games centre, cafés and shops. The Auckland Town Hall is on the other side of the square.

Collectively, the locations bordering Aotea Square – the Town Hall, Aotea Centre and Force Entertainment Centre – are known as The Edge.

Auckland Town Hall **⓫**

Queen St. **☎** *(09) 309 2677.* ◯ *Mon–Fri.* ● *public hols.* ♿

THE WEDGE-SHAPED Edwardian Town Hall, built in 1911, is Auckland's prime historic building. It has been used extensively as an administrative and political centre, as well as a cultural venue. During work to restore it to its original design, the building was gutted of non-original materials and strengthened structurally.

The Concert Chamber, Council Chamber and main street foyer were meticulously restored, a process which included using vintage glass to reconstruct windows that had disappeared over the years. The Great Hall, an excellent concert facility, is a replica of the Neues Gewandhaus in Leipzig, Germany, which was destroyed by Allied bombing during World War II.

Auckland Town Hall

Sky Tower ⑫

OPENED IN AUGUST 1997, Auckland's 328-m (1,076-ft) Sky Tower, a splendid tourist, broadcasting and telecommunications facility, has taken over from Sydney's AMP Tower as the tallest building in the southern hemisphere. The tower, which is part of Harrah's Sky City, is visited by almost one million people a year. From its four observation levels, visitors are able to see about 82 km (50 miles) into the distance.

VISITORS' CHECKLIST

Cnr Victoria & Federal sts. ☎
0800 759 2489. ☐ 8:30am till
late daily. 🌐 🚻 🍴 🛍 🏧
W www.skycity.co.nz

The **93-m (305-ft)** high spire weighs 150 tonnes and is the main telecommunications and broadcasting mast in the region.

The **sky deck** offers 360-degree views through seamless glass, and is the country's highest public viewing area.

The **outdoor observation level** features high-powered binoculars that offer a close-up view of Auckland and its surrounding areas.

Orbit, Sky Tower's revolving restaurant, makes a full revolution every 60 minutes.

Observation Levels
Visitors enjoy fantastic views of the city of Auckland and its environs from the tower's indoor and outdoor observation levels.

The **floors** above and below the centre pod house telecommunications facilities.

The **main observation level** offers free multilingual audio guides, live weather forecasts and touch-screen computers.

The **lower observation level** contains the Sky Stop Café and Bar.

The **structure** of the tower has been designed to withstand winds gusting to 200 km/h (125 mph) and earthquakes measuring 7.0 on the Richter Scale.

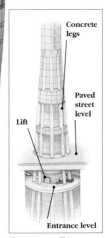

Concrete legs

Paved street level

Lift

Entrance level

Entrance to Tower
Entry to Sky Tower's lifts is through an underground gallery.

The Sky Tower at Night
The Sky Tower is an even more visible landmark at night. Over Christmas, it is lit in different colours that make its observation pod resemble a flying saucer.

Old Government House, New Zealand's first wooden mansion

Old Government House **⓭**

Cnr Waterloo Quadrant and Princes St. *Closed to public.*

THE CLASSICAL Old Government House was the seat of government until 1865 when the capital was moved to Wellington. It was also the residence of New Zealand's governor-general until 1969. Royalty used to stay here, and Queen Elizabeth II broadcast her Christmas speech from upstairs in 1953. It is now a part of the University of Auckland, housing the staff common room, council reception suite and apartments for visiting academics.

Located within walking distance of the central business district, Old Government House, designed by William Mason and completed in 1856, appears to be made of stone. Like its British prefabricated predecessor, however, it is built from wood. A big coral tree and a Norfolk pine at the southern edge of the lawn are said to have been planted by Sir George Grey during his second term as governor from 1861 to 1867.

Old Arts Building and Clock Tower **⓮**

Princes St. *Closed to public.*

ALSO PART OF the university buildings, the Old Arts Building and Clock Tower face Albert Park, a summer gathering place for students. Designed by Chicago-trained architect R A Lippincott, it was completed in 1926. Lippincott's brother-in-law, Walter Burley Griffin, was the designer of Canberra in Australia. The clock tower that crowns the building was inspired by the Tom Tower of Christ Church in Oxford, England, and has come to symbolize the university. The building's octagonal interior is vaulted and galleried with a mosaic floor and piers. A major reconstruction was undertaken between 1985 and 1988, which won an Institute of Architects award.

From the rear of the Old Arts Building, the Barracks Wall runs for 85 m (280 ft) to the back of the Old Choral Hall. Built in 1847, it is the only remnant of the wall which enclosed an area, including Albert Park, where British troops were stationed until 1870. The basalt stone wall was quarried from the slope of Mount Eden, now known as Eden Garden.

University of Auckland's Old Arts Building and Clock Tower

Auckland Art Gallery **⓯**

Cnr Wellesley & Kitchener sts.
📞 *(09) 307 7700.* ⭘ *daily.*
🌑 *public hols.* 🎟 *some exhibits.*
♿ 🛍 🍴 🖥 📷

VISITORS INTERESTED in art should add the Auckland Art Gallery to their itinerary. Designing the 1887 French Renaissance-style building must have been a challenge to the architectural firm of Grainger and D'Ebro, as it occupies a rising corner site. The gallery originally housed civic offices and the public library, but today it is solely a gallery, mainly devoted to showcasing the development of New Zealand art.

Entrance to the New Gallery, Auckland Art Gallery

The collection of around 11,500 works includes international as well as national art. The gallery also organizes exhibitions on a regular basis. The New Zealand collection contains works from many of the nation's most prominent artists, including Frances Hodgkins, Colin McCahon and Ralph Hotere. The Mackelvie Collection, named after a self-made man who lived in Auckland between 1865 and 1871, is mainly of non-New Zealand paintings, as is the Grey Collection.

The New Gallery, almost next door to the Auckland Art Gallery, was a former telephone exchange. Refurbished by architect David Mitchell, it adds 30 per cent more space to the existing gallery and focuses on contemporary art. Wedged between these two is the commercially run Gow Langsford Gallery.

Auckland Domain and Winter Gardens ⑯

The Domain. 📞 (09) 306 7067. ◯ daily. ● Easter Sun, 25 April, 25 Dec. 🖼 ♿ 💳 🚻 🛈

The Sky City Starlight Symphony playing at the Auckland Domain

CENTRAL AUCKLAND has been built around a number of extinct volcanoes, including 14 volcanic cones, many of which are now parks. The oldest park is the Auckland Domain, situated within walking distance of both the city centre and the Parnell area. Tuff rings created by volcanic activity thousands of years ago can still be seen in its contours.

Land for the city's 1.35-sq-km (0.50-sq-mile) park was set aside in 1840, in the early years of European settlement. In 1940, a carved Maori memorial palisade was installed around a totara tree on Pukekaroa knoll. This enclosure commemorates Maori leader Potatu Te Whero Whero, who made peace with the neighbouring tribes on the site a hundred years earlier.

Nearby is a sports field where the tuff rings form a natural amphitheatre. The field is used for free outdoor concerts over the summer that attract large crowds.

The large, shady Auckland Domain is also a popular place with walkers and picnickers. Several of the large trees in the park were seedlings from a nursery set up in 1841 to grow and distribute European plants and trees. The formal gardens feature many sculptures. The best known are the three bronze sculptures in the free-form pond. The central, male figure represents Auckland and the two females represent wisdom and fertility of the soil.

Statue at the Winter Gardens

The Winter Gardens, a legacy from the Auckland Exhibition of 1913, consist of two glasshouses joined by a courtyard that contains a large water lily and lotus pool. The dome-roofed areas contain a wide variety of plants. In recent years, a scoria quarry behind the Winter Gardens has been converted into a fernery. Ferns are a dominant feature of the New Zealand landscape and there are more than 100 varieties in the fernery. The gardens are a popular venue for wedding and other photography.

The Domain's best-known structure is the Auckland War Memorial Museum (see pp76–7). Made of reinforced concrete and faced with Portland stone, the museum has bronze detailing. The façade contains plaques that list the battles of World War I, while at the rear of the building, added by R F and M K Draffin in 1960, there are lists of World War II battles.

One of the two glasshouses at the Winter Gardens

Auckland War Memorial Museum ⑰

Museum cenotaph

BUILT IN 1929 to commemorate the end of World War I, in which 16,697 New Zealanders died, the museum's Neo-Classical façade evokes the Greek temples that many servicemen saw from the decks of warships in the Mediterranean. The design of the cenotaph in front of the museum is based on newsreel footage, shown at the beginning of movies in the 1920s, of the tomb of the unknown soldier in London. Besides providing visitors with an introduction to New Zealand's history, people and landscape, the museum also contains a renowned collection of Maori treasures and Pacific artifacts and holds Maori cultural performances.

Aerial view of the museum located in the Auckland Domain

Museum Lobby
The lobby features tall columns reminiscent of the Parthenon in Greece. Light filters through the stained-glass ceiling above the lobby.

"Origins" features the bones of extinct animals, such as dinosaurs and moa, many of which were discovered in caves around the country.

Garden

Ground floor

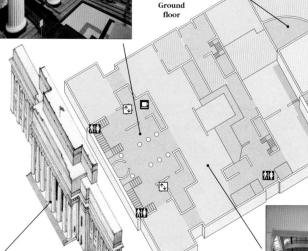

The museum entrance evokes the temples of Greece.

STAR EXHIBITS

★ Maori Treasures

★ World War I Sanctuary

★ Maori Treasures
This gallery showcases a superb collection of Maori artifacts, such as the waka *(canoe) in the foreground and a traditional carved meeting house.*

Discovery Centres
The two Discovery Centres, "Weird and Wonderful" and "Treasures and Tales", are colourful, interactive areas where children can learn about anything from whale skeletons to computers.

VISITORS' CHECKLIST

The Domain. 🔔 0800 256 873.
🚌 Explorer bus, Satellite Link
bus. ⏱ 10am–5pm daily. ● 25
Dec. 💷 donation (none for war
memorials); Maori cultural show.
♿ 🛗 📷 🚻 🏪
🌐 www.akmuseum.org.nz

Level 2

Library

MUSEUM GUIDE
The museum's collection is housed on three levels. The ground level is dedicated to the people of New Zealand, both of Maori and European descent, and the Pacific region. The first level provides information on the land, while the top level focuses on New Zealand at war and how these experiences have forged the country's identity.

"Scars on the Heart" contains exhibits depicting the two world wars, including a re-creation of a World War I front trench.

Level 1

Spitfire Gallery
This area features early fighter planes. A high percentage of Royal Air Force pilots during World War II came from New Zealand, including its Supreme Commander, Keith Park.

"Oceans" helps visitors discover marine life with a rock pool and replicas of a beach and the Poor Knights Islands marine reserve.

KEY TO FLOORPLAN

▦	Adminstration
▦	City
▦	Discovery centres
▦	Library
▦	Maori and Pacific
▦	Natural history
▦	Other exhibits
▦	Special exhibition halls
▦	War exhibits

★ World War I Sanctuary
The stained-glass ceiling above the entrance lobby shows the coat of arms of all British dominions and colonies during World War I. On the balcony are badges of the units, regiments and corps in which New Zealanders served.

Auckland's central business district and suburbs ▷

Further Afield

B EYOND AUCKLAND'S CITY CENTRE, visitors are offered
a range of places to visit and a variety of things to
do. Harbours, beaches and islands are prime attractions, not only for their superb scenic views but also for
sea sports, such as kayaking, surfing and sailing. The
city is well known for its beautiful parks and gardens
which provide peaceful retreats; some offer visitors a
chance to walk through bush and wilderness. Families
with young children will find Kelly Tarlton's Underwater World and Antarctic Encounter, Rainbow's End
Adventure Park and the Auckland Zoological Gardens
enjoyable. Across the harbour, Devonport makes for a
pleasant outing for the day, with its many restaurants
and art and crafts shops.

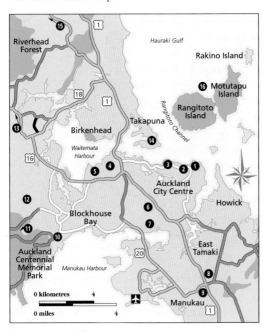

A view of Auckland City from
Tamaki Drive

Tamaki Drive ❶

T AMAKI DRIVE, east of the
city, shows Auckland at
its best. The road crosses
Hobson Bay and closely
follows the water's edge past
Okahu Bay, Mission Bay and
St Heliers Bay. The views
across Waitemata Harbour
towards Rangitoto Island and
Devonport are stunning.

Many of the city's most
prestigious homes are located
on Tamaki Drive, or just off it,
and many tourist buses make
a small detour to go through
nearby Paritai Drive, the
most expensive real estate
in Auckland. Small, fine
sandy beaches, such as the
one at Mission Bay, are a
major attraction along Tamaki
Drive. These beaches serve
as a base for family outings,
swimmers and sunbathers.

Mission Bay got its name
from Mission House when
the area was developed in
the 1920s. Built in 1859, the
house was part of Bishop
Selwyn's Melanesian Mission
School. When the school was
transferred to Norfolk Island
in 1867, the house was used
for different purposes. It is
now an up-market restaurant.

SIGHTS AT A GLANCE

KEY

   Auckland city

   Park, forest or reserve

   Motorway

   State highway

   Other roads

   Auckland International Airport

Cyclists enjoying the sun on
Tamaki Drive

Rangitoto Island dominates Auckland's harbour horizon

Tamaki Drive ends at the St Heliers Shopping Centre. Instead of turning right into St Heliers Bay Road, it is worthwhile to continue along Cliff Road, leading to Ladies Bay. The viewing platform at the top of the cliff offers a superb panorama of the Hauraki Gulf. Directly below the platform, but far enough from viewers not to be intrusive, is one of New Zealand's few nudist beaches. At other beaches along Tamaki Drive, nudity is prohibited.

Learning to windsurf

Savage Memorial Park ❷

LOCATED OFF Tamaki Drive, the Savage Memorial Park was named after one of New Zealand's prime ministers, Michael Joseph Savage (1871–1940), of the Labour Party. The gardens, which have formal arrangements, also contain concrete fortifications that date from World War II.

The area occupied by the gardens was originally a historic Maori *pa*, and its shoreline was renowned for

its plentiful supply of mussels. Originally named Tokapur-ewha, Maori for "mussel rocks", the area has since been renamed Bastion Point.

It is best known for a Maori protest staged in 1979 after the government had razed a local Maori village to develop Bastion Point as a prime residential zone. A 506-day occupation was organized to protest against the appropriation of the site, followed by ten years of litigation. In 1990, the land was finally returned to the Ngati Whatua tribe. The nearby 900-sq-m (9,690-sq-ft) Orakei Marae is the tribe's meeting house. Smaller ones can be found around the Kaipara Harbour and at Helensville, on the North Shore.

Riding through the Plexiglas tube at Kelly Tarlton's Underwater World

Kelly Tarlton's Underwater World and Antarctic Encounter ❸

23 Tamaki Drive. (09) 528 0603. Downtown Centre, 74, 75, 76. daily. 25 Dec. no flash. Antarctic Encounter.

TAMAKI DRIVE's best-known tourist attraction is Kelly Tarlton's Underwater World and Antarctic Encounter. Visitors ride on a moving walkway through a Plexiglas tunnel inside a tank, with fish swimming around the sides. The tunnel winds past two marine aquariums, one devoted to reef fish and the other to sharks and stingrays. The Antarctic Encounter features a replica of the Cape Evans 1910 hut of South Pole explorer Robert F Scott (1868–1912), complete with ice and winds. A highlight is a ride in a heated Snow Cat through a typical subantarctic landscape, past a penguin colony, and under the ice to a subantarctic aquarium.

Museum of Transport and Technology ❹

Great North Rd, Western Springs. Customs St, 45. (09) 846 0199. daily. 25 Dec.

Early aircraft at the Museum of Transport and Technology

THE MUSEUM of Transport and Technology (MOTAT) has a collection of about 300,000 items, 20 per cent of which can be seen in various buildings and halls on two sites within walking distance of the Auckland Zoological Gardens. Exhibits vary from dental equipment and under-wear to 19th-century houses.

The focal point is a collection of 30 rare and historic aircraft. These include home-made planes by New Zealander Richard Pearse, believed by many New Zealanders to have preceded the Wright brothers in being the first person to fly (*see p246*). Also of interest is the Solent flying boat ZK-AMO *Aranui*, a luxurious aircraft that flew around the South Pacific from 1949 until 1960. An electric tram runs approximately every 20 minutes from the entrance of MOTAT to the zoo gates.

Corrugated iron elephant at the zoo

Auckland Zoological Gardens ❺

Motions Rd, Western Springs. Customs St, 45. (09) 360 3800. daily. 25 Dec.

NEW ZEALAND'S isolated geographical position means that its fauna has developed differently from that of most countries. A lack of predators, for example, has resulted in many flightless birds. With the exception of bats, there are no native mammals. There is no better place to learn about the country's varied and unusual wildlife than at Auckland Zoo. The zoo houses saddlebacks, tuis, kakas and kakarikis, besides the nocturnal kiwis.

The zoo's population, which is not limited to native animals, is presented in natural settings. Primates such as squirrel monkeys and macaques can be seen at close range in a rainforest. Zebras and giraffes roam on an African savanna with Zulu huts and interconnected habitats. A wetlands environ-ment features baboons as well as hippopotamuses.

One Tree Hill ❻

Manukau Rd.

ONE TREE HILL, a dormant volcanic cone and once the site of the largest pre-historic Maori settlement in the region, was named after the solitary tree which was

One Tree Hill, formerly the site of a large Maori fortification

planted on its summit in 1640. Since then, a succession of single trees on the summit have been attacked by protesters wanting to draw attention to various issues. The last, a Monterey pine, was removed in October 2000 by city council workers as it was unstable. Its most famous predecessor was a native totara tree, cut down in 1852 by a party of workmen angry at the non-arrival of rations.

Surrounding the hill is Cornwall Park, named after the Duke and Duchess of Cornwall, and donated to the city by Sir John Campbell during their royal tour in 1901.

Acacia Cottage, Auckland's oldest wooden home, was built in 1841 by Sir John Campbell. It was relocated in 1920 from Shortland Street to Cornwall Park, where Sir John once had a farm.

Acacia Cottage, in Cornwall Park

At the base of the park, near the entrance, is the **Auckland Observatory**. It has telescopes for viewing the stars, and aspects of space and astronomy are shown at the Stardome Planetarium.

🏚 **Acacia Cottage**
Cornwall Park. ⬜ Mon–Fri.
🌑 public hols.
🏛 **Auckland Observatory**
One Tree Hill Domain. 📞 (09) 624 1246. ⬜ daily. 🎦 ♿ ✉
Stardome and telescopes. 📷

Highwic ❼

40 Gillies Ave, Epsom. 🚌 Link bus.
📞 (09) 524 5729. ⬜ Wed–Sun.
🌑 Good Fri, 25 Dec. 🎦

Built in 1862, Highwic was the home of Alfred Buckland, a stock and station owner. The house was built in stages, with the front part

Water ride at Rainbow's End Adventure Park

showing more detail than the rest. The house, with its elaborate decoration and diamond pane windows, is an example of Carpenter Gothic Revival architecture. The extensive landscaped gardens are also worth a visit.

Auckland Regional Botanic Gardens ❽

Hill Rd, Manukau City. 📞 (09) 303 1530. ⬜ daily. ♿ 🎦 ✉

These gardens, which sprawl over 640 sq km (250 sq miles), contain more than 10,000 species of New Zealand native and introduced plants, as well as a comprehensive collection of ornamental plants. They have been established to help people with selections of plants for their own gardens. Guided tours are held on the first Sunday of every month.

Rainbow's End Adventure Park ❾

Cnr Great South & Wiri Station rds, Manukau City. 🚌 Central Auckland, 47. 📞 (09) 262 2030. ⬜ daily. 🌑 25 Dec. 🎦 ♿ 🍴 ✉ 📷

Lots of rides and entertainment are available at this large amusement park. The most popular attraction is a roller coaster that takes people up more than 30 m (98 ft) in the air, hurls them down through a complete loop, round a corner and through a double corkscrew. Among the other attractions are the Motion Master Virtual Theatre, featuring dinosaurs, an enchanted forest ride, a minigolf course, family go-karts, water rides and the Goldrush, that takes visitors on a thrilling ride through an abandoned gold mine in a runaway mining cart.

SIR JOHN LOGAN CAMPBELL

Sir John Logan Campbell (1817–1912) was one of New Zealand's pioneering entrepreneurs. On 21 December 1840, he set up a tent at the bottom of Shortland Street that served as Auckland's first shop. When he died at the age of 95, he was the city's most prominent businessman. Apart from trading and farming, he was involved in shipping, brewing, timber, the export of kauri gum, flax and manganese, newspaper publishing and banking. He was also a member of New Zealand's parliament, captain of the militia, and a founding member of the Mechanics Institute and the Northern Club. Today, "the father of Auckland" is best remembered for donating his farm, Cornwall Park (see p83), to the city.

**Totem pole at the entrance to the
Arataki Visitors Centre**

Titirangi ⑩

Road map E2. 🏛 *3,400*. 🚌

SITUATED TO THE west of
Auckland city, the small
settlement of Titirangi offers
superb views of the Waitakere
Ranges and the 390-sq-km
(150-sq-mile) Manukau Harbour to the south. The village,
which is home to a number
of artists and writers, has a
reputation for being trendy.
Its main street is lined with
cafés and restaurants. The
main landmark is the Spanish-
style Lopdell House, opened
in 1930, which houses an art
gallery, small theatre and
restaurant. The square in front
of the nearby library is transformed into an art and crafts
market on the last Sunday of
the month from 9am to 12pm.

Titirangi is the gateway
to the Auckland Centennial
Memorial Park in the Wai-
takere Ranges. Formed by
volcanic action about 1.7
million years ago, the park
has about 250 km (155 miles)
of walking tracks, suitable for
people of all levels of fitness.
It attracts over two million
visitors a year.

The **Arataki Visitors
Centre**, 5 km (3 miles)
beyond Titirangi, has well-
organized displays on the
area's logging history and
attractions, and also stocks
detailed maps of the ranges,
books, audio tapes and posters. Large timber decks
around the building allow
good views of the harbour.
Across the road from the
centre is the Arataki Nature
Trail, a self-guided walk.

🏠 **Arataki Visitors Centre**
Scenic Drive. 📞 *(09) 817 8470.*
🕐 *daily.*

Piha ⑪

Road map E2. 🏛 *2,500*. 🚌

PRIZED BY LOCALS but not
well known to tourists,
Auckland's rugged, wind-
swept west coast beaches are
within easy reach of Auckland
and are well worth visiting.
Because they are exposed to
the Tasman Sea, however,
swimmers and surfers need to
exercise care as the currents
can be treacherous and conditions often change rapidly.

Piha is the most popular of
the beaches because of its
heavy surf. It is also the most
gentrified. Here,
many "baches",
New Zealand's
traditional ram-
shackle holiday
homes, have made
way for architect
designed mansions.
The Piha Surf Life
Saving Club serves as
a community centre
over the summer.

ENVIRONS: The bleakest, yet
perhaps grandest, stretch of
coast is at **Whatipu**, south of
Piha at the entrance to the
Manukau Harbour. A sand bar
visible from the beach partly

blocks the harbour. It was
here that the HMS *Orpheus*
was shipwrecked on 7 February 1863. Of the 259 officers
and crew of the 1,727-tonne
corvette, only 70 survived
the disaster.

Just south of Piha, **Karekare** has several idyllic picnic
spots and a swimming hole
at the base of a waterfall. Its
beach achieved some fame as
the location for the award-
winning film *The Piano*.

To the north of Piha is
Bethells Beach, inhabited by
Maoris for several centuries;
some 75 sites have been
recorded here by archaeologists. Ihumoana Island, just
off the beach, is the area's
best-preserved island *pa*.
Although not as spectacular
as Cape Kidnappers (*see
p147*), a headland at
Muriwai Beach, be-
yond Bethells, is
home to a colony
of around 2,000
Australasian gannets,
which originally
nested on offshore Motutara
Island. Barriers and viewing
platforms allow visitors to
observe the birds without
disturbing them. The best
time to see the gannets is
between July and December.

**Gannet at
Muriwai**

View of Piha from the parking lot at the top of the road

Henderson ⑫

Road map E2. 🏃 *4,600.* 🚌

THE VINEYARDS AT Henderson, an hour's drive from Auckland city, have become a popular weekend destination for Aucklanders and visitors alike. Many of the wineries sell food, ranging from a snack to a complete meal, and offer free wine tastings.

Family-owned Babich Wines has a picnic and *pétanque* area overlooking its vineyards. The winery has a reputation for award-winning vintages, such as Babich Patriarch, but also produces

Outdoor eating area at Babich Wines in Henderson

inexpensive wines. New Zealand's second largest winery, Corbans Wine, established by Lebanese immigrants in 1902, is another popular destination, as is Montana Wines, which produces more than 150 varieties – half of the country's total output. Its Deutz Marlborough Cuvée, made under an arrangement with Champagne Deutz, won the 1998 Sparkling Wine of the Year award at the International Wine Challenge in London. Soljans Estate Winery features a pleasant picnic area and offers visitors tours. Its premium varieties include Chardonnay. Visitors can obtain details of Henderson's vineyards at the Auckland visitor centre.

Kumeu ⑬

Road map E2. 🏃 *1,800.* 🚌

ANOTHER POPULAR weekend pursuit of Aucklanders is lunch at a vineyard restaurant followed by shopping for fresh fruit and vegetables from a roadside stall on the way home. At Kumeu, a wine

Locally grown fruit and vegetables for sale at Kumeu

as well as fruit growing district, where a high percentage of the people involved in the wineries and orchards are from Yugoslavia, visitors are spoilt for choice.

Kumeu River Wines should be included in every wine safari. Specializing in regionally grown grapes, Kumeu River's Chardonnay has made the top 100 Wines of the World list of the United States *Wine Spectator* magazine five times. The House of Nobilo, with 4,000 tonnes of grapes crushed in 1998, is the country's fourth largest winery. It also sells wines from Selaks Wines, which it purchased in 1998.

Matua Valley Wines produces a broad range of good quality wines, has pleasant grounds with picnic facilities, and boasts the top winery restaurant in Auckland, the Hunting Lodge (see p318).

FILM MAKING IN NEW ZEALAND

New Zealand's coastal scenery has not escaped the notice of location finders in the movie industry. The beach scenes in Jane Campion's *The Piano*, winner of the 1994 Palme d'Or at Cannes and Oscars for Best Original Screenplay and Best Supporting Actress, were shot at Karekare. Bethells Beach features in *Xena: Warrior Princess* and *Hercules: The Legendary Journeys*. Numerous television series, such as *Black Beauty*, movies and commercials have also been filmed along the New Zealand coast. International interest has spawned a burgeoning domestic film industry. Over 120 feature films have been produced in the country since 1940. Lee Tamahori's *Once Were Warriors* was released in 1994 in cinemas around the world. Local director Peter Jackson's *Lord of The Rings* trilogy, the first part being shot in 1999–2000, is set to eclipse all previous New Zealand motion pictures in terms of scale and budget.

Shooting a film on a New Zealand beach

Well-preserved Victorian buildings on Devonport's waterfront

Devonport ⓮

Road map E2.  17,500. 🚗 🚢

AUCKLANDERS OFTEN think of their city's southern and western (except Titirangi) quadrants as underprivileged, while the eastern and northern quadrants are seen as affluent. Although oversimplified, this picture is not completely inaccurate. The North Shore, the suburban area north of the Harbour Bridge, is relatively wealthy and blessed with a string of beaches that also function as launching pads for sailing boats and dinghies.

Devonport is a ten-minute ferry ride from Auckland's Ferry Building (see p71). It is the only North Shore suburb with a distinctly historical flavour. With many of its villas found along the waterfront, a stroll along King Edward Parade provides an impression of the suburb's Victorian architecture, as well as views of Auckland's central business district across Waitemata Harbour. From Victoria Wharf, where the ferries arrive, it is a five-minute walk to the cafés, restaurants and book shops of Victoria Road. Mount Victoria and North Head, both extinct volcanoes, are accessible by car and offer good views.

Devonport has a long military history. Its association with the Royal New Zealand Navy dates back to 1841 and there are approximately 2,200 staff currently stationed at the local base. Devonport's naval heritage can be viewed at the **Navy Museum** which houses a collection of photographs, uniforms, weapons and other related memorabilia.

Further north, **Takapuna** has its own popular beach. Brasserie-style restaurants, cafés and shops are found along Hurstmere Road.

🏛 Navy Museum
Spring St. 📞 (09) 445 5186.
🕐 daily. 🌑 public hols. 🈚
donation. 📷 on request. 📷

Orewa ⓯

Road map E2. 🏘 (including Hibiscus Coast) 28,000. 🚗 ℹ 214A Hibiscus Coast Hwy, (09) 426 0076.

BEACH HOUSES and motels line the main road through this small seaside town, 40 minutes' drive north of Auckland. Orewa's main attraction is its beach, a 3-km (2-mile) long stretch of sand. The beach is suitable for swimming, surfing and boating. Easterly winds from the sea also attract windsurfers.

ENVIRONS: Just north of Orewa, a small road off State Highway 1 leads to **Puhoi**, New Zealand's earliest Bohemian settlement. A tiny calvary shrine beside the road leading to the settlement is a reminder of the settlers' background. The local pub also doubles as a museum of the pioneers of the area. The nearby Church of St Peter and St Paul, built in 1881, features a Bohemian painting.

About 48 km (30 miles) north of Auckland, Waiwera is best known for its thermal resort, **Waiwera Hot Pools**. The popular complex has 26 indoor and outdoor pools of varying temperatures, private spas, water slides and picnic areas. The natural springs deliver up to 1 million litres (0.2 million gallons) of water per day.

🈚 Waiwera Hot Pools
State Hwy 1. 📞 0800 924 937.
🕐 daily. 🌑 🍴 📷 📷

Hauraki Gulf Islands ⓰

Road map E2. 🚢 ℹ Department of Conservation, Ferry Building, Quay St, Auckland, (09) 379 6476.

THE HAURAKI GULF ISLANDS are among the most beautiful in the world. Some of the 65 islands are popular spots for recreational activities. Others, with their rare bird sanctuaries and unspoiled stands of native trees and plants, are protected for conservation. Three of the islands in the gulf – Waiheke, Great Barrier and Kawau – are maritime suburbs with permanent communities and facilities.

The beach at Orewa, popular with swimmers and windsurfers

Sir George Grey's historic home, Mansion House, on Kawau Island, Hauraki Gulf

Waiheke Island has gained an "alternative" reputation because of its organic farms and artisans. Apart from its white sand beaches, its vineyards and olive groves are attractive to visitors.

Electricity on **Great Barrier Island**, the furthermost island in the Hauraki Gulf, is provided by windmills and diesel generators, while most refrigerators use kerosene. Drinking water comes from rain collected on roofs. The island is dominated by Mount Hobson, standing at 620 m (2,034 ft), and Ruahine, 410 m (1,345 ft). Visitors may spot a kaka, the New Zealand parrot, or a brown teal duck while on a tramping trip.

Regular boats to **Kawau Island** leave from Sandspit at Warkworth. The island is best known for Mansion House, built in 1846, the home of former New Zealand governor Sir George Grey. Sir George imported a variety of animal species, such as kookaburras and peacocks. Several, such as the parma wallaby, thought to be extinct in Australia, can still be seen.

Rangitoto has a highly visible presence in the gulf. The volcano erupted about 600–700 years ago to form an island. Now, the 260-m (850-ft) high lava slopes are covered in native trees and shrubs. Vegetation includes mosses, mangroves, ferns, tree daisies, orchids, coastal pohutukawa, manuka and rewa. There are good walks, including one to the summit. Alternatively, visitors can use a tractor-drawn train.

Brown kiwi with egg

Rakino is popular with weekenders. A hotchpotch of houses sit perched on striking ridges. Its beaches are suitable for swimming and it is a favourite stop for yachts.

Little Barrier Island, a wildlife sanctuary, has 30 native and 19 introduced species of birds breeding on it. They include the brown kiwi, kaka and bellbird. Flora includes 370 native species, with 90 ferns. It is prohibited to land on Little Barrier but it is possible to visit the island with a permit.

Gazetted in 1975, Goat Island Marine Reserve is also known as the Leigh Marine Reserve. The sheltered channel between Goat Island and the mainland provides an opportunity to see red moki, moray eel, snapper and blue cod, as well as marblefish and kelpfish. Crayfish, a favourite on the dinner table of up-market restaurants, is often found in the reserve.

The channel is only about 2 to 5 m (7 to 17 ft) deep and diving is possible straight from the beach. Underwater visibility fluctuates from 2 to 15 m (7 to 50 ft) and is at its best in the warmer months from January to June.

Waiheke Island
7,000. *Artworks, Korora Rd, Oneroa, (09) 372 9999.*

Great Barrier Island
1,000. *Claris Airport, (09) 429 0033.*

Kawau Island
200.

Visitors watching birds at the Leigh Marine Reserve

SHOPPING IN AUCKLAND

SHOPS IN Auckland cater for the needs of most shoppers. However, the city is quite spread out and it pays to do some research first. Shops in downtown Auckland are predominantly European in character; in other areas they have a more Pacific or Asian flavour. Shoppers in search of local items should consider pure wool products, such as hand-knitted sweaters or cuddly toys made

Greenstone pendant

from possum fur. The New Zealand fashion scene is lively and creative, and local designers such as Zambesi, Karen Walker, Anne Mardell, and Trelise Cooper have outlets in all the smart shopping areas. Jewellery, pottery, glass and other crafts are of a high standard and are worth buying. Specialized retailers sell items such as crayfish, which they will package for outbound travellers.

SHOPPING HOURS

TYPICAL BUSINESS hours are 9am to 6pm, with many stores open on Saturday and Sunday. Most large supermarkets are open until 9pm. Dairies (convenience stores) are sprinkled throughout the suburbs and sell a wide range of groceries and other items, as do most gas stations.

DUTY-FREE SHOPPING

THE NEW ZEALAND government adds 12.5 per cent Goods and Services Tax (GST) to sales items. Visitors to New Zealand can avoid paying this tax, as well as other government duty, by purchasing duty-free goods on arrival and departure at

the airport or at the large duty-free shop, **DFS Galleria**, in the city. This results in savings of 30 per cent on average. Items purchased at the shop have to be collected at the airport. Besides the usual cigarettes and alcohol, sheepskin goods, *paua* shell jewellery, oval black pearls, and finely crafted woodwork using local timbers are popular items with tourists.

SHOPPING AREAS

QUEEN STREET is the major banking and commercial centre. However, the restoration of Charles Bohringer's Civic Theatre (1929), the Force Entertainment Centre and shopping complexes such as **Atrium on Elliot**,

Interior of an Outdoor Heritage outlet in the city

the **BNZ Tower Shopping Centre** and **Downtown Shopping Centre** have revitalized the central business district as a shopping and entertainment centre. Book stores such as **Whitcoulls** and **Dymocks**, CD and record shops such as **Marbecks Record Shop**, woollen clothing and couture boutiques, and numerous souvenir stores are also

The country's largest duty-free shop, DFS Galleria, located at the Old Customhouse

located downtown. Nautical-type clothing and souvenirs, sought after during the 2000 America's Cup Regatta, can be purchased at the **National Maritime Museum Shop**.

Newmarket is Auckland's prime shopping area. Shops along Broadway include **Country Road**, **Outdoor Heritage** and **Living and Giving**. Parnell and Ponsonby retailers specialize in luxury goods, such as delicatessen food, clothing, art, ceramics and glassware.

MARKETS

Fresh fruit on sale at one of Auckland's markets

SHOPPERS WHO are more interested in typically New Zealand goods at lower prices should go to **Victoria Park Market**, a former rubbish destructor building built in 1905. Today, the site houses shops and stalls selling anything from souvenirs to snacks. There are also three licensed restaurants and a food court at the complex.

Saturday morning's **Otara Market**, open from 6am to 12pm, offers yams, green bananas, *hangi* (Maori food cooked on heated stones) and other local produce.

DIRECTORY

SHOPPING CENTRES

Atrium on Elliot
Elliot St.
(09) 300 3290.

BNZ Tower Shopping Centre
127 Queen St.
(09) 309 6949.

DFS Galleria
Old Customhouse,
Cnr of Albert &
Customs sts.
0800 388 937.

Downtown Shopping Centre
Queen Elizabeth II Square,
Cnr of Albert &
Customs sts.
(09) 978 5065.

Dress-Smart Factory Outlet
151 Arthur St, Onehunga.
(09) 622 2400.

Queen's Arcade
Cnr of Queen &
Customs sts.
(09) 358 1777.

MARKETS

Otara Market
Newbury St & Te Puke o
Tara Community Hall.
(09) 274 0830.

Victoria Park Market
210 Victoria St West.
(09) 309 6911.

FOOD AND WINE

Accent on Wine
347 Parnell Rd,
Parnell.
(09) 358 2552.

Gourmet Food Store
22 Remuera Rd,
Newmarket.
(09) 522 0040.

Lovrich Wines and Spirits
346 Dominion Rd,
Mt Eden.
(09) 630 7853.

Pandoro Italian Bakery
427 Parnell Rd,
Parnell.
(09) 358 1962.

Pasta Italia
56 Brighton Rd, Parnell.
(09) 373 3735.

CLOTHES

Country Road
246 Queen St.
(09) 358 1334.
157 Broadway,
Newmarket.
(09) 524 9685.

Karen Walker
15 O'Connell St.
(09) 309 6299.
6 Balm St, Newmarket.
(09) 522 4286.

Living and Giving
277 Broadway,
Newmarket
(09) 522 1270.

National Maritime Museum Shop
Viaduct Basin.
(09) 373 0800.

Outdoor Heritage
75 Queen St.
(09) 309 6571.
217 Broadway,
Newmarket.
(09) 522 0607.

Workshop
Cnr of Vulcan Lane and
High St.
(09) 303 3735.
4 Teed St, Newmarket.
(09) 524 6844.

BOOKS AND MUSIC

Borders
291–297 Queen St.
(09) 309 3377.

Dymocks
Atrium on Elliot,
21 Elliot St.
(09) 379 9919.

Magazzino
123 Ponsonby Rd,
Ponsonby.
(09) 376 6933.

Marbecks Record Shop
15 Queen's Arcade.
(09) 379 0444.

Real Groovy Records
438 Queen St.
(09) 302 3940.

Whitcoulls
210 Queen St.
(09) 356 5400.

Women's Bookshop
105 Ponsonby Rd.
(09) 376 4399.

SOUVENIRS AND OTHERS

Breen's Sheepskin Specialists
Southpac Tower,
6 Customs St.
(09) 373 2788.

Höglund Art Glass Gallery
285 Parnell Rd, Parnell.
(09) 300 6238.

OK Gift Shop
Downtown Shopping
Centre, Cnr of Albert &
Customs sts.
(09) 303 1951.

ENTERTAINMENT IN AUCKLAND

REFLECTING Auckland's ethnic diversity, events staged in the city range from a Puccini opera to a Maori dance performance. Many of these take place at venues in the central business district. The Aotea Centre, Auckland Town Hall, Imax Cinema and several cinemas are all on Queen Street. The restored Civic Theatre Centre is worth a visit for architectural reasons alone.

Busker in Queen Street

Bordering Queen Street, Fort Street and Karangahape Road, commonly known as K-Road, offer alternative entertainment in the form of strip clubs and massage parlours. K-Road is also known for its many nightclubs. Harrah's Sky City Casino features more than 100 gaming tables and 1,000 machines. In the suburbs, multiplex cinemas, sports parks and nightclubs are the main entertainment venues.

Interior of the refurbished Civic Theatre Centre

INFORMATION

THE ENTERTAINMENT section of *The New Zealand Herald* should be checked first for events in the city. It carries cinema listings and information about concerts, ballets and theatre performances. The Auckland City Council also publishes a free quarterly brochure, *Auckland Alive & Happening*, available at tourist information centres. It contains an extensive overview of cultural and sporting events. The country's largest booking agency, **Ticketek**, lists events on its website.

THEATRE

THE TWO MAIN venues, the **Aotea Centre** and the **Auckland Town Hall**, are part of the complex known as The Edge *(see p72)*. This is where the biggest musicals and productions are staged. The renovated Great Hall in the Auckland Town Hall (*see p72*) is renowned for its acoustics. Many of the shows presented in these venues feature international artistes.

DANCE

NEW ZEALAND HAS a small dance community. Its leading contemporary dance choreographers are Mary Jane O'Reilly, Michael Parmenter, and Douglas Wright.

At present, the Footnote Dance Company is the country's only full-time contemporary dance company. Based in Wellington, the troupe regularly performs in Auckland, as does the classical Royal New Zealand Ballet, which also has its home in the capital. However, the Black Grace Dance Company is Auckland-based. Regular tours by overseas dance and ballet companies enrich the dance calendar.

Annabel Reid of the Royal New Zealand Ballet in *Raymonda*

MUSIC

FOR CLASSICAL MUSIC, the New Zealand Symphony Orchestra (NZSO) and the Auckland Philharmonia Orchestra (APO) have a good reputation. The 33-member APO is unusual in that the musicians own the orchestra. Most concerts are held at the Aotea Centre and the Auckland Town Hall. Both the NZSO and the APO also perform at the free "Symphony under the Stars" and "Opera in the Park" concerts at Auckland Domain *(see p75)*. These events attract more than 100,000 people.

Many pubs in Auckland have live bands which play most nights, including the Powerstation, Judder Bar, and The Dogs Bollix, a popular Irish pub.

Fireworks during a symphony performance at the Auckland Domain

The Pounamu Maori Performance Group giving a cultural show

CULTURAL PERFORMANCES

A T THE Auckland War Memorial Museum (*see pp76–7*), visitors are able to witness authentic Maori ceremonies and dances. During the shows, which are staged twice daily, talented singers and dancers from the Pounamu Maori Performance Group present the *haka*, the fierce war dance of the men, the *poi* dances of the women (*see pp28–9*), as well as various other traditional songs and dances. Each show lasts about 45 minutes.

Visitors can also get to see Pacific Island culture at the Pasifika Festival, held at Western Springs, on the outskirts of Auckland, in March every year (*see p40*). The festival features the traditional arts and culture of the various Pacific Island communities.

CLUBS

A LTHOUGH THEATRES throughout the country feature one-off performances by local and visiting comedians, the **Classic Comedy & Bar** claims to be the only venue in New Zealand that is dedicated to stand-up comedy.

The city's main nightclub strip is on Karangahape Road. Venues that are popular with young people include **Sinners Nightclub**, which can accommodate up to 1,000 people on busy

nights, **Calibre**, **The Box** and **The Ministry Nightclub**. The well-known international franchise, **Planet Hollywood**, attracts a wider age range than most other clubs. Gay clubs include **Legend** and **Surrender Dorothy**.

FILM

M ULTIPLEX CINEMAS are found throughout Auckland. The larger multiplexes, such as the **Village Force Cinemas**, show blockbuster movies, often before they are screened in Europe. Newmarket's **Rialto Cinema**, on the other hand, regularly screens foreign titles for the more sophisticated movie buff. The **Imax Cinema** (*see p72*), part of an international chain of wide-screen cinemas, features a good variety of panoramic films.

The highlight of the cinematographic year is the New Zealand Film Festival, held in July. Auckland filmgoers get to enjoy a wide selection of local and international films over several days.

Façade of the Imax Cinema along Queen Street

DIRECTORY

BOOKING TICKETS

Ticketek
((09) 307 5000.
w www.ticketek.co.nz

THEATRES

Aotea Centre
Queen St.
((09) 309 2677.

Auckland Town Hall
Queen St.
((09) 309 2677.

Civic Theatre Centre
Cnr Queen and Wellesley sts.
((09) 377 3315.

CLUBS

Calibre
179 Karangahape Rd.
((09) 303 1673.

Classic Comedy & Bar
321 Queen St.
((09) 373 4321.

Legend
335 Karangahape Rd.
((09) 377 6062.

Planet Hollywood
291–297 Queen St.
((09) 308 7827.

Sinners Nightclub
373 Karangahape Rd.
((09) 308 9985.

Surrender Dorothy
3/175 Ponsonby Rd.
((09) 376 4460.

The Box
35 High St.
((09) 303 1336.

The Ministry Nightclub
17 Albert St.
((09) 373 3664.

CINEMAS

Imax Cinema
291–297 Queen St.
((09) 979 2400.

Rialto Cinema
169 Broadway, Newmarket.
((09) 529 2218.

Sky City Theatre
Cnr Wellesley and Hobson sts.
((09) 912 6267.

Village Force Cinemas
((09) 915 2222.

NORTHLAND

*S*TRONG MAORI ROOTS, *early European settlements, a subtropical climate and enchanting scenery – these make Northland both the cradle of the nation and one of its favourite playgrounds. Northland is where Europeans first made their presence felt in New Zealand. It is a region with a history of bloodshed and raw frontier emotions, but is today dominated by holiday fun.*

The long history of Maori occupation in Northland is evident in the hillside *pa* sites and shellfishing grounds around the coast. Maori culture *(see pp28–9)* continues to be extensively practised in this region and many Maori tribes live here.

Early post-European history in Northland includes both the licentious whalers, who earned Russell its title of "hell-hole of the Pacific" *(see p100)*, and missionaries, who brought Christianity to the country. The brothels and taverns have now disappeared, but buildings like Pompallier House are reminders of early Christian influences.

Historically, Waitangi House, where the Treaty of Waitangi was signed *(see pp46–7, 102–103)*, is of prime importance. Cape Reinga *(see p106)* is a drawcard, because of its location at the top of the country where the Pacific Ocean and Tasman Sea merge, and also because of its significance in Maori mythology as the place where the spirits of the dead depart the country for Hawaiki.

Visitors to Northland will be impressed by its natural beauty: gently rolling farmland, white sand beaches, massive sand dunes and rock formations. In a world where scenic spots are often spoiled due to countless visitors, Northland stands out. In its forests, with gigantic kauris that are up to 2,000 years old, it is still possible to walk for hours without encountering a single fellow tramper. The region also offers a variety of other activities, such as fishing, diving, kayaking, tobogganing and horseback riding.

Diving near the wreck of the *Rainbow Warrior* (see p51) off Matauri Bay

◁ **Wild flowers and rolling hills of the Northland landscape**

Exploring Northland

NORTHLAND'S CHARM lies in its unspoiled, simple character. The region is blessed with two contrasting coastlines, which offer endless scope for outdoor recreation. As the site of first permanent contact between Maoris and Europeans, the region is also rich in history and has many well-preserved historic sites. There are three main bases from which visitors can explore the region: Paihia, which has its own attractions but is close to historic Russell, Waitangi and Kerikeri, and the beautiful Bay of Islands; Kaitaia, which attracts day-trippers to the Aupori Peninsula, Mangonui and Ahipara; and Opononi and Omapere, which have wonderful beaches and are close to Rawene, a historic settlement on Hokianga Harbour.

CAPE REINGA ⑬
North Cape
TE PAKI
KARATIA
1
Great Exhibition Bay
NINETY MILE BEACH ⑭
⑮ AUPORI PENINSULA TOUR
● HOUHORA
WAIPAPAKAURI ●
AWANUI ●
KAITAI ⑫
Abipara Bay
● AHIPARA
HEREKI
OP
Hokian Harbo

0 kilometres   20
0 miles   20

Pohutukawa trees and bays around Whangarei Heads

TOP OUTDOOR ACTIVITIES

The places shown here have been selected for their recreational activities. Conditions vary depending on the weather and the time of year, so exercise caution and, if in doubt, seek local advice.

	CRUISING	GAME FISHING	KAYAKING	SAILING	SCUBA DIVING	SNORKELLING	SWIMMING	TRAMPING
Cape Reinga								●
Kai-Iwi Lakes			●	●			●	
Kaitaia								●
Ninety Mile Beach						●	●	●
Omapere	●		●	●		●	●	
Opononi	●		●	●		●	●	
Paihia	●	●	●	●	●	●	●	
Russell	●	●	●	●	●	●	●	
Tutukaka	●	●	●	●	●	●	●	
Waipoua Forest								●
Whangarei	●	●	●	●			●	●

SEE ALSO
- *Where to Stay* p299
- *Where to Eat* p319

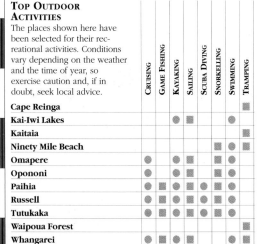

Painting an ancestral figure on the meeting house at Waitangi

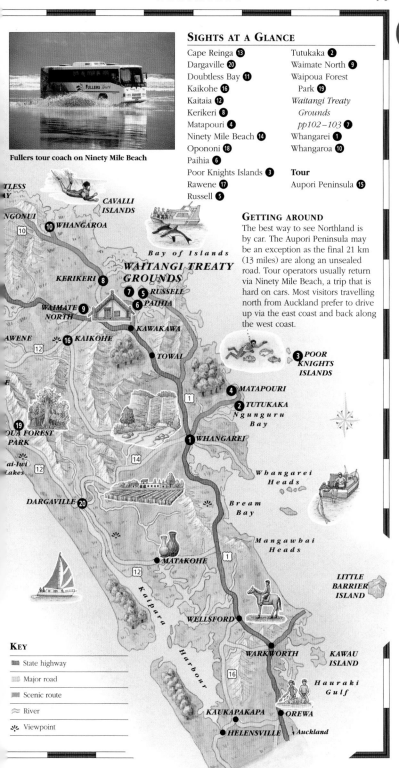

Fullers tour coach on Ninety Mile Beach

Sights at a Glance

Cape Reinga 13
Dargaville 20
Doubtless Bay 11
Kaikohe 16
Kaitaia 12
Kerikeri 8
Matapouri 4
Ninety Mile Beach 14
Opononi 18
Paihia 6
Poor Knights Islands 3
Rawene 17
Russell 5
Tutukaka 2
Waimate North 9
Waipoua Forest Park 19
Waitangi Treaty Grounds pp102–103 7
Whangarei 1
Whangaroa 10

Tour

Aupori Peninsula 15

Getting Around

The best way to see Northland is by car. The Aupori Peninsula may be an exception as the final 21 km (13 miles) are along an unsealed road. Tour operators usually return via Ninety Mile Beach, a trip that is hard on cars. Most visitors travelling north from Auckland prefer to drive up via the east coast and back along the west coast.

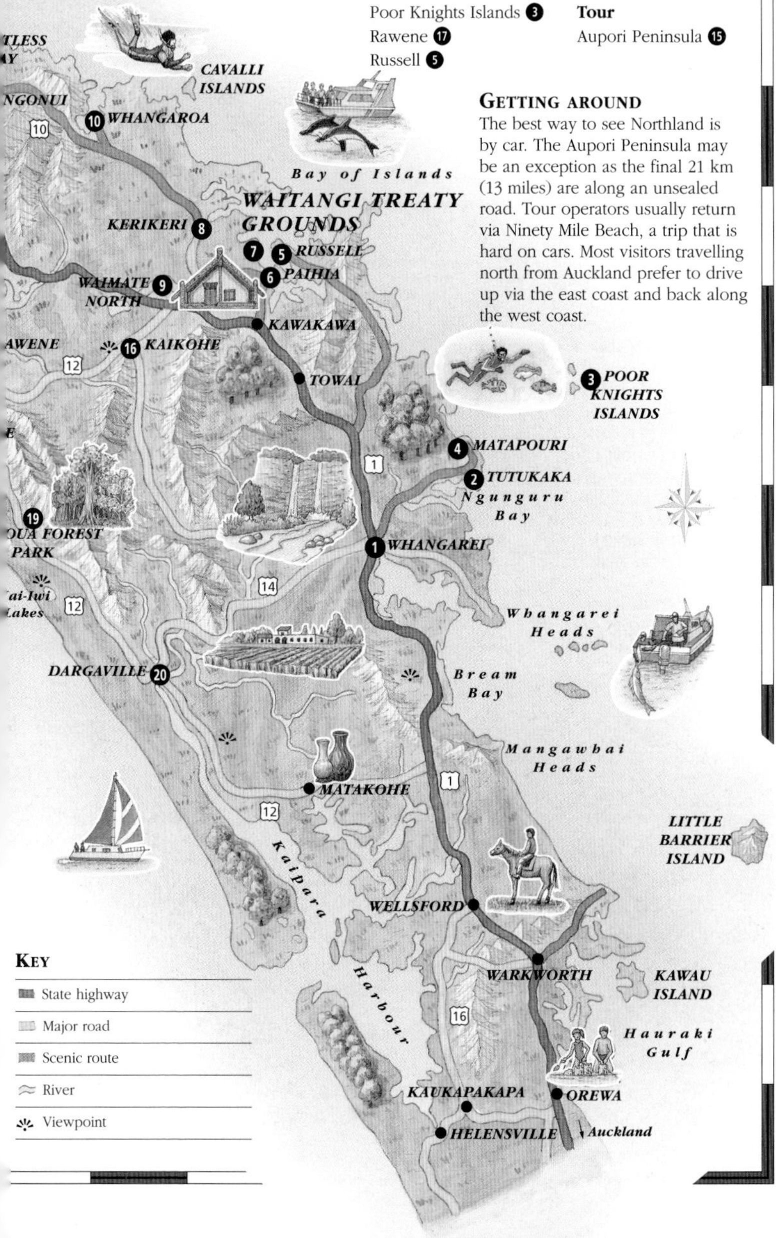

CAVALLI ISLANDS
10 WHANGAROA
Bay of Islands
WAITANGI TREATY GROUNDS
KERIKERI 8
7 5 RUSSELL
6 PAIHIA
WAIMATE NORTH 9
KAWAKAWA
16 KAIKOHE
TOWAI
3 POOR KNIGHTS ISLANDS
4 MATAPOURI
2 TUTUKAKA
Ngunguru Bay
1 WHANGAREI
Whangarei Heads
Bream Bay
DARGAVILLE 20
Mangawhai Heads
MATAKOHE
Kaipara Harbour
LITTLE BARRIER ISLAND
WELLSFORD
WARKWORTH
KAWAU ISLAND
Hauraki Gulf
KAUKAPAKAPA
OREWA
HELENSVILLE
Auckland
KEY
State highway
Major road
Scenic route
River
Viewpoint

The Town Basin on the waterfront at Whangarei

Whangarei ❶

Road map E1. 🏃 *47,000.* ✈
🚉 🚌 ⓘ *Tawera Park, 92 Otaika Rd, (09) 438 1079.*

T HE NORTHERNMOST city in New Zealand and the only one in Northland, Whangarei is a three-hour drive from Auckland. The city lies between forested hills and a deep harbour. The combination of fertile soil and temperate climate is reflected in the city's lush gardens and in the surrounding farmlands and orchards.

Whangarei's historic Town Basin, in the heart of the city, has been redeveloped in a colonial theme. Its cafés, restaurants, art galleries, museums and speciality shops make it a popular gathering place for locals and visitors. It is also one of the most popular destinations for yacht sailors wandering the world, who come here to avoid the cyclonic storms common in the South Pacific over the summer. The Town Basin and local marinas are often full with visiting yachts coming to refit.

A giant sundial marks the location of the Town Basin's **Clapham Clock Museum**, which houses more than 1,600 items donated by A Clapham, who made many of the clocks himself. The oldest, an English lantern clock, dates from 1720. The collection also includes Biedermeier wall clocks, grandfather and Black Forest clocks, and a *staartklok* (literally a "tail clock" because of the shape of its winding mechanism) from Friesland in the Netherlands. To avoid the deafening sound of the hundreds of time-pieces marking the hour simultaneously, the clocks have been set at different times.

Visitors who are in the area for fishing or snorkelling should first visit the **Museum of Fishes** to get an overview of what can be encountered offshore. There are hundreds of mounted fish, including game fish, such as a 412-kg (908-lb) blue marlin and a 40-kg (88-lb)

Clapham Clock Museum exhibit

broadbill swordfish. Shark species include the hammerhead and tiger shark. The museum also has live displays, with snapper, pack horse lobsters and eels (including "Eel McPherson"). The excellent shell collection by Dave Hayward comprises several thousand specimens.

For those looking for more challenging activities, there are many tramping opportunities around Whangarei. The Parahaki Scenic Reserve, on the eastern side of the city, has good bush walks. The war memorial at the summit of Parahaki Mountain can be reached via Memorial Drive or by two tracks from Mair Park or Dundas Road, for a superb panoramic view of the city and harbour. There are Maori pits and old gum-digging workings on all the walks, and a trail leads to a historic Maori *pa* site nearby.

Whangarei Falls, known as the most photogenic waterfalls in New Zealand, lie northeast of the Parahaki Scenic Reserve in the suburb of Tikipunga, 5 km (3 miles) north of the town centre. The 26-m (86-ft) high waterfall drops over basalt cliffs. There are natural pools and picnic spots, plus two viewing platforms that provide excellent views of the falls.

🏛 **Clapham Clock Museum**
Town Basin, Quayside. 📞 *(09) 438 3993.* ⬜ *daily.* 🖼 ♿ 🎬 ⓘ
🏛 **Museum of Fishes**
6 Quayside. 📞 *(09) 438 5681.* ⬜ *daily.* ● *25 Dec.* 🖼 ♿ 🎬 *by arrangement.* ⓘ

Tutukaka ❷

Road map E1. 🏃 *520.* 🚌 ⓘ
Whangarei Deep Sea Anglers Club, Marina Rd, (09) 434 3818.

O N THE COASTAL loop road, a short distance from Whangarei, Tutukawa is a well-known base for diving trips to the Poor Knights Islands and for big game fishing. The Whangarei Deep Sea Anglers Club is based here

The picturesque Whangarei Falls

Yachts moored at the marina in Tutukaka's sheltered harbour

and the sheltered, natural harbour is alive with yachts and fishing boats.

A popular diving site off the coast between Tutukaka and Matapouri is an artificial reef created by sinking the *Tui*, a former naval ship, on 20 February 2000. Another attraction off the coast is shark diving. Clients (who have to be certified divers) are locked inside an aluminium cage, which is then lowered into the water near the sharks.

Poor Knights Islands ❸

Road map E1. **🛈** *Department of Conservation, Tarewa Park, 92 Otaika Rd, Whangarei, (09) 430 2007.*

Aᴮᴼᵁᵀ 24 km (15 miles) from the coast at Tutukawa are the Poor Knights Islands. Once a favourite spot for fishermen, the area around these two islands was established as a marine reserve in 1981. Although landing on the islands is prohibited without a special permit from the Department of Conservation, the surrounding waters are accessible to divers. Well-known mariner Jacques Cousteau considered the reserve one of the world's top five diving sites because of its exceptional water clarity and

the variety of its sea life. The area benefits from a sub-tropical current that makes it warmer than the surrounding coastal waters, and promotes a profusion of tropical and temperate marine life. Eroded volcanic rock has created a seascape of tunnels, arches and caves where divers can view fish and sponges. The best time for scuba diving in this haven is from January to May. Boats leave daily from Tutukawa Marina.

Reptiles such as geckos and tuataras can be found on both islands, which are thought to be the world's only nesting spot for Buller's shearwaters.

Matapouri ❹

Road map E1.

Lᴼᶜᴬᵀᴱᴰ ᴬ sʜᴼᴿᵀ distance north of Tutukawa on the coastal loop road, Matapouri has one of Northland's most beautiful beaches. Tucked between headlands and dotted with islets, Matapouri's calm waters and white sands make it a popular place for swimming and snorkelling.

A walking track connects the beach with Whale Bay, 2 km (1.2 miles) north. Lookout points on the track offer magnificent views of the coastline and ocean.

Diving in the marine reserve at Poor Knights Islands

Aerial view of the Bay of Islands ▷

The churchyard, Christ Church, Russell

Russell **5**

Road map E1. **A** 1,000. **☐** **☐**
i The Wharf, (09) 403 7596.

AT THE TURN of the 19th century, Russell, then known as Kororareka, served as a shore station for whalers. It became a lawless town, earning the title "Hell-hole of the Pacific". It was renamed Russell in 1844 in honour of the British colonial secretary of the day. Today, the quiet town·is involved in tourism, fishing, oyster farming and cottage industries.

Formerly known as the Captain Cook Memorial Museum, the **Russell Museum** features a working model of Captain Cook's *Endeavour* and memorabilia from American author Zane Grey, who helped establish the Bay of Islands as a game fishing centre in the late 1920s. There is also a collection of early settlers' relics.

Christ Church, built in 1836, is the country's oldest surviving church. One of the contributors to the church was Charles Darwin, author of *The Origin of Species*, who visited New Zealand in 1835.

Stately **Pompallier House** was built on the waterfront between 1841 and 1842 to house the Marist mission's Gaveaux printing press. The building later became much neglected, until it passed to the New Zealand Historic Places Trust in 1968 and was restored to its original state in 1993. The country's oldest standing industrial building, it now houses a printing company, which still uses the original printing press, and a book bindery.

Flagstaff Hill serves as a reminder of Russell's turbulent past. It was here that Hone Heke (1810–50) cut down the British shipping signal flagpole in 1844 *(see p61)*.

Paihia restaurant sign

🏛 **Russell Museum**
2 York St. **[** (09) 403 7701.
◯ daily. **●** 25 Dec. 🖼 🚻 🚹
🚹 **Christ Church**
Church Rd. **[** (09) 403 7707.
🚹 11am Sun.
🚻 **Pompallier House**
The Strand. **[** (09) 403 9015.
◯ daily. **●** Good Fri, 25 Dec.
🖼 🚻 garden only. 🚹 🚹

Paihia **6**

Road map E1. **A** 1,850. **☐** **☐**
i Marsden Rd, (09) 402 7345.

STARTING LIFE as a mission post in 1823, Paihia now joins places such as Russell and Tutukaka as a base for deep-sea game fishing. When fishermen in the Bay of Islands discover rare or unusual species in their nets, these are dropped off at the **Aquatic World Aquarium**. Here, visitors can also learn about fish commonly found in the area, such as snapper or parrot fish. The aquarium also boasts an extensive and successful sea horse breeding programme. Located beside the bridge over the Waitangi River, in an old sailing ship, **Kelly Tarlton's Museum of Shipwrecks** houses over 1,000 artifacts from ships that have sunk around the coast of New Zealand.

🐟 **Aquatic World Aquarium**
Marsden Rd. **[** (09) 402 6220.
◯ daily. **●** 25 Dec. 🖼 🚻 🚹
🏛 **Kelly Tarlton's Museum of Shipwrecks**
[(09) 402 7018. **◯** daily. **●** 25 Dec. 🖼 🚻 🚹

Kelly Tarlton's Museum of Shipwrecks

Leisure Activities in the Bay of Islands

Fishing club logo

A FAVOURABLE climate, an irregular coastline lapped by the Pacific Ocean and some 150 islands dotted around its aquamarine waters combine to make the Bay of Islands one of New Zealand's most popular playgrounds. The region has been a favourite tourist destination since the 1930s when a road connecting Northland with Auckland to the south was built. The Bay of Islands' reputation is based primarily on deep-sea fishing, but today visitors also have the opportunity to experience other water sports, such as swimming, kayaking, sailing, diving and water-skiing. Tour operators tempt visitors by adding new attractions, such as scenic flights, paragliding and horse trekking.

GAME FISHING

Deep-sea game fishing is a year-round activity in the Bay of Islands. The most prolific game fish is the striped marlin, which may weigh up to 120 kg (265 lb). Many other species, which can be caught using both heavy and light tackle, are abundant in the bay's waters. Deep-sea fishing charters usually include accommodation, food, tackle and bait. No licence is required for ocean fishing.

Anglers increasingly are tagging and releasing the fish they catch, such as this striped marlin.

The Rowe family, keen anglers of the Bay of Islands Swordfish Club, with their prize catch

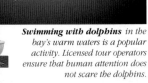

Swimming with dolphins in the bay's warm waters is a popular activity. Licensed tour operators ensure that human attention does not scare the dolphins.

Kayaking guided tours range from paddling up sheltered waters to kayaking on the open sea.

Paragliding, one of several airborne sports introduced in the Bay of Islands, is an excellent way to appreciate the beauty of the bay.

Leisure cruises include Paihia's Cream Trip. The boat used to collect cream from outlying dairy farms but now drops off mail and takes visitors on cruises.

Waitangi Treaty Grounds **❼**

Tatooed figure on meeting house

WAITANGI EARNED its pivotal place in New Zealand's history on 6 February 1840 when the Treaty of Waitangi was signed *(see pp16, 46–7)* in front of the house of James Busby (1800–71), the British Resident in New Zealand. The Residency, renamed the Treaty House, became a national memorial in 1932. The Treaty House and its grounds are a gathering point for Maoris and government leaders each year on 6 February, Waitangi Day.

Aerial View of Waitangi Treaty Grounds
The grounds are surrounded by a beautiful coastline, tidal estuary, mangrove, forest and native bush.

Visitor Centre
An audiovisual presentation every half hour describes the events surrounding the signing of the Treaty of Waitangi. There are also displays on the major personalities involved and copies of the Treaty documents. A shop sells souvenirs, Maori carvings and books.

Waikokopu Café *(see p319)*

Waitang

Kelly Tarlton's Museum of Shipwrecks *(see p100)*

Te Tii Marae

Bay of Islands Yacht Club

PAIHIA

Tau Hemare Drive

Copthorne Resort Waitangi *(see p299)*

A coastal walk takes visitors past unusual pillow lava rock, which fractured into hexagonal shapes as it erupted under water.

Car Park

Canoe House

HOBSON BEACH

0 metres 200

0 yards 200

★ Maori War Canoe
Carved from three kauri trees, this 35-m (114-ft) long canoe, named Ngatokimatawhaorua after the canoe in which Kupe discovered New Zealand (see p43), carries up to 120 warriors. It is launched each year on Waitangi Day.

STAR SIGHTS

★ Maori Meeting House

★ Maori War Canoe

★ Treaty House

Mangrove Forest Boardwalk
A boardwalk takes visitors through a mature mangrove forest to the Haruru Falls at the end of the tidal Waitangi River.

★ Treaty House
Prefabricated in Australia, the Treaty House (see p47), was the home of the first British Resident in New Zealand. It was the venue for important political events up to 1840.

Hutia Creek

ver

Waitangi
Golf Course

Flagstaff

★ Maori Meeting House
Opened on 6 February 1940 to commemorate the centennial of the Treaty, the meeting house (Te Whare Runanga) contains beautiful Maori wall carvings.

Treaty Grounds
A ceremonial celebration of the signing of the Treaty of Waitangi is held each year on the grounds in front of the Treaty House.

The Stone Store, St James Church and Kerikeri Mission House

Kerikeri 8

Road map E1. 4,200.

THE PRETTY TOWN of Kerikeri is noted for its subtropical climate, citrus and kiwifruit orchards, historic buildings, and an art and craft trail.

The Kerikeri Basin is home to New Zealand's oldest surviving stone building, the **Stone Store**, built in 1835 as part of the **Kerikeri Mission House**, New Zealand's oldest surviving wooden house. Intended as a storehouse, the Stone Store gradually turned into a general store and, from the 1960s, a souvenir shop. Its merchandise includes hand-forged nails and other products in keeping with its history. The Kerikeri Mission House was the second European mission station to be set up in New Zealand, in 1819, under the protection of the Maori chief Hongi Hika *(see p61)*; the first mission was established near the entrance to the Bay of Islands five years earlier. Constructed in 1821, the building came into the hands of the Kemp family in 1832 and was left to the New Zealand Historic Places Trust in 1974. Restored, it looks much as it did in the 1840s. On the slope behind is **St James Church**, constructed in 1878 of native timbers such as kauri and puriri.

Above the Basin are the remnants of Kororipo Pa, a Maori fortification. The strategic base of Hongi Hika, the *pa* is best known as an assembly point for war parties in the 1820s. Across the river from the *pa* is **Rewa's Village**, a reconstructed pre-European Maori fishing village built from native materials, those used before the missionaries came. It provides an introduction to traditional buildings such as a *marae* (gathering place) and *pataka* (communal raised storehouse). There are two ancient canoes at the village.

Stone Store
The Basin. (09) 407 9236. daily. by arrangement.
Kerikeri Mission House
The Basin. daily. 25 Dec. by arrangement.
St James Church
The Basin. daily.
Rewa's Village
1 Landing Rd. (09) 407 6454. daily. Good Fri, 25 Dec. by arrangement.

Waimate North 9

Road map E1. 700.

NOT FAR FROM Kerikeri is Waimate North, a missionary community in the 1830s. It was also the site of New Zealand's first large English-style farm. It is now best known for **Te Waimate Mission,** the sole survivor of three mission houses built in 1832 and first occupied by the Clarke family. It is furnished with missionary period furniture and early tools.

Te Waimate Mission
Te Ahu Ahu Rd. (09) 405 9734. Sat–Mon. public hols.

Whangaroa 10

Road map E1. 530.

A SMALL, SCENIC settlement with a beautiful harbour, Whangaroa is best appreciated from the summit of St Paul, a rock formation which dominates the town. The surrounding hills were once covered in huge kauri trees, which have long since been turned into ship masts and timber. Yugoslavs worked the Matauri Bay gumfields in the late 19th century, extracting resin *(see p108)*.

Today, Whangaroa Harbour has become well known for its big game fishing, cruises, diving and snorkelling.

Doubtless Bay 11

Road map D1.

SAID TO BE THE first landfall for the explorer Kupe *(see pp43–4)*, Doubtless Bay was an important base for whalers in the early days of European settlement. The bay encompasses a wide crescent of golden beaches, including Cable Bay and Cooper's Beach, popular with swimmers and snorkellers. The fishing village of Mangonui, situated on the bay's estuary, has many historic buildings.

Te Waimate Mission, one of New Zealand's oldest wooden buildings

Art and Crafts

ART AND CRAFTS are well developed in Northland, often with a strong local flavour in the use of colours and motifs. Ironically, the best-known artist was not a New Zealander but Austrian architect and painter Hundertwasser, who spent much of his time in New Zealand until his death in March 2000. Visitors to Kawakawa, south of Paihia and Russell, can visit a grass-roofed Hundertwasser-designed toilet

Northland pottery

block. Local artist Chris Booth is known for sculptures that feature large stones – not the sort of art piece that is easily transported. There are many outlets in the area, however, that offer paintings, prints, bone carvings and traditional greenstone (jade) items. In Kerikeri, an art and craft trail leads visitors through shops selling a variety of individually handcrafted and decorated pieces of high quality.

SWAMP KAURI CARVING

Swamp kauri is turned by local artisans into items ranging from small bowls to dining sets. The timber is milled from the remnants of huge trees which fell into swamplands 30,000–50,000 years ago.

This kauri staircase in Awanui, north of Kaitaia, came from a tree estimated to be 11 m (36 ft) in circumference and 1,087 years old when it fell 50,000 years ago.

Part of a stone sculpture *by Northland artist Chris Booth, which forms the entrance to Auckland's Albert Park.*

Plaited floor mats, baskets and hats *made from flax, a swamp plant, are popular souvenirs. Flax weaving is a traditional Maori skill.*

Wood, bone or greenstone *are carved by crafts people like Hohepa Renata, who use their own designs or traditional Maori ones.*

Carved wooden mask

Pottery *is produced in a variety of techniques, including glazing methods from Japan.*

Kaitaia ⓬

Map D1. 👥 *5,300.* 🚌 ℹ *Jaycee Park, South Rd, (09) 408 0879.*

THE LARGEST TOWN in the Far North, Kaitaia is a good base for day trips in the area. It is home to the **Far North Regional Museum**, which has the earliest authenticated European artifact left in New Zealand – a 1,500-kg (3,300-lb) wrought-iron anchor, lost in a storm in Doubtless Bay by J F M de Surville, the French explorer, in 1769.

🏛 **Far North Regional Museum**
6 South Rd. ☎ *(09) 408 1403.*
○ *Mon–Fri.* ● *Public hols.* 💰 📷 ♿ 🚶 *on request.* 🛍

Cape Reinga ⓭

Map D1.

REINGA, meaning "underworld", refers to the Maori belief that this is where the spirits of the dead leave for the journey to Hawaiki. The roots of an old pohutukawa tree at the tip of the cape are said to be the departure point for these spirits. Looking out from Cape Reinga over the Columbia Bank, visitors can see the Tasman Sea converge with the Pacific Ocean. The cape is not the very end of the country; the northernmost point is on North Cape.

Ninety Mile Beach ⓮

Map D1.

A MISNOMER, Ninety Mile Beach is, in fact, only 96 km (60 miles) long. The longest beach in the country, this area is almost like a desert, with sand dunes that can reach 143 m (470 ft) high fringing the beach. It was once a forested region, but the kauri trees were destroyed by inundations of water during successive Ice Ages. Pine trees have been planted to stabilize the dunes. Surf fishing and digging for shellfish are popular activities.

Aupori Peninsula Driving Tour

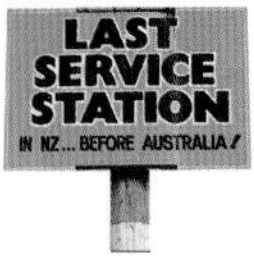
LAST SERVICE STATION
IN NZ... BEFORE AUSTRALIA!

Gas station sign

CALLED "THE TAIL OF THE FISH" by Maoris, Aupori Peninsula is a thin strip of land no more than 12 km (7 miles) wide between Ninety Mile Beach on the west coast and a number of beaches and bays along the east coast. The unspoilt beaches and coastline, together with high year-round temperatures, make this region an appealing holiday destination. The peninsula offers swimming, walking, sand tobogganing and fishing.

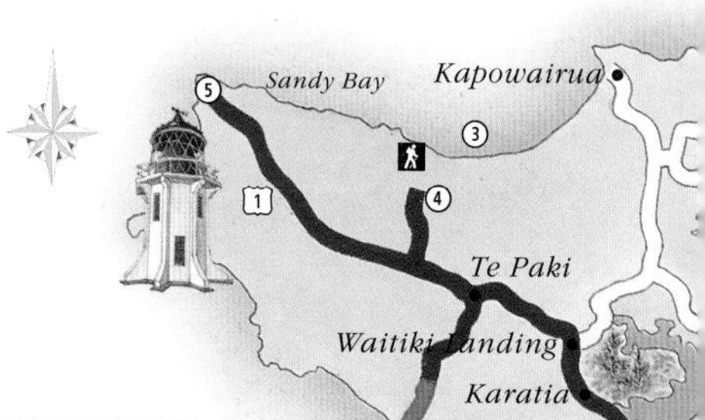
Sandy Bay
Kapowairua
Te Paki
Karatia
The Bluff
1
3
4
5
0 kilometres 6
0 miles 6

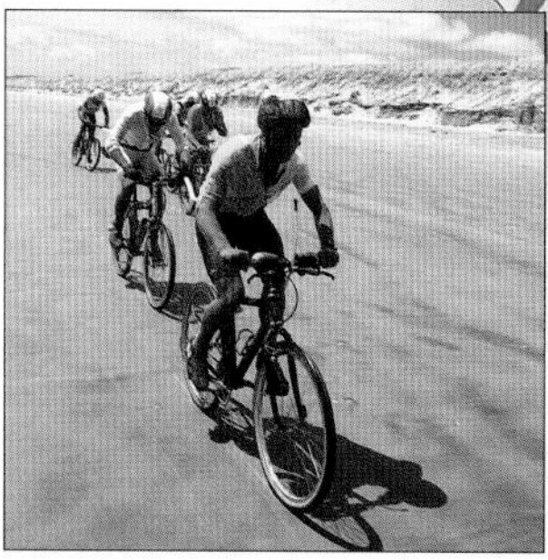

Ninety Mile Beach ⑥
The hard sand on the beach makes it a popular driving track for cars and farm bikes, as well as for cycling and marathons.

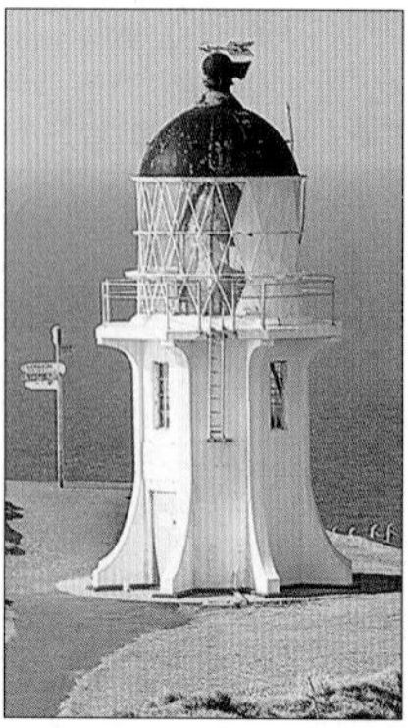

Cape Reinga Lighthouse ⑤
Visible from a distance of 48 km (26 nautical miles) offshore, the solitary, whitewashed Cape Reinga Lighthouse is New Zealand's northernmost lighthouse.

KEY

- Tour route
- Scenic route
- Other roads
- 🚶 Walking track

Wagener Museum ①
A carved entrance leads visitors into the museum. The 50,000 exhibits range from washing machines to stuffed animals. The Subritzky Homestead, a pioneer home from 1860, is nearby and is open to visitors.

North Cape

KAIKAI CENIC SERVE

Rarawa Beach ②
Sparkling white silica sand makes Rarawa Beach one of the most attractive beaches on the east coast.

Great Exhibition Bay

Spirits Bay ③
This sacred Maori area is the starting point for the 28-km (17-mile) walking track to Cape Reinga.

Henderson Bay

Pukenui

Houhora Heads

Mohutangi

Hukatere

WAIPAPAKAURI BEACH

DIGGING FOR SHELLFISH

Gathering *kai moana* (seafood) is not just a Maori tradition. Many other New Zealanders fish from boats or the shore, dive for fish, or dig in the sand for shellfish to supplement their diet. At Ninety Mile Beach, people are likely to be searching for *tuatua*, a shellfish that occurs in large quantities in the area. The daily limit a person can collect is 150 and each shellfish must be at least 125 mm (5 inches) long. More difficult to find, *paua* (abalone) are also gathered along the beach. The daily limit per person is ten.

Digging for *tuatua* at Ninety Mile Beach

Te Paki Reserve ④
Tobogganing off the massive sand dunes is the main attraction here but there is also a pleasant 40-minute walk to the beach.

TIPS FOR DRIVERS

Length: 210 km (130 miles).
Stopping-off points: There are places to stay and eat between Kaitaia and Waitaki Landing. The final 21-km (13-mile) drive to the lighthouse follows an unsealed road. As an alternative to return-ing on State Hwy 1, 4WD vehicles can access Ninety Mile Beach at Te Paki, 16 km (10 miles) south of Cape Reinga Lighthouse, and exit near Waipapakauri Beach. Trips should be made two hours before or after high tide. Visitors are advised to take a coach tour, as rental car companies do not allow drivers to follow this route.

Boatshed Café and Gallery at Rawene

Kaikohe ⑯

Road map E1. 🚶 *4,100.* ▣ 🛈
112 Broadway Rd, (09) 401 1693.

A SERVICE CENTRE for farms in the area, Kaikohe is best known for the **Ngawha Hot Springs** (Waiaraki Pools). While such hot springs have been turned into major tourist attractions in places such as Rotorua (*see pp134–5*), they are mainly a local feature in Kaikohe, where most visitors and the attendant are on first-name terms. Outsiders are welcome, and if they can accept the springs' unadorned character, they will enjoy the hot spring waters with temperatures between 32 and 42 °C (90 and 108 °F).

Kaikohe's **Pioneer Village**, an indoor and outdoor museum, is a collection of houses and artifacts related to the district's early European history. A conducted tour takes visitors to attractions from the 1862 Old Court-house to the Maioha Cottage (1875), the Utakura Settlers Hall (1891) and Alexander's Sawmill (1913). There are also vintage vehicles, a fire station, a bush railway and a small railway station. From a hill-side monument to Chief Hone Heke (grand-nephew of the old chief), there are fine views of both coasts.

🚶 **Ngawha Hot Springs**
Off State Hwy 12. 📞 *(09) 401 0116.*
◯ *daily.* ● *public hols.* 🈯
🏛 **Pioneer Village**
Recreation Rd. 📞 *(09) 401 0816.*
◯ *daily.* ● *Good Fri, 25 Dec.* 🈯
🚻🈯🛈

Rawene ⑰

Road map D1. 🚶 *520.* 🛥 🛈
Boatshed Café and Gallery, The Esplanade, (09) 405 7728.

T HIS QUAINT village, which has shops jutting out over the water, was home to James Reddy Clendon (1800–72), the first US Consul in New Zealand. He later became Hokianga's Resident Magistrate. **Clendon House**, now owned by the New Zealand Historic Places Trust, was probably built after 1866.

The ferry across Hokianga Harbour links with an alternative route to Kaitaia, via Broadwood and Herekino.

🏛 **Clendon House**
The Esplanade. 📞 *(09) 405 7874.*
◯ *Sat–Mon.* ● *May–Oct & public hols.* 🈯

Opononi ⑱

Road map D1. 🚶 *600.* ▣ 🚌 🛈
Hokianga Information Centre, State Hwy 12, (09) 405 8869.

I N THE MINDS OF many New Zealanders, the small beach town of Opononi is forever linked to that of its most famous visitor, Opo. This dolphin became a national celebrity when it spent the summer of 1955 playing with children and performing tricks with beach balls. Sadly, it was killed by unknown dynamite fishers. A sculpture by Christchurch artist Russell Clark marks the dolphin's grave outside Opononi's pub. A video of Opo can be viewed at the Hokianga Information Centre.

Diagonally across the road from Opo's statue is the wharf, which is the starting point for a short boat trip to see, at close range, the giant sand dunes on the far side of Hokianga Harbour.

Sculpture of Opo the dolphin at Opononi

THE EARLY KAURI GUM INDUSTRY

As the immigrants of the 19th century rapidly depleted the country's native forests of kauri trees, a new industry began to emerge. Resin, exuded by the trees, became a valuable commodity in the production of varnish. To reveal the location of lumps of resin, long rods were poked into the ground near dead trees, a job mostly carried out by Yugoslav immigrants. By 1885, 2,000 people were employed in this trade. Many of these people later turned to growing vegetables and to viticulture near Auckland.

Today, lumps of kauri gum, known as amber, are popular souvenir items. The gum is carved and polished and made into pendants and other small items. Sometimes insects or fern fragments can be seen trapped inside the finished items.

Polished kauri gum

Tane Mahuta, New Zealand's largest kauri tree

Waipoua Forest Park ⑲

Road map D1. 🏠 *Waipoua Forest,*
(09) 439 3011.

WAIPOUA FOREST PARK IS
well worth a visit
because of its magnificent
kauri trees. Being in the
presence of a tree that has
entered its third millennium is
a memorable experience, as
photos seldom capture the
grandeur of these trees. Local
Maoris have christened the
country's largest living kauri
Tane Mahuta, "the god of the
forest". Reached by an easy
5-minute walk from the road
through the park, the tree is
51m (168 ft) high, has a girth
of 14 m (46 ft) and a volume
of 244.5 cu m (8,635 cu ft).
Department of Conservation
experts estimate the tree to be
about 1,500 years old. Four
other known giant trees in
the forest are at least 1,000
years old. The park also
contains around 300 species
of trees, palms and ferns.

Dargaville ⑳

Road map E1. 🏠 *4,900.* 🚐
🛈 *Normandy St, (09) 439 8360.*

DARGAVILLE IS THE nation's
kumara capital and
many road stalls with honesty
boxes offer the opportunity to
buy these sweet potatoes.
The **Dargaville Maritime
Museum** is not just of interest
to sailors. Apart from Maori
canoes, ship models and
other nautical items, the display materials range from old
photos of the local Yugoslav
Social Club to memorabilia
from the Northern Wairoa
Scottish Society and a pig
skull from New Mexico.

🏛 **Dargaville Maritime
Museum**
Harding Park. 📞 *(09) 439 7555.*
◻ *daily.* ● *25 Dec.* 📷 ♿ ✔ ⊡

ENVIRONS: Located 45 km (28
miles) south of Dargaville, the
Matakohe Kauri Museum
gives visitors an insight into
kauri trees, especially after a
trip through Waipoua Forest
Park. The museum illustrates
the role these mammoth trees
played in New Zealand's
pioneering history. A steam
sawmill, with mannequins
representing local settler
families, shows how the
logs were milled.
Within the main museum
building there is also kauri
furniture, carvings and timber
panels as well as an extensive
collection of carved and
polished kauri gum. Outside
is a kauri post office from
1909, a 6-room fully furnished
early 20th-century home and
an 1867 pioneer church.
The **Kai-Iwi Lakes**, 34 km
(21 miles) north of Dargaville,
may lack the excitement of
west coast beaches, but they
are well frequented by local
families and visitors. Comprising the Waikere, Taharoa and
Kai-Iwi, these brilliant blue
lakes are popular with swimmers, water-skiers, fishermen
and picnickers.

🏛 **Matakohe Kauri Museum**
Church Rd, Matakohe. 📞 *(09) 431
7417.* ◻ *daily.* ● *25 Dec.* 📷 ♿
✔ *by arrangement.* 🍽 ⊡

Boat exhibit in the Dargaville Maritime Museum

THE CENTRAL NORTH ISLAND

S*TRETCHING FROM AUCKLAND down to Taranaki, Manawatu and Wairarapa, this area includes beautiful and varied natural and man-made sights: snow-capped volcanoes, geothermal features, trout-filled lakes and rivers, mountain ranges, sandy beaches, fertile farmlands, prolific orchards and vineyards, and extensive forests. It is also a major centre of Maori history and culture.*

Cutting a swathe from White Island in the north to Mount Ruapehu in the south, the Taupo Volcanic Zone *(see pp62–3)*, is testimony to underground forces that have fashioned the central plateau. Rotorua has a range of thermal attractions: geysers, bubbling mud pools, multicoloured silica terraces, steaming lakes and streams and hot mineral pools. Lakes dotting the plateau offer excellent fishing, while rivers flowing from them are used for white-water rafting and jet-boating. In winter there is downhill skiing on the slopes of Mount Ruapehu in Tongariro National Park.

Steep, rugged, bush-clad ranges stretch 300 km (186 miles) from the volcanic plateau to the East Cape, separating the temperate area to the west from the warm, dry east coast region. Farming and forestry are well established in the Bay of Plenty, King Country and Waikato. Dairy farmers compete with horticulturists for the best land, while sheep, cattle and deer roam larger paddocks on hills clear-felled of their native forest in the 19th and early 20th centuries. The Coromandel Peninsula, gripped by gold fever in the latter half of the 19th century, is now home to alternative lifestylers and artists inspired by its natural beauty. The curving Bay of Plenty, the scenic East Cape and the beaches of Gisborne offer excellent swimming, fishing and surfing.

The entire region is rich in Maori history, and Rotorua is the main centre for Maori cultural experiences. The Waikato-based Maori King Movement *(see p115)* began here in 1858, shortly before battles waged between the government and Maoris over land.

Maori cultural performance at Rotorua

◁ **Kiwifruit orchard at Te Puke**

Exploring the Central North Island

The central North Island contains a wide range of landscapes and activities. Hamilton, the region's largest town, is set among lush farmland close to the western surf beaches of Raglan and the mysterious Waitomo Caves. North of Hamilton, the rugged Coromandel Peninsula flows into sandy, unspoilt Bay of Plenty beaches, the East Cape and the east coast, all popular spots for fishing and water sports. Hawke's Bay is famous for its Art Deco buildings, orchards and vineyards. Geothermal attractions stretch from lunar-landscaped White Island to the volcano Ruapehu, the North Island's best skiing location. At the bottom of the region, Tongariro National Park offers a wilderness experience.

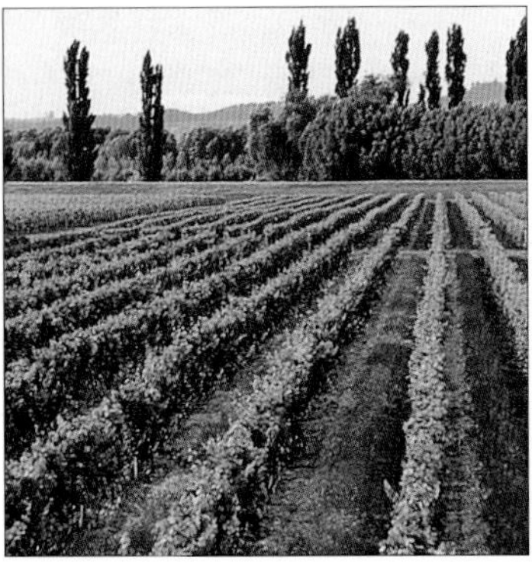

Hawke's Bay vineyard

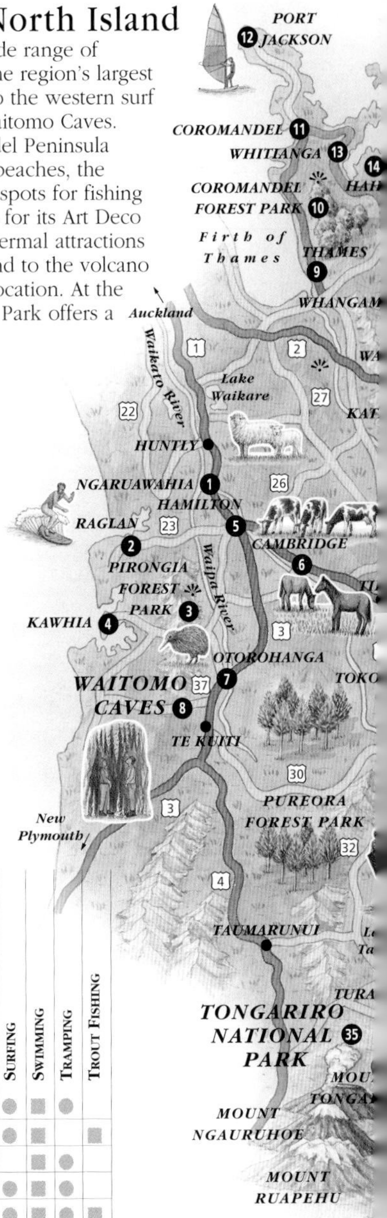
PORT JACKSON 12
COROMANDEL 11
WHITIANGA 13
COROMANDEL FOREST PARK 10
Firth of Thames
THAMES 9
Auckland
Waikato River
Lake Waikare
HUNTLY
NGARUAWAHIA 1
HAMILTON
RAGLAN
2
5
CAMBRIDGE
6
PIRONGIA FOREST PARK 3
Waipa River
KAWHIA 4
OTOROHANGA
7
WAITOMO CAVES 8
TE KUITI
PUREORA FOREST PARK
New Plymouth
TAUMARUNUI
TONGARIRO NATIONAL PARK 35
MOUNT NGAURUHOE
MOUNT RUAPEHU
1
2
22
27
26
23
3
37
30
32
4
0 kilometres 40
0 miles 40

Key

- State Highway
- Major road
- Scenic route
- River
- Viewpoint

Top Outdoor Activities

The places shown here have been selected for their recreational activities. Conditions vary depending on the weather and the time of year, so exercise caution and, if in doubt, seek local advice.

	Game Fishing	Golf	Scuba Diving/Snorkelling	Skiing	Surfing	Swimming	Tramping	Trout Fishing
Coromandel		■	●		●	■	●	
Gisborne	●	■	●		●	■		■
Mayor Island	●		●			■	●	
Mount Maunganui/Tauranga	●	■			●	■	●	
Opotiki		■			●	■	●	■
Raglan		■	●		●	■	●	
Rotorua		■				■	●	■
Taupo		■				■		■
Te Urewera National Park						■	●	■
Tongariro National Park		■		■		■	●	■
Turangi		■				■	●	■
Whitianga	●	■	●		●	■	●	

SIGHTS AT A GLANCE

Cambridge **6**
Cape Kidnappers **38**
Coromandel **11**
Coromandel Forest Park **10**
Gisborne **27**
Hahei **14**
Hamilton **5**
Hastings **37**
Katikati **17**
Kawhia **4**
Mayor Island **20**
Mount Maunganui **19**
Napier pp144–7 **36**
Ngaruawahia **1**
Opotiki **24**

Orakei Korako
  Geyserland **31**
Otorohanga **7**
Pirongia Forest Park **3**
Port Jackson **12**
Raglan **2**
Rotorua pp132–7 **28**
Taupo **33**
Tauranga **18**
Te Puke **21**
Te Urewera National Park **26**
Thames **9**
*Tongariro National Park
  pp140–41* **35**
Turangi **34**

Waihi **16**
Waimangu Volcanic Valley **29**
Waiotapu Thermal
  Wonderland **30**
Wairakei Park **32**
Waitomo Caves pp118–19 **8**
Whakatane **22**
Whangamata **15**
White Island **23**
Whitianga **13**

Tours
East Cape **25**
Hawke's Bay Vineyards **39**

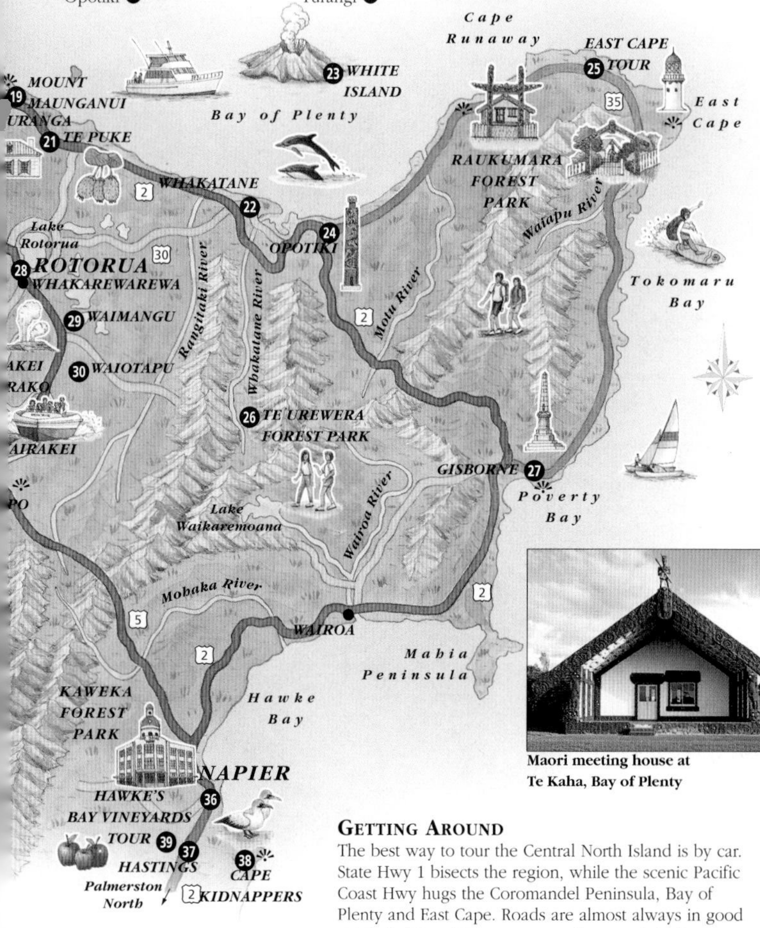

Maori meeting house at
Te Kaha, Bay of Plenty

GETTING AROUND

The best way to tour the Central North Island is by car.
State Hwy 1 bisects the region, while the scenic Pacific
Coast Hwy hugs the Coromandel Peninsula, Bay of
Plenty and East Cape. Roads are almost always in good
repair, but in winter snow may close roads in the
vicinity of Tongariro National Park. A passenger train
service links Auckland with Wellington, with stops at
Hamilton and other main towns. Local buses and tour
companies operate throughout the region.

SEE ALSO

• *Where to Stay* pp300–303

• *Where to Eat* pp320–22

Ngaruawahia ❶

Road map E2. 🏠 6,500. 🚌 ℹ️
160 Great South Rd, Huntly, (07)
828 6406. 🏯 *Ngaruawahia Regatta*
(Sat closest to St Patrick's Day,
17 Mar).

Sᴵᴛᴜᴀᴛᴇᴅ ᴡʜᴇʀᴇ ᴛʜᴇ Waikato
and Waipa rivers meet at
the edge of the central Waikato Basin, Ngaruawahia is
one of the oldest and most
historic settlements in Waikato
and an important centre of
Maori culture. On the northeastern bank of the river, off
River Road, is one of the
Maori people's most important locations – Turangawaewae Marae, "the footstool" or
home of the Waikato Tainui
tribe. Turongo House, located
within the *marae*, is the
official residence of the
reigning Maori monarch, Te
Arikinui Dame Te Atairangi-
kaahu. Although Turanga-
waewae Marae is considered
too sacred for tourism, and
visitors are likely to be referred to Rotorua where Maori
cultural experiences are
widely available, the *marae*
is open to the public for the
annual Ngaruawahia Regatta
on the river, which features
waka (canoe) racing, tribal
dance competitions and other
activities *(see p40)*.
 Mount Taupiri, 6 km
(4 miles) north of Ngaruawahia, provides excellent
views of the Waikato Basin
for those who walk the loop
track to its summit. However,
care must be taken to avoid a
large sacred ancestral burial

The single-plume Bridal Veil Falls southeast of Raglan

ground on the side of the hill
facing State Highway 1.
 In the Hakarimata Reserve
on the slopes of the Hakarimata Range to the north of
Ngaruawahia, native rimu and
kauri trees grow beside three
well-marked tracks, which
offer excellent tramping and
views of the Waikato Basin.

**Eɴᴠɪʀᴏɴs: Waingaro Hot
Springs**, 42km (26 miles)
west of Ngaruawahia, features
four open-air mineral water
pools ranging in temperature
from 32 to 42 °C (90 to 108
°F) as well as private spa
pools. New Zealand's longest
hot water hydroslide as well
as bumper boats offer plenty
of excitement. A range of
accommodation options is
available at the springs.

🏠 **Waingaro Hot Springs**
Waingaro Rd. 📞 *(07) 825 4761.*
⭕ *daily.* 🏊

Raglan ❷

Road map E2. 🏠 3,100. 🚌 ℹ️
7 Bow St, (07) 825 0556. 🏯 *Raglan*
Surf Classic (Mar).

Wᴀɪᴋᴀᴛᴏ's only seaside
resort on the west coast,
Raglan is a small, pleasant
town with welcoming shady
trees in the main street.
Raglan fills with visitors
during summer, attracted to
the water sports available in
its tranquil harbour, its good
swimming beaches and its
excellent surfing. Te Kopua
Beach and Te Aro Aro Bay,
close to Raglan, are popular
for swimming, while Whale
Bay, a ten-minute drive south
along the coast, is famous
worldwide among surfers for
its left-hand break.
 The 25-km (15-mile) drive
south along Raglan's narrow
coastal Whaanga Road pro-
vides breathtaking views of

Turangawaewae Marae, Ngaruawahia, home of the Maori queen

the rugged coastline and the swells of the Tasman Sea.

Abput 21 km (13 miles) southeast of Raglan, on the road to Kawhia, an easy ten-minute walk through dense bush leads to the Bridal Veil Falls. The 55-m (180-ft) water-fall plunges in a single plume from a rock cleft to a deep pool below. A steep track continues to the base of the falls and an even more dramatic vantage point.

Mount Pirongia, an extinct volcanic peak

Whale Bay, Raglan, world famous for its surfing

Pirongia Forest Park ❸

Road map E3. ☐ *18 London St, Hamilton, (07) 838 3363.*

THIS PARK, comprising four separate forest areas south and southeast of Raglan, con-tains an extensive network of trails, from easy walks on the lower peaks to more strenu-ous hikes higher up. At 959 m

(3,146 ft), Mount Pirongia, an ancient volcano lying south-east of Raglan, is the most obvious landmark in the park; its dramatic skyline and dark green forest contrast strongly with the surrounding farm-land. Closer to Raglan, 756-m (2,480-ft) Mt Karioi rises sharply from the coastline. Tracks lead to both peaks.

During the summer months it is advisable to carry drink-ing water on the tracks as natural supplies are difficult to find. A number of native birds can be seen along the tracks and around the park's margins. Several native fish species and a huge variety of aquatic invertebrates can be found in the park's streams.

A hut on Mount Pirongia – Pahautea – sleeps six to eight people. Hut tickets are avail-able from the Department of Conservation in Hamilton. There are picnic areas at the end of both Corcoran and Grey roads and a camping area alongside Kaniwhaniwha Stream, which is also an excellent trout fishing spot.

Kawhia ❹

Road map E3. ♗ *650.* ☐ *57 Maniapoto St, Otorohanga, (07) 873 8951.*

LOCATED ON THE coast 55 km (34 miles) to the south of Raglan, along winding but scenic back roads, the small settlement of Kawhia com-prises a jumble of cottages on the north side of Kawhia Harbour, 5 km (3 miles) from the Tasman Sea. The harbour is remote, splendid and huge, its shoreline twisting and turning for 57 km (35 miles).

In former times, Maoris prized the harbour and the fertile valleys running down to it and fought over rights to the area. The Maori migration canoe Tainui, which last plied the coastline eight centuries ago, is buried on the slopes behind the Anaukiterangi meeting house. Stones placed 23 m (75 ft) apart above the bow and stern mark its position. The canoe was once moored to a pohutukawa tree, Tangi te Korowhiti, on the shore at the end of Karewa Street. Now a large clump of pohutukawas, the tree is still revered by the Tainui people as signifying the beginning of their associ-ation with Aotearoa.

The large Kawhia harbour on the west coast

MAORI KING MOVEMENT

Queen Te Atairangikaahu

This movement grew in the 1850s out of a realization among Maoris that intertribal feuding assisted the Pakeha (white people) to acquire Maori land. In 1858, several tribes chose a paramount king in the hope that the dignity and *mana* (respect) that would accrue to him would promote peaceful co-existence with the government and settle land conflicts. Instead, the government interpreted the Maori King Movement as a form of rebellion. Attitudes hardened and spawned the Waikato land wars of the 1860s *(see pp47–8)*. Queen Te Atairangi-kaahu, the sixth monarch in the line, was proclaimed in 1966. Today, the monarch's role is essentially cultural and spiritual, although this is becoming more important as the place of Maoris in New Zealand society is reassessed.

Hamilton ❺

Road map E2. 🏛 118,000. ✈ 10 km (6 miles) S of city. 🚌 🚆 Cnr Bryce & Anglesea sts, (07) 839 3580. 🎪 New Zealand Hot Air Balloon Fiesta (mid-Apr); National Agricultural Fieldays (Jun).

New Zealand's fifth largest metropolitan area and largest inland city, Hamilton straddles a meandering section of the mighty Waikato River, at 425 km (264 miles) the longest in the country. The city has grown from a 19th-century military settlement into a bustling centre servicing the Waikato region, a huge undulating plain. Attractive parks and gardens, bisected by footpaths, border the river, and bridges connect the east and west banks. The **MV Waipa Delta** paddleboat cruises the river three times daily from its landing in central Hamilton, offering the best views of the area.

Perched on five levels above the river, the **Waikato Museum of Art and History** features a large collection of New Zealand art, Waikato history and history of the local Tainui people. On permanent display is an impressive war canoe, Te Winika.

The **Hamilton Gardens**, located at the southern end of the city, are Hamilton's most popular visitor attraction. Set along a scenic stretch of the Waikato River, they include pavilions showcasing Japanese, Chinese and English gardens as well as seasonal attractions.

Hamilton hosts two major annual events – the Hot Air Balloon Fiesta, which attracts balloonists from around the world, and the National Agricultural Fieldays at nearby Mystery Creek, one of Australasia's largest agricultural trade shows (see p41).

🚢 MV Waipa Delta
Memorial Park Jetty, Memorial Drive. 📞 (07) 854 9415. ◯ daily. 🎫
♿ 🍴

🏛 Waikato Museum of Art and History
1 Grantham St. 📞 (07) 838 6606. ◯ daily. ● 25 Dec. 🎫 ♿ 📷 📖

🌺 Hamilton Gardens
Cobham Drive. 📞 (07) 856 3200. ◯ daily. ♿

Cambridge ❻

Road map E3. 🏛 13,500. ✈ 15 km (9 miles) E of city. 🚆 Cnr Queen & Victoria sts, (07) 823 3456.

Fifteen minutes' drive south of Hamilton, Cambridge lies amid farmland, home to New Zealand's thoroughbred horse industry. Known as "the town of trees" because of its avenues of oak and elm, the town has a charming village green and pretty gardens. The domain around Lake Koutu, fringed by exotic trees and native bush, is a popular place for walks and picnics.

Cambridge is also known for its contemporary art and crafts outlets; one, the large,

Items for sale at the Cambridge Country Store

award-winning **Cambridge Country Store**, is located in a church built in 1898. The town's numerous antique shops and galleries are another major attraction.

Visitors can also view a potpourri of architectural styles at St. Andrew's church and the public buildings along Victoria Street and the roads branching off it.

🎁 Cambridge Country Store
92 Victoria St. 📞 (07) 827 8715. ◯ daily. ● 25 Dec. ♿ 📷

Otorohanga ❼

Road map E3. 🏛 2,600. 🚉 🚌 🚆 57 Maniapoto St, (07) 873 8951.

Fifty kilometres (31 miles) south of Hamilton lies Otorohanga, a small provincial town whose main attraction is the **Otorohanga Kiwi House**. Three kiwi species are bred at the zoological park and 300 birds, representing 29 species, can be viewed in a massive walk-through aviary. In addition to kiwis, these include native pigeons, tuis, silvereyes, parakeets and saddlebacks. Geckos, wetas, and the ancient tuatara reptile are also on display.

Otorohanga, being the closest town, is regarded as the gateway to the Waitomo Caves (see pp118–19).

🦜 Otorohanga Kiwi House
20 Alex Telfer Drive. 📞 (07) 873 7391. ◯ daily. ● 25 Dec. 🎫 ♿ 🌙 Nocturnal House. 🍴

Glassware at the Cambridge Country Store

The MV **Waipa Delta** cruising on the Waikato River

Stock-Stud Heartland

Holstein-Friesian cow

ONE OF THE most fascinating sights on the drive between Hamilton and Cambridge is of wooden-railed fences behind which young thoroughbred horses cavort, growing strong on the best pasture and supplementary feed their owners can provide. Set back from the road are signposted stud stables where the horses are housed and trained. Another common sight is of black and white cows grazing on dappled green fields. New Zealand's thoroughbred racehorse and dairy cattle stud industries are concentrated in the Waikato region, where a mild, wet climate produces lush cattle pasture and the rolling plains are ideal for exercising and training racehorses.

THOROUGHBRED HORSES

Waikato is renowned internationally for its racing progeny, and the yearling export industry earns the country more than NZ$100 million annually. Some 60 stallions are available for breeding purposes at 18 Waikato commercial thoroughbred studs, the most sought after of these sires mating 100–150 mares.

Thoroughbred yearlings and foals on a Waikato stud farm

New Zealand Horse Magic, 6 km (4 miles) south of Cambridge, showcases a collection of horse breeds and features an informative hour-long show. Thoroughbred stud tours are also available at other stud farms in the area.

Waikato-bred horses have won Australia's Melbourne Cup, the pinnacle of the Australasian racing season, 18 times.

New Zealand's main dairy breeds – Holstein-Friesian, Jersey and Ayrshire – can be found in Waikato, although the Holstein-Friesian predominates. The average New Zealand cow produces 3,420 litres (752 imperial gallons) of milk a year.

New Zealand's thoroughbred industry is showcased to the world each February at the yearling sale held at Karaka on the southern outskirts of Auckland.

Waitomo Caves ●8

Glowworm Cave logo

THE AREA KNOWN as Waitomo consists of a 45-km (28-mile) network of underground limestone caves and grottoes linked to the Waitomo River. A chamber of the Glowworm Cave was the first to be explored, in 1887, but most caves remain untouched. Apart from touring the Glowworm and Aranui caves, famous for their glowworm grottoes and fantastic limestone formations, visitors can enjoy a range of cave-based adventure activities, including abseiling into a limestone shaft and cave system, and black-water rafting, an adventure sport unique to New Zealand. The 2.5 km (1.5 miles) of caves accessible to the public have superb lighting, good paths, handrails and informative local guides.

Waitomo Walkway
A 5-km (3-mile) walk over farmland and through native bush takes visitors past typical limestone karst features such as outcrops and sinkholes.

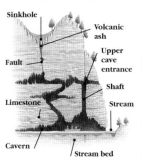

Black-water Rafting
Equipped with wet suits, helmets, lights and "cave rafts" (inner tubes), these black-water rafters drift in darkness along an underground river in the Ruakuri Cave.

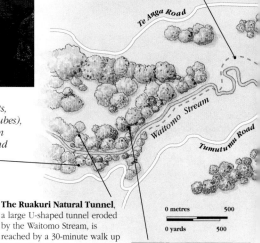

KEY

═══	Road
══	River
▪ ▪	Walking track

The Ruakuri Natural Tunnel, a large U-shaped tunnel eroded by the Waitomo Stream, is reached by a 30-minute walk up the Ruakuri Gorge.

0 metres   500

0 yards   500

FORMATION OF THE WAITOMO CAVES

Caves are formed through the erosion of layers of limestone by water flowing underground. The cave systems in the Waitomo area have developed in fractured limestone, up to 100 m (330 ft) thick, along or adjacent to major fault lines *(see p20)* where percolation of groundwater is particularly high. Surface water flowing down cracks in the limestone created an underground drainage system which gradually increased in size and complexity. Inside the Waitomo caves, dripping water containing dissolved limestone has formed stalactites on the cave roofs, stalagmites on the floors, and other fascinating formations.

Sinkhole
Volcanic ash
Upper cave entrance
Fault
Shaft
Limestone
Stream
Cavern
Stream bed

★ Aranui Cave
The high chambers, magnificent formations and pale brown, pink and white shades of the huge stalactites are the finest to be seen in Waitomo's caves.

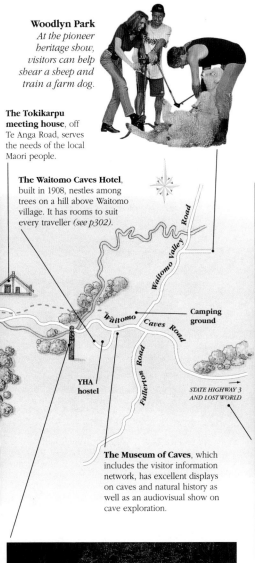

Woodlyn Park
At the pioneer heritage show, visitors can help shear a sheep and train a farm dog.

The Tokikarpu meeting house, off Te Anga Road, serves the needs of the local Maori people.

The Waitomo Caves Hotel, built in 1908, nestles among trees on a hill above Waitomo village. It has rooms to suit every traveller *(see p302).*

Camping ground

YHA hostel

STATE HIGHWAY 3 AND LOST WORLD

The Museum of Caves, which includes the visitor information network, has excellent displays on caves and natural history as well as an audiovisual show on cave exploration.

Lost World
The Lost World Adventure involves a 100-m (330-ft) abseil descent into a huge limestone shaft followed by an amazing caving expedition through the Mangapu Cave system.

STAR SIGHTS

★ **Aranui Cave**

★ **Glowworm Cave**

★ **Glowworm Cave**
A walk through the three levels of the cave – the Banquet Chamber, Pipe Organ and Cathedral – is capped by a tranquil boat ride through the magical Glowworm Grotto.

Karaka Bird Hide on the Firth of Thames

Thames ❾

Road map E2. 👤 7,000. ✈️ 2 km (1.2 miles) S of town. 🚌 ℹ️ 206 Pollen St, (07) 868 7284.

LOCATED AT THE southeastern corner of the Firth of Thames, against hills that 100 years ago rang to the sound of battery stamps pounding quartz ore to extract gold, Thames is the principal town of the Coromandel region, servicing surrounding farmland and a swelling coastal population. It is the gateway to the Coromandel Peninsula and an ideal base from which to explore the Coromandel Forest Park wilderness area. Many of the buildings in the town owe their grandeur to wealth generated during the gold-mining era.

Hard against a hillside at the northern end of the town is the **Thames Gold Mine and Stamper Battery** where ore is processed by a traditional battery. A tour through 100 m (330 ft) of intersecting tunnels provides an insight into early mining techniques. The **Thames Historical Museum** features relics from the town's past, including the pioneering foundries that sprang up to support the mining industry, while the **Thames School of Mines and Mineralogical Museum** features 5,000 mineral samples and equipment used to process quartz ore and extract gold. Mine managers were taught in the school's classroom from 1885 to 1954.

A large World War I memorial, off Waiotahi Creek Road, stands on a hill above the town to the north, and affords panoramic views of the town, the Firth of Thames, and the Hauraki Gulf beyond. At the small Karaka Bird Hide, built among mangroves off Brown Street on the edge of town, visitors can see a variety of migratory wading birds, especially in the period between high and low tides.

Entrance to the Thames Gold Mine and Stamper Battery

🎫 **Thames Gold Mine and Stamper Battery**
Cnr State Hwy 5 & Moanatairi St. 📞 (07) 868 8514. 🔲 daily. 🔴 Good Fri, 25 Apr, 25 Dec. 🎟️ 🔲 not in mine.

🏛️ **Thames Historical Museum**
Cnr Pollen & Cochrane sts. 📞 (07) 868 8509. 🔲 daily. 🎟️ 🔲

🏛️ **Thames School of Mines and Mineralogical Museum**
Cnr Cochrane & Brown sts. 📞 (07) 868 6227. 🔲 daily. 🔴 Mon (Jun–Aug), Good Fri, 25 Dec. 🎟️

ENVIRONS: Along the Firth of Thames' southern edge, 85 sq km (33 sq miles) of rich, intertidal mud flats provide another excellent habitat for migratory wading birds, such as gulls, shags, oystercatchers and pied stilts, and opportunities to observe them. The **Miranda Shorebird Centre,**

established by the Miranda Naturalists' Trust, can arrange tours to see the birds as well as accommodation. Nearby is the Miranda Hot Springs, a thermal pool complex.

🦅 **Miranda Shorebird Centre**
East Coast Rd, Pokeno. 📞 (09) 232 2781. 🔲 daily. 🔴 25 Dec. 🎟️ donation. 🔲

Coromandel Forest Park ❿

Road map E2. ℹ️ Kauaeranga Valley, Thames, (07) 867 9080.

THIS PARK stretches for 100 km (62 miles) along the peninsula's interior, but the most accessible portion is the forested Kauaeranga Valley, with its well-developed network of short walks, longer tramps and picnic areas.

The valley was a major source of kauri timber from the 1870s to the 1920s. Remains of dams, trestle bridges and river booms, used to flush kauri logs into the Kauaeranga River, are evident.

Anglers can fish for trout in the valley's streams where the keen-eyed may also find gemstones. The Kauaeranga Visitor Centre, 13 km (8 miles) northeast of Thames, provides details of walks and tramps that comprise the Kauaeranga Kauri Trail, a pack track made by kauri bushmen, as well as the various types of accommodation available in the park.

Trampers in the Kauaeranga Valley, Coromandel Forest Park

Coromandel Gold Fever

Gold nugget

THE FIRST significant gold find on the Coromandel Peninsula occurred in October 1852 near Coromandel Town. Three hundred diggers rushed to the area. Further discoveries near Thames in 1867 attracted 5,000 men into the surrounding hills. Soon Thames became a boom town and its population mushroomed to 18,000. Miners thronged the town on Saturdays, three live theatres were seldom closed, and more than 100 hotels sold liquor. But by the 1870s the Thames goldfields were in decline and interest had shifted southeast to Karangahake Mountain and to Waihi. By 1912, Waihi's Martha Mine had become one of the world's largest *(see p124)*. The mines all closed eventually, but new gold-bearing zones found within old fields prompted large-scale mining operations to begin once more at the open mining pit at Waihi in 1988.

Candles provided light and indicated the presence of gas.

A mallet and pick were used to loosen gold-bearing rock.

Canvas bags held any nuggets that were extracted.

Model of a miner at the Thames Gold Mine and Stamper Battery

GOLD-MINING RELICS

Old gold mines, shafts, mine dumps and abandoned mining machinery are dotted around Thames. The mining school and mineralogical museum, as well as the gold mine tours on offer, are further reminders of the town's gold-mining history. Coromandel gold had to be laboriously extracted from the ground with pick and shovel.

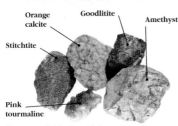

Orange calcite

Goodlitite

Amethyst

Stitchtite

Pink tourmaline

Coromandel is also rich in semi-precious gemstones. It is still possible to stumble across agate on some of the beaches north of Thames.

This classroom in the Thames School of Mines provided practical instruction to gold-miners working the quartz fields.

Fossicking for gold in the old gold mines is a popular pastime but care must be taken when entering old mines that they are structurally safe.

The Imperial Hotel, one of a number of fine colonial hotels in Thames built at the height of the town's gold-rush prosperity.

Coromandel ⑪

Road map E2. 🏠 1,500. ✈ 3 km (2 miles) S of town. 🚌 ⓘ 355 Kapanga Rd, (07) 866 8598.

COROMANDEL TOWN, as it is referred to by those wishing to distinguish it from the peninsula itself, is a quiet fishing and crafts town about an hour's drive north of Thames. It owes its name to the 1820 visit of HMS *Coromandel*, which called to load kauri spars for the British Royal Navy. Mining featured prominently in the town's formative years *(see p121)*, and fine examples of Victorian and colonial architecture are a legacy of that era. The laid-back atmosphere and beauty of the area make it a haven for artists and crafts people, and an ideal place in which to tramp, swim, fish, sail or simply relax.

One of Coromandel's most popular attractions is the **Driving Creek Railway and Potteries**, built by well-known New Zealand potter Barry Brickell to convey clay and wood to his kiln, and to service a kauri forest replanting project. The narrow-gauge mountain railway takes visitors in specially designed carriages on a one-hour round trip through native forest and tunnels and across bridges to a viewpoint high above Coromandel.

The **Coromandel Gold Stamper Battery** and a 100-year-old gold-processing museum, featuring a large working water wheel, lie at the end of Buffalo Road to

Water-powered bicycle at the Waiau Waterworks

the north of the town. The **Coromandel School of Mines and Historical Museum** has displays of early gold-mining and kauri logging, geological specimens, an old jailhouse and other items of town history.

🚆 Driving Creek Railway and Potteries
Driving Creek Rd. 📞 (07) 866 8703. ⏰ daily. ● 25 April, 25 Dec. 📷 ♿ ⓘ

⚒ Coromandel Gold Stamper Battery
Buffalo Rd. 📞 (07) 866 8113. ⏰ Summer: daily; Winter: Thurs–Mon. ● 25 Dec. 📷 ♿

🏛 Coromandel School of Mines and Historical Museum
841 Rings Rd. ⏰ Summer: daily; Winter: Sat & Sun. ● 25 Dec. 📷 ♿

ENVIRONS: The delightful **Waiau Waterworks**, 9 km (5.5 miles) from Coromandel Town, showcases artist Chris Ogilvie's genius for inventing

water-powered art forms and gadgets that amaze both children and adults. One of Coromandel's most innovative attractions, the waterworks is set in park-like gardens.

Just east of the waterworks is a turn-off to Castle Rock. At 525 m (1,722 ft), it is the core of an old volcano on the "backbone" of the peninsula. A drive through pine forest takes visitors to the start of a 45-minute walk. The last few metres are a strenuous climb, but panoramic views make it worthwhile. Further along the road is the Waiau Kauri Grove where magnificent kauris, protected for more than 100 years, are to be seen ten minutes' walk along a track on the left side of the road.

🎋 Waiau Waterworks
309 Rd. 📞 (07) 866 7191. ⏰ mid-Sep–June: daily. 📷 ♿ ⓘ

Coastline between Coromandel Town and Port Jackson

Port Jackson ⑫

Road map E2. 🏠 10. ⓘ 355 Kapanga Rd, Coromandel Town, (07) 866 8598.

AT THE TIP of the peninsula, 56 km (35 miles) north of Coromandel, Port Jackson's long, lupin-backed beach comes as a surprise. The road, which is unsealed from the small settlement of Colville, the last supply point, ends at Fletcher's Bay, 6 km (4 miles) further on, a pretty pohutukawa-shaded cove with good fishing.

The Coromandel Walkway, a 7-km (4.5-mile) track, leads from Fletcher's Bay to Stony Bay and takes about three hours to complete. Port Jackson, Fletcher Bay and Stony Bay all have camping grounds with toilets, cold showers and barbecue pits.

The unique Driving Creek Railway

Boats at sheltered Whitianga harbour

Whitianga ⓭

Road map E2. 👥 3,500. ✈ 3 km (2 miles) SW of town. 🚌 ℹ 66 Albert St, (07) 866 5555.

WHITIANGA sits on the innermost recess of Mercury Bay which was named by Captain Cook *(see p46)* when he observed a transit of the planet Mercury on his 1769 visit to the area. Whitianga provides safe boat launching, ideal during the big game fishing season from November to April. Major fishing contests occur in February and March. The tiny Mercury Bay Boating Club, at the west end of Buffalo Beach, earned world fame when it spearheaded Auckland financier Michael Fay's unsuccessful 1988 challenge to the San Diego Yacht Club for the America's Cup.

Boating club logo

The **Mercury Bay Museum** occupies a disused dairy factory opposite the wharf on The Esplanade. It documents the Polynesian chief Kupe *(see p45),* whose descendants are said to have occupied the town for more than 1,000 years. A short ferry ride across the narrow harbour entrance takes visitors to Ferry Landing, the original site of Whitianga, where there are walks, lookouts and craft outlets. Whitianga Rock, upstream of Ferry Landing, was formerly a *pa* site of the Ngati Hei tribe.

Whitianga's Buffalo Beach is named after an 1840 shipwreck. The British ship *Buffalo*, which had delivered convicts to Australia and was to return to Britain with kauri spars, was blown by a storm onto the beach and destroyed. A cannon from the ship is mounted at the RSA Memorial Park in Albert Street.

At the northeast tip of the headland, 1.5 km (1 mile) from Ferry Landing, is Shakespeare Lookout, named after the bard. Here also, a memorial to Cook stands above Lonely Bay and the 3-km (2-mile) sweep of Cooks Beach.

Wave action at Flaxmill Bay, at the southwest end of Front Bay, has undercut the rock to form a natural soundshell.

The **Te Whanganui-A-Hei Marine Reserve** at Cathedral Cove covers 9 sq km (4 sq miles) and extends from Cooks Bluff to Hahei Beach. It was established in 1992 to restore the area's marine environment to its former rich and varied condition. No fishing or gathering of shellfish is allowed, although visitors may swim, dive and sail in the reserve.

🏛 Mercury Bay Museum
The Esplanade. ⏰ 11am–3pm Sun, Tue & Thu. ● Public hols. 📷 ♿

Hahei ⓮

Road map E2. 👥 200. 🚌 General Store, Hahei Beach Rd.

HAHEI IS THE start of a two-hour return walk to Cathedral Cove, where a dramatic, cathedral-shaped cavern, accessible at low tide, cuts through a white headland. Reasonable fitness is required to reach the cove but panoramic cliff-top views make the effort worthwhile. Hahei's beach is sheltered by offshore islands and tinged pink with broken shells. The area is popular with divers.

At Hot Water Beach, 6 km (4 miles) south of Hahei, visitors can dig their own thermal spa in the sand between low and mid-tides. Spades are available for hire.

Visitors soaking in hot springs in the sand at Hot Water Beach, Hahei

Whangamata **⑮**

Road map E2. 👥 4,100. 🚌
🛈 606 Port Rd, (07) 865 8340.

THE TOWN OF Whangamata, meaning "obsidian harbour", was named after the dark, glass-like volcanic rock that has washed ashore from Mayor Island, 30 km (19 miles) from the mainland. The town is often referred to as "the surfing capital of New Zealand" because of the size of the waves in the area, particularly its sandbank surf break known as "the bar". Its surf is also popular with swimmers who enjoy large waves and with surf-fishers. Other superb surfing beaches in the vicinity include Onemana and Opoutere to the north of the town and Whiritoa on the coast to the south.

The hills and valleys behind Whangamata, a short drive from the town, offer many

Whangamata Beach, one of New Zealand's best surf beaches

outdoor activities. Within the Tairua Forest lie the Wentworth Valley, Taungatara Recreation Reserve and Parakiwai Valley. These are crisscrossed with walking tracks that make the most of stony streams and pockets of native bush. A popular walk takes in the "Luck at Last" gold mine and the remains of ore processors, water races, buildings and even a baker's oven. Walk details are available from the Whangamata information centre and forestry company Carter Holt Harvey, which may close access when it is conducting forestry operations. The Wharekawa Wildlife Refuge, 15 km (10 miles) north of Whangamata, is a conservation area based on the Opoutere sandspit. The refuge is home to oyster-catchers and dotterels.

Martha Mine at Waihi

Waihi **⑯**

Road map E2. 👥 4,500. 🚌
🛈 Seddon St, (07) 863 6715.

THE HISTORY of Waihi has been linked with gold since Robert Lee and John McCrombie discovered a gold-bearing quartz reef in 1878. The **Martha Mine**, established on the site in 1882 and worked continuously until 1952, was the most important and successful of many in the district (see pp120–21). In 1988, it reopened, with concessions to operate until 2007. Substantial amounts of gold are extracted from the mine each week. Bookings are essential for tours conducted by the Waihi Gold Mining Company.

The **Goldfields Railway** operates vintage diesel and steam trains on 7 km (4 miles) of track between Waihi and Waikino, gateway to the Karangahake gold fields. The Karangahake Gorge Historic Walkway, a 5-km (3-mile) loop along the gorge past old bridges, abandoned mining equipment and mining shafts,

is clearly signposted from the road. Waihi Beach, 11 km (7 miles) east of the town, is one of the most popular beaches along the coast.

⛏ Martha Mine
Seddon St. 📞 (07) 863 9880. ◯
Mon–Fri. 🎫 donation. ♿ 🚻
booking essential.

🚂 Goldfields Railway
Wrigley St. 📞 (07) 863 8251. ◯
daily. ⬤ 25 Dec. 🎫 ♿ 🖥 🎁

Katikati **⑰**

Road map E2. 👥 4,000. 🛈 34 Main
St, (07) 549 1658.

ENTHUSIASTIC IRISH colonizer George Vesey Stewart bought Katikati and its surrounding land in the 1870s and sold it to 406 "refined and educated" Ulster families. Unfamiliar with the hard work needed to break in their land, these immigrants initially resented Stewart, but the district has since proved itself ideal for horticulture and dairy farming. Today, Katikati has earned a reputation as an open-air "art gallery". More than 30 murals and other pieces of art decorate its buildings, streets and parks, all of them the work of local artists. **Sapphire Springs**, set in a bush reserve 6 km (4 miles) from the town, has a number of freshwater thermal springs for swimming or soaking.

Street sculpture, Katikati

♨ Sapphire Springs
Hot Springs Rd. 📞 (07) 549 0768.
◯ daily. 🎫 🖥

Mural on a building at Katikati

Coromandel's Artisan Lifestyle

Hand-blown glass bowl

THE EVER-CHANGING sea, beautiful valleys and rugged forest interior of the Coromandel Peninsula not only offer a quiet alternative to city life but provide constant inspiration to a large number of artists and crafts people. Here painters farm, potters paint and raise silkworms, and weavers rear their own sheep for wool. Since their arrival in the early 1960s, many of these "alternative lifestylers" have turned to art and crafts to support their nature-based lifestyle, honing their talents to produce a large number of attractive items for sale in retail outlets throughout New Zealand. The Coromandel Craft Trail leaflet, available at visitor centres, directs visitors to tucked-away studios where they can see artists at work and buy items direct at studio prices.

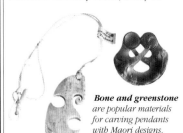

Bone and greenstone *are popular materials for carving pendants with Maori designs.*

Retail outlets *in Thames and Coromandel Town, such as Weta Art, sell a wide range of Coromandel and other New Zealand-made crafts.*

Pottery items *are either thrown on a wheel or, like these pieces, hand-sculpted and glazed in a multitude of colours.*

Barry Brickell at Driving Creek Potteries

COROMANDEL'S CRAFTS

Although the initial surge of artistic pursuits on the peninsula in the early 1960s focused on clay, crafts quickly diversified to include carving (in wood, bone and greenstone), kauri furniture, weaving, knitting, jewellery, leadlight glass work, hand-made knives and garden décor.

Colville Store, *one of the peninsula's most unusual retail outlets, 26 km (16 miles) north of Coromandel Town, is owned by an 80-member co-operative.*

Alternative lifestylers *often choose to raise young children in supportive community environments where they grow organic produce, paint, sculpt and make crafts.*

Tauranga ⑱

Road map E2. 🏘 *including Mount Maunganui, 90,600.* ✈ *3 km (2 miles) E of town.* 🚌 ℹ *95 Willow St, (07) 578 8103.*

THE LARGEST CITY in the western Bay of Plenty and an important commercial centre and port, Tauranga lies along a section of the sprawling Tauranga Harbour, a plain thought to have been flooded at the end of the last Ice Age. On its seaward side, the city is sheltered by Matakana Island and to the west by the Kaimai Range.

In recent years, Tauranga has experienced rapid growth. Its benign climate and coastal location are not only attractive to retired New Zealanders, but to anyone who enjoys year-round outdoor activities. Recreational and competitive boating, surfing and deep-sea fishing are its major attractions. It is also a popular venue for jet-skiing, water-skiing, wind-surfing, parasailing and diving. The Strand, in the centre of town, is the main shopping and restaurant area.

Originally a flax-trading and missionary town, Tauranga was the scene of fierce fighting during the New Zealand land wars in the 1860s *(see pp47–8)*. Many of the troops involved in a significant battle at Gate Pa, 5 km (3 miles) south of the city, were stationed at Monmouth Redoubt, a military camp built by British troops in 1864 to stop supplies reaching the Waikato Maori King Movement *(see p115)*. Well-preserved earthworks and heavy artillery, are still in place.

The Elms Mission House, built in stages between 1838 and 1847 by the Reverend Alfred Brown, is one of New Zealand's oldest homes. The grounds contain gardens and several buildings, including an 1839 free-standing library.

Tauranga's other attractions include 50 km (31 miles) of beach and foreshore reserve and 27 km (17 miles) of public walkways around the coastal areas, estuary and inland reserves.

🏛 The Elms Mission House
Cnr Mission & Chapel sts. ℹ *(07) 577 9772.* ⬜ *grounds: daily; house & library: tours by arrangement.* 🏠 *house & library.*

ENVIRONS: McLaren Falls Park, off State Highway 29 on the road to Hamilton, has walks through picturesque native bush interspersed with thousands of introduced trees. A river and Lake McLaren offer swimming. On scheduled days throughout the year, top white-water action occurs downstream on the Wairoa River when floodgates on the hydro-controlled waterway are opened.

🌿 McLaren Falls Park
McLaren Falls Rd. ℹ *Tauranga District Council, (07) 577 7000.* ⬜ *daily.* ♿

Beach at Mount Maunganui from "The Mount"

Mount Maunganui ⑲

Road map E2. 🏘 *including Tauranga, 90,600.* ✈ *3 km (2 miles) S of town.* 🚌 ℹ *Salisbury Ave, (07) 575 5099.*

THE TOWN OF Mount Maunganui, built on a narrow peninsula at the mouth of Tauranga Harbour, is the main port for the central North Island timber industry. Overshadowing the town is the 232-m (761-ft) cone-shaped Mount Maunganui. A walk to the summit and back takes 90 minutes and provides views of Maori fortifications dating from when "The Mount", as it is commonly called, was a *pa* site. At the top, unobstructed views up and down the coast can be seen. At the bottom are the **Mount Maunganui Hot Salt Water Pools**, which are heated by a natural thermal resource.

Magnificent Ocean Beach extends east from The Mount to Papamoa and beyond, creating an ideal summer playground for surfers and swimmers. In high seas, a blowhole at Moturiki Island, off Marine Parade, shoots spray skywards.

♨ Mount Maunganui Hot Salt Water Pools
Adams Ave. ℹ *(07) 575 0868.* ⬜ *daily.* 🏊♿🚻

Game fishing competition, Tauranga

Mayor Island ⑳

Road map F2. *35 km (22 miles) from Tauranga Harbour.* 🚢 *from Tauranga or Whangamata.* ☎ *(07) 577 0531.*

MAYOR ISLAND is rather hilly and bush-clad and there are very few landing places around its steep cliffs. The highest peak, Opauhau, reaches 354 m (1,161 ft) above a roughly circular island 4 km (3 miles) across. Two lakes, one green and the other black, lie within a crater crowning the summit of what is a dormant volcano rising from the sea floor.

The island's most striking feature is black obsidian, a natural glass formed by rapid cooling of silica-rich lava. In pre-European times, Maoris prized obsidian and fought battles over the island.

An 18-km (11-mile) walking track circles the island while other paths cross the interior. All sea life is protected within a marine reserve on the northern coastline. A camping ground and cabins provide accommodation, but visitors must take adequate food and water as supplies on the island are limited. Game fish in the vicinity of the island include tuna, marlin, kingfish and mako sharks. The largest fish are caught between late December and early May.

Tour in kiwi-carts through Kiwifruit Country

Te Puke ㉑

Road map F3. 🏠 *6,500.* 🚌
ℹ️ *130 Jellicoe St, (07) 573 9172.*

TE PUKE is another town originally settled with Irish folk by Ulsterman George Vesey Stewart *(see p124)* in the 1880s. Early farming of sheep and cattle in the area was hampered by "bush sickness," a cobalt deficiency that dogged farming in many central North Island regions until it was identified in the 1930s and corrected with cobaltized fertilizers. With an

Entrance to Kiwifruit County

ideal climate for sheep, cattle and dairy farming, these land uses predominated until interest in horticulture strengthened in the 1960s.

Pioneering horticulturists experimented with what was then known as the Chinese gooseberry, and developed an international market for it under a new name – kiwifruit. Since then Te Puke has been hailed as "the kiwifruit capital of the world". All aspects of the industry, from cultivation to processing, are displayed at the export kiwifruit orchard and horticultural park **Kiwifruit Country**, 6 km (4 miles) southeast of Te Puke.

Longridge Park, 8 km (5 miles) south of Te Puke, is a large farm designed to show the diversity of New Zealand farming. Tours of the park take in deer, sheep and pigs, as well as groves of avocado, kiwifruit and pine trees. Children can get up close to young animals and hand-feed 60-year-old eels. Visitors can also explore the stunning natural beauty of the bush-clad Kaituna River during a 30-minute jet-boat ride.

🥝 **Kiwifruit Country**
85 Young Rd. ☎ *(07) 573 6340.*
◯ *daily.* ● *25 Dec.* 🎫 &
📷 *obligatory.* 🍴 ▣ ▢
🥝 **Longridge Park**
State Hwy 33, Paengaroa, Te Puke. ☎
(07) 533 1818. ◯ *daily.* ● *25 Dec.*
🎫 *rides.* & 📷 *obligatory.* ▣ ▢

KIWIFRUIT

Before kiwifruit *(Actinidia chinensis)* became an international marketing success, it was known in New Zealand as the Chinese gooseberry after its country of origin. The first plant was grown in Te Puke in 1918, but it was not until the mid-1930s that Te Puke grower Jim McLoughlin planted the first orchard and sold fruit on the local market. Offshore markets were sought as more kiwifruit were grown. In the late 1960s, the industry was propelled to success by a combination of good marketing and the discovery that refrigerated kiwifruit remains in good condition for up to six months. In the late 1970s, many horticulturists became millionaires almost overnight. Since 1998, the yellow-fleshed, tropical-flavoured Zespri Gold variety has supplemented the traditional emerald green-centred Hayward variety.

Kiwifruit from Te Puke

Fishing at the mouth of the Whakatane River

Whakatane ㉒

Road map F3. 🏃 *14,000*. 🚌
🛈 *Boon St, (07) 308 6058.*

R ESTING IN THE coastal heart of the eastern Bay of Plenty, Whakatane is one of New Zealand's sunniest locations. The town enjoys more than 2,500 sunshine hours a year, making it ideal for a wide range of marine activities. These include fishing in the Whakatane River and viewing and swimming with dolphins. Dolphins Down Under, in The Strand, takes visitors on a voyage out into the Bay of Plenty to swim with dolphins.

The **Whakatane District Museum and Gallery** gives an insight into the lifestyles of early Maori and European settlers. It contains a pictorial history of the district as well as displays of Maori artifacts.

There are several excellent local walkways. One, the Nga Tapuwae O Toi Walkway, provides beautiful views of the sea and coastal pohutu-kawa trees. Access to the

route, which takes seven hours to complete the entire circuit, is from Seaview Road above the town. The first landmark is Kapu te Rangi ("ridge of heaven"), the site of some of the country's oldest known earthworks.

🏛 Whakatane District Museum and Gallery
11 Boon St. 📞 *(07) 307 9805.*
🕐 *Tue–Sun.* 🏷 *donation.* ♿

ENVIRONS: Whale Island, 10 km (6 miles) north of the harbour entrance, is a wildlife refuge. Excursions are organized by the Department of Conservation over the Christmas–New Year period. Bookings can be made at the Whakatane Visitor Centre.

East of Whakatane, idyllic **Ohope Beach** stretches 12 km (7.5 miles) from Otarawairere, its western extremity, to the mouth of tidal Ohiwa Harbour. The harbour is an important source of both fish and shellfish.

White Island ㉓

Road map F2. *46 km (28 miles) from Whakatane.*

N EW ZEALAND'S most active volcano, White Island lies at the northern end of the Taupo–Rotorua volcanic fault line *(see pp62–3).* It can be reached by boat or helicopter or simply viewed from the air. The island's terrain is likened to that of the moon or Mars and many visitors rate it as one of the country's best attractions. The island was

mined for sulphur until 1914, when a night-time eruption killed all miners on the island. Remains of mining activities can be seen. A large gannet colony has established on the island and suffers no ill-effects from the ash fall-out.

Old suphur mining equipment on White Island

Opotiki ㉔

Road map F3. 🏃 *4,150*. 🚌 🛈 *Cnr St John & Elliott sts, (07) 315 8484.*

S ITUATED AT THE confluence of the Waioeka and Otara rivers, Opotiki is the gateway to the East Cape and the last major town before Gisborne. In 1865, at Opotiki, the Reverend Carl Sylvius Völkner was hanged and then decapitated by Maoris convinced he passed information about their movements and fortifications to Governor George Grey *(see p74).* Hiona St Stephen's Anglican Church, where the incident took place, lies at the northern end of the Church Street business area. A key is held across the road at the **Opotiki Historical and Agricultural Society Museum**, which is jammed with early settlers' items.

An excellent example of a warm, temperate rainforest is Hukutaia Domain, which can be reached from the western end of Waioeka Bridge along Woodlands Road. The reserve is home to more than 2,000 native tree species, including a 2,000-year-old hollow puriri *(Vitex lucens)* where the bones of important Maoris were once interred.

🏛 Opotiki Historical and Agricultural Society Museum
123 Church St. 📞 *(07) 315 5193.*
🕐 *daily.* ● *Good Fri, 25 Dec.* 🏷 ♿

Ohope Beach, Whakatane's best surf beach

Maori Migration and Settlement

ACCORDING TO LEGEND, three migration canoes travelling from Hawaiki landed in the eastern Bay of Plenty in the 14th century *(see p43)*: the Mataatua at Whakatane and the Arawa and Tainui at Whanga-paraoa Bay, west of East Cape. Muriwai's Cave at Whakatane is testament to Muriwai's arrival on the Mataatua: she is believed to have had

Cave of Muriwai

supernatural powers and lived hermit-like in the cave. Mild weather and abundant seafood encouraged Maoris to settle along the coastal margins. Maoris continue to form a high proportion of the population in the Bay of Plenty area, and red-framed Maori meeting houses, important spiritually and as decision-making centres, dot the countryside.

MAORI ART AND CULTURE

The meeting houses and other Maori works of art seen along the coast reflect Maori history, belief in gods and ancestral spirits, and a hierarchical, tribal social structure. Maori culture was primarily a wood culture. Wood was crafted into objects for economic, social and religious purposes, and embellished with symbols and motifs *(see pp28–9)*.

Meeting houses, like the beautifully carved Tukaki at Te Kaha, are usually symbolic of a male tribal ancestor. His head is represented by the mask below the gable figure, while the wide, sloping bargeboards represent his arms.

Elements of Maori artistry have been incorporated into Christian churches, such as the intricate woven panels, carved wooden wall panels and rafter patterns at St Mary's Church at Tititiki.

The haka, a vigorous rhythmic posture dance formerly per-formed by warriors to steel their resolve for war, is taught in schools along the coast.

This ornately carved gateway guards the entrance to coastal Omaio Marae.

A prominent carving in the main street of Opotiki is indicative of a renaissance in Maori arts, culture and traditions that took hold in the 1980s and 1990s.

East Cape Tour ㉕

Pohutukawa flower

SKIRTING THE RUGGED hills of the East Cape peninsula, this section of the Pacific Coast Highway offers exceptional scenery. From Opotiki northeast to East Cape, the road clings to rocky coastline cloaked with pohutukawa trees. The second part of the route heads south to Gisborne along an inland farming route with secondary roads providing access to the coast. Most beaches and bays are suitable for swimming, fishing and diving. There are also opportunities for jet-boating, horse trekking and tramping. Maori *marae* and churches dot the route.

Te Araroa Pohutukawa ③
On the foreshore at Te Araroa grows Te Waha-o-Rerekohu ("the mouth of Rerekohu"), believed to be the largest pohutukawa tree in the country. It has 22 trunks.

Raukokore Church ②
Built in 1894, this small, wooden Anglican church, with its distinctive roofline, stands lonely sentinel between road and sea.

Motu River ①
The Motu River, banked by steep hills and forest, is a magnificent setting for rafting and jet-boating. There is also excellent fishing at its mouth.

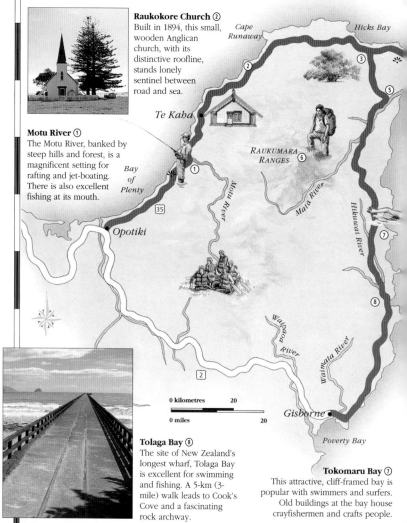

Cape Runaway

Hicks Bay

Te Kaha

Bay of Plenty

RAUKUMARA RANGES ⑥

Motu River

Mata River

Hikuwai River

Opotiki

35

Waiapu River

Waimata River

0 kilometres   20

0 miles   20

Gisborne

Poverty Bay

Tolaga Bay ⑧
The site of New Zealand's longest wharf, Tolaga Bay is excellent for swimming and fishing. A 5-km (3-mile) walk leads to Cook's Cove and a fascinating rock archway.

Tokomaru Bay ⑦
This attractive, cliff-framed bay is popular with swimmers and surfers. Old buildings at the bay house crayfishermen and crafts people.

Tips for Drivers

Length: *334 km (207 miles)*
Stopping-off points: *There is a spectacular view from the Maraenui Hill Lookout 36 km (22 miles) from Opotiki. Towns on the route are small, but most offer food and accommodation. Permission to climb Mount Hikurangi must be obtained from Ngati Porou Outdoor Pursuits, Gisborne (06) 867 8436. Bookings for jet-boating on the Motu River can be made at the Opotiki Information Centre* (see p128).

East Cape Lighthouse ④
A gravel road along a picturesque coastline leads to New Zealand's most easterly lighthouse. The view from the lighthouse is well worth the climb up the 600 steps to reach it.

Tikitiki's St Mary's Church ⑤
Built in 1924 to commemorate Maori servicemen killed in World War I, St Mary's Church at Tikitiki is one of the most ornate Maori churches in the country *(see p129)*.

Mount Hikurangi ⑥
The first place in mainland New Zealand to see the sun each day, Mount Hikurangi is sacred to Maoris and permission must be obtained to climb it.

Key

- Tour route
- Other roads
- River
- Viewpoint

Star of Canada **wheelhouse, Gisborne Museum and Arts Centre**

Te Urewera National Park ㉖

Road map F3. 🚌 ℹ *Aniwaniwa Visitor Centre, State Hwy 38, Waikaremoana, (06) 837 3803.*

This is New Zealand's fourth largest national park and the biggest tract of untouched native forest remaining in the North Island. For centuries its dense rainforest sheltered the industrious and resilient Tuhoe people. At the centre of Te Urewera lies the 243-m (797-ft) deep Lake Waikaremoana ("the lake of rippling waters"), formed 2,200 years ago by a landslide. A 46-km (28-mile) track around the lake, one of the country's Great Walks *(see p334)*, takes three to four days to complete. Booking through the Aniwaniwa Visitor Centre is essential. There are also many beautiful short walks into the park from the main road.

Gisborne ㉗

Road map F3. 👥 *35,000.* ✈ *4 km (2.5 miles) NW of town.* 🚌 ℹ *209 Grey St, (06) 868 6139.* 🎉 *Wine and Food Festival (last week of Oct).*

Gisborne is renowned for its warm summers, its farming, viticulture and horticulture, its surf beaches at Midway, Wainui and Makorori, and its history. A monument and reserve on Kaiti Hill are named in honour of Captain James Cook who made his first New Zealand landfall at Gisborne's Kaiti Beach *(see p46)* on 9 October 1769.

The **Gisborne Museum and Arts Centre** houses fine Maori and European artifacts and an extensive photographic collection. On the bank of the Taruheru River, but part of the museum complex, rests the salvaged wheelhouse from the *Star of Canada*, which sank off Kaiti Beach in 1912. Young Nick's Statue, at the mouth of the Turanganui River, commemorates cabin boy Nicholas Young, the first crewman on board Cook's ship, the *Endeavour*, to sight New Zealand.

🏛 **Gisborne Museum and Arts Centre**
Kelvin Park, Stout St. ☎ *(06) 867 3832.* ○ *daily.* ● *Good Fri, 25 Dec.* ♿ *except in* Star of Canada. 📽 🛍

Environs: Eastwoodhill Arboretum, 35 km (22 miles) west of Gisborne, contains a world-renowned collection of exotic trees and shrubs in a rambling park setting. Set among lush native bush and abundant birdlife, **Morere Hot Springs,** 60 km (37 miles) south of Gisborne, has both hot and cold pools as well as walking tracks.

🌳 **Eastwoodhill Arboretum**
2992 Wharekopae Rd. ☎ *(06) 863 9003.* ○ *daily.* ● *Good Fri, 25 Dec.* 🎫 ♿ 👤 *by arrangement.*
🏞 **Morere Hot Springs**
State Hwy 2. ☎ *(06) 837 8856.* ○ *daily.* 🎫 ♿ 🛍

Tall trees in the Eastwoodhill Arboretum, Gisborne

Rotorua ㉘

Situated on the southern shore of a lake of the same name, Rotorua is the North Island's most popular tourist destination. Despite the pungent, rotten egg smell of hydrogen sulphide gas emanating from countless bores and ground fissures, the town's hot and steamy thermal activity, healing mineral pools, and surrounding lakes, rivers and crystal springs are major attractions. Rotorua is also a major centre of Maori culture, offering Maori art, architecture, song and dance and colourful evening entertainment to the visitor.

Government Gardens and the Rotorua Museum of Art and History

♣ Government Gardens
Queens Drive.

The formal Government Gardens are laid out in front of the stately Tudor-style Bath House. They comprise a series of trimmed croquet and bowling greens and formal flower gardens dotted with steaming thermal pools. The 1927 Arawa Soldiers' Memorial, a short distance north of the Bath House, symbolizes the history of contact between Pakehas and local tribes. At its base is the Arawa migration canoe, from which Rotorua's Arawa people trace their descent.

🏛 Rotorua Museum of Art and History
Queens Drive. ☎ (07) 349 4350.
◯ daily. ⬤ 25 Dec. 🅿 ♿ ground level. 🄳 🄸 🄳 🄳

Maori artifacts are plentiful in Rotorua's museum, situated within the magnificent Bath House building in the Government Gardens. Some of the most important of these are bargeboards from Rotoiti's Houmaitawhiti meeting house, carved in 1860. Also on display is 19th-century

palisading from the Maori settlement of Ohinemutu and a curious female pumice figure, Pani, a *kumara* goddess depicted in the act of giving birth; most Maori fertility gods are male.

The story of the Bath House itself is shown in "Taking the Cure", in a section of the building painstakingly restored to its original condition. History, mythology and geology are combined in a dramatic 15-minute film to explain Rotorua's geothermal activity and Maori history. The highlight of the film is a re-enactment of the 1886 Tarawera Eruption.

♣ Orchid Gardens
Hinemaru St. ☎ (07) 347 6699.
◯ daily. ⬤ 25 Dec. 🄼 ♿ 🄳 🄳

Orchids, New Zealand ferns, tropical plants and a water organ – comprising choreographed fountains, light and music – are displayed at the Orchid Gardens. At the Microworld display, cameras enable visitors to get close-up views of living insects.

🏊 Polynesian Spa
Hinemoa St. ☎ (07) 348 1328.
◯ daily. 🄼 ♿ 🄳

Year after year, visitors from around the world return to the Polynesian Spa's mineral waters, which vary in temperature from 33 °C (92 °F) to 43 °C (110 °F). Radium and Priest waters, both acidic and cloudy, are sourced from an underground spring while alkaline Rachel water is piped to the spa from nearby. Adults have access to a large mineral pool, while a large, heated, freshwater pool, with a small water slide and shallow end for toddlers, is available for families. Users can regulate the temperature in the spa's private pools. Aix massage (massage under jets of water) is available in the luxury spa area.

SPA CITY

"Cripples throw away their crutches and the gouty man regains his health," a government report proclaimed in 1903, referring to Rotorua's mineral waters. Two mineral waters were used in a succession of 19th-century and early 20th-century spas, the largest being the Bath House, opened in 1908. The waters were considered "stimulating and tonic in reaction". Today, on the shores of Lake Rotorua, Queen Elizabeth Hospital uses hot mineral waters to relieve pain, relax muscles and stimulate joint movement.

Mineral pool at Polynesian Spa

St Faith's Anglican Church

carvings, woven wall panels and painted scrollwork. There are several graves of interest next to the church, including that of Seymour Mills Spencer (1810–98) who preached to the Arawa for 50 years, and Captain Gilbert Mair (1843–1923).

🔼 St Faith's Anglican Church

Ohinemutu. ⬤ daily. ⬆ 9am Sun; 10am Wed.

Built in 1910, the Tudor-style St Faith's is the second church built at Ohinemutu, a Maori village on the shores of the lake around which Rotorua grew. An etched-glass window in the chapel at the far end of the church depicts Christ dressed in a *korowai* (chief's cloak) and appearing to walk on the waters of Lake Rotorua. The interior is richly embellished with Maori

🔼 Tamatekapua

Ohinemutu.

The magnificent Tamate-kapua meeting house, built in 1873, is the main gathering place of the Arawa tribe. Located opposite St Faith's, it was named for an earlier house that stood on Mokoia Island and the captain of the Arawa migration canoe. The figure at the base of the centre post is Ngato-roirangi, the canoe's navigator, whom myth-ology credits with bringing thermal activity to the region.

Carving at Tamatekapua

VISITORS' CHECKLIST

Road map E3. 🏠 67,000. ✈ State Hwy 30, 10 km (6 miles) NE of city. 🚉 Railway Rd, 2 km (1.2 miles) NW of city. 🚌 🚏 🛈 1167 Fenton St, (07) 348 5179. ⬤ 8am–6pm daily. ⬤ 25 Dec. 🎉 New Zealand International Two-Day Walk (Mar); Rotorua Marathon (May); Rotorua District Garden Festival (Nov). 🖳 www.rotoruanz.co.nz

🏕 Kuirau Park

Kuirau Rd.

Within Kuirau Park there are a number of boiling mud pools, steam vents and small geysers. A small aquarium with a collection of tropical fish, free thermal foot pools, picnic areas, well-kept gardens and a small, warm lake are other attractions within the domain.

Visitors will appreciate a scented garden in the park, and during weekends and school holidays fairground rides are available in the grounds for young children.

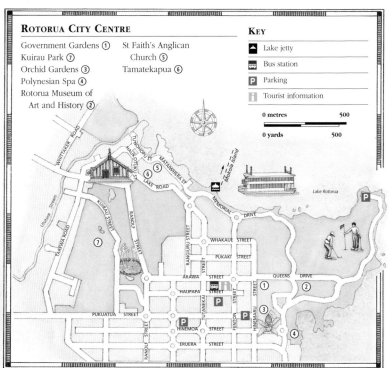

ROTORUA CITY CENTRE

Government Gardens ①
Kuirau Park ⑦
Orchid Gardens ③
Polynesian Spa ④
Rotorua Museum of Art and History ②
St Faith's Anglican Church ⑤
Tamatekapua ⑥

KEY

⛴ Lake jetty
🚌 Bus station
🅿 Parking
🛈 Tourist information

0 metres 500
0 yards 500

Greater Rotorua

Figure at Tamaki Maori Village

Many of Rotorua's best attractions lie outside the city centre, around Lake Rotorua and the ten other magnificent bush-fringed lakes that make up the Rotorua Lakes district. Complementing the lakes are geothermal wonders, bubbling springs, crystal-clear trout streams and mighty, unspoiled native forests. The rivers and lakes are renowned for their trout, and make a beautiful setting for boating, camping and tramping. Thrill-seekers can take four-wheel drive tours and ride horses to remote forest locations. Visitors can also enjoy Maori cultural experiences and observe the farming and livestock displays.

Visitors viewing trout at Rainbow Springs Park

Lake Rotorua and Mokoia Island from Mount Ngongotaha

🎋 Lake Rotorua

This nearly circular lake is the largest of the lakes around Rotorua and is a popular venue for windsurfing and kayaking. It can be enjoyed by hover shuttle, paddle steamer, speedboat or water scooter. Mokoia Island, in the centre of the lake, is famous for the love story of Hinemoa, who defied her family's wishes and swam at night to the island to be with the young chief Tutanekai, who played his flute to guide her. There are 4 km (2.5 miles) of walking tracks on the island and a thermal bathing pool.

🏛 Skyline Skyrides

Fairy Springs Rd. **(** (07) 347 0027.
☐ daily. 🕎 & 🍴 🛍
Mount Ngongotaha towers 778 m (2,552 ft) above the city and lake. The Skyline lookout, at 487 m (1,598 ft), can be reached by gondola, and gives unmatched views of the city, lakes and countryside. An exciting way to

descend the mountain, by day or night, is by luge (a short, raised toboggan). A 2-km (1.2-mile) scenic ride suits most people, while a shorter and steeper ride provides the adrenalin rush sought by others. Chairlifts return riders to the start.

🎋 Rainbow Springs Park

Fairy Springs Rd. **(** (07) 347 9301.
☐ daily. 🕎 & 🍴 🛍
The park's two attractions, Rainbow Springs and Rainbow Farm, are linked by an under-road pedestrian walkway. Visitors can feed

some of the thousands of rainbow, brown, brook and tiger trout in the crystal-clear freshwater streams and fern-fringed pools at Rainbow Springs, and view tuataras, kiwis and other birds in a walk-through aviary. At Rainbow Farm, visitors are given an insight into New Zealand's farming history and lifestyle and an opportunity to participate in farming activities, such as bottle feeding a lamb, milking a cow, or bidding on a sheep at a mock auction.

🐑 Agrodome Leisure Park

Western Rd, Ngongotaha. **(** (07) 357 4350. ☐ daily. 🕎 & 🍴
🍴 🛍
Founded in 1972, this family business offers a broad range of farming-related as well as adventure activities. There are three live sheep shows daily, at which champion rams are introduced on stage, and sheep shearing and sheep dog trials are demonstrated. Visitors can also tour the sheep and cattle farm, feeding and handling the animals. The souvenir shop specializes in quality woollen clothing and sheepskin rugs.

Adventure activities on offer in the park include bungy jumping, jet-boating and zorbing (rolling downhill inside a large plastic "ball").

Live sheep show at the Agrodome Leisure Park

⚑ Hell's Gate

State Hwy 33. 〖 *(07) 345 3151.*
〇 *daily.* 📷 🅿 🚻 💲
Sixteen km (10 miles) from
Rotorua, at Tikitere, Hell's
Gate is famous for its fero-
cious volcanic activity. Drifting, wraith-like mists part to
reveal a fierce and spectacular
thermal valley that includes
the Kakahi Falls, the largest
hot waterfall in the southern
hemisphere, and New Zea-
land's largest boiling whirl-
pool. Another cauldron of
water, the Sulphur Bath, is
purported to cure septic cuts,
bites and some skin ailments.
The whole area has excellent
pathways and barriers and is
well signposted.

♣ Whakarewarewa Forest Park

Off State Hwy 5.
This 40-sq km (15-sq mile)
multipurpose forest adjoining
the Whakarewarewa thermal
area *(see pp136–7)* contains
majestic groves of redwoods,
firs and other plantation trees.
Forest walks can take from 30
minutes to all day. There are
also mountain biking and
horse tracks, a nature trail
and picnic area.

**Horse riding in Whakarewarewa
Forest Park**

⚐ Tamaki Maori Village

State Hwy 5. 〖 *(07) 346 2823.* 〇
daily. ● *25 Dec.* 📷 🅿 💲
Visitors are introduced to
Maori customs and traditions
at this replica of a pre-
European Maori village. Daily
tours include sampling a
hangi, in which selected
foods are cooked on hot
rocks in an authentic earth
oven. Prior to the evening
cultural performance, visitors
are challenged at the entrance
by a fierce Maori "warrior" in

**A Maori "warrior" greets visitors
at the Tamaki Maori Village**

traditional dress. Overnight
stays can be arranged during
which visitors listen to Maori
myths and legends and
experience the village's
cultural life. Education workshops are also conducted on
traditional Maori carving and
weaving, performing arts,
weaponry and warfare, and
Maori food and health.

⚑ Blue and Green Lakes

Tarawera Rd.
Eleven km (7 miles) southeast
of Rotorua are the stunning
Blue and Green Lakes (Tikitapu and Rotokakahi). The
narrow isthmus that divides
the lakes provides a good
vantage point to compare
their contrasting hues. Lake
Rotokakahi is sacred to
Maoris and is not accessible,
but Lake Tikitapu is the scene
of many summer activities.

⚐ Buried Village

Tarawera Rd. 〖 *(07) 362 8287.* 〇
daily. ● *25 Dec.* 📷 🅿 💲
Fifteen minutes' drive from
Rotorua and 2.5 km (1.5
miles) from Lake Tarawera is
what remains of the village of
Te Wairoa, devastated by the
eruption of Mount Tarawera
in 1886. A walk through park-
land takes in the excavations
of several sites and a museum
explains the drama of the
eruption to visitors. A bush
walk leads to the Te Wairoa
waterfalls where visitors can
feed large rainbow trout.

TARAWERA ERUPTION

Months of underground rumbling culminated early in the
morning of 10 June 1886 in the eruption of Mount Tarawera, which left a deep crater *(see pp62–3)*. Lasting about
three hours, the blast spread along a 17-km (10-mile) rift
and killed 153 people. The eruption hurled red-hot
volcanic bombs and pieces of solidified lava 14 km (8.5
miles), and the Maori villages of Te Ariki, Te Wairoa and
Moura were buried under 20 m (65 ft) of mud. The
explosion's roar was heard in Christchurch and Auckland.
The famous Pink and White Terraces, massive fan-like
silica terraces, acknowledged as the eighth wonder of the
world, were completely obliterated. Information on guided
walks to the crater and on scenic flights over it can be
obtained from the Rotorua information centre *(see p133)*.

**Painting by Charles Blomfield of the Pink Terraces,
around 1890**

Whakarewarewa Thermal Area

Maori carving

THE GEOTHERMAL AREA at Rotorua's southern edge, commonly referred to as Whaka, comprises two separate areas – the New Zealand Maori Arts and Crafts Institute and the Whakarewarewa Thermal Village. The Institute's attractions include Maori carving and weaving, cultural performances, examples of Maori buildings and fortifications, and the geysers Pohutu and Prince of Wales Feathers. At the Thermal Village, visitors can see a meeting house, cooking and bathing pools and a cemetery. At both venues, guides take visitors on an educational journey that unravels the mystery of Maori ways.

★ **Te Aronui-a-Rua Meeting House**
Visitors are greeted with a Maori "challenge" at Te Aronui-a-Rua meeting house at the Arts and Crafts Institute.

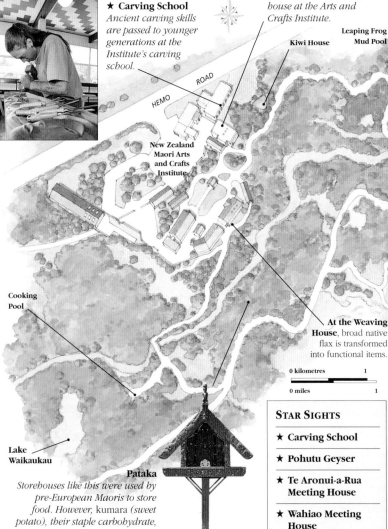

★ **Carving School**
Ancient carving skills are passed to younger generations at the Institute's carving school.

Kiwi House

Leaping Frog Mud Pool

HEMO ROAD

New Zealand Maori Arts and Crafts Institute

Cooking Pool

At the Weaving House, broad native flax is transformed into functional items.

| 0 kilometres | | 1 |
| 0 miles | | 1 |

Lake Waikaukau

Pataka
Storehouses like this were used by pre-European Maoris to store food. However, kumara (sweet potato), their staple carbohydrate, was stored in pits in the ground.

STAR SIGHTS

★ **Carving School**

★ **Pohutu Geyser**

★ **Te Aronui-a-Rua Meeting House**

★ **Wahiao Meeting House**

★ Pohutu Geyser
Pohutu ("Big Splash") is the largest geyser and typically erupts 10–25 times a day up to 30 m (98 ft) high, depending on wind strength and direction.

At Puarenga Stream, village children dive from a bridge for coins thrown by tourists.

TYRON ST

Prince of Wales Feathers Geyser

VISITORS' CHECKLIST

New Zealand Maori Arts and Crafts Institute Hemo Rd. *(07) 348 9047.* Summer: 8am–6pm daily; Winter: 8am–5pm daily. Cultural performance, 12:15pm daily plus 6:30pm in summer.
Whakarewarewa Thermal Village 34 Tyron St. *(07) 349 3463.* 8:30am–5pm daily. 25 Dec. no video in meeting house.

★ Wahiao Meeting House
Tourists, including children, join in a cultural performance outside Wahiao meeting house.

Whakarewarewa Thermal Village

Geyser Flat, a 1-sq-km (0.4-sq-mile) silica terrace, is home to more than 500 thermal features, including seven geysers.

Above-ground Cemetery
At Whakarewarewa Thermal Village, the dead are buried above ground in vaults to keep the remains out of the steaming earth.

The Brainpot, a symmetrical silica basin, is said to have been used to cook the heads of enemies.

VOLCANIC FEATURES

The volcanic activity at Whakarewarewa is a reminder of how the earth is still changing and how the pressure of volcanic gases and heat below the surface can break through in spectacular and often dangerous ways. Here, superheated steam escapes from a vast chamber of boiling water through narrow vents in roaring towers of spray; mud pools boil and heave as gas and hot water seek to escape to the surface, and steam and gases are discharged in hot pools beside mineral-coloured silica flats.

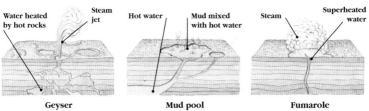

Water heated by hot rocks — Steam jet

Geyser

Hot water — Mud mixed with hot water

Mud pool

Steam — Superheated water

Fumarole

Waimangu Volcanic Valley ❷⑨

Road map E3. **【** (07) 366 6137.
⭕ daily. 📷 ♿ to bus stop & boat
cruise. 🍴 🏠

CREATED ON 10 June 1886 as a result of the Tarawera Eruption *(see p135)*, Waimangu is the only hydrothermal sytem in the world wholly formed within historic times. It offers an easy, mostly downhill, 90-minute walk past a succession of geothermal features at the southern end of the 17-km (10-mile) rift created by the eruption.

The 38,000-sq-m (409,032-sq-ft) Frying Pan Lake, claimed to be the world's largest hot water spring, emits steam over its entire area and is dominated by the red-streaked Cathedral Rocks. The lake was formed by an eruption in 1917 that buried a nearby tourist hotel.

The pale blue steaming water and delicate silica clay terracing of the Inferno Crater should not be missed, even though it requires a short detour from the main path. The water reaches 80 °C (176 °F) in the lake and rises and falls 8 m (26 ft) over a 38-day cycle.

At the end of the walk lies Lake Rotomahana, submerging what remains of the Pink and White Terraces *(see p135)*. Across the water stands Mount Tarawera. A boat excursion follows a shoreline scarred by craters, fumaroles and geysers. Unusual thermal plants grow along the lake's edge. Visitors need to allow two to three hours for the volcanic valley walk and the boat cruise.

Inferno Crater at Waimangu Volcanic Valley

Champagne Pool at Waiotapu Thermal Wonderland

Waiotapu Thermal Wonderland ❸⓪

Road map E3. **【** (07) 366 6333. ⭕
daily. 📷 ♿ main area. 🚻 🅿 🏠

THIS IS THE country's most colourful and diverse geothermal area and is home to the reliable Lady Knox Geyser, named in 1904 after Governor-General Lord Ranfurly's daughter. Primed with soap powder, it shoots water and steam up to 21 m (69 ft) into the air at 10:15am daily.

Other main attractions include the Artist's Palette, a panorama of hot and cold pools, boiling mud pools and hissing fumaroles in a variety of ever-changing colours, and the Champagne Pool, with its ochre-coloured petrified edge. The Primrose Terraces are also naturally tinted and have delicately formed lacework patterns. Walks through the geothermal area, over boardwalks and along clearly signposted paths, take from 30 to 60 minutes.

Orakei Korako Geyserland ❸①

Road map E3. **【** (07) 378 3131.
⭕ daily. 🚻 🅿 🏠

ORAKEI KORAKO, or "The Hidden Valley", as it is known, lies at the southern end of Lake Ohakuri, fed by the Waikato River as it flows northward from Lake Taupo. Reaching the valley's geothermal attractions requires a boat trip across the lake to the imposing Emerald Terrace, the largest silica feature of its kind in the country. Beyond is a 45-minute walk taking in a geyser, more silica terraces, mud pools, hot springs and a cave. Cabin accommodation is available at the lake's edge, where there are also boats for hire.

Jet-boating rapids on the Waikato River

Wairakei Park ❸②

Road map E3.

TEN KILOMETRES (6 miles) north of Taupo is the area loosely referred to as Wairakei Park. The star attraction is the Huka ("foam") Falls, where the Waikato River is channelled through a narrow rock chute before hurtling over an 11-m (36-ft) bluff to a foaming cauldron below. Access down the Waikato River from Taupo to the Huka Falls is possible by jet-boat, or by the more sedate paddlewheeler, built in 1908. A 7-km (4 -mile) path leads from the falls down the right-hand side of the river to the Aratiatia Rapids, also accessible by road. Floodgates to the dam above the rapids are opened several times a day to allow kayaking and jet-boating.

At **Craters of the Moon**, at the end of Karapiti Road, 2 km (1.2 miles) south of Wairakei, steaming craters and boiling mud pits can be viewed free of charge among a bush-covered landscape.

The country's only prawn farm, off Huka Falls Road, uses geothermally heated river water to raise giant prawns for its restaurant, Prawn Works Bar and Grill *(see p321)*. Tours of the farm are conducted hourly.

Taupo ㉝

Road map E3. 🏠 *21,300.* ✈ *8 km (5 miles) S of town.* 🚌 *Gascoigne St Travel Centre.* 📞 *(07) 376 0027.* 🛈 *30 Tongariro St, (07) 378 9000.* 🎣 *Lake Taupo International Fishing Tournament (late Apr).*

THE TOWN OF Taupo lies at the northeastern end of Lake Taupo, New Zealand's largest lake, formed by a volcanic explosion in AD 186 *(see pp62–3)*. White pumice beaches and sheltered rocky coves surround the lake, which covers 619 sq km (239 sq miles). On a clear day, the distant volcanic peaks of Mounts Tongariro and Ngauruhoe and the snow-capped Ruapehu provide a spectacular backdrop to the lake.

Taupo services surrounding farms and forests and an important tourist industry. All year round the town attracts large numbers of holidaymakers who come for its excellent lake and river fishing, sailing and water sports, and local geothermal attractions. There is a wealth of accommodation in the town, much of it with lakeside views, and good dining and shopping. Many hotels have their own hot pools.

The wide selection of outdoor activities available includes bungy jumping, boating and rafting, horse riding, mountain biking, tandem skydiving, flightseeing and golf. The bungy, set in majestic surroundings above the Waikato River off Spa Road, is a big drawcard. Details of the many operators offering outdoor recreation may be obtained from the information centre in Taupo.

Turangi ㉞

Road map E3. 🏠 *5,500.* 🚌 🛈 *Ngawaka Place, (07) 386 8999.*

LOCATED AT THE southeastern end of Lake Taupo on the banks of the Tongariro River, Turangi was a small fishing retreat until it was developed into a town in 1964 to accommodate workers for the Tongariro Hydro-Electricity Scheme. It remains an excellent resort area for anglers, and is also a popular base for trampers, white-water rafters, kayakers and skiers.

South of Turangi is the **Tongariro National Trout Centre**, a hatchery and research facility. Ova collected from wild female trout

Trimming pine trees in a pine forest near Turangi

are fertilized to breed trout for research purposes and to release in other areas. A self-guided 15-minute walk takes viewers through the hatchery and alongside a stream to an underwater viewing chamber where trout may be seen in their natural environment.

↗ **Tongariro National Trout Centre**
State Hwy 1. 🕐 *daily.* ♿

TROUT FISHING PARADISE

World-famous Lake Taupo and its surrounding lakes – Kuratau, Hinemaia, Rotoaira and Otamangakau – are fed by numerous rivers and streams well-stocked with rainbow and brown trout. Fishermen frequently stand shoulder to shoulder at the mouth of the Waitahanui River to form the "picket fence" fishing phenomenon. Line fishing from boats on Lake Taupo or from the shore is effective from November until March, as trout feed upon smelt spawning close to shore. In late summer, trout congregate after dark where streams flow into the lake, providing excellent fly-fishing. River fishing is best from May till October. A special fishing licence, available from sports shops and information centres, is required in the Taupo Fishing District.

Fishing at the mouth of the Waitahanui River

Tongariro National Park ⑮

A T THE SOUTHERN END of Lake Taupo lies the magnificent 7,600-sq-km (2,930-sq-mile) Tongariro National Park. The three active volcanic mountains which form its nucleus, Ruapehu, Ngauruhoe and Tongariro *(see pp62–3)*, were given to the government in 1887 by Tukino Te Heuheu IV, a Ngati Tuwharetoa chief. The park, which is surrounded by access roads, serves as a winter playground for skiers and snowboarders and a year-round wilderness walking, tramping and mountain climbing area. The park was the first in the world to achieve UNESCO World Heritage status for both its natural (1990) and cultural value (1993).

Bust of Tukino Te Heuheu IV

★ **Whakapapa Ski Field**
The largest developed ski area in New Zealand, Whakapapa has a sophisticated chairlift system and more than 30 groomed trails catering to all levels of skiers and snowboarders.

Grand Chateau Hotel
This luxury hotel, built in 1929 on the lower slopes of Mount Ruapehu, offers outstanding mountain and valley views (see p302).

★ **Mount Ruapehu**
In summer, visitors can climb to the crater of Mount Ruapehu, the North Island's tallest mountain, from the highest Whakapapa chairlift.

KEY

▬▬▬	State highway
═══	Minor road
⚍⚍⚍	River
– ‐ –	4 WD track
▬ ▬	Walking track
▬ ▬	Park boundary
– –	Restricted area
ℹ	Tourist information
Ⓐ	Camp site
🏕	Picnic area
⛷	Skiing

Round the Mountain is a four- to five-day tramp around Ruapehu for those seeking solitude, magnificent mountain views and a back-country experience.

Mountain biking is prohibited in the park but is allowed in the Rangataua Forest Conservation Area.

STAR SIGHTS
★ **Emerald Lakes**
★ **Mount Ruapehu**
★ **Whakapapa Skifield**

Map labels:

National Park
Mang Road
47
48
Tonga
Whakapapa Village
Makatote River
MOUNT RUAPEHU
2,797 m (9,176 ft)
Crater La
Mangaturuturu River
Round the Mountain Track
Mangawhero River
Ohakune Mountain Road
Ohakune
Mangawhero Falls
R A N G A T A U A   F O R E S T
Dreadnought Road
49
4

The Turoa Ski Resort is renowned for its expansive ski areas, long runs and vertical drops.

0 kilometres	5
0 miles	5

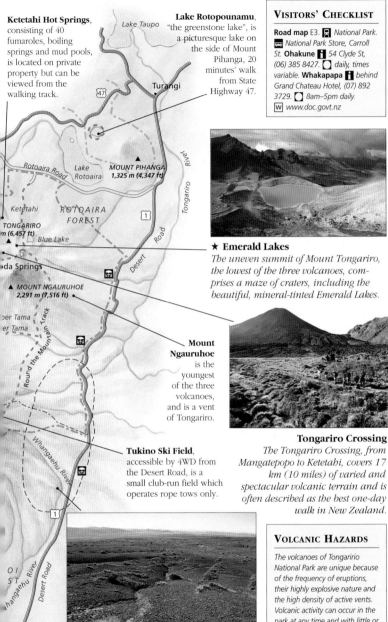

Ketetahi Hot Springs, consisting of 40 fumaroles, boiling springs and mud pools, is located on private property but can be viewed from the walking track.

Lake Rotopounamu, "the greenstone lake", is a picturesque lake on the side of Mount Pihanga, 20 minutes' walk from State Highway 47.

VISITORS' CHECKLIST

Road map E3. 🚻 *National Park.* 🚌 *National Park Store, Carroll St.* **Ohakune** ℹ️ *54 Clyde St, (06) 385 8427.* ⏰ *daily, times variable.* **Whakapapa** ℹ️ *behind Grand Chateau Hotel, (07) 892 3729.* ⏰ *8am–5pm daily.* 🌐 *www.doc.govt.nz*

Lake Taupo

Turangi

47

Rotoaira Road

Lake Rotoaira

▲ MOUNT PIHANGA 1,325 m (4,347 ft)

Ketetahi

ROTOAIRA FOREST

1

Tongariro River

Desert Road

TONGARIRO m (6,457 ft) ▲

Blue Lake

da Springs

▲ MOUNT NGAURUHOE 2,291 m (7,516 ft) •

er Tama

er Tama

Round the Mountain Track

Whangaehu River

O I
S T

Whangaehu River

Desert Road

1

• Waiouru

⛺

★ **Emerald Lakes**
The uneven summit of Mount Tongariro, the lowest of the three volcanoes, comprises a maze of craters, including the beautiful, mineral-tinted Emerald Lakes.

Mount Ngauruhoe is the youngest of the three volcanoes, and is a vent of Tongariro.

Tongariro Crossing
The Tongariro Crossing, from Mangatepopo to Ketetahi, covers 17 km (10 miles) of varied and spectacular volcanic terrain and is often described as the best one-day walk in New Zealand.

Tukino Ski Field, accessible by 4WD from the Desert Road, is a small club-run field which operates rope tows only.

VOLCANIC HAZARDS

The volcanoes of Tongariro National Park are unique because of the frequency of eruptions, their highly explosive nature and the high density of active vents. Volcanic activity can occur in the park at any time and with little or no warning. Anyone intending to tramp or climb on the upper slopes of the volcanoes needs to check the current volcanic alert status and exclusion zones with the nearest visitor centre and read any recommended safety information for the area before starting out.

Rangipo Desert
Temperature extremes on the eastern side of the volcanoes have produced a desolate landscape of gravel fields and hardy alpine vegetation. The area is used mainly for army training.

Skiers at Whakapapa on Mount Ruapehu looking towards Mounts Ngauruhoe and Tongariro ▷

Street-by-Street: Napier 🕉

Wall panel, Municipal Theatre

Perched on the edge of the Pacific Ocean, this elegant city is a memorial to a 1931 earthquake and fire that destroyed most buildings and killed many people. The quake raised marshland and the harbour bed, providing new farmland and room for urban development. During rebuilding, an earthquake-proof building code was enforced and architects adopted the then fashionable Art Deco style. Today, the city's Art Deco buildings, with their pastel colours, bold lines and elaborate motifs, are internationally renowned.

Napier Mall
Traffic bollards and seats topped with Art Deco motifs enhance pedestrian-friendly Emerson Street.

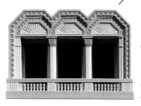

★ Desco Centre
Purpose-built in 1922 as Napier's Central Fire Station, and refurbished in Art Deco style after the earthquake, it now houses the Art Deco Trust and Art Deco Shop.

The Municipal Theatre, built in 1938, is noted for its Egyptian-style columns and door lintels, and for the leaping nude wall panels flanking the stage in the auditorium.

The Public Trust Building's massive columns and internal oak fittings escaped earthquake damage.

Countrywide Bank
This 1932 building has charming balcony windows framed by angular arches decorated with sunbursts and zigzags.

ART DECO TRUST

The Art Deco Trust is responsible for protecting, enhancing and promoting Napier's Art Deco buildings, keeping a register of them and maintaining worldwide links with other Art Deco groups. It also organizes Art Deco walks and publishes information on Art Deco tours. A highlight is the annual Art Deco Weekend, held in mid-February, a light-hearted celebration of the Art Deco style.

A couple dressed for an Art Deco Weekend

0 metres 50
0 yards 50

KEY

– – –   Suggested route

STAR SIGHTS

★ A & B Building

★ Desco Centre

The Napier Antique Centre, built in 1932, is one of four buildings in Napier ornamented with Maori motifs.

VISITORS' CHECKLIST

Road map F4. 🏠 *55,700.* ✈
5 km (3 miles) NW of city. 🚉 🚌
Munro St. ℹ *100 Marine Pde,
(06) 834 1911.* ◯ *8:30am–5pm
Mon–Fri; 9am–5pm Sat & Sun.*
⬤ *25 Dec.* **Art Deco walks** *Art
Deco Trust, Desco Centre, 163
Tennyson St, (06) 835 0022.*
Ⓦ *www.hb.co.nz/artdeco*

Daily Telegraph Building
Built in 1932, this building is well endowed with Art Deco motifs – sunbursts, zigzags, ziggurats and fountain-like flowers.

Criterion Hotel
Leadlight glass was a favourite form of decoration in the 1930s, as shown in the window in the hotel's stairwell.

The ASB Bank's interior features fine examples of Maori carving and rafter patterns.

Masonic Hotel
Completed in 1932, the hotel features an unusual first-floor loggia built over the street.

CATHEDRAL LANE

TREET

BROWNING STREET

HASTINGS STREET

HERSCHELL ST

THE DOME

MARINE   PARADE

★ A & B Building
This Napier landmark, built in 1936 to house the Silver Slipper Nightclub, has a beautifully restored elevator.

Exploring Napier

Statue of Pania

WITHIN EASY walking distance of Napier's inner-city Art Deco buildings is the ocean front Marine Parade, fringed by Norfolk pines. The floral clock, Tom Parker Fountain, statue of Pania (a maiden of local legend), Soundshell, Colonnade and Sunken Gardens, all on the seaward side of Marine Parade, add considerably to the city's charm. To the north, Bluff Hill, notable for its steep, tortuous roads and lovely old wooden homes, is the city's only high ground. Beyond it, the bustling port of Ahuriri is the site of the first European settlement in the area.

Dolphins in an aerobatic show at Marineland

🐟 Aquarium

Marine Parade. ☎ (06) 834 1404. ○ *daily.* ⌂

A wide range of live marine and freshwater creatures, from sharks and stingrays to sea horses, swim amid a deep-sea shipwreck. Visitors can watch divers hand-feed the fish at 3:15pm daily. There are plans to upgrade the aquarium to a national environmental education and research facility and eco-tourist entertainment centre.

🦡 Opossum World

157 Marine Parade. ☎ (06) 835 7697. ○ *daily.* ● *1 Jan, 25 Dec.* ⌂ ⟨ ⟩ ⌂ ⌂

This attraction focuses entirely on possums, with static and interactive displays of the marsupial in its natural environment, the ecological damage it has caused, and the possum fur industry. Visitors can test their marksmanship in a simulated night hunt. Products made from possum fur and hide are on sale.

🐬 Marineland

290 Marine Parade. ☎ (06) 834 4027. ○ *daily.* ● *25 Dec.* ⌂ ⌂

⌂ ⌂ ⌂

Two shows daily (at 10:30am and 2pm) feature Marineland's famous performing dolphins supported by a cast of otters, seals, sea lions and penguins. Visitors can arrange to swim with the dolphins (wetsuits are provided) or to feed them. In a special recovery workshop at the site, visitors can help to feed, weigh and care for injured penguins and other seabirds found in the wild by members of the public.

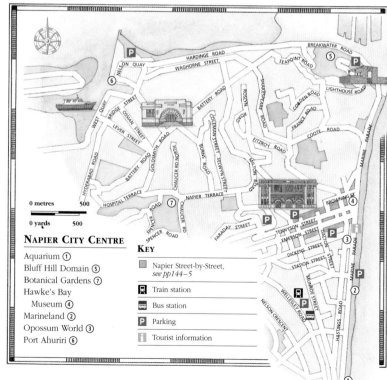

NAPIER CITY CENTRE

Aquarium ①
Bluff Hill Domain ⑤
Botanical Gardens ⑦
Hawke's Bay
  Museum ④
Marineland ②
Opossum World ③
Port Ahuriri ⑥

KEY

▣ Napier Street-by-Street, *see pp144–5*

🚉 Train station

🚌 Bus station

🅿 Parking

ℹ Tourist information

🏛 Hawke's Bay Museum

65 Marine Parade/9 Herschell St.
📞 *(06) 835 7781.* ⏰ *daily.*
⏰ *25 Dec.* ♿ 📷 📱

Housed in an Art Deco building, the museum has extensive collections of Maori treasures, fine art, applied and decorative arts and textiles, as well as artifacts relating to the daily lives of Hawke's Bay's early settlers. Through audiovisual displays and ephemera, visitors can also experience the devastation of the 1931 earthquake.

♣ Bluff Hill Domain

Lighthouse Rd.

Prior to the 1931 earthquake, Napier comprised an oblong mass of hills (Scinde Island) surrounded almost entirely by water. A stroll or drive to the 102-m (335-ft) high lookout within Bluff Hill Domain will recreate this feeling if visitors imagine much of the low-lying area south of the hill covered in water. What were gun emplacements are now vantage points from which to view the Kaweka and Ruahine ranges to the west, the Mahia Peninsula to the northeast, and Cape Kidnappers to the southeast.

🚂 Port Ahuriri

At Port Ahuriri, 4 km (2.5 miles) from Napier's centre, visitors can watch boys fishing and fishing fleets being unloaded or enjoy the port's restaurants. A beach boardwalk meanders to the harbour entrance at Perfume Point, crafts and antiques are on sale, and one of the largest working model railways is displayed at Trainworld on the corner of Bridge and Waghorne streets. The Rothmans Building, one of the most beautiful Art Deco buildings in Napier, is in nearby Ossian Street.

♣ Botanical Gardens

Spencer Rd.

Located on a hill in the middle of the city, the gardens form a charming oasis. Apart from a spacious aviary, there are well-kept lawns bordered by flower beds, groves of stately trees, and a stream with ornamental bridges.

View north towards Napier from Te Mata Peak

Hastings 🟠37

Road map F4. 🏃 *28,400.* ✈ *25 km (15 miles) N of town.* 🚌 🚉 *Caroline Rd.* ℹ️ *Russell St North, (07) 873 5526.* 🎪 *Harvest Hawke's Bay (first weekend of Feb); Hastings Blossom Festival (Sep).*

Situated on the Heretaunga Plains, 20 km (12 miles) south of Napier, Hastings is the centre of a large fruit growing and processing industry, including wine making *(see pp148–9)*. Rebuilt after the 1931 earthquake, it is the only city in New Zealand with streets laid out on the American block system. It has some fine Spanish Mission buildings, the most notable being the Hastings Municipal Theatre.

Hawke's Bay apples

Between Hastings and the eastern coastline, Te Mata Peak rises 399 m (1,309 ft). Maori legend describes the Te Mata ridgeline as the body of chief Te Mata O Rongokako, who choked and died eating his way through the hill, a task set him by the beautiful daughter of another chief. From Hastings the "bite" that killed him can be clearly seen, as can his body, which forms the skyline.

Cape Kidnappers 🟠38

Road map F4.

Maoris believe that the crescent-shaped bay and jagged promontory of Cape Kidnappers, 30 km (19 miles) south of Napier, represent the magical jawbone hook used by Maui to pull the North Island from the sea like a fish. In October 1769, Captain Cook anchored off the headland *(see p46)* naming it Cape Kidnappers after some Maoris attempted to carry off his Tahitian translator.

At the cape, up to 15,000 young and mature yellow-headed Australasian gannets surf wind currents metres from onlookers before flopping in ungainly fashion onto nests. The best time to see them is from early November to late February. Access is closed during the early nesting phase between July and October. At low tide, visitors can walk 8 km (5 miles) along the beach to the colony. Guided tours by coach, tractor-trailer and quad bike are also available.

Australasian gannets at Cape Kidnappers Gannet Reserve

Hawke's Bay Vineyard Tour 39

Wine
barrel race

Hawke's bay's long sunshine hours, wide range of growing microclimates, and variety of soil types have allowed more than 30 wineries to develop all the classical grape varieties to a high standard. Traditionally a fruit-growing area, Hawke's Bay's fruit is sourced from varied vineyard and orchard sites, and wines are made using both modern and traditional techniques. The success of the region's wine is not only evident in its international awards, but in one of New Zealand's most important wine events, the annual Harvest Hawke's Bay, celebrated during the first weekend of February.

Mission Estate Winery ①
Established in 1851 by a group of French Catholic missionaries, early vintages were produced for sacramental purposes. Today, this historic winery, nestled on a hill overlooking sweeping vineyards, offers wine sales, winery tours, a gourmet restaurant and a craft gallery.

Clearview Estate Winery ⑨
Established in 1989 by Tim Turvey and Helma van den Berg, this gently sloping coastal vineyard produces small quantities of hand-made wines sold only from the winery, by mail order, or enjoyed at its seaside restaurant *(see p320).*

0 kilometres   4

0 miles   4

Te Mata Estate Winery ⑧
The oldest winery still operating in New Zealand (vines were planted on the lower slopes of Te Mata peak in 1892) and one of its most prestigious and successful, Te Mata produces mainly red wines, which can be purchased at its restored winery.

Vidal of Hawke's Bay ⑦
Anthony Vidal, an immigrant from Spain, established his winery in a stable in 1905. Urban development has encompassed the site but Vidals continues to produce good wines. Sales, tastings and a brasserie are available.

Sileni Estates ⑥
Located within an area of red-metal soils, massive investment has produced a showcase winery incorporating a gourmet food store, wine education centre and restaurant/café.

KEY

▬▬▬	Tour route
═══	Other roads
▓▓▓	River

Park Estate Winery ②
Formerly a traditional orchard, Park Estate has established niche markets for three very different beverages: grape wines, fruit wines from feijoa, boysenberry, kiwifruit and apple, and natural fruit juices. Orchard and winery tours, wine tasting and dining are available. A shop sells fresh fruit and homemade produce.

Fruitbowl of New Zealand

Hawke's Bay's warm, sunny summers and crisp winter frosts have been exploited by generations of horticulturists, who have earned the region its unofficial title of "fruitbowl of New Zealand". While apples are the largest crop – more than half of the country's 17 million export cartons are filled here – pears, peaches, nectarines, apricots, plums, cherries and kiwifruit are also important. At Pernel Fruitworld, a large orchard on the outskirts of Hastings with its own packhouse, some 85 varieties of pip and stone fruits are grown. Tours are conducted hourly, fruit is available to taste, and a museum traces the history of the fruit industry.

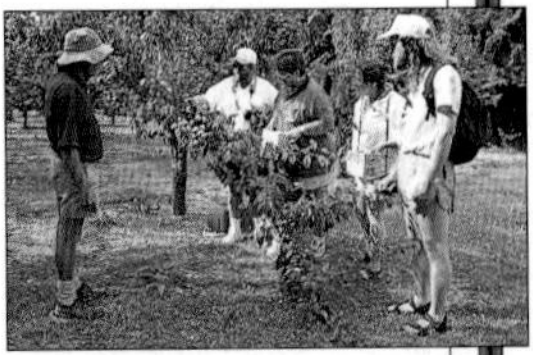

Orchard tour at Pernel Fruitworld

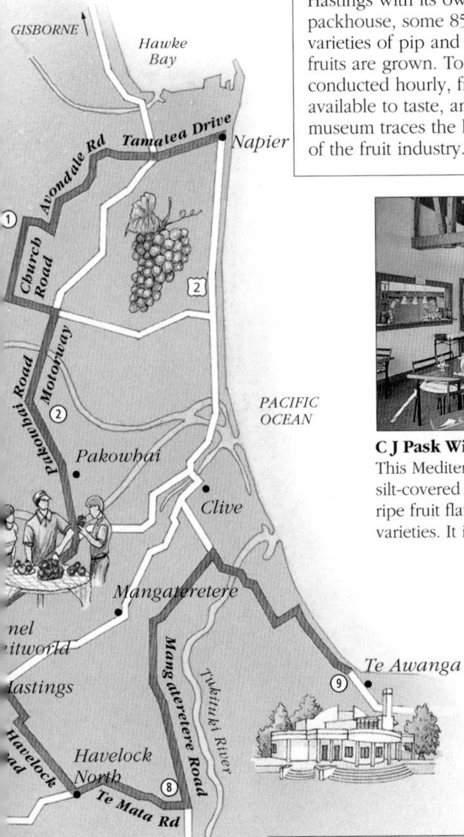

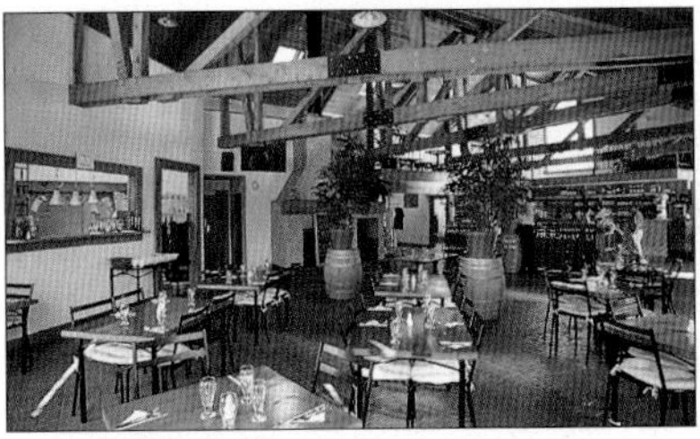

C J Pask Winery ③
This Mediterranean-style winery, located in a stony, silt-covered river bed, produces grapes with very ripe fruit flavours across a range of premium varieties. It is one of the region's best wineries.

Te Awa Farm Winery ④
Named "River of God" for the enormous aquifer beneath the Hawke's Bay plains that is tapped to irrigate crops, Te Awa makes fine Bordeaux-blend red wines, which can be savoured at its restaurant.

Tips for Drivers

Visiting three or four wineries in one day will allow time to taste and discuss the wines. Many wineries offer tours and most offer tastings and sales. Some have indoor and outdoor eating facilities, although booking is advisable. Information on the facilities at each listed winery can be obtained at the Napier Visitor Information centre (see p145).

Visitors planning to visit a greater number of wineries and make the most of tasting opportunities may prefer to take one of the many tours available.

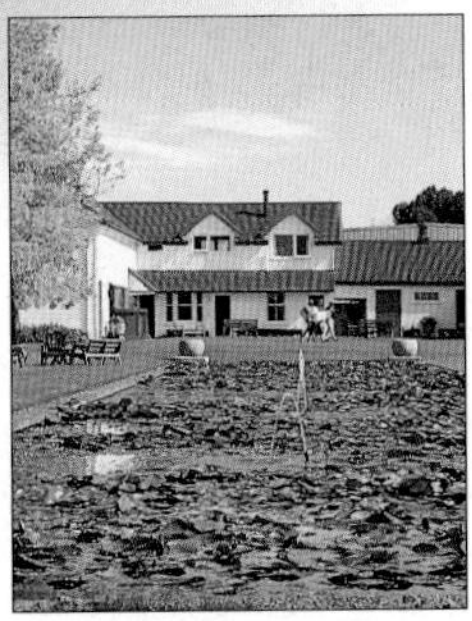

Ngatarawa Wines ⑤
A large rectangular lily pond and stable buildings housing the winery make an attractive setting that is more than matched by Ngatarawa's wines. The vineyard also has a pleasant picnic area and a *pétanque* court.

WELLINGTON AND THE SOUTH

EUROPEAN SETTLERS ARRIVING *in the mid-1800s and making their way north of Wellington, now New Zealand's capital city, quickly found themselves in the middle of virgin rainforest. The recent history of much of the area covered by Wellington and the South is linked to the massive clearance of the land through milling and burning of forest during the late 19th century.*

In their thousands, ancient giant trees covered potentially rich pastoral land acquired from the Maoris. Between the 1870s and 1910s, the area became the site of the country's biggest forest clearance programme as settlers poured in from overseas and demand for farmland grew. Sawmills, closely linked with the new rail network, sprang up throughout the district. Small towns along the railway enjoyed periods of importance before the sawmillers moved on. By 1907, however, milling output in the lower half of the North Island had passed its peak, to be superseded by the rich, rolling farmlands and rural lifestyles that have been a feature of the area ever since.

Although Taranaki, Wanganui and Manawatu are among the most productive and intensively farmed areas in New Zealand, these days diversity is the rule rather than the exception for the lower North Island. The exploitation of natural gas fields off the Taranaki coast, for example, has put an additional string to the region's economic bow.

Tourists are drawn to the compact lower North Island because of its mild climate, wild coastline, stunning beaches, scenic rivers, national parks, mountain ranges, ski fields, vineyards, and rich Maori heritage.

Harbour-fringed Wellington, situated at the bottom of the North Island, is the area's main city, and the centre of government, business, and the performing arts. The numerous small towns that radiate from it to the north, servicing local farms, are charming, friendly stopover points for travellers.

The Beehive and Parliament Buildings in Wellington, New Zealand's capital city

◁ Mount Taranaki, also known as Mount Egmont, in the centre of Egmont National Park

Exploring Wellington and the South

Wairarapa, the Kapiti Coast, Horowhenua, Manawatu, Wanganui and Taranaki are all within a day's drive of Wellington. The contrast between the arty, political capital city and the areas immediately to its north is striking. Within an hour, the country's rural heartland shows itself and the numerous small, sleepy towns become apparent. Dairy and sheep farms continue to feature strongly in the region, but visitors can also see newer forms of land use, such as ostrich farms and vineyards. The Egmont and Whanganui national parks await the more adventurous.

Sheep farm near Martinborough

Top Outdoor Activities

The places shown here have been selected for their recreational activities. Conditions vary depending on the weather and the time of year, so exercise caution and, if in doubt, seek local advice.

	Golf	Jet-Boating	Kayaking	Sailing	Surfing	Swimming	Tramping	Windsurfing
Egmont National Park						●	●	
Manawatu Gorge			●				●	
Masterton	●		●			●	●	
New Plymouth	●	●	●	●	●	●	●	●
Oakura					●	●		●
Opunake					●	●		●
Palmerston North	●					●		
Paraparaumu	●	●	●	●	●	●	●	●
Sugarloaf Islands						●		
Waikanae	●	●	●			●	●	
Wanganui	●	●	●			●		
Wellington	●	●	●	●	●		●	●
Whanganui National Park			●			●	●	
Whanganui River		●	●	●		●	●	

Sights at a Glance

See Also

Key

🚾 Motorway

🚾 State Highway

🚾 Major road

〜 River

🔆 Viewpoint

GETTING AROUND

The area is well served by rail, bus and air services, and an extensive, well-maintained road network. The country's mild climate ensures roads in the region are usually passable throughout the year. Wellington's state-of-the-art airport serves both international and domestic travellers, while increasing numbers of international cruise liners make use of the city's port. Several times a day, ferries, including those carrying cars, trucks and railway carriages, take travellers from Wellington across Cook Strait to the South Island and back again. A fast ferry service is also available.

16 WHANGANUI NATIONAL PARK

Taupo

50

4 WHANGANUI **15** RIVER

TAIHAPE

Napier

3

14 WANGANUI

WAIPUKURAU

2

Rangitikei River

54

3

2

1

56

13 PALMERSTON NORTH

52

Manawatu River

57

LEVIN

2

51

8

OTAKI

MOUNT BRUCE NATIONAL **12** WILDLIFE CENTRE

KAPITI ISLAND NATURE RESERVE **6** **7**

WAIKANAE **5**

Ruamahanga River

MASTERTON

PARAPARAUMU **4**

11

3

PAEKAKARIKI FEATHERSTON

GREYTOWN

2

PORIRUA **2** UPPER HUTT

9

1

MARTINBOROUGH

WELLINGTON **1**

LOWER HUTT

Lake Wairarapa

10

53

2 MARINE DRIVE TOUR

Palliser Bay

0 kilometres 20

0 miles 20

Cook Strait

Cape Palliser

Lambton Harbour marina in Wellington

Wellington: Cultural Capital

Poster for a comedy

KNOWN PRIMARILY AS the home of New Zealand's parliament and its public servant population, Wellington transformed itself during the 1980s and 1990s into a vibrant, culture-driven hot spot. Tucked around one of the world's most picturesque harbours, the capital city is intimate, sophisticated, arty and packed with national treasures. It is home to the Museum of New Zealand Te Papa Tongarewa *(see pp164–5)*, the Royal New Zealand Ballet, the New Zealand Symphony Orchestra, the National Business Review New Zealand Opera, the Chamber Music New Zealand and the New Zealand School of Dance. The city's strong arts scene combines an international flavour with an intrinsic Pacific identity.

Professional theatre, *strongly supported by Wellingtonians, can be enjoyed at several venues, including Downtown, Circa and Bats.*

The numerous public and private galleries *in Wellington are well patronized and exhibit local and international works of art. Dealer galleries, such as the Peter McLeavey Gallery, play a significant role in bringing the best of New Zealand art onto the market.*

The kiwi and the fern, *both symbols of New Zealand, formed the logo for the New Zealand International Festival of the Arts in 2000.*

"WELLYWOOD"

Film making in New Zealand began on a large scale only in the 1960s and 1970s. Today, film production is a multimillion dollar industry in New Zealand. With much of the industry based in studios around Wellington, and international stars now often working there, the city has earned the nickname "Wellywood".

The city is also the home town of director Peter Jackson, whose international film credits include *Meet the Feebles*, *Brain Dead* and *The Frighteners*. Much of the film work for these, as well as the making of J R R Tolkien's *The Lord of The Rings* trilogy, directed by Jackson, has been carried out in Wellington. The Wellington International Film Festival, held every July, attracts large crowds.

Film making at one of the many locations around the city

The New Zealand Symphony Orchestra, based in Wellington, performs regularly throughout the country. The orchestra accompanied New Zealand-born diva, Dame Kiri Te Kanawa, to welcome the dawn of the new millennium at Gisborne.

Percussion instruments, including assorted percussive junk, were drummed in a high-energy performance of rhythmic power.

BOOKS AND WRITERS

The emphasis on formal education, especially by Scottish immigrants who settled in Dunedin in the late 1800s, resulted in the demand that education in the new country be "free, secular and compulsory". Today, the early value placed on book learning by those settlers, many of them barely literate, has resulted in a national literacy rate of around 99 per cent. New Zealand-based reading programmes and books for children are exported around the world.

In Wellington, annual literary festivals, writers and readers programmes, and readings by local and visiting authors, are able to attract sponsorship as well as big audiences. Internationally recognized writers from Wellington include UK-based poet Fleur Adcock and novelists Maurice Gee, Elizabeth Knox and Vincent O'Sullivan *(see p31).*

Author Linda Burgess at her book launch

A scaffold "cube" formed the setting for the band's players and instruments.

INTERNATIONAL FESTIVAL OF THE ARTS

Held biennially in Wellington in early autumn, the New Zealand International Festival of the Arts is the country's largest performing arts festival. The New Zealand percussion group, Strike, was among the local and international artistes who performed at the festival in 2000.

The Royal New Zealand Ballet conducts national and international tours from its base in the capital city. Stephen Wellington and Nadine Tyson are shown here in a pas de deux from Raymonda.

The WestpacTrust Stadium is the leading venue for one of the mainstays of New Zealand culture – sport. Rugby, cricket and soccer, as well as concerts, are held in the 40,000-seat state-of-the-art stadium.

Wellington ①

WELLINGTON'S COMPACT CENTRAL business district lies between the city's foothills and its mountain-encircled harbour. Partly built on land developed during reclamation projects begun in the mid-1800s, the area today is the working environment of the country's politicians and the national government infrastructure. Foreign embassies, the Court of Appeal, National Archives, National Library, Museum

Statue in Plimmers Lane

of New Zealand Te Papa Tongarewa and the head offices of local and international businesses are among the institutions and organizations in its precincts. The city is known for its stylish shops, café culture, restaurants and galleries, with an atmosphere that is both stimulating and unhurried.

Lunching outdoors at the Astoria on Lambton Quay

🚆 Lambton Quay

Wellington's premier shopping street, Lambton Quay runs through the heart of New Zealand's political and commercial life. Its lively 1,100-m (3,600-ft) route is lined with arcades, plazas and elevated walkways. Most of Lambton Quay and its seaward parts are sited on reclaimed land. Plaques set at intervals along its footpaths identify the lay of the shoreline before the mid-1800s. While steep steps lead up to the slopes on the west, side streets on the east offer flat access to the redeveloped harbourfront (*see pp160–63*).

⛪ Cathedral Church of St Paul

Mulgrave St. 🕻 (04) 473 6722. ◯ Mon–Sat. ♿
Known as Old St Paul's, the Cathedral Church of St Paul is an outstanding example of an early English Gothic-style cathedral adapted to colonial conditions and materials. Consecrated in 1866, the cathedral is made entirely of wood, including its nails.

⛪ Wellington Cathedral of St Paul

45 Molesworth St. 🕻 (04) 472 0286. ◯ daily. 🎟 📷 behind church. ♿
After a building programme spread over several decades, including a number of exterior and interior design changes and reversals, the Wellington Cathedral of St Paul was finally completed in 1998. Standing in the parliamentary precinct opposite the Law Courts and the National Library, the Romanesque-style cathedral houses unique displays of etched and stained-glass windows, memorials to historic events, and a 2,500-pipe organ. The Lady Chapel, formerly a parish church on the Kapiti coast north of Wellington, was relocated to the site in 1998 to complete the cathedral complex.

Stained-glass window

Art in the Galleria of the Parliament Buildings

🏛 Parliament Buildings

Molesworth St. 🕻 (04) 471 9999. ◯ daily. ● 1 & 2 Jan, 6 Feb, Good Fri, 25 & 26 Dec. 🚫 ♿ 🎟 🛈
New Zealand's Parliament is made up of three main buildings: the Edwardian Neo-Classical style Parliament Building opened in 1918; the Parliamentary Library, completed in 1899; and the Beehive, occupied since 1977. Only the Beehive is not open to the public. The three buildings stand alongside each other on the site that has housed the country's parliament since 1865, 400 m (1,300 ft) away from the earthquake fault line which runs through Wellington. Key historic trees have been retained in the beautifully landscaped grounds, which also feature a rose garden.

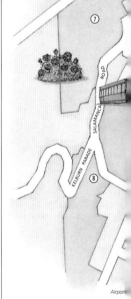

Airport

KEY

🟦	Wellington Street-by-Street, *see pp160–61*
🚉	Train station
🚌	Bus station
⛴	Ferry terminal
🅿	Parking
🛈	Tourist information

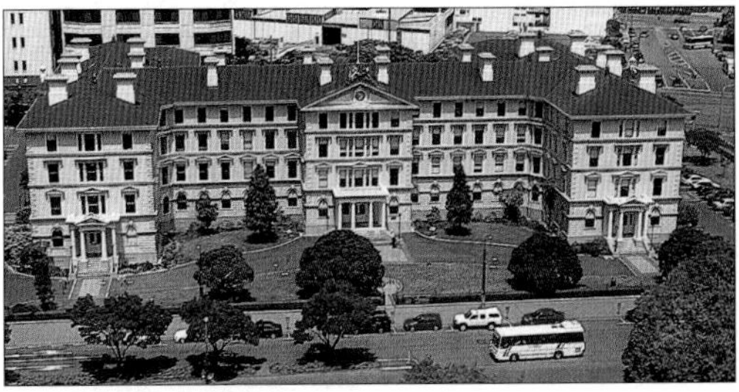

Old Government Buildings

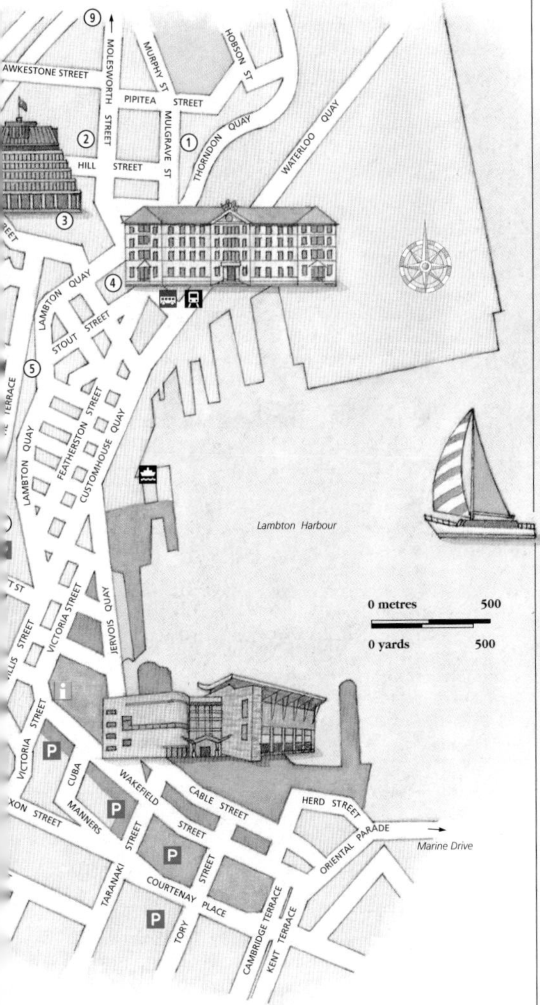

Wellington City Centre

Cathedral Church of St Paul ①
Katherine Mansfield Museum ⑨
Kelburn Cable Car ⑥
Lambton Quay ⑤
Old Government Buildings ④
Parliament Buildings ③
Victoria University ⑧
Wellington Botanic Garden ⑦
Wellington Cathedral of St Paul ②

Visitors' Checklist

Road map D5. 👥 *414,000.*
✈ *8 km (5 miles) S of city.*
🚆 *Bunny St (btw Featherston St & Waterloo Quay).* 🚆 🚌 *Platform 9, Wellington Railway Station, Waterloo Quayside.*
⛴ *Aotea Quay Terminal.*
ℹ *Cnr of Wakefield and Victoria sts, (04) 801 4000.*
🎭 *New Zealand International Festival of the Arts (Mar).*
[W] *www.wcc.govt.nz*

Old Government Buildings

15 Lambton Quay. ☎ *(04) 472 7356.* ○ *daily.* ● *Easter Sun, 25 Apr, four days over New Year.* ♿ 🚶 🍴 ☕ 🛍

The largest wooden building in the southern hemisphere, and one of the largest such buildings in the world, the Old Government Buildings were built in the 1870s in a style imitating stone. Used in the early 1900s by New Zealand's parliamentary cabinet and then by various government departments until 1990, the restored buildings are now occupied by Victoria University's Law School. The original cabinet room on the ground floor and historic displays on the first floor are open to the public.

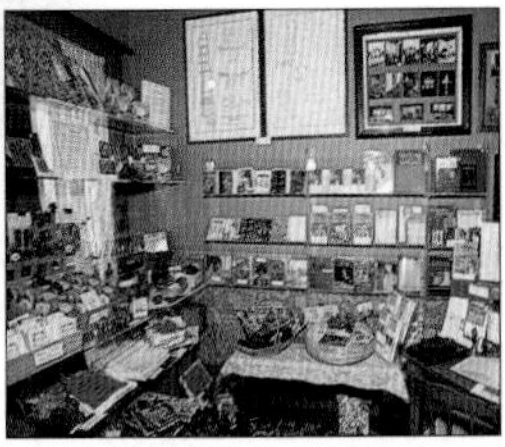

Items for sale in the Katherine Mansfield Museum

Katherine Mansfield Museum

25 Tinakori Rd. ☎ *(04) 473 7268.* ○ *daily.* ● *Good Fri, 25 Dec.* 💲 📷 🚶 *by arrangement.* 🛍

This 1888 villa is the birthplace and childhood home of Katherine Mansfield *(see p31)*, possibly the country's most famous author. It contains period photographs, excerpts from Mansfield's writing, and antique furniture.

Exploring Wellington

Water lilies in Botanic Garden

A VIBRANT, INNER-CITY AREA bordered to the north by a green belt, central Wellington encompasses late Victorian mansions, student flats, tiny former workers' cottages, the Prime Minister's residence, an historic cemetery and the main motorway in and out of the city.

At the end of the 19th century, as the number of overseas settlers increased, land near the foreshore became scarce, and steeper, less accessible land above the city was utilized for housing. Today, a walk around the suburb of Thorndon to higher points shows how a community has spread onwards and upwards from its original concentration in the port area.

Cable car climbing to the top of the Botanic Garden

Kelburn Cable Car
Cable Car Lane, 280 Lambton Quay. (04) 472 2199. ☐ daily. fares.
Opened in 1902 to link the newly developed hill suburbs with the city, the cable cars used on the route have been powered by electricity since 1933. Stops along the way include Victoria University, with access to the Botanic Garden and Carter Observatory at the top. The Kelburn terminus, which is the final stop, offers a sweeping view of the city and harbour.

Wellington Botanic Garden
Glenmore St. (04) 801 3071. ☐ daily.
Established in 1868, the garden is a mix of protected native forest, conifer plantings and plant collections. A major seasonal bedding programme includes a massed display of 30,000 tulips in spring and early summer. The Lady Norwood Rose Garden has 106 formal beds, including recent introductions and old favourites. The Begonia House features tropical and temperate plants, a lily pond, seasonal displays of orchids, and a collection of epiphytic and carnivorous plants. The garden's information hub, the Treehouse Visitor Centre, can be accessed via a tower lift. The more hardy can get to the centre via a steep path.

The **Carter Observatory**, New Zealand's national observatory, stands in the Botanic Garden complex near the terminus of the cable car.

Astronomical displays, audio-visual shows, a planetarium and an historic refracting telescope are special features.

Carter Observatory
40 Salamanca Rd, Kelburn. (04) 472 8167. ☐ daily.

The ivy-covered Hunter Building at Victoria University

Victoria University
Kelburn Parade. (04) 472 1000.
With 15,000 students enrolled in over 50 departments and schools, Victoria University is the fourth largest of New Zealand's eight universities and three Maori tertiary institutions. Opened in 1899, Victoria University's main campus has occupied its Kelburn site overlooking downtown Wellington since 1904. The Law School, as well as the School of Architecture and Design, are among the campuses located in the city.

Lady Norwood Rose Garden in the Wellington Botanic Garden

Suburban Hillside Villas

OFTEN APPEARING to cling precariously to the sides of hills, accessible only by cable car or long flights of steep steps, hillside villas are a striking feature of Wellington's older city suburbs such as Oriental Bay, Mount Victoria, Thorndon and Kelburn. These ubiquitous New Zealand homes evolved during the late 19th and early 20th centuries from simple, flat-fronted single-storey colonial cottages with verandahs running across the front, to two-storey houses with projecting faceted bay windows. The villas were traditionally made of timber from New Zealand's kauri forests, roofed with corrugated iron, and decorated with mass-produced components ordered from catalogues. Other features included the use of stained glass, large double-hung sash windows and balustraded porches or verandahs.

Painted window surrounds

HARBOURFRONT SUBURBS

Wellington's early settlers were forced by a shortage of flat land to build on the hills bordering the harbour. Many original villas, as well as those restored and adapted as family homes, can be seen during a walk or drive through Wellington's harbourfront suburbs.

Wooden villas on the hillside overlooking Oriental Bay

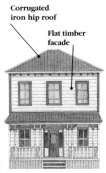

Corrugated iron hip roof
Flat timber facade

Flat-fronted, hip-roofed villa with long verandah

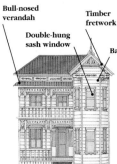

Bull-nosed verandah
Double-hung sash window
Timber fretwork
Bay window

Gabled hip-roofed villa with faceted bay window

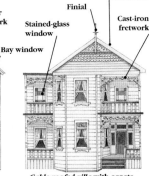

Finial
Gable roof
Stained-glass window
Cast-iron fretwork

Gable-roofed villa with ornate cast-iron decoration

Late 19th-century villas constructed for middle-income families usually had a living area (the "parlour"), three or four bedrooms and a central hallway, with a single bathroom and kitchen area to the rear. Toilet (often referred to as the "long drop") and laundry ("wash house") facilities were usually housed in rudimentary dwellings in garden areas behind the house.

Parlour at the 1888 villa in Thorndon where Katherine Mansfield was born *(see p157)*

Street-by-Street: The Harbourfront

Silver fern globe

THE AREA BETWEEN Lambton Harbour and Clyde Quay Wharf on Wellington's harbourfront stands entirely on reclaimed land. It covers a site once central to Wellington's waterfront industry, and can be covered on foot within an hour. Echoes of the commercial sailing ships and liners that once dominated the area remain in the Museum of Wellington, City and Sea. In spring and summer, dragon boat competitions are held opposite the Museum of New Zealand Te Papa Tongarewa. The Civic Square, with its open spaces and nearby public buildings, such as the Town Hall, is a favourite meeting place for Wellingtonians and visitors alike.

Courtenay Place
Lined with bars, clubs, restaurants and theatres, Courtenay Place provides a taste of the city's nightlife (see p163).

Circa Theatre
This refurbished building is a focal point of the city's contemporary theatre scene (see p154).

0 metres   100
0 yards   100

The Overseas Terminal is where passengers arriving on overseas liners first set foot in Wellington. It also houses facilities for conferences and exhibitions, as well as licensed restaurants.

★ Museum of New Zealand Te Papa Tongarewa
The museum offers visitors interactive experiences of New Zealand's Maori heritage, national history and natural environment as well as art treasures (see pp164–5).

STAR SIGHTS

★ **Museum of New Zealand Te Papa Tongarewa**

★ **Museum of Wellington, City and Sea**

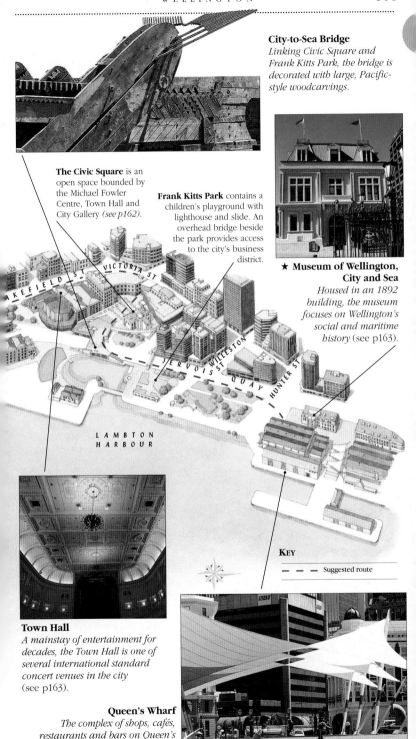

City-to-Sea Bridge
Linking Civic Square and Frank Kitts Park, the bridge is decorated with large, Pacific-style woodcarvings.

The Civic Square is an open space bounded by the Michael Fowler Centre, Town Hall and City Gallery *(see p162).*

Frank Kitts Park contains a children's playground with lighthouse and slide. An overhead bridge beside the park provides access to the city's business district.

★ **Museum of Wellington, City and Sea**
Housed in an 1892 building, the museum focuses on Wellington's social and maritime history (see p163).

VICTORIA ST

AKEFIELD ST

JERVOIS QUAY

WILLESTON ST

HUNTER ST

LAMBTON HARBOUR

KEY

––– Suggested route

Town Hall
A mainstay of entertainment for decades, the Town Hall is one of several international standard concert venues in the city (see p163).

Queen's Wharf
The complex of shops, cafés, restaurants and bars on Queen's Wharf is a popular entertainment hub for nearby office workers.

The Harbourfront

Steel nikau palm

THE HARBOURFRONT is dominated by the City-to-Sea bridge, a pedestrian-only right of way above one of the main roads into Wellington. Bordered on one side by Wellington's wharves and on the other by office blocks, the bridge leads from steps within the Civic Square complex to Frank Kitts Park and the waterfront, a lagoon and further on to the Museum of New Zealand Te Papa Tongarewa (*see pp164–5*). The bridge is a public art space in its own right, featuring works by leading New Zealand sculptors.

Contemporary exhibit at the City Gallery

♣ Civic Square

Wakefield St. 🛈 *(04) 802 4860.* ⬭ *daily.* ♿

The heart of the city's cultural scene, this extensive paved, plaza-style courtyard was opened in the early 1990s, making use of an area that was previously a busy street. The pink and beige square is an open space that features various sculptures and provides a link to a number of institutions bordering it. These include the Public Library, Visitor Information Centre, City Council Buildings, City Gallery and the capital's main concert venues, the Town Hall and Michael Fowler Centre.

The square harkens back to its previous role as a thoroughfare. It brings together Wellington's central business district with the city's cultural and social side: the Museum of New Zealand Te Papa Tongarewa, the Opera House, theatres, cinemas and shops, as well as the bars and restaurants of the city's main night-time entertainment area, Courtenay Place. The square has become a well-used and central meeting place for Wellingtonians. Visitors to the square will often find themselves among street theatre performers and at outdoor concerts, exhibitions and rallies of all kinds.

🏛 City Gallery

Civic Square. 🛈 *(04) 801 3952.* ⬭ *daily.* 🗓 *international exhibitions.* ♿ 🖼

Housed in a striking Art Deco building fitted with original kauri doors, marble finishes, handrails and steel windows, the building that for decades served as the city's Public Library is now home to the country's leading, and often most controversial, art gallery.

Primarily an exhibition space, with no permanent collection of its own, the gallery has nonetheless developed a distinctive character, specializing in bringing to Wellington the best contemporary art and design shows from within New Zealand and around the world. Exhibitions held at the gallery have covered a diverse range of media and subjects, including painting, sculpture, film and video, industrial and graphic design and architecture.

An addition to the ground floor of the building is the Michael Hirschfelt Gallery. Named after a former head of the New Zealand Labour Party, this small gallery concentrates mainly on promoting the work of up-and-coming artists.

Neil Dawson's ferns sculpture suspended in the Civic Square

⚡ Michael Fowler Centre

Wakefield St. **(** (04) 801 4242.
🔘 daily. 📷 for concerts. ♿ 📷
by arrangement. 🔢

Designed by Christchurch's
Sir Miles Warren and named
after a former mayor and
prominent architect, the
semicircular complex is internationally renowned for its
ability to distribute sound
throughout its 2,550-plus
seat concert chamber. Rock
concerts, conventions and
even political rallies are
staged in what has become
the city's premier concert hall.
Many events associated with
the increasingly popular
biennial New Zealand International Festival of the Arts
(see pp40, 154–5), which
attracts thousands of local
and overseas visitors to
Wellington, are held here.

The Victorian-tiled lobby of the
Town Hall

♨ Town Hall

Wakefield St. **(** (04) 801 4242.
🔘 daily. 📷 for concerts. ♿ 📷
by arrangement. 🖥

Restoration of the Town Hall,
a sedate 1904 Edwardian
brick building with a Roman-
style portico, has returned the
Town Hall to much of its former glory. Restoration work
included seismic strengthen-
ing of the building, restoring
the floor's Victorian tiles,
uncovering wrought-iron
balustrades, manufacturing
lights and fittings from original samples, and repairing
the auditorium's pressed zinc
ceiling. The hall's magnificent
main staircase is now a major
attraction. The 2,000-seat
"shoe box" auditorium is regarded as one of the world's
leading venues for the performance of classical music.

Courtenay Place, a prime night-time entertainment area

🍴 Courtenay Place

Lined with a concentrated
strip of sophisticated nightclubs, trendy cafés and
restaurants, and professional
theatres, Courtenay Place and
the streets leading from it
form the night-time entertainment heart of the city.

With nearly every cuisine
style and price range available, from budget eating
outlets to award-winning
restaurants, Courtenay Place
is the venue to meet visitors,
mix with locals, and eat
and dance the whole night
away. Live music inside cafés
and bars is matched by a
lively street scene, where
crowds thread their way
through buskers and per-
formers that add to the area's
relaxed atmosphere.

🏛 Museum of Wellington, City and Sea

Queens Wharf. **(** (04) 472
8904. 🔘 daily. ⬤ 25 Dec.
📷 ♿ 📷 by arrangement.
📷

Housed in a building
constructed in 1891, the
Museum of Wellington,
City and Sea used to be
essentially a maritime
museum. It is now
dedicated to recording
not only Wellington's
maritime past but also
its social legacy. The
museum uses model
ships, ships' instru-
ments, relics from
wrecks, maritime
paintings, old maps
and sea journals, as
well as holographic
re-creations and videos to tell
the story of Wellington in the
context of its harbour and
surrounding coast.

One of the most interesting
exhibits in the museum's
collection of ship models is
that of the inter-island ferry,
the *Wahine*, in the process
of sinking off the Wellington
suburb of Seatoun in April
1968 during a storm. A photograph exhibit documents the
tragedy. There is also a model
of the sinking of the *Titanic*.

Visitors to the museum can
get a good perspective of
Wellington from a three-
dimensional model of the
harbour. There is also an
education room for children,
with activities and computers.

Façade of the Museum of Wellington,
City and Sea

Museum of New Zealand Te Papa Tongarewa

Museum logo

Wᴛʜ ᴇxʜɪʙɪᴛɪᴏɴ sᴘᴀᴄᴇ equivalent to three football fields, the Museum of New Zealand Te Papa Tongarewa ("Our Place") is one of the largest national museums in the world. Committed to telling the stories of all cultures in New Zealand, home to the National Art Collection, and with ample gallery space for touring exhibitions, the museum opened on its waterfront site in 1998. Te Papa's collections include a number of significant Maori works of art and treasures, as well as a unique 21st-century carved meeting house.

Mountains to Sea
The amazing variety of New Zealand's animals and plants, from kiwis to kauris, are revealed in exhibits featuring the natural world.

"Awesome Forces" help visitors experience the powerful forces shaping the country's landscape.

Level 2

Future Rush
In Time Warp, the museum's entertainment heart, visitors will enjoy this interactive visit to a super-modern house in the year 2055.

Level 1

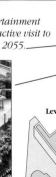

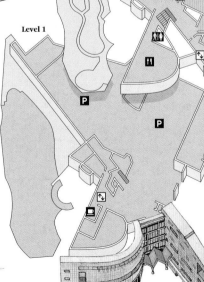

Bush City
Visitors step into the open air to experience native bush, wetlands, a volcanic landscape, a waterfall and a lagoon right in the centre of the city. They can explore a glowworm cave and dig for dinosaur fossils.

Sᴛᴀʀ Exʜɪʙɪᴛs

★ **Mana Whenua**

★ **Te Marae**

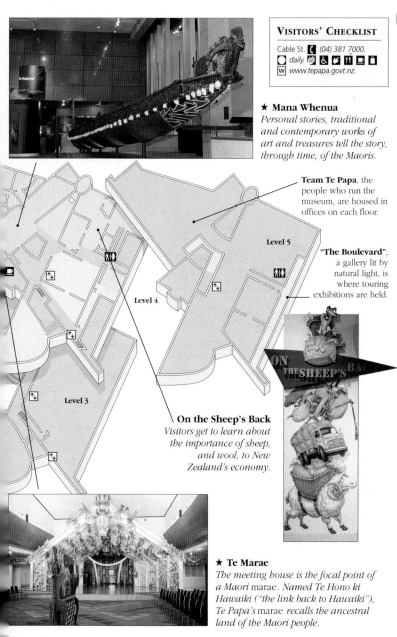

VISITORS' CHECKLIST

Cable St. ☎ *(04) 381 7000.*
◯ *daily.* 🅿 ♿ 🅲 🚻 🖥 📷
🆆 *www.tepapa.govt.nz.*

★ Mana Whenua
Personal stories, traditional and contemporary works of art and treasures tell the story, through time, of the Maoris.

Team Te Papa, the people who run the museum, are housed in offices on each floor.

Level 5

"The Boulevard", a gallery lit by natural light, is where touring exhibitions are held.

Level 4

Level 3

On the Sheep's Back
Visitors get to learn about the importance of sheep, and wool, to New Zealand's economy.

★ Te Marae
The meeting house is the focal point of a Maori marae. *Named Te Hono ki Hawaiki ("the link back to Hawaiki"), Te Papa's* marae *recalls the ancestral land of the Maori people.*

KEY TO FLOORPLAN

▓	Art
▓	History
▓	Maori
▓	Nature
▓	Sea
▓	Time warp

GALLERY GUIDE
The first of the high-tech interactive exhibitions begins on Level 2, which also provides access to Bush City. Level 3 has space for touring exhibitions, while Maori, Pacific Island and European cultural exhibits are concentrated on Level 4. Level 5 contains more gallery space as well as the museum's library, reading room and research facilities. Works from the National Art Collection are spread throughout the museum.

Marine Drive Tour ❷

Hugging the coastline from Oriental Bay, south-east of the city centre on the inner harbour, to Owhiro Bay on the outer shoreline facing Cook Strait, this route is undoubtedly one of New Zealand's best coastal drives. It is both picturesque on cloudless days and awe-inspiring when Wellington's famous southerly gales whip up pounding waves. The route takes visitors past numerous small bays and sheltered, sandy beaches. It also passes through several suburbs where wooden villas *(see p159)* perch on what seem precarious sites high above the road, and around steep, uninhabited hillsides covered with trees that come down to the water's edge.

Owhiro Bay ⑩
Tourers can turn right at this bay and return to the city via Happy Valley Road or continue onto the 4-km (2.5-mile) Red Rocks Coastal Walk, where a pod of 80–150 male seals takes up residence each year.

Island Bay ⑨
Descendants of Italian immigrants, who settled here in the early 1900s, are among those seen fishing in Cook Strait and beyond.

CITY CENTRE

Lyall Bay ⑧
Bordered by Wellington's airport, this bay is used all year round by surfers and swimmers. On a clear day, the South Island's snow-covered mountain ranges can be seen.

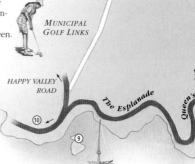

Cambridge

GOVERNMENT HOUSE

Adelaide Road

WELLINGTON ZOO

MUNICIPAL GOLF LINKS

HAPPY VALLEY ROAD

The Esplanade

Queen's Drive

Lyall

| 0 kilometres | 1 |
| 0 miles | 1 |

KEY

▬▬ Tour route

═══ Other road

☼ Viewpoint

Oriental Bay [1]
This is an area of cafés and fashionable restaurants and a favourite spot for joggers and swimmers. Across from the sandy beach, stately Victorian villas share the hillside with modern apartment blocks.

Tips for Drivers

Length: *30 km (19 miles).*
Stopping-off points: *There are glorious views at all points along the route. Several parking areas allow visitors to leave their cars and stroll along the bays. Eating places include the famous Chocolate Fish Café at Scorching Bay, whose waiting staff have official permission to serve customers seated across the road on the waterfront.*

Mahanga Bay [3]
One of the smallest and most sheltered bays along the route, Mahanga Bay is fringed with pine trees.

Evans Bay [2]
This sheltered bay is a popular spot for yachting. It also contains a marina.

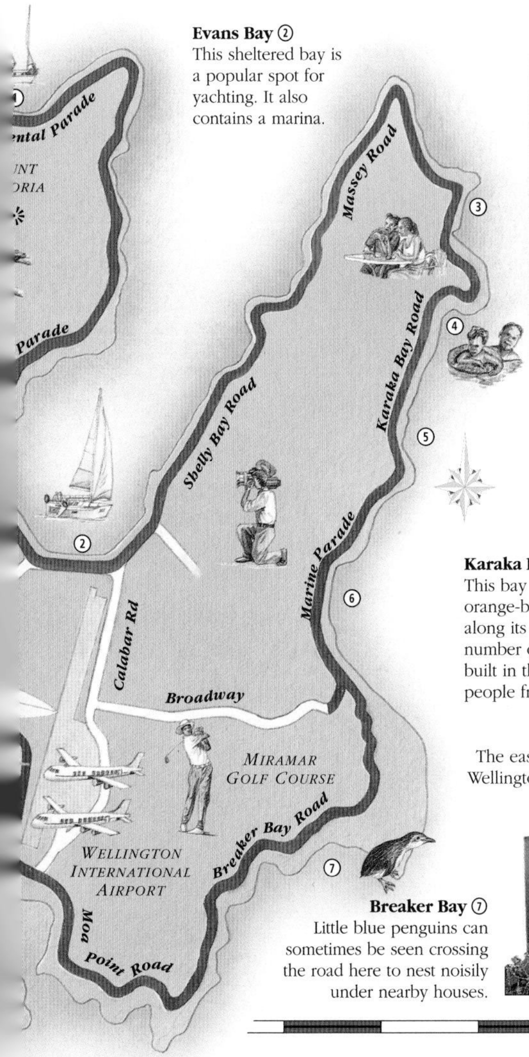

Scorching Bay [4]
Popular with swimmers, this beach allows good views towards Somes and Ward islands and Cook Strait. The seaside suburb of Eastbourne is opposite.

Karaka Bay [5]
This bay is named after the native orange-berried karaka trees found along its edge. It has a pier and a number of wooden summer houses built in the early 1900s by wealthy people from out of town.

Worser Bay [6]
The eastern suburbs are the home of Wellington's thriving international film industry *(see p154)*.

Breaker Bay [7]
Little blue penguins can sometimes be seen crossing the road here to nest noisily under nearby houses.

Old trams at the Tram Museum, Paekakariki

Paekakariki ❸

Road map E4. 🚶 *1,700.* 🚉 🚌 🚏
ℹ️ *Coastlands, Paraparaumu,*
(04) 298 8195.

Sᴛᴜᴀᴛᴇᴅ ᴏɴ the Kapiti
Coast, 40 minutes'
drive north of Wellington
on State Highway 1,
Paekakariki is the first
of four townships
spaced evenly along
40 km (25 miles) of
sweeping, sandy
coastline. A main
attraction at Paekaka-
riki is Queen Elizabeth
Park, which encom-
passes a stunning coast-
line, sand dunes, streams,
peat swamps and bush walks.
A tram ride from McKays
Crossing north of Paekakariki
takes visitors through the 6.4-
sq km (2.5-sq mile) park.

At the **Tram Museum** in
the park, visitors can view
historical displays of some of
the trams and trolley buses
that once crossed Wellington's
streets, and observe aged
trams being refurbished.

Boy with calf at Lindale

🏛 **Tram Museum**
Queen Elizabeth Park. 📞 *(04) 298*
5139. ⬜ *Sat & Sun.* ⬛ *25 Dec.*
♿ ♿

Paraparaumu ❹

Road map E4. 🚶 *12,000.* 🚉 🚉
🚌 🚌 ℹ️ *Coastlands, (04) 298*
8195.

Tʜᴇ ᴍᴀɪɴ ᴄᴇɴᴛʀᴇ on the
Kapiti Coast, Paraparaumu
has a shorefront shopping
complex, cafés and restaurants. It also has a developed

beach, with a park and playgrounds. The town is the
departure point for boat trips
to Kapiti Island.

The area's major attraction
is the **Southward Car Museum**, which holds the largest
collection of vintage and
veteran vehicles in the
southern hemisphere.
The collection of bi-
cycles includes an
1863 bone shaker.
Marlene Dietrich's
limousine is one of
more than 250
classic and quirky
vehicles dating
from 1895. Racing
boats, home-made
vehicles, motor cycles, early
motoring curios and traction
engines are also housed on
the site. A highlight is a 1950

Cadillac Gangster Special,
once owned by an employee
of Al Capone and Lucky
Luciano. It boasts a bomb-
proof floor, armour-plated
doors, bulletproof windows,
and a hinged windscreen for
firing from inside.

The **Lindale Tourist and
Agricultural Centre**, set
around a New Zealand farm,
is a good place to bring
children. The centre offers
sheep shearing demonstra-
tions as well as hands-on
opportunities to milk a cow,
bottle-feed lambs and goats,
play with chickens and baby
deer, and observe exotic
species like llama and emu.
There are farm walks, a golf
driving range and helicopter
rides for the more active.

A fully operational dairy
factory, which produces the
award-winning gourmet
Kapiti Cheese and Kapiti Ice
Cream is located on the site,
along with galleries, shops
and eating places.

🏛 **Southward Car Museum**
Otaihanga Rd, Paraparaumu North.
📞 *(04) 297 1221.* ⬜ *daily.* ⬛
Good Fri, 25 Apr, 25 Dec. ♿ ♿
🎞 💻 🚻

🍽 **Lindale Tourist and
Agricultural Centre**
State Hwy 1, Paraparaumu North.
📞 *(04) 297 0916.* ⬜ *daily.* ♿ ♿
🎞 🍴 💻 🚻

Vintage cars at the Southward Car Museum

Waikanae ❺

Road map E4. 🚶 8,600. 🚗 🚌 🚆
ℹ️ *Aputa Place, (04) 904 5768.*

NESTLED BETWEEN the foothills of the Tararua Range and the Kapiti Coast, Waikanae is primarily a retirement centre, known for its craft shops and magnificent gardens. Burnard Gardens, recognized as one of New Zealand's most formally designed English-style gardens, is located here.

The **Kapiti Coast Museum**, housed in a former post office in Waikanae, contains extensive collections of wireless and telephone equipment.

🏛 **Kapiti Coast Museum**
9 Elizabeth St. 📞 *(04) 293 2359.*
⏰ *Sat, Sun & public hols.* 📷 *by arrangement.*

View of Kapiti Island from the mainland

Kapiti Island Nature Reserve ❻

Road map E4. 🚢 *Paraparaumu.*
ℹ️ *Department of Conservation, Stout St, Wellington, (04) 472 7356.*

KAPITI ISLAND, lying about 6 km (4 miles) from the mainland, dominates the Kapiti Coast. The 10-km (6-mile) long island has been a protected wildlife reserve since 1897. Access to the island is very limited although a permit to visit by charter boat can be obtained from the Department of Conservation in Wellington. All parties are met by the resident ranger. Trips around the island, and diving or fishing in the surrounding waters can be done at any time. Making their home on the island are birds rare or absent from the mainland, such as saddlebacks and takahe. Less rare, but twice as cheeky, are the wekas, which are likely to steal anything that is left unattended by visitors.

Otaki ❼

Road map E4. 🚶 7,600. 🚗 🚌 🚆
ℹ️ *239 State Hwy 1, (06) 364 7620.*

BEFORE THE EUROPEAN settlers' arrival in 1840, Otaki was heavily populated by Maoris. It had the finest Maori church, Rangiatea Church, in New Zealand. Built in 1851, the church was destroyed by fire in 1995. Construction of a replica of the church on the site began in 1998.

ENVIRONS: Just south of Otaki is the **Hyde Park Museum and Craft Village**. The museum has Maori artifacts from pre-European days, colonial memorabilia and exhibits from present-day New Zealand. Included are a Royal Room with displays from the 1953 visit of Queen Elizabeth and Prince Phillip, old farm machinery and a grocery shop with over 3,000 items marked at 1937 prices.

South of the town, the 19-km (12-mile) Gorge Road leads to **Otaki Forks** and the **Tararua Forest Park**. Along the way are walking tracks.

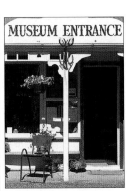

Entrance to the Hyde Park Museum, Otaki

🖼 **Hyde Park Museum and Craft Village**
Te Horo, State Hwy 1. 📞 *(04) 298 4515.* ⏰ *Tue–Sun.* 📷 ♿

Levin ❽

Road map E4. 🚶 15,400.
🚗 🚌 🚆

LEVIN SITS ON a fertile plain that is one of the largest vegetable-producing areas in the country. Its main street, lined with shops that service its farming hinterland, epitomizes much of traditional small town New Zealand. Owner-operated outlets on the outskirts of the town offer "pick-your-own" freshly grown produce direct from the fields and orchards.

TE RAUPARAHA

Kapiti Island was once the base of Te Rauparaha (1768–1849), chief of the Ngati Toa tribe and one of the greatest Maori generals of his era. After years of warfare in the Waikato and Taranaki areas, he moved to Kapiti Island in the 1820s, dominating the southwestern part of the North Island and the north of the South Island until the 1840s. He is credited with composing the well-known *haka* (war chant) often performed by the All Blacks before international rugby matches.

Watercolour (1840) by Isaac Coates

Kamate. Kamate.
Ka Ora. Ka Ora.
Tenei te tangata
*   puhuruhuru*
Nana nei i tiki mai
I whakawhiti te ra.
Upane. Upane.
Whiti te ra.

It is death. It is death.
It is life. It is life.
This is the hairy person
Who caused the sun to
   shine.
Abreast. Keep abreast.
The rank. Hold fast.
Into the sun that shines.

Hay rolled into bales, ready for storing, on a farm near Martinborough

Featherston ⑨

Road map E4. 🏃 2,600. 🚌 🚑
🚐 ⓘ Old Courthouse, Main St,
(06) 308 8051.

SITUATED AT the foot of the
Rimutaka Range, Feather-
ston is the southern gateway
to the Wairarapa area for
those arriving from the Wellington side of the divide.
Known for its antique shops
and colonial buildings, it also
houses several museums,
including the **Fell Engine
Museum**, home to the
world's only surviving and
lovingly restored Fell engine.
Running on three rails, these
ingenious locomotives used
to climb up and over the
Rimutaka Range in the district's early days.

🏛 **Fell Engine Museum**
Cnr Fitzherbert and Lyon sts.
📞 (06) 308 9379. ◯ Sat & Sun,
school hols. 🈺 ♿

ENVIRONS: On the right side
of the road from Wellington,
before reaching Featherston,
a signpost points the way to a
lookout. This is the best spot
for visitors to get splendid
views across **Lake Wairarapa**
to the ranges of Haurangi
(Aorangi) Forest Park and
Palliser Bay. The lake is home
to internationally recognized
wetlands that are the third
largest in New Zealand.
   South of the lake is **Cape
Palliser** where, next to a
public road, visitors can find
the country's largest breeding
colony for the New Zealand
fur seal, one of nine fur seal
species found worldwide.
Seals can be seen throughout
the year, with breeding from
November to January.
   Another spectacular sight
in the area is the **Putangirua
Pinnacles**, formed in the past
120,000 years by heavy rain
eroding an ancient gravel
deposit. Some of the pinnacles may be 1,000 years old.

Martinborough ⑩

Road map E5. 🏃 1,500. 🚑
ⓘ Kitchener St, (06) 306 9043.
🍷 Toast Martinborough (Nov).

ESTABLISHED IN 1881 by Irish
immigrant John Martin,
Martinborough was once
reliant for its prosperity on
the surrounding farming
community. Since the late
1970s, the town has become
internationally known for
its grape growing and wine
making (see pp34–5). It is
now a fashionable weekend
destination for wine lovers
and those attracted by its
cafés, bars, restaurants and
thriving arts community. Most
of the area's 20 boutique
wineries are within walking
distance of Martinborough's
picturesque town square.

ENVIRONS: New Zealand's first
commercial wind farm, **Hau
Nui Wind Farm**, lies 21 km
(13 miles) southeast of
Martinborough. Operated by
Wairarapa Electricity, the
farm's seven turbines are a
surreal sight ranged along a
540-m (1,770-ft) ridge. Although on private land, they
can be seen from a nearby
public viewing area that has
an information kiosk.

Visitors enjoying the wine at the Grapevine in Martinborough

Masterton ⓫

Road map E4. 🚶 22,800. 🚉 🚌
🚌 ℹ️ 5 Dixon St, (06) 378 7373.
🎫 Golden Shears (Mar).

A N HOUR'S DRIVE from both
Wellington and Palmer-
ston North, Masterton is Wairarapa's largest town, and
home to the annual Golden
Shears event. Masterton's
Henley Lake Park, opened in
1988, has an artificial lake
containing four small islands.
It is popular with families and
anglers attracted by the trout
regularly released into it.
Queen Elizabeth Park, close
to the town centre on the
main road leading north of
the town, has trees planted by
settlers in 1877. Facilities
include a boating lake, aviary,
aquarium and deer park. A
pioneer cemetery is located
behind the park.

Flights in vintage aircraft,
including a Tiger Moth,
T6 Harvard and Proctor 5,
are available at the **Hood
Aerodrome**, a flight training
and skydiving venue. It also
houses a flying museum.

🏛 Hood Aerodrome
South Rd. ℂ (06) 377 3804. ◯ by
arrangement. 🏷 donation. ♿

ENVIRONS: On the road from
Featherston to Masterton is
the picturesque village of
Greytown. Settled in 1854, it
is the oldest town in Wairarapa and has the most
complete street of wooden

**Agricultural implements at the
Cobblestone Museum**

Victorian architecture in New
Zealand. Greytown is home
to the **Cobblestone Mu-
seum**. Located on the site of
coach stables built in 1856 for
the Wellington mail service,
the museum houses colonial
buildings, vehicles, agricultural equipment and a
working saddlery. It has
relocated and restored
buildings, complete
with memorabilia of
the days of the
early settlers.

The **Tararua
Forest Park**, located
within the rugged Tara-
rua Range, can be
accessed at Holdsworth, 15
km (9 miles) from State
Highway 2, via Norfolk Road

just south of Masterton. The
park has bush walks ranging
from easy to difficult. Grassy
flats beside the Atiwhakatu
Stream are ideal for picnics
and barbecues.

🏛 Cobblestone Museum
169 Main St. ℂ (06) 304 9687.
◯ daily. 🏷 ♿ 🚻

Mount Bruce National Wildlife Centre ⓬

Road map E4. ℂ (06) 375 8004.
◯ daily. ⬤ 25 Dec. 🏷 🚌 ♿ 🚻

A DMINISTERED BY the Department of Conservation,
this centre, located 30 km (19
miles) north of Masterton,
gives visitors the chance to
get close to and learn about
some of New Zealand's most
threatened native birds. Priority species, including the
saddleback, stitch-
bird, kokako and
takahe, live in un-
crowded aviaries.
Bush walks to view
ancient plant species
lead through a last
remnant of forest known
as the "Forty Mile Bush",
containing native rimu,
rata and kamahi. Other
attractions include the
nocturnal kiwi, tuatara,
and eels sunning themselves
on the mud near the bridge
over the centre's river.

**Kokako at
Mount Bruce**

GOLDEN SHEARS COMPETITION

One of the biggest sheep shearing competitions in the
world, the Golden Shears competition is held in Masterton from the Thursday to the first Saturday of March each
year. Initiated by the Wairarapa District Young Farmers
Club, the competition was originally envisaged to form
part of the local Agricultural and Pastoral Show. Since the
inaugural competition in 1961, the Golden Shears has
become a national institution, attracting hundreds of
competitors from around the world and thousands of
observers. The competition reached its peak during the
1960s and 1970s when seats to the event were sold out
12 months in advance. Although several smaller shearing
competitions are now held around the country, the
Golden Shears remains the pre-eminent show in New
Zealand. Sheep shearing has also entered the world of
professionalism: prize money has risen over the years,
corporate sponsorship has become the norm, and many
shearers adopt fitness and training programmes not
dreamed of in the early days of the event.

Sheep shearer in competition

Palmerston North ⑱

Institute of Rugby sign

FROM THE MID-1960s, pastoral farming has been the stimulus for the development of Palmerston North, Manawatu's largest town. Lying in the centre of a broad, fertile coastal plain stretching from the Tasman Sea across to the Tararua and Ruahine ranges, the city is a major crossroad for the southern part of the North Island, with three main roads converging near it. New Zealand's second largest university, Massey University, and several colleges and research institutes are based here, giving Palmerston North a pleasant university town atmosphere.

1926 poster in the New Zealand Rugby Museum

♣ The Square
ℹ *(06) 354 6593.*
Laid out in 1866, this tranquil, leafy garden zone at the heart of the city provides welcome relief to the busy commercial centre. Originally bisected by New Zealand's main trunk railway, The Square's clipped lawns, flower beds, trees and shrubs, floral clock, ornamental ponds and fountains, war memorial and chiming clock tower attract large numbers of visitors all year round. The shops and buildings surrounding The Square reflect the diversity of styles in New Zealand's architectural history.

⛫ Manawatu Art Gallery
398 Main St. **ℂ** *(06) 355 5000.*
⭕ *daily.* ⬤ *25 Dec.*
First opened in 1959 as the Palmerston North Art Gallery, the gallery was renamed and rehoused in a modern, spacious building near The Square in 1977. Visitors will

be greeted at the entrance by local artist Paul Dibble's striking sculpture, *Pacific Monarch*, which is reputedly the largest bronze work cast in New Zealand.

The gallery's strength lies in its collection of recent art, particularly that from the 1970s, but it also houses a permanent collection of paintings, sculpture, prints, drawings, photographs and ceramics by prominent New Zealand artists. There is a regularly changing programme of exhibitions of New Zealand and international art and crafts. About 30 exhibitions are held every year. There are usually five being shown at any one time.

⛫ New Zealand Rugby Museum
87 Cuba St. **ℂ** *(06) 358 6947.* ⭕
daily. 🚫 ♿ 📷 *by arrangement.*
A turnstile previously installed at the gates of Wellington's famous Athletic Park allows visitors into the New Zealand Rugby Museum, located a few blocks from The Square. Founded in 1968, the museum contains exhibits and memorabilia relating to the history of rugby in New Zealand from the first game played in the country, at Nelson in 1870, to the present. There are also exhibits from every other country where rugby is played. The paraphernalia on display includes caps, jerseys,

trophies, badges, autographed balls, ties, posters and photographs. Famous international games can be watched on video. Also on display is a broken protestor's shield, a legacy of the bitter 1981 tour to New Zealand by the South African Springbok rugby team. The tour divided the country and caused organized demonstrations and bloody protests against South Africa's racist apartheid system.

⛫ Massey University
Tennant Drive. **ℂ** *(06) 356 9099.* ♿
Five km (3 miles) south of the city, the eclectic mixture of old homesteads and modern buildings that make up Massey University are set in superb countryside. On the Massey History Walk, part of the City Heritage Trail, visitors can look at these and some of the city's older sites and buildings. The world's first university-based Institute of Rugby and New Zealand's only university aviation school are both located here.

ENVIRONS: North of the city, the Manawatu River runs through the imposing **Manawatu Gorge**. The river defies geographical logic by rising on the eastern slopes of the Tararua Range, then turning back on itself in order to reach the Tasman Sea to the west. The gorge is a favourite place for jet-boating.

There are a number of beautiful gardens around the city. One, the Cross Hill Gardens, a 45-minute drive north, has one of New Zealand's largest and most varied collections of rhododendrons.

Sculpture by Paul Dibble in front of the Manawatu Art Gallery

Science Centre and Manawatu Museum

Reclining mermaid

THE SCIENCE CENTRE AND MANAWATU MUSEUM is the only regional museum in New Zealand that integrates hands-on science exhibitions with an area's social, cultural and artistic heritage. The Tangata Whenua Gallery, beginning on the ground floor and continuing on the first floor, forms the heart of the complex and recalls the long occupation of the region by the Maoris. A water area and "Kids Own" section on the ground floor are popular with children, while galleries on the first floor mainly feature changing displays of history, culture and natural history.

VISITORS' CHECKLIST

Te Awe Awe Complex, 396 Main St. ((06) 355 5000. ○ daily. ● Good Fri, 25 Dec. ☒ Science Galleries. ♿

Ivory Carving
Part of an exhibition, this exquisite carving features a Chinese mythological animal.

The Science Galleries have exhibits on the human body, light and communications.

Level 1

★ **Hot Air Balloon**
Visitors can activate a blower inflating a balloon with heated air, to show how hot air causes lift.

"Kids Own" features tunnel adventures, a frozen shadows wall, and an ultraviolet room.

Ground floor

"Slices of Lives" depicts Manawatu and its people.

AgResearch Conservatory
This features samples of the plant kingdom, including New Zealand native and exotic species.

KEY TO FLOORPLAN

☐	Kids Own
☐	Science Galleries
☐	Museum Galleries

Entrance

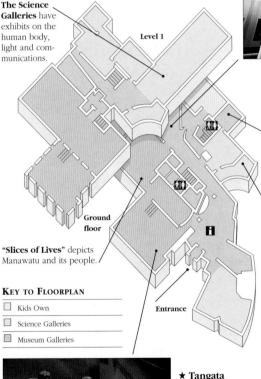

★ **Tangata Whenua Gallery**
These 19th-century carved palisade posts are among the Maori treasures exhibited in the gallery.

STAR SIGHT

★ **Hot Air Balloon**

★ **Tangata Whenua Gallery**

The Pohangina River flowing through Manawatu's farmland ▷

Wanganui ⓮

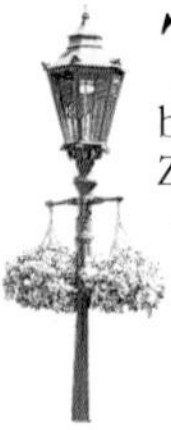

Hanging flower baskets

THE AREA AROUND Wanganui (which has retained its Maori spelling) was first settled by Maoris about AD 1100. By 1840 the New Zealand Company, unable to provide sufficient land in the Wellington district for the steady flow of new colonists, began to negotiate with Maoris for land in Wanganui. The town became a distribution centre for the area extending to Waitotara in the west, Marton in the east and Taumarunui in the north. Less than an hour by road to Palmerston North and only two and a half hours to Wellington, Wanganui's thriving arts centre sits alongside a variety of export-oriented industries.

Victoria Avenue

The preserved buildings, cinema, gaslights, wrought-iron street furniture and palm trees make Victoria Avenue, Wanganui's central city shopping area, a charming spot for visitors. From December to March, 1,000 floral baskets are hung on streetlights and verandahs to celebrate the Wanganui in Bloom festival.

Durie Hill

Via Anzac Parade. ☎ *(06) 345 8525.*
◯ *daily.* 🎟

Located opposite the city bridge at the end of Victoria Avenue, Durie Hill is known for an historic elevator which rises 66 m (216 ft) inside the hill to the summit. Opened in 1919, it is one of only two such elevators in the world. A pedestrian tunnel leads to the elevator. It takes about a minute to rise to the summit.

A climb up the spiral staircase inside the 34-m (110-ft) Durie Hill Memorial Tower, a short distance from the top of the elevator, allows panoramic views of Wanganui, Mount Taranaki/Egmont to the northwest *(see pp180–81)*, Mount Ruapehu to the east *(see pp140–41)*, and the Tasman Sea. The World War I memorial, opened in 1925, is constructed from blocks of fossilized seashell rock taken from quarries up the river.

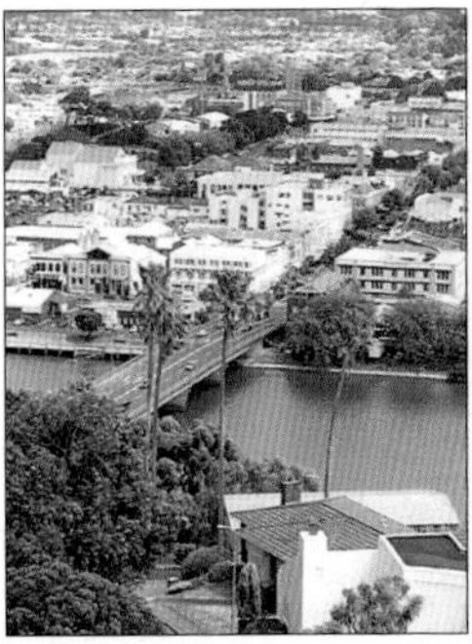

View of Wanganui and the city bridge from Durie Hill

Whanganui Regional Museum

Queens Park. ☎ *(06) 345 7443.*
◯ *daily.* ● *Good Fri, 25 Dec.* 🎟
🚫📷 ♿ 🛍

Among the treasures displayed in the Whanganui Regional Museum, visitors will find paintings of Maori subjects by Gottfried Lindauer (1839–1926), who managed to avoid service in the Austro-Hungarian army by settling in New Zealand, and Te Mata-o-Hoturoa, a *waka* (Maori war canoe) carved from a single totara tree. Established in 1895, the museum preserves and exhibits materials recording the geology, natural and social history of the city and surrounding region.

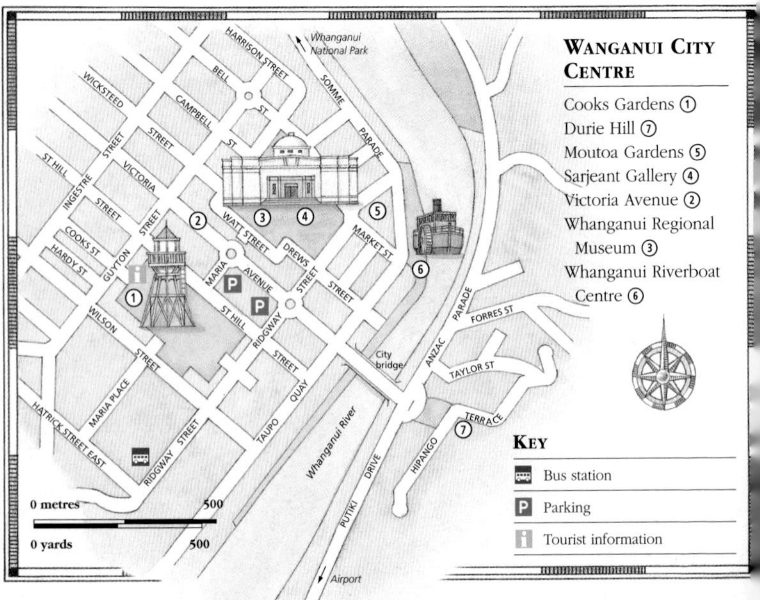

WANGANUI CITY CENTRE
Cooks Gardens ①
Durie Hill ⑦
Moutoa Gardens ⑤
Sarjeant Gallery ④
Victoria Avenue ②
Whanganui Regional Museum ③
Whanganui Riverboat Centre ⑥
KEY
Bus station
Parking
Tourist information
Whanganui National Park
HARRISON STREET
BELL ST
SOMME PARADE
WICKSTEED STREET
CAMPBELL ST
STREET
VICTORIA
ST HILL
INGESTRE STREET
WATT STREET
DREWS STREET
MARKET ST
COOKS ST
HARDY ST
GUYTON STREET
MARIA AVENUE
ST HILL STREET
RIDGWAY STREET
WILSON STREET
MARIA PLACE
HATRICK STREET EAST
RIDGWAY STREET
TAUPO QUAY
Whanganui River
City bridge
ANZAC PARADE
FORRES ST
TAYLOR ST
TERRACE
HIPANGO
PUTIKI DRIVE
Airport
0 metres 500
0 yards 500

🏛 Sarjeant Gallery

Queens Park. 📞 (06) 349 0506.
⭘ daily. ● Good Fri, 25 Dec.
♿ 🅿

This gallery features a highly regarded collection of New Zealand oil paintings, watercolours and prints from the 19th and 20th centuries. It houses the Denton photography collection and World War I posters and cartoons.

♣ Moutoa Gardens

Market Place.

Located at the site of the settling of Wanganui as a town, the beautiful Moutoa Gardens feature monuments set within mature specimen trees and flower beds. In recent years, the gardens have become a political rallying point, and are sometimes occupied by local Maori groups protesting about land issues.

Moutoa Gardens statue

♣ Cooks Gardens

Maria Place.

A leading outdoor venue, Cooks Gardens contain the country's only wooden velodrome and an attractive old bell tower. It was here, in 1962, that New Zealander Peter Snell ran the mile in under four minutes, breaking the record held by Roger Bannister of Great Britain.

▣ Whanganui Riverboat Centre

Taupo Quay. 📞 (06) 347 1863.
⭘ daily. 📷 🚫 inside. ♿ 🅿

This centre houses the salvaged and restored paddle steamer *Waimarie*. Built in London in 1899, it plied the Whanganui River for 50 years. The centre's museum has photographs and memorabilia of the riverboat era.

The *Waimarie* on the Whanganui River

Whanganui River ⑮

Road map E3–E4. 🚌 Wanganui Department of Conservation, cnr of Ingestre and St Hill sts, (06) 345 2402.

THE WHANGANUI RIVER is the longest navigable and the third longest river in New Zealand. The 290-km (180-mile) river begins its journey high up on Mount Tongariro in the centre of the North Island, and meanders its way down through the Whanganui National Park to Wanganui and the Tasman Sea.

Up until the 1920s there was a regular river boat service carrying passengers, mail and freight into the interior, and a thriving tourist trade operated between Mount Ruapehu and Wanganui. Today, the river, with its deep gorges and sheer cliffs, is New Zealand's most canoed waterway. Its 239 listed rapids offer a variety of challenges. The main entry and exit points for journeys on the river by canoe, raft or jet-boat are Taumarunui, Pipiriki and Wanganui. The 145-km (90-mile) journey from Taumarunui to Pipiriki takes about five days by canoe. From October to April, visitors must obtain hut and campsite passes from the local Department of Conservation or other sales outlets.

The river can also be followed by road from Wanganui to Pipiriki. Good side tracks lead to historic sites, early Maori villages, waterfalls and lookouts.

Whanganui National Park ⑯

Road map E3. 🚌 Department of Conservation, cnr of Ingestre and St Hill sts, Wanganui, (06) 345 2402.

ESTABLISHED IN 1987, the three main sections of the park lie within the catchment of the Whanganui River. Broadleaf podocarp forest surrounding the river forms the heart of the park. Tree ferns and riverside plants are also a feature, as is the birdlife. The river is rich in fish.

Visitors can choose from a variety of energetic activities, include canoeing, kayaking, rafting, jet-boating, and tramping. There is also fishing and hunting for deer and goats. For a more leisurely trip, visitors can board large vessels which ply the lower reaches of the river.

The Whanganui River flowing through Whanganui National Park

New Plymouth

T HE PRINCIPAL CENTRE of the Taranaki region, New Plymouth is situated around the only deep-water port on New Zealand's west coast, sandwiched between surfing beaches along the North Taranaki Bight. The massive cone of Mount Taranaki/ Egmont towers behind the city. Agriculture, with a strong emphasis on dairying, as well as aquaculture, floriculture, horticulture and forestry are among the mainstays of the local economy. The area is also the base for the country's major oil, gas and petrochemical industries. New Plymouth is recognized for its many beautiful parks, gardens and reserves, and is an ideal base from which to explore Egmont National Park *(see pp180–81)*.

Fountain in Pukekura Park

Stained-glass windows in St Mary's Church

🔒 St Mary's Church
37 Vivian St. 📞 (06) 758 3111.
⭕ daily. ✝ most days. ♿
Consecrated in 1848, St Mary's Anglican Church is the oldest stone church in New Zealand. It is a fine example of 19th-century architecture, and has some outstanding stained-glass windows. The headstones of children, settlers, soldiers and clergymen in the grounds of the church recall the poignant story of the difficulties faced by the city's earliest settlers. Several Maori chiefs are also buried there.

🏛 Taranaki Museum
Ariki St. 📞 (06) 758 9583.
⭕ daily. ♿ 📷
One of the oldest museums in New Zealand, the Taranaki Museum had its origins in the Mechanics Institute, opened in the embryonic settlement of New Plymouth in 1847. The museum has wildlife exhibits, including moa and whale skeletons, and comprehensive collections of colonial items, paintings and Maori art and artifacts.

🏚 Richmond Cottage
Ariki St. 📞 (06) 758 9583.
⭕ Jun–Aug: Fri–Sun & pub hols; Sept–May: Mon, Wed, Fri–Sun & pub hols. 📷 ♿
Richmond Cottage, constructed in 1853 of stone instead of the customary timber, was the residence of several prominent early Taranaki families. Many of the artifacts and furnishings in the cottage belonged to these former settler owners. During the 1880s, the cottage offered accommodation to seaside holiday-makers.

♣ Pukeariki Landing
Ariki St. ⭕ daily.
An oasis of green in the central city, Pukeariki Landing opened in 1990 when train tracks previously fronting the coastline were removed. This attractive park stands where surfboats, which carried people and supplies from ships, used to come ashore.

🏛 Govett-Brewster Art Gallery
Queen St. 📞 (06) 758 5149.
⭕ daily. 🚫 1 Jan, Good Fri, 25 & 26 Dec. 📷 specific exhibits. ♿ 📼 📷
Opened in 1970 as a contemporary art museum – a novel concept in New Zealand and the Asia-Pacific region at the time – the Govett-Brewster Art Gallery was the gift of local benefactor Monica Brewster. She stipulated in her deed of gift that the gallery must always have a director of national standing and the ability to acquire art works with "minimal influence from local politicians".

Today, it is New Zealand's only contemporary art museum with a permanent collection. Its main strengths lie in its collection of abstract art from the 1970s and 1980s, including works by Patrick Hanly, Michael Illingworth and Colin McCahon, and in its contemporary sculpture. The gallery serves as the site of the Len Lye Archive and contains the kinetic sculptures, paintings and films of this internationally renowned New Zealand artist, painter and film-maker (1901–80). The gallery also conducts frequent lectures on art.

TARANAKI'S GARDENS AND PARKS

Taranaki's parks, reserves and gardens are a highlight of the district and a drawcard for visitors. Long hours of sunshine, high rainfall, a mild climate, rich volcanic soils and shelter from prevailing winds combine to create ideal gardening conditions. Rhododendrons, azaleas and camellias suit Taranaki's conditions perfectly, and this is reflected in the large numbers of such species grown successfully throughout the region, along with roses, magnolias, irises and various native plants. From the end of October until the end of the first week of November, about 100 home gardens, both small and large, open their gates for public viewing in the annual Taranaki Rhododendron Festival, now into its second decade. Visitors may enjoy tea at some of these gardens and buy plants.

Rhododendrons in bloom

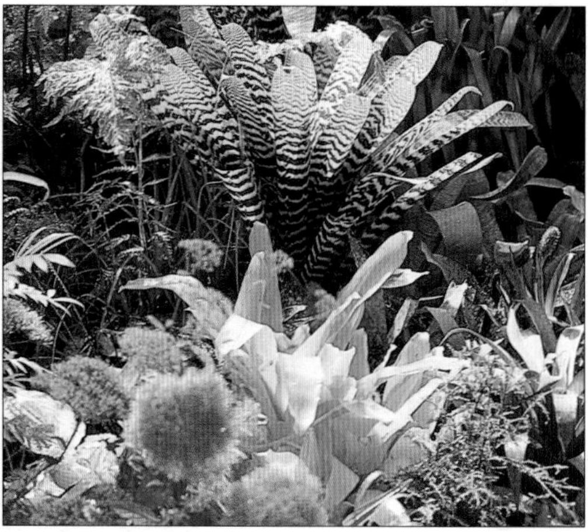

Fernery at Pukekura Park

Visitors' Checklist

Road map D3. 👥 *68,000.* ✈ *12 km (7.5 miles) NE of city.* 🚌 *Queen St.* ℹ *Cnr Leach & Liardet sts, (06) 759 6080.* 🎉 *Taranaki Rhododendron Festival (late Oct–early Nov), Festival of Lights (late Dec–early Feb).*

Pukekura Park

Liardet St. 🕐 *daily.* ♿

Opened in 1876 and only a ten-minute walk from the city centre, the dominant theme of Pukekura Park is water. Paths lead through dense native bushland, native and exotic trees, and fern gullies beside freshwater lakes and streams. A fernery, fountain, waterfall, water wheel, playground and boats for hire are other attractions. From the Tea House across the main lake there is a dramatic view of Mount Taranaki/Egmont.

During the Festival of Lights, held from Christmas to early February, Pukekura Park is transformed at night into a fairyland by thousands of coloured lights strung through its walkways and plantings.

Brooklands Park

Brooklands Park Drive. 🕐 *daily.* ♿

Adjoining Pukekura Park, Brooklands is an English-style park with sweeping lawns and formal gardens. Originally a private family estate, it was bequeathed to the city in 1934. Highlights include an enormous 2,000-year-old puriri tree, 300 varieties of rhododendron, and a children's zoo. The Bowl of Brooklands, an outdoor soundshell in a bush and lake setting, is the site of concerts and other entertainment.

The park also contains a colonial hospital, the Gables, built in 1847. The beautiful beach stone building failed as a hospital, attracting only 55 patients, and is now an art gallery and medical museum.

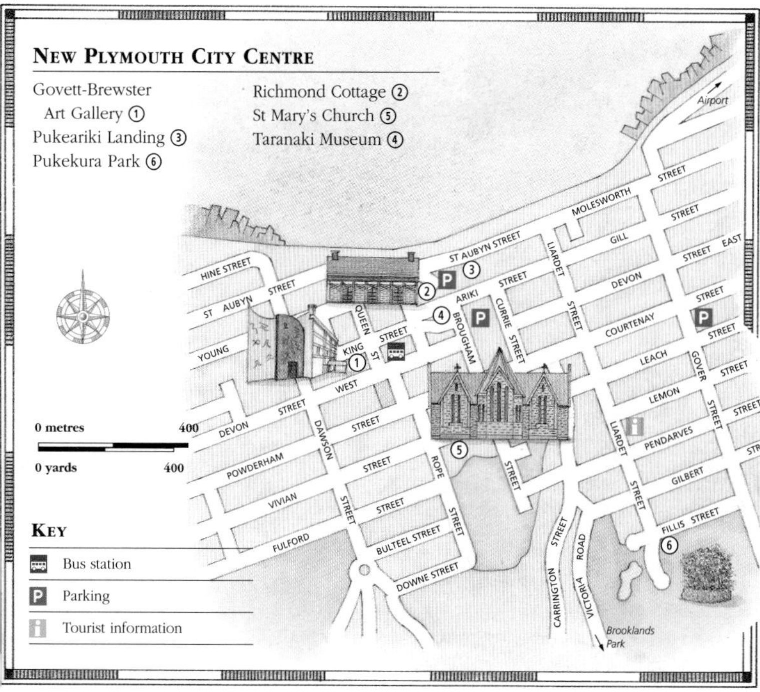

Egmont National Park ⑱

EGMONT NATIONAL PARK is one of the most easily accessed parks in New Zealand. The centrepiece is the solitary 2,518-m (8,261-ft) Mount Taranaki/Egmont, a dormant volcano. Ice and snow permanently cover the peak and upper slopes of this majestic and almost symmetrical mountain. Although weather conditions can change rapidly in the park, a 150-km (93-mile) network of tracks offers excellent climbing, skiing and tramping for the fit and well prepared. The park also has many tracks suitable for the average walker.

Tramper on the mountain

Huts
Walking tracks link the huts in the park. Hut passes can be bought from information centres and Department of Conservation offices.

Native trees
The wet mountain climate, combined with periods of dry, hot weather, promote luxurious vegetation. Native trees are abundant on the lower slopes.

Puniho Track
This loop makes a superb day walk (6–8 hours), but also leads to the Around-the-Mountain Circuit at Holly Hut or north of Kahui Hut.

Oakura River

Mango

Dover Track

Po

P O U A K A I R A N G E

Stony River

Puniho Track

Kahui

Kahui Track

Oaonui Track

Waiaua Gorge

Brames Fal

Ihaia Track

Waiaua River

Taungatara Track

Lak

0 kilometres 3
0 miles 3

WALKS IN EGMONT NATIONAL PARK

The park includes an extensive network of walking tracks leading to the summit or around the mountain. Shorter tracks start off from the three roads heading up the mountain. These range from easy to difficult and take from 30 minutes to several hours. The popular Around-the-Mountain Circuit, which takes up to five days for the full trip, can be accessed at several points and walked in sections at different times. Vegetation in the park ranges from tall rimu and kamahi trees at lower altitudes, to dense subalpine shrubs and an alpine herbfield complete with plants unique to the park. The park is also rich in insect and bird life.

Tramper on one of the park's tracks

KEY

═══ Minor road

〜〜 River

-- - Park boundary

- - Walking track

ℹ Tourist information

Ⓐ Hut

🏞 Picnic area

VISITORS' CHECKLIST

Road map D3. 🚌 *Stratford Depot, Miranda St.* ℹ️ *North Egmont Visitors Centre, (06) 756 0990; Dawson Falls Display Centre, (025) 430248; Stratford Area Office, Department of Conservation, Stratford, (06) 765 5144.* Ⓦ *www.doc.govt.nz*

Mount Taranaki/Egmont

Mount Taranaki/Egmont is believed to have formed after a volcanic eruption more than 70,000 years ago. Sacred to local Maoris, the mountain last erupted in 1775.

The North Egmont Visitors Centre has interesting displays on the park and the mountain, an audiovisual show and café.

Egmont Road

Signs at Egmont Village point to the 16-km (10-mile) Egmont Road which brings visitors into the northern area of the park. There are picnic areas along the way within the park.

EGMONT VILLAGE

Waiwhakaiho River

Egmont Road

Ngatoro Track

Veronica Track

△ Maketawa

Curtis Falls

Manganui River

Track

TaranakilEgmont 518 m (8,261 ft)

Pembroke Road

Summit Track

Waingongoro △

Patea River

STRATFORD

Waingongoro River

e Dive

Manaia Road

KAPONGA

Winter Climbing

Several ice and snow routes lead to the summit from the northern slopes. In winter, climbers need to be properly equipped.

The Dawson Falls Display Centre has exhibits on the park's flora and fauna, and a model of its volcanic features.

Dawson Falls

Dropping 18 m (59 ft) down an ancient lava flow, the waterfall can be reached via a 20-minute walk from the Dawson Falls Display Centre.

View of one of the Sugar Loaf Islands

Oakura ⑲

Road map D3. 🏘 *1,000.*

Sᴵᴛᴜᴀᴛᴇᴅ ᴏɴ a beautiful
stretch of Taranaki coastline 15 km (9 miles) west of
New Plymouth, Oakura is one
of a number of small, scenic
towns typifying the rural
aspect of New Zealand. It has
the traditional fixtures of such
towns – the main street row
of shops, service station, recreation grounds, churches,
pubs and war memorial. A
train carriage restaurant in the
main street is a novelty. The
Crafty Fox, a neighbouring
shop, sells works by the
many artists and crafts people
who live in the area.
　The beach at Oakura is well
known for its beautiful sun-
sets (in Maori, Oakura means
"the place of flashing red-
ness"). It is also a prime spot
for swimming, windsurfing
and surfboarding.

Sugar Loaf Islands Marine Park ⑳

Road map D3. ⛴ *from Lee
Breakwater, New Plymouth.*

Esᴛᴀʙʟɪsʜᴇᴅ ᴀs a marine
protected area in 1991,
the Sugar Loaf Islands lie
between 700 m (2,300 ft) and
1.5 km (1 mile) off New Plymouth's Port Taranaki breakwater. The stacks and reefs
that make up the islands are
the oldest volcanic features in
Taranaki. They consist of
eroded andesitic domes produced around 1.75 million
years ago, lying at depths of
between 5 m (16 ft) and 30 m

(98 ft). Of the eleven islands,
or groupings of islands, the
two largest are Motumahanga
and Moturoa, located at the
northern end of the park.
They are often referred to as
the "outer islands". Four
rocky islets close to the mainland at Paritutu are known as
the "inner islands".
　The islands support a
wealth of wildlife and plants.
Among them are 80 recorded
types of fish, at least 19
species of birdlife, rare and
endangered native and introduced plants and 33 species
of sponge. Fur seals are
present on the islands all year
round, with common and
Hector's dolphins and killer,
pilot and humpback whales
also seen at times.
　Although the best way to
explore the islands is by
charter boat, Round Rock,
one of the "inner islands", can
be accessed on foot from the
beach during mid- to low
tide. Snapper Rock, another
"inner island", is accessible
from the shore only when the
spring tides are very low.
　The relatively deep water,
wide variety of marine life
and spectacular underwater
scenery make the park a
popular venue for divers.
Visibility often reaches 20 m
(65 ft) during the summer and
autumn months. Recreational
fishing is also very popular in
the park, although there are
fishing restrictions. Blue cod,
kingfish and snapper are
among the most frequently
caught species. Game fishing
further offshore for tuna,
marlin and mako shark
usually takes place during
summer and early autumn.

Cape Egmont ㉑

Road map D3.

Tᴀʀᴀɴᴀᴋɪ's most westerly
point, Cape Egmont is
characterized by strong winds
and choppy seas. The solitary
landmark is the Cape Egmont
lighthouse, transferred from
Mana Island near Wellington
in 1881. Powered by diesel
generators until 1951, it now
operates on electricity.
　Located 30 km (19 miles)
offshore from the cape, the
Maui field produces gas,
which is processed at Oaonui,
9 km (6 miles) northwest of
the town of Opunake. At the
site of the processing plant, a
visitor centre provides details
of the history of oil exploration in the Taranaki region.
There are also scale models
of ships and oil rigs. Visitors
can use the binoculars at the
centre to get a good view of
one of the platforms, Maui A,
35 km (21.5 miles) offshore.

**Steps leading up to the Cape
Egmont lighthouse**

Opunake ㉒

Road map D3. 🏘 *1,600.* 🚌
ℹ *Tasman St, (06) 761 8663.* 🎪
Opunake Beach Carnival (Jan).

Tʜᴇ ᴛʜʀɪᴠɪɴɢ ᴄᴇɴᴛʀᴇ of a
rich dairying district,
Opunake is the largest town
on the west side of Mount
Taranaki/Egmont. The beach
at Opunake, situated along
the small, sheltered Middleton
Bay, is regarded as Taranaki's
best beach. It teems with
tourists attracted to its safe
swimming and its surfing
during the summer months.

Opunake Beach, a safe swimming spot along the Taranaki coast

The Opunake Walkway takes visitors around the beautiful coastline and beach front, as well as around the nearby Opunake Lake, an excellent spot for canoeing, yachting and other water sports. Other points along the way include two old cemeteries. The 7-km (4-mile) route can be accessed from a number of points along the way.

Hawera ❷

Road map D3. 🚶 9,000. 🚌
🚹 55 High St, (06) 278 8599.

PART OF Taranaki's rural heartland, Hawera boasts a number of interesting places for visitors. The 38,000-sq-m (409,000-sq-ft) **Hollard Gardens** were laid out in the late 1920s by farmer Bernard Hollard and presented to the Queen Elizabeth II National Trust in 1982. The gardens are at their most colourful from September to November.

At the interactive visitor centre at **Dairyland**, visitors can take a simulated tanker ride to collect milk from surrounding farms and compare 19th-century dairying methods with those practised today. The centre relates the history of dairying, innovations and technological breakthroughs. It also celebrates the lives of those involved over the years in what is still New Zealand's largest export industry. Dairy delicacies are available on site from the region's only revolving café,

from where visitors can also enjoy excellent views of Mount Taranaki/Egmont. Across the road is Kiwi Dairies. Not open to the public, it is the largest single-site, multiproduct milk processing plant in the world.

Hawera and its surroundings can be viewed from the top of the town's water tower, built after a series of fires in the 1880s, one of which razed most of the main street. In 1914, a month after the tower was erected, an earthquake caused it to list 0.75 m (2.5 ft) to the south. The fault has now been reduced to 8 cm (3 inches).

Cow statue outside Dairyland

The **Tawhiti Museum**, claimed to be the best private museum in the country, recreates many aspects of early life in South Taranaki. Housed in the town's former cheese factory, exhibits range from the early land wars to the

development of the fledgling dairy industry. The life-like figures in the exhibits, modelled on the faces of local volunteers, were cast at the museum's on-site workshops. A bush railway takes passengers on a reconstruction of the logging railways that used to operate in Taranaki.

🌸 **Hollard Gardens**
Manaia Road, N of Kaponga.
📞 (06) 764 6544. ⏰ Sep–Mar: daily.
📷 ♿
🏛 **Dairyland**
Cnr State Hwy 3 & Whareroa Rd.
📞 (06) 278 4537. ⏰ daily. 📷
♿ 🍴 ♿
🏛 **Tawhiti Museum**
401 Ohangai Rd. 📞 (06) 278 6837.
⏰ variable. 📷 ♿ 🎫 by arrangement. 📷 📷

Stratford ❷

Road map D3. 🚶 5,700. 🚌
🚹 Broadway South, (06) 765 6708.

LYING TO THE east of Mount Taranaki/Egmont, 40 km (25 miles) south of New Plymouth, Stratford is named after Shakespeare's birthplace, Stratford-upon-Avon, and many of its streets are named after Shakespearean characters. The **Taranaki Pioneer Village** in the town comprises restored or re-created buildings, including a school house, jail, railway station and about 50 other buildings that relate the area's local and provincial history.

🚩 **Taranaki Pioneer Village**
Stratford South. 📞 (06) 765 5399.

Life-size exhibits in the Tawhiti Museum, Hawera

THE SOUTH ISLAND

Introducing the South Island

UNPARALLELED SCENIC VARIETY awaits the visitor to the South Island. The snow-capped Southern Alps dominate the island, dividing it in two and contributing to a vast adventure playground of mountains, glaciers, lakes, rivers and fiords. Golden sand beaches, waterways and vineyards dominate the sun-soaked north. Along the narrow West Coast, waves from the Tasman Sea pound wild beaches. To the east is the patchwork Canterbury Plains and the rich, rolling farmland of Otago and Southland. Christchurch, New Zealand's English "garden city", and Picton in the picturesque Marlborough Sounds, are the two main entry points to the South Island.

LOCATOR MAP

In Mount Cook National Park (see pp250–51), *the highest peaks in New Zealand soar above the crest of the Southern Alps and over the surrounding subalpine park. The park is one of the country's most popular centres for skiers, climbers and photographers.*

Mount Cook glacier landing

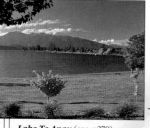

Lake Te Anau (see p279), *facing the glacier-carved mountains of Fiordland National Park, is one of the longest lakes in New Zealand and is popular with trout and salmon anglers.*

Fishing in Lake Te Anau

OTAGO AND SOUTHLAND *(see pp252–289)*

St Paul's Cathe in the Octag

The Octagon (see p258), *an attractive eight-sided garden area in the centre of Dunedin, is surrounded by imposing public buildings and a statue of the Scottish poet Robert Burns.*

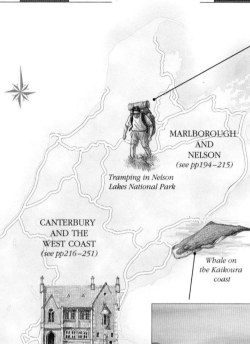

MARLBOROUGH
AND
NELSON
(see pp194–215)

*Tramping in Nelson
Lakes National Park*

CANTERBURY
AND THE
WEST COAST
(see pp216–251)

*Whale on
the Kaikoura
coast*

**Nelson Lakes
National Park**
(see p210), *at the
northern tip of the
Southern Alps, is
dominated by the twin
glacier-formed lakes,
Rotoiti and Rotoroa.*

*Provincial
Council Buildings*

0 kilometres   50

0 miles   50

The Kaikoura coast (see pp206–
207) *is the only place in New Zealand
where a pod of sperm whales can be
seen throughout the year. Eco-tourism
companies take visitors out to sea in
an open boat to spot the whales and
other marine life.*

*Moeraki
Boulders*

The Provincial Council Buildings in
Christchurch (see p224) *are considered the
finest example of secular Gothic archite-
ture in New Zealand and are the city's
most historic buildings.*

The Moeraki Boulders (see p265), *a group of perfectly
round, smooth, grey boulders of various sizes, are
scattered haphazardly along the seashore
and near the cliffs behind the beach.*

Southern Splendour

THE OVERWHELMING IMPRESSION a visitor has of the South Island is its scenic diversity: the bush-clad inlets of the Marlborough Sounds, golden sand beaches of Nelson, sweeping plains of Canterbury, snow-covered mountains of the alpine chain, dripping rainforests of the West Coast, rugged tussocklands and rolling farmland of Otago and Southland and the fiords of the southwest. No less varied is the climate. Only three hours of driving separate the wet west coast and the dry east coast.

Mitre Peak, the centrepiece of Fiordland National Park, is the world's highest sea cliff.

Abel Tasman National Park's golden sand beaches contrast with the deep green of the forest (see pp212–13). The coastal walk in this park is one of the most popular in New Zealand.

Sheep need supplementary feed, such as hay, during the coldest winter months.

SOUTHERN ALPS
Stretching almost the entire length of the South Island, the mighty Southern Alps and its various alpine environments were formed by the upward thrust of the Pacific Continental Plate *(see p20).*

The West Coast region, occupying a narrow strip of land between the Tasman Sea and the Southern Alps, has the highest rainfall in New Zealand. It also has some of the best examples of untouched rainforest, as shown here on the Milford Track (see p281).

On Banks Peninsula, the craters of past volcanoes, created by lava flows, are today's harbours of Lyttelton and Akaroa.

The Marlborough Sounds, *in the north of the South Island, were produced by the drowning of an extensive river system* (see pp200–201).

Mountains and glaciers combine to produce spectacular scenery and numerous opportunites for outdoor activities.

The rocks of the Southern Alps, folded and raised by titanic forces, and eroded by wind, rain and ice, are a striking sight from the air or road.

The Sutherland Falls in Fiordland, once thought to be the highest in the world, plunge 580 m (1,900 ft) in three cascades.

The lakes on the eastern side of the Alps, such as Lake Ohau shown here, are the direct result of glacial gouging.

Lake Tekapo and other eastern lakes are a milky blue, caused by ice rasping against rocks to produce fine powder.

BRAIDED RIVERS

Weaving sinuous strands of water from the mountains to the sea, the braided rivers of the South Island's east coast are, globally, rare ecosystems. Over thousands of years the largest rivers, among them the Rakaia, Waimakariri, Rangitata and Waitaki, have carried rocks and shingle from the Southern Alps and deposited this debris to create the fertile Canterbury Plains. On the river flats lives the wrybill, the only bird in the world with a sideways turning beak. The world's rarest wader, the black stilt, breeds on shingle "islands" in the rivers of the Mackenzie Basin *(see p249)*.

The sinuous strands of the Waimakariri River cross the Canterbury Plains

Wildlife Colonies

Beware of Wildlife sign

WITH A SMALLER POPULATION, there is less human pressure on wildlife in the South Island than in the North Island, and this is reflected in the number of wildlife colonies scattered around the mainland which are accessible to tourists. New Zealand has been described as "the seabird capital of the world" because of the number of species that either visit or breed along its coasts. A lack of predators has also led inland birds to be more fearless, and therefore more visible, than birds in most other countries. Marine mammals abound and tour operators guarantee an almost 100 per cent chance of seeing these animals in their natural habitat.

__The white heron__ breeds only in a coastal swamp near Okarito in September–October but is often seen in other estuaries along the coast.

__The royal albatross__ has one of the greatest wingspans – up to 3 m (10 ft) – of any seabird. The world's only mainland breeding colony is at Taiaroa Head on the Otago Peninsula (see p264). Here a four-month-old chick is being weighed.

The black stilt, an endangered wader, can be seen along the braided rivers of the Mackenzie Basin and at visitor hides *(see p249)*.

The blue penguin, the smallest of all penguins, can survive near populated areas, such as Oamaru *(see p267)*, feeding on fish close to shore.

Bottlenose dolphins, known to swim as fast as 40 km/h (25 mph), prey on inshore bottom-dwelling species. A pod has taken up year-round residence in Doubtful Sound *(see p282)*.

The Fiordland crested penguin, a rare native species, has a characteristic yellow stripe over each eye. It comes ashore each June and makes its way to the Fiordland rainforest to breed.

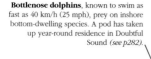

Okarito Lagoon
O

Haast

Lake

Milford Sound

Lake Wanaka

Twiz

Lake Hawea

Doubtful Sound

Queenstown

Lake Wakatipu

Oama

DU

Invercargill

Oi Pe

STEWART ISLAND

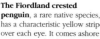

__The kiwi__, although primarily nocturnal, can be seen during twilight hours foraging in the forest on Stewart Island (see pp286–7).

__The yellow-eyed penguin__, the world's rarest species, is mostly concentrated on the Otago Peninsula (see p265). In the evening, they can be seen patrolling the beach.

Fur seals *haul out on rocky shorelines at several sites. At Cape Foulwind (see p232) there is a breeding colony where pups can be seen in spring and summer.*

Wading birds, *such as pied stilts (shown here), congregate in large numbers to methodically feed on rich tidal mud flats around the coastline.*

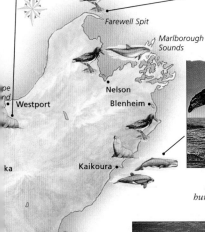

Farewell Spit

Marlborough Sounds

Nelson
Westport
Blenheim

Kaikoura

RISTCHURCH

Akaroa
Banks
Peninsula

Sperm whales, *which can be viewed off the Kaikoura coast (see p207), are specialized for hunting the deep sea, diving to depths of 1,000 m (3,280 ft) to feed mainly on large squid.*

Hector's dolphin, *a small species found exclusively in New Zealand, spends most of its time close to the shore, in pairs or small groups.*

0 kilometres   75

0 miles   75

KEY

Black stilt		Kiwi	
Blue penguin		Royal albatross	
Bottlenose dolphin		Sperm whale	
Fiordland crested penguin		Wading bird	
Fur seal		White heron	
Hector's dolphin		Yellow-eyed penguin	

WILDLIFE WATCHING

It is important to cause as little disturbance as possible, especially when animals are breeding, and to be very patient. Seal mothers can attack if people come between them and their pups, yellow-eyed penguins will not come ashore to feed their young if disturbed, and dolphins do not always welcome people swimming with them. It is best to view wildlife with an experienced guide who is well versed in wildlife etiquette, skilled at finding the animals and who can provide interesting and informative commentary.

Adventure Sports Paradise

Q UEENSTOWN IS TAGGED as New Zealand's top adventure tourism destination because of the many adrenaline-pumping sports on offer in and around the town. The area's mountains, lakes and rivers and generally dry climate combine to create conditions ideal for outdoor

Snowboarder

pursuits, while daredevil New Zealanders continue to pioneer ever more thrilling sports for the enjoyment of visitors. Strict regulations and highly trained operators reduce the risks involved in speeding through inches of water, leaping off bridges, skiing at remote sites and free-falling from airplanes, and explain New Zealand's excellent safety record.

Jet-boats – *propellerless power boats specially designed in New Zealand for use in 10-cm (4-inch) deep water – take visitors at breakneck speed down narrow river gorges.*

QUEENSTOWN AND SURROUNDINGS

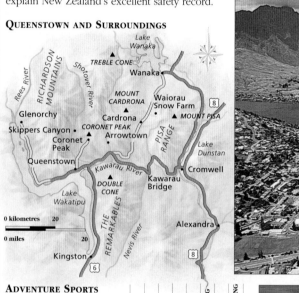

Lake Wanaka
TREBLE CONE
Wanaka
RICHARDSON MOUNTAINS
Shotover River
Rees River
MOUNT CARDRONA
Waiorau Snow Farm
8
Glenorchy
Cardrona
MOUNT PISA
Skippers Canyon
CORONET PEAK
PISA RANGE
Coronet Peak
Arrowtown
Queenstown
Lake Dunstan
Kawarau River
Cromwell
DOUBLE CONE
Kawarau Bridge
Lake Wakatipu
THE REMARKABLES
Alexandra
0 kilometres 20
Nevis River
0 miles 20
Kingston
6
8

ADVENTURE SPORTS AROUND QUEENSTOWN

These places are all within 70 km (44 miles) of Queenstown and offer a range of activities. Adventure sports tour operators provide transport, equipment and qualified instructors.

	BUNGY JUMPING	HANG-GLIDING	JET-BOATING	MOUNTAIN BIKING	SKIING	TANDEM PARAPENTING	TANDEM SKYDIVING	WHITE-WATER RAFTING
Cardrona Alpine Resort					■	●		
Coronet Peak			■		■	●		●
Kawarau Bridge	●							
Kawarau River			●					■
Queenstown (*see p274*)	●					■	●	
Remarkables			■		■	●	■	●
Shotover River			●					■
Skippers Canyon	●	●						
Treble Cone					●	■		
Waiorau Snow Farm					●			
Wanaka (*see p269*)				■		■	●	■

Downhill skiing *at the commercial ski fields near Queenstown is rated the best in the country.*

KEY

▬▬▬ State highway

══ Minor road

〜 River

Mountain biking *allows riders, either independently or as part of a guided tour, to explore off-road routes that were traditionally walked.*

Queenstown, Lake Wakatipu and the Remarkables from the Skyline Gondola lookout on Bob's Peak.

White-water rafting *through the narrow gorges and thundering rapids of the Kawarau and Shotover rivers is a heart-pounding, exhilarating and drenching experience.*

The preparation area where ankles are strapped and adjustments made to the length of the cord to suit the weight of the bungy jumper.

BUNGY JUMPING

This was made famous by New Zealander A J Hackett, who dived from the Eiffel Tower in 1986 suspended by a rubber cord strapped to his ankles. Bungy jumping options now range from plummeting 104 m (340 ft) from a bridge towards a narrow river gorge – for a wet or dry dip – to hurtling earthward from "The Ledge" on Bob's Peak above Queenstown.

A jumper dives off the platform before soaring upwards again on the end of the bungy cord.

Cross-country skiing *is a speciality of the Waiorau Snow Farm in the Pisa Range near Wanaka, which also hosts cross-country racing and ski-jumping competitions during the ski season.*

Tandem parapenting *(or paragliding) – plunging off a hill with a guide, strapped to a rectangular parachute – is a safer option than the "ultimate" tandem activity, tandem skydiving – jumping out of an airplane with an instructor attached to one's back followed by a parachute descent to ground.*

MARLBOROUGH AND NELSON

THE WARM CLIMATE of the *Marlborough and Nelson region has always attracted visitors. Landscapes vary from wild coast, golden beaches, drowned valleys and dry inland mountains to lush, forested ranges. Known for its horticulture, the area is New Zealand's largest wine producer and a major source of fresh seafood. Along with heritage sites, its national parks are an added attraction.*

Archaeological evidence dates Maori occupation of the region to at least AD 1200. Early Polynesian navigators, Kupe *(see p43)* and Rakaihautu, are also known to have spent time here. In 1642, Dutch explorer Abel Tasman sailed into Golden Bay *(see p46)*. A confused and ultimately fatal confrontation with the Maoris that left four of the crew dead, made the Dutch reluctant to revisit the area. James Cook's later visits to Queen Charlotte Sound in the 1770s, fortunately proved more successful *(see p46)*.

Following the signing of the Treaty of Waitangi in 1840 *(see pp46–7)*, the New Zealand Company established its Nelson settlement in 1842 *(see pp208–209)*. In 1858, Nelson was declared New Zealand's second city, a year before Marlborough gained identity as a separate province. The region splits neatly into halves, Marlborough in the east and Nelson in the west. Marlborough's contrasts are perhaps greater, from the sinuous waterways of the Marlborough Sounds in the north, to the sheep farms and grape-growing region of southern Marlborough, and further south to the coastal spectacle of Kaikoura.

In northern Nelson is the Golden Bay region, sheltered from the open sea by Farewell Spit and isolated behind the national parks of Abel Tasman and Kahurangi. Nelson city and Motueka sit on the shores of Tasman Bay. The rich hinterland, peopled by artists, vintners and horticulturists, extends south to the Southern Alps and the region's third national park, Nelson Lakes.

The weekend market at Nelson

◁ Golden sand beach at Totaranui in Abel Tasman National Park

Exploring Marlborough and Nelson

THE NORTHERN REGION of the South Island beckons visitors with its sunny climate, inviting coastline, food, wines, marine reserves and three national parks: Nelson Lakes, Abel Tasman and Kahurangi. Marine life watching at Kaikoura *(see p207)*, winery tours *(see pp204–205)* and Nelson's Wearable Art Awards *(see p211)* are the best-known attractions. Nelson is home to craft artisans and is an excellent base for boating and adventure tours. Walking, tramping and cycling tracks are spread throughout the national parks and other areas, including the Marlborough Sounds, a unique geographical feature of the region *(see pp200–201)*.

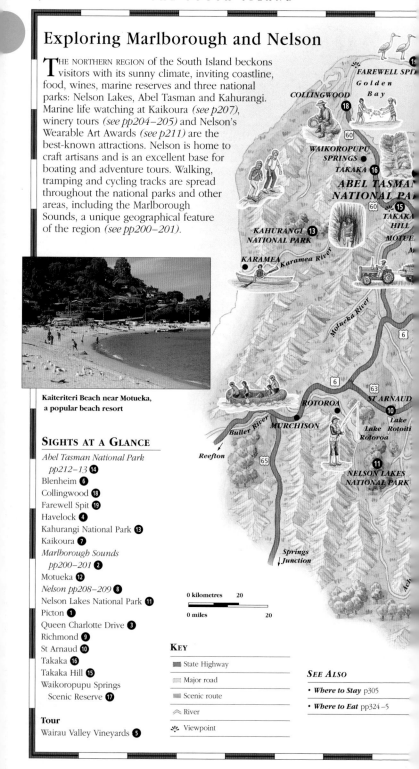

Kaiteriteri Beach near Motueka, a popular beach resort

SIGHTS AT A GLANCE

Abel Tasman National Park
  pp212–13 **14**
Blenheim **6**
Collingwood **18**
Farewell Spit **19**
Havelock **4**
Kahurangi National Park **13**
Kaikoura **7**
Marlborough Sounds
  pp200–201 **2**
Motueka **12**
Nelson pp208–209 **8**
Nelson Lakes National Park **11**
Picton **1**
Queen Charlotte Drive **3**
Richmond **9**
St Arnaud **10**
Takaka **16**
Takaka Hill **15**
Waikoropupu Springs
  Scenic Reserve **17**

Tour

Wairau Valley Vineyards **5**

FAREWELL SPIT **19**
Golden Bay
COLLINGWOOD **18**

WAIKOROPUPU SPRINGS
TAKAKA **16**
ABEL TASMAN NATIONAL PARK
TAKAKA HILL **15**
MOTUEKA

KAHURANGI NATIONAL PARK **13**

KARAMEA *Karamea River*

Motueka River
6

ROTOROA
MURCHISON
Buller River
Reefton
65
6
63
ST ARNAUD **10**
Lake Rotoiti
Lake Rotoroa
11
NELSON LAKES NATIONAL PARK

Springs Junction

0 kilometres 20
0 miles 20

KEY

State Highway
Major road
Scenic route
River
Viewpoint

SEE ALSO

• *Where to Stay* p305

• *Where to Eat* pp324–5

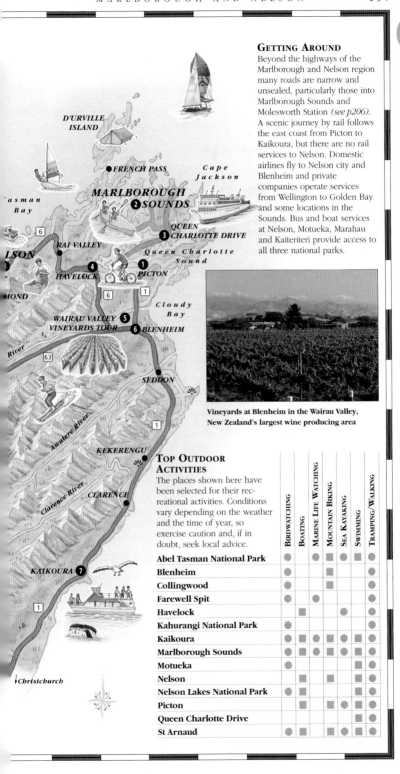

GETTING AROUND

Beyond the highways of the Marlborough and Nelson region many roads are narrow and unsealed, particularly those into Marlborough Sounds and Molesworth Station *(see p206)*. A scenic journey by rail follows the east coast from Picton to Kaikoura, but there are no rail services to Nelson. Domestic airlines fly to Nelson city and Blenheim and private companies operate services from Wellington to Golden Bay and some locations in the Sounds. Bus and boat services at Nelson, Motueka, Marahau and Kaiteriteri provide access to all three national parks.

Vineyards at Blenheim in the Wairau Valley, New Zealand's largest wine producing area

TOP OUTDOOR ACTIVITIES

The places shown here have been selected for their recreational activities. Conditions vary depending on the weather and the time of year, so exercise caution and, if in doubt, seek local advice.

	BIRDWATCHING	BOATING	MARINE LIFE WATCHING	MOUNTAIN BIKING	SEA KAYAKING	SWIMMING	TRAMPING/WALKING
Abel Tasman National Park	●		●	■	●	■	●
Blenheim	●						●
Collingwood	●			■			●
Farewell Spit	●		●				●
Havelock		■			●		●
Kahurangi National Park	●						●
Kaikoura	●	■	●	■	■	■	●
Marlborough Sounds	●	■	●	■	●	■	●
Motueka	●					■	●
Nelson		■		■		■	●
Nelson Lakes National Park	●	■				■	●
Picton		■		■	■	■	●
Queen Charlotte Drive						■	●
St Arnaud	●	■		■	●	■	●

Picton ❶

Road map D4. 🏠 4,000.
✈ Koromiko, 9 km (6 miles) S of
town. 🚌 🚆 ⛴ 🛈 Picton
foreshore, (03) 573 7477.

Set in the upper reaches of
Queen Charlotte Sound,
Picton is the South Island
terminus for the ferries that
cross Cook Strait. The buzz
of port and railway activity
dominates this pretty town
nestled between the sea and
the hills. Ferries and water
taxis mingle with pleasure
boats in the region, popular
for its safe anchorages.

Picton's wide streets and
historic buildings along the
waterfront reflect the town's
European beginnings. For-
merly known as Waitohi,
Picton was chosen to become
the port for the Wairau district, and in 1859 became the
capital of the newly
formed province of
Marlborough. That
status shifted to Blen-
heim in 1866. An inter-
island ferry service was
first mooted in 1899 and
the first rail and car ferry
began operating in 1962.

Picton is a good base to
explore the history of the
Marlborough region. The
Picton Museum tells stories
of the whaling era, beginning in the 1820s, and of the
1770s visit of Captain James
Cook to the outer sound.

At each end of the fore-
shore, the scow *Echo* and
the sailing ship *Edwin Fox*
provide a fascinating look at
New Zealand's shipping
history. Built in 1905, the

Whaling exhibits at Picton Museum

Echo is an old cargo scow
that shipped around 14,000
tonnes of freight per year between Blenheim and Wellington. The *Edwin Fox*, the last
Australian convict ship in existence, is an internationally
significant link to the era of
colonial settlement, having
brought convicts to Aus-
tralia and migrants to
New Zealand. Built from
teak in India in 1853,
it is now being pre-
served in a dry dock
beside a purpose-
built museum.
A number of
walks and
cycling tracks in
Picton begin
near the *Echo* or at Shelly
Beach on Picton Harbour
where a lookout affords
excellent views of the town.
A short uphill walk from the
Echo leads to Victoria Domain, a bushy reserve named
after Queen Victoria. A longer
walk past Bob's Bay passes a
panoramic view of Queen
Charlotte Sound and leads to
The Snout, the headland
between Picton and Waikawa
bays. The Maoris know the
Snout as Te Ihumoeoneihu
(nose of the sand worm). The
Tirohanga and Essons Valley
tracks allow exploration of the
forest behind the town.

**Maori club,
Picton Museum**

🏛 **Picton Museum**
London Quay. 📞 (03) 573 8283.
🕐 daily. ● Good Fri, 25 Dec. 🅿
🏛 **Echo**
Shelly Beach. 📞 (03) 573 7498.
🕐 Summer: daily; Winter: by
appointment. ● 25 Dec. 🅿 🛈

**The *Edwin Fox*, formerly a
convict transport ship**

🏛 **Edwin Fox**
Dunbar Wharf. 📞 (03) 573 6868.
🕐 daily. ● Good Fri, 25 Dec. 🅿 🛈

Environs: A 20-minute drive
northeast of Picton leads to
Karaka Point, a narrow
peninsula once occupied by a
pa. A short walk leads down
to the water with signs
explaining the earthworks
encountered on the way. At
Koromiko, about 9 km (6
miles) south of Picton, the
Koromiko Store offers
salmon, emu and ostrich
products and the chance to
feed ostrich and emu chicks
or to watch eggs hatching.

🛈 **Koromiko Store**
State Hwy 1. 📞 (03) 573 6676.
🕐 daily.

Marlborough Sounds ❷

See pp200–201.

Queen Charlotte Drive ❸

Road map D4.

The best-known road in the
Marlborough Sounds,
Queen Charlotte Drive is a
scenic route connecting
Picton and Havelock. With
stopovers, it can take up to
half a day to complete the
35-km (21.5-mile) journey on
the sealed but narrow and
winding road. Leaving Picton,
the Queen Charlotte Drive
passes lookout points above

the town and at Governors Bay, 8 km (5 miles) from Picton, with excellent views up and down Queen Charlotte Sound. Beaches and pleasant picnic and swimming areas can be found along the route that passes through the picturesque settlements of Ngakuta and Momorangi bays. At Ngakuta Bay, **Sirpa Alalääkkölä's Art Studio** showcases her large, bright paintings, many of them inspired by the Sounds.

Continuing west, a turn-off 12 km (8 miles) from Governors Bay leads to historic Anakiwa, where the Queen Charlotte Track begins *(see pp200–201)*. A shelter and picnic area are provided and an easy stroll along the track leads through beech forest to Davies Bay.

The Queen Charlotte Drive route continues through Linkwater with the road following the waters of the Mahakipawa Arm, the innermost reaches of Pelorus Sound. The walking tracks and viewpoint at Cullen Point provide another perspective on the waterways below, before the road's final descent into Havelock.

A restaurant in Havelock advertising green lip mussels

Greenstone carved in Havelock

🏛 **Sirpa Alalääkkölä Art Studio**
Phillips Rd, Ngakuta Bay. 📞 (03) 573 7775. ⬜ by appointment.

Havelock ❹

Road map D4. 🏠 500. 🚌 ⛴ ℹ️
65A Main Rd, (03) 574 2114.

THE SELF-STYLED green lip mussel capital of the world, the village of Havelock receives a growing number of visitors attracted by its history and the success of its mussel farming industry. Havelock was established in the 1850s on the Nelson–Blenheim track near the uppermost navigable reaches of Pelorus Sound. Timber milling and gold mining were its first industries, while today fishing and aquaculture (the cultivation of shellfish) are major industries.

The main street still retains something of its pioneer character. Highlights of a walk around the waterfront are the stately 1880s home of timber miller William Brownlee, the stone St Peter's Church, and the old primary school (now a hostel) attended by Lord Ernest Rutherford *(see pp19, 210)* in the 1870s. A number of cafés can be found in the town along with many interesting shops selling antiques, jewellery, carvings, crafts, and Maori art.

Tours and activities as diverse as sea kayaking and pig hunting begin in Havelock, with the scenic mail run (where mail is delivered by boat) being perhaps the easiest and most popular way to get to the outer sounds. The **Havelock Museum** preserves relics from the pioneer era and Rutherford's time.

🏛 **Havelock Museum**
Main St. 📞 (03) 574 2176.
⬜ daily. ● 25 Dec.
💰 donation.

ENVIRONS: Nine km (6 miles) west of Havelock, **Canvastown** was established in 1864 following the region's first gold rush. A tent city grew here, attracting several thousand miners. Flood-prone fields and severe overcrowding meant many miners

left shortly after the gold fields in the West Coast were opened.

A further 11 km (7.5 miles) west, along State Highway 6, the road crosses the Pelorus River at **Pelorus Bridge Scenic Reserve**. Spared destruction after development of a town failed to proceed, the reserve is the last remnant of riverplain forest that formerly covered much of lowland Marlborough. A network of tracks allows visitors to explore the rich forest and river banks, with a suspension bridge, swimming holes and waterfalls. Other facilities include a shop, café, cabins and caravan park with electric powered sites. River cruises and nature tours are also available. Some of the walks are accessible by wheelchair.

Pelorus Bridge Scenic Reserve, a popular swimming and picnic area

Marlborough Sounds **2**

THE MARLBOROUGH SOUNDS region is a mass of bays, inlets and hidden coves with numerous walking tracks, wildlife, historical sites and unsurpassed views. Picton and Havelock are the Sounds' main towns *(see pp198–9)*.

Mushroom on walking track

Launch services from these two towns provide the best access to the secluded bays and accommodation by the sea. The best ways to explore the Sounds are by bicycle, sea kayak, or on foot.

Cyclists on the road exploring the Sounds

D'Urville Island
Accessible by water taxi, the island was once an important source of argillite, a hard sandstone used in tool making by Maoris. Today, farming is the main occupation with fishing, diving, kayaking and mountain biking popular pursuits.

French Pass
This picturesque fishing and farming village takes its name from the narrow and treacherous strait between the mainland and D'Urville Island.

```
0 kilometres    5
0 miles         5
```

Tennyson Inlet is cloaked in native forest. Natural beauty abounds in this quiet inlet where picnic areas and campsites are found along the shoreline.

HOW THE SOUNDS WERE FORMED

The Sounds region appears as a series of ridges rising above the water but is, in fact, valleys drowned by the ocean. A combination of changing sea levels (due to world climate changes), movement along faults in the region, and tilting of the landmass downwards and towards the northeast, has caused inundation by the sea. The last significant surge in sea level was at the end of an Ice Age about 12,000 years ago, and gives the area its current sinuous coastline.

Drowned valleys at Elaine Bay, Tennyson Inlet

STAR SIGHTS

★ **Motuara Island**

★ **Outer Queen Charlotte Sound**

★ **Queen Charlotte Track**

Map labels: Waitai Road, Main Road, Clay, French Pass, Admiralty Bay, Port Ligar Road, Maud Island, French Pass Road, Nydia Track, Te Wairoa, Nydia Bay, Pelorus Sound, Kenepuru Road, Havelock, Linkwater, Queen Charlotte Drive, 6, BLEN

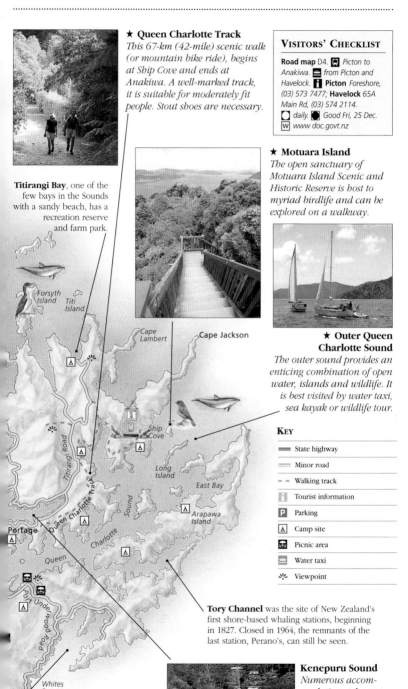

★ Queen Charlotte Track
This 67-km (42-mile) scenic walk (or mountain bike ride), begins at Ship Cove and ends at Anakiwa. A well-marked track, it is suitable for moderately fit people. Stout shoes are necessary.

Titirangi Bay, one of the few bays in the Sounds with a sandy beach, has a recreation reserve and farm park.

★ Motuara Island
The open sanctuary of Motuara Island Scenic and Historic Reserve is host to myriad birdlife and can be explored on a walkway.

★ Outer Queen Charlotte Sound
The outer sound provides an enticing combination of open water, islands and wildlife. It is best visited by water taxi, sea kayak or wildlife tour.

KEY

▬▬▬	State highway
▬▬▬	Minor road
– – –	Walking track
🛈	Tourist information
🅿	Parking
⬟	Camp site
🞐	Picnic area
▤	Water taxi
⚡	Viewpoint

Tory Channel was the site of New Zealand's first shore-based whaling stations, beginning in 1827. Closed in 1964, the remnants of the last station, Perano's, can still be seen.

Kenepuru Sound
Numerous accommodation styles are available in this quiet waterway where walking, fishing and camping are popular.

Port Underwood was a strategic whaling station in the 1830s. Today, its main attraction is White's Bay, with its swimming beach and old cable station.

Sea kayaking at Abel Tasman National Park *(see pp212–13)* ▷

Wairau Valley Vineyard Tour **5**

Chardonnay grapes

WELL KNOWN FOR its Sauvignon Blanc, the Wairau valley is New Zealand's largest and best known wine region. In the early 1970s, grape planting was begun by Montana Wines *(see p206)*. Now, nearly 50 wineries operate in the area. The wines of the Wairau are celebrated with the annual Wine Marlborough festival each February. South of Blenheim, at the Montana winery, is the Montana Brancott Visitor Centre covering all aspects of the wine experience.

Vineyards in the Blenheim region backed by the Richmond Range

CLOUDY BAY

CELLAR DOOR OPEN

Cloudy Bay ⑨
This is one of Marlborough's most successful exporting wineries, with a reputation for fine Sauvignon Blanc, Chardonnay and Pinot Noir. Tastings and sales are available daily.

Allan Scott Wines and Estates ⑧
One of the pioneers of grape growing in Marlborough, this vineyard offers wines characteristic of the region: Chardonnay, Sauvignon Blanc and Riesling.

STONELEIGH
Vineyards

MARLBOROUGH
RIESLING
1999

WINE OF NEW ZEALAND
PRODUCED AND BOTTLED BY
STONELEIGH VINEYARDS LTD
JACKSONS ROAD, BLENHEIM
5% vol.   750

Stoneleigh Vineyards ⑦
Built on a former riverbed, the vineyard is named after the stones covering the area. Sunlight reflected from the stones speeds the ripening process of the grapes. Chardonnay, Riesling, Sauvignon Blanc, Pinot Noir and Cabernet Sauvignon wines are produced here.

Hunters Wines ⑥
This is one of the region's most awarded wineries. Red, white and sparkling wines are available, including Sauvignon Blanc, Pinot Noir, Cabernet/Merlot, sparkling Brut and Chardonnay.

KEY

▨	Tour route
▬	Other roads
▭	River

Ponder Estate ①
Producing award-winning Sauvignon Blanc and Chardonnay wines, the owners of Ponder Estate are also pioneers of olive growing in New Zealand. The white wines and olive oil are for sale in the estate's Shed Gallery. Mike Ponder's well-known works of art are also on display.

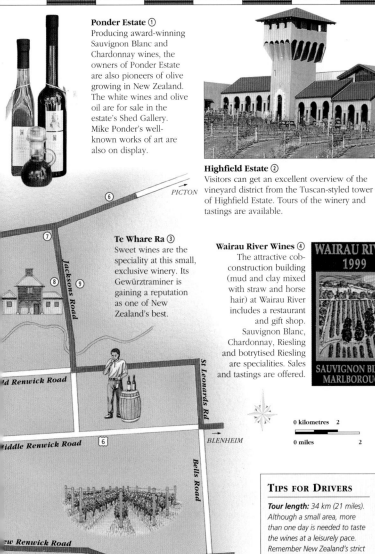

Highfield Estate ②
Visitors can get an excellent overview of the vineyard district from the Tuscan-styled tower of Highfield Estate. Tours of the winery and tastings are available.

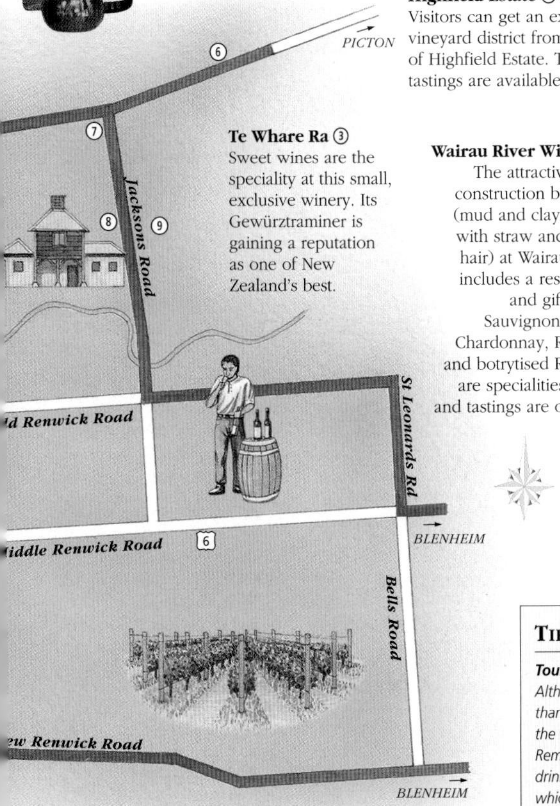

PICTON
6
7
8
9
Jacksons Road
St Leonards Rd
ld Renwick Road
iddle Renwick Road
6
BLENHEIM
Bells Road
ew Renwick Road
BLENHEIM
0 kilometres 2
0 miles 2

Te Whare Ra ③
Sweet wines are the speciality at this small, exclusive winery. Its Gewürztraminer is gaining a reputation as one of New Zealand's best.

Wairau River Wines ④
The attractive cob-construction building (mud and clay mixed with straw and horse hair) at Wairau River includes a restaurant and gift shop. Sauvignon Blanc, Chardonnay, Riesling and botrytised Riesling are specialities. Sales and tastings are offered.

WAIRAU RIVER
1999
SAUVIGNON BLANC
MARLBOROUGH

Le Brun Family Estate ⑤
This winery specializes in *méthode traditionelle* sparkling wines. Tours of the winery and underground cellar are available. Wine can be purchased at the wine shop.

Tips for Drivers

Tour length: *34 km (21 miles). Although a small area, more than one day is needed to taste the wines at a leisurely pace. Remember New Zealand's strict drink driving laws, something which makes a guided tour a wise choice. Enquire about these at the Blenheim Visitor Centre* *(see p206).*
Starting point: *Blenheim is a logical choice to begin and end the tour, which is a circle with a short side trip. Road conditions are good throughout.*
Stopping-off points: *Besides restaurants at the wineries, Renwick and Blenheim offer many eating choices. Fruit stalls abound in summer, with December a good time for cherries.*

The Clock Tower in Seymour Square, Blenheim

Blenheim ❻

Road map D5. 🏛 *20,500.* ✈ *6 km (4 miles) W of city.* 🚌 📍
ℹ *2 High St, (03) 578 9904.*
🎪 *Wine Marlborough (second Sat of Feb); Hunters Garden Marlborough (second weekend of Nov).*

THE LARGEST TOWN in the Marlborough region, Blenheim's importance in the Wairau Valley has grown along with the development of the wine industry in Marlborough *(see pp204–205)*. The annual food and wine festival is a major attraction. A number of art and crafts people also live and work in Blenheim and its environs.

In the city centre, Seymour Square has a fountain, pretty gardens and the Clock Tower. The **Millennium Art Gallery** houses works by local artists and sculptors, while the **Marlborough Historical Society's Museum and Archive** are set beside the heritage streetscape of Brayshaw Park on the southern edge of town. The park has a miniature railway, boating pond and reconstructed colonial village, giving some insight into colonial Blenheim. Nearby is **Wither Hills Farm Park** where a network of foot and cycling tracks have been developed for visitors within the working farm. The tracks are well marked and require average fitness.

🏛 Millennium Art Gallery
Cnr Seymour and Alfred sts. 📞 *(03) 579 2001.* ◯ *daily.* ● *1 Jan, 25 Dec.*
🎨 *donation.* ♿ 📷

🏛 Marlborough Historical Society's Museum and Archive
Arthur Baker Place. 📞 *(03) 578 1712.* ◯ *Tues–Sun.* ● *25 Dec.*
🎨 ♿

♣ Wither Hills Farm Park
Redwood St. 📞 *Blenheim Visitor's Centre, (03) 578 9904.* ◯ *daily.*

ENVIRONS: South of Blenheim is the **Montana Brancott Visitor Centre**. One-hour tours include insights into the wine process, tastings, audiovisual shows, views of two barrel halls and an interactive "aroma wheel".

Further south, in the Awatere valley, **Molesworth Station**, New Zealand's largest farm, can be explored when the road through it opens each summer. The 59-km (37-mile) road journey through high country, passes historic cob houses, wide river valleys and mountains.

🏛 Montana Brancott Visitor Centre
State Hwy 1. 📞 *(03) 578 2099.* ◯ *daily.* ● *Good Fri, 25 Apr, 25 Dec.*
♿ 📷 🍴 🛍 📷

🌾 Molesworth Station
ℹ *Department of Conservation, (03) 572 9100.* ◯ *Dec–Feb.* 🎨

Kaikoura ❼

Road map D5. 🏛 *3,100.* 🚌 📍
ℹ *Westend St, (03) 319 5641.* 🎪 *Kaikoura Seafest (first Sat in Oct); Kaikoura Races (Mon after Labour Day).*

THE NAME Kaikoura means "meal of crayfish" and reflects the importance of the sea throughout the area. Captain Cook sailed past the Kaikoura Peninsula in 1770, because of the reticence of the local Maoris.

The first European settlers were whalers, beginning in 1842. The town's current tourism boom is also based on whales and other marine wildlife. The visitor centre has extensive displays and an audiovisual show. Whale tooth carvings can be seen at historic **Fyffe House**, a colonial cottage from the whaling days. Nearby, at the beachfront, is the Garden of Memories with a walkway encased with pairs of whale ribs.

Above town, Scarborough Street has a lookout point, a remnant *pa* and the Gold Gallery with wall sculptures gilded with gold leaf.

On the southern edge of town, guided tours can be taken at the **Kaikoura Wine Company** and at **Maori Leap Cave**, a limestone cave formed by the sea, full of stalagmites. Six km (4 miles) south of town is Fyffe Country Inn which has pleasant gardens and a gallery showcasing local art. Inland roads lead to Mount Fyffe, where superb views can be obtained from the walking tracks through the forest and mountains.

Whale tooth carving

🏵 Fyffe House
62 Avoca St. 📞 *(03) 319 5835.*
◯ *Summer: daily; Winter: Thu–Mon.* ● *Good Fri, 25 Dec.* 🎨 *Adults.*

🍷 Kaikoura Wine Company
State Hwy 1. 📞 *(03) 319 4440.* ◯ *daily.* ● *Good Fri, 25 Dec.* 📷 🍴

🏛 Maori Leap Cave
State Hwy 1. 📞 *(03) 319 5023.*
◯ *daily.* ● *25 Dec.* 🎨 📷 🍴 📷

Picnickers on the Kaikoura coast

Watching Marine Life at Kaikoura

IN THE LATE 1980s, the popularity of observing marine life in Kaikoura led to a tourism boom that transformed the town into one of New Zealand's premier visitor destinations. The main attraction is sperm whales, seen as they rest on the surface between dives, as well as orca and numerous dolphin species. Through the services of several eco-tourism companies in Kaikoura, the habits of whales and seals and the antics of the acrobatic

Stained-glass souvenir

dusky dolphins can be observed from the shore or air and both in and on the water. The special richness of Kaikoura's marine life is explained by the presence of very deep water and the mixing of warm and cold ocean currents there, which forces nutrients to the surface. Species of seabirds found in Kaikoura include the royal albatross, wandering albatross, grey petrel, Antarctic fulmer, and black-browed mollymawk.

WHALE WATCHING

Most whales seen at Kaikoura are toothed whales, a group of marine mammals that includes dolphins. Unlike baleen whales, which feed by filtering plankton, toothed whales hunt their prey, including fish, krill and giant squid, sometimes at great depths.

Tourists get a close-up view from the Whale Watch® boat

Tour operators offer opportunities to visitors to get close to the marine life.

Swimming with dusky dolphins, inquisitive, playful creatures, is a memorable experience.

New Zealand fur seals can be observed at a colony at Obau Point, 23 km (14 miles) north of Kaikoura.

Fresh seafood is a speciality of Kaikoura's restaurants. The abundance of scallops, fish, crayfish and prawns is celebrated annually in October with the Kaikoura Seafest.

Mollymawks are one of the marine bird species to be seen within easy reach of the shores of Kaikoura.

Nelson ⓬

Statue of Abel Tasman

Nʟᴇʟsᴏɴ ᴡᴀs ᴛʜᴇ second settlement developed by the New Zealand Company. The first settlers arrived in February 1842, but in 1844 the company failed. Some settlers persisted, and in 1853 Nelson became the capital of a province of the same name. A royal decree in 1858 made the small town New Zealand's second city. Today, Nelson is renowned as a vibrant art, crafts and festival centre with a superb climate. The compact city centre includes numerous galleries, craft shops and heritage attractions. A memorial to Dutch navigator Abel Tasman can be seen at Tahunanui, a popular swimming beach close to the centre of the city.

View of Nelson from Auckland Point

♣ Anzac Park
Cnr Rutherford and Halifax sts.
The beautifully landscaped Anzac Park, with its pretty flowerbeds, tall palms and cenotaph is Nelson's main war memorial. A horse-drawn passenger carriage, the "city bus", ran alongside the park until 1901, using a section of New Zealand's first railway line. Auckland Point nearby was once the site of Matangi Awhio Pa. Maoris living there sold produce to the first Europeans. The site is now being revegetated and a winding track to the summit provides excellent views over the city.

♣ Centre of New Zealand
Cnr Milton & Hardy sts.
An easy walk beginning at the Botanical Reserve – where the country's first rugby game was played in 1870 – leads up a hill to a marker and lookout known locally as "the centre of New Zealand". The hill provides good views of the city, harbour, Maitai Valley and the Maitai River, which flows through the city into the harbour. A pathway follows the river downstream through pleasant parklands and past Riverside Pool, a modern heated pool within a historic façade, to the visitor centre.

⏛ Suter Art Gallery
208 Bridge St. 【 (03) 548 4699.
⬡ daily. ⬤ 25 Dec. ⬚⬚⬚⬚
One of New Zealand's oldest galleries (1899), the Suter Art Gallery holds a nationally important permanent collection, including paintings by Sir Tosswill Woolaston (one of the founders of New Zealand modern art), Frances Hodgkins, Colin McCahon, (see p30) and contemporary Nelson painter, Jane Evans. It also houses the collection of Andrew Suter, the city's bishop from 1866 to 1891. He donated the assortment of early colonial paintings, including many by the colonial watercolourist John Gully, to the people of Nelson. The gallery also supports changing exhibitions, live performances, films and recitals. The variety of material it holds makes the Suter Art Gallery an ideal place to explore the region's visual arts.

♣ Queens Gardens and Albion Square
One of the city's heritage precincts, the main focus is the Queens Gardens. Some of the trees date back to the 1850s although the gardens were formally established in 1887. Albion Square borders the gardens and was once the political centre of Nelson when provincial government buildings dominated the square. Some historic relics and buildings remain, such as a powder magazine, trout hatchery and fire station. A still-in-service 1864 post box and surveyors' test chain complete the picture.

⛪ Church Hill
Trafalgar Square.
Church Hill is dominated by the Anglican Christ Church Cathedral, the third church built on a site which has also been a survey base, *pa*, fort and immigration barracks. Church Hill is linked to Trafalgar Street by the impressive granite Cathedral Steps, one of many gifts to the city by Thomas Cawthron, a noted philanthropist. Panels explain the history of Church Hill and some of its notable trees, while the remains of the old fort are visible near the cathedral entrance.

Christ Church Cathedral on Church Hill

Fresh flowers at the Nelson weekend market

🅰 Nelson Market

Montgomery Square. 📞 (03) 546-6454. 🕐 8am–1pm Sat, 9am–1pm Sun. 🚫 1 Jan, 25 Dec. 🅶 🅿

On weekends the car park at Montgomery Square is transformed into a colourful marketplace. Vendors of plants, toys, crafts, organic produce and foods, ranging from sushi to Dutch cheeses, arrive before sunrise to set up their stalls. Shoppers and buskers

bring the market to life, creating a busy spectacle that has become a key part of life in Nelson and of visits there.

🚽 Trafalgar Street South

Nelson's main street, Trafalgar, extends south of the cathedral to Trafalgar Street South. It leads to Fairfield Park and a small cemetery with graves of some early settlers. The inscriptions on the headstones give an idea of the hardships endured during Nelson's early years.

Within walking distance of the park are two colonial era houses, Melrose and Fairfield. Melrose House (around 1878) is a truly grand home in the Italianate style. A feature of Fairfield House (1873) is its viewing tower, a replica of one used by its original owner, Arthur Atkinson, for astrological purposes. The garden contains some plantings made by the Dalai Lama during his 1996 visit to New Zealand. From Fairfield House a steep track climbs to a viewpoint on the Grampian Range.

VISITORS' CHECKLIST

Road map D4. 🏠 52,000. ✈ 15 km (9 miles) SW of city. 🚌 27 Bridge St. 🛈 Cnr Halifax & Trafalgar sts, (03) 548 2304. 🎵 Winter Music Festival (Jul); Nelson Arts Festival (Sep–Oct); Sealord Summer Festival (Dec–Jan). 🖥 www.nelson.net.nz

🚽 South Street

To the west of Church Hill is the historic precinct of South Street comprising a collection of workers' cottages built between 1863 and about 1867. Sixteen cottages remain intact and many have been restored for use as accommodation or to house craft galleries.

Former workers' cottages in the historic South Street precinct

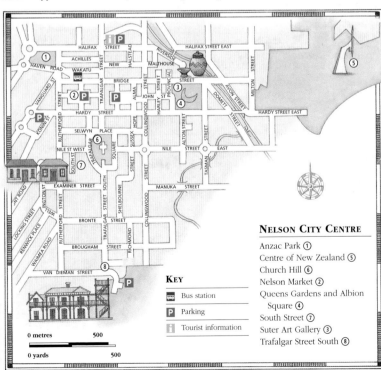

NELSON CITY CENTRE

KEY

🚌 Bus station
🅿 Parking
🛈 Tourist information

0 metres   500

0 yards   500

Richmond ⑨

Road map D4. 🏠 *10,000.*
✈ *Nelson, 8 km (5 miles) W of town.*
🚹 *Gladstone Rd, (03) 544 4793.*
📷 *Chelsea Flower and Garden
Show (Mar).*

T HIS BUSY TOWN serves the
productive horticultural
lands to its south and west.
Highlights are the Wash-
bourne Gardens, complete
with 1862 jailhouse, and the
Redwood Stables restaurant,
built using bricks from New
Zealand's first racing stables.
Visitors can observe the art of
glass making at **Höglund Art
Glass** where Ola and Marie
Höglund create their re-
nowned glassware.

ENVIRONS: Six km (4 miles)
southwest of Richmond, at
Brightwater, is a memorial to
New Zealand's best known
scientist, Lord Ernest Rutherford *(see p19)*, born here in
1871. Also at Brightwater is
the **McGlashen Pottery**.
Continuing southwest to
Wakefield is a historic church,
St John's (1846).

🏛 **Höglund Art Glass**
Lansdowne Rd. 【 *(03) 544 6500.*
○ *daily.* ● *Good Fri, 25 Dec.* 🚹
🏛 **McGlashen Pottery**
128 Ellis St, Brightwater. 【 *(03) 542
3585.* ○ *daily.* ● *Good Fri, 25 Apr,
25 Dec.* 🚹

**The South Island's oldest church,
St John's, at Wakefield**

St Arnaud ⑩

Road map D5. 🏠 *200.* 🚌
🚹 *View Rd, (03) 521 1806.*
📷 *Power Boat Championships (Mar).*

A PPROXIMATELY 90 minutes'
drive from Blenheim or
Nelson is the small town of St
Arnaud, nestled on the shore
of Lake Rotoiti, a trout fishing,
boating and water-skiing

Lake Rotoiti in Nelson Lakes National Park

paradise. The nearby Lake
Rotoroa also has good trout
fishing but is more secluded
and quiet. St Arnaud is the
gateway to Nelson Lakes
National Park and the closest
town to the **Rainbow Ski
Area**, where the terrain is
suitable for novice and inter-
mediate snowboarders and
skiers. In summer, the ski
field road continues through
to Hanmer Springs *(see p231)*.

🎿 **Rainbow Ski Area**
Wairau Valley. 【 *(03) 521 1861.*
○ *June – Oct daily.* 🎿 🖳 🚹

Nelson Lakes
National Park ⑪

Road map C5. 🅿 🚌 🚹 *View Rd,
(03) 521 1806.*

T HE TWIN, glacier-formed
lakes Rotoiti and Rotoroa
dominate this 960 sq-km (370
sq-mile) park at the northern
tip of the Southern Alps. A
water taxi is the easiest form
of access to the area of high
passes, forests, valleys and
basins. The lakes and rivers
are popular for kayaking,
sailing, boating, swimming
and trout fishing. Winter
pastimes include climbing
and ski touring. There are
many trails for trampers and
walkers, including the well-
known 80-km (50-mile)
Travers–Sabine Circuit that
includes two major valleys,
an alpine pass, the wetland
Howard–Speargrass area and
both main lakes. The two-day
return walk along Robert
Ridge to the beautiful Lake
Angelus is also very pleasant
but has high altitudes.

Motueka ⑫

Road map D4. 🏠 *6,600.* 🚌 🚹
20 Wallace St, (03) 528 6543.

M OTUEKA has a diverse
horticultural industry
and is the country's most
prolific orcharding area.
Kiwifruit, apples, berries,
hops, pears, and grapes are
some of the produce grown
here. The town is also a base
for trips to the Abel Tasman
and Kahurangi national parks.

ENVIRONS: Kaiteriteri, 14 km
(9 miles) north of Motueka, is
known for its stunning golden
beaches. South of Motueka
are the coastal villages of
Tasman and Mapua. Inland is
Upper Moutere village,
established in the 1840s by
German settlers. Each village
has its own artists, shops,
wineries, eating places and
boutique accommodation.

Kahurangi
National Park ⑬

Road map C4. 🚹 *20 Wallace St,
Motueka, (03) 528 6543.*

A GREAT VARIETY of native
animals and plants live in
the 4,510 sq-km (1,740 sq-
mile) park. A highlight is the
Heaphy Track, a four- to six-
day walking track. Kayaking,
hunting, caving, tramping,
rafting and fishing are all
popular activities here. Alpine
plants can be seen growing
here near the Cobb Reservoir.
The major gateway is Mot-
ueka, but the park can also
be accessed from Murchison,
Tapawera, Karamea *(see p232)*
and Golden Bay *(see p214)*.

The Nelson Arts Scene

A COMBINATION OF a warm climate and a relaxed environment has attracted many artists to Nelson, making it one of New Zealand's most vibrant arts regions. Its history of artistic endeavour is long. Today, Nelson abounds with opportunities to explore art in the many galleries and studios of glass-blowers, painters, jewellers, textile artists, woodworkers and

Hand-blown glass vase

ceramic artists. The Suter Art Gallery *(see p208)* is noted for its extensive collection of historical and contemporary works. The Nelson region is also becoming known for music and performance events, such as the Wearable Art Awards and the Nelson School of Music Festival. Nelson's Provincial Museum houses a photographic display chronicling Nelson and New Zealand's early colonial beginnings.

CERAMICS

A variety of fine raw clays and glaze materials has long attracted ceramic artists to Nelson. A large number of pottery outlets showcase the work of talented potters, and many nationally recognized crafts people choose Nelson as a living and working base.

Ron McGlashen at work in his ceramic studio at Brightwater

Handmade tiles adorn the doorway of a tile shop in Mapua

Glassware in Nelson is made by combining modern design ideas with traditional glass-blowing methods (see p210). The result is colourful creations, each one handcrafted and unique.

Artists in Nelson have long been inspired by their surroundings. A nationally important collection can be seen at the Suter Art Gallery (see p208).

The Wearable Art Awards is the highlight of the annual Nelson Arts Festival, showcasing vivid "artwear" from around the world (see p38).

Three-dimensional art, designed to be viewed from many sides, is popular in Nelson. Some pieces are practical, others whimsical. Local sculptors have been commissioned to provide works for public areas.

Art and craft galleries are a common sight in the region

Abel Tasman National Park ⑭

NEW ZEALAND'S smallest national park, at 225 sq km (87 sq miles), Abel Tasman has a mild climate, golden beaches and sandy estuaries fringed by natural forest. The park is best known for its Coast Track which can be walked one way, with the return trip made on a launch or water taxi. A large number of camp sites and huts are available along tracks in the park to break the journey. Due to the park's popularity in summer, it is necessary to book huts before visiting. Abel Tasman is also one of New Zealand's better sea kayaking destinations and a day spent drifting in a slowly filling estuary or watching seals, penguins, dolphins or birdlife from these quiet craft will not be forgotten.

Oystercatcher in the park

Aerial view of Abel Tasman National Park

★ Wainui Falls
Nelson's finest accessible falls are reached via an easy 45-minute walk from a small car park on the road to Totaranui.

★ Harwood's Hole
A 45-minute walk from Canaan car park (see p214) leads to the entrance of the 176-m (577-ft) vertical marble shaft known as Harwood's Hole. It is dangerous to get too close to the chasm as the sides may be unstable.

The Inland Track, more rugged than its coastal counterpart, is a three-day walk from Tinline Bay to Wainui Bay. Drinking water should be carried on the track.

STAR SIGHTS

★ Harwood's Hole

★ Totaranui

★ Wainui Falls

VISITORS' CHECKLIST

Road map D4. 🚌 to Marahau
and Totaranui daily from Nelson
and Motueka. 🚤 water taxi and
launch services from Kaiteriteri
and Marahau. ℹ️ 20 Wallace St,
Motueka, (03) 528 6543.
🌐 www.doc.govt.nz

★ Totaranui
*A main arrival point for visitors to northern
Abel Tasman National Park, Totaranui's
sandy beaches and azure waters are a
prime attraction (see p214).*

**The Tonga Island Marine
Reserve** covers 12 km (8 miles)
of coastline. Established to restore
the marine environment to its
natural state, no fishing from
boats or the shore is allowed.

Granite Rocks
*Granite is a common feature
of the park, and was once
extracted at Tonga Quarry.*

Coast Track
*The 51-km (32-mile) long
Coast Track from Marahau to
Wainui meets four estuaries
only negotiable at low tide.*

Falls River is about a
one-hour walk from
Torrent Bay. The
track follows Tregidga
Stream and passes
Cascade Falls before
ending at Falls River.
A further 15-minute
walk up rocks leads
to the main falls.

KEY

▬▬▬	State highway
═══	Minor road
～～	River
– –	Walking track
▪▪▪	Park boundary
– –	Marine Reserve boundary
ℹ️	Tourist information
🅿️	Parking
⛺	Camp site
🌺	Viewpoint

0 kilometres   4

0 miles   4

Marahau
*The southern gateway to Abel
man National Park, Marahau
he base for water taxis serving
the coast. Outdoor pursuits
available at Marahau include
sea kayaking, walking and
swimming with seals.*

View from Takaka Hill looking towards Motueka and Nelson

Takaka Hill ⑮

Road map D4.

TAKAKA HILL IS commonly referred to as "the marble mountain" because of its large marble deposits that contrast sharply with the granite hills of adjoining Abel Tasman National Park. There are many caves and sinkholes to explore in the area, including **Ngarua Caves** near the summit of Takaka Hill, where a lookout offers views north to D'Urville Island and east towards Nelson city. Tours of the caves are available and bones of moa *(see pp23)* can be seen. Visible below the caves is Marahau's golden beach *(see p213)*, where marble from a local quarry was shipped to Wellington for use in New Zealand's Parliament Building.

To the west of Ngarua Caves, Canaan Road leads to Canaan car park, the starting point for walking tracks, including the Rameka Track, one of Nelson's better mountain bike rides. An easy walk leads to the impressive Harwood's Hole *(see p212)*, a 176-m (577-ft) vertical shaft. A short steep side track leads to the Harwood Lookout with a fine viewpoint inland to the Tablelands in Kahurangi National Park *(see p211)*.

To the east of Ngarua Caves is Hawkes Lookout. A short walk leads to a platform perched over a precipitous 500-m (1,640-ft) drop to the forest at Riwaka Resurgence.

🦇 Ngarua Caves
📞 (03) 528 8093. ⭕ Summer: daily. Winter: school hols. 🈲 ♿ 🚫 📷

Takaka ⑯

Road map D4. 🏘 1,230. ✈ 6 km (4 miles) N of town. 🚌 ℹ Willow St, (03) 525 9136.

TAKAKA IS the main shopping and business area for the Golden Bay region and an access point to Abel Tasman National Park *(see pp212–13)*. The townspeople are a mix of "alternative lifestylers" and farming folk. Dairy farming is one of the largest industries in the region. The **Golden Bay Museum** is

excellent, and best known for its displays on Abel Tasman and the story of Golden Bay's many mining ventures. It also has an adjacent gallery. Several artists near Takaka show their work – painted gourds, pottery and wood or stone sculptures – to visitors.

At **Bencarri Farm Park**, home to tame eels and farm animals, rare species such as yaks, llamas and alpacas are bred. Riverside walking and picnics in a valley at the park are other attractions.

🏛 Golden Bay Museum
Commercial St. 📞 (03) 525 9990. ⭕ daily. ⭕ Sun in winter, public hols. 🈲 ♿ 🚫

🐾 Bencarri Farm Park
McCallum's Rd. 📞 (03) 525 8261. ⭕ Summer: daily. ⭕ 25 Dec. 🈲 ♿ limited. 📱 📷

ENVIRONS: Beyond the beach at **Pohara**, 10 km (6 miles) from Takaka, is a memorial to Dutch navigator Abel Tasman, with a lookout platform and display. After the memorial, the road leads to **Wainui Bay**. Several coastal walks and one to Wainui Falls *(see p212)* begin there. Beyond Wainui Bay the road climbs to Abel Tasman National Park, descending finally to the sea and golden sands of Totaranui. A camp ground and visitor centre with a shop operate here over the summer.

Painted gourd

Llamas at Bencarri Farm Park

Waikoropupu Springs Scenic Reserve ⓱

Road map D4.

NORTH OF TAKAKA on State Highway 60, a turnoff leads to the Waikoropupu Springs Scenic Reserve. The waters here are exceptionally clear, coming from an underground cave system that is connected to the features encountered on Takaka Hill and at Riwaka Resurgence *(see p214)*. In the past it was a place of ceremonial blessings for Maoris.

Divers in the ice cold, clear waters of Waikoropupu Springs

The springs are best viewed using a large fixed periscope set on a viewing platform. An easy walk through beautiful forest leads to the platform.

Beyond the springs (at the end of the road), the Pupu Walkway is a track that follows the line of a water race built to serve a gold mining claim. An impressive piece of engineering, the water race was later used (and still is) to generate electric power. The walk is about 3-km (2-miles) long.

Collingwood ⓲

Road map D4. 🏃 500. 🚌

A QUIET VILLAGE at the mouth of the Aorere River, Collingwood was designated a port of entry in the 1850s gold rush and was considered as the site for New Zealand's

capital city. Despite several devastating fires, the courthouse, post office, original cemetery and Anglican St Cuthbert's Church remain to remind visitors of the town's fleeting moment of glory.

Collingwood acts as the base for tours to Farewell Spit and for buses serving the Heaphy Track in Kahurangi National Park *(see p210)*.

ENVIRONS: Within 20 km (12 miles) of Collingwood is the beautiful Kaituna Track with river views and lush forest, the Te Anaroa Caves, a 350-m (1,148-ft) limestone cave system with glowworms and shellfish fossils, and the Aorere, New Zealand's first major gold field. Quartz, silver and gold were mined here. The workings can be explored by a walking track with views over the valley.

Farewell Spit ⓳

Road map D4. 🛈 *Visitor Centre and Café, (03) 524 8454.* ⭕ *daily.* 🖥 🚻

AT THE NORTHERN tip of the South Island, a 25-km (16-mile) sandspit sweeps eastward into the sea. Farewell Spit is a nature reserve with restricted access and has been designated a Wetland of International Importance.

In late spring, tens of thousands of migratory waders arrive from the northern hemisphere, joining the year-round residents before returning home in autumn to breed.

Early gold workings at Aorere, near Collingwood

Black swans, Canadian geese, Australasian gannets, Caspian terns, oystercatchers, black shags and eastern bartailed godwits are amongst the species to be seen in summer. As the region is a protected area, the only way to visit the spit is on a guided tour with one of the licensed tour operators based in Collingwood.

ENVIRONS: Immediately to the west of the spit is **Puponga Farm Park**, with walking tracks and viewpoints. Visitors can also participate in the activities on a working farm. A short walk from the Farewell Spit visitor centre and café leads to Fossil Point on the wild ocean beach. Further west is the easy climb to Pillar Point lighthouse and the Old Man Range, while at the end of the road a short track crosses a series of dunes to Wharariki Beach, with rock pools, birds, seals and the towering Archway Islands nearby.

🌺 **Puponga Farm Park**
Collingwood–Puponga Main Rd.
📞 *(03) 525 8026.* ⭕ *daily.* 🖥

Tourist bus at Farewell Spit

Tourists climbing the sand dunes at Farewell Spit

CANTERBURY AND THE WEST COAST

*C*ANTERBURY AND THE WEST COAST, *stretching from the Tasman Sea in the west to the Pacific Ocean in the east, is characterized by sharp and sudden distinctions of geology, flora and climate. The combined area contains four national parks and New Zealand's highest mountain. Christchurch, the largest city in the South Island, is an ideal base from which to explore the various subregions.*

When large-scale European settlement of Canterbury began in 1850, both Canterbury and the West Coast were dominated by the Ngai Tahu tribe. By 1860, the bulk of the tribe's land had been acquired by the government in a series of dubious sales transactions, leaving the Ngai Tahu impoverished and unable to participate equally in the new settler economy. It was not until 1997 that the Ngai Tahu received compensation from the New Zealand Government.

While pastoral farming was the key to the development of Canterbury in the 1850s, it was the discovery of gold in the 1860s that brought European settlement to the West Coast. Today, "the Coast" retains a rustic mystique, a product of its mining heritage, powerful landscapes of rugged mountains and glaciers, lush rainforest, rushing rivers and sombre lakes, as well as its isolation from the rest of New Zealand.

The West Coast climate is wet, with prevailing westerly air-flows bringing frequent heavy rain as moisture-laden air is forced up and over the Southern Alps. By contrast, Canterbury is relatively dry, with warm, blustery winds commonly sweeping down the eastern side of the alps and over the Canterbury Plains.

The plains are carved into a patchwork of grazing and crop paddocks, backed by tussock vegetation and forest-covered mountain ranges. They merge to the north and south with rolling farmland, interspersed with wide, braided rivers. The inland region is a large, dry, open basin of austere beauty, over which New Zealand's highest mountains loom.

Climbers on the summit of Mount Cook

◁ The daffodil woodland in Hagley Park, Christchurch, a popular springtime rendezvous

Exploring Canterbury and the West Coast

CANTERBURY AND THE WEST COAST's distinctive landscapes are dominated by the Southern Alps through which there are only two roads and one railway line. To get the best out of the region, and particularly to appreciate the beauty of its varied geology, flora and fauna, a willingness to don sturdy shoes and set out on foot is necessary. For the independent outdoor enthusiast, the opportunities are enormous, and for those who prefer to be guided through the wilderness, commercially run adventure tourism activities are available at most key locations.

Inner-city tram in Christchurch

SIGHTS AT A GLANCE

TOP OUTDOOR ACTIVITIES

The places shown here have been selected for their recreational activities. Conditions vary depending on the weather and the time of year, so exercise caution and, if in doubt, seek local advice.

	Fishing	Golf	Mountain Biking	Mountain Climbing	Skiing/Heli-Skiing	Tramping	Walking	White-Water Rafting
Arthur's Pass National Park				▣	●	▣	●	
Banks Peninsula	●	▣	●			▣	●	
Franz Josef Glacier				▣	●	▣	●	
Hanmer Springs	●	▣	●		●	▣	●	●
Hokitika	●	▣				▣	●	
Karamea	●	▣	●			▣	●	●
Lake Ohau	●				▣		●	
Lake Tekapo	●	▣			●		●	
Lewis Pass	●				▣	▣	●	
Mount Cook				●	▣	▣	●	
Mount Hutt		▣			●		●	
Paparoa National Park	●					▣	●	
Port Hills			●				●	
Rakaia	●	▣					●	▣
Reefton	●		●			▣		
Westport	●	▣						

Okarit
Lagoo

FRANZ J
Gillespies   GLAC
Point
FOX GLACIER ●

WESTLAN
NATIONA
PARK
Haast   M
    C

6

LAK
PUKA

LAKE OHAU **27**
TWI

KEY

▬ Motorway

▬ State Highway

▬ Major road

▬ Scenic route

〜 River

✲ Viewpoint

Getting Around

Numerous bus operators link all parts of the region, but the most convenient way to get around is by car. The roads are good, although care is needed in winter on the alpine routes, and some sights are accessible only via gravel roads. Many areas are easily visited by day trips from Christchurch, including Banks Peninsula, Hanmer Springs, Arthur's Pass and mid-Canterbury's ski fields. The four and a half hour trip from Christchurch to Greymouth on the TranzAlpine railway is a relaxing way to see the region's diverse scenery.

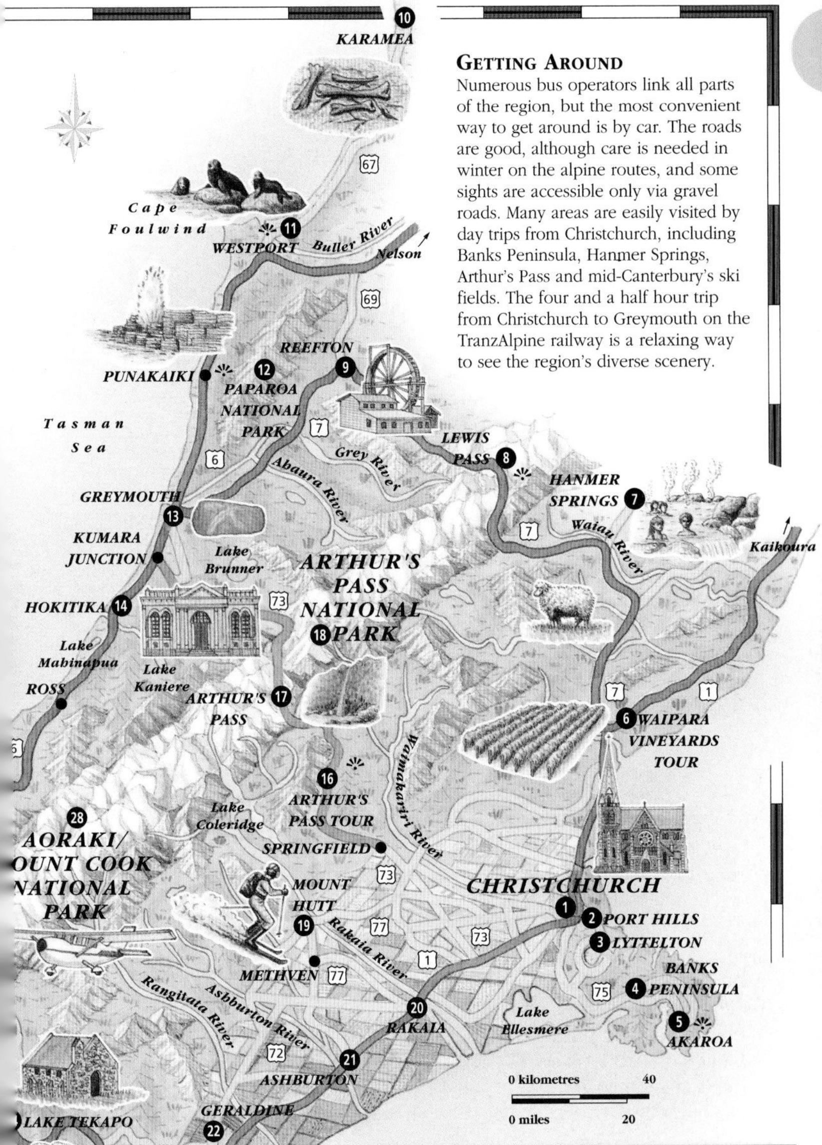

10 KARAMEA
67
Cape Foulwind
11 WESTPORT
Buller River
Nelson
69
REEFTON 9
PUNAKAIKI
12 PAPAROA NATIONAL PARK
Tasman Sea
7
6
LEWIS PASS 8
Grey River
Abaura River
HANMER SPRINGS 7
GREYMOUTH 13
KUMARA JUNCTION
Lake Brunner
Waiau River
Kaikoura
ARTHUR'S PASS NATIONAL PARK 18
73
HOKITIKA 14
Lake Mahinapua
Lake Kaniere
ROSS
ARTHUR'S PASS 17
1
6 WAIPARA VINEYARDS TOUR
Waimakariri River
16 ARTHUR'S PASS TOUR
28
Lake Coleridge
AORAKI/ MOUNT COOK NATIONAL PARK
SPRINGFIELD
MOUNT HUTT 19
CHRISTCHURCH 1
2 PORT HILLS
3 LYTTELTON
Rakaia River
METHVEN
77
BANKS 4 PENINSULA
75
Rangitata River
Ashburton River
20 RAKAIA
Lake Ellesmere
5 AKAROA
72
21 ASHBURTON
0 kilometres 40
0 miles 20
GERALDINE 22
LAKE TEKAPO

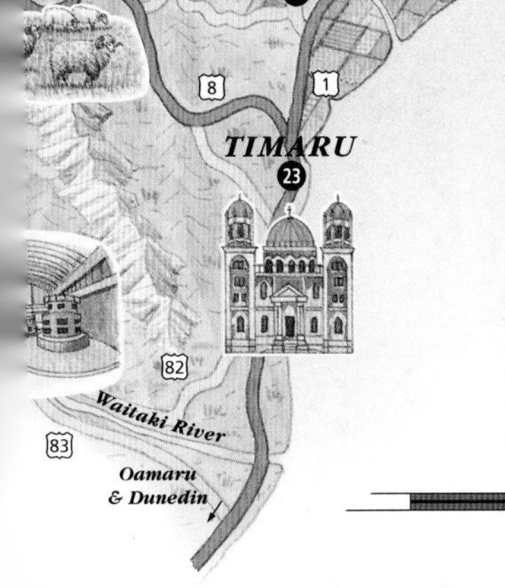

8
TIMARU 23
82
Waitaki River
83
Oamaru & Dunedin

Lake Tekapo, a popular venue for water sports

Christchurch

Christchurch's resident Wizard

CANTERBURY'S provincial capital, Christchurch, is the largest city in the South Island and the principal gateway to its scenic wonders. Laid out as the capital of the Canterbury Settlement in 1850, the city has many notable buildings and monuments that recall its colonial heritage, as well as many parks and gardens. It is often thought of as a conservative city, a reflection of its origins as a Church of England settlement modelled on 19th-century English society. Although it has essentially been an agricultural market town for much of its history, it now has all the trappings of a modern city, including an increasingly sophisticated restaurant, café and arts scene.

Timber ceiling in Christ Church Cathedral

🚌 Cathedral Square

Lying in the heart of the city, Cathedral Square is dominated by the Anglican Christ Church Cathedral. Other historic buildings surround the square: the Renaissance-style Old Chief Post Office (built in 1879), the former Government Building (1911), the ornate Edwardian Regent Theatre (1905), and the Gothic Press Building (1909) *(see p27)*, which houses the city's daily newspaper. An 1867 statue of Canterbury's founder, John Robert Godley, faces the cathedral. The steps in front of the cathedral attract many eccentrics, including Christchurch's resident Wizard, who appears most summer lunchtimes to cast "spells" and pontificate.The square is closed to traffic.

🏛 Christ Church Cathedral

Cathedral Square. 📞 *(03) 366 0046.* ⬤ *daily.* 📷 🚻 *daily except Sat.* ♿ 🚻 🛍 🛒

Begun in 1864 and completed in 1904, Christ Church Cathedral was built as the focal point of the new Anglican settlement of Canterbury, and it remains the city's most important landmark. It was designed by English architect George Gilbert Scott in the Gothic Revival style. Noted local architect Benjamin Mountfort supervised the completion and also had considerable influence over the design. Built of Canterbury stone and native timbers, this impressive building has many notable features, including detailed wood and stone carvings around the high altar and main pulpit. Other works of art depict the history of Canterbury's settlement, the city's connection with Antarctic exploration and military campaigns through the world wars. The tower's 134 steps can be climbed for an excellent view of the city, Port Hills, Canterbury Plains and distant Southern Alps.

GODLEY AND THE CANTERBURY SETTLEMENT

John Robert Godley (1814–61) is regarded as the founder of Canterbury although he spent only three years in the new province. With Edward Gibbon Wakefield, founder of the New Zealand Company *(see p47)*, he formed the Canterbury Association in 1848, which then purchased 1,210 sq km (470 sq miles) of land for the creation of a Church of England-dominated province in New Zealand. A slice of England was to be transplanted on Canterbury's far shores. English newspapers commented on the "respectability" of the so-called "Canterbury Pilgrims" who set sail on four ships, the *Randolph, Charlotte Jane, Cressy* and *Sir George Seymour*, in September 1850. Within three years of its founding, Canterbury was governing itself as one of New Zealand's six provinces. Godley returned to England in 1852.

Statue of Godley in Cathedral Square

| 0 metres | | 500 |
| 0 yards | | 500 |

KEY

▦	Christchurch Street-by-Street *see pp222–3*
🚌	Bus station
P	Parking
🛈	Tourist information
- -	Inner-city tram route

VISITORS' CHECKLIST

Road map C6. 🏙 310,000. ✈
10 km (6 miles) NW of city. 🚂
1 Clarence St. 🚌 123 Worcester
St. 🚆 Cathedral Square. 🅸
Old Chief Post Office Building,
Cathedral Square, (03) 379 9629.
📷 Showtime Canterbury (Nov);
Summertimes Festivals (Dec–Mar)
W www.Christchurchnz.net

🐬 Southern Encounter Aquarium

33 Cathedral Square. 📞 (03)
377 3474. ☐ daily. 🎫 ♿
📅 school hols. 🛍 🚻

This small aquarium, situated
in the old Regent Theatre
building in Cathedral Square,
specializes in the aquatic life
of the South Island. Fish in
the aquarium are regularly
returned to the wild and replaced with fresh stock.

Punting on the Avon River in Christchurch

🌿 Avon River

Cashel St & Oxford Terrace.

The Avon River, which gently
meanders through the city, is
Christchurch's greatest natural
asset and one of its main
attractions. Its grassy banks,
weeping willows, old oak
trees, ducks, and bridges linking the city's main streets lure
office workers and visitors
alike to its banks in summer.
A walk along the Avon River
bank from Victoria Square to
the Bridge of Remembrance
takes visitors past the Law
Courts, the Floral Clock, the
Provincial Council Buildings
and a 1917 statue of Antarctic
explorer Robert Scott sculpted
by his widow, Kathleen.

Another great way to enjoy
the river is to take a boat trip.
Punts operate from various
landings along the river,
including near the Town Hall
and Thomas Edmonds Band
Rotunda (see p222).

🌿 Victoria Square

Formerly the city's marketplace, Victoria Square is a
beautifully landscaped
expanse of green north of
Cathedral Square. Focal points
of the square are the Floral
Clock, statues of Queen
Victoria (1901) and James
Cook (1932), and the much
photographed Bowker and
Ferrier fountains. The Parkroyal Hotel and Town Hall
provide the backdrop to the
square. The Town Hall, built
in 1972, on the banks of the
Avon in Kilmore Street,
features a pleasing combination of glass, marble, and
still and flowing water. A
block away, on Victoria
Street, is the Christchurch
Casino, recognizable by its
stylized roulette wheel façade.

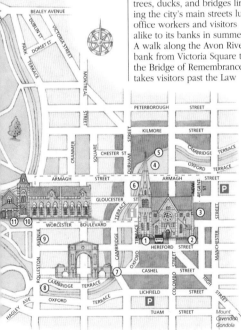

CHRISTCHURCH CITY CENTRE

Victoria Square

Street-by-Street: Christchurch

Rose window, Christ Church Cathedral

THE STREETS SURROUNDING Cathedral Square are laid out in a grid pattern bordered by four broad avenues. The formality of the layout is broken by the quaint Avon River which winds serpentine through the inner city and adjacent parks. Christchurch's many Gothic Revival and Edwardian buildings, pretty parks and landscaped river bank support the oft-repeated description of Christchurch as the most English of cities outside England. The city is easily navigated on foot or bicycle. Yellow buses offer free inner-city transport and a tram route stops at the city's main historic and cultural attractions.

New Regent Street
This charming pedestrian-only area was built in the Spanish Mission style in 1932. The city tram regularly rumbles through.

The Thomas Edmonds Band Rotunda has been refurbished as a restaurant.

Floral Clock
Established in 1955, the clock is replanted twice a year with over 5,000 plants to give spring and summer displays.

Victoria Square, with its Avon River boundary, clipped lawns, formal plantings and many trees, is a peaceful oasis in the city.

The Town Hall, built in 1972 by noted local architects Warren and Mahoney, is the city's principal venue for the performing arts.

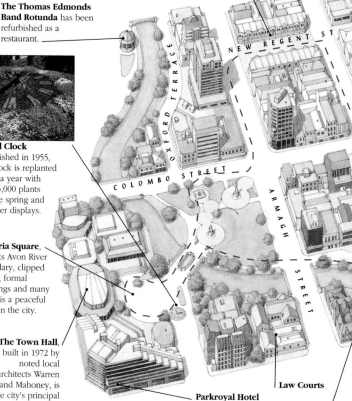

Parkroyal Hotel

Law Courts

★ Provincial Council Buildings
These buildings, built between 1858 and 1865, feature fine stained-glass windows, a delicately stencilled ridge-and-furrow ceiling and mosaic tile work.

STAR SIGHTS

★ **Christ Church Cathedral**

★ **Provincial Council Buildings**

★ Christ Church Cathedral
Built between 1864 and 1904, this impressive building dominates Cathedral Square, and contains many works of art that illustrate the history of Canterbury.

Old Government Building

Press Building
(see p27)

Christchurch Tram
A fleet of restored trams takes passengers on a 3-km (2-mile) route past many significant city centre sights (see pp220–21).

City Mall, a pedestrian-only precinct spanning parts of High and Cashel streets, is an exciting and diverse complex of large department stores, shopping arcades and fashion boutiques.

COLOMBO STREET

HEREFORD STREET

CITY MALL

WORCESTER STREET

OXFORD TERRACE

Avon River

KEY

- - - Suggested route

| 0 metres | 100 |
| 0 yards | 100 |

Southern Encounter Aquarium
(see p221)

Oxford Terrace
This is Christchurch's popular bar and café strip.

Bridge of Remembrance
The bridge's stone archway commemorates the gunners from Canterbury who served in World Wars I and II and subsequent conflicts.

Stone legislative chamber of the Provincial Council Buildings

♛ Provincial Council Buildings

Cnr of Armagh & Durham sts.
[(03) 366 1100. **◐** Summer: daily;
Winter: Mon –Sat. **●** public hols.
& limited. **✓**

Designed by Christchurch architect Benjamin Mountfort, the Provincial Council Buildings are claimed to be the finest example of secular Gothic Revival architecture in New Zealand. They are also the only council buildings to have survived from the period 1853–76 when the country was governed by elected provincial councils.

The buildings were constructed in three stages. The first two, from 1858 to 1861, saw the creation of a mainly wooden building. The third involved the construction of a stone council chamber, completed in 1865, the high point of this notable complex.

♛ Bridge of Remembrance

Cnr of Cashel St & Oxford Terrace.

A commemoration of New Zealand soldiers who served in various arenas of war, the bridge stands at the head of City Mall, the city's central shopping area. The large stone archway over the bridge, built in 1923, underwent extensive refurbishment in the early 1990s.

⊞ Canterbury Museum

Rolleston Ave. **[** (03) 366 8379. **◐**
daily. **●** 25 Dec. **✍** donation. **&**

Built between 1869 and 1876, Canterbury Museum is considered to be one of Mountford's most successful adaptations of the Gothic style for secular purposes. The museum has a comprehensive selection of genuine Antarctic relics as well as one of the finest mounted bird displays in the southern hemisphere. Other halls feature oriental art, furniture and fashions through the ages, a reconstruction of a 19th-century Christchurch street, and a Maori cultural section, including displays of the extinct moa and the bird's early Polynesian hunters.

Moa skeleton, Canterbury Museum

♛ Christ's College

Rolleston Ave. **[** (03) 366 8705.
◐ daily. **●** buildings: school hols.
✓ by arrangement. **&** partial.

At Christ's College, a modern-day reminder of Christchurch's English heritage, the sons of Canterbury's élite are educated in crisp blazers along English public school lines amid Gothic Revival buildings dating back to 1863. Visitors can view the principal buildings and witness public school life by taking an organized tour.

⊞ Arts Centre

Cnr of Rollerston Ave & Worcester Boulevard. **[** (03) 366 0989. **◐**
daily. **●** 25 April, 25 Dec. **&**
ground floor. **✓** 11am. **‖ ▯ ▤**
weekends. **📷** Instant Kiwi World
Buskers Festival (mid-Jan).

Located in the old University of Canterbury buildings, the Arts Centre is Christchurch's art and crafts hub (see p227).
The complex houses more than 40 permanent galleries, studios and speciality shops, as well as theatre and ballet venues and eating places. A bustling outdoor market is held every weekend throughout the year.
Construction of the Gothic Revival-style buildings began in 1877. Although designed by a succession of architects, including Mountford, who was responsible for the Clock Tower building, Great Hall and Classics block, and assembled piecemeal over the next 46 years, the buildings were linked by quadrangles and cloisters that lend unity to the whole complex.

Weekend market at the Arts Centre in Christchurch

🏛 Robert McDougall Art Gallery

Botanic Gardens. **(** (03) 365 0915. **◯** daily. **●** Good Fri, 25 Dec. **&**
Located behind the Canterbury Museum, in the Botanic Gardens, this is the city's principal art gallery. It houses a collection of 4,500 New Zealand and international works of art, which are complemented by touring exhibitions. Its large permanent display features Dutch, French, Italian and British paintings, drawings, prints, sculpture and ceramics.

The New Zealand collection, especially of Canterbury works, is one of the most comprehensive in the region. It includes works by Canterbury landscape artist William Sutton (see p30), as well as other leading New Zealand painters, including Doris Lusk, Colin McCahon and Rita Angus. The contemporary art annexe is part of the Arts Centre. A new gallery, about 500 m (1,640 ft) towards Cathedral Square, is to be completed in 2003.

🚣 Antigua Boat Sheds

Cnr of Cambridge Terrace & Rolleston Ave. **(** (03) 366 5885. **◯** daily. **●** 25 Dec. **✍** **□**
The Antigua Boat Sheds, on the banks of the Avon River, have been providing people with river recreation since 1882. Here, canoes and paddle boats can be hired for trips through the city or upstream to the Botanic Gardens. They are the only surviving commercial boat sheds of the five or six that once offered boats for hire.

🏵 Mona Vale

Mona Vale Rd. **(** (03) 348 9659. **◯** daily. **▯**
Mona Vale, one of Christchurch's historic homes, built between 1899 and 1900, is situated among sweeping lawns, mature trees and landscaped gardens to the northwest of Hagley Park. The Avon River meanders through the property. Visitors are invited to stroll through the gardens, feed the ducks or take punt rides. The imposing homestead was almost demolished in the

Mona Vale on the banks of the Avon River

1960s, but a public appeal for funds led to its purchase by the city. The gardens are open to the public, and morning and afternoon teas and lunches are available at the homestead.

🌿 Hagley Park

((03) 366 1701. **◯** daily. **&**
Hagley Park, a vast green expanse in the heart of Christchurch, serves as the city's lungs. Within its boundaries are a golf course, sports grounds, tree-lined walking and cycling tracks, artificial lakes, and the Botanic Gardens (see pp226–7). When the early colonists laid out the site for their new town, they set aside 2 sq km (0.80 sq mile) for a public park, and in 1856 an ordinance was passed declaring it "reserved forever" for public recreation and enjoyment. By the early 1870s, the settlers had replaced the park's native flora with European plants, grasses and trees.

🏛 International Antarctic Centre

Orchard Rd. **(** (03) 358 9896. **◯** daily. **●** 25 Dec. **✍** **&** **☐** **□** **▯**
About 20 minutes from the centre of the city, located near the airport to the west, is the International Antarctic Centre, the base for the New Zealand, United States and Italian Antarctic programmes. Its visitor centre has a range of exhibits on the exploration and geology of Antarctica. Visitors can also take rides on Antarctic vehicles.

🚠 Christchurch Gondola

10 Bridle Path Rd. **(** (03) 384 0700. **◯** daily. **✍** **&** **🍴** **□** **▯**
Southeast of the city, the Christchurch Gondola takes passengers from a terminal in the Heathcote Valley to the rim of an extinct volcano at the top of the Port Hills. From the summit there are outstanding 360-degree views of the city, Banks Peninsula, Canterbury Plains and the Southern Alps in the distance.

A boat operator offering punting in Hagley Park

Botanic Gardens

THE BOTANIC GARDENS, founded in 1863, contribute to Christchurch's reputation as New Zealand's garden city. The gardens' conservatories, rose and bulb beds, rock and water gardens, English lawns and woodland are largely enclosed in the loop of the Avon River, and the proximity of flowing water to all sections makes the gardens particularly tranquil. The area fringing the eastern side of the Botanic Gardens is Christchurch's creative and artistic heart. The city's museum, civic art gallery, ballet company, professional theatre and Arts Centre are located here.

"Taking Flight" sculpture

★ **Conservatory Complex**
Of the complex's six glass-houses, one of the most notable is Cuningham House, built in 1923, which houses tropical plants.

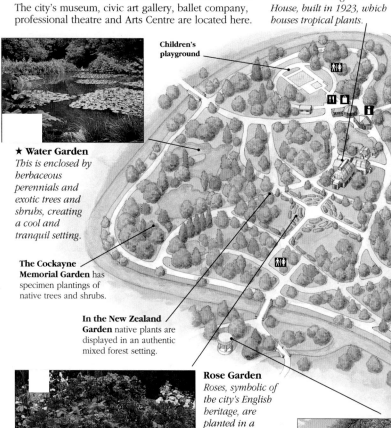

Children's playground

★ **Water Garden**
This is enclosed by herbaceous perennials and exotic trees and shrubs, creating a cool and tranquil setting.

The Cockayne Memorial Garden has specimen plantings of native trees and shrubs.

In the New Zealand Garden native plants are displayed in an authentic mixed forest setting.

Rose Garden
Roses, symbolic of the city's English heritage, are planted in a formal garden in front of the Conservatory Complex.

Daffodil Woodland and Bandsmen's Memorial Rotunda
The area surrounding the rotunda was planted with 16,000 bulbs in 1933, and in spring is a blaze of yellow.

STAR FEATURES

★ Conservatory Complex

★ Water Garden

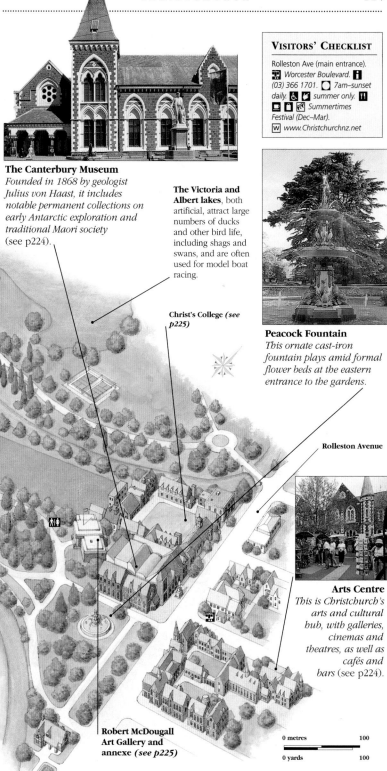

The Canterbury Museum
Founded in 1868 by geologist Julius von Haast, it includes notable permanent collections on early Antarctic exploration and traditional Maori society (see p224).

The Victoria and Albert lakes, both artificial, attract large numbers of ducks and other bird life, including shags and swans, and are often used for model boat racing.

Christ's College (see p225)

VISITORS' CHECKLIST

Rolleston Ave (main entrance).
Worcester Boulevard.
(03) 366 1701. 7am–sunset daily. summer only.
Summertimes Festival (Dec–Mar).
www.Christchurchnz.net

Peacock Fountain
This ornate cast-iron fountain plays amid formal flower beds at the eastern entrance to the gardens.

Rolleston Avenue

Arts Centre
This is Christchurch's arts and cultural hub, with galleries, cinemas and theatres, as well as cafés and bars (see p224).

Robert McDougall Art Gallery and annexe (see p225)

0 metres   100
0 yards   100

Sign of the Takahe, on Dyers Pass Road above Christchurch

Port Hills ❷

Road map C6.

THE PORT HILLS separate Christchurch from Lyttelton Harbour, and were formed as the result of the eruption of the now extinct Lyttelton volcano. Their tussock-covered slopes and volcanic outcrops flank the southern part of the city. Because of their proximity to the city they are extremely popular with walkers, runners, rock climbers and mountain bikers.

The Port Hills are also easily accessed by car, thanks to the work of early 20th-century conservationist

Lyttelton Timeball Station

and politician Harry Ell, who strove for the creation of a road around the summit of the volcano. The first stretch of the Summit Road was opened in 1938.

Ell's vision included the creation of a series of rest houses along the Port Hills, the most impressive of which is the Sign of the Takahe, completed in 1949. Nestled in the hill suburb of Cashmere, this imposing Gothic building is now a restaurant *(see p325)*. Another Ell legacy, the Sign of the Kiwi, is a popular resting place for people using the Summit Road.

The many tracks on the Port Hills provide striking views of Lyttelton Harbour, the Canterbury Plains and the Southern Alps. The summit of the Port Hills can also be accessed via the Christchurch Gondola *(see p225)*.

Lyttelton ❸

Road map C6. 🏔 4,000. 🚌 ℹ️ 20 Oxford St, (03) 328 9093.

LYTTELTON WAS the landing place of the Canterbury Pilgrims, brought out by the Canterbury Association to populate the new province in 1850, and was named after Lord Lyttelton, the chairman of the Association. In 1867, a rail tunnel was drilled through the volcanic rock of the Port Hills to provide a link between Lyttelton's port and Christchurch, and a road tunnel was completed in 1964. The town's port is one of the busiest in New Zealand.

The **Lyttelton Museum** has interesting displays of local maritime history and relics from the colonial past, as well as a small section on Antarctic exploration.

The **Lyttelton Timeball Station** stands sentry over the town, as it has done since its construction in 1875. Each day at 1pm the large black ball hanging from its tower was lowered to signal Greenwich Mean Time to the ships in the harbour. Its function was replaced by radios in 1934, but it remains in working order. A ferry service across the harbour to Quail and Ripapa islands and the small township of Diamond Harbour operates from the Lyttelton docks.

🏛 **Lyttelton Museum**
Gladstone Quay. 📞 *(03) 328 8516.*
⬜ *Tue, Thu, Sat & Sun.* ⬛ *25 Dec.*
💷 *donation.* ♿ *ground floor.*
🎯 **Lyttelton Timeball Station**
Reserve Terrace. 📞 *(03) 328 7311.*
⬜ *Summer: daily; Winter: Mon–Thu.*
⬛ *25 Dec.* 💷 ✔️

Banks Peninsula ❹

Road map C6.

FORMED BY the eruptions of the Lyttelton and Akaroa volcanoes, Banks Peninsula was, until some 25,000 years ago, an island. Reminders of this dramatic geological past are everywhere on the peninsula, including rocky volcanic outcrops, craggy headlands, deep valleys and precipitous bluffs. The Summit Road allows excellent views of this striking scenery.

The peninsula has been settled by Maoris for 1,000 years, and until the 1820s was a place of prosperity and security for the Ngai Tahu tribe. That changed as a result of internecine and intertribal fighting, conflict which contributed indirectly to the

Maori and Colonial Museum and meeting house at Okains Bay

Laverick's Bay, Banks Peninsula

decision taken by the British government to install a governor and sign the Treaty of Waitangi (*see pp46–7*).

Among the peninsula's many attractions are its beautiful bays and picturesque villages, including Pigeon Bay, Okains Bay, Laverick's Bay and Le Bons Bay. There are many walking tracks, ranging from the five-hour Pigeon Bay Walkway to the two- to four-day Banks Peninsula Track, which traverses private farmland and the coastline of many of the remote eastern bays.

At Okains Bay is the **Maori and Colonial Museum**, which houses an extensive collection of Maori artifacts, including an 1867 Maori *waka* (canoe) which is still used each year during the Waitangi Day celebrations on 6 February (*see p39*).

Also worth a visit is the boutique **Barry's Bay Cheese Factory**, which continues the peninsula's long tradition of cheese making. Just as popular for its good wine, food and picturesque rural setting is the French Farm Winery and Restaurant (*see p325*).

⌂ Maori and Colonial Museum
1146 Okains Bay Rd. ▐ (03) 304 8611. ☐ daily. ● 25 Dec. ▨ ▮ ▮
⌂ Barry's Bay Cheese Factory
State Hwy 75. ▐ (03) 304 5809. ☐ daily. ● 25 Dec. ▮

Akaroa ❺

Road map C6. ⋔ 750. ▣ ▮
80 Rue Lavaud, (03) 304 8600.

THIS ATTRACTIVE small town, nestled at the head of Akaroa Harbour, is the oldest town in Canterbury, and was founded by a small band of French settlers in 1840. With its many French-influenced historic buildings, narrow streets, French and English street signs and place names, cosmopolitan shops and picturesque harbourfront location, it has a relaxed and charming ambience. Among the many reminders of Akaroa's French heritage is **Langlois-Eteveneaux House**, believed to have been prefabricated in France and erected in Akaroa in 1845. It is part of the **Akaroa Museum** complex, which also includes the town's old courthouse, opened in 1880. The museum exhibits cover natural and regional history and architecture. A self-guided walk through the town covers 43 historic sites, including the 1880 **Lighthouse**.

A safe swimming beach lies at the centre of the town. Harbour cruises operate from the main wharf, and visitors may see Hector's dolphins, little blue penguins and seal colonies. A number of walking tracks lead up to the surrounding volcanic saddles and peaks, affording panoramic views of the harbour. Akaroa also boasts an active art and crafts community, and its many shops and galleries offer a variety of local wares.

⌷ Langlois-Eteveneaux House and Akaroa Museum
71 Rue Lavaud. ▐ (03) 304 7614. ☐ daily. ● 25 Dec. ▨ ▮ ▮ ▮
⌷ Lighthouse
▐ (03) 304 5099. ☐ public hols & by arrangement. ▨ donation. ▮ ground floor. ▮

JEAN FRANÇOIS LANGLOIS

The man primarily responsible for Akaroa's French heritage was whaler Jean François Langlois. In August 1838, he conceived the idea of a French colony and attempted to buy most of the peninsula from the local Ngai Tahu people. The following year he returned to France to gain support for his plan, and formed the Nanto-Bordelaise Company as the vehicle for his colonizing ambitions.

Langlois-Eteveneaux House

French navy captain Charles Lavaud was dispatched to provide protection for the 57 colonists who landed at Akaroa in August 1840. However, French ambitions were thwarted by the British who, in the interim, had signed the Treaty of Waitangi and, upon hearing of the settlers' impending arrival, rushed to appoint two magistrates to Akaroa. Despite the assertion of British sovereignty, the settlers stayed, although by 1842 Langlois was back in France. The Nanto-Bordelaise Company was bought out by the New Zealand Company in 1849, opening the way for large-scale British migration to the settlement.

Waipara Vineyard Tour ❻

Cabernet grapes

The Waipara district is a relatively new wine-growing region, with the first vineyards planted only in the 1980s. However, it has emerged quickly as a promising area, and many of its vineyards have won awards for their wines. Canterbury has over 30 vineyards, but Waipara, about 65 km (40 miles) north of Christchurch, is the area of most rapid development. Wine-tasting tours can be arranged through the Christchurch visitor information centre *(see p221)*, including a tour in a Clydesdale-drawn wagon.

Pegasus Bay ①
This winery crushed its first grapes in 1991, but has already won many awards. Its wine-tasting venue has a charming garden setting overlooking the surrounding countryside.

Daniel Schuster Wines ⑨
Established in 1988, this vineyard produces high-quality Chardonnay and Pinot Noir. It is open for wine tasting by appointment.

Mountford Vineyard ⑧
Mountford produces top-of-the-range Chardonnay and Pinot Noir. A beautiful homestead overlooks the vineyard.

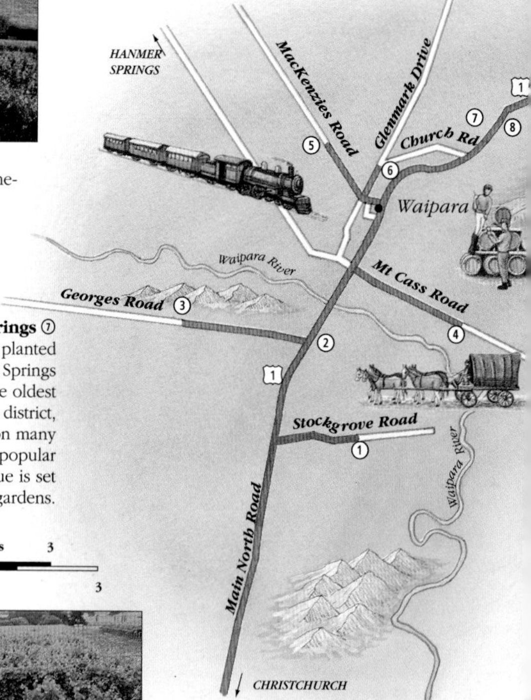
HANMER SPRINGS
MacKenzies Road
Glenmark Drive
Church Rd
Waipara
Waipara River
Georges Road
Mt Cass Road
1
Stockgrove Road
Main North Road
CHRISTCHURCH
0 kilometres 3
0 miles 3

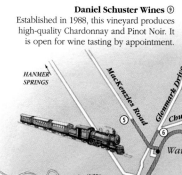

Waipara Springs ⑦
With its first vines planted in 1982, Waipara Springs is one of the oldest vineyards in the district, and has won many awards. Its popular wine-tasting venue is set in pleasant gardens.

Glenmark Wines ⑥
Glenmark's vines were planted in 1981, making it the district's first winery. Its wines have won many awards, and can be tasted in a pleasant, rustic setting.

Chancellor Wines ④
Chancellor has produced grapes for other vineyards since 1982 and did not produce under its own label until 1995. It is open for wine tasting by appointment.

Torlesse Wines ⑤
Torlesse uses both Waipara and Marlborough grapes to produce a wide range of wines, including Gewürztraminer, Cabernet Sauvignon, Sauvignon Blanc and Chardonnay.

Canterbury House Vineyards ②
One of the newest additions to Waipara's wine industry, it is distinguished by a huge stone winery building next to State Highway 1.

Fiddlers Green ③
Producing its first vintage in 1998, this is another of Waipara's newcomers. However, its Riesling and Sauvignon Blanc wines have already won awards.

KEY

▬▬▬ Tour route

▬▬▬ Other roads

═══ River

Hot pool complex at Hanmer Springs

Hanmer Springs ❼

Road map C5. 650. 🅿 ℹ
Amuri Ave, (03) 315 7128.

THIS SMALL alpine village, 385 m (1,260 ft) above sea level, is best known for the extensive **Hanmer Springs Thermal Reserve**. Although hot springs were first discovered in the area in 1859, they were officially opened only in 1883. Today, the complex includes 11 thermal and freshwater pools of varying temperatures, including private pools and a children's water slide area.

Surrounding the hot pools is a 168-sq-km (65-sq-mile) forest park, which offers a variety of activities, including walks ranging from the short Conical Hill walk (one hour return) to the longer Mount Isobel walk (five to six hours return), and excellent mountain biking opportunities. At the Waiau Ferry Bridge, 5 km (3 miles) from the village, tourist operators offer bungy jumping, jet-boating and rafting down the Waiau River.

🅷 Hanmer Springs Thermal Reserve
Amuri Ave. 【 *(03) 315 7511.*
🔾 *daily.* ● *25 Dec.* 🅰 🅱 ▢

Lewis Pass ❽

Road map C5.

LEWIS PASS marks the crossing point on State Highway 7 over the South Island's Main Divide. The surrounding 183-sq-km (70-sq-mile) Lewis Pass National Reserve offers a

range of unguided outdoor activities, including tramping, fishing and hunting.

Just over the pass, **Maruia Springs Thermal Resort** has a small complex of outdoor hot pools in a natural setting, with views of the surrounding bush and mountain peaks.

🅷 Maruia Springs Thermal Resort
State Hwy 7. 【 *(03) 523 8840.*
🔾 *daily.* ● *25 Dec.* 🅰 🅱 🅷

Reefton ❾

Road map C5. 1,200. 🅿
ℹ *67 Broadway, (03) 732 8391.*

FOUNDED IN 1872, Reefton takes its name from the gold-bearing quartz reefs in the area. The town's gold-mining heritage is evident in the many historic remains of the 1870s boom dotted around the region, especially in the beech forest-clad Victoria Forest Park. A network of tracks provides opportunity for exploration on foot or on mountain bike.

A heritage walk around Reefton takes in many historic buildings, including the **School of Mines**, which operated from 1887 to 1970 as part of a network of similar schools around New Zealand. Two km (1.2 miles) from Reefton, the **Black's Point Museum** exhibits relics from the gold-mining era.

🅷 School of Mines
Shiel St. 【 *(03) 732 8391.* 🔾
by arrangement. 🅰 🅱 🅲
🏛 Black's Point Museum
State Hwy 7. 【 *(03) 732 8391.*
🔾 *Wed–Sun.* ● *25 Dec.* 🅰 🅱

KAIKOURA
North Road   Reeces Road
⑨

Karamea ⑩

Road map C4. 🚶 700. 🚌
ℹ Market Cross, (03) 782 6652.
🎭 Wearable Art Awards (Sep),
Whitebaiters Ball (Oct).

SETTLED BY EUROPEANS in
1874, Karamea is a small,
sprawling beachside village
that lies at the northern end
of the West Coast's State
Highway 67. Nestled in a
basin dominated by dairy
farming and fringed by the
Kahurangi National Park,
Karamea is best known as the
exit point for the Heaphy
Track, which emerges from
the forest 15 km (9 miles) to
the north. A number of short
walking tracks are based
around the Heaphy exit point,
including the 40-minute Nikau
Loop and the 90-minute Scotts
Beach walk.

About 26 km (16 miles) to
the northeast of Karamea is
the **Oparara Basin**, featuring
impressive limestone formations and a 15-km (9-mile)
system of caves enveloped by
dense forest. Much of the
gravel road to the basin is
narrow and winding, but can
be undertaken in a 2WD
vehicle. The highly fragile
Honeycomb Caves system,
first explored in 1980, is
accessible only with a guide,
and contains the remains of
about 50 species, including
the extinct moa and New
Zealand eagle. Areas that can
be explored without a guide

Cows, cabbage trees and beach near Karamea

are the Oparara Arch, 43 m
(141 ft) high and 219 m (719
ft) long, which is reached
after a 20-minute walk on a
good track through the forest,
and the Box Canyon and
Crazy Paving caves. It is
essential to carry a good
torch. For the highly adventurous, local tourist operator
The Last Resort (see p307)
runs grades four and five
white-water rafting trips
down the Karamea River.

Karamea is also a base for
walkers using the increasingly
popular three- to five-day
Wangapeka Track. The
Fenian Track is an historic
gold-miners' route, and the
four-hour return walk leads to
the former mining settlement
of Adams Flat.

🌴 Oparara Basin

State Hwy 67. 📞 (03) 782 6617.
🌐 Honeycomb Caves. 🎫 obligatory
at Honeycomb Caves.

Westport ⑪

Road map C5. 🚶 5,300. ✈ 3 km (2
miles) N of town. 🚌 ℹ 1 Brougham
St, (03) 789 6658.

ALTHOUGH WESTPORT'S origins
lie in the gold rush of the
1860s, coal has been its life-
line for much of its history.
Until 1954, coal from mines in
the surrounding mountains
was shipped out through the
town's once busy port at the
head of the Buller River, but
today the bulk is taken by
train to Lyttelton on the east
coast (see p228). The **Coal
Town Museum** at Westport
has extensive exhibits

reconstructing aspects of the
region's coal-mining heritage.

Westport is a base for a
number of outdoor activities.
Among the most popular is
underground rafting in the
Nile River Canyon area. This
can be done only with a
guide and involves floating in
inner tubes through glow-
worm grottos and caverns
before emerging into the
open to float down the
Waitakere River rapids and
Nile River Canyon. The Metro
Cave, which has dramatic
limestone stalactite and
stalagmite formations, can be
explored on foot.

**Seals at Tauranga Bay, near
Westport**

Westport's North Beach and
Carter's Beach are both
popular swimming and surfing spots, as is the scenic
Tauranga Bay. On the Cape
Foulwind Walkway at the
edge of Tauranga Bay is a
breeding colony of fur seals
(see p191). The walkway,
which takes three hours
return, crosses rocky granite
bluffs, grassy downs, swampy
streams and sandy beaches.

🏛 Coal Town Museum

Lower Queen St. 📞 (03) 789 8204.
🕐 daily. ⬤ 25 Dec. 🎫 ♿

**Nikau Loop at the exit to the
Heaphy Track**

West Coast Coal-Mining Heritage

Miner's Hall near Runanga, Greymouth

COAL WAS FIRST discovered on the West Coast by explorer Thomas Brunner in 1848. The largest of the early mines were on the Denniston and Stockton plateaus, north-east of Westport, where large-scale exploitation began in 1878. The task of extracting coal from the rugged, mountainous terrain was hazardous, and necessitated some striking feats of engineering. The most famous was the Denniston Incline, a gravity-powered rail system under which laden coal trucks were lowered 520 m (1,700 ft) down the mountainside on a steel cable. Empty wagons were pulled back up by the weight of full wagons. The incline closed in 1967, but during its 87 years of operation it carried 13 million tonnes of coal off the Denniston Plateau. The coal industry continues to be important to the West Coast economy, with over 1.5 million tonnes exported from the coalfields each year.

EARLY MINING TOWNS

Several mining settlements sprang up in the 19th century to support the coal industry, but they are little more than ghost towns today. The 120-km (75-mile) self-guided Buller Coalfields Heritage Trail leads through many mining relics, including the once thriving towns of Denniston, Stockton and Millerton. Information on the trail is available at the information centre in Westport.

Coal wagon on steel tracks for transporting coal in and out of the mine

The entrance, carefully reinforced to prevent collapse

Coal miners at the entrance to the Rewanui coal mine

This aerial ropeway is used to lower coal from the opencast Stockton mine down to the coastal settlement of Ngakawau, where it is loaded onto trains bound for the port of Lyttelton on the east coast.

Coal wagons like this one in the Coal Town Museum were used to bring coal down from the mountainous coalfields.

Among the many relics that remain at Denniston, the marshalling point for coal from all over the plateau, are retaining rock walls where coal would be screened before being lowered down the incline, and parts of machinery.

Paparoa National Park ⓬

Road map C5. 🅿 🛈 *State Hwy 6, Punakaiki, (03) 731 1895.*

Founded in 1987, this 300-sq-km (115-sq-mile) park contains varied and dramatic scenery, the most famous of which are the Pancake Rocks and blowholes near the small coastal settlement of Punakaiki. Bands of limestone, separated by thin bands of softer mudstone, which has been worn away by thousands of years of rain, wind and sea spray, have created the layered formations of the Pancake Rocks. Over hundreds of thousands of years, caverns have also been formed as carbon dioxide-bearing rainwater has gradually eaten into cracks in the limestone. During high seas, these subterranean caverns become blowholes as the waves surge in under huge pressure and explode in a plume of spray. The Pancake Rocks and blowholes are easily accessible from the main highway, including by wheelchair, via the short Dolomite Point walk.

Other short walks as well as longer tramps are available in the park, including the 15-minute Truman Track through subtropical forest to a wild coastline featuring caverns, a blowhole and waterfall, and the two-hour walk to a huge limestone structure known as "the ballroom overhang". A two- to three-day tramp through the heart of the park follows a pack track, built in 1867 to avoid dangerous travel along the isolated and rugged coastline.

Greymouth ⓭

Road map C5. 🛤 *13,500.* 🚌 ✈ 🛈 *Cnr Herbert & Mackay sts, (03) 768 5101.*

The largest town on the West Coast, Greymouth occupies the site of what was once Mawhera Pa. Although colonial government agents purchased the majority of the West Coast in 1860 for £300, the land under modern Greymouth remained a Maori reserve. Greymouth was laid out in 1865. Around this time, gold was being found in large quantities in the area, and coal had been discovered 17 years earlier. When the gold boom ended, coal mining ensured the district's continued survival. However, the Grey River mouth, which has served the town as a port, has also delivered misfortune. Repeatedly throughout its history, Greymouth has been submerged by flood waters, including twice in 1988. Since then a flood wall has been erected, popularly called "the great wall of Greymouth".

Greymouth's **History House Museum** has a large collection of historical photographs giving insight into the town's heritage. The **Left Bank Art Gallery** features an important greenstone collection, crafted in both contemporary and traditional designs, and hosts a major exhibition every two years. It also displays local art works.

Like other West Coast towns, Greymouth offers a range of adventure tourism activities, including floating

Left Bank Art Gallery

through the Taniwha Caves on inflated tubes, and dolphin watching along the coast. The Grey River system is known for good fishing.

🏛 **History House Museum**
Gresson St. 📞 *(03) 768 4028.* ◐ *Summer: daily; Winter: Mon–Fri.* ● *25 Dec.* 📷 ♿
🏛 **Left Bank Art Gallery**
1 Tainui St. 📞 *(03) 768 0038.* ◐ *daily.* ● *25 Dec, 1 Jan.* 📷 ♿ *by arrangement.* 🅿

Pancake Rocks at Dolomite Point, Punakaiki

Street in Shantytown, a replica gold-mining town

ENVIRONS: One of Greymouth's most popular attractions is **Shantytown**, 11 km (7 miles) south. This elaborate replica gold-mining town includes a 1913 steam train which travels through native bush to a working sawmill and gold claim where visitors can try gold panning, guaranteed of finding at least a few specks of gold.

Lake Brunner, a restful, scenic spot surrounded by bush-clad mountains 42 km (26 miles) from Greymouth, is excellent for trout fishing, boating and water sports. The lake area is serviced by the small township of Moana, which features a **Kiwi House and Conservation Park** with a collection of rare native birds and exotic animals.

Shantytown
Rutherglen Rd. ((03) 762 6634.
◯ daily. ● 25 Dec. ⊠ & ⑪ ◻
♣ **Kiwi House and Conservation Park**
Dobsons Rd. ((03) 738 0405.
◯ daily. ⊠ & ✆

Hokitika ⑭

Road map C5. ⚄ 3,600. ✈ 2 km (1.2 miles) N of town. ⊟ ⑈
Carnegie Library, Hamilton St, (03) 755 6166. ⚅ Wildfoods Festival (Mar).

W ITH ITS wide streets, notable historic buildings and excellent local craft studios, Hokitika is perhaps the West Coast's most attractive town. Little more than a shanty town in 1864, by 1866 Hokitika had become a thriving commercial centre thanks to gold. Its river port bustled with ships bearing miners flocking from the

goldfields of Australia, but it was a treacherous harbour where a ship went down every 10 weeks in the years 1865 and 1866. The wreck of one such ship is on the self-guided Hokitika Heritage Trail, which includes 22 historic buildings and sights. The most impressive of these is the 1908 Carnegie Library, now the home of the town's information centre and the **West Coast Historical Museum**. The museum has comprehensive displays on gold-mining and an informative audiovisual display of the town's history. It also houses a collection of rare books about the West Coast.

Westland's Water World is a small aquarium specializing in native fish species, including the adult version of the tiny whitebait for which the

Hokitika clock tower

West Coast's rivers are renowned. The remarkable Glowworm Dell, on the northern edge of the town, is worth a visit after dark. The best time to view the lights exuded by these carnivorous larvae is on a wet night.

🏛 **West Coast Historical Museum**
Carnegie Library, Hamilton St.
((03) 755 6898. ◯ daily. ●
25 Dec. ⊠ &
↣ **Westland's Water World**
Sewell St. ((03) 7555 251. ◯
daily. ● 1 Jan, 25 Dec. ⊠ & ✆

ENVIRONS: There are a number of scenic areas around Hokitika. **Lake Mahinapua**, 10 km (6 miles) south, and **Lake Kaniere**, 20 km (12 miles) east of the town, are peaceful retreats, popular for boating, fishing, swimming and bush walking. The Lake Kaniere Walkway is 13 km (8 miles) and takes about four hours.

Ross township, 28 km (17 miles) south of Hokitika, has a small local museum devoted to its colourful gold-mining history. Walks take visitors past old gold mine workings. New Zealand's biggest gold nugget was discovered here in 1909, and the area – said still to contain many millions of dollars worth of gold – is again being mined.

GREENSTONE

Nephrite jade *(pounamu)*, locally known as greenstone, is a hard, opaque, emerald stone. Formed in alpine fault lines under intense heat and pressure, greenstone boulders are eventually flushed from the eroding mountains into West Coast rivers. Greenstone holds great spiritual significance for

Artisan at the Mountain Jade Greenstone Factory

the Maori people. Long before European colonization, tribes sent missions to search for the precious stone, later bartering it for food and other items. It was the hardest material known to Maoris and was used for making tools, weapons and items of personal adornment. In 1997, ownership of the greenstone resource on the West Coast was handed back to the South Island Ngai Tahu tribe as part of a major Treaty of Waitangi settlement *(see p51)*.

Westland National Park ⑮

STRETCHING FROM the top of the Southern Alps in the east, where it shares a common boundary with Aoraki/Mount Cook National Park, to the Tasman Sea in the west, this 1,175-sq-km (450-sq-mile) national park is renowned for its mountain peaks (which reach a height of 3,500 m or 11,500 ft), dramatic glaciers, dense rainforest, coastal lagoons and beautiful lakes. Although the park contains about 60 glaciers, the most famous are the Franz Josef and the Fox. Despite the intrusions of the West Coast gold rush of the 1860s and pastoral farming on the river flats, the area has remained largely unspoiled.

Warning sign, Fox Glacier

Ski touring
This is one of the best ways to experience the glaciers in the park. Ski-plane and helicopter tours also allow stunning views.

Gillespies Beach, a historic gold-mining settlement 20 km (12 miles) from Fox Glacier, offers walks along an early miners' track and to a fur seal colony along the beach.

TASMAN SEA

Gillespies Point

Gillespies Cook River Road

Lak Gau

Cook River

Cook Fla

KARANGARUA FOREST

Karangarua River

6

COPLAND RANG

Copland Track

Copland Rive

★ **Lake Matheson**
On clear, still mornings, Mount Cook and Mount Tasman are reflected in the lake, which is enveloped by forest.

The Copland Valley Track, accessible from State Highway 6, is popular with trampers. For experienced climbers, the track continues over the Copland Pass and ends at Mount Cook village.

ROCKY RANGE

HOOKER R

KEY

▬▬	State highway
═══	Minor road
═══	River
‑ ‑	Walking track
‑ ‑	Park boundary
ℹ	Tourist information
🏞	Picnic area

STAR SIGHTS

★ **Fox Glacier**

★ **Franz Josef Glacier**

★ **Lake Matheson**

Lowland rainforest
The park's extremely high rainfall (5,000 mm or 200 inches a year at Franz Josef village) supports lush, densely ferned lowland podocarp forest, featuring local species.

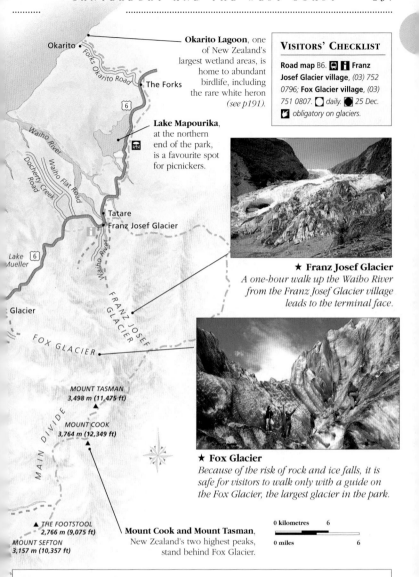

Okarito Lagoon, one of New Zealand's largest wetland areas, is home to abundant birdlife, including the rare white heron *(see p191)*.

Lake Mapourika, at the northern end of the park, is a favourite spot for picnickers.

VISITORS' CHECKLIST

Road map B6. 🚌 🛈 Franz Josef Glacier village, *(03) 752 0796;* Fox Glacier village, *(03) 751 0807.* ◯ *daily.* ● *25 Dec.* 🚠 *obligatory on glaciers.*

★ Franz Josef Glacier
A one-hour walk up the Waiho River from the Franz Josef Glacier village leads to the terminal face.

★ Fox Glacier
Because of the risk of rock and ice falls, it is safe for visitors to walk only with a guide on the Fox Glacier, the largest glacier in the park.

Mount Cook and Mount Tasman, New Zealand's two highest peaks, stand behind Fox Glacier.

MOUNT TASMAN
3,498 m (11,475 ft)

MOUNT COOK
3,764 m (12,349 ft)

THE FOOTSTOOL
2,766 m (9,075 ft)

MOUNT SEFTON
3,157 m (10,357 ft)

0 kilometres   6
0 miles   6

MOVEMENT OF A GLACIER

Snowline
Crevasses
Subglacial stream
Melted ice
Layers of snow and ice
Equilibrium line
Terminus
River gravel

A glacier is a large body of ice that forms on land and moves slowly downhill at a rate of about 1.5 m (5 ft) a day. Glaciers are fed by snow accumulating in high-altitude basins (névés) where it condenses to form bluish ice. This ice field flows downhill under its own weight, cracking into a jumble of deep crevasses and collecting moraine (debris) which scours the mountain sides to form U-shaped valleys. The glacier ends at a terminal where the ice melts.

The Franz Josef and Fox glaciers, both about 13 km (8 miles) long, are unique in that they descend from regions of perpetual snow to rainforest close to the coast.

Hot-air ballooning on the Canterbury Plains ▷

Arthur's Pass Driving Tour ⓰

Arthur's pass road is the highest and most spectacular highway across the Southern Alps. From Springfield, the road climbs steeply to the 945-m (3,100-ft) Porters Pass before travelling through wide, tussock-covered basins hemmed by mountains and past dramatic limestone outcrops. Entering the eastern flank of Arthur's Pass National Park, the road is enveloped by mountain beech forest. It then climbs to the 924-m (3,030-ft) Arthur's Pass summit, before descending steeply on the western side of the Southern Alps.

Porters Pass and Lake Lyndon ①
This area is characterized by distinctive dryland native fauna. Lake Lyndon is a good bird-watching spot in summer and is also popular with anglers.

Porter Heights Ski Field ②
This is the closest ski area to Christchurch and one of six ski fields along State Highway 73. Other than Porters, all are small fields run by local ski clubs where visitors are welcome.

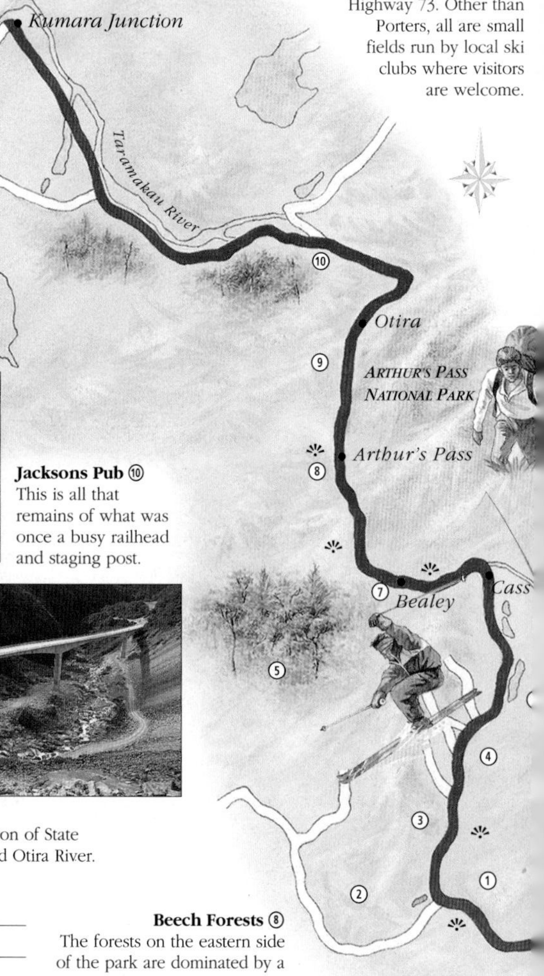
Kumara Junction
Hokitika
Taramakau River
Otira
Arthur's Pass National Park
Arthur's Pass
Bealey
Cass

OPEN
FOOD
BAIT

Jacksons Pub ⑩
This is all that remains of what was once a busy railhead and staging post.

Otira Viaduct ⑨
Completed in 1999, this section of State Highway 73 spans the rugged Otira River.

Key

- Tour route
- Other roads
- River
- Viewpoint

Beech Forests ⑧
The forests on the eastern side of the park are dominated by a canopy of mountain beech, and thus are dramatically different from the dense and varied forests on the western side.

Castle Hill ③
The large limestone rock formations of Castle Hill are eerily impressive, and very popular with rock climbers. The area has historical significance to Maoris as a seasonal food-gathering spot and as part of the route used by Maoris to reach the West Coast.

Tips for Drivers

Tour length from Springfield to Kumara Junction: *160 km (100 miles). This is an alpine route that is sometimes closed after snow, and drivers should check conditions.*
Stopping-off points: *There are many scenic viewpoints and lay-bys along the route. Arthur's Pass is the only township offering services between Kumara and Springfield, although there are hotels at Jacksons and Bealey.*

Cave Stream ④
This 360-m (1,180-ft) limestone cave takes about two hours to navigate, and requires sturdy footwear, warm clothing and a good torch.

Craigieburn Forest Park ⑤
The beech-covered hills in the park are popular spots for walking, picnicking and mountain biking.

Lake Pearson ⑥
Lake Pearson and nearby Lake Grasmere are both good trout fishing spots. Lake Pearson is also known for its beautiful mountain reflections.

Bealey Spur ⑦
A rustic cluster of holiday homes marks Bealey Spur, at the fringe of Arthur's Pass National Park.

ringfield

0 kilometres 20
0 miles 20

The road to Arthur's Pass

Arthur's Pass ⓱

Road map C5. 👥 *50.* 🚆 🚌 🚍
ℹ *State Hwy 73, Arthur's Pass, (03) 318 9211.*

The tiny village of Arthur's Pass is nestled in the Bealey Valley about 5 km (3 miles) east of the summit of Arthur's Pass. It was originally the camping site of contractors engaged to push the road through from Christchurch to the West Coast in 1865–6. In 1908, workers at Arthur's Pass village and at Otira, on the western side of the Main Divide, began construction of the 8-km (5-mile) Otira rail tunnel. In 1912, the population of Arthur's Pass had swelled to about 300, comprised mainly of tunnel workers. It took 10 years for the two ends of the tunnel to meet, and another five years before the first train travelled through it. A number of tunnellers' cottages remain in the village, now used as private holiday homes.

Since the 1920s, the village has been a base for day-trippers from Christchurch and Greymouth, walkers, trampers, and mountaineers, as well as skiers who enjoy the splendid views and low-key atmosphere of the nearby Temple Basin ski field. It is also the headquarters of Arthur's Pass National Park *(see pp242–3).*

An original tunneller's cottage at Arthur's Pass village

Arthur's Pass National Park ⑱

Alpine plant

STRADDLING THE Southern Alps 153 km (95 miles) from Christchurch and 98 km (60 miles) from Greymouth, the 1,170-sq-km (450-sq-mile) Arthur's Pass National Park, the sixth largest in the country, is a place of huge geological and climatic contrasts. On the western side of the alps, where the rainfall is high, the park is clad in dense and varied rainforest through which steep, boulder-strewn rivers rush; on the drier eastern side, mountain beech forests and tussock-covered river flats predominate. Sixteen mountain peaks in the park exceed 2,000 m (6,560 ft). The park offers the well-equipped outdoor enthusiast superb mountain climbing and tramping opportunities, as well as many shorter walks suitable for people of all ages and fitness levels.

★ **Dobson Nature Walk**
This 30-minute walk on the Arthur's Pass summit gives an excellent introduction to the area's alpine and subalpine plants, which bloom from November to February.

Bealey Valley
A tramping track leads from State Highway 73 through mountain beech forest to the beautiful Bealey Valley. It takes about three to four hours' return to complete the walk.

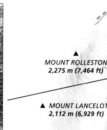

Otira Track
Otira River
ARTHUR'S PASS
924 m (3,030 ft)
Upper Tv
▲ MOUNT ROLLESTON
2,275 m (7,464 ft)
Bealey River
Bridal Ve
Walk
▲ MOUNT LANCELOT
2,112 m (6,929 ft)
Cons Tre
Scotts Track
Punc
Mt A
AVALANCHE PEAK ▲
1,833 m (6,014 ft)
Avalanche
Peak Track
Ar
Pa

★ **Devil's Punchbowl Waterfall**
Although the top of this 131-m (430-ft) waterfall can be seen from the main road, a one-hour walk from Arthur's Pass village takes visitors to the base of the falls.

Crow River

▲ MOUNT BEALEY
1,836 m (6,024 ft)

Waimakarin River

Keas
These cheeky, inquisitive alpine parrots are sometimes seen in Arthur's Pass village, pecking the rubber from around car windscreens.

STAR SIGHTS

★ **Devil's Punchbowl Waterfall**

★ **Dobson Nature Walk**

VISITORS' CHECKLIST

Road map C5. 🚊 🚌
ℹ️ Arthur's Pass village, (03) 318
9211. ⏱ daily. ⬤ 25 Dec.
♿ in village only; not on tracks.
🍴 🚻 📷
🌐 www.doc.govt.nz

Temple Basin

*Trampers can enjoy great
views of Temple Basin's
mountains and valleys.
In winter, the ski field is
accessible only by foot.*

FLORA AND FAUNA IN ARTHUR'S PASS NATIONAL PARK

As well as the impressive mountain beech forests in the east and mixed rainforest in the west, the park contains a wide variety of alpine and subalpine plant species, including tussock, snow grass, alpine daisies and herbs, sedge and ourisia. The park is also rich in birdlife, and species such as the paradise shelduck, bellbird, silvereye, fantail, kea and rifleman are often seen or heard. The area is home to a number of rare species, including the alpine rock wren, blue duck and spotted kiwi.

Blue ducks

MOUNT TEMPLE
1,913 m (6,276 ft)

MOUNT AIKEN
1,859 m (6,099 ft)

▲
MOUNT OATES
2,041 m (6,696 ft)

▲ **MOUNT WILLIAMS**
1,718 m (5,636 ft)

...ingtha River

Edwards River

0 kilometres   5

0 miles   5

KEY

▰▰▰	State highway
══	Minor road
≈≈	River
= =	Walking track
——	TranzAlpine route
– –	Tunnel
ℹ️	Tourist information
Ⓐ	Camp site
🏕	Picnic area
⛷	Skiing
⚹⚹	Viewpoint

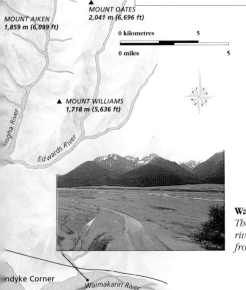

Waimakariri River

*The sinuous strands of this mighty
river transport rock and shingle
from the Southern Alps (see p189).*

...ndyke Corner

Waimakariri River

...EALEY SPUR ▲
...m (3,018 ft)   Bealey Spur

TIPS FOR WALKERS

*The valleys, alpine passes and
scree- and tussock-covered
mountainsides of the park offer
a range of graded walks, from
short, easy strolls to demanding
climbs. However, the climate in
the park is highly changeable
and many routes rudimentary, so
it is important for tramping and
climbing parties to register their
intentions with the visitor centre
at Arthur's Pass village.*

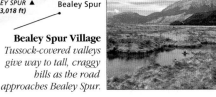

Bealey Spur Village

*Tussock-covered valleys
give way to tall, craggy
hills as the road
approaches Bealey Spur.*

Mount Hutt ski field with Lake Coleridge in the distance

Mount Hutt ⓳

Road map C6. 🚌 🛈 *Main St, Methven, (03) 302 8955.* 📷
New Zealand Walking Festival (Apr).

Mᴏᴜɴᴛ ʜᴜᴛᴛ, in the foothills of the Southern Alps, is Canterbury's largest ski field, and claims to have the longest ski season in Australasia (early June to mid-October). The ski field is served by nine lifts and tows, as well as artificial snow-making facilities. From the 2,075-m (6,808-ft) mountain, there are excellent views over the Canterbury Plains.

Enᴠɪʀᴏɴs: The town of **Methven** serves as Mount Hutt's après-ski centre in winter, and reverts in summer to a typical New Zealand farming town. The 42-sq km (16-sq mile) Mount Hutt Conservation Area, 14 km (9 miles) west of the town, has a number of short walking tracks through native forest dominated by mountain beech. The Rakaia Gorge, about 16 km (10 miles) north of Methven, is popular for jet-boating. A 5-km (3-mile) walkway traverses its edge.

Rakaia ⓴

Road map C6. 🚌 *800.* 🚌 📷
Rakaia Salmon Fishing Competition (end Feb).

Lᴏᴄᴀᴛᴇᴅ ᴏɴ ᴛʜᴇ southern bank of the Rakaia River, the small farming settlement of Rakaia claims to be "the salmon capital of New Zealand". A large fibreglass

fish in the middle of the township celebrates the excellent salmon and trout fishing to be had at various spots along the river.

Bridge over the Rakaia Gorge, a popular place for jet-boating

Ashburton ㉑

Road map C6. 🚌 *16,000.* 🚌 🚌
🛈 *The Green, East St, (03) 308 1050.* 📷 *Wheels Week (May).*

Asʜʙᴜʀᴛᴏɴ sᴛʀᴀᴅᴅʟᴇs the Ashburton River and is the principal town in the farming district of mid-Canterbury. The town was named after Lord Ashburton, a member of the Canterbury Association, which settled the province in the 1850s. Although originally dry and tussock covered, irrigation has allowed agriculture to flourish. The well-laid out town has historic brick buildings and many mature trees, including some in the Ashburton Domain. Worth a visit is the **Ashford Craft Village**, which produces and sells a variety of high quality craft work and has a museum housing spinning wheels.

🏠 Ashford Craft Village
427 West St. 📞 *(03) 308 9085.* 🕐
daily. ⬤ *Public hols.* 🚫 *in factory.*
♿ 📷 *required in factory.* 🖥 🔲

Geraldine ㉒

Road map C6. 🚌 *2,000.* 🚌 🛈
34 Talbot St, (03) 693 1006. 📷
Geraldine Festival of Arts (Nov).

Tʜɪs ᴀᴛᴛʀᴀᴄᴛɪᴠᴇ small farming town is a popular stopping point for travellers heading south to the Mackenzie Country. First known as Talbot Forest, then Fitzgerald, and finally Geraldine, in 1866, it began as a sheep run and base for sawmillers. Talbot Forest now refers to the stand of lowland podocarp forest which provides a backdrop to Geraldine. The town has retained many of its historic buildings, such as the 1908 Post Office, which can be viewed on a self-guided walking trail.

Locally produced fruit wines, juices and condiments can be sampled at **Barker's Berry Barn**. The **Vintage Car and Machinery Museum** has cars dating from 1907 to 1953 and tractors from 1874 as well as a large amount of early agricultural machinery.

🏠 Barker's Berry Barn
76 Talbot St. 📞 *0508 227 537.*
🕐 *daily.* ⬤ *25 Dec.* ♿ 🔲
🏛 Vintage Car and Machinery Museum
178 Talbot St. 📞 *(03) 693 6756.*
🕐 *daily.* ⬤ *1 Jan, 25 & 26 Dec.*
📷 ♿ 📷 *by arrangement.*

Enᴠɪʀᴏɴs: The town is a good base for exploring the forests and rivers of mid-Canterbury, including Peel Forest, 22 km (13 miles) north of Geraldine, the Mount Somers Conservation Area, 47 km (29 miles) north, and the Orari, Waihi and Te Moana gorges, 15 km (9 miles) north, which are good spots for swimming, rafting and picnicking.

The Post Office in Geraldine, built in 1908

High Country Farming

WHEN THE "Canterbury Pilgrims" arrived in 1850 to establish their new settlement, they quickly saw the potential of pastoral farming, and the runholders – the farmers who grazed Canterbury's extensive plains, downs and interior – soon became a powerful economic and political force. Although land reform in the late 19th century saw the great estates broken

The hardy merino

up, large high country stations covering many thousands of square kilometres have remained a feature of farming in New Zealand, particularly in Canterbury. Good roads and modern communications have reduced the isolation and harshness of station life, but it remains a unique existence defined by the climate and the topography of the high country and the annual cycle of farming.

THE ANNUAL CYCLE

Stock graze the tussock-covered mountainsides over the summer, and are mustered down to lower ground before winter. This task takes several days and is carried out on horseback or on foot with the aid of teams of highly trained sheepdogs. As shearing, lambing and weaning are completed, stock are released back to the high country for the summer.

Mustering sheep

Shearing is done by skilled teams of contractors, often using manual blade shears which leave a protective layer of wool on the sheep's back. The dominant breed farmed on high county farms is the fine-woolled and hardy merino.

Selling and buying sheep is a serious business at local livestock auctions as sheep farmers seek to buy stock that will improve the quantity and quality of their wool and meat production.

Fodder crops, such as hay and silage, are grown on the farms as supplementary feed for sheep during the cold winter months.

Merino wool from the high country farms of the South Island is very fine, and is used to make luxury knitwear and fine suiting fabrics.

Roast lamb served with vegetables such as baked potatoes and beans remains a favourite traditional meal.

Timaru ㉓

Painting by Goldie in the Aigantighe

ABOUT HALFWAY BETWEEN Christchurch to the north and Dunedin to the south, Timaru is built on rolling hills marking the edge of the Canterbury Plains and is the largest town in South Canterbury. Its name derives from Te Maru, meaning "a place of shelter", denoting its historical importance as a safe haven for Maori canoes travelling the coast. It was a whaling station from 1838. The town centre is built on 0.5 sq km (0.2 sq mile) of land acquired by early settlers George and Robert Rhodes, although settlement did not begin in earnest until 1859. Today, Timaru has the appearance of a sturdy and well-appointed provincial capital, with many notable buildings gracing its commercial heart.

Aigantighe gallery and grounds

🏖 Caroline Bay
 🚫 not in piazza.

From 1877, when Timaru's artificial port was first created, the white sand of Caroline Bay accumulated to form a safe and popular swimming beach. The port flanks the southern end of the beach. Behind the beach is an extensive grassed area, including a children's playground, an aviary, tennis courts and a mini-golf course. The bay is linked to the central city on the hill above by a piazza – a series of staircases and terraced platforms. To the north of the bay are the Benevue Cliffs and the 1877 Timaru Lighthouse, which is still in use.

🏛 Sacred Heart Basilica
7 Craigie Ave. 📞 (03) 684 4263.
⭕ daily. 🕇 daily. ♿

Arguably the most impressive of the many distinguished buildings in Timaru, Sacred Heart Basilica was designed by architect Francis William Petre and built in 1910–11. Its twin towers and large dome overlook the main route south through the city, and house an equally majestic interior featuring stencilled ceilings, large white pillars and stained-glass windows. Petre also designed the Catholic cathedrals in Christchurch and Dunedin.

🏛 Aigantighe
49 Wa-iti Rd. 📞 (03) 688 4424.
⭕ Tue–Sun. ● 1 Jan, Good Fri, 25 Dec. 🚫 ♿ 🅿 by arrangement.

This charming gallery, pronounced "egg and tie" ("at home" in Scottish Gaelic) is housed in a 1908 building bequeathed to the city by Alexander and Helen Grant, Scottish immigrants who had farmed in the Mackenzie Country. It opened as an art gallery in 1956, with much of its collection donated by the Grant family. Its permanent collection includes works by New Zealand and British painters, as well as English and continental china. The well-laid out gallery sits amid a restful garden, which features a permanent exhibition of stone sculptures.

🏛 St Mary's Anglican Church
Church St. 📞 (03) 688 8377.
⭕ Mon–Sat. ● Good Fri, 25 Dec.
🕇 daily. ♿ 🅿

The foundation stone for St Mary's Anglican Church was laid in 1880, and its nave was consecrated in 1886. The interior of the church features high ribbed ceilings, many fine stained-glass windows, intricate wooden carvings and sturdy columns.

Many of the art pieces and plaques in the church bear the names of influential colonial families in South Canterbury. Steps in the tower can be climbed for an excellent view of the city.

RICHARD PEARSE

Inventor, aviator and farmer, Richard Pearse (1877–1953) has for decades been at the centre of debate about who was the first to achieve powered flight. Pearse was born near Temuka, north of Timaru, and although ridiculed in his lifetime, has been posthumously recognized as an inventive genius. In his farm workshop he constructed a monoplane of bamboo, aluminium, wire and canvas. His first flight in the aircraft is said to have covered 46–91 m (150–300 ft), ending with a crash into a hedge. No records were kept of the flight, but there is some eyewitness evidence that it occurred on 31 March 1903 – about nine months before the 13 December 1903 flight of Orville and Wilbur Wright, officially regarded as the first in the world. Some people even put the date at 1902.

Replica of Pearse's monoplane

Roses in the Timaru Botanical Gardens

♣ Timaru Botanical Gardens

Queen St. 🔲 *(03) 684 8199.* 🔲 *daily.* 🔲
Set aside as a public park in 1864, the gardens have several notable features, including a 1913 statue of Scottish poet Robert Burns, a cabbage tree believed to date from pre-European times, and a 1911 band rotunda. The existing conservatory complex, built in 1983, houses desert, tropical and subtropical collections.

🏛 South Canterbury Museum

Perth St. 🔲 *(03) 684 2212.* 🔲 *Tue –Sun.* 🔲 *1 Jan, 25 Dec.* 🔲 🔲
This octagonal-shaped museum, opened in 1966, is the main regional museum.

Its collections cover the natural history of the area, the early whaling industry and European settlement. The development of the city is shown in a series of photographs. A highlight is a replica of the airplane built by Temuka farmer Richard Pearse, who is believed to have successfully flown in 1903, possibly before the Wright brothers in the US. The plane is suspended from the ceiling at about the height at which Pearse is thought to have flown.

ENVIRONS: Temuka, about 18 km (11 miles) north of Timaru, is the service centre for a rich farming hinterland, and is also the home of the well-known **Temuka Pottery** works, which makes a wide range of high-quality household ceramics.

State Highway 8 to Tekapo passes through the small township of Pleasant Point, where the **Pleasant Point Railway and Historical Museum** retains a 2-km (1.2-mile) section of the old

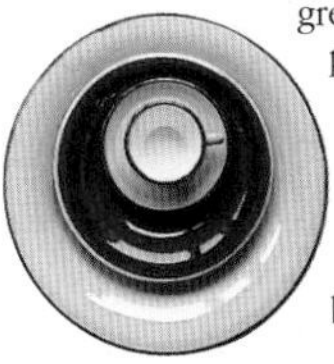

Temuka pottery

VISITORS' CHECKLIST

Road map C6. 🏠 *27,500.*
✈ *12 km (7 miles) N of city.*
🚉 🚌 🛈 *14 George St, (03) 688 6163.* 🎭 *Caroline Bay Carnival (Dec–Jan); Fish Fest (third Sun in Feb).*

Timaru to Fairlie line, established in 1875 and closed in 1968. Two steam locomotives ply the track on school and public holidays. The road winds through rolling green farmland and passes through the small towns of Cave, Fairlie and Kimbell, and the turn-off to Mount Dobson Ski Field, before reaching Burke Pass, the entrance to the Mackenzie Country.

🏺 Temuka Pottery

Thomas St. 🔲 *(03) 615 7719.* 🔲 *daily.* 🔲 *Good Fri, Easter Sun, 25 Apr, 25 Dec.* 🔲 *in factory.* 🔲 *obligatory.*

🚉 Pleasant Point Railway and Historical Museum

Main Rd. 🔲 *(03) 686 2269.* 🔲 *variable.* 🔲 🔲

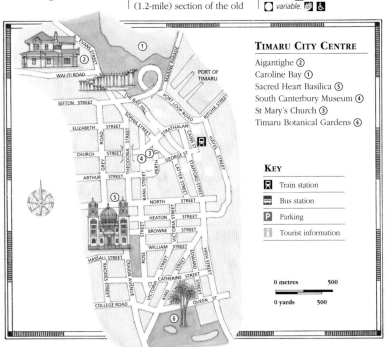

TIMARU CITY CENTRE

Aigantighe ②
Caroline Bay ①
Sacred Heart Basilica ⑤
South Canterbury Museum ④
St Mary's Church ③
Timaru Botanical Gardens ⑥

KEY

🚉	Train station
🚌	Bus station
🅿	Parking
🛈	Tourist information

| 0 metres | 500 |
| 0 yards | 500 |

Lupins on the shores of Lake Tekapo

Lake Tekapo ㉔

Road map B6. 🏔 300. 🚌 ℹ *Kiwi Treasures, State Hwy 8, (03) 680 6686.*

LAKE TEKAPO is a place of exceptional beauty and clarity. The remarkable blue of the lake is caused by "rock flour" – finely ground particles of rock brought down by the glaciers at the head of the lake and held in suspension in the melt water. The lake is a very popular venue for fishing, boating, kayaking, swimming and hang-gliding.

On the lake front stands the Church of the Good Shepherd. The foundation stone of this stone-and-oak church was laid in 1935 by the Duke of Gloucester. The front window of the church creates a perfect frame for a view of the lake. Next to the church is a bronze statue of a sheep dog, erected in 1968 as a tribute to the important role played by these animals in the development of high country farming.

Because of the purity of the atmosphere above Lake Tekapo, the University of Canterbury has an observatory atop Mount John to the west of the township. There is a popular walkway to the top of the mountain (about three hours return). Cowan's Hill Track (about two hours) also provides good views of the lake and mountains.

Lake Tekapo town is a good base for skiing at Mount Dobson, about 30 km (18 miles) away, while the town's small tourist airport is also a base for scenic flights over Mount Cook. Lake Alexandrina, 10 km (6 miles) from Tekapo, is renowned for its trout fishing and is also a popular swimming spot.

⛪ Church of the Good Shepherd
Pioneer Drive. 📞 *(03) 680 6871.* 🕐 *daily.* ⬤ *25 Dec, weddings.* 🕐 *variable.* 📷 *donation.* ♿ ✉

Lake Pukaki ㉕

Road map B6.

LIKE LAKE TEKAPO, Lake Pukaki is a place of majestic scenery. State Highway 8 hugs the southern tip of the lake, and a large and popular lay-by and picnic area allows stunning views of Mount Cook and the Southern Alps. The lake is fed by the Tasman River, which flows off the Tasman Glacier. It has been artificially raised as part of the Upper Waitaki hydroelectricity network and is linked by canals to Lake Tekapo and Lake Ohau. On a clear day, Mount Cook is reflected in the waters of the lake.

The **Mount Cook Salmon Farm** on the Pukaki–Tekapo canal sells fresh salmon and offers tours.

Glentanner Park Centre, about 20 km (12 miles) south of Mount Cook village, on the shores of Lake Pukaki, is a major base for flightseeing over Mount Cook and the surrounding peaks. A range of other outdoor activites run from the centre, including horse trekking, mountain biking, boat trips, hunting and fishing. The centre is set amid Glentanner Station, a

Glentanner Park Centre, backed by the Southern Alps

182-sq-km (70-sq-mile) high country farm. Short tours of the farm allow visitors to see sheep shearing and sheepdog demonstrations.

⚓ Mount Cook Salmon Farm
Heritage Trail. 🕻 *(025) 390 038.*
⭘ *daily.* 🌮 ⚹ 🗹 🎲
♣ Glentanner Park Centre
State Hwy 80. 🕻 *(03) 435 1855.*
⭘ *daily.* 🌮 *for activities.* ⚹ *some activities.*

Twizel ㉖

Road map B6. 🏃 *900.* 🗃 🚹
Market Place, (03) 435 0689.

TWIZEL WAS BUILT in 1969 as a construction town for the Upper Waitaki hydro-electric development scheme. Once the hydro scheme was completed, the local people successfully fought to retain the town, and began to exploit its proximity to excellent fishing and boating lakes, and to Mount Cook 61 km (37 miles) away. Lake Ruataniwha, a man-made lake just south of Twizel, is popular for water sports. It has an international standard rowing course

Black stilt

and is the site of national rowing events every year. From Lake Ruataniwha, a sealed back road leads to Lake Benmore, a 75-sq km (29-sq mile) hydroelectric dam that has also become a favourite boating destination.

One of Twizel's most important attractions is the **Kaki Visitor Hide**. The kaki, or black stilt, is one of the rarest wading birds in the world, and the species has been subject to intensive conservation management since 1981 *(see p190)*. Visitors can take tours to view captive breeding birds from specially designed hides.

🦅 Kaki Visitor Hide
Wairepo Rd. 🕻 *Department of Conservation, (03) 435 0802.*
⭘ *daily.* ⬤ *25 Dec.* 🌮 ⚹
🎲 *obligatory.*

Clay cliffs at Omarama

ENVIRONS: South of Twizel, on State Highway 8, lies the small town of **Omarama**. The town has gained a worldwide reputation for gliding because of its strong northwest thermal updraughts.

About 10 km (6 miles) west of the town are the **Clay Cliffs**, a set of steep, high pinnacles separated by deep, narrow ravines. The cliffs are believed to have been frequented by early Maoris travelling into the Mackenzie Country to hunt. Although privately owned, the cliffs are protected by covenant, and are accessible to the public.

🏔 Clay Cliffs
Henburn Rd. 🕻 *(03) 438 9780.*
⭘ *daily.* 🌮

Lake Ohau ㉗

Road map B6.

ABOUT 30 KM (18 miles) to the west of Twizel, Lake Ohau is a popular swimming, fishing and boating spot. The six native forests which surround the lake – the Ohau, Temple, Dobson, Huxley, Hopkins and Ahuriri – also provide excellent tramping and walking opportunities. Many huts are scattered in the forests for the use of more adventurous trampers.

The Ohau ski field, overlooking the western side of the lake, is a commercial ski field serviced by basic facilities, such as a T-bar and platter lift.

UPPER WAITAKI HYDRO DEVELOPMENT SCHEME

The power stations of the Upper Waitaki and Mackenzie Country provide about one-third of New Zealand's hydro-electricity. The idea of harnessing the water resources of the region was first mooted in 1904, and today the vast scheme includes the Tekapo A and B power stations, Ohau A, B and C stations, and Benmore, Aviemore and Waitaki stations. An important feature of the scheme is 58 km (36 miles) of man-made canals, which pool the resources of Lakes Tekapo, Pukaki and Ohau, along which there is an attractive scenic drive. The lakes created by the hydro scheme have become popular venues for water sports.

Lake Benmore from the adjacent hills

Aoraki/Mount Cook National Park ㉘

Mount Cook lily

AORAKI/MOUNT COOK National Park takes its name from Aoraki/Mount Cook, which at 3,764 m (12,349 feet) is New Zealand's highest mountain. It is sacred to the Ngai Tahu tribe of the South Island, and Maori legend has it that the mountain and its companion peaks were formed when a boy named Aoraki and his three brothers came down from the heavens to visit Papatuanuku (Earth Mother) in a canoe. The canoe overturned, and as the brothers moved to the back of the boat they turned to stone. The 700-sq-km (270-sq-mile) area was designated a national park in 1953 and includes 19 peaks over 3,000 m (9,842 feet). Glaciers cover 40 per cent of the park.

Flightseeing
Scenic flights operate from Glentanner Park Centre and Mount Cook airstrip. They fly a range of routes over the park, and many include a landing on a glacier.

★ **Mount Cook**
A premier mountaineering destination, Mount Cook was first climbed in 1894 by New Zealanders Tom Fyfe, George Graham and Jack Clarke.

DOUGLAS PEAK
3,085 m (10,120 ft)

MOUNT TASMAN ▲
3,498 m (11,475 ft)

MOUNT HICKS ▲
3,216 m (10,550 ft)

▲ MOUNT DAM
3,411 m (11,1?

AORAKI/MOUNT C
3,764 m (12,349 ft)

Copland Pass is a high-altitude mountain-eering route across the Southern Alps. From the pass the route travels down the Copland River through Westland National Park *(see pp236–7)* before emerging on State Highway 6.

THE FOOTSTOOL
2,766 m (9,075 ft) ▲

MOUNT SEFTON ▲
3,157 m (10,357 ft)

Hooker

Valley Track

HOOKER GLACIER

MOUNT COOK RANGE

TASMAN GLAC

Hooker River

Tasman Valley Road

Tasman River

MUELLER GLACIER

SEALY RANGE

Mount Cook

Mount Cook Road

80

The Hermitage
First built in 1895, but rebuilt and expanded over the years, The Hermitage is the only hotel in Mount Cook National Park (see p307).

STAR SIGHTS
★ Mount Cook
★ Tasman Glacier

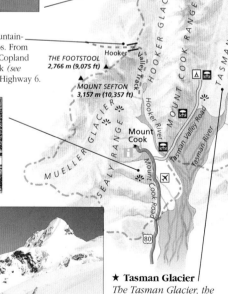

★ **Tasman Glacier**
The Tasman Glacier, the largest in New Zealand, is 29 km (18 miles) long and 1.6 km (1 mile) wide. Heli-skiing is a popular way to experience the glacier.

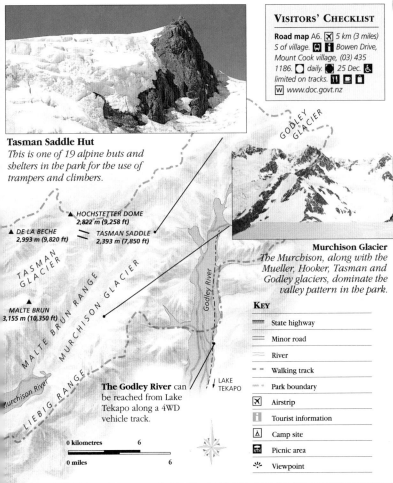

Tasman Saddle Hut
*This is one of 19 alpine huts and
shelters in the park for the use of
trampers and climbers.*

HOCHSTETTER DOME
2,822 m (9,258 ft)

▲ **DE LA BECHE**
2,993 m (9,820 ft)

TASMAN SADDLE
2,393 m (7,850 ft)

Murchison Glacier
*The Murchison, along with the
Mueller, Hooker, Tasman and
Godley glaciers, dominate the
valley pattern in the park.*

▲ **MALTE BRUN**
3,155 m (10,350 ft)

The Godley River can
be reached from Lake
Tekapo along a 4WD
vehicle track.

KEY

▬▬	State highway
═══	Minor road
≈≈	River
– – –	Walking track
– ·· –	Park boundary
✕	Airstrip
ℹ️	Tourist information
⛺	Camp site
🏞️	Picnic area
☀️	Viewpoint

0 kilometres   6
0 miles   6

WALKS FROM MOUNT COOK VILLAGE

There are several walking tracks in the
vicinity of Mount Cook village which are
well formed and signposted. They are
suitable for people who do not have any
climbing experience.

Kea Point and Governors Bush are short
walking trips which focus on the park's
vegetation and birdlife. Longer walks from
the village include the Sealy Tarns, Hooker
Valley, Red Tarns and Wakefield tracks.
Although these tracks are well marked,
the ground is rough in places and it is
advisable to wear stout shoes or boots and
to carry a walking stick. A warm sweater
or jacket is needed for places exposed to
the wind, even during summer.

Brochures on the walks, giving descriptions and walking times, are available at
the visitor centre in the village.

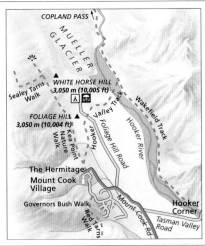

WHITE HORSE HILL
3,050 m (10,005 ft)

FOLIAGE HILL ▲
3,050 m (10,004 ft)

The Hermitage
Mount Cook Village

Governors Bush Walk

OTAGO AND SOUTHLAND

WITH ITS HIGH, SNOW-CAPPED MOUNTAINS, *lush rainforests, dry tussocklands, deep glacial lakes, spectacular beaches and rugged coastlines, the Otago and Southland region is one of extreme natural beauty. Set among the area's untamed wilderness and historic settlements is Queenstown, a world centre for adventure sports and one of New Zealand's foremost tourist destinations.*

Before the arrival of the first Europeans, the Maoris settled in coastal areas where seafood was plentiful, although they also hunted, and collected greenstone *(pounamu)*, in the rugged interior. The first Europeans also looked to coastal areas for an environment that would be easy to tame. Members of the Free Church of Scotland were the first to settle the area in an organized way, making Dunedin the centre of their new land. Hopes of an idyllic enclave were dashed in the early 1860s with the discovery of gold.

Gold-miners poured into the inhospitable lands of what is now known as Central Otago, in search of an elusive fortune. The money gold brought to the region saw it leap ahead, and for a time Dunedin became New Zealand's commercial capital. The legacy of the gold mining era lives on in the humblest of stone cottages on remote and rugged landscapes as well as in the splendid buildings that adorn the streets of Dunedin. The region's natural legacy also lives on in many areas, such as the Mount Aspiring and Fiordland national parks, which remain relatively untapped. They are beautifully complemented by other natural attractions, such as Stewart Island and the Catlins area on the southeast coast, while the farmlands that have been tamed provide an attractive contrast. Such is the variety on offer, that each corner of the region provides its own attractions, making exploration very rewarding.

The Octagon in the heart of Dunedin

◁ **Reflections in the Mirror Lakes, Fiordland National Park**

Exploring Otago and Southland

THE GEOGRAPHY, CLIMATE and scenery of the Otago and Southland region vary greatly over relatively short distances. To the west, the land rises steeply from the coast through thick rainforest to 3,000-m (9,900-ft) high mountain peaks in the space of only 40 km (25 miles) – features that make the Fiordland and Mount Aspiring national parks so spectacular. To the east of these peaks, the ranges and valleys of Central Otago provide a stark contrast. The interior is dry and rugged. Vivid blue lakes nestle among tussock-covered hills and snow-capped mountains to create the scenery and adventure playground that has made resorts such as Queenstown so popular. From the lakes, the land drops down to the eastern and southern coasts and hinterland where extra rainfall has produced fertile farmland to feed the cities of Dunedin and Invercargill.

White-water rafting, Shotover River, Queenstown

SIGHTS AT A GLANCE

Arrowtown 12
Bluff 19
Cromwell 13
Dunedin pp256–7 1
Fiordland National Park pp278–9 15
Glenorchy 11
Gore 18
Haast 9
Invercargill pp284–5 17
Kingston 14
Lake Hawea 6
Lindis Pass 5
Moeraki Boulders Scenic Reserve 3
Mount Aspiring National Park pp270–71 8
Oamaru pp266–7 4
Otago Peninsula 2
Queenstown pp274–5 10
Stewart Island 20
Wanaka 7

Tours
Catlins 21
Doubtful Sound 16

Milford Sound
Tasman Sea
DOUBTFUL SOUND 16
15
FIORDLAND NATIONAL PARK
Lake Manapouri
Dusky Sound
Lake Hauroko
Lake Poteriteri
0 kilometres 25
0 miles 25

TOP OUTDOOR ACTIVITIES

The places shown here have been selected for their recreational activities. Conditions vary depending on the weather and the time of year, so exercise caution and, if in doubt, seek local advice.

	Aerial Sightseeing	Bungy Jumping	Jet-Boating	Paragliding	Skiing	Tramping/Walking	White-Water Rafting	Wildlife Watching
Catlins						■		■
Dunedin	●					■		■
Fiordland National Park	●					■		■
Haast						■		■
Invercargill	●					■		■
Milford Sound	●					■		■
Mount Aspiring National Park	●					■		■
Oamaru						■		■
Otago Peninsula						■		■
Queenstown	●	■	●	■	●	■	●	
Stewart Island	●					■		■
Te Anau	●		●			■		■
Wanaka	●	■	●	■	●	■	●	

KEY

- Motorway
- State Highway
- Major road
- Scenic route
- River
- Viewpoint

The bright blue Lake Hawea, one
of the largest southern lakes

SEE ALSO

- *Where to Stay* pp308–309

- *Where to Eat* p327

GETTING AROUND

Road travel is the main means of getting around the region.
There is a range of bus services along the main routes, and
for those who choose to drive the state highways are good
and generally not too busy, apart from peak holiday periods.
Some roads, such as State Hwy 94 to Milford, require care
because of the mountainous terrain. There are domestic
airports at Dunedin, Invercargill and Queenstown, while
Dunedin also handles some flights from Australia. A daily rail
service along the east coast links the main towns.

Street-by-Street: Dunedin ●

St Paul's Cathedral
St Paul's has the only vaulted stone ceiling in New Zealand (see p258).

Statue of Robert Burns

Dunedin has close historical links with the Scottish city of Edinburgh. Not only is Dunedin the old Gaelic name for Edinburgh, but many of its street names are Scottish and several Scottish traditions have been preserved since the first Presbyterian settlers arrived in 1848. The Octagon, so-called because of its eight sides, gives the city a central focus. Surrounding it, and within a few blocks, are a number of Victorian and Edwardian public buildings, which are among the finest in the country. Visitors can also enjoy the many cafés and restaurants dotted around the area.

Stuart Street Terrace Houses
Built around 1900 as town residences for country folk, these terrace houses are now popular locations for restaurants, boutiques and professional offices.

Dunedin Public Art Gallery *(see p258)*

First Church *(see p259)*

Otago Early Settlers Museum
Early means of transport feature prominently in the museum, including one of the country's first steam engines (see p259).

MORAY PLACE

STREET

BURLINGTON STREET

RATTRAY ST

CUMBERLA

Queens Gardens

STAR SIGHTS

★ **Dunedin Railway Station**

★ **The Octagon**

0 metres   300
0 yards   300

KEY

– – – Suggested route

The Municipal Chambers
Built in 1880 at a time when Dunedin was revelling in the fortune brought by the gold rush, the building is topped by a 47-m (155-ft) high tower (see p258).

VISITORS' CHECKLIST

Road map B7. 120,000.
25 km (16 miles) S of city centre. Limited international flights to and from Australia.
Anzac Ave. Intercity, St Andrew St. 48 The Octagon, (03) 474 3300. Dunedin Festival (3rd week of Feb), Rhododendron Festival (3rd week of Oct).
www.cityofdunedin.com

★ The Octagon
The Octagon is a popular gathering place for small groups who lunch under the trees, and for bigger crowds during festivals and exhibitions.

The Otago Daily Times Building, an interesting piece of 1930s Art Deco architecture, is the home of New Zealand's oldest newspaper.

Law Courts *(see p259)*

Prison *(see p259)*

★ Dunedin Railway Station
Perhaps the finest stone structure in the country, the station has a 37-m (120-ft) high square tower, three huge clock faces and a covered carriageway (see pp260–61).

Central Dunedin

Bronze penguin

ONE OF THE joys of exploring Dunedin is that there is a great deal to see in a relatively small area. Its buildings are among the most interesting and architecturally diverse in the country. Many that have survived from Dunedin's heyday following the 1860s gold rush, when the city was the country's commercial centre, are within walking distance of the centre. Others are to the north of the city *(see pp262–3)* in proximity to Dunedin's many beautiful parks and gardens. The flat central city, which remains the retail hub, is surrounded by hills, which afford a splendid view of the city and harbour below.

St Paul's Cathedral

🌺 The Octagon

When the site of the settlement of "New Edinburgh" was first surveyed in 1846 by its Edinburgh-based surveyors, The Octagon was planned as the focal point. More than 150 years later, The Octagon continues to fulfil that role. It has watched over a passing parade of festivals, protests, parties and royal visits, as well as seeing local troops and sporting heroes alike waved off and welcomed.

This small oasis in the heart of the city – a popular lunchtime spot – is surrounded by a number of fine buildings. A large bronze statue of Scottish poet Robert Burns, erected in 1887, has a prominent place in front of St Paul's Cathedral. Burns' nephew, the Reverend Thomas Burns, was spiritual leader for the first group of Scottish settlers to arrive in Dunedin in 1848.

🏛 Municipal Chambers

48 The Octagon. 📞 *(03) 477 4000.*
⭕ *Mon–Fri.* ⚫ *public hols.* 📷
inside. ♿ *public areas.*
Completed in 1880, the Municipal Chambers is an excellent example of the use of Oamaru stone *(see pp266–7)*. It has undergone considerable restoration and refurbishment both inside and out. It is home to the Council Chambers, where city councillors meet, and features a number of reception and meeting rooms. It also houses the Dunedin Visitor Centre. The Dunedin Convention Centre and the 2,200-seat Town Hall are located behind it.

✝ St Paul's Cathedral

The Octagon. 📞 *(03) 477 2336.*
⭕ *daily.* ✝ *daily except Sat.* ♿
📷 *Summer.*
Consecrated in 1919, the Anglican St Paul's stands high above The Octagon on an elevated site, with a broad staircase leading to its doors. It owes its prominent position in a predominantly Presbyterian settlement to the generosity of Johnny Jones, an early whaler and trader. The cathedral, which replaced a smaller church built on the site in 1863, has many fine architectural details, including a vaulted stone ceiling.

🏛 Dunedin Public Art Gallery

30 The Octagon. 📞 *(03) 477 4000.*
⭕ *daily.* ⚫ *Good Fri, 25 Dec.* 📷
📷 ♿ 📷 🔲
This modern gallery, designed to harmonize with The Octagon's historic buildings, has one of the best collections of European art in the country. It also has sections on early and contemporary New Zealand arts, including works by the world-renowned Impressionist Frances Hodgkins *(see p30)*.

Entrance foyer of the Dunedin Public Art Gallery

0 metres   300

0 yards   300

KEY

🔲 Dunedin Street-by-Street
see pp 256 – 7

🚆 Train station

🚌 Bus station

🅿 Parking

ℹ Tourist information

🛈 First Church

415 Moray Place. 🕿 (03) 477 7118.
◯ daily. ✝ Sunday only. ♿ 🖼

The flagship of the Presbyterian Church in Otago, First Church, consecrated in 1873, is considered to be architect Robert Lawson's greatest contribution to Dunedin's rich architectural heritage. Of note are its rose window, wooden ceiling and 56-m (184-ft) high spire. The church has undergone considerable restoration work to repair its weathered exterior. Bell Hill, the area on

The Law Courts in Central Dunedin

which First Church stands, had to be lowered by about 12 m (40 ft) in order to accommodate the building.

🎭 Law Courts

41 Stuart St. *Closed to the public.*

These were completed in 1902 to a design by government architect John Campbell. Local Port Chalmers bluestone with lighter Oamaru stone distinguishes the building. Just around the corner, in complete contrast, is the red brick Dunedin Prison, another Campbell design which mimics many aspects of London's

New Scotland Yard, although on a smaller scale. Completed in 1895, it also served as the Dunedin Police Station until a new building was commissioned in the mid-1990s.

🏛 Otago Early Settlers Museum

31 Queens Gardens. 🕿 (03) 477 5052. ◯ daily. ⊗ Good Fri, 25 Dec.
🖼 ♿ 🎁 🖼

As its name suggests, this museum provides a unique window on the lives of the province's early settlers. The displays are many and varied, from early photographs and household goods to implements and vehicles, including two large steam locomotives, one of which dates back to the 1870s. The museum is housed in two adjoining buildings, one a former art gallery, built in the early 1900s, the other a former bus station built in Art Deco style.

Map key

ROBERT LAWSON

Many of Dunedin's finest Victorian and Scottish Edwardian-style buildings are attributed to architect Robert Lawson (1833–1902). The Scottish-born Lawson had trained as an architect in his home country before migrating to Melbourne, where he found little work, and instead made a living from gold-mining and journalism. He took up his profession again in 1861 and the following year won a competition for the design of First Church in Dunedin. Lawson moved to Dunedin and so began a successful association with the city. His list of

First Church

credits includes the Municipal Chambers, Otago Boys High School (a handsome bluestone building completed in 1884) and Knox Church in George, which was consecrated in 1876. However, it was his initial Dunedin design, First Church, which many consider to be his masterpiece.

Dunedin Railway Station

Frieze with cherub and foliage

Dunedin's railway station is one of New Zealand's finest historic buildings and one of the best examples of railway architecture in the southern hemisphere. Although not large by international standards, the station's delightful proportions lend it an air of grandeur. Opened in 1906, the Flemish Renaissance-style building was designed by New Zealand Railways architect George Troup, whose detailing on the outside of the building earned him the nickname "Gingerbread George".

★ Exterior Stonework
Beige Oamaru limestone (see pp266–7) detailing provides a striking contrast to the darker Central Otago bluestone on the walls and the finely polished Aberdeen granite of the columns.

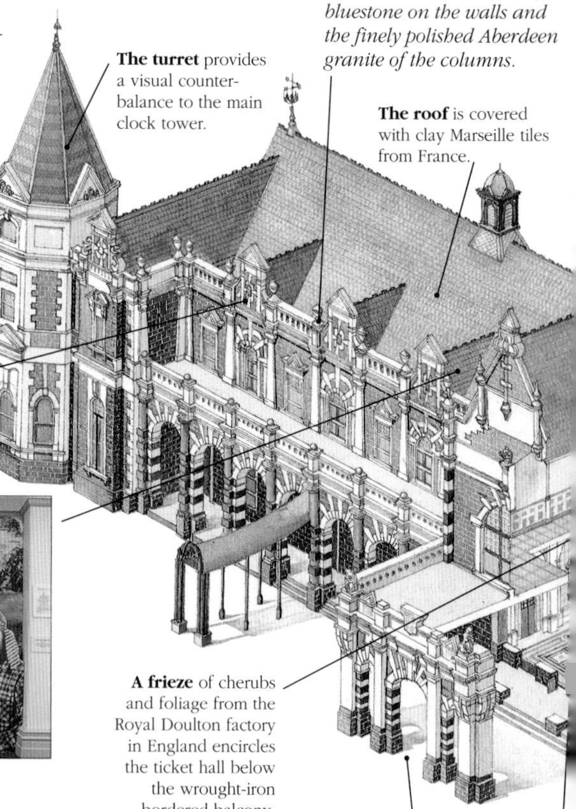

The turret provides a visual counterbalance to the main clock tower.

The roof is covered with clay Marseille tiles from France.

Dormer windows projecting from the sloping gable roof are typical Flemish architectural features.

New Zealand Sports Hall of Fame
This features imaginative displays recounting the exploits and achievements of famous New Zealanders.

A frieze of cherubs and foliage from the Royal Doulton factory in England encircles the ticket hall below the wrought-iron bordered balcony.

Main entrance

Ticket Windows
The ticket windows are ornately decorated with white tiles and a crest featuring the old New Zealand Railways logo.

STAR FEATURES

★ **Exterior Stonework and Carvings**

★ **Mosaic Floor**

★ **Stained-glass Windows**

★ Stained-glass Windows

Two imposing stained-glass windows on the mezzanine balcony depict approaching steam engines, lights blazing, facing each other across the ticket hall.

VISITORS' CHECKLIST

Anzac Ave. *(03) 477 4449.*
◻ *8am–6pm Mon–Fri,*
9am–6pm Sat, Sun & public
hols. ● *25 Dec.* ⬥ 🛈

Finely carved sandstone lions on each corner of the clock tower guard the cupola behind them.

The clock tower rises 37 m (120 ft) above street level.

Staircase

Complete with wrought-iron balustrades and mosaic tiled steps, a staircase sweeps up from the ticket hall to the balcony above.

The platform behind the station is still an arrival and departure point for travellers, as well as visitors taking the Taieri Gorge Railway *(see p262).*

★ Mosaic Floor

More than 725,000 Royal Doulton porcelain squares form images of steam engines, rolling stock and the New Zealand Railways logo.

North Dunedin and Environs

Dunedin's city centre is enclosed by hills to the north and west, and by water – the Otago Harbour and Pacific Ocean – to the east and south. In the north of the city are several green areas, most notably the Botanic Gardens at the foot of Signal Hill, and several historic buildings. A road along the narrow, scenic harbour leads to lookout points providing panoramic views of the city, harbour and peninsula.

🦌 Signal Hill

Signal Hill Rd via Opoho Rd.
⬜ daily. ♿

To the north of the city, the road up Signal Hill leads to a monument built in 1940 to mark 100 years of British sovereignty in New Zealand. From here visitors can get excellent views of the central city, upper harbour and parts of the Otago Peninsula.

♣ Dunedin Botanic Gardens

Opoho Rd. 📞 (03) 471 9275.
⬜ daily. ♿ 🏧 🍴 📷 🎁
Rhododendron Festival (late Oct).

Dunedin's extensive Botanic Gardens were the first to be established in New Zealand, in 1868. The area's varied topography and microclimates are used to grow a diverse range of plants. The flat lower gardens are home to the more formal displays – lawns interspersed with trees and native bush and formal flower gardens – and to the Edwardian Winter Garden, first opened in 1908. On the hill, the upper gardens include more than 3,000 rhododendron varieties in the world-renowned Rhododendron Dell. These provide a springtime feast for the eyes.

🏛 Otago Museum

419 Great King St. 📞 (03) 477 2372.
⬜ daily. ● Good Fri, 25 Dec. 🎟
donation. ♿ 📷 2pm on weekends.
🍴 🎁

The displays in the large, Classical-style Otago Museum, opened in 1877, introduce visitors to the region's human and natural history. There are halls dealing with pre-European Maori life, Pacific culture, marine life, and archaeology of the ancient world. The museum also houses one of New Zealand's leading maritime exhibitions and a quaint Victorian-style "Animal Attic". Particularly exciting for children is the interactive Discovery World science centre.

🦌 Tunnel Beach Walkway

Blackhead Rd. ⬜ daily. ● Aug–Oct.

Located 7 km (4 miles) south of the city, Tunnel Beach is named after the tunnel cut through sandstone cliffs in the 1870s by Edward Cargill so that his family could get down to the pretty beach below. The short but steep walkway to the beach gives breathtaking views of the sandstone cliffs which have been spectacularly sculpted by wind and sea.

University of Otago clock tower

⛪ University of Otago

Leith St. 📞 (03) 479 1100. ⬜
Mon–Fri. ● public hols. ♿ grounds
& public areas.

Founded in 1869, the University of Otago – New Zealand's oldest university – plays a crucial role in the life of the city. The bluestone clock tower registry building dates from 1878 (see p26), while the semi-detached houses close to its northern end were built in 1879 to house the university's first four professors. The grounds are a pleasant place to wander.

🦌 The Organ Pipes

Mount Cargill Rd.

Strange multi-sided basalt columns, known as "the organ pipes", are a reminder of Dunedin's volcanic past. Reaching them requires a walk of at least an hour from a signpost on Mount Cargill Road, north of the city. The panoramic views are a bonus.

🚂 Taieri Gorge Railway

Anzac Avenue. 📞 (03) 477 4449.
⬜ Summer: departs 2:30pm daily;
Winter: departs 12:30pm daily. ●
25 Dec. 🎟 ♿ 🍴 🎁

Departing from Dunedin Railway Station, the train takes passengers on a 60-km (38-mile) four-hour trip west of the city. Opened in 1879, the line passes through the relative greenery of Dunedin's coast, then climbs through a steep-sided river gorge to the arid grasslands and rocky outcrops of the Strath Taieri. It cuts through ten tunnels and crosses bridges and viaducts up to 47 m (155 ft) above the Taieri River.

Rhododendrons in bloom in the Dunedin Botanic Gardens

Olveston House

David Theomin

OLVESTON, a 35-room Jacobean-style mansion, was completed in 1906 for David and Marie Theomin and their children, Edward and Dorothy. Dorothy left the house and its contents to the city and it remains as it was when the family lived in it. Olveston's grand drawing room, dining room, library, billiard room and great hall contain fine furniture and many treasures collected by the Theomins, who were keen travellers.

VISITORS' CHECKLIST

42 Royal Terrace. (03) 477 3320. daily. 25 Dec. ground floor. obligatory; hourly 9:30am–4:00pm.

Exterior Stonework
The double-brick house gets its warm exterior colour from a cladding of Moeraki pebbles with Oamaru stone highlights (see pp266–7).

The kitchen is dominated by a kauri dresser filled with blue and white Delft ware and a kauri table.

Library

★ Dining Room
Attractive features are the oak panelling, semicircular stained-glass windows and richly embossed wallpaper.

The Billard Room has a full-size table and adjustable overhead lights.

Main entrance

Card Room

Dutch gables and projecting windows add architectural interest to the exterior of Olveston.

The Drawing Room, used for entertaining and music, has the only decorated ceiling in the house.

★ Great Hall
A centre for receptions, the hall has oak joinery, printed hessian wall covering featuring acanthus leaves, and a collection of porcelain.

STAR FEATURES

★ Dining Room

★ Great Hall

Otago Peninsula ❷

THE 24-KM (15-MILE) LONG Otago Peninsula offers a wide variety of attractions, including rare and unusual wildlife, historic buildings, woodland gardens and spectacular harbour and coastal scenery. The 64-km (40-mile) round trip, taking the "high" Highcliff Road, which runs over the top of the peninsula, on the outward journey, and returning via the "low" Portobello Road along the coast, can take from 90 minutes to a full day. The Highcliff Road offers the best views of the surrounding waters.

Yellow-eyed penguin

🏰 Larnach Castle
Camp Rd. 📞 (03) 476 1616.
◯ daily. ● 25 Dec. 🎟 ∅ inside.
♿ ground floor. ▯ ▯

Located 20 km (12 miles) from central Dunedin along the "high" road, Lanarch Castle is New Zealand's only castle. Built between 1871 and 1885 for financier, businessman and politician, William J M Larnach, the grand stone mansion, set in 2 sq km (0.8 sq mile) of bush and gardens, is built along Scottish baronial lines. It has many fine features, including elaborately carved and decorated ceilings and a large, hanging staircase, the product of the many English and Italian artisans brought to Dunedin to work on the building. There is also a ballroom, added as a complete wing as a birthday present for Larnach's daughter. Visitors can climb up the narrow stone steps for a view from the top of the tower. Accommodation is available next to the castle (see p308).

From Larnach Castle, the road down to Portobello goes past the turn-off to Lovers Leap and the Chasm, where the surging surf has created a blowhole and natural rock bridge some 220 m (720 ft) below. On the side road to these features are three circular lime kilns from the 1860s used to produce mortar for brickwork.

🔭 Royal Albatross Centre
Taiaroa Head. 📞 (03) 478 0499.
◯ daily. ● 25 Dec. 🎟 ♿ visitor centre only. 📷 except Tue; tours obligatory. ▯ ▯

The prominent Taiaroa headland at the mouth of Otago Harbour is home to the world's only mainland royal albatross colony. Opened in 1989, the centre contains excellent displays of these large birds. During the nesting period, guides take visitors to an observatory where the birds can be seen nesting and flying when the conditions are right. A colony of Stewart Island shags can also be seen from the observatory.

Black and white royal albatrosses at Taiaroa Head

Taiaroa Head's other main attraction is the Armstrong disappearing gun, a 15-cm (6-inch) diameter naval defence gun installed in 1886 during the "Russian scare". Designed to pop out of the ground, fire and then recoil back into its pit, it is the only one of its kind in the world still in working order in its original position.

Larnach Castle viewed from the gardens

Homestead in the Glenfalloch Woodland Gardens

🌿 Glenfalloch Woodland Gardens

430 Portobello Rd. 📞 (03) 476 1006. ☐ daily. 💵 donation. ♿ lower gardens. 📷 ☐

On the "low road", 10 km (6 miles) from Dunedin, the Glenfalloch Woodland Gardens – glenfalloch means "hidden glen" – have been attracting visitors since the 1870s. An elegant homestead, built in 1871, tearooms and a pottery, where pieces that are made on the spot are sold, are sheltered in grounds containing mature trees, shrubs, and a stream. The gardens are ablaze with rhododendrons and azaleas in spring, and in summer they are noted for their colourful displays of fuchsias.

Visitors to Glenfalloch can enjoy several short walking tracks through the trees and woodland gardens. They can also hand-feed peacocks and other semi-tame birds which wander freely in the grounds.

🐟 WestpacTrust Aquarium

Hatchery Rd. 📞 (03) 479 5826. ☐ daily. ● 25 Dec. 💵 ♿ 📷 ☐

Portobello is a peaceful little harbourside settlement with shops and a tavern. Its main claim to fame is the Westpac-Trust Aquarium, formerly the Portobello Aquarium and Marine Biological Station, which is part of the University of Otago's marine research centre. Located at the end of a small peninsula near Portobello, the aquarium features marine life peculiar to the region as well as a "touch tank" for children with starfish, crabs and sea anemones.

⛩ Otakou

Off Harrington Point Rd. ☐ daily. 🚫 inside.

Otakou is the site of one of the earliest Maori settlements in the area, and it was this word which was anglicized to Otago to give the surrounding province its name. The local church and meeting house were built to commemorate the 1940 centenary of the signing of the Treaty of Waitangi (see pp46–7). What appear to be carvings are actually moulded concrete.

Maori church and meeting house at Otakau

🐧 Penguin Place

Harrington Point Rd. 📞 (03) 478 0286. ☐ daily. 💵 📷 obligatory, bookings essential. ☐ 📷

The road to Taiaroa Head passes Penguin Place, an award-winning venture to save the yellow-eyed penguin, the world's rarest species of penguin. Yellow-eyed penguins are found only on the Otago Peninsula and other isolated east coast areas of Otago and Southland. An ingenious system of camouflaged trenches at Penguin Place allows visitors to view nesting yellow-eyed penguins at close range without disturbing them. The birds are most active at dusk.

Moeraki Boulders Scenic Reserve ❸

Road map B7.

T HE MOERAKI BOULDERS, 78 km (49 miles) north of Dunedin on State Highway 1, have long been the subject of legend and curiosity. Almost perfectly spherical, with a circumference of up to 4 m (13 ft), the grey boulders lie scattered along a 50-m (164-ft) stretch of the beach. They were formed on the sea bed about 60 million years ago as lime salts gradually accumulated around a hard core.

Maori legend claims that the boulders were the food baskets or Te Kaihinaki of the Araiteuru canoe, one of the great ancestral canoes that brought the Maoris to New Zealand from Hawaiki. The canoe was wrecked while on a greenstone gathering trip. It is said that the *kumara* on board became rough rocks, the food baskets became smooth boulders, and the wreck turned into a reef.

It is not unusual to see small black and white Hector's dolphins playing in the surf near the boulders. A nearby café and restaurant service the flow of visitors.

The tiny, picturesque fishing village of Moeraki, a former whaling station established in 1836, can be seen on the opposite side of the bay from the reserve.

Spherical boulders on the beach at Moeraki

Street-by-Street: Oamaru ❹

Warehouse window

THE MAIN TOWN OF NORTH OTAGO and service centre for a rich agricultural hinterland, Oamaru is a pretty town with wide, tree-lined streets, well-kept gardens, galleries, beaches, colonies of rare penguins, and the best preserved collection of historic public and commercial buildings in New Zealand. The buildings were fashioned in the 1880s from Oamaru stone, a local cream-coloured limestone which is easily cut, carved and moulded. They present a fascinating picture of a prosperous period when grain stores and warehouses were designed to be as grand as the public and commercial buildings which surrounded them.

★ Forrester Gallery
Ornately carved Corinthian columns distinguish this 1882 building, which formerly housed the Bank of New South Wales.

Courthouse
Built in 1883 and still in use, the Courthouse features a Neo-Classical portico with Corinthian columns.

Meeks Grain Elevator Building (1883)

National Bank (1871)

HUMBER ST

THAMES ST

ITCHIN STREET

OAMARU STONE

★ North Otago Museum
Exhibits in the museum, built in 1882, include displays on the quarrying and use of Oamaru stone.

Oamaru's first Post Office, a small Italianate building with a squat clock tower, was built in 1864.

Colonial Bank (1878)

St Luke's Anglican Church (1865–1913) contains fine interior wood-carving.

STAR SIGHTS

★ **Forrester Gallery**

★ **New Zealand Loan and Mercantile Warehouse**

★ **North Otago Museum**

Waitaki District Council
Originally Oamaru's second post office (1883), the building's 28-m (92-ft) clock tower was added in 1903.

Criterion Hotel
Built in 1877, this hotel went "dry" in 1906 during prohibition. Now restored, it serves patrons in a Victorian pub atmosphere.

Harbour Board Office (1876)

Harbour Street
At the heart of the port area, this street is lined with 19th-century warehouses, commercial buildings and grain stores.

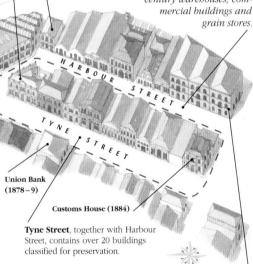

HARBOUR STREET

TYNE STREET

Union Bank (1878–9)

Customs House (1884)

Tyne Street, together with Harbour Street, contains over 20 buildings classified for preservation.

0 metres 100
0 yards 100

KEY

– – – Suggested route

★ **New Zealand Loan and Mercantile Warehouse**
This three-storey Victorian warehouse, built in 1882 for New Zealand's largest stock and station agency, was designed to hold up to 100,000 sacks of grain.

View of Oamaru and the harbour from Lookout Reserve

Exploring Oamaru
Apart from its historic harbour precinct, Oamaru has several scenic and natural attractions. The 1-km (0.6-mile) South Hill Walkway above the harbour leads to Lookout Reserve. The Graves Walkway, a two- to three-hour return walk, follows the coastline to a sandy beach and tidal platforms where seals can be seen. Further on is Bushy Beach where a viewing hide allows visitors to see blue and yellow-eyed penguins.

🐧 **Oamaru Blue Penguin Colony**
Waterfront Rd. 📞 *(03) 433 1195.* ◯ *daily.* 📷 🚫 *no flash.* ♿ 🏪
At Friendly Bay, an old quarry in Oamaru's harbour, visitors can see penguins leave at dawn to feed at sea, and return at dusk past a special viewing area. The greatest number of birds (100–150) is visible in December.

🌺 **Oamaru Public Gardens**
Chelmer St. ◯ *daily, until sunset.*
Established in 1876, these contain traditional features such as rose gardens, ponds, an azalea lawn and rhododendron dell. A band rotunda, summerhouse, aviary, peacock house and marble fountain are other attractions.

🏛 **Totara Estate**
State Hwy 1. ℹ *(03) 434 7169.* ◯ *1–4pm Sun, 10–4pm school & public hols.* 📷 ♿ 🏪
About 8 km (5 miles) south of Oamaru, this is where New Zealand's first shipment of frozen mutton to England in 1882 was processed, heralding the beginning of New Zealand's most important industry. Limestone buildings house displays on the history of the meat industry.

Stone woolshed at Morven Hills Station, Lindis Pass

Lindis Pass ❺

Road map B6.

THE MAIN INLAND link between Otago and the Waitaki Basin, the Lindis Pass climbs through rocky gorges before reaching the tussock-covered hills of a Department of Conservation reserve near the summit. Early Maoris, like today's holiday-makers, used the route in summer to get to Lakes Wanaka and Hawea.

In 1858, John McLean, the first European to settle in the area, established the 2,000-sq-km (772-sq-mile) Morven Hills Station. Many of the original buildings can still be seen about 15 km (9 miles) south of the summit. These include McLean's original homestead and a massive stone woolshed, built about 1880, which was capable of holding up to 1,500 sheep.

Lake Hawea ❻

Road map B6. 🏃 1,100. 🎭 Hawea Picnic Day & Races (28 Dec).

TUCKED AMONG hills and mountains, the bright blue waters of Lake Hawea make it one of the most beautiful of the southern lakes. The lake, which is 410 m (1,345 ft) ⋅

deep in places, is separated from the equally beautiful Lake Wanaka by a narrow, 35-km (22-mile) isthmus, known as "the neck".

Lake Hawea is a popular holiday haven. There are many free camping spots around its shores. It is also well known for its excellent trout and land-locked salmon fishing and for various boating activities. The small town of Hawea on the lake's southern shores is the main base for outdoor activities.

Wanaka ❼

Road map B6. 🏃 3,000. 🛈 Ardmore St, (03) 443 1233. 🎭 Wanaka Snow Festival (Aug).

LOCATED AT THE southern end of the lake, Wanaka is one of the country's favourite holiday spots. The willow-lined shores and bays of Lake Wanaka are popular in summer for boating, fishing and water-skiing, while in winter skiers and snowboarders flock to the local ski areas. Snow-capped peaks provide a beautiful lake setting, and these natural attractions also bring hikers and walkers to the many breathtaking tracks in the nearby Mount Aspiring National Park (see pp270–71).

Aside from the area's natural features, there is plenty to visit and see around the town. One of the chief attractions, the **New Zealand Fighter Pilots Museum**, located at Wanaka Airport, is home to a variety of World War II fighter aircraft, such as

the Spitfire, Hurricane, P51 Mustang, Vought Corsair, a Japanese Nakajima "Oscar" (the only such plane left in the world) and several rare Russian Polikarpovs. Illustrated displays explain the role of New Zealand fighter pilots and crews in several theatres of war. Visitors can also see aircraft being restored in the maintenance hangar. "Warbirds Over Wanaka", a major airshow involving military aircraft, is held every second Easter in even years. It features aircraft from New Zealand as well as overseas in acrobatic displays and mock battles. Wanaka's open skies and dramatic alpine scenery provide a spectacular backdrop.

Next to Wanaka Airport is the **Wanaka Transport Museum**. Its large private collection of more than 13,000 items includes memorabilia, such as toys and

Stuart Landsborough's Puzzling World

models, as well as military vehicles and aircraft. A special exhibit is a huge Russian Antonov AN-2, the world's largest single engine biplane.

Another of Wanaka's attractions, **Stuart Landsborough's Puzzling World**, is based around "The Great Maze", 1.5 km (1 mile) of three-dimensional wooden passages and under- and overbridges. Other attractions include a Hologram Hall, the Tumbling Towers/Tilted House, and the Puzzle Centre where you can sit down with a cup of coffee and try to solve one of the many challenging puzzles on display.

Like many other parts of Central Otago, Wanaka's climate is proving ideal for grape growing. **Rippon Vineyard**, started in 1974 just 4 km (2.5 miles) from the

Fishing on the shores of Lake Hawea

Rippon Vineyard on the shores of Lake Wanaka

centre of town, is one of the pioneering growers and wine makers of the region. It produces a range of wines, including Sauvignon Blanc, Riesling, Chardonnay, Pinot Noir and Osteiner.

New Zealand Fighter Pilots Museum

Wanaka Airport. ((03) 443 7010. ◯ daily. ● 25 Dec.

Wanaka Transport Museum

State Hwy 6. ((03) 443 8765. ◯ daily. ● 25 Dec. by arrangement.

Stuart Landsborough's Puzzling World

State Hwy 6. ((03) 443 7489. ◯ daily.

Rippon Vineyard

Mt Aspiring Rd. ((03) 443 8084. ◯ daily. ● 25 Dec. wine tasting. Music Festival (6 Feb).

ENVIRONS: Twenty-five km (16 miles) south of Wanaka is the tiny township of **Cardrona**, consisting of a few cottages and a hotel dating back to 1863 *(see p309)*.

The surrounding Cardrona Valley, a popular route for gold-miners in the 1860s, is now better known for the well-equipped Cardrona Alpine Resort on the south-eastern slopes of Mount Cardrona, and for cross-country skiing at the nearby Waiorau Snow Farm *(see pp192–3, 335)*.

The **Treble Cone Ski Area**, 20 km (12 miles) southwest of Wanaka, off Mount Aspiring Road, has uncrowded slopes to suit skiers of all abilities *(see pp192–3, 335)*. Guided back country heli-skiing over the Harris, Richardson and Buchanan mountains is another option. Skiers and snowboarders are flown to some of the best out-of-the-way ski spots in the area.

WANAKA'S OUTDOOR ATTRACTIONS

Wanaka is a recreational centre with a wide variety of outdoor pursuits in both summer and winter. Fishing is a popular activity on the lake shore, along rivers and from charter vessels. Waterborne adventures include kayaking, jet-boat and cruise boat trips, white-water sledging on small purpose-designed boards, and canyoning. There are several good walks which leave from or near the township, as well as longer hikes in the nearby Mount Aspiring National Park *(see pp270–71)* for more serious, well-equipped hikers. Horse riding, mountain biking and quad bike motorcycle tours are other ways of exploring Wanaka's back country areas.

Within easy distance of Wanaka lie two commercial downhill ski areas, Treble Cone and Cardrona, as well as the Waiorau Snow Farm cross-country ski area and heli-skiing in the surrounding mountains. From Wanaka Airport, flightseeing tours are available, or, for the more adventurous, acrobatic flights in Tiger Moths or World War II Mustangs.

Skiers on a chairlift at Treble Cone Ski Area, southwest of Wanaka

Mount Aspiring National Park ⓪

Alpine plant

NEW ZEALAND's third largest national park after Fiordland and Kahurangi, Mount Aspiring National Park enjoys World Heritage status as part of the Southwest New Zealand World Heritage Area, which stretches from Mount Cook to the southern tip of Fiordland. Within the park's 3,500-sq km (1,350-sq mile) area, the scenery ranges from snow- and glacier-clad mountains to rugged rock faces, spectacular forested valleys and picturesque river flats. The park, close to the tourist centres of Queenstown and Wanaka, is a popular walking, tramping and climbing destination.

Exploring the park
Opportunities to explore the park on foot are varied, and range from short walks from the road to back country circuits for fit trampers.

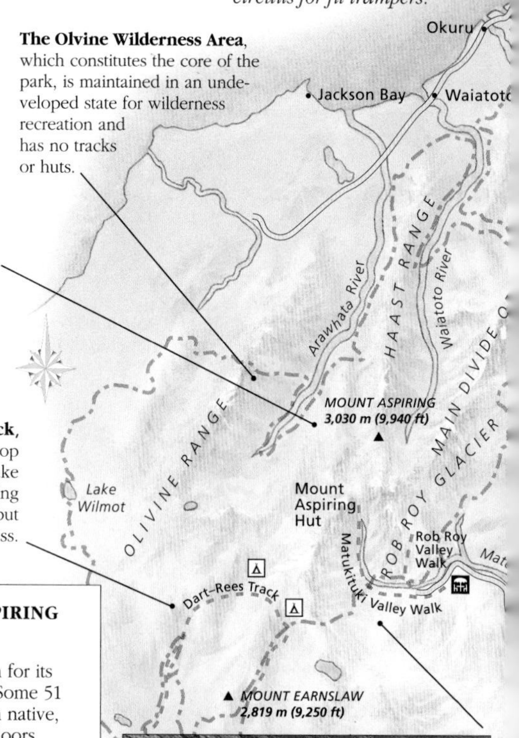

The Olvine Wilderness Area,
which constitutes the core of the park, is maintained in an undeveloped state for wilderness recreation and has no tracks or huts.

★ **Mount Aspiring**
Because of its pyramid shape, Mount Aspiring is often described as New Zealand's "Matterhorn".

The Dart–Rees Track,
a challenging four- to five-day loop track reached from the head of Lake Wakatipu, offers outstanding mountain and valley scenery but requires a high standard of fitness.

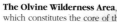

Okuru

Jackson Bay • Waiatotｏ

Arawhata River

Waiatoto River

HAAST RANGE

MAIN DIVIDE

MOUNT ASPIRING
3,030 m (9,940 ft) ▲

OLIVINE RANGE

Lake
Wilmot

Mount
Aspiring
Hut

ROB ROY GLACIER

Rob Roy
Valley
Walk

Dart–Rees Track

Matukituki Valley Walk

Mate

▲ MOUNT EARNSLAW
2,819 m (9,250 ft)

BIRDLIFE IN MOUNT ASPIRING NATIONAL PARK

Rock wren

This park is known for its abundant birdlife. Some 51 species, 38 of them native, inhabit the valley floors, riverbeds, forests, subalpine scrub and high alpine regions. Especially symbolic of the park are the kea, rock wren and blue duck. The kea, whose call may be heard echoing through the valleys, is an inquisitive bird well known for its interest in trampers' equipment and food. The hardy little rock wren lives high in the hills in one of the harshest environments in the park, while pairs of blue ducks can be seen feeding on vegetation and insects in the park's swift mountain streams, especially in the hanging valleys.

Matukituki Valley
A track up the west branch of the river from the end of the road takes trampers to the head of the valley and to some challenging climbing in the Mount Aspiring area.

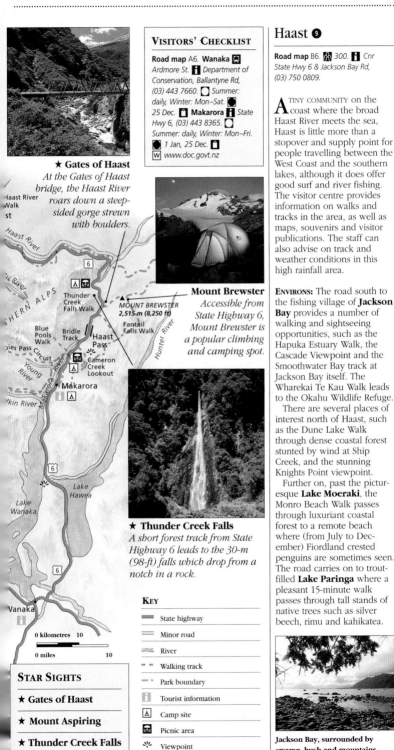

★ **Gates of Haast**
At the Gates of Haast bridge, the Haast River roars down a steep-sided gorge strewn with boulders.

Mount Brewster
Accessible from State Highway 6, Mount Brewster is a popular climbing and camping spot.

★ **Thunder Creek Falls**
A short forest track from State Highway 6 leads to the 30-m (98-ft) falls which drop from a notch in a rock.

Haast ❾

Road map B6. 🚶 300. 🛈 Cnr
State Hwy 6 & Jackson Bay Rd,
(03) 750 0809.

A TINY COMMUNITY on the coast where the broad Haast River meets the sea, Haast is little more than a stopover and supply point for people travelling between the West Coast and the southern lakes, although it does offer good surf and river fishing. The visitor centre provides information on walks and tracks in the area, as well as maps, souvenirs and visitor publications. The staff can also advise on track and weather conditions in this high rainfall area.

ENVIRONS: The road south to the fishing village of **Jackson Bay** provides a number of walking and sightseeing opportunities, such as the Hapuka Estuary Walk, the Cascade Viewpoint and the Smoothwater Bay track at Jackson Bay itself. The Wharekai Te Kau Walk leads to the Okahu Wildlife Refuge.

There are several places of interest north of Haast, such as the Dune Lake Walk through dense coastal forest stunted by wind at Ship Creek, and the stunning Knights Point viewpoint.

Further on, past the picturesque **Lake Moeraki**, the Monro Beach Walk passes through luxuriant coastal forest to a remote beach where (from July to December) Fiordland crested penguins are sometimes seen. The road carries on to trout-filled **Lake Paringa** where a pleasant 15-minute walk passes through tall stands of native trees such as silver beech, rimu and kahikatea.

Jackson Bay, surrounded by swamp, bush and mountains

KEY

▬▬▬	State highway
═══	Minor road
～～	River
▪ ▪ ▪	Walking track
▬ ▬ ▬	Park boundary
🛈	Tourist information
Ⓐ	Camp site
🏕	Picnic area
☀	Viewpoint

STAR SIGHTS

★ **Gates of Haast**

★ **Mount Aspiring**

★ **Thunder Creek Falls**

Milford Sound in Fiordland National Park ▷

Queenstown ❶

Bungy jumping sign

SITUATED ON THE northeast shore of Lake Wakatipu, backed by the Remarkables range, Queenstown enjoys one of the most scenic settings in the world. Since the 1970s, it has developed from a sleepy lakeside town into a leading international resort and a world centre for adventure sports, including bungy jumping *(see pp192–3)*. Like most towns in the area, Queenstown was established during the 1860s gold rushes. Although the pace of development in Queenstown has been dictated by the demands of tourism, it still has the feel of a small town and proudly maintains its links with the days of the gold boom.

TSS *Earnslaw* on Lake Wakatipu

🐟 Lake Wakatipu

There is no mistaking Lake Wakatipu's glacial origins, although Maori legend has it that the lake was formed by the imprint of a sleeping demon burnt to death by the lover of a beautiful Maori girl

captured by the demon. Because his heart did not perish and still beats, the level of the lake rises and falls as much as 7 cm (3 inches) every five minutes. Lake Wakatipu, which is the second largest of the southern glacial lakes,

after Te Anau, is up to 380 m (1,246 ft) deep in places.

The steep, rugged slopes of the Remarkables drop down to the lake's edge, leaving downtown Queenstown snuggled on one of the few pieces of relatively flat land in the area. Most private residences and many hotels have been banished to the surrounding hills. During the mining boom, the lake was the principal means of communication, but today it is a focus for recreational activities.

🍀 Queenstown Gardens

Park St. ⬭ *daily.* ♿

Set on a glacial moraine peninsula, the Queenstown Gardens are within walking distance of the town centre. They are surrounded by stands of large fir trees and contain broad lawns and rose beds. The gardens provide a quiet oasis in an otherwise busy tourist town, and are particularly attractive in autumn. An ice skating rink, sporting greens, a children's park, and a walkway around the point are other attractions.

⛴ TSS *Earnslaw*

Steamer Wharf. 🎧 *(03) 442 7500.* ⬭ *daily.* 🎫 ♿ *main deck.* 📷 🚻

The TSS (Twin Screw Steamer) *Earnslaw* is a wonderful relic of the mining boom when paddle steamers and other craft plied Lake Wakatipu, the principal means of communication. Launched in 1912, the 51-m (168-ft) vessel, affectionately known as "the lady of the lake", is still powered by its original twin 500-hp coal-fired steam engines. Its interior is finished with wood and brass.

A number of cruises depart from Queenstown all year round, from 90-minute cruises to four-hour dinner cruises in the warmer months. Visitors can also take daytime or evening excursions across the lake to the **Walter Peak High Country Farm**. Here they can enjoy refreshments at the Colonel's Homestead Restaurant, go horse trekking or watch displays of various aspects of high country life, such as sheep shearing and sheep dogs in action.

ADVENTURE CAPITAL OF NEW ZEALAND

Queenstown offers a range of adventures, from outdoor experiences to total adventure packages *(see pp192–3, 334–9)*. Summer activities are centred around the lake and in the many rivers nearby, in particular the Dart, Shotover and Kawarau, where jet-boat trips and white-water rafting offer

White-water rafting on the Shotover River

exciting rides through narrow, rocky canyons. In winter, two ranges within 30 km (19 miles) of Queenstown – the Remarkables and Coronet Peak – provide great skiing. The town's reputation as New Zealand's adventure capital, however, rests on its many airborne activities: bungy jumping, ranging from the 43-m (141-ft) high Kawarau Bridge to the 134-m (440-ft) high Nevis highwire bungy; hang-gliding from the area's mountainous terrain; tandem parapenting from Bob's Peak; and tandem skydiving.

Underwater World

Maintown Pier. ☎ (03) 442 8437.
○ daily. 🎫 🛍

Built beneath the Maintown Pier, Underwater World provides a unique opportunity to see life below the lake surface. From a viewing lounge 5 m (16 ft) under the lake, visitors can view brown and rainbow trout peacefully swimming alongside massive New Zealand long-finned eels, which are often visited by diving black teal ducks.

The Mall

The best way to see Queenstown is on foot and the best place to start is at The Mall, a popular meeting place for visitors and a pedestrian-only street dominated by restaurants, cafés and souvenir shops. The Mall leads directly down to the Maintown Pier from which boats depart for cruises on the lake.

A number of old colonial buildings remain in The Mall, including Eichardt's Tavern at the waterfront end, which dates back to 1871.

Skyline Gondola

Brecon St. ☎ (03) 442 7860.
○ daily. 🎫 ♿ 🍴 ☕ 🛍

The gondola up to Bob's Peak is synonymous with Queenstown. It rises 450 m (1,476 ft) in the space of just 730 m (2,400 ft) and provides breathtaking panoramic views of the Remarkables, Lake Wakatipu and Queenstown from the observation deck at the top. Visitors can choose to eat at the restaurant or café, take walks in the area, watch parapenters float down from the peak or take a ride downhill on the luge – a short, raised toboggan.

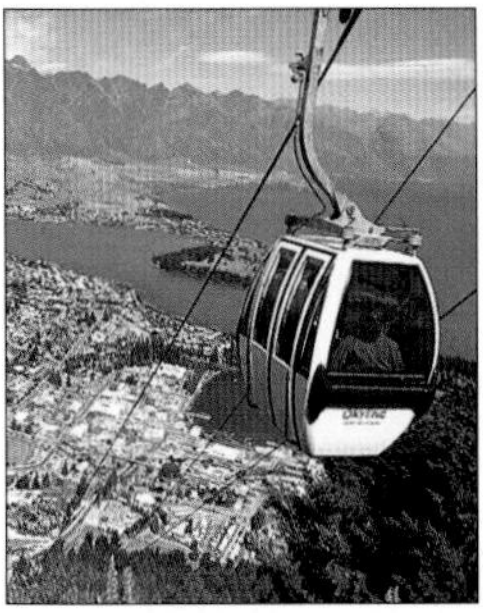

Skyline Gondola

Visitors' Checklist

Road map A6. 👥 7,500
✈ *6 km (4 miles) E of town.*
🚌 *Steamer Wharf.* [i] *Cnr Camp & Shotover sts, (03) 442 4100; 0800 668 888.*
🎉 *Winter Festival (Jul).*
[W] *www.queenstown-nz.co.nz*

Kiwi and Birdlife Park

Brecon St. ☎ (03) 442 8059. ○ daily. ● 25 Dec. 🎫 📷 Kiwi House. ♿ *one house.* 📖 🛍

Queenstown's Kiwi and Birdlife Park, located below the gondola terminal, is home to several kiwis and other endangered native birds. The birds are either part of national breeding programmes, where young birds are produced for release into the wild, or are being rehabilitated after injury.

A major attraction is the nocturnal Kiwi House where visitors can see this flightless bird. Other species on view in natural, parklike surroundings include native owls, large alpine parrots known as keas, parakeets, and the black stilt, a rare wader *(see p249)*.

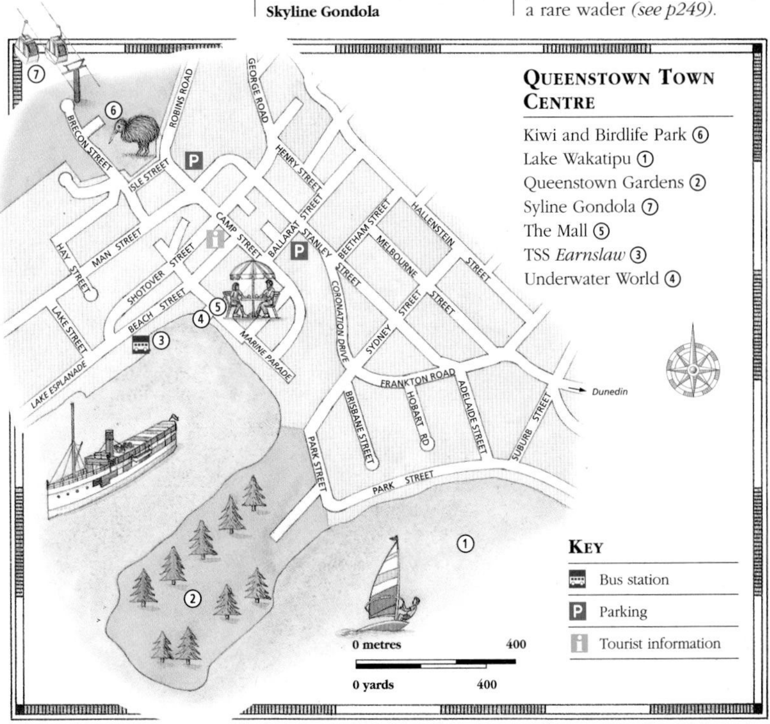
QUEENSTOWN TOWN CENTRE
Kiwi and Birdlife Park ⑥
Lake Wakatipu ①
Queenstown Gardens ②
Syline Gondola ⑦
The Mall ⑤
TSS Earnslaw ③
Underwater World ④
ROBINS ROAD
GEORGE ROAD
BRECON STREET
ISLE STREET
HENRY STREET
HALLENSTEIN STREET
CAMP STREET
BALLARAT STREET
STANLEY STREET
BEETHAM STREET
MELBOURNE STREET
HAY STREET
MAN STREET
SHOTOVER STREET
BEACH STREET
LAKE STREET
LAKE ESPLANADE
MARINE PARADE
CORONATION DRIVE
SYDNEY STREET
FRANKTON ROAD
BRISBANE STREET
HOBART RD
ADELAIDE STREET
SUBURB STREET
PARK STREET
Dunedin
KEY
Bus station
Parking
Tourist information
0 metres 400
0 yards 400

Glenorchy ⓫

Road map A6. 🚶 360. ℹ️ *Cnr Mull & Oban sts, (03) 442 9937.*

Gᴌᴇɴᴏʀᴄʜʏ ɪꜱ ᴀ small, tran-quil township at the head of Lake Wakatipu, 44 km (27 miles) or 40 minutes' drive from Queenstown. The town stands in the shadow of snow-capped peaks with names such as Mount Chaos and Mount Head which rise steeply above the Rees and Dart river valleys.

The town is the transit point for trampers entering the valleys, which are part of the Mount Aspiring National Park *(see pp270–71)*, and which are among New Zealand's Great Walks. For the serious tramper, there is a 77-km (48-mile) loop track which con-nects both valleys via the 1,447-m (4,747-ft) Rees Sad-dle. Although it takes four to five days and requires proper equipment, it is possible to enjoy a few hours' return walk up either valley. Flight-seeing and horse trekking are also available at Glenorchy.

Arrowtown ⓬

Road map B6. 🚶 1,700. ℹ️ *Buckingham St, (03) 442 1824.* 🎏 *Autumn Festival (Apr).*

Nᴇꜱᴛᴌᴇᴅ ᴀᴛ ᴛʜᴇ foot of rug-ged hills 20 km (12 miles) from Queenstown, Arrowtown is the most pictur-esque and best preserved gold-mining town in the area. In 1862, a small band of min-ers, including William Fox and John O'Callaghan, dis-covered gold in the Fox River and within weeks they had

Lake Hayes near Arrowtown

recovered 113 kg (250 lb) of the precious metal. Arrow-town's population peaked at more than 7,000 and is one of the few boom towns not to have either become a ghost town or been overrun by more modern development. The main street, partly lined with deciduous trees, has many old colonial shops and buildings at one end and, at the other, tiny miners' stone cottages dating back to the 1860s and 1870s.

Chinese miners played a big part in Arrowtown's history after 1865, when they were invited to fill the vacuum created by European miners who had left for the West Coast gold rush. Their legacy is Arrow-town's **Chinese Settlement** with its pre-served and restored stone buildings, including tiny cottages, a stone outhouse and a stone store.

The **Lakes District Museum** chronicles both Arrowtown and Queens-town's past, focusing on gold-miners and their innovations.

Stone cottage at the Chinese settlement

It includes a display on New Zealand's first hydroelectric plant, built in 1886 in what is now the ghost town of Bul-lendale. Other displays cover local geology, agriculture, sawmilling and domestic life of the gold rush period. The museum doubles as Arrow-town's visitor centre.

♨ Chinese Settlement
Buckingham St. 【 (03) 442 1824. ◯ *daily.* &.
🏛 Lakes District Museum
Buckingham St. 【 (03) 442 1824. ◯ *daily.* ● *25 Dec.* 📷 & ☑ 🄰

Eɴᴠɪʀᴏɴꜱ: Near to Arrowtown is the much-photographed **Lake Hayes**, at its best in autumn. The road from Arrowtown to Queenstown passes the access road to Coronet Peak which heads 7 km (4 miles) up to great views from the ski area. **Macetown** is a popular destination for 4WD vehicles. A 26-km (16-mile) return journey from Arrowtown takes visitors up a steep, gold-bearing gorge. Ghost town relics include the remains of old stone buildings and a gold stamping battery.

Gibbston Valley Wines is a good example of the vine-yards that have sprung up in the area *(see pp34–5)*. Euro-pean varieties thrive in the hot summer days and cool evenings. Gibbston's wine is stored in a cool underground cave, and tours and wine tastings are available.

🍷 Gibbston Valley Wines
State Hwy 6. 【 (03) 442 6910. ◯ *daily.* ● *Good Fri, 25 Dec.* & ☑ 📷 *cave.* 🍴 ☐ 🄰

The main street of Arrowtown

Cromwell

Road map B7. 3,000.
47 The Mall, (03) 445 0212.

CROMWELL survived the gold era to become a service town in one of New Zealand's leading fruit growing areas. In the 1980s, an electricity generating dam built down river created nearby Lake Dunstan, flooding much of Cromwell's quaint and historic main street, although several of the more notable buildings were relocated stone by stone to a new site. Cromwell now makes its living from farming, horticulture and tourism.

ENVIRONS: Gold-mining relics in the area include **Bendigo**, a ghost town 4 km (2 miles) off State Highway 8, the main road between Cromwell and Lindis Pass. By 1866 Bendigo was all but deserted until a rich gold-bearing quartz reef was found, and mined for more than 50 years.

A loop track above Bendigo leads to **Logantown** and **Welshtown**, two associated settlements deserted in the 1880s. It is wise to keep to the tracks because there are many old unmarked mine shafts throughout the area.

The **Goldfields Mining Centre** in the Kawarau Gorge, 5 km (3 miles) from Cromwell, offers visitors working exhibitions of gold-mining techniques.

🏛 Goldfields Mining Centre
Kawarau Gorge, State Hwy 6.
(03) 445 1038. daily.
25 Dec.

THE GOLD RUSH

The Otago gold rush began with the discovery of gold in Gabriel's Gully in 1861, near the present-day town of Lawrence, 92 km (57 miles) west of Dunedin. A tent town sprang up and prospectors soon began pushing further inland. Finds in the Dunstan area around Cromwell and Alexandra followed in 1862, with discoveries in the Wakatipu region soon after. Tens of thousands braved hot, dry summers, cold, harsh winters and starvation in search of a quick fortune. New discoveries were made in other corners of the province, but by the late 1860s the focus had shifted to the West Coast. With the main fields well picked over,

more sophisticated methods, such as sluicing, dredging and quartz reef mining, were needed to extract gold. Gold-mining continued well into the 1900s and, more recently, modern methods have led to large-scale mining operations in the area.

Arrowtown miners at their claim in the 1860s

Kingston ⑭

Road map A7. 65. Kingston to Queenstown Yacht Race (Jan).

FOR A LONG TIME the little settlement of Kingston served as a railhead and steamer terminal for travellers heading towards Lake Wakatipu from the south. Nowadays, its main claim to fame is the **Kingston Flyer**, a restored vintage steam train with several coaches and staff in period costume which takes passengers on a 75-minute return trip.

🚂 Kingston Flyer
Kingston Railway Station. (03) 248 8848. Oct–Apr: daily. May–Sep.

ENVIRONS: To the south of Kingston, on State Highway 6, is **Lumsden**, well known for the trout-filled rivers which crisscross the countryside surrounding the town. Just before Lumsden, State Highway 94 branches west to Te Anau, Manapouri and Fiordland National Park, and east to the farming area of Gore.

The vintage steam train Kingston Flyer on a short "flight" from Kingston

Fiordland National Park ⑮

Fiordland crested penguin

FIORDLAND NATIONAL PARK'S 21,000 sq km (8,100 sq miles) make it the largest of New Zealand's National Parks, while its special geology, landscape, flora and fauna have earned it a place in the Southwest New Zealand World Heritage Area. It is a region dominated by forest and water. Its 14 fiords and five major lakes – the work of Ice Age glaciers – flanked by steep mountains clad with thick, temperate rainforest, make the interior virtually inpenetrable except along its 500 km (310 miles) of tracks. Fiordland National Park is also known for its wildlife, especially its marine mammals and native birds, including the Fiordland crested penguin.

★ **Doubtful Sound**
This fiord extends 40 km (25 miles) from the foot of the main mountain divide to the open waters of the Tasman Sea (see pp282–3).

HOW THE FIORDS WERE FORMED

Although named otherwise, Milford Sound, Doubtful Sound and the other sounds are, in fact, fiords. Sounds are flooded river valleys whereas fiords are valleys carved by the tremendous pressure and power of glaciers during successive Ice Ages, then later flooded by the sea as the ice melts and sea levels rise.

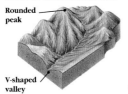

Rounded peak

V-shaped valley

10 million years ago, intense pressure in the earth's crust caused the most recent uplift in the area, forming peaks and V-shaped valleys.

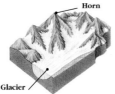

Horn

Glacier

2 million years ago, the mountains were covered by glaciers. Ridges and peaks became sharper and valleys became U-shaped.

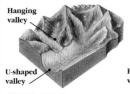

Hanging valley

U-shaped valley

20,000–12,000 years ago, the ice melted as the Ice Age receded, leaving the tributaries of rivers as hanging valleys above the main valley.

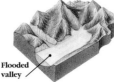

Flooded valley

6,000 years ago, at the end of the last Ice Age, the sea reached its present levels, flooding the valleys and leaving the peaks exposed.

DOUBTFUL SOUND

DUSKY SOUND

STAR SIGHTS

★ **Cleddau Valley**

★ **Doubtful Sound**

★ **Mitre Peak**

Dusky Sound
This sound can be reached on an overnight cruise from Lake Manapouri or, for experienced climbers, via the 10-day Dusky Track.

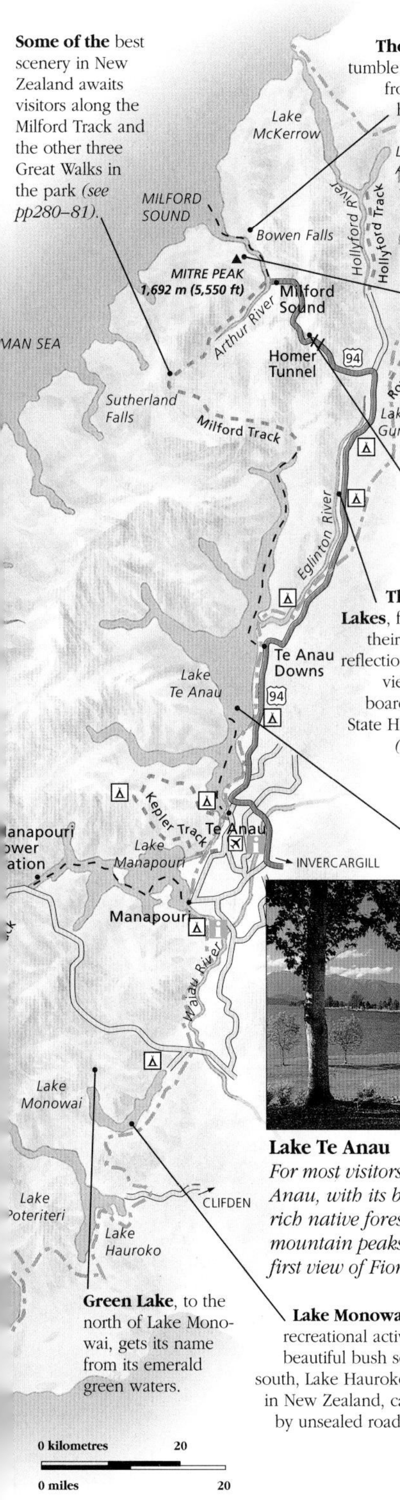
Lake McKerrow
Lake Alabaster
MILFORD SOUND
Bowen Falls
Hollyford River
Hollyford Track
MITRE PEAK
1,692 m (5,550 ft)
Milford Sound
Arthur River
MAN SEA
Homer Tunnel
94
Routeburn Track
Lake Gunn
Sutherland Falls
Milford Track
Eglinton River
Te Anau Downs
Lake Te Anau
94
Kepler Track
Te Anau
Lake Manapouri
anapouri
ower
ation
INVERCARGILL
Manapouri
Waiau River
Lake Monowai
Lake Poteriteri
Lake Hauroko
CLIFDEN
0 kilometres 20
0 miles 20

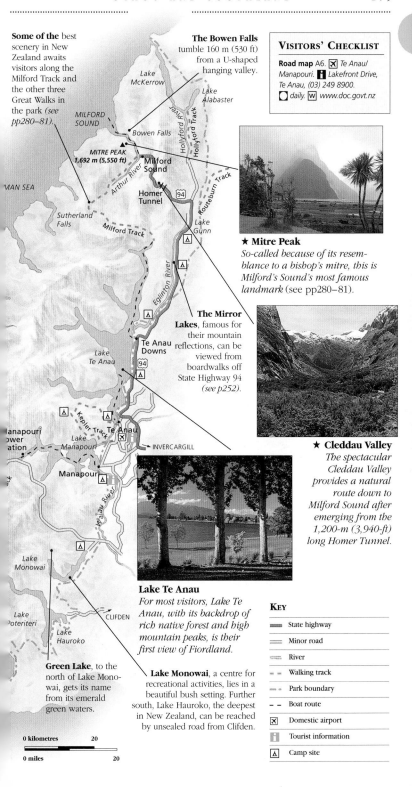

Some of the best scenery in New Zealand awaits visitors along the Milford Track and the other three Great Walks in the park *(see pp280–81).*

The Bowen Falls tumble 160 m (530 ft) from a U-shaped hanging valley.

Visitors' Checklist

Road map A6. ✈ *Te Anau/ Manapouri.* ℹ *Lakefront Drive, Te Anau, (03) 249 8900.* ◯ *daily.* W *www.doc.govt.nz*

★ Mitre Peak
So-called because of its resemblance to a bishop's mitre, this is Milford's Sound's most famous landmark (see pp280–81).

The Mirror Lakes, famous for their mountain reflections, can be viewed from boardwalks off State Highway 94 *(see p252).*

★ Cleddau Valley
The spectacular Cleddau Valley provides a natural route down to Milford Sound after emerging from the 1,200-m (3,940-ft) long Homer Tunnel.

Lake Te Anau
For most visitors, Lake Te Anau, with its backdrop of rich native forest and high mountain peaks, is their first view of Fiordland.

Green Lake, to the north of Lake Monowai, gets its name from its emerald green waters.

Lake Monowai, a centre for recreational activities, lies in a beautiful bush setting. Further south, Lake Hauroko, the deepest in New Zealand, can be reached by unsealed road from Clifden.

Key

- State highway
- Minor road
- River
- Walking track
- Park boundary
- Boat route
- Domestic airport
- Tourist information
- Camp site

Exploring Fiordland National Park

Church near Te Anau

W ITH MOUNTAINS rising 2,750 m (9,020 ft), sheer rock walls climbing 1,200 m (3,940 ft) from deep fiords, and waterfalls tumbling 160 m (530 ft), Fiordland's spectacular landscape attracts visitors from around the world. Sealers were the first to exploit the area's natural resources, and from 1792 to the 1820s hundreds of thousands of fur seals were slaughtered. Since then, human impact has been minimal. Until 1953, when State Highway 94 (the Milford Road) was completed, the only way to Milford Sound was by boat or via the Milford Track. Today, visitors arrive by the busload, and those with the time, fitness and equipment can experience the area by walking one of the famous tracks.

Sheep drive on the road to Milford Sound

Te Anau

Road map A7. 🚶 *1,800*. 🚌 *Miro St.* ℹ️ *Lakefront Drive, (03) 249 8900.*

Te Anau, on the southeastern shore of Lake Te Anau, is Fiordland's commercial centre (primarily deer farming and tourism) and a good base for exploring Fiordland National Park. The lake, the largest in the South Island, is 61 km (38 miles) long and 417 m (1,370 ft) deep, the result of glacial action. It is a popular venue for boating and fishing.

🐾 Te Anau Caves

ℹ️ *Fiordland Travel Visitor Centre, Lakefront Drive, Te Anau.* 📞 *(03) 249 7416.* ⏰ *daily.* 🎫 ⊘

At the Te Anau Caves, reached by a boat trip across Lake Te Anau, is a combination of carefully formed walkways and punts allow visitors to

explore a series of magical limestone grottos. The caves are home to thousands of tiny New Zealand glowworms, which use their tiny light – the result of a chemical reaction – to attract insects for food. Return trips, which depart several times a day, take two and a half hours.

🐾 The Milford Road

The 121-km (75-mile) road to Milford Sound from Te Anau has earned World Heritage Highway status for its beauty and scenic variety. This includes lush lakeside forest, rugged mountains, cascading alpine rivers and picturesque walks. Although Milford Sound can be reached by road in three hours, there are many side trips possible along the way to make the drive more memorable.

Te Anau Downs, 30 km (19 miles) from Te Anau, is the departure point for the boat to the Milford Track. From here there is a 45-minute forest walk to Lake Mistletoe. Further on, the Mirror Lakes are a short five-minute walk from the road across a boardwalk. On a calm day, beautiful reflections of the surrounding scenery are visible in the lakes (*see p252*). Nearby is a curious section of road, known as "the avenue of the

NEXT 35 km

Sheep warning sign, Milford Road

disappearing mountain", where a mountain directly in front appears to shrink.

At Lake Gunn, about 46 km (29 miles) from Te Anau Downs, an easy 45-minute loop through beech forest is suitable for all ages and for people in wheelchairs. The Divide, a short distance away, marks the start of the Routeburn Track, which leads overland to Lake Wakatipu. A three-hour return walk to Key Summit gives rewarding views. The nearby Hollyford Valley also makes a scenic trip.

Nineteen km (12 miles) east of Milford Sound is the 1,200-m (3,940-ft) long Homer Tunnel, started in 1935 but not completed until 1954. Leaving the tunnel, the road slopes very steeply downhill to the Milford side where there are spectacular views along the Cleddau Valley. The Chasm, a few kilometres from the tunnel, can be reached by a 20-minute walk to where the Cleddau River drops 22 m (72 ft) through a series of unusual rock formations.

🐾 Milford Sound

Road map A6. 🚶 *170*.

Milford Sound, a 16-km (10-mile) long fiord is Fiordland's best-known attraction. Its most famous landmark is Mitre Peak, a pyramid-shaped mountain rising 1,692 m (5,550 ft) straight from the deep fiord. Although scenic flights are available, the

Te Anau Caves

grandeur of Milford Sound can be best appreciated by boat. Trips pass unusual geological features, such as Lion Mountain, the Elephant and Copper Point, as well as waterfalls: the Bowen Falls drop 160 m (530 ft) into the water, and the Stirling Falls 146 m (480 ft). Fur seals, dolphins, and the occasional Fiordland crested penguin can be seen along the way.

An Underwater Observatory at Milford Sound allows visitors to see the unusual black coral, red coral, anemones, starfish and fish that live in the fiord. High rainfall means there is a 3–4 m (10–13 ft) layer of fresh water above the underlying salt water.

Fur seals at the entrance to Milford Sound

Apart from day trips on Milford Sound, full-day and overnight cruises take visitors out of the sound to the open Tasman Sea, with stops at other fiords, such as Dusky Sound. Cruises often combine fishing and diving excursions.

THE FOUR GREAT WALKS

Trampers on the Milford Track

Fiordland National Park is probably the best place in New Zealand for trampers. Its four major walking tracks – the Milford, Hollyford, Routeburn and Kepler (*see pp278–9*) – can be walked independently or with a guided group from late October to April. Advance booking is essential for the Milford and Routeburn tracks (*see pp334–5*), while all tracks require advance purchase of hut or campsite passes.

The spectacular 55-km (34-mile) **Milford Track**, which takes four days, climbs through the Clinton Valley to the Mackinnon Pass. It passes the Sutherland Falls before dropping down to Milford Sound. The 60-km (37-mile) **Hollyford Track**, which takes four to five days, follows the Hollyford River to the West Coast through lowland forest beneath snow-capped peaks. The 39-km (24-mile) **Routeburn Track** usually takes three days. It climbs through forest to spectacular subalpine terrain before crossing the Harris Saddle and descending the Routeburn Valley towards Lake Wakatipu. The **Kepler Track**, a three- to four-day 67-km (42-mile) loop, skirts Lake Te Anau, then climbs to panoramic views from Mount Luxmore before descending to Lake Manapouri.

Typical alpine plant

Aerial view of Milford Sound

A Trip to Doubtful Sound ⑯

D
OUBTFUL SOUND was named by Captain James
Cook in 1770, on his voyage to New Zealand
when, looking at the narrow entrance to the sound,
he was doubtful that he could safely get his vessel
in and out. The 40-km (25-mile) long fiord is
Fiordland's second largest and, at 421 m (1,380 ft),
the deepest. It is a remote, unspoilt wilderness of
mountain peaks, fiords and rainforest which
supports a rich array of bird and marine life, including crested penguins, fur seals and bottlenose
dolphins. Getting there is an adventure in itself,
involving two boat trips and a coach ride over a
mountain pass, with a side trip deep underground
to the huge Manapouri Power Station generator hall.

Lake Manapouri ①
The trip to Doubtful Sound
begins at the Pearl Harbour
marina on the Waiau River,
which feeds into Lake Manapouri. The lake, which is
forested to the shoreline, covers
142 sq km (55 sq miles) and is
dotted with 34 islands.

New Zealand Fur Seals ⑩
Colonies of New Zealand's
most common seal can
be seen on the islands
dotting the entrance to
Doubtful Sound.

*TASMAN
SEA*

*Secretary
Island*

Thompson Sound

⑩

*Bauza
Island*

Bradshaw Sound

Crooked Arm

⑨

Malaspina Reach

⑧

Hall Arm

⑦

⑥

Bottlenose Dolphins ⑨
A resident pod of bottlenose dolphins may
be seen playing in the waters at Malaspina
Reach. They grow up to 4.5 m (15 ft).

Commander Peak ⑧
To the left at the head of Hall Arm,
Commander Peak is one of many
awe-inspiring bush-clad peaks that
visitors see during a cruise of
Doubtful Sound's flooded glacial
valleys *(see p278)*.

Deep Cove ⑦
The peaceful waters of Deep
Cove hide the 10-km (6-mile)
tunnel under the mountains from
the Manapouri Power Station.

Manapouri Power Station

The Manapouri Power Station is a man-made wonder that takes advantage of the difference in height of the mountains between Lake Manapouri and Doubtful Sound to act as a natural dam. Water is chanelled through vertical penstocks into seven generators housed in a huge underground room. The water then flows out a 10-km (6-mile) tunnel to Deep Cove. The electricity generated is used to power the Comalco Aluminium Smelter 171 km (106 miles) to the south, at Bluff.

Underground machine hall

Tips for Travellers

This trip takes eight hours and can only be undertaken with a commercial tour operator. Winter is the best time of the year for clear views and little rain, but the busiest time for tours is spring and summer. Although light refreshments are served along the way, it is advisable to take along something else to eat. Insect repellent, warm clothing and a waterproof jacket are also essential items.

Boat trips: *Fiordland Travel Visitor Centre, Manapouri, (03) 249 6602.*

Manapouri Power Station [2]
Coaches take visitors down a 2-km (1.2-mile) spiral access tunnel to the machine hall which is carved out of solid granite 213 m (700 ft) under the mountains at West Arm.

Moss Gardens [4]
Dozens of species of moss growing on a rock face show how plant life can get a foothold in all sorts of terrain in this high rainfall environment.

Wilmot Pass Road [3]
The 22-km (13-mile) Wilmot Pass Road, completed in May 1965 to facilitate the building of the Manapouri Power Station tailrace at Deep Cove, cost more than $2 per cm ($5 per inch) to build.

Cleve Garth Falls [5]
The 365-m (1,200ft) high Cleve Garth Falls make a breathtaking entrance from a mountain ridge high above the Wilmott Pass Road.

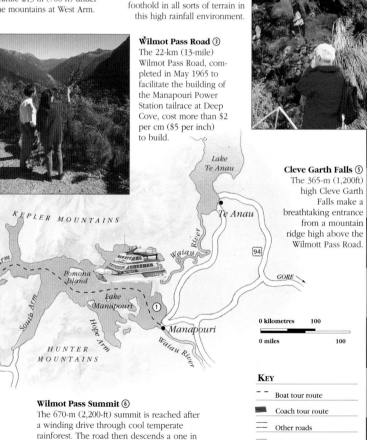

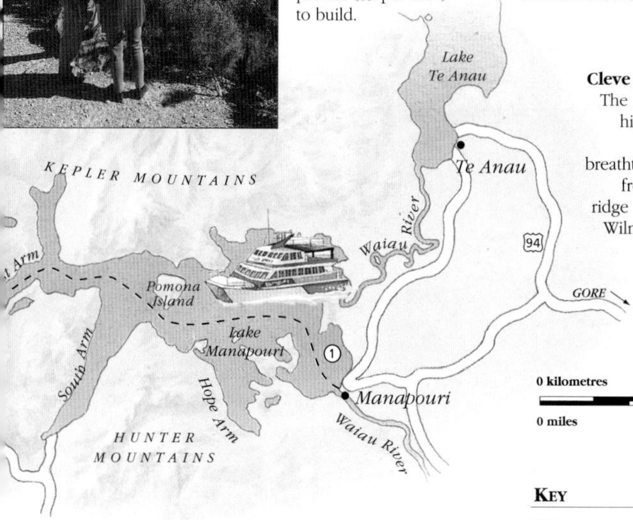
Lake Te Anau
Te Anau
KEPLER MOUNTAINS
Waiau River
94
GORE
t Arm
Pomona Island
Lake Manapouri
1
South Arm
Hope Arm
Manapouri
Waiau River
HUNTER MOUNTAINS

0 kilometres 100

0 miles 100

Key

- - Boat tour route

Coach tour route

Other roads

River

Wilmot Pass Summit [6]
The 670-m (2,200-ft) summit is reached after a winding drive through cool temperate rainforest. The road then descends a one in five slope to Deep Cove.

Invercargill ⑰

Water Tower

N EW ZEALAND's southernmost city, and the commercial hub of Southland, Invercargill is a well-planned city with wide, tree-lined streets and many parks and reserves. Settled in the 1850s and 1860s by Scottish immigrants, the city's cultural links with Scotland are reflected in the streets named after Scottish rivers and in its many historic buildings. To the west of the city are several sheltered beaches and walking tracks.

VISITORS' CHECKLIST

Road map A7. ▓ 54,000. ✈
2 km (1.2 miles) W of city. ⊞ ⊞
Leven St. ℹ 108 Gala St, (03)
214 6243. ◯ daily. ● 25 Dec.
▨ Invercargill Summer Festival
(early Jan); Garden Festival (Feb).
ⓦ www.southland.org.nz

♣ Queen's Park

Gala St. 📞 (03) 214 6243.
The best-known reserve in the city centre is the 0.8 sq km (0.3 sq mile) Queen's Park, a botanical reserve featuring formal gardens, including rose gardens and the extensive Steans Memorial Winter Garden. There is also a small wildlife park containing deer and wallabies, an aviary, and a challenging 18-hole golf course.

⿴ Southland Museum and Art Gallery

108 Gala St. 📞 (03) 214 6243.
◯ daily. ● 25 Dec. ♿ ✒ by
arrangement. ▣ ▯
Apart from its three art exhibition galleries, the Southland Museum and Art Gallery, housed in a pyramid-shaped building near the entrance to

Tuatara at the Southland Museum and Art Gallery

Queen's Park, contains displays outlining the area's human and natural history. It also features a tuatarium where visitors can see several of New Zealand's "living fossil" *(see p22)* at close range. The "Roaring Forties Experience" at the Subantarctic Islands Interpretive Centre provides an accessible introduction to New Zealand's five remote island reserves, which lie hundreds of kilometres to the south of Invercargill.

▦ Water Tower

Leet St.
A distinctive landmark in the city, the 42-m (138-ft) high red brick water tower, completed in 1889 for the Public Works Department, is a fine example of Neo-Romanesque industrial design of the time.

▦ Dee and Tay Streets

Invercargill's early prosperity resulted in the construction of many fine commercial buildings and churches. At the northern end of Dee Street lies the former Dee Street Hospital, the oldest public hospital buildings in New Zealand, and the quaint former Porter's Lodge, built around 1866 and reputed to be the oldest house in Invercargill. Nearby is St Paul's Presbyterian Church, whose square tower houses a set of bells manufactured in Italy from captured guns. Further down, the 1901 red brick Alexander Building

INVERCARGILL CITY CENTRE

Anderson Park Art Gallery ⑤
Dee and Tay Streets ④
Queen's Park ①
Southland Museum and
    Art Gallery ②
Water Tower ③

KEY

	Train station
🚌	Bus station
P	Parking
ℹ	Tourist information

0 metres   500
0 yards   500

Queenstown
Anderson Park Art Gallery ⑤
VICTORIA AVENUE
GALA STREET
LEET STREET
YARROW STREET
SPEY STREET
DON STREET
ESK STREET
TAY STREET
MERSEY STREET
LEVEN STREET
DEE STREET
KELVI STREET
DEVERSON STREET
JED STREET
DOON STREET
QUEENS DRIVE
Bluff
Gore

Anderson Park Art Gallery and gardens

is noted for its eclectic style, while the Grand Hotel opposite has fine iron balconies.

At the intersection of Dee Street and Tay Street (Invercargill's main street) stands the impressive Troopers' Memorial flanked by three elegant bank buildings, erected between 1876 and 1926. In Tay Street is the imposing Renaissance-style Civic Theatre, completed in 1906, and St John's Anglican Church, noted for its stained-glass windows and timber barrel-vaulted ceiling. The Lombardy-style First Presbyterian Church, also in Tay Street, features an unusual square 32-m (105-ft) tower.

🏛 Anderson Park Art Gallery

McIvor Rd. **📞** *(03) 215 7432.*
◯ *1:30–5pm daily.* **●** *Good Fri, 25 Dec.* **◌** *donation.* **∅** *inside.*
♿ *ground floor.* **📷** *by arrangement.*
Five km (3 miles) north of the city centre, this beautiful Georgian-style house built in 1925, set in 0.2 sq km (0.08 sq mile) of gardens and native bush, houses a fine collection of New Zealand art.

First Presbyterian Church in Tay Street

Gore ⑱

Road map B7. **🏘** *8,500.* **🚉** *Main St.*
🚌 **ℹ** *Cnr Hokonui Drive & Norfolk St, (03) 208 9908.* **🎸** *New Zealand Gold Guitar Awards (May–Jun).*

LYING 66 km (41 miles) north of Invercargill, Gore has varied claims to fame: brown trout in the Mataura River and its tributaries (symbolized by a large trout statue in the middle of the town), sheep (the town is surrounded by fertile farmlands and thrives as an agricultural service town), moonshine whisky, and a reputation as the country music capital of New Zealand (country music devotees come each May for the New Zealand Gold Guitar Awards).

Boys with flounder

The Gore Information Centre incorporates the **Gore Historical Museum** and the **Hokonui Moonshine Museum**. The latter covers the colourful period in the past when whisky was made illegally in the Hokonui Hills behind Gore.

Fifteen km (9 miles) west of Gore on State Highway 94 is the **Old Mandeville Airfield** where the Croydon Aircraft Company lovingly restores vintage aircraft and offers flights to visitors.

🏛 Gore Historical Museum and Hokonui Moonshine Museum
Cnr Hokonui Drive & Norfolk St.
📞 *(03) 208 9908.* **◯** *daily.* **●** *25 Dec.* **♿** **📷**
✕ Old Mandeville Airfield
📞 *(03) 208 9755.* **◯** *daily.* **●** *25 Dec.* **♿** **📷** *by arrangement.*

Bluff ⑲

Road map A7. **🏘** *2,000.* **🚌** *Gore St.* **⛴** *Stewart Island Wharf.* **🎣** *Bluff Oyster & Seafood Festival (mid-Apr).*

BLUFF IS New Zealand's southernmost export port and the departure point for ferries to Stewart Island. It is also the base for fishing fleets which cruise the south and west coasts for fish and crayfish as well as the famous "Bluff oysters". Unique to New Zealand, the oysters are harvested during a limited season each autumn.

Bluff has a long history of human occupation, with Maori settlement dating back to the 13th century. The town is named after the 265-m (870-ft) high Bluff Hill which overlooks Foveaux Strait towards Stewart Island, which lies 32 km (20 miles) away. Beneath the hill is Stirling Point – the end of State Highway 1 – where there is a much photographed international signpost. Several walks, including the Foveaux Walkway and the Glory Track, pass through native forest. A 45-minute climb up the hill gives panoramic views of the Foveaux Strait, surrounding coast and inland areas.

The **Bluff Maritime Museum** contains interesting exhibits tracing the history of whaling, muttonbirding and oyster harvesting, as well as development of the port and the Stewart Island ferry.

🏛 Bluff Maritime Museum
243 Foreshore Rd. **📞** *(03) 212 7534.*
◯ *daily.* **●** *25 Dec.* **📷** **♿** **📷** *by arrangement.* **📷**

International signpost at Stirling Point, Bluff

Stewart Island ⑳

Stewart Island logo

ACCORDING TO Maori legend, Stewart Island, New Zealand's third largest island, was the anchor of Maui's canoe (the South Island) when he pulled the great fish (the North Island) from the sea. Separated from the South Island by the shallow, 32-km (20-mile) Foveaux Strait, Stewart Island can be reached by boat or plane. Its unspoilt inlets and beaches, bush-clad hills, rugged coastline and variety of native birdlife combine to make the 1,746-sq-km (674-sq-mile) island a naturalist's paradise. First settled in the 1800s by European sealers, whalers and miners, today's small population makes a living from fishing and tourism.

Halfmoon Bay from Observation Rock

Oban

Oban, Stewart Island's only settlement, sits snugly around the picturesque, protected shores of Halfmoon Bay. It is easy to explore the town on foot but a 90-minute bus tour along Oban's 20 km (12 miles) of road takes visitors past the main points of interest in and around the town.

From Oban many short tracks lead through beautiful bush to places of scenic or historic interest, and to lookouts with stunning views, including Observation Rock, which provides splendid views over Paterson Inlet towards Ulva Island. On a clear, summer night it is easy to see why Maoris named Stewart Island "the land of the glowing skies". Several beautiful beaches also lie within walking distance to the north and east of the town.

The island offers a range of accommodation options, such as backpacker inns, beach houses, motels, bed and

breakfasts, and the century-old South Sea Hotel. The 20-seat Gumboot Theatre in Miro Crescent is the venue for a number of productions, including the long-running one-woman show "A Day in the Life of a Stewart Islander".

The Rakiura Museum in Ayr Street, which is open daily, provides a fascinating insight into Stewart Island's past, such as its seafaring history and relics of whaling, sealing, tin mining and timber milling.

Boat charters are also available from Oban, catering for a whole range of interests, including fishing, sightseeing

South Sea Hotel on the shores of Halfmoon Bay

and wildlife spotting. Trips in glass-bottom boats allow visitors to see octopuses and crayfish and a variety of fish and prawns up close. For the more adventurous, there is diving, kayak hire and guided sea kayak excursions.

🐟 Paterson Inlet

Over the hill from Halfmoon Bay is the 16-km (10-mile) long Paterson Inlet, which extends deep into the hinterland. Charter boats and water taxis can be hired in Oban for sightseers, divers and those wanting to catch their own fish. These trips are also a great opportunity to view various seabirds, including yellow-eyed and little blue penguins and molly-mawks, as well as seals and dolphins.

🦅 Ulva Island

Located in the centre of Paterson Inlet, Ulva Island is a 10-minute trip by water taxi from the main wharf at Oban. Rats and possums have been eradicated from the island, creating a sanctuary where visitors can get a close look at native New Zealand birds. The remains of an old sawmill and whaling station are also accessible. Walks on the island range from 15 minutes to three hours.

Muttonbird Islands

STEWART ISLAND

🦅 Ocean Beach

"Kiwi spotting" (viewing kiwis at night in their natural habitat) is an experience unique to Stewart Island. Licensed tour operators take small groups by boat to the Neck in Little Glory Bay, then on foot through the bush to Ocean Beach where the Stewart Island brown kiwi can be seen feeding on washed-up kelp as darkness falls.

🦅 Big Glory Bay

Salmon and mussel farming have become important industries in Paterson Inlet. A boat trip takes visitors to a salmon farm at Big Glory Bay, past seal colonies and shag rookeries, with a stopover at Ulva Island on the way.

🦅 Muttonbird Islands

Muttonbirds, or sooty shearwaters, breed on Stewart Island's many offshore islands after a round-the-world migration. Long a source of food, oil and feather down for Maoris, young birds are harvested each April by descendants of the Rakiura Maori. By day, Ackers Point lighthouse gives panoramic views of the islands, and at night during the breeding season (October to April), visitors can hear the muttonbirds returning to land. Some tour operators are licenced to take visitors to the islands to view the birds.

VISITORS' CHECKLIST

Road map A7. 🚶 *400.* ✈ *from Invercargill (20 mins).* ⛴ *from Stewart Island Wharf, Bluff (60 mins).* ℹ *Main Rd, Oban, (03) 219 1218.* 🔓 *daily, times variable Jun–Aug.* ● *25 Dec.* 🌐 *www.stewartisland.co.nz*

Muttonbird (sooty shearwater) leaving its burrow

🦅 Codfish Island

Codfish Island, about 3 km (2 miles) off the northwest coast of Stewart Island, was once a European settlement. The island has been cleared of introduced fauna and is now a protected sanctuary for some 60 species of birds, including the rare and endangered kakapo, a large, flightless, nocturnal parrot.

MOUNT ANGLEM
980 m (3,215 ft) ▲

North-West Circuit

RUGGEDY MOUNTAINS

Freshwater River

THOMSON RIDGE

Southern Circuit

Duck Creek

MOUNT ▲ RAKEAHUA
681 m (2,234 ft)

ADAMS HILL
401 m (1,316 ft)

▲ DOUGHBOY HILL
446 m (1,463 ft)

TIN RANGE

Gorge Creek

Blaikies River

Lords River

Rakeahua River

Heron River

Foveaux Strait

▲ BLUFF

Port William

Rakiura Track

Horseshoe Point
Ackers Point

Carter Passage

The Neck
Little Glory Bay

0 kilometres   10

0 miles   10

KEY

River	
Ferry route	
Walking track	
✖ Airstrip	
⛴ Ferry	
ℹ Tourist information	

WALKING THE ISLAND

Stewart Island has a number of well-maintained tracks that take visitors into some of New Zealand's most beautiful bush. From Oban, a three-hour return walk through coastal forest to Ackers Point Lighthouse goes past one of New Zealand's oldest buildings, Ackers Cottage, built in 1835, while the four-hour Horseshoe Point walk leads past the Moturau Moana native garden, then on to Horseshoe Bay. The Ryan's Creek Track is a three- to four-hour loop through coastal forest above Paterson Inlet.

For the fitter visitor, there is the Rakiura Track, a popular three-day circuit, and the 10- to 14-day North-West and Southern Circuits. For these longer walks, Great Walks hut and camp passes must be obtained from the visitor centre in Oban.

Tramper on the Rakiura Track, north of Oban

Tour of the Catlins ㉑

NATURAL CURIOSITIES and beauty combine to make this southeastern corner of the South Island a scenic treasure. Fossilized trees, beautiful waterfalls, golden beaches, high cliffs and secret caves are all part of a unique mix of attractions in this area, commonly referred to as the Catlins after one of the early landowners of the 1840s. A varied coastline of cliffs and golden sand surf beaches provides a home to a wide range of wildlife, from rare Hector's dolphins to penguins, seals and sea lions. The area is made all the more spectacular by the ancient forests of rimu, matai, totara, beech and miro which reach almost to the sea, and which are filled with the sounds of native birds.

Gallery sign, Papatowai

Curio Bay ②
The fossilized remains of a 160 million-year-old forest from the Jurassic period can be seen on a rock platform at low tide.

Waipapa Point ①
A picturesque spot but the site of New Zealand's worst shipping disaster when the SS *Tararua* ran aground on a hidden reef in 1881, with the loss of 131 lives.

0 kilometres 5

0 miles 5

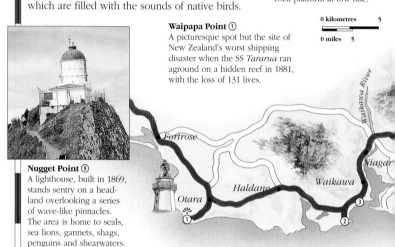

Waikawa River

Fortrose

Niagar

Haldane

Waikawa

Otara

Nugget Point ⑨
A lighthouse, built in 1869, stands sentry on a headland overlooking a series of wave-like pinnacles. The area is home to seals, sea lions, gannets, shags, penguins and shearwaters.

TIPS FOR DRIVERS

Tour length: 172 km (107 miles) from Invercargill to where the tour rejoins State Hwy 1 at Balclutha. About 60 km (37 miles) of the route is on unsealed roads, so care is required. It is well worth allowing at least a day to complete the journey because of the number of side tracks and walks taking visitors to the many sights.

Stopping-off points: Most accommodation on this route is on a small scale. There are motels at Chaslands, Papatowai and Owaka, and camping grounds, backpackers hostels and homestays dotted around the area. Food and refreshments are available at numerous places along the route.

Jack's Blowhole ⑧
Sea water surges through a subterranean tunnel before spraying out of this 60-m (197-ft) deep blowhole, located in the middle of cliff top pastures.

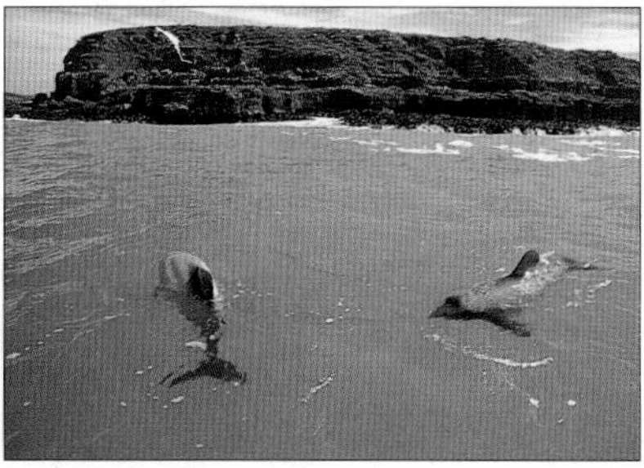

Porpoise Bay ③
Little black and white Hector's dolphins are often seen playing here in the surf as the waves break along this long, curving beach.

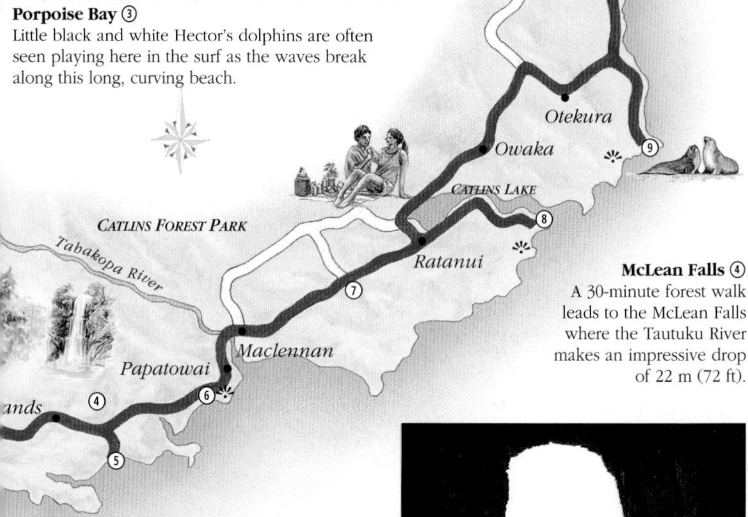
Balclutha
Romahapa
Otekura
Owaka
9
CATLINS LAKE
8
CATLINS FOREST PARK
Tahakopa River
Ratanui
7
Maclennan
Papatowai
6
4
5

McLean Falls ④
A 30-minute forest walk leads to the McLean Falls where the Tautuku River makes an impressive drop of 22 m (72 ft).

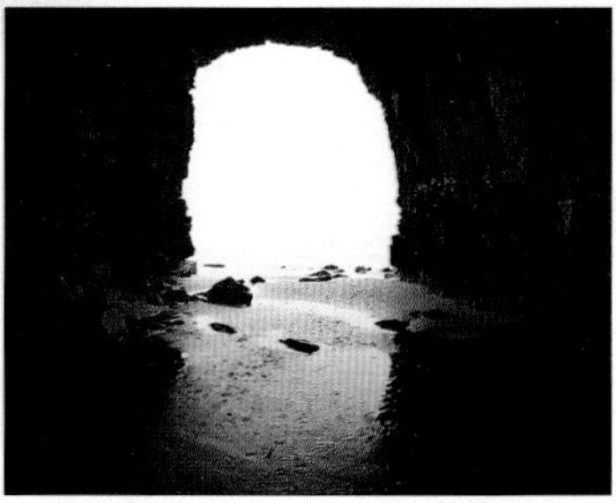

Cathedral Caves ⑤
The caves, accessible only at low tide, can be reached after a 40-minute walk through forest and along a beach. The opening of the largest cave is 30 m (98 ft) high.

Lake Wilkie ⑥
This small forest lake is only a short distance from the road but there is a 20-minute loop walk around it with some good examples of the large tree species found in the area.

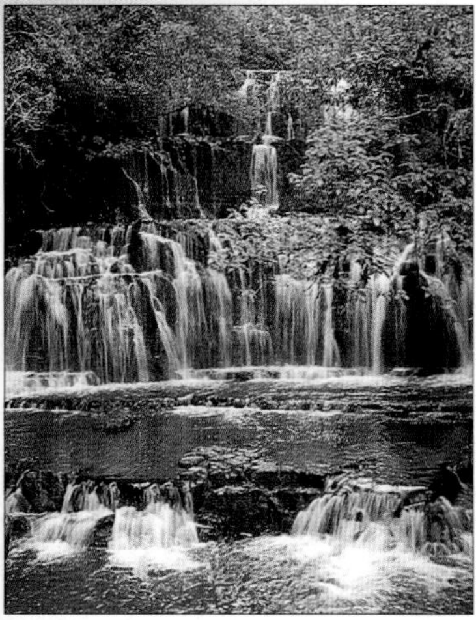

Purakaunui Falls ⑦
A ten-minute walk through beech and podocarp forest leads to a viewing platform overlooking these attractive waterfalls where the river drops 20 m (65 ft) over a series of wide terraces.

KEY

- Tour route
- Other roads
- River
- Viewpoint

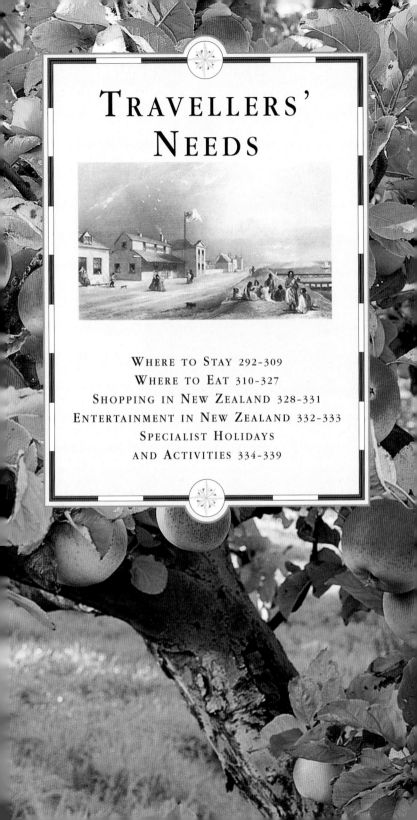

TRAVELLERS' NEEDS

WHERE TO STAY

NEW ZEALAND offers a variety of accommodation to suit all budgets. At the top end of the range, five-star hotels and wilderness lodges provide luxury accommodation. Mid-range hotels, motels and motor lodges, self-catering apartments, country pubs, farmstays, and bed and breakfasts cater for travellers on a more modest budget. For those on a

Auckland hotel doorman

very tight budget, camping grounds and backpacker hostels offer good value. Away from the larger cities and resorts, the choice of accommodation can be limited, although there are motels and camping grounds in virtually all locations. The listings on pages 296–309 give full descriptions of different types of accommodation throughout New Zealand to suit all budgets.

Parkroyal Hotel in Victoria Square, Christchurch *(see p306)*

GRADINGS AND FACILITIES

THE ONLY independent accommodation grading system in New Zealand is Qualmark, which was established by the Automobile Association and Tourism New Zealand in 1994. Qualmark grades hotels, motels and camping grounds on a star system. One star indicates that the premises meet basic standards of cleanliness, comfort and hospitality, while five stars denote that the facility is among the best in New Zealand. Qualmark plans to introduce a grading system for backpacker hostels in 2002. The Qualmark system is voluntary, however, and many accommodation establishments choose not to participate in it.

    Many of the large chain hotels are air conditioned, but the New Zealand climate does not generally warrant air conditioning. Hot showers and heating are provided in all types of accommodation. Linen is also provided in

hotels and motels. In backpacker hostels and camping grounds, linen is not always provided but can usually be hired for a reasonable fee.

PRICES

PRICES VARY according to the style of accommodation, facilities and services. Luxury lodges start at about NZ\$600 a night, while a room in a backpacker hostel can be as low as NZ\$30 a night. Most motels are in the range of NZ\$50 to NZ\$100

per unit, while bed and breakfast hotels cost between NZ\$50 and NZ\$100 per person. Off-season discounts are often available, and it is a good idea to ask about these when making bookings.

BOOKINGS

IT IS ADVISABLE to book accommodation in advance, especially at peak holiday times (December to February). During winter, hotels and motels in ski resort towns are often fully booked during school holidays (two weeks in both early July and in late September–early October). Bookings can be made directly to the accommodation provider, either by fax, telephone or via the Internet, through travel agents or at one of New Zealand's 100 visitor information centres.

    In most cases, a credit card number will be requested when a booking is arranged. It is wise to ask about cancellation policies when

Edwardian façade of the Southern Cross in Dunedin *(see p308)*

◁ **An apple orchard in the Hawke's Bay area**

Huka Lodge on the banks of the Waikato River *(see p302)*

making bookings as some premises will debit the credit card one night's accommodation if a cancellation is made at short notice. If additional services are required, such as children's cots, inform the accommodation provider when making a booking.

CHILDREN

TRAVELLING with children in New Zealand is easy, with cots and baby-sitting services generally available on request. However, children are not welcome at some exclusive lodges and bed and breakfasts. The definition of a "child" among hotels varies, ranging from under 12 to 17 years. Children enjoy special rates only if they are the third or subsequent occupant of a room and do not request an extra bed. Rooms advertised as "triple" rooms normally contain one double bed and a single one, while "quad" rooms have two double beds.

DISABLED TRAVELLERS

NEW ZEALAND law stipulates that all new buildings as well as old buildings undergoing major renovation must provide "reasonable and adequate" access for the disabled. Most facilities have wheelchair access. It is best to check in advance.

LUXURY LODGES

OFTEN LOCATED near a lake, river or beach, such lodges provide breathtaking scenery, elegant surroundings and high quality service for a limited number of guests at any one time. Three New Zealand lodges that have won international acclaim are Huka Lodge located on the Waikato River near Taupo *(p302)*, Solitaire Lodge on a bush-covered peninsula of Lake Tarawera not far from Rotorua *(p301)*, and Wharekauhau Country Estate at Palliser Bay in Wairarapa *(p303)*.

Qualmark hotel grading sign

Many lodges specialize in fishing, hunting and other outdoor activities, and hosts often have extensive knowledge of the local environment. The tariff at the most exclusive lodges can be as high as NZ$1,900 a night, including meals and alcohol.

CHAIN HOTELS

SEVERAL INTERNATIONAL luxury hotel chains, including the **Hyatt**, **Millennium**, **Novotel**, **Parkroyal** and **Sheraton**, are represented in New Zealand. Other chains include the **Copthorne**, **Scenic Circle** and **Pacifica**, which offer a reliable standard of accommodation in the main cities and resorts of New Zealand. Chain hotels offer a full range

of services, including a television, telephone, minibar and bathroom *en suite* in all rooms, as well as room service and restaurants. Some also have sports, business and conference facilities. For hotel listings, see pp296–309.

COUNTRY PUBS

THESE ARE found throughout rural New Zealand and range in style from basic, inexpensive accommodation to "boutique" lodgings in renovated historic buildings. Prices vary greatly depending on the location and facilities, but can be as low as NZ$45 a night. Linen is provided and bathrooms may be private or shared. Some country pubs also provide backpacker accommodation and meals.

Typical wooden country pub accommodation

Last Resort backpacker lodge at Karamea *(see p307)*

SELF-CATERING APARTMENTS

THIS STYLE of accommodation is not widely available in New Zealand, but can be found in the main cities and at major resort towns such as Queenstown. With spacious rooms and kitchen facilities, self-catering apartments are popular with corporate travellers seeking both comfort and independence. Prices vary depending on the length of stay.

For travellers wishing to spend a week or more in one location, a good option is to rent a holiday home. These can range in quality from a luxurious home to a tiny, rustic cottage known in New Zealand as a "bach" (pronounced "batch"). Real estate agents in the area are the best source of information about available holiday homes.

MOTELS AND MOTOR LODGES

MOTELS ARE THE most common form of visitor accommodation in New Zealand, and even small towns have at least one. They are particularly suitable for large families or groups because they are spacious and have their own cooking facilities. They usually contain one or two bedrooms, a lounge, kitchen and bathroom, and have a television set, radio and telephone. Smaller units, where guests sleep in the lounge, are called studios. Larger motels and motor lodges are similar to hotels, with swimming pools,

laundry facilities, restaurants and room service.

Travellers can save money by purchasing a motel accommodation pass for one of the local chains, such as **Best Western** or **Golden Chain** *(see p295)*.

BACKPACKER HOSTELS AND YOUTH HOSTELS

NEW ZEALAND has more than 250 backpacker hostels in scenic locations around the country. These are clearly signposted along the main roads. Hostels offer clean, tidy and inexpensive accommodation, and are excellent places to meet other travellers and exchange up-to-date information as things change quickly. Prices can be as low as NZ$15 per person for a shared room and NZ$30 for a single room.

Another option for low-budget travellers is the **Youth Hostel Association** (YHA)

Accommodation sign in Marlborough

(see p295), which has a chain of 56 hostels in strategic locations. Despite the name, youth hostels cater for travellers of all ages. They usually offer separate male and female dormitories, as well as twin, double and family rooms for those wanting more privacy. Linen and blankets are provided. Youth hostels also have well-equipped communal kitchens and comfortable lounges for relaxation. However, bathroom facilities in most hostels are shared.

It is not necessary to be a member of the Youth Hostel Association to stay at a hostel, but non-members incur a surcharge of NZ$3 a night in addition to the regular fee.

FARMSTAYS AND HOMESTAYS

FARMSTAYS offer visitors the chance to gain an insight into everyday farming life. Guests stay either in the farmhouse or in separate quarters, and share meals with their hosts. Bathroom facilities may be either shared with the family or separate. In many cases, guests are able to participate in some farming activities.

Homestays are located in both urban and rural areas, and, like farmstays, guests stay in the family home or in adjacent quarters and share meals with their hosts. Tariffs range from NZ$100 to NZ$400 a double per night.

Holiday-makers at a farmstay in Manawatu

Maui Rentals campervan on tour in the South Island

CAMPING GROUNDS

CAMPING GROUNDS (also called holiday parks and motor camps) offer a cheap way of travelling. Some contain sites for tents and caravans only, while others have basic cabins fitted with bunk beds, or tourist flats with full cooking and bathroom facilities. Many have children's playgrounds and games rooms, and are located beside beaches, lakes or rivers in scenic locations.

Typical motor camp sign

Camping grounds have shared washing and laundry facilities, and fully equipped communal kitchens. At some, shops sell basic foodstuffs and supplies. It is wise to book during the main New Zealand holiday period, from Christmas until the end of January, but not necessary during off-peak periods. Most camping grounds charge about NZ$7 a night per person for a camp site and from about NZ$30 for a double cabin.

CAMPERVANS

A POPULAR way to see the country is in a self-drive campervan. Two-, four- and six-berth vans are available, complete with amenities *(see p359)*. Rental charges vary according to the season.

Generally, campervan travellers stop at camping grounds for the night where they can hire a site with electric power. In remote locations, travellers can park in a rest area near the roadside. Many camping grounds have "dump stations" for the disposal of sewage effluent.

DIRECTORY

LUXURY HOTELS AND LODGES

Southern Crossings
Private Bag 93-236, Parnell, Auckland.
((09) 309 5912.
@ nzdesign@southern-crossings.co.nz

New Zealand Lodge Association
41 Towey St, Oamaru.
((04) 434 7939.
W www.lodgesofnz.co.nz

CHAIN HOTELS

Copthorne
W www.stay.with-us.com

Hyatt
W www.hyatt.com

Millennium
W www.stay.with-us.com

Novotel
W www.novotel.com

Pacifica
W www.pacificalodges.co.nz

Parkroyal
W www.parkroyal.com.au

Scenic Circle
W www.scenic-circle.co.nz

Sheraton
W www.sheraton.com

MOTELS

Best Western NZ
PO Box 74-346, Auckland 5.
(0800 237 893.

Golden Chain NZ
PO Box 5341, Christchurch.

((03) 358 0821.
@ res@mchg.co.nz

BACKPACKER AND YOUTH HOSTELS

Budget Backpacker Hostels NZ
99 Titiraupenga St, Taupo.
((07) 377 1568.
W www.backpack.co.nz

VIP Backpacker Resorts NZ
PO Box 80021, Greenbay, Auckland.
((09) 827 6016.
W www.vip.co.nz

Youth Hostel Association of New Zealand
PO Box 436, Christchurch.
((03) 379 9970.
W www.stayyha.com

FARMSTAYS

New Zealand Farm Holidays
PO Box 74, Kumeu, Auckland.
(0800 803 276.
W www.nzaccom.co.nz

New Zealand Home and Farmstay Co
PO Box 66, Geraldine.
((09) 810 9175.

BED AND BREAKFAST HOTELS

New Zealand Federation of Bed and Breakfast Hotels
123 Grey St, Palmerston Nth. ((06) 358 6928.
W www.nzbnbhotels.com

Choosing a Hotel

THE HOTELS in this guide have been selected for their good value, excellent facilities and location. This chart lists the hotels by region, starting with Auckland. The colour codes of each region are shown on the thumb tabs. This list also highlights the various facilities on offer at each establishment. For restaurant listings, see pages 316–27.

	CREDIT CARDS	NUMBER OF ROOMS	RESTAURANT/CAFÉ	CHILDREN'S FACILITIES	FAMILY ROOMS
AUCKLAND					
CITY: *Aspen Lodge* @ aspenlodge@xtra.co.nz 62 Emily Place. **Road map** E2. ((09) 379 6698. FAX (09) 377 7625. Affordable accommodation in the inner city. The manager organizes sightseeing tours and the lodge provides complimentary coffee. 📶 ♿	ⓢ	AE DC MC V	28		●	▓
CITY: *Auckland City Hotel* @ aucklandcityhotel@xtra.co.nz 131 Beach Rd. **Road map** E2. ((09) 303 2463. FAX (09) 358 2489. Opposite Auckland's railway station, this hotel is close to the waterfront and various tourist attractions. 📶 24 TV 📶 🅟	ⓢ	AE DC MC V	60	▓		▓
CITY: *Auckland Peninsula Hotel* Elm St, Avondale. **Road map** E2. ((09) 828 1179. FAX (09) 828 3496. Private gardens, an in-house casino and a solarium are among the attractions of this suburban hotel. 📶 24 TV 📶 Ⓨ 🏊 🍽 🅟	ⓢ	AE DC MC V	50	▓		▓
CITY: *City Backpackers Hotel* @ reservations@city_backpacker.hotel.co.nz 38 Fort St. **Road map** E2. ((09) 307 0181. Budget accommodation in city red-light district but within walking distance of all inner-city tourist attractions. Clean rooms. 📶 📶 ♿	ⓢ	AE DC MC V	35	▓	●	▓
CITY: *Georgia Parkside Backpackers* @ bacpacgeorgia@xtra.co.nz 189 Park Rd, Grafton. **Road map** E2. (09) 309 9560. FAX (09) 309 8999. Budget accommodation in an early 20th-century house across the road from Auckland Domain. Between the city and Newmarket. 📶 🅟	ⓢ	MC V	12			▓
CITY: *Mount Albert Motor Inn* @ dickbarb@ihug.co.nz 743 New North Rd, Mt Albert. **Road map** E2. ((09) 846 4959. FAX (09) 846 9462. Close to the city centre, this motel has a quiet ambience with a pleasant garden and an outdoor spa for guests. TV 🅟 ♿ 🅟	ⓢ	DC MC V	14		●	▓
CITY: *The Brown Kiwi* @ enquiries@brownkiwi.co.nz 7 Prosford St, Ponsonby. **Road map** E2. (& FAX (09) 378 0191. Built in 1900, this two-storey refurbished colonial home has a kitchen, laundry facilities and garden. Within walking distance of Ponsonby's many restaurants and cafés. 📶 🅟	ⓢ	BC MC V	9			▓
CITY: *Acapulco Motel* 20 Shelly Beach Rd. **Road map** E2. ((09) 376 5246. FAX (09) 378 1528. These self-contained units are close to amenities and the city bus stop. Near tourist attractions such as the Maritime Museum and Victoria Park Market. More than 50 restaurants nearby. 📶 TV 📶 Ⓨ 🅟	ⓢⓢ	AE DC JCB MC V	15		●	▓
CITY: *Bavaria B&B Hotel* @ bavaria@xtra.co.nz 83 Valley Rd, Mt Eden. **Road map** E2. ((09) 638 9641. FAX (09) 638 9665. This German-owned hotel offers excellent personal service and home-cooked breakfast. Close to the airport and city sights. 📶 📶 🅟	ⓢⓢ	AE BC JCB MC V	11		●	▓
CITY: *City Towers Serviced Apartments* @ reservations@citytowers.co.nz 2 Maungawhau Rd, Newmarket. **Road map** E2. ((09) 520 6186. FAX (09) 524 6512. Spacious apartments in the prime shopping district. Well-priced considering the space and central location. 📶 TV 📶 🅟	ⓢⓢ	AE DC MC V	33		●	▓
CITY: *Ellerslie International Motor Inn Ltd* @ accom@eimi.co.nz Cnr Ellerslie/Panmure Hwy & Wilkinson Rd, Ellerslie. **Road map** E2. ((09) 525 1909. FAX (09) 525 1465. Well-appointed motel with in-house video system. Close to the southern motorway and airport. 📶 TV 📶 🅟 ♿ 🅟	ⓢⓢ	AE DC MC V	36	▓	●	▓
CITY: *Kiwi International Airport Hotel* 150 McKenzie Rd, Mangere. **Road map** E2. ((09) 256 0046. FAX (09) 256 0047. A convenient location for travellers, the hotel offers a 24-hour airport shuttle, round-the-clock reception and a spa pool. 📶 TV 🅟 ♿ 🅟	ⓢⓢ	AE DC MC V	86	▓	●	▓

<table>
<tr><td>

Price categories for a standard double room per night, inclusive of Goods and Service Tax (GST) of 12.5%. Breakfast is usually charged separately.
$ under NZ$100
$$ NZ$100–NZ$150
$$$ NZ$150–NZ$200
$$$$ NZ$200–NZ$250
$$$$$ over NZ$250

</td><td>

CREDIT CARDS
AE American Express; *BC* Bankcard; *DC* Diners Club; *JCB* Japanese Credit Bureau; *MC* Master Card/Access; *V* Visa.
RESTAURANT/CAFÉ
Hotel restaurant or dining room usually open to non-residents unless otherwise stated.
CHILDREN'S FACILITIES
Child cots and a baby-sitting service available.
FAMILY ROOMS
Hotels with rooms to accommodate the whole family. Self-contained chalets and cabins are common in New Zealand.

</td></tr>
</table>

	CREDIT CARDS	NUMBER OF ROOMS	RESTAURANT/CAFÉ	CHILDREN'S FACILITIES	FAMILY ROOMS
CITY: *New President Hotel* **$$** 27–35 Victoria St West. **Road map** E2. (09) 303 1333. FAX (09) 303 1332. Value-for-money, mid-range accommodation in the central city. A wide range of facilities and good service. *limited.*	AE DC MC V	97	■	●	■
CITY: *Park Towers* @ rec@parktowers_hotel.co.nz **$$** 3 Scotia Place. **Road map** E2. (09) 309 2800. FAX (09) 302 1964. A mid-range hotel, Park Towers is within walking distance of the city nightclubs and Myers Park. It is close to dozens of restaurants along Upper Queen Street and Karangahape Road.	AE DC MC V	80	■	●	■
CITY: *Rydges Auckland* W sales_auckland@rydges.com **$$** Cnr Federal and Kingston sts. **Road map** E2. (09) 375 5900; (0800) 755 900. Close to tourist spots, Rydges Auckland provides reasonably priced rooms with a wide range of facilities that include a restaurant.	AE DC MC V	188	■	●	
CITY: *Barrycourt Motor Inn* @ barrycourt@xtra.co.nz **$$$** 10/20 Gladstone Rd. **Road map** E2. (09) 303 3789. FAX (09) 377 3309. Situated in fashionable Parnell, five minutes from downtown Auckland. Private spa pool, satellite TV, good harbour and city views in tranquil surroundings.	AE DC JCB MC V	107	■	●	■
CITY: *Birdwood House* @ info@birdwood.co.nz **$$$** 41 Birdwood Crescent, Parnell. **Road map** E2. (09) 306 5900. FAX (09) 306 5909. This restored 1914 Arts and Crafts Edwardian bungalow is located in the heart of Parnell, close to shops and restaurants. Very friendly, unobtrusive service.	MC V	5			
CITY: *Centra Auckland Hotel* **$$$** 128 Albert St. **Road map** E2. (09) 302 1111. FAX (09) 302 3111. Centrally located with excellent facilities for business people but suitable for tourists too. Good service and four levels of shops.	AE DC MC V	352	■	●	■
CITY: *Cornwall Park Motor Inn* @ cornwallpark@xtra.co.nz **$$$** 317 Manukau Rd. **Road map** E2. (09) 638 6409. FAX (09) 638 6407. This small motel is located in a quiet area close to the airport. Walking distance to Cornwall Park and One Tree Hill.	AE DC MC V	20			■
CITY: *Novotel Auckland* **$$$** 8 Customs St. **Road map** E2. (09) 377 8920. FAX (09) 302 0993. Close to Auckland's waterfront, downtown shopping areas and the casino. Good views towards Rangitoto Island from the restaurant.	AE DC JCB MC V	188	■	●	
CITY: *The Devereux Boutique Hotel* **$$$** 267 Remuera Rd. (09) 524 5044. FAX (09) 524 5080. @ the.devereux.hotel@xtra.co.nz This boutique hotel from the 1890s is renowned for its wide choice of breakfast items. Located in the affluent suburb of Remuera, the hotel is quiet with a large garden.	AE DC MC V	12			■
CITY: *Hyatt Regency* @ auckland@hyatt.co.nz **$$$$** Cnr Princes St and Waterloo Quadrant. **Road map** E2. (09) 366 1234. FAX (09) 303 2932. Excellent service, very central and with a reputation for good quality, innovative food.	AE DC JCB MC V	274	■	●	■
CITY: *Aachen House* @ info@aachenhouse.co.nz **$$$$$** 39 Market Rd, Remuera. **Road map** E2. (09) 520 2329. FAX (09) 524 2898. Luxury accommodation with good, personal service. Aachen House is very well appointed with a collection of Dutch-Indonesian antiques. Private restaurant and large conservatory.	AE DC MC V	9			

For key to symbols see back flap

	CREDIT CARDS	NUMBER OF ROOMS	RESTAURANT/CAFÉ	CHILDREN'S FACILITIES	FAMILY ROOMS
Price categories for a standard double room per night, inclusive of Goods and Service Tax (GST) of 12.5%. Breakfast is usually charged separately. **(S)** under NZ\$100 **(S)(S)** NZ\$100–NZ\$150 **(S)(S)(S)** NZ\$150–NZ\$200 **(S)(S)(S)(S)** NZ\$200–NZ\$250 **(S)(S)(S)(S)(S)** over NZ\$250	**CREDIT CARDS** *AE* American Express; *BC* Bankcard; *DC* Diners Club; *JCB* Japanese Credit Bureau; *MC* Master Card/Access; *V* Visa. **RESTAURANT/CAFÉ** Hotel restaurant or dining room usually open to non-residents unless otherwise stated. **CHILDREN'S FACILITIES** Child cots and a baby-sitting service available. **FAMILY ROOMS** Hotels with rooms to accommodate the whole family. Self-contained chalets and cabins are common in New Zealand.				

CITY: *Carlton Hotel* @ sales@carlton_auckland.co.nz **(S)(S)(S)(S)** Mayoral Drive. **Road map** E2. (*(09) 366 3000*. **FAX** *(09) 366 0121*. An imposing atrium, superb Japanese restaurant, fabulous views over Waitemata Harbour and close proximity to the town centre make the Carlton a popular luxury hotel. 🛏 24 TV ▤ 🏊 Ŷ 🌊 🍴 🔆 ᴿ P	AE DC JCB MC V	469	■		■
CITY: *Sheraton Auckland Hotel* **(S)(S)(S)(S)** 83 Symonds St. **Road map** E2. (*(09) 379 5132*. **FAX** *(09) 377 4075*. Centrally located with excellent service for tourists and business people. The restaurant is highly rated. 🛏 24 TV ▤ 🏊 Ŷ 🍴 🔆 ᴿ P	AE DC MC V	410	■	●	■
GREATER AUCKLAND: *North Shore Motels & Holiday Park* **(S)** 52 Northcote Rd, Takapuna. **Road map** E2. (*(09) 418 2578*. **FAX** *(09) 480 0435*. @ info@nsmotels.co.nz Choice of motel units, tourist flats, leisure lodges, cabins, dormitories and tent sites. 🛏 TV 🏊 🔆 🔆 ᴿ P	MC V	90		●	■
GREATER AUCKLAND: *Albany Country Home* **(S)(S)** 57 Ngarahana Ave, Albany. **Road map** E2. (*(09) 413 9580*. **FAX** *(09) 413 9583*. @ fordham@nznet.gen.nz This modern colonial-style house has stained-glass windows, great views of Auckland's upper harbour and a quiet country setting. 🛏 🌊 🔆 P	AE DC MC V	2		●	■
GREATER AUCKLAND: *Fitzroy House* **(S)(S)** Port Fitzroy, Great Barrier Island. **Road map** E2. (*(09) 429 0091*. **FAX** *(09) 429 0492*. Two 1901 cottages surrounded by walkways through native bush. Each cottage sleeps six. Canoes available. 🛏 🌊 P	MC V	6		●	■
GREATER AUCKLAND: *Greenmead Farm Cottage* @ jabat@magic.gen.nz **(S)(S)** 115 Bethells Rd, RD1, Henderson. **Road map** E2. (*(09) 810 9363*. **FAX** *(09) 810 9122*. A well-maintained two-bedroom cottage that offers a rural alternative. Close to the west coast beaches and vineyards. 🛏 TV 🌊 P		2		●	■
GREATER AUCKLAND: *Harpoon Hill* @ jan.murray@xtra.co.nz **(S)(S)** Great Barrier Island. **Road map** E2. (& **FAX** *(09) 429 0337*. Modern, fully self-contained cottage with a garden full of native trees. Sea views. Friendly service and a peaceful environment. 🛏 TV 🌊		1			
GREATER AUCKLAND: *Esplanade Hotel* **(S)(S)(S)** 1 Victoria Rd, Devonport. **Road map** E2. (*(09) 445 1291*. **FAX** *(09) 445 1999*. The newly refurbished Esplanade Hotel combines traditional ambience with upgraded facilities. Close to Devonport town. 🛏 TV 🌊 Ŷ 🔆 P	AE DC MC V	16	■		
GREATER AUCKLAND: *Rangiwai Lodge* W www.accommodation-nz.com **(S)(S)(S)** 29 Rangiwai Rd, Titirangi. **Road map** E2. (& **FAX** *(09) 817 8990*. This lodge suits tourists who want to combine visits to the city with tramping in the Waitakere Ranges and the west coast. 🛏 🌊 P	MC V	4			
GREATER AUCKLAND: *Villa Cambria Bed & Breakfast Inn* **(S)(S)(S)** 71 Vauxhall Rd, Devonport. **Road Map** E2. (*(09) 445 7899*. **FAX** *(09) 446 0508*. A traditional boutique hotel, with pleasant ambience. A courtesy car to the ferry that links Devonport to central Auckland is provided. The beach is a short walk away. 🛏 🌊 🔆 P	AE MC V	5			
GREATER AUCKLAND: *The Peace and Plenty Inn* **(S)(S)(S)(S)** 6 Flagstaff Terrace, Devonport. **Road map** E2. (*(09) 445 2925*. **FAX** *(09) 445 2901*. @ peaceandplenty@xtra.co.nz Boutique hotel with gourmet breakfast and well-appointed rooms. Close to ferry link to the city. 🛏 TV 🌊 🔆 P	AE DC MC V	6			■
GREATER AUCKLAND: *Glenora Estate* @ glenora.estate@xtra.co.nz **(S)(S)(S)(S)(S)** 160 Nick Johnstone Drive, Oneroa, Waiheke Island. **Road map** E2. (*(09) 372 5082*. **FAX** *(09) 372 5087*. French farm-style luxury accommodation with sea views. Glenora is a popular wedding spot with a *pétanque* (boules) court, native bush and an olive grove. 🛏 TV 🌊 Ŷ 🔆 🔆 P	AE DC MC V	3			

NORTHLAND

DARGAVILLE: *Waipoua Lodge* @ tony@waipoualodge.co.nz — $$ — AE BC DC MC V — 3
State Hwy 12, RD6. **Road map** E1. & FAX (09) 439 0422.
Simple cottages with friendly service. The licensed restaurant that forms part of the lodge has a good reputation.

KAITAIA: *Historic Kaitaia Hotel & Flame Grill* — $ — AE BC DC MC V — 36
15 Commerce St. **Road map** D1. (09) 408 0360.
Low-cost, simple accommodation in central Kaitaia in a hotel built in 1837. The restaurant offers fresh crayfish.

KAITAIA: *Houhora Chalets and Motor Lodge* — $ — AE DC MC V — 6
RD4, Kaitaia. **Road map** D1. (09) 409 8860. FAX (09) 409 8864.
Quiet, self-contained units at the tip of New Zealand. Close to Wagner Park, a good base for trips to Cape Reinga and Northland.

KERIKERI: *Palm Grove Cottage Motels* — $$$ — AE DC MC V — 6
Kerikeri Rd. **Road map** E1. & FAX (09) 407 8484.
These self-contained cottages are set in a large garden with water features. A short drive from historic tourist sights.

PAIHIA: *Peppertree Lodge* — $ — MC V — 56
15 King's Rd. **Road map** E1. & FAX (09) 402 6122.
Budget rooms and dormitories with a central kitchen. Meeting point for mostly younger tourists. Clean with a friendly atmosphere.

PAIHIA: *The Park Lodge on Paihia* @ parklodge@xtra.co.nz — $$ — AE DC MC V — 39
Cnr Seaview & McMurray rds. **Road map** E1. (09) 402 7826. FAX (09) 402 8500.
A five-minute walk to town, the lodge has extensive grounds, including a camping site. There is a saltwater pool for guests.

PAIHIA: *Pioneer On the Waterfront* @ pioneer@xtra.co.nz — $$$$ — AE DC MC V — 11
Marsden Rd. **Road map** E1. (09) 402 7924. FAX (09) 402 7656.
These serviced apartments are very spacious. Each has a washing machine, gas barbecue and private balcony.

PUKENUI: *Pukenui Lodge Motel* w www.pukenuilodge.co.nz — $ — AE MC V — 9
Cnr Wharf and Main Rd North. **Road map** D1. (09) 409 8837. FAX (09) 409 8704. New Zealand's northernmost hotel. Separate youth hostel. Fishing and tours to Ninety Mile Beach and Cape Reinga.

RUSSELL: *Mako Lodge & Fishing Charters* — $$ — AE DC MC V — 3
Te Wahapu Rd. **Road map** E1. & FAX (09) 403 7770. @ mako.lodge_charters @xtra.co.nz Close to Russell town, the location offers the option to go fishing or sightseeing on an 8-m (27-feet) vessel. Free use of a kayak and dinghy. Pets can be accommodated upon request.

RUSSELL: *Kimberley Lodge* @ kimlodge@ihug.co.nz — $$$$$ — AE DC MC V — 5
Cnr York & Pitt sts. **Road map** E1. (09) 403 7090. FAX (09) 403 7239.
Luxury mansion with personal service and professional chef. Offers good views towards Paihia. The hotel staff will arrange seaplane flights, sea kayaking and charter yachts for guests.

TUTUKAKA: *Pacific Rendezvous* — $$ — AE DC MC V — 30
Motel Rd, RD3. **Road map** E1. (09) 434 3919. FAX (09) 434 3919.
Self-contained units set in extensive grounds. The motel has a mini shop and its own beach with good fishing spots.

WAITANGI: *Copthorne Resort Waitangi, Bay of Islands* — $$ — AE DC MC V — 145
Tau Henare Drive. **Road map** E1. (09) 402 7411. FAX (09) 402 8200.
One of the largest accommodation options in the region. Within walking distance of Waitangi National Trust grounds.

WHANGAREI: *The Grand Hotel* — $ — AE BC DC MC V — 28
2 Bank St. **Road map** E1. (09) 438 4279. FAX (09) 438 4276.
Dating back to the 19th century, the Grand's claim to fame is Queen Elizabeth's stay here in 1953. The hotel has 3 bars.

WHANGAREI: *Quality Hotel* @ quality.whangarei@xtra.co.nz — $$ — AE DC MC V — 95
9 Riverside Drive. **Road map** E1. (09) 438 0284. FAX (09) 438 4320.
Offers a wide range of facilities for business people as well as tourists, from a sauna to cable TV. The hotel offers a special rate for corporate bookings.

For key to symbols see back flap

<table>
<tr><td colspan="2">

Price categories for a standard double room per room, inclusive of Goods and Service Tax (GST) of 12.5%. Breakfast is usually charged separately.
$ under NZ$100
$$ NZ$100–NZ$150
$$$ NZ$150–NZ$200
$$$$ NZ$200–NZ$250
$$$$$ over NZ$250

</td></tr>
</table>

CREDIT CARDS
AE American Express; BC Bankcard; DC Diners Club; JCB Japanese Credit Bureau; MC Master Card/Access; V Visa.

RESTAURANT/CAFÉ
Hotel restaurant or dining room usually open to non-residents unless otherwise stated.

CHILDREN'S FACILITIES
Child cots and a baby-sitting service available.

FAMILY ROOMS
Hotels with rooms to accommodate the whole family. Self-contained chalets and cabins are common in New Zealand.

		CREDIT CARDS	NUMBER OF ROOMS	RESTAURANT/CAFÉ	CHILDREN'S FACILITIES	FAMILY ROOMS
THE CENTRAL NORTH ISLAND						
CAMBRIDGE: *Riverside Motor Lodge* @ riverside@clear.net.nz 7 Williamson St. **Road map** E3. ((07) 827 6069. FAX (07) 827 3068. Set in spacious grounds with lovely views and close to a river walk. Golf club and jet-boat operator nearby.	$	AE DC MC V	34	■	●	■
COROMANDEL: *Jacaranda Lodge* @ jacarandacoromandel@xtra.co.nz 3195 Tiki Rd. **Road map** E2. (& FAX (07) 866 8002. Located on a small, peaceful farm with beautiful gardens. A great opportunity to see native birds and trees.	$	MC V	6		●	■
COROMANDEL: *Karamana Homestead* @ karamana@xtra.co.nz 84 Whangapoua Rd. **Road map** E2. ((07) 866 7138. FAX (07) 866 7477. One of the oldest buildings in Coromandel town, full of antique furniture. The old-world charm is complemented by excellent food and complimentary pre-dinner drinks for guests.	$$	MC V	4		●	■
GISBORNE: *Champers Motor Lodge* @ champers.gisborne@xtra.co.nz 811 Gladstone Rd. **Road map** F3. ((06) 863 1515. FAX (06) 863 1520. Close to a golf course in landscaped grounds with a children's playground. Modern and friendly.	$	AE DC MC V	14		●	■
GISBORNE: *Pacific Harbour Motor Inn* Cnr of Read's Quay & Pitt St. **Road map** F3. ((06) 867 8847. FAX (06) 867 4586. A modern motor inn close to picturesque Gisborne Port, bars, restaurants and town centre.	$$	AE DC MC V	25			■
GISBORNE: *Acton Estate Lodge* @ acton.estate@actrix.gem.nz 577 Back Ormond Rd. **Road map** F3. ((06) 867 9999. FAX (06) 867 1116. Historic mansion on a large scenic estate. Tranquil ambience amid the trees and garden.	$$$$$	AE DC MC V	6	■		
HAHEI: *The Church Accommodation and Dining* 87 Hahei Beach Rd. **Road map** E2. ((07) 866 3533. FAX (07) 866 3055. @ hahei4ch@voyager.co.nz A wonderful atmosphere exists in the church-style dining and lounge area built from recycled timber. Chalets are set in extensive gardens.	$$	MC V	7	■		
HAMILTON: *The Flying Hedgehog* 1157 Victoria St. **Road Map** E2. ((07) 839 2800 FAX (07) 834 0098. Friendly, clean backpacker hostel close to central Hamilton. Papier-mâché animals and wooden fish decorations are a nice touch.	$	MC V	10			■
HAMILTON: *Le Grand Hotel* @ legrandhotel@xtra.co.nz Cnr Victoria & Collingwoods sts. **Road map** E2. ((07) 839 1994. FAX (07) 839 7994. Built in 1926 as an office block, this central Hamilton building was converted in 1994 into a European-style hotel.	$$	AE DC MC V	38	■		■
HAMILTON: *Novotel Tainui Hamilton* 7 Alma St. **Road map** E2. ((07) 838 1366. FAX (07) 838 1367. Situated in central Hamilton on the banks of the Waikato River, the spacious rooms have stunning views.	$$$	AE DC MC V	177	■	●	■
MOUNT MAUNGANUI: *Main Beach Hotel* 23 Marine Parade. **Road map** E2. (& FAX (07) 574 4050. This boutique motel is close to shopping, restaurants and hot pools. Across the road from the beach.	$$	AE DC MC V	4		●	■
MOUNT MAUNGANUI: *Oceanside Motel Lodge* @ oceanlodge@xtra.co.nz 1 Maunganui Rd. **Road map** E2. ((07) 575 5371. FAX (07) 575 0486. Large, modern lodge with harbour and ocean views, close to town centre and Mount Maunganui.	$$	AE DC MC V	60	■	●	■

NAPIER: *Shoreline Motel* @ shorelinemotel@xtra.co.nz (\$)(\$)
377 Marine Parade. **Road map** F4. **(** (06) 835 5222. **FAX** (06) 835 5955.
Fabulous sea views in well-appointed units. Studio units have freshwater
spas.
AE DC MC V — 28

NAPIER: *County Hotel* @ countyhotel@xtra.co.nz (\$)(\$)(\$)
12 Browning St. **Road map** F4. **(** (06) 835 7800. **FAX** (06) 835 7797.
Close to the city centre and beach, this Art Deco hotel has been
beautifully restored.
AE DC MC V — 12

NAPIER: *Mon Logis Hôtel Privé* @ monlogis@xtra.co.nz (\$)(\$)(\$)
415 Marine Parade. **Road map** F4. **(** & **FAX** (06) 835 2125.
French-style ambience with home-cooked cuisine and personal service.
Bookings essential for five-course formal dinners. Close to Marine Parade
attractions. Tariff includes breakfast.
AE DC MC V — 4

NAPIER: *Mangapapa Lodge* @ mangapapa.lodge@xtra.co.nz (\$)(\$)(\$)(\$)(\$)
466 Napier Rd. **Road map** F4. **(** (06) 878 3234. **FAX** (06) 878 1214.
One of Napier's most prestigious properties, this lodge was once the
home of canned-food magnate, Sir James Wattie. The food, wine and
service are excellent.
AE DC JCB MC V — 10

RAGLAN: *Raglan Wagon Cabins* (\$)
611 Wainui Rd, Raglan. **Road map** E2. **(** (07) 825 8268.
Old railway wagons renovated into accommodation units are scattered
across a hillside with dramatic sea views.
MC V — 17

ROTORUA: *Funky Green Voyager* (\$)
4 Union St. **Road Map** E3. **(** (07) 346 1754. **FAX** (07) 350 1100.
This small, well-kept backpacker hostel offers double rooms and prides
itself on its cleanliness.
— 11

ROTORUA: *Namaste Point* @ namaste.point@xtra.co.nz (\$)(\$)
187 Te Akau Rd, Okere Falls. **Road map** E3. **(** (07) 362 4804. **FAX** (07) 362 4060.
Secluded, private retreat on the shores of Lake Rotoiti. Meals by
arrangement. Good fishing. Canoes are available.
MC V — 3

ROTORUA: *Wylie Court Motor Lodge* @ wyliroto@fc-hotels.co.nz (\$)(\$)
345 Fenton St. **Road map** E3. **(** (07) 347 7879. **FAX** (07) 346 1494.
The Campbell tartan and rockwork are themes running through this
lodge, a ten-minute walk from a redwood forest. Some suites have
mezzanine floors.
AE DC MC V — 36

ROTORUA: *Royal Lakeside Novotel* @ rotorua@novotel.co.nz (\$)(\$)(\$)
9–11 Tutanekai St. **Road map** E3. **(** (07) 346 3888. **FAX** (07) 347 1888.
Built in 1996, the hotel is close to the lake and central city area, shops
and restaurants.
AE DC JCB MC V — 199

ROTORUA: *The Prince's Gate Hotel* @ princes.gate@clear.net.nz (\$)(\$)(\$)
Arawa St. **Road map** E3. **(** (07) 348 1179. **FAX** (07) 348 6215.
Chandeliers, panelled walls and ornate staircases in this 1897 building
lend a charm absent in modern hotels.
AE DC MC V — 50

ROTORUA: *Millennium Hotel* @ millennium.rotorua@cdlhms.co.nz (\$)(\$)(\$)(\$)(\$)
Cnr Eruera & Hinemaru sts. **Road map** E3. **(** (07) 347 1234. **FAX** (07) 348 1234.
Native rimu timber frames the hotel lobby, creating a warm, friendly
atmosphere in this 4-star deluxe hotel.
AE DC MC V — 227

ROTORUA: *Solitare Lodge* @ solitaire@wave.co.nz (\$)(\$)(\$)(\$)(\$)
Ronald Rd, Lake Tarawera. **Road map** E3. **(** (07) 362 8208. **FAX** (07) 362 8445.
Solitaire Lodge is tucked away on a promontory above remote Lake
Tarawera. Privacy, seclusion and scenic beauty are hallmarks of a stay at
this luxury resort.
AE DC JCB MC V — 10

TAUPO: *Courtney Motel* @ reservations@courtneymotel.co.nz. (\$)
15 Tui St. **Road map** E3. **(** (07) 378 8398. **FAX** (07) 378 9789.
This quiet motel is close to Lake Taupo and has two- and three-bedroom
suites. Ten-minute walk to town.
AE DC MC V — 12

TAUPO: *Wairakei Resort* (\$)(\$)
Wairakei. **Road map** E3. **(** (07) 374 8021. **FAX** (07) 374 8485.
A large hotel with 9-hole golf course, squash court, billiard room, tennis
courts, table tennis and indoor bowling area. Across the road from the
18-hole Wairakei golf course.
AE DC MC V — 187

For key to symbols see back flap

Price categories for a standard double room per night, inclusive of Goods and Service Tax (GST) of 12.5%. Breakfast is usually charged separately.
- $ under NZ$100
- $$ NZ$100–NZ$150
- $$$ NZ$150–NZ$200
- $$$$ NZ$200–NZ$250
- $$$$$ over NZ$250

CREDIT CARDS
AE American Express; BC Bankcard; DC Diners Club; JCB Japanese Credit Bureau; MC Master Card/Access; V Visa.

RESTAURANT/CAFÉ
Hotel restaurant or dining room usually open to non-residents unless otherwise stated.

CHILDREN'S FACILITIES
Child cots and a baby-sitting service available.

FAMILY ROOMS
Hotels with rooms to accommodate the whole family. Self-contained chalets and cabins are common in New Zealand.

	CREDIT CARDS	NUMBER OF ROOMS	RESTAURANT/CAFÉ	CHILDREN'S FACILITIES	FAMILY ROOMS
TAUPO: Copthorne Manuels Resort Hotel $$$ 243 Lake Terrace. **Road map** E3. ☎ (07) 378 5110. **FAX** (07) 378 5341. @ copthorne.manuels@clear.net.nz Luxury Mediterranean-style hotel on Lake Taupo's shores. Most rooms have panoramic lake and mountain views.	AE DC MC V	71	●	●	■
TAUPO: Huka Lodge $$$$$ Huka Falls Rd. **Road map** E3. ☎ (07) 378 5791. **FAX** (07) 378 0427. Visiting royalty regularly stay in this secluded retreat that is consistently ranked as one of the world's best.	AE DC MC V	20	●	●	■
TAURANGA: Bell Lodge @ bell.lodge@host.co.nz $ 39 Bell St. **Road map** E3. ☎ (07) 578 6344. **FAX** (07) 578 6342. Motel and backpacker lodge accommodation is offered in this quiet location with good parking. Free shuttle rides into Tauranga city and Mount Maunganui.	MC V	16		●	■
TAURANGA: Hotel Armitage @ hotel.armitage@xtra.co.nz $$ 9 Willow St. **Road map** E3. ☎ (07) 578 9119. **FAX** (07) 577 9198. The Armitage has a wide range of facilities and is close to central Tauranga, the Rose Gardens, Monmouth Redoubt and the Mission House.	AE DC MC V	81	●	●	■
TE KUITI: Tapanui Country Home @ tapanui@xtra.co.nz $$ 1714 Oparure Rd, Te Kuiti (near Otorohanga). **Road map** E3. ☎ (07) 877 8549. **FAX** (07) 877 8541. A magnificently appointed home set in hill country amid stunning limestone outcrops. Panoramic views.	MC V	3	●		
THAMES: Adventure Backpacker Coromandel $ 476 Pollen St. **Road map** E2. ☎ & **FAX** (07) 868 6200. A bar and nightclub operate on Friday and Saturday nights in this historic Art Deco building. Staff organize adventure tours of the area.	DC MC V	15	●	●	■
TONGARIRO NATIONAL PARK: Skotel @ skotel@clear.net.nz $$ Whakapapa Village. **Road map** E3. ☎ (07) 892 3719. **FAX** (07) 892 3777. Relaxed atmosphere. Close proximity to Mount Ruapehu with excellent views.	AE DC MC V	50	●	●	■
TONGARIRO NATIONAL PARK: Powderhorn Chateau $$$ Mangawhero Terrace, Ohakune. **Road map** E3. ☎ (06) 385 8888. **FAX** (06) 385 8925. @ powderhorn@xtra.co.nz Close to Turoa ski field with open fireplaces in restaurants and natural timber finish to create a warm atmosphere.	AE DC MC V	30	●	●	■
TONGARIRO NATIONAL PARK: The Grand Chateau $$$ Whakapapa Village. **Road map** E3. ☎ (07) 892 3809. **FAX** (07) 892 3704. The Grand Chateau's massive proportions have made it a New Zealand icon. It has been graced by royalty.	AE DC MC V	73	●	●	■
WAINGARO: Brooklands Country Estate $$$$$ Waingaro Rd. **Road map** E2. ☎ (07) 825 4756. **FAX** (07) 825 4873. @ relax@brooklands.net.nz Luxurious hospitality on an 8 sq-km (3-sq mile) farm.	AE DC MC V	10	●	●	■
WAITOMO: Waitomo Caves Hotel ⓦ www.waitomo_hotel.co.nz $$ Lemon Point Rd. **Road map** E3. ☎ (07) 878 8204. **FAX** (07) 878 8205. Grand old hotel built in 1910, with an Art Deco addition in the 1930s. Rooms range from backpacker style to luxurious.	AE DC MC V	25	●	●	
WHAKATANE: White Island Rendevous $ 15 The Strand East. **Road map** F3. ☎ (07) 308 9500. **FAX** (07) 308 0303. Close to the waterfront and built with a marine theme, this new motel is close to central Whakatane.	AE DC MC V	10	●	●	■

WHAKATANE: *Livingston Inn Motel* @ livingstoninn@xtra.co.nz ⓈⓈ — AE DC MC V — 15
42 Landing Rd. **Road map** F3. 【 *(07) 308 6400.* FAX *(07) 308 5665.*
Built in 1996 and set back from the road, each self-contained unit
has its own spa pool. 🔧 TV ➳ 🔲 ⓵ P

WHANGAMATA: *Garden Motor Lodge* ⓈⓈ — AE DC MC V — 18
245 Port Rd. **Road map** E2. 【 & FAX *(07) 865 9580.*
Each modern unit has its own garden. An indoor barbecue is available
for guests along with free use of boogie boards. 🔧 TV ➳ ⓵ P

WHANGAMATA: *La Dolce Vita Mediterranean* ⓈⓈ — MC V — 3
107 Beverly Terrace. **Road map** E2. 【 *(07) 865 7916.* FAX *(07) 865 7918.*
An outstanding but moderately priced, vibrant Mediterranean-style
boutique hotel. Attention to detail is superb. 🔧 24 TV ➳ 🍴 ⓵ P

WHITIANGA: *Oceanside Motel* W www.whitianga.co.nz/oceanside ⓈⓈⓈ — AE DC MC V — 9
32 Buffalo Beach Rd. **Road map** E2. 【 *(07) 866 5766.* FAX *(07) 866 4803.*
This motel with panoramic sea views is close to safe swimming and is a
short walk from shops and restaurants. 🔧 TV

WHITIANGA: *Waterfront Motel* @ atwaterfront@mercurybay.co.nz ⓈⓈⓈ — MC V — 11
2 & 4 Buffalo Beach Rd. **Road map** E2. 【 *(07) 866 4498.* FAX *(07) 866 4494.*
Superb views and close to shops and restaurants. Rooms are spacious
and quiet. For those seeking to maximize the view, there is a third-storey
penthouse. 🔧 TV ➳ 🔲 ⓵ P

WELLINGTON AND THE SOUTH

FEATHERSTON: *Fernside* W www.fernside.co.nz ⓈⓈⓈⓈⓈ — AE MC V — 4
RD1, Featherston. **Road map** E4. 【 *(06) 308 8265.* FAX *(06) 308 9172.*
On the main highway but set back in a mature garden, Fernside offers
luxury accommodation at the top end of the price range, where nothing
is too much trouble. 🔧 24 TV ➳ 🍸 ⓵ 🔲 P

GREYTOWN: *The Green Man* Ⓢ — MC V — 9
53 Main St, Greytown (near Featherston). **Road map** E4. 【 *(06) 304 9569.* FAX
(06) 304 8238. A cheerful country-style pub with a restaurant and budget
accommodation. Serves boutique beers and local wines. ➳ P

LEVIN: *The Fantails* Ⓢ — BC MC V — 3
40 MacArthur St. **Road map** E4. 【 *(06) 368 9011.* FAX *(06) 368 9279.*
Bush surrounds this bed and breakfast that also offers self-contained
apartments. Evening meals feature organic food. 🔧 TV ➳ ⓵ P

MARTINBOROUGH: *Shadyvale* @ huntavale@wise.net.nz ⓈⓈ — MC V — 2
Hinakura Rd. **Road map** E5. 【 & FAX *(06) 306 9374.*
Two guest houses at opposite ends of the main house, plus views of the
Tararua Range and a solar-heated pool make rural Shadyvale a popular
bed and breakfast destination. 🔧 ➳ 🔲 P

MARTINBOROUGH: *Wharekauhau Country Estate* ⓈⓈⓈⓈⓈ — AE DC MC V — 12
Western Lake, Palliser Bay. **Road map** E5. 【 *(06) 307 7581.* FAX *(06) 307 7799.*
W www.wharekauhau.co.nz Internationally acclaimed luxury hideaway.
Price includes breakfast and dinner. 🔧 24 TV ➳ 🍸 🍴 🔲 ⓵ P

NEW PLYMOUTH: *Heritage Lodge* Ⓢ — AE DC MC V — 9
115 Coronation Ave. **Road map** D3. 【 *(06) 758 5216.* FAX *(06) 758 5215.*
All units have their own kitchen for self-catering in this friendly lodge
priced at the lower end of the market. 🔧 TV ➳ P

NEW PLYMOUTH: *Pukekura Lodge Motel* Ⓢ — AE DC MC V — 6
52 Victoria Rd. **Road map** D3. 【 *(06) 758 2310.* FAX *(06) 757 5408.*
On the edge of the magnificent Pukekura Gardens, this family-owned
motel has comfortable rooms and a friendly atmosphere. 🔧 TV ➳ P

PALMERSTON NORTH: *Coachman Hotel and Motel* Ⓢ — AE BC DC MC V — 73
134 Fitzherbert Ave. **Road map** E4. 【 *(06) 356 5065.* FAX *(06) 356 6692.*
A large-scale hotel/motel, the Coachman offers inexpensive rooms with
all the trimmings. 🔧 TV ▤ ➳ 🍸 ♨ 🍴 ⓵ P

PALMERSTON NORTH: *King Street Backpackers* Ⓢ — — 70
95 King St. **Road map** E4. 【 *(06) 358 9595.*
Ultra cheap accommodation in an old hotel in the middle of town,
especially designed for backpackers. Payment by cash only. ➳

For key to symbols see back flap

Price categories for a standard double room per night, inclusive of Goods and Service Tax (GST) of 12.5%. Breakfast is usually charged separately.
$ under NZ$100
$$ NZ$100–NZ$150
$$$ NZ$150–NZ$200
$$$$ NZ$200–NZ$250
$$$$$ over NZ$250

Credit Cards
AE American Express; *BC* Bankcard; *DC* Diners Club; *JCB* Japanese Credit Bureau; *MC* Master Card/Access; *V* Visa.

Restaurant/Café
Hotel restaurant or dining room usually open to non-residents unless otherwise stated.

Children's Facilities
Child cots and a baby-sitting service available.

Family Rooms
Hotels with rooms to accommodate the whole family. Self-contained chalets and cabins are common in New Zealand.

	Credit Cards	Number of Rooms	Restaurant/Café	Children's Facilities	Family Rooms
Palmerston North: *Supreme Motor Lodge* $ 665 Pioneer Hwy. **Road map** E4. ☎ *(06) 356 5265.* [FAX] *(06) 356 5267.* This well-appointed lodge offers two-storey studio apartments with their own kitchens for self-catering. 🛏 [TV] 🚭 🏊 🏋 🗝 ♿ [P]	AE DC MC V	47	■	●	■
Palmerston North: *The Gables* [W] www.friars.co.nz $ 179 Fitzherbert Ave. **Road map** E4. ☎ & [FAX] *(06) 358 3209.* Comfortable, separate apartments attached to a gracious, two-storeyed 1920s English-style home. [TV] 🚭 ♿ [P]	AE MC V	5			
Wanganui: *Bignell Street Motels* $ 86 Bignell St. **Road map** E4. ☎ *(06) 344 2012.* [FAX] *(06) 344 2011.* Budget-priced, centrally situated accommodation offering bed and breakfast and other meals on request. Has a games room and a children's playground. 🛏 [TV] 🚭 ♿ [P]	AE DC MC V	8		●	■
Wanganui: *Rutland Arms Inn* [W] www.rutland_arm.co.nz $$ Cnr Victoria Ave and Ridgway St. **Road map** E4. ☎ *(06) 347 7677.* [FAX] *(06) 347 7345.* Small bed and breakfast with excellent range of facilities. Close to town centre. Price includes breakfast. 🛏 [TV] 🚭 🍸 🗝 [P]	AE DC MC V	8	■	●	■
Wellington: *Hotel Willis Lodge* [@] willis.lodge@xtra.co.nz $ 318 Willis St. **Road map** E5. ☎ *(04) 384 5955.* [FAX] *(04) 384 5952.* On the quiet side of Central Park, the hotel offers good facilities. It is a short walk to town via the southern reaches of arty Cuba Street, or to the university and Botanic Gardens past Victorian villas and student hang-outs up steeply winding Devon Street. 🛏 [TV] 🚭 🗝 ♿ [P]	AE DC MC V	24	■	●	■
Wellington: *St George's Hall Summer Hotel* [@] reservations@george.co.nz $ 1 Boulcott St. **Road map** E5. ☎ *(04) 473 9139; 0800 909 707.* An Art Deco building and formerly one of the better hotels in town, this central hotel is now a student hostel and between November and February offers rooms for budget travellers. [TV] 🚭 ♿ [P]	AE DC MC V	180			■
Wellington: *Trekkers Hotel* [@] info@trekkers.co.nz $ 213 Cuba St. **Road map** E5. ☎ *(04) 385 2153.* [FAX] *(04) 382 8873.* Accommodation ranges from dormitory-style beds to motel units in this large, vibrant, mid-town hotel, popular with travellers. 🛏 [TV] 🚭 ♿ [P]	AE BC DC MC V	107	■	●	■
Wellington: *Eight Parliament Street* [@] grasenack@xtra.co.nz $$ 8 Parliament St. **Road map** E5. ☎ *(04) 499 0808.* [FAX] *(04) 479 6705.* Boutique bed and breakfast in a wooden, self-contained, former workers' cottage in the historic suburb of Thorndon. 🚭 [P]	MC V	3			
Wellington: *Halswell Lodge* [@] reserve@halswell.co.nz $$ 21 Kent Terrace, Courtenay Place. **Road map** E5. ☎ *(04) 385 0196.* [FAX] *(04) 385 0503.* Established hotel/motel. Comfortable and close to Te Papa, Oriental Bay and inner city. 🛏 [TV] 🚭 ♿ [P]	AE BC DC MC V	35		●	■
Wellington: *The Terrace Villas* [@] terracevillas@actrix.co.nz $$ 202 The Terrace. **Road map** E5. ☎ *(04) 473 3971.* [FAX] *(04) 920 2030.* Centrally located, these self-contained apartments are set in restored late 19th-century villas. Close to town and the university. 🛏 [TV] 🚭 ♿ [P]	AE DC MC V	40		●	
Wellington: *The Lighthouse* [@] bruce@sportwork.co.nz $$$ 326 The Esplanade, Island Bay. **Road map** E5. ☎ *(04) 472 4177.* [FAX] *(04) 472 4177.* Not a real lighthouse but a quirky "folly" bed and breakfast on Wellington's dramatic south coast. Close to the airport. 🛏 🚭 [P]	MC V	2			■
Wellington: *Parkroyal Wellington* [W] www.parkroyal.com.au $$$$ Cnr Grey and Featherston sts. **Road map** E5. ☎ *(04) 472 2722.* [FAX] *(04) 472 4724.* In the central business district, with a good selection of restaurants. International standards. 🛏 [24] [TV] ❄ 🚭 🍸 🏊 🏋 🗝 ♿ [P]	AE DC MC V	233	■	●	■

MARLBOROUGH AND NELSON

BLENHEIM: *Chateau Marlborough* @ chatmarlb@xtra.co.nz $$
Cnr Henry and High sts. **Road map** D5. (*(03) 578 0064.* **FAX** *(03) 578 2661.*
The motel overlooks Seymour Square in the centre of Blenheim.
Executive and studio suites cater for families.
AE DC MC V — 30

BLENHEIM: *The Marlborough* @ TheMarlborough@marlborough.co.nz $$$
20 Nelson St. **Road map** D5. (*(03) 577 7333.* **FAX** *(03) 577 7337.*
A modern luxury hotel in central Blenheim with large rooms and an
extensive art collection.
AE DC MC V — 28

BLENHEIM: *Hotel d'Urville* w www.durville.co.nz $$$$
52 Queen St. **Road map** D5. (*(03) 577 9945.* **FAX** *(03) 577 9946.*
Small hotel in an historic building. Each room has a different theme.
Personal service and an excellent restaurant.
AE DC MC V — 9

COLLINGWOOD: *Twin Waters Lodge* @ twinwaters@xtra.co.nz $$
Totara Ave. **Road map** D4. (*(03) 524 8014.*
This beautifully designed lodge sits between a calm estuary and a beach.
Facilities include private decks and a guest lounge.
MC V — 3

KAIKOURA: *The Old Convent* @ o.convent@xtra.co.nz $$
Mt Fyffe Rd. **Road map** D5. (*(03) 319 6603.* **FAX** *(03) 319 6690.* Self-contained
This renovated convent offers an historic atmosphere and mountain
views. Superb French cuisine. Tariff includes breakfast.
AE BC MC V — 17

KAIKOURA: *Fyffe Country Inn* @ fyffe@xtra.co.nz $$$
State Hwy 1. **Road map** D5. (*(03) 319 6869.* **FAX** *(03) 319 6865.*
Luxury accommodation in mud brick and timber buildings,
complemented by a country garden and innovative cuisine. Superb
mountain views. Tariff includes breakfast.
AE DC MC V — 7

MARAHAU: *Abel Tasman Marahau Lodge* $$
Marahau Beach (near Abel Tasman National Park). **Road map** D4. (*(03) 527
8250.* **FAX** *(03) 527 8256.* @ jan@AbelTasmanMarahauLodge.co.nz Self-contained
or studio rooms. Attractive landscaping. Outdoor spa.
DC MC V — 8

MARLBOROUGH SOUNDS: *French Pass Motels* @ adventure@seasafaris.co.nz $$
RD 3, Rai Valley. **Road map** D4. (& **FAX** *(03) 576 5204.*
Intimate, chalet-style waterfront units provide easy access to services and
activities in French Pass. Personalized service is a plus.
MC V — 3

MARLBOROUGH SOUNDS: *Raetihi Lodge* w www.raetihi.co.nz $$$
Double Bay, Kenepuru Sound. **Road map** D4. (*(03) 573 4300.* **FAX** *(03) 573
4323.* Off the beaten track, but with easy air and water taxi access, this
waterfront retreat is relaxing and comfortable.
AE MC V — 14

NELSON: *Rutherford Hotel Nelson* $$$
Trafalgar Square. **Road map** D4. (*(03) 548 2299.* **FAX** *(03) 546 3003.*
@ enquiries@rutherfordhotel.co.nz Nelson's premier hotel in the central city,
with a variety of rooms.
AE DC MC V — 115

NELSON: *The Honest Lawyer Hotel* @ thl@ts.co.nz $$$
1 Point Rd, Monaco. **Road map** D4. (*(03) 547 8850.* **FAX** *(03) 547 8868.*
The stone architecture and estuary setting make this hotel unique. The
rooms are well-appointed and there is a complimentary guest pantry.
AE DC MC V — 11

PICTON: *Jasmine Court* w www.jasminecourt.co.nz $$$
78 Wellington St. **Road map** D4. (*(03) 573 7110.* **FAX** *(03) 573 7211.*
The hosts of this centrally located but quiet inn offer high quality service,
including ferry pick-ups. Tariff includes breakfast.
AE DC MC V — 9

ST ARNAUD: *Alpine Lodge* @ enquiries@alpinelodge.co.nz $$
Main Rd. **Road map** D5. (*(03) 521 1869.* **FAX** *(03) 521 1868.*
The Alpine Lodge offers comfortable rooms on the edge of the beech
forest of Nelson Lakes National Park.
AE DC MC V — 32

TAKAKA: *Sans Souci Inn* @ reto@sanssouciinn.co.nz $
Richmond Rd. **Road map** D4. (& **FAX** *(03) 525 8663.*
Mediterranean architecture creates a pleasing effect here. Sans Souci is a
few minutes walk from Pohara Beach and close to many attractions of
eastern Golden Bay.
AE MC V — 7

For key to symbols see back flap

<table>
<tr><td colspan="2">

Price categories for a standard double room per night, inclusive of Goods and Service Tax (GST) of 12.5%. Breakfast is usually charged separately.
$ under NZ$100
$$ NZ$100–NZ$150
$$$ NZ$150–NZ$200
$$$$ NZ$200–NZ$250
$$$$$ over NZ$250

</td></tr>
</table>

CREDIT CARDS
AE American Express; *BC* Bankcard; *DC* Diners Club; *JCB* Japanese Credit Bureau; *MC* Master Card/Access; *V* Visa.
RESTAURANT/CAFÉ
Hotel restaurant or dining room usually open to non-residents unless otherwise stated.
CHILDREN'S FACILITIES
Child cots and a baby-sitting service available.
FAMILY ROOMS
Hotels with rooms to accommodate the whole family. Self-contained chalets and cabins are common in New Zealand.

CANTERBURY AND THE WEST COAST

	CREDIT CARDS	NUMBER OF ROOMS	RESTAURANT/CAFÉ	CHILDREN'S FACILITIES	FAMILY ROOMS
AKAROA: *Akaroa Village Inn* W www.akaroa.co.nz $$ 81 Beach Rd. **Road map** C6. ((03) 304 7421. FAX (03) 304 7423. The inn overlooks Akaroa waterfront and is close to shops and cafés. Suites range from moderate to expensive.	AE DC JCB MC V	40		●	■
ARTHUR'S PASS: *The Chalet* W www.arthurspass.co.nz $$ State Hwy 73. **Road map** C5. ((03) 318 9236. FAX (03) 318 9200. The Chalet has a rustic, alpine lodge ambience, befitting its location in the mountain village of Arthur's Pass.	AE JCB MC V	10	■		■
CHRISTCHURCH: *Croydon House Bed and Breakfast Hotel* $ 63 Armagh St. **Road map** C6. ((03) 366 5111. FAX (03) 377 6110. W www.croyden.co.nz Delightfully renovated private hotel located near the city centre. Rooms are cheerful and bright. Price includes cooked breakfast. Tea- and coffee-making facilities are available.	MC V	12		●	■
CHRISTCHURCH: *Windsor Bed and Breakfast Hotel* $ 52 Armagh St. **Road map** C6. ((03) 366 1503. FAX (03) 366 9796. W www. windsorhotel.co.nz A well-maintained 1907 building, located between the city centre and Hagley Park. Rooms are basic but clean.	AE DC JCB MC V	40			■
CHRISTCHURCH: *Hotel Grand Chancellor* W www.grandc.co.nz $$$ 161 Cashel St. **Road map** C6. ((03) 379 2999. FAX (03) 379 9989. The tallest hotel in Christchurch, well located just beyond the City Mall. Spacious, well-appointed rooms. The hotel also caters for conferences.	AE DC JCB MC V	171	■	●	■
CHRISTCHURCH: *Rydges Hotel* @ reservations_christchurch@rydges.com $$$ Cnr Worcester St and Oxford Terrace. **Road map** C6. ((03) 379 4700. FAX (03) 379 5357. Imposing curved building located just one block from Cathedral Square and overlooking the Avon River.	AE DC JCB MC V	209	■	●	■
CHRISTCHURCH: *Parkroyal Christchurch* $$$$$ Cnr Durham and Kilmore sts. **Road map** C6. ((03) 365 7799. FAX (03) 365 0082. Luxurious hotel with well-appointed rooms, spacious atrium, a variety of restaurants and professional staff.	AE DC JCB MC V	298	■	●	■
FOX GLACIER: *Fox Glacier Hotel* @ fox.resorts@xtra.co.nz $ 6 Cook Flat Rd. **Road map** B6. ((03) 751 0839. FAX (03) 751 0868. A charming old wooden building with accommodation in a wide price range, from low budget to fully serviced rooms.	AE DC MC V	85	■		■
FOX GLACIER: *Glacier Country Hotel* @ glacier_country@xtra.co.nz $$ State Hwy 6. **Road map** B6. ((03) 751 0847. FAX (03) 751 0822. Well-appointed hotel with bush backdrop in the centre of Fox Glacier village.	AE DC MC V	51	■		■
FRANZ JOSEF GLACIER: *Terrace Motel* @ terrace.motel@xtra.co.nz $ 1 Cowan St. **Road map** B6. ((03) 752 0130. FAX (03) 752 0190. The motel has spacious, modern and well-equipped rooms. The proprietors are friendly and helpful.	MC V	10		●	■
FRANZ JOSEF GLACIER: *Franz Josef Glacier Hotel* $$$$ State Hwy 6. **Road map** B6. ((03) 752 0728. FAX (03) 752 0709. @ franz.josef@scenic-circle.co.nz Full-service hotel in Franz Josef village with rooms across a wide price range.	AE DC JCB MC V	177	■		■
GREYMOUTH: @ rosewoodnz@xtra.co.nz $ 20 High St. **Road map** C5. ((03) 768 4674. FAX (03) 768 4694. Pleasant, spacious, clean rooms in a tastefully renovated character home, near the town centre. Friendly hosts will pick up guests.	MC V	5			■

	Price	Credit Cards	Number of Rooms			
GREYMOUTH: *Quality Hotel Kings* @ quality.kings@cdlhms.co.nz ⓈⓈⓈ 32 Mawhera Quay. **Road map** C5. ☎ *(03) 768 5085.* **FAX** *(03) 768 5844.* Good quality rooms in a central location that overlooks the Grey River. Close to shops and services. ▮ 24 TV ▮ ▮ ▮ ▮ & P		AE DC MC V	102	▮	●	▮
HANMER SPRINGS: *Drifters Inn* W www.driftersinn.co.nz Ⓢ 2 Harrogate St. **Road map** C5. ☎ *(03) 315 7554.* **FAX** *(03) 315 7235.* Directly opposite the Hanmer Springs Thermal Resort. Cooking facilities are provided in a guest kitchen. Tariff includes breakfast. ▮ TV & P		AE DC MC V	26			▮
HANMER SPRINGS: *Albergo Hanmer Bed and Breakfast* ⓈⓈ 88 Rippingale Rd. **Road map** C5. ☎ & **FAX** *(03) 315 7428.* W www.albergo.8m.com A boutique bed and breakfast establishment with luxuriously appointed rooms. ▮ TV ▮ & P		MC V	3	▮	●	
HOKITIKA: *Southland Hotel* @ southland@clear.net.nz ⓈⓈ 111 Revell St. **Road map** C5. ☎ *(03) 755 8344.* **FAX** *(03) 755 8258.* Located in the town centre on the site of the historic Hokitika Hotel, with views over the Tasman Sea. ▮ TV ▮ ▮ ▮ ▮ P		AE DC JCB MC V	23	▮	●	▮
HOKITIKA: *Villa Polenza Boutique Lodge* ⓈⓈⓈⓈ Brickfield Rd. **Road map** C5. ☎ *(03) 755 7801.* **FAX** *(03) 755 7901.* Luxurious accommodation in a modern Italian-style villa on the outskirts of Hokitika. Tariff includes breakfast. ▮ ▮ ▮		MC V	3			▮
KARAMEA: *Karamea Village Hotel* @ karamea.info@xtra.co.nz Ⓢ Cnr Waverley St and Wharf Rd. **Road map** C4. ☎ & **FAX** *(03) 782 6800.* Historic hotel dating from 1876. Facilities range from shared backpackers' rooms to modest, clean serviced hotel rooms. ▮ 24 TV ▮ ▮ & P		MC V	13	▮	●	▮
KARAMEA: *The Last Resort* @ lastresort@xtra.co.nz ⓈⓈ 71 Waverley St. **Road map** C4. ☎ *(03) 782 6617.* **FAX** *(03) 782 6820.* A rambling, rustic yet chic complex with rooms across a wide price range. ▮ 24 TV ▮ ▮ ▮ ▮ & P		AE DC MC V	31	▮	●	▮
LAKE TEKAPO: *The Godley* @ tekapo@xtra.co.nz ⓈⓈⓈ State Hwy 8. **Road map** B6. ☎ *(03) 680 6848.* **FAX** *(03) 680 6873.* This is the largest hotel in Lake Tekapo, with wonderful views over the lake. Price includes bed, breakfast and dinner. ▮ TV ▮ ▮ ▮ & P		AE DC JCB MC V	82	▮	●	▮
LAKE TEKAPO: *Lake Tekapo Lodge* ⓈⓈⓈⓈ 24 Aorangi Crescent. **Road map** B6. ☎ *(03) 680 6566.* **FAX** *(03) 680 6599.* Small boutique lodge purpose-built of adobe brick blocks, with sweeping views over the lake. Friendly, helpful hosts. ▮ TV ▮ & P		AE DC JCB MC V	4			
METHVEN: *Brinkley Village Resort* @ brinkley@xtra.co.nz ⓈⓈ Barkers Rd. **Road map** B6. ☎ *(03) 302 8885.* **FAX** *(03) 302 8862.* Large complex in an attractive country setting with a tennis court. Has self-contained rooms and apartments. ▮ TV ▮ ▮ P		AE DC MC V	80	▮	●	▮
MOUNT COOK: *Glentanner Park Centre* Ⓢ State Hwy 80. **Road map** C6. ☎ *(03) 435 1855.* **FAX** *(03) 435 1854.* Budget accommodation, with great views of Mount Cook National Park. Includes self-contained cabins and dormitory beds. ▮ ▮		AE DC JCB MC V	14	▮		
MOUNT COOK: *The Hermitage* W www.sphc.com.au ⓈⓈ Mount Cook Village. **Road map** B6. ☎ *(03) 435 1809.* **FAX** *(03) 435 1879.* The only hotel in Mount Cook National Park, the sprawling complex has facilities to suit a wide range of budgets. ▮ 24 TV ▮ ▮ P		AE DC JCB MC V	212	▮	●	▮
PUNAKAIKI: *Punakaiki Cottage Motels* Ⓢ Dickinson Parade. **Road map** C5. ☎ *(03) 731 1008.* **FAX** *(03) 731 1118.* Small motel complex located on the beach front, just a few minutes walk from the Pancake Rocks. ▮ TV ▮ & P		AE DC MC V	6		●	▮
TIMARU: *Grosvenor Hotel* @ grosvenortimaru@xtra.co.nz ⓈⓈ 26 Cains Terrace. **Road map** C6. ☎ *(03) 688 3129.* **FAX** *(03) 684 8381.* A grand historic building dating back to 1875, located in the commercial centre of Timaru. ▮ 24 TV ▮ ▮ P		AE DC MC V	43	▮	●	▮
WESTPORT: *Chelsea Gateway Motor Lodge* Ⓢ 330 Palmerston St. **Road map** C5. ☎ *(03) 789 6835.* **FAX** *(03) 789 6379.* This modern complex in the centre of Westport has self-contained units with kitchen facilities. ▮ TV ▮ ▮ & P		AE DC MC V	20		●	▮

For key to symbols see back flap

Price categories for a standard double room per night, inclusive of Goods and Service Tax (GST) of 12.5%. Breakfast is usually charged separately.
$ under NZ$100
$$ NZ$100–NZ$150
$$$ NZ$150–NZ$200
$$$$ NZ$200–NZ$250
$$$$$ over NZ$250

CREDIT CARDS
AE American Express; *BC* Bankcard; *DC* Diners Club; *JCB* Japanese Credit Bureau; *MC* Master Card/Access; *V* Visa.
RESTAURANT/CAFÉ
Hotel restaurant or dining room usually open to non-residents unless otherwise stated.
CHILDREN'S FACILITIES
Child cots and a baby-sitting service available.
FAMILY ROOMS
Hotels with rooms to accommodate the whole family. Self-contained chalets and cabins are common in New Zealand.

		CREDIT CARDS	NUMBER OF ROOMS	RESTAURANT/CAFÉ	CHILDREN'S FACILITIES	FAMILY ROOMS

OTAGO AND SOUTHLAND

CROMWELL: *Golden Gate Lodge* @ ggl@voyager.co.nz — $
Barry Ave. **Road map** B7. ((03) 445 1777. FAX (03) 445 1776.
Well-appointed hotel/restaurant/conference complex in a central location between Wanaka and Queenstown. Great base to explore both areas.
| | | AE DC MC V | 47 | ■ | ● | ■ |

DUNEDIN: *97 Motel Moray* @ bookingsa@97motel.co.nz — $$
97 Moray Place. **Road map** B7. ((03) 477 2050. FAX (03) 477 1991.
An excellent budget option a few minutes' walk from The Octagon. Friendly and well run with comfortable rooms.
| | | AE DC MC V | 40 | | | |

DUNEDIN: *Pacific Park Hotel* @ pacpark@earthlight.co.nz — $$
22–24 Wallace St. **Road map** B7. ((03) 477 3374. FAX (03) 477 1434.
On the edge of Dunedin's green belt with great views over the city and harbour. A choice of hotel rooms or motel units.
| | | AE DC JCB MC V | 58 | ■ | ● | ■ |

DUNEDIN: *Southern Cross Hotel* @ southern.cross@scenic-circle.co.nz — $$
Cnr Princes and High sts. **Road map** B7. ((03) 477 0752. FAX (03) 477 5776.
Well-appointed centrally located hotel/casino. Partly housed in an old hotel building. Luxury suites available.
| | | AE DC JCB MC V | 141 | ■ | ● | ■ |

GORE: *Croydon Lodge* @ thelodge@esi.co.nz — $$
Queenstown Hwy. **Road map** B7. ((03) 208 9029. FAX (03) 208 9252.
Set in extensive gardens with a 9-hole, par-3 golf course. The well-appointed rooms have recently been redecorated. Award-winning restaurant and gardens.
| | | AE DC MC V | 37 | ■ | ● | ■ |

INVERCARGILL: *Birchwood Manor Motel* @ birch@birchwood.co.nz — $
189 Tay St. **Road map** A7. ((03) 218 8881. FAX (03) 218 8880.
This modern motel offers spacious units with tasteful décor and furnishings. Breakfast available.
| | | AE DC MC V | 15 | | ● | ■ |

INVERCARGILL: *Gerrard's Hotel* — $
3 Leven St. **Road map** A7. ((03) 218 3406. FAX (03) 218 3003.
An Historic Places Trust building built in 1896 as a railway hotel. The rooms are tastefully appointed.
| | | AE DC JCB MC V | 10 | | ● | ■ |

INVERCARGILL: *Ascot Park Motel* — $$
Cnr Tay St and Racecourse Rd. **Road map** A7. ((03) 217 6195. FAX (03) 217 7002. One of Invercargill's leading hotels, with a reputable restaurant. Indoor spa and sauna.
| | | AE DC MC V | 96 | ■ | ● | ■ |

MANAPOURI: *Manapouri Lakeview Motor Inn* — $
Cathedral Drive. **Road map** A7. ((03) 249 6652. FAX (03) 249 6650.
@ manapouri@clear.net.nz A great budget option with a range of rooms and prices. Lake views from most rooms.
| | | MC V | 55 | ■ | ● | ■ |

OAMARU: *Armada Motor Inn* — $
500 Thames Hwy. **Road map** B7. ((03) 437 0017. FAX (03) 437 0297.
Comfortable accommodation and restaurant complex. Facilities include a heated swimming pool, sauna and spa.
| | | AE DC MC V | 22 | ■ | ● | ■ |

OAMARU: *Pen-y-bryn* W www.penybryn.co.nz — $$$$$
41 Towey St. **Road map** B7. ((03) 434 7939. FAX (03) 434 9063.
This 1889 house features a billiard room, library and antiques. Tariff includes breakfast, dinner and drinks.
| | | AE BC DC MC V | 5 | | | |

OTAGO PENINSULA: *Larnach Lodge* @ larnach@larnachcastle.co.nz — $$$
Camp Rd. **Road map** B7. ((03) 476 1616. FAX (03) 476 1574.
Boutique-style accommodation next to Larnach Castle. Rooms are decorated in Scottish and Victorian themes.
| | | AE DC MC V | 18 | ■ | ● | ■ |

Hotel	Price	Cards	Rooms			
QUEENSTOWN: *Goldfields Motel* @ goldfieldsmotel@xtra.co.nz 57 Frankton Rd. **Road map** A6. ☎ *(03) 442 7211.* FAX *(03) 442 6179.* The Swiss-style family-run main house provides bed and breakfast while cosy A-frame chalets offer a self-service option. 🛏 [TV] 🚭 [P]	$	AE DC MC V	15		●	■
QUEENSTOWN: *A-Line Hotel* @ aline@es.co.nz 27 Stanley St. **Road map** A6. ☎ *(03) 442 7700.* FAX *(03) 442 4715.* A good, middle-of-the-range option only a few hundred metres from town, with lake and mountain views. 🛏 [TV] 🚭 🍸 ≋ 🔒 ♿ [P]	$$	AE DC JCB MC V	82	■	●	■
QUEENSTOWN: *Quality Resort Terraces* @ quality.terraces@cdlhms.co.nz Frankton Rd. **Road map** A6. ☎ *(03) 442 7950.* FAX *(03) 442 8066.* Pleasant rooms and apartments with excellent views of Lake Wakatipu and the mountains. Close to town. 🛏 [24] [TV] 🚭 🍸 ≋ ♿ [P]	$$	AE DC JCB MC V	85	■	●	■
QUEENSTOWN: *Millennium* @ central.res@cdlhms.co.nz Cnr Frankton Rd & Stanley St. **Road map** A6. ☎ *(03) 441 8888.* FAX *(03) 441 8889.* Attractively appointed rooms in modern hotel a few minutes walk from town. Lake and mountain views. 🛏 [24] [TV] ▤ 🚭 🍸 🏋 🔒 ♿ [P]	$$$	AE DC JCB MC V	240	■		
QUEENSTOWN: *The Heritage Hotel* @ rosannac@dynasty.co.nz 91 Fernhill Rd. **Road map** A6. ☎ *(03) 442 4988.* FAX *(03) 442 4989.* A top-class hotel close to central Queenstown. Indoor and outdoor spa. Elegant rooms. 🛏 [24] [TV] 🚭 🍸 🏋 🔒 ♿ [P]	$$$$	AE DC JCB MC V	178	■	●	■
RIVERTON: *Riverton Rock Guest House* @ kiwiwalks@riverton.co.nz 136 Palmerston St, Riverton (near Invercargill). **Road map** A7. ☎ *(03) 234 8886.* FAX *(03) 234 8816.* A real old-world feel. Each room is tastefully decorated with its own Victorian theme. Close to Riverton beach. 🛏 🚭 🔒 [P]	$	AE DC MC V	7		●	■
STEWART ISLAND: *South Sea Hotel* Waterfront, Oban. **Road map** A7. ☎ *(03) 219 1059.* FAX *(03) 219 1120.* Country pub atmosphere. Choice of motel units or simple hotel rooms right on the waterfront. [TV] 🔒 ♿ [P]	$	AE MC V	26	■	●	■
STEWART ISLAND: *Stewart Island Lodge* Halfmoon Bay, Oban. **Road map** A7. ☎ & FAX *(03) 219 1085.* [W] www.stewartisland.lodge.co.nz A luxurious top-flight homestay. Tariff includes breakfast and dinner. Fresh local foods. 🛏 🚭 🔒 ♿ [P]	$$$$	AE DC MC V	5	■		
TE ANAU: *Luxmore Hotel* Main St. **Road map** A7. ☎ *(03) 249 7526.* FAX *(03) 249 7272.* Comfortable, modern hotel with good facilities in the heart of Te Anau. Adjacent to the main tourist departure points. 🛏 [TV] 🚭 ♿ [P]	$$	AE DC MC V	148	■	●	■
TE ANAU: *Quality Hotel* @ quality.teanau@cdlhms.co.nz 20 Lakefront Drive. **Road map** A7. ☎ *(03) 249 7421.* FAX *(03) 249 8037.* A pleasant 10-minute walk along the waterfront to town. Spacious rooms, many with lake and mountain views. 🛏 [TV] 🚭 🍸 🔒 ♿ [P]	$$	AE DC JCB MC V	94	■	●	■
TE ANAU: *Centra Te Anau* @ centra.teanau@xtra.co.nz Lakefront Drive. **Road map** A7. ☎ *(03) 249 7411.* FAX *(03) 249 7947.* Middle-of-the-range hotel, handy to town, boats and tourist operators. Indoor and outdoor spa. Excellent views. 🛏 [TV] 🚭 🔒 ♿ [P]	$$$	AE DC MC V	112	■	●	■
WANAKA: *Cardrona Hotel* @ info@cardrona_hotel.co.nz Cardrona Valley. **Road map** B6. ☎ *(03) 443 8153.* FAX *(03) 443 8163.* Gold-rush period hotel dating back to 1863. Quaint restaurant, bar and courtyard. Spa and sauna for guest use. 🛏 [TV] 🚭 🍸 🔒 ♿ [P]	$	AE MC V	9	■	●	■
WANAKA: *The Moorings* 17 Lakeside Rd. **Road map** B6. ☎ *(03) 443 8479.* FAX *(03) 443 8489.* Modern motel/apartment complex just across the lakefront. Close to restaurants and shops. Great views. 🛏 [TV] 🚭 🔒 ♿ [P]	$$	AE DC MC V	14		●	■
WANAKA: *Edgewater Resort* @ edgewater@xtra.co.nz Sargood Drive. **Road map** B6. ☎ *(03) 443 8311.* FAX *(03) 443 8323.* Resort-style accommodation. Sumptuous hotel rooms and fully appointed apartments. Spa, sauna and tennis courts. 🛏 [TV] 🚭 🔒 [P]	$$$	AE DC JCB MC V	105	■	●	■
WANAKA: *Wanaka Motor Inn* @ wanaka@bigfoot.com Mount Aspiring Rd. **Road map** B6. ☎ *(03) 443 8216.* FAX *(03) 443 9108.* Comfortable 3-star hotel with Scandanavian-style wood-lined rooms. Studios or larger suites. 🛏 [TV] 🚭 🔒 [P]	$$$	AE DC JCB MC V	35	■	●	■

For key to symbols see back flap

WHERE TO EAT

NEW ZEALAND'S restaurants and cuisine have both undergone a revolution in the past 20 years. Whereas eating in restaurants was once reserved for special occasions and usually included a traditional European meal, such as roast lamb and vegetables, New Zealand now has a wide variety of eating places to suit all tastes and all budgets. Although plainer fare is still available, the country's multicultural population has meant that restaurants serving traditional food sit alongside those offering cuisine from

Café sign, Martinborough

almost every corner of the world, especially in the larger towns. Influences from Asia and the Pacific have been particularly significant. New Zealand restaurants make good use of home-grown produce, such as fresh fish, oysters, mussels, crayfish (rock lobsters), beef, lamb and venison, as well as vegetables and fruit. These can all be enjoyed with a glass of New Zealand wine *(see pp314–15)*. A popular tourist experience is a Maori *hangi*, where food is wrapped and cooked on heated rocks under the ground.

The Icon Restaurant at the Museum of New Zealand Te Papa Tongarewa in Wellington *(see p324)*

TYPES OF RESTAURANTS

NEW ZEALAND'S MAJOR cities have a vibrant restaurant scene ranging from formal dining to a multitude of casual cafés. Diners can experience haute cuisine or eat in a café offering cheaper, simpler food. Some eateries feature courtyard, garden or pavement seating. Ethnic restaurants range from Chinese, Cambodian and Malaysian, to Turkish and Greek. Some high-quality restaurants can be found in provincial and rural areas. Many vineyard restaurants serve ploughman's lunches with seating among the vines as well as more formal meals in picturesque restaurant settings. Pubs often offer food, although a pub meal tends to be cheaper and more basic. A typical meal might

include steak and chips or fish and chips.

A meal in a café or ethnic restaurant can cost less than NZ$15 per person. Restaurant prices range from NZ$25 to more than NZ$100 per person for a three-course meal. A range of fast-food chains, such as McDonalds, KFC and Burger King, have franchises in New Zealand, and the traditional takeaway meal of fish and chips remains very popular. Fish and chip shop specialities, such as Bluff oysters or whitebait fritters, are recommended.

EATING HOURS AND RESERVATIONS

MOST RESTAURANTS serve lunch from 12 to 2pm and dinner from 6 to 10pm. Establishments may open earlier on the weekend for

brunch. Some cafés are open for breakfast and close later than restaurants. Late-night and 24-hour cafés are gaining in popularity.

Bookings are usually necessary at more formal restaurants. Cafés and bars vary in their booking policies, with some eateries taking reservations and others operating on a casual basis. It pays to ring and check booking policies to avoid disappointment.

PAYING AND TIPPING

THE MAJORITY OF restaurants and cafés accept credit cards, though it is a good idea to check when booking. Some restaurants will not accept personal cheques or traveller's cheques. Government taxes are included in the menu prices and there are no service charges. New Zealand's egalitarian society

Seafood buffet at Sheraton Auckland Hotel *(see p298)*

Tables outside a café at Mount Maunganui

means tipping is not compulsory, although a tip will be appreciated for very good service and a quality meal. Patrons can leave tips in cash on the table or include them in credit card payments.

CHILDREN

Most restaurants cater for children. If travelling with very young children, it is best to check with the restaurant to ensure that children are welcome. An option in busy cafés is to book early before large numbers of adult diners arrive. Chinese, Greek and other ethnic restaurants tend to have more relaxed attitudes towards children. Fast-food chains can be found in most cities and towns, and children usually enjoy a meal of fish and chips at the park or beach. Families staying in motels with equipped kitchens may find that a trip to a local supermarket provides a break from having to take small children to eat out in restaurants.

WHEELCHAIR ACCESS

Government regulations require building owners to ensure that new and re-developed buildings are accessible by wheelchair. Facilities that comply with the code display an international symbol. Most restaurants also now provide toilet facilities for the disabled. However, as in most countries, it is wise to phone ahead to ensure facilities are accessible.

VEGETARIANS

Tourist offices should be able to provide details about vegetarian restaurants which are sprinkled throughout the cities and main towns, including resort areas. Many restaurants offer some vegetarian meals and will usually be happy to adapt menus, especially in areas where there is an abundance of home-grown produce. Most Asian restaurants also offer vegetarian food on their menus.

Vineyard café sign

ALCOHOL AND OTHER DRINKS

Licensed restaurants and bars serve a range of alcohol, including wine, beer and spirits. Most cafés are also fully licensed but may offer a more limited range of alcohol. Many restaurants and cafés highlight New Zealand wines and boutique beers. Restaurants in wine-growing areas usually specialize in wine from that region. BYO restaurants offer diners the opportunity to bring the wines they wish to drink with their meal. Tap water is usually safe in the larger centres. Bottled still or sparkling water and fresh fruit juices are also popular.

DRESS

Dress is informal compared to many other parts of the world. It is unlikely that a jacket or tie will be needed, although visitors may feel more comfortable formally dressed at the up-market restaurants. Informal but tidy dress is appreciated at less formal restaurants. Street fashion is the rule at most inner-city cafés.

SMOKING

An increasing number of restaurants are becoming smoke-free, in line with world trends. Other restaurants have smoking and non-smoking areas. Most restaurants will ask where you want to sit when you arrive at the restaurant. It is better for visitors to specify their preference upon booking.

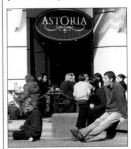

The Astoria at Lambton Quay, Wellington

BYO RESTAURANTS

BYO means to "bring your own" alcohol. Instead of a full liquor licence, restaurants may have a BYO licence that allows diners to bring their own alcohol. This is cheaper than purchasing alcohol on the premises, although a small fee may be charged for corkage. It is also usual to bring bottled wine to a BYO restaurant, and acceptable to take along a few bottles of beer to a curry restaurant. Some fully licensed restaurants do allow diners to bring their own wine, but it is recommended to check when booking.

What to Eat in New Zealand

NEW ZEALAND HAS a reputation for producing tasty dishes in a clean environment. Deep seas and rich soils provide a variety of high-quality raw ingredients. Meat animals are pasture-fed rather than grain-fed, and both lamb and beef are renowned for their rich flavour. New Zealand's long coastline means seafood is fresh and abundant, with fish, rock lobsters, oysters and scallops featured on many menus. A large variety of fresh fruit and

Olive oil

vegetables complement these dishes. While pies and roast lamb remain popular with New Zealanders, the emergence of a new breed of local chefs has led to exciting new styles of cooking. A growing tourist industry has also attracted many international chefs to New Zealand's restaurants. The development of Maori-owned tourist ventures provides an ideal opportunity to enjoy traditional Maori specialities, such as the *hangi (see p135).*

Rewarewa **Vipers bugloss** **Rata**

New Zealand Honeys
Honeys include delicious varieties made from the nectar of native honeysuckles and trees.

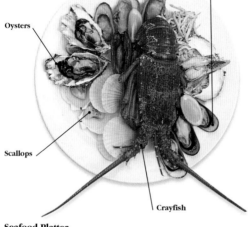

Oysters

Mussels

Scallops

Crayfish

Seafood Platter
Crayfish (rock lobster), mussels, oysters and scallops can be enjoyed at many restaurants.

Beef Fillet
Grass-fed New Zealand beef is served here as grilled fillets with vegetables.

Groper
Groper is a premium fish widely available as either steaks or fillets.

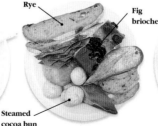

Rye

Fig brioche

Steamed cocoa bun

Fish and Chips
Fish and chips are a popular takeaway meal, and also feature on children's menus.

Speciality Breads
A wide variety of breads is available, thanks largely to European immigrants.

Mussel Chowder
This chowder is made from green-lipped mussels found only in New Zealand waters.

Venison
Venison (cervena), a gamey meat, is usually cooked quickly and served rare with light, interesting sauces.

Lamb Cutlets
New Zealand lamb is famous for its rich flavour. Here lamb cutlets are served rare with gravy and garnish.

Roast Lamb
Roast lamb, served with vegetables such as kumara (sweet potato), remains a favourite traditional meal.

Pavlova
Pavlova, made from egg whites and sugar, is often served with kiwifruit.

Asparagus
Asparagus is one of many fresh vegetables popular in New Zealand restaurants.

Mixed Leaf Salad
Salads made from a variety of fresh leaves are available on most menus.

Hokey Pokey Ice Cream
This ice cream contains chunks of confectionery made from golden syrup and sugar.

Mixed Berries
Fresh strawberries, raspberries and blueberries are delicious served with cream.

Stone Fruit
Tree-ripened cherries, peaches and apricots are abundant in season.

Brie

**Kikorangi
blue**

Kapiti goat

Pacific red

**Washed rind
cheese**

**Linkwater
cheddar**

Cheeses
A selection of New Zealand cheeses is a good way to end a meal. A wine and cheese party is a common feature of the New Zealand social scene.

SOME COMMON CONFUSIONS

In New Zealand, french fries are commonly called chips. To confuse matters further, packets of potato chips are also called chips or chippies. Ketchup is referred to as tomato sauce. An invitation to "tea" in New Zealand means the host is asking the guest to come to an evening meal or dinner. An invitation to "drop in and have a cup of tea" means the guest is being invited to morning or afternoon tea, an event that is likely to be very casual.

What to Drink in New Zealand

Corbans Noble Riesling label

Traditionally, NEW ZEALANDERS have been a nation of beer drinkers, with wine consumption viewed as a foreign custom. However, the meteoric rise of New Zealand's wine industry, which has scooped many international awards, means wine has enjoyed a dramatic rise in popularity over the last 20 years. New Zealand's temperate maritime climate is ideal for maximizing grape ripeness and the production of premium, intensely flavoured wines. There are about 300 wineries throughout the country, most near the coast *(see pp34–5)*. In-depth guides on wines, vineyards and vineyard restaurants are available at larger book shops or can be found at www.nzwine.com.

Wine tasting at C J Pask Winery, Hastings *(see pp148–9)*

WHITE WINE

Huia Sauvignon Blanc   **Palliser Sauvignon Blanc**

Chardonnay and Sauvignon Blanc are regarded as New Zealand's most outstanding white wines, with critics naming New Zealand Sauvignon Blanc as the world's finest. New Zealand's white wines, produced by both modern and traditional methods, are known for their fruit flavours. There is also a fascinating range of Chardonnays to choose from: cheaper Chardonnays fermented in stainless steel tanks and bottled young to more expensive Chardonnays fermented and aged in oak barrels. Most vineyards produce at least one example. Riesling is growing in popularity, with New Zealand Riesling often described as similar to the light and elegant German style.

SWEET WHITE WINE

New Zealand sweet wines are also winning international recognition and awards. The most interesting of these sweet wines are made from botrytis-affected grapes, with the Marlborough region emerging as a leading producer of the finest wines *(see pp204–205)*. However, the weather conditions needed to produce botrytis-type wines occur irregularly in New Zealand, and therefore prices for these luscious dessert wines tend to be somewhat higher than other wine varieties.

Cave cellar at Gibbston Valley Wines *(see p276)*

WINE TYPE	REGIONS	RECOMMENDED PRODUCERS
Chardonnay	All key wine regions	Church Road, Clearview, Cloudy Bay, Corbans, Hunters, Morton Estate Wines, Vavasour
Chenin Blanc	Gisborne, Hawke's Bay	Collard Brothers, The Millton Vineyard
Gewürztraminer	Central Otago, Gisborne, Hawke's Bay, Marlborough	Brookfields, Chifney Wines, Dry River, Eskdale, Gatehouse, Lawson's Dry Hills, Stonecroft
Muller-Thurgau	Gisborne, Hawke's Bay, Marlborough	Corbans Gisborne Winery, Pleasant Valley Wines, Vidal of Hawke's Bay, Villa Maria
Pinot Gris	Canterbury, Marlborough	Brookfields, Dry River, Margrain, Martinborough Vineyard
Riesling	Canterbury, Central Otago, Hawke's Bay, Marlborough, Nelson, Wairarapa	Allan Scott Wines and Estates, Collards, Cooper's Creek, Corbans, Framingham Wine Company, Grove Mill, Martinborough Vineyard, Neudorf, Stoneleigh
Sauvignon Blanc	Canterbury, Gisborne, Hawke's Bay, Marlborough	Cloudy Bay, Grove Mill, Hunters, Jackson Estate, Nautilus, Palliser, Selaks, Villa Maria
Sémillon	Gisborne, Hawke's Bay, Marlborough	Collards, Huntaway, Kim Crawford, Pleasant Valley, Vidal of Hawke's Bay
Sweet wines	Central Otago, Gisborne, Hawke's Bay, Marlborough	Church Road, Cooper's Creek, Cottage Block, Dry River, Framingham Wine Company, Villa Maria

SPARKLING WINE

NEW ZEALAND sparkling wines are world class and have won a number of awards. Deutz Marlborough Cuvée was voted "Sparkling Wine of the Year" in the Great Wine Challenge held in Britain in 1998. Visitors should be aware that there are two types of sparkling wine. At the bottom end of the market, "bubblies" are carbonated wines and tend to be rather sweet. However, the middle and top ends of the market feature *méthode traditionnelle* labels made by bottle fermentation methods. Marlborough is regarded as the country's top region for bottle-fermented *méthode traditionnelle*, although other regions in the country are now also gaining a reputation for producing high quality products.

Huia Marlborough Brut

WINE REGIONS OF NEW ZEALAND

Auckland	Cabernet Sauvignon, Chardonnay, Merlot, Pinot Noir
Northland	Cabernet Sauvignon, Chardonnay, Merlot
Waikato and Bay of Plenty	Cabernet Sauvignon, Chardonnay, Chenin Blanc, Sauvignon Blanc
Gisborne	Chardonnay, Muller-Thurgau, Muscat, Sémillon
Hawke's Bay	Cabernet, Chardonnay, Chenin Blanc, Merlot, Sauvignon Blanc, Sémillon
Wairarapa	Chardonnay, Pinot Noir, Riesling, Sauvignon Blanc
Nelson	Chardonnay, Pinot Noir, Riesling, Sauvignon Blanc
Marlborough	Chardonnay, Pinot Noir, Riesling, Sauvignon Blanc
Canterbury	Chardonnay, Pinot Gris, Pinot Noir, Riesling
Otago	Chardonnay, Pinot Noir, Riesling, Sauvignon Blanc

RED WINE

ALTHOUGH NEW ZEALAND is still primarily known for its white wines, its red wines are gaining in importance as wine makers select better sites, perfect their viticulture methods and as vines mature, making them more stable. Pinot Noir is the most widely planted red variety, but Cabernet Sauvignon, Merlot and Cabernet Franc are also well suited to New Zealand's soil and climatic conditions. Wine makers frequently blend red wines from different areas and provinces.

Alana Estate Pinot Noir

Clearview Estate's popular seaside restaurant, Hawke's Bay *(see pp148–9)*

WINE TYPE	REGIONS	RECOMMENDED PRODUCERS
Cabernet Sauvignon	Auckland, Hawke's Bay, Northland, Waikato	Benfield, Brookfields, Church Road, Delamere, Esk Valley, Goldwater, Morton Estate, Villa Maria
Merlot	Auckland, Gisborne, Hawke's Bay, Marlborough	Arahura, Babich, Church Road, C J Pask, Clearview Estate, Corbans, Delegates, Esk Valley, Villa Maria
Pinotage	Auckland, Gisborne, Hawke's Bay, Marlborough	Cottle Hill Winery, Kerr Farm Vineyard, Landmark Estate Wines, Ohinemuri Estate Wine, Pleasant Valley
Pinot Noir	Canterbury, Central Otago, Hawke's Bay, Marlborough, Nelson, Wairarapa	Ata Rangi, Black Ridge, Cloudy Bay, Cooper's Creek, Dry River, Martinborough Vineyard, Rippon Vineyard

BEER

BEER REMAINS A very popular drink in New Zealand and beers such as Steinlager and Kiwi Lager have won international recognition. There are about 64 breweries in the country producing styles that range from light lagers to draft beers and malt ales. Beer is usually served chilled and is available on tap in bars and hotels. Low-alcohol beers as well as overseas bottled and canned beers are available in supermarkets, bottle stores, bars and restaurants.

Steinlager

OTHER DRINKS

NEW ZEALAND'S CLIMATE, which ranges from subtropical to alpine, allows the cultivation of a large variety of fresh fruit for juicing, including its famous kiwifruit *(see p127)*. Its apples are made into cider. Other bottled drinks and mineral waters are also widely available. A local speciality is Lemon and Paeroa, a lemon-flavoured mineral water from Paeroa in the Coromandel Peninsula. Coffee and tea are other popular drinks with New Zealanders.

Kiwifruit

Choosing a Restaurant

These restaurants have been selected across a wide price range for their good value, facilities and location. Entries are arranged alphabetically within price categories by area. The colour-coded thumb tabs indicate the regions on each page of the chart. Most restaurants in New Zealand have non-smoking sections and soon all may be totally non-smoking.

	Credit Cards	Children's Facilities	Reservation Recommended	Vegetarian	BYO
Auckland					
City: ***Dizengoff*** [$] 256 Ponsonby Rd. **Road map** E2. ☎ *(09) 360 0108.* Interesting, healthy food with an emphasis on Jewish cuisine. Dizengoff closes at 5pm, so is primarily a breakfast and lunch venue. The chopped liver is wonderfully rich and garlicky. ● *25 Dec.* ♿ ⛱	AE DC MC V			●	
City: ***Bowmans*** [$][$] 597 Mount Eden Rd. **Road map** E2. ☎ *(09) 638 9676.* This Mount Eden restaurant has an informal atmosphere and many customers are local regulars. The mainly European food is of good quality and in generous portions. ● *Sun, Mon & 25 Dec.* ♿	AE DC MC V	●	■	●	
City: ***Java Room*** [$][$] 317 Parnell Rd. **Road map** E2. ☎ *(09) 366 1606.* Predominantly Asian food that is varied and interesting, ranging from Malaysian prawn dishes to Indian curries. Small corkage fee per person for BYO. ● *25 Dec.* ♿ ⛱	AE DC MC V	●	■	●	
City: ***Saigon Vietnamese Restaurant*** [$][$] 450 Karangahape Rd. **Road map** E2. ☎ *(09) 379 5559.* Simple Vietnamese restaurant featuring authentic Vietnamese specialities. Casual atmosphere. ● *Mon.*	MC V	●		●	■
City: ***Shahi Café*** [$][$] 115 Parnell Rd. **Road map** E2. ☎ *(09) 377 7898.* Well-priced, tasty food and a small wine list. Fixed-priced menus and Asian food available. The owner runs two other virtually identical cafés at 26 Jervois Rd, Ponsonby, and at 1/1 Milford Rd, Milford. BYO allowed for small corkage fee.	AE DC MC V			●	
City: ***Armadillo Lounge and Bar*** [$][$][$] 531 Karangahape Rd. **Road map** E2. ☎ *(09) 303 3515.* A relaxed, casual restaurant specializing in hearty meals. Friendly and efficient service. Roast pork with crackling a speciality. Popular for functions. ● *25 Dec.* ♿ 🍸 ♫	AE DC MC V	●		●	
City: ***Bella*** [$][$][$] 165 Ponsonby Rd. **Road map** E2. ☎ *(09) 360 2656.* Serving traditional Italian food with a New Zealand flavour, Bella is known for the best risotto in town. The restaurant occupies a great spot in Ponsonby. Good, friendly service and an above average wine list. ● *Sun L & 25 Dec.* ☰ ♿ ⛱ 🍸	AE DC MC V		■	●	
City: ***City Café*** [$][$][$] 20 Lorne St. **Road map** E2. ☎ *(09) 309 6960.* A small restaurant that is particularly popular for lunch. Try the salads, curries and daily specials. BYO allowed for small corkage fee. ● *Sat & Sun, 25 Dec.* ♿ ⛱	AE DC MC V	●		●	
City: ***GPK*** [$][$][$] 234 Dominion Rd. **Road map** E2. ☎ *(09) 623 1300.* GPK's reputation is based on "gourmet pizzas" with toppings such as tandoori chicken with banana. However, the restaurant also serves fish, meat, risotto and many other choices. There is another GPK located at 262 Ponsonby Rd, Ponsonby. ● *25 Dec.* ♿ ⛱ 🍸	AE DC MC V			●	■
City: ***La Bocca and La Bocca di Mare*** [$][$][$] 251 Parnell Rd. **Road map** E2. ☎ *(09) 375 0083.* These two restaurants at one location offer Italian food and seafood. Both are of good quality. La Bocca di Mare is closed over winter. BYO allowed for corkage fee. ⛱	AE DC MC V		■	●	

Price categories are for a three-course meal for one, not including drinks, inclusive of Goods and Service Tax (GST) charges of 12.5%.
Ⓢ under NZ $25
ⓈⓈ NZ$25–NZ$35
ⓈⓈⓈ NZ$35–NZ$50
ⓈⓈⓈⓈ NZ$50–NZ$70
ⓈⓈⓈⓈⓈ over NZ$70

CREDIT CARDS
AE American Express; BC Bankcard; DC Diners Club; JCB Japanese Credit Bureau; MC Master Card/Access; V Visa.
CHILDREN'S FACILITIES
Small portions and/or high chairs available.
VEGETARIAN
Vegetarian selections are available on the menu.
BRING YOUR OWN
A BYO listing allows diners to bring their own wine or beer to the restaurant, a cheaper option than purchasing them on the premises. A small fee may be charged for corkage.

	CREDIT CARDS	CHILDREN'S FACILITIES	RESERVATION RECOMMENDED	VEGETARIAN	BYO
CITY: *Masala* ⓈⓈⓈ 169 Ponsonby Rd. **Road map** E2. ((09) 378 4500. Masala's menu is excellent and the restaurant is a good choice for Indian aficionados. Large vegetarian selection. Busy location that can be a bit noisy. BYO allowed for small corkage fee per person. ▦ Ⓨ	AE DC MC V			●	▦
CITY: *Musical Knives* ⓈⓈⓈ 272 Ponsonby Rd. **Road map** E2. ((09) 376 7354. Organic vegetarian food and organic wine in a formal setting. Very high quality, recommended even for meat lovers. ● *Mon.* ▤ ▦	AE DC MC V		▦	●	
CITY: *Ramses Restaurant and Bar* ⓈⓈⓈ 435 Khyber Pass. **Road map** E2. ((09) 522 0619. Award-winning food with a Mediterranean theme. Good service, rooftop parking. The vegetarian food is organic. ● *Sat L & Sun.* ▤ ▤ Ⓨ ♪	AE DC MC V		▦	●	
CITY: *Sun World* ⓈⓈⓈ 56 Wakefield St. **Road map** E2. ((09) 373 5336. This restaurant is particularly popular with the local Chinese community and seats more than 200. Large menu of Cantonese-style dishes. Popular for *yum cha* lunches. ▤ ▤ Ⓨ	AE MC V			●	
CITY: *Tribeca* ⓈⓈⓈ Foundation Building, 8 George St. **Road map** E2. ((09) 379 6359. The menu offers ample choice of fusion-style dishes that combine elements of different ethnic backgrounds. The restaurant has a quiet courtyard in the back. ▤ ▦ Ⓨ	AE DC MC V		▦	●	
CITY: *Zest Restaurant* ⓈⓈⓈ City Life Hotel, 171 Queen St. **Road map** E2. ((09) 367 1234. With one of the most comprehensive wine lists in New Zealand, Zest is a good choice for wine lovers and also for those who appreciate fresh, healthy food. Centrally located. ● *Sat & Sun L.* ▤ ▤ Ⓨ	AE DC MC V	●		●	
CITY: *Anglesea Grill* ⓈⓈⓈⓈ Cnr of Ponsonby Rd & Anglesea St. **Road map** E2. ((09) 360 4551. Excellent reputation primarily based on their seafood specialities, including chowder and Thai fishcakes. There are a few non-fish dishes as well. BYO allowed for $7 corkage charge. ● *Sat–Tue L, Sun.* ▤ ▦ Ⓨ	DC V	●	▦	●	
CITY: *Berlin* ⓈⓈⓈⓈ 423 Mount Eden Rd. **Road map** E2. ((09) 630 6602. This traditional European restaurant has made no concessions to the latest culinary trends and has been serving German fare, from marinated herring to pork sausages, for years. Excellent service. ● *Sun.*	AE DC MC V	●	▦	●	▦
CITY: *Cibo* ⓈⓈⓈⓈ 91 St Georges Bay Rd. **Road map** E2. ((09) 309 2255. A popular haunt of advertising executives, Cibo has an excellent courtyard in a converted industrial building. ● *Sun.* ▤ ▦ Ⓨ	AE BC MC V		▦	●	
CITY: *Cin Cin on Quay* ⓈⓈⓈⓈ 99 Quay St. **Road map** E2. ((09) 307 6966. Ⓦ www.cincin.co.nz A popular gathering place for the well-heeled, Cin Cin has a good reputation for friendly and professional staff at a great waterfront location in the Ferry Building. The chicken salad is excellent. ▤ ▤ ▦ Ⓨ	AE DC MC V	●	▦	●	
CITY: *Hammerheads Seafood Restaurant* ⓈⓈⓈⓈ 19 Tamaki Drive. **Road map** E2. ((09) 521 4400. Hammerheads offers good sea views over the Hauraki Gulf. The food is excellent, especially the seafood platter. The wine list includes a number of fine French wines. ▤ ▦ Ⓨ	AE DC MC V	●	▦	●	

Price categories are for a three-course meal for one, not including drinks, inclusive of Goods and Service Tax (GST) charges of 12.5%.
$ under NZ $25
$$ NZ$25–NZ$35
$$$ NZ$35–NZ$50
$$$$ NZ$50–NZ$70
$$$$$ over NZ$70

Credit Cards
AE American Express; *BC* Bankcard; *DC* Diners Club; *JCB* Japanese Credit Bureau; *MC* Master Card/Access; *V* Visa.
Children's Facilities
Small portions and/or high chairs available.
Vegetarian
Vegetarian selections are available on the menu.
Bring Your Own
A BYO listing allows diners to bring their own wine or beer to the restaurant, a cheaper option than purchasing them on the premises. A small fee may be charged for corkage.

Restaurant	Credit Cards	Children's Facilities	Reservation Recommended	Vegetarian	BYO
City: *Kermadec Fresh Ocean Restaurant* $$$$ 1st Floor, Viaduct Quay Building, Cnr Lower Hobson and Quay sts. **Road map** E2. ☎ *(09) 309 0412.* This restaurant and brasserie next door are owned by a fishing company with a good reputation for fresh produce. Private Japanese dining rooms are part of the complex. ▤ ♿ ⛱ 🍸	AE DC JCB MC V	●	■	●	
City: *Rikka Newmarket* $$$$ 73 Davis Crescent. **Road map** E2. ☎ *(09) 522 5277.* Japanese food, including excellent *sashimi.* The restaurant's décor is very smart. Rikka Newmarket's location makes it an ideal spot to conclude a shopping expedition. ▤ 🍸	AE DC MC V	●	■	●	
City: *The French Café* $$$$ 210 Symonds St. **Road map** E2. ☎ *(09) 377 1911.* The French Café has been around for decades, yet seems capable of continually reinventing itself. Known for its innovative food and comprehensive wine list. ● *Sun, Mon & Sat.* ▤ ♿ ⛱ 🍸	AE DC MC V		■	●	
City: *Toto Italian Restaurant* $$$$ 53 Nelson St. **Road map** E2. ☎ *(09) 302 2665.* Modern Italian food in a traditional setting. Pleasant ambience with good food and service. Popular with Television New Zealand executives who work nearby. Live opera music some nights. ● *25 Dec– 3 Jan.* ⛱ 🍸 ♫	AE DC MC V	●	■	●	
City: *Veranda Bar and Grill* $$$$ 11/279 Parnell Rd. **Road map** E2. ☎ *(09) 309 6289.* This top Parnell restaurant is not cheap but the food is of an unusually high standard with an extensive wine list, including top French vintages. Popular for special occasions. ● *Sun & 25 Dec.* ▤ 🍸	AE DC MC V	●	■	●	
City: *Wildfire Bar and Restaurant* $$$$ Shed 22, Princes Wharf. **Road map** E2. ☎ *(09) 377 6869.* [FAX] *(09) 353 7590.* This busy restaurant features a selection of fish, meats, poultry and sausages on small spits which are carried by waiters to guests and carved at the table. ● *25 Dec.* ▤ ♿ ⛱ 🍸	AE DC MC V	●	■	●	
City: *Antoines* $$$$$ 333 Parnell Rd. **Road map** E2. ☎ *(09) 379 8756.* Established for more than 25 years, Antoines has a reputation for excellent traditional French food and superb service. ⛱	AE DC MC V		■	●	
Greater Auckland: *Allely House, Selaks Vineyard Restaurant* $$$ Cnr Old North Rd & State Hwy 16, Kumeu. **Road map** E2. ☎ *(09) 412 7206.* This 1902 villa is popular for indoor or patio dining. Large range of choices from a blackboard menu. Live music on Sunday. ♿ ⛱ 🍸	AE DC MC V	●	■	●	■
Greater Auckland: *Shamrock Cottage* $$$ 73 Selwyn Rd, Howick. **Road map** E2. ☎ *(09) 534 6861.* A small restaurant in a historic cottage that provides good quality New Zealand cooking. Good service and interesting ambience. BYO allowed for small corkage fee. ● *Sun & Mon.* ⛱	AE DC MC V	●	■	●	
Greater Auckland: *The Hunting Lodge* $$$$ Waikoukou Valley Rd, Waimauku (7 km (4 miles) from Kumeu). **Road map** E2. ☎ *(09) 411 8259.* This well-known restaurant with an excellent reputation is located on Matua Valley Estate in a scenic rural area. The wine list features Matua's top wines. ● *Mon & Tues (Jan–Nov).* ⛱ ♿ 🍸	AE DC MC V		■	●	
Greater Auckland: *Vinnies* $$$$ 166 Jervois Rd, Herne Bay. **Road map** E2. ☎ *(09) 376 5597.* Arguably Auckland's top restaurant. Vinnies has a reputation for innovative food and has won many awards. Its degustation menu is famous among local gourmets. ⛱ ♿ 🍸	AE DC MC V	●	■	●	

NORTHLAND

HELENSVILLE: *Steak House & Chicken Inn* $$$
138 Victoria St. **Road map** E2. ((09) 439 8460.
Steak is a speciality at this cheerful restaurant. The outdoor courtyard is popular in summer. Knowledgeable, friendly staff. ● 25 Dec.

| | AE MC V | ● | ▨ | ● | |

KAITAIA: *Beachcomber Restaurant* $$
The Plaza, 222 Commerce St. **Road map** D1. ((09) 408 2010.
The Beachcomber specializes in fresh, local seafood. The menu also features a selection of vegetarian dishes. ● Sun & 25 Dec.

| | AE DC MC V | ● | ▨ | ● | ▨ |

KAITAIA: *Henry VIII Restaurant* $$
Cnr North Rd & Kohuhu St. **Road map** D1. ((09) 408 2800. FAX (09) 408 0306.
This centrally located restaurant has been open for 45 years and has had the same Swiss chef all that time. He specializes in French cuisine.

| | AE DC JCB MC V | ● | ▨ | ● | |

KERIKERI: *The Black Olive* $
Kerikeri Rd. **Road map** E1. ((09) 407 9693.
A pizza restaurant with toppings ranging from orthodox to Cajun chicken and mango chutney. Takeaway and delivery available. ● 25 Dec.

| | MC V | ● | ▨ | ● | ▨ |

KERIKERI: *Marsden Estate Vineyard Restaurant* $$
Wiroa Rd, RD3. **Road map** E1. ((09) 407 9398.
Innovative, European-inspired food is served at this lunch-only restaurant. The courtyard is popular in summer. The restaurant serves Marsden Estate wines. ● D & 25 Dec.

| | DC MC V | ● | | | |

KERIKERI: *The Kina Kitchen* $$$
Village Mall, Kerikeri Rd. **Road map** E1. ((09) 407 7669.
With seafood and venison specialities, this casual establishment is popular with locals and tourists alike. The restaurant has a courtyard setting. Small charge for BYO. ● Mon (Mar–Nov).

| | AE DC MC V | ● | ▨ | ● | ▨ |

PAIHIA: *Swiss Café and Grill* $$
48 Marsden Rd. **Road map** E1. ((09) 402 6701. FAX (09) 402 8278.
Reminiscent of Switzerland in décor and menu, this restaurant has waterfront views. ● Mid-Jun to mid-Jul.

| | BC MC V | ● | ▨ | ● | ▨ |

PAIHIA: *The Park Lodge on Paihia* $$
Cnr Seaview & McMurray Rd. **Road map** E1. ((09) 402 7826. FAX (09) 402 8500.
This restaurant is primarily used by hotel guests but anyone is welcome. Apart from buffet meals, there are specials of the day.

| | AE DC MC V | ● | ▨ | ● | |

RUSSELL: *Gannet Restaurant* @restaurant@gannets.co.nz $$$
Town Square. **Road map** E1. ((09) 403 7990.
Specialities include fresh fish and excellent meat dishes at this restaurant serving New Zealand fare. Multilingual staff speak German, Dutch, French and Italian. ● Jun to mid-Aug, 25 Dec.

| | AE DC MC V | ● | ▨ | | |

RUSSELL: *The Gables Restaurant* $$$$
The Strand. **Road map** E1. (& FAX (09) 403 7618.
A waterfront restaurant in historic Russell specializing in fresh seafood. High level of personal service and excellent food.

| | AE DC MC V | ● | ▨ | ● | |

WAITANGI: *Waikokopu Café* @ waikokopucafe@xtra.co.nz $$
Treaty Grounds. **Road map** E1. ((09) 402 6275. FAX (09) 402 6276.
An award-winning café with an interesting menu. BYO allowed for corkage fee. Children's play area. ● 25 Dec.

| | DC MC V | ● | | ● | ▨ |

WHANGAREI: *Killer Prawn* $$$
Bank St. **Road map** E1. ((09) 430 3333. FAX (09) 430 3131.
Seafood is a speciality at this centrally located restaurant. Well-trained staff give outstanding service. ● Sun, Good Fri, 25 Dec.

| | AE DC MC V | ● | ▨ | ● | |

WHANGAREI: *Reva's on the Waterfront* W www.revas.co.nz $$
31 Quayside, Town Basin. **Road map** E1. ((09) 438 8969. FAX (09) 438 0172.
Housed in a traditional building on the waterfront, Reva's is well known for its pizza. ● Sun & public hols.

| | AE DC MC V | ● | ▨ | ● | |

WHANGAREI: *The New Water St Brasserie* $$$
24 Water St. **Road map** E1. ((09) 438 7464. FAX (09) 438 7460.
Run by a husband and wife team, the menu has a variety of innovative dishes. BYO allowed for small corkage fee. ● Sun & Mon.

| | AE MC V | ● | ▨ | ● | ▨ |

For key to symbols see back flap

<table>
<tr><td colspan="2">Price categories are for a three-course meal for one, not including drinks, inclusive of Goods and Service Tax (GST) charges of 12.5%.
$ under NZ $25
$$ NZ$25–NZ$35
$$$ NZ$35–NZ$50
$$$$ NZ$50–NZ$70
$$$$$ over NZ$70</td></tr>
</table>

CREDIT CARDS
AE American Express; BC Bankcard; DC Diners Club; JCB Japanese Credit Bureau; MC Master Card/Access; V Visa.
CHILDREN'S FACILITIES
Small portions and/or high chairs available.
VEGETARIAN
Vegetarian selections are available on the menu.
BRING YOUR OWN
A BYO listing allows diners to bring their own wine or beer to the restaurant, a cheaper option than purchasing them on the premises. A small fee may be charged for corkage.

	CREDIT CARDS	CHILDREN'S FACILITIES	RESERVATION RECOMMENDED	VEGETARIAN	BYO

THE CENTRAL NORTH ISLAND

	CREDIT CARDS	CHILDREN'S FACILITIES	RESERVATION RECOMMENDED	VEGETARIAN	BYO
CAMBRIDGE: *Souter House* $$$ 19 Victoria St. **Road map** E3. ((07) 827 3610. FAX (07) 827 4885. Fine dining restaurant set in an 1875 Victorian home built by Captain William Souter. Souter House has won awards for its beef and lamb specialities. ● 26 Dec. ▤ & ▦	AE DC MC V	●	▮	●	▮
COROMANDEL: *Success Café* $$ 104 Kapanga Rd. **Road map** E2. (& FAX (07) 866 7100. Success Café serves fresh local seafood, including oysters and chowder made from Hauraki Gulf mussels. ● Tue & Wed. & ▦	MC V	●	▮	●	▮
COROMANDEL: *Peppertree Restaurant and Bar* $$$ 31 Kapanga Rd. **Road map** E2. ((07) 866 8211. FAX (07) 866 7391. Local snapper is used in a variety of exciting ways. Courtyard dining or fire-warmed interior for cooler nights. ● 25 Dec. & ▦ ▮ ♫	AE DC MC V	●	▮	●	▮
GISBORNE: *Café Villagio* $$ 57 Balance St. **Road map** F3. ((06) 868 1611. FAX (06) 867 9701. Game, seafood and vegetarian dishes are specialities in this modern café-style restaurant. ● Sun & Mon D. & ▦	AE DC MC V	●		●	▮
GISBORNE: *The Marina* $$$ 1 Vogel St. **Road map** F3. (& FAX (06) 868 5919. Originally built as a ballroom for a young woman's 21st birthday, The Marina specializes in crayfish, which may be chosen live from the tank. ▤ & ▦ ▮	AE DC MC V	●	▮	●	▮
GISBORNE: *Wharf Café and Bar* $$$ 60 The Esplanade. **Road map** F3. (& FAX (06) 868 4876. Occupying a converted warehouse on Gisborne's wharf, this café has a predominantly seafood menu. Live music in summer. & ▦ ▮	AE DC MC V	●	▮	●	▮
HAMILTON: *Barzurk Gourmet Pizza Bar* $ 250 Victoria St. **Road map** E2. ((07) 834 2363. Wood-fired cooked pizzas are served with salads in this busy restaurant. The pastas and desserts are also good. ● 25 & 26 Dec, 1 Jan. & ▦ ▮	AE DC MC V	●		●	
HAMILTON: *Tables on the River* $$$ 12 Alma St. **Road map** E2. ((07) 839 6555. FAX (07) 839 6400. Award-winning Mediterranean-style food. Balcony tables above the Waikato River create a lovely atmosphere. ● Sun. ▤ & ▦ ▮	AE DC MC V	●	▮	●	▮
HAMILTON: *The Narrows Landing* $$$ 431 Airport Rd, Tamihere. **Road map** E2. ((07) 858 4001. FAX (07) 858 4499. Located in a picturesque park by the Waikato River. Game dishes available, including emu, venison and pheasant. ● 25 Dec. & ▦ ▮	AE DC MC V	●	▮	●	
MOUNT MAUNGANUI: *Thai-phoon Restaurant* $ 14A Pacific Ave. **Road map** E2. (& FAX (07) 572 3545. Good, cheap, tasty Thai food in tasteful surroundings right in the centre of the town. ● Mon. & ▦ ▮	MC V		▮		▮
NAPIER: *Clearview Estate Winery* $$ 194 Clifton Rd, Te Awanga. **Road map** F4. ((06) 875 0150. FAX (06) 875 1258. This popular seaside winery restaurant has a menu featuring local produce. Lunch only. ● D, Easter, Tue–Thur (Jun–Aug). & ▦ ▮	AE MC V	●	▮	●	▮
NAPIER: *Deano's Bar and Grill* $$ 255 Marine Parade. **Road map** F4. ((06) 835 4944. FAX (06) 835 4387. Steak is a speciality here. A free drink is served with each main meal. Friendly, intimate environment. ● Mon L & 25 Dec. & ▦ ▮	AE DC MC V	●	▮		

NAPIER: *Anatole's* $$$
12 Browning St. **Road map** F4. **(** *(06) 835 7800/0800.* **FAX** *(06) 835 7797.*
Over the years Anatole's has won many awards for its beef and lamb
dishes. Casual by day, fine dining in the evening. **🕭 ⊞ ⅄**
AE DC MC V

NAPIER: *Pierre sur le Quai* $$$
60 West Quay. **Road map** F4. **(** *(06) 834 0189.*
A wide range of seafood and fish dishes prepared with a French
influence. Intense, interesting flavours. **●** *Sun, Mon (Jun–Aug).* **🕭 ⊞ ⅄**
AE DC MC V

OHAKUNE: *Fat Pigeon Garden Café* $
2 Tyne St. **Road map** E3. **(** *(06) 385 9423.*
Diners may eat outside in a garden where birds can be seen. Fillet steak
and fresh fish are specialities. **●** *Mon–Thu (Dec–Feb).* **🕭 ⊞ ⅄**
MC V

OHAKUNE: *Sassi's Bistro* $$
7 Miro St. **Road map** E3. **(** & **FAX** *(07) 385 8758.*
A convivial atmosphere and wide-ranging menu ensure dining
satisfaction at this restaurant, open year round. **🕭 ⊞ ⅄**
AE DC MC V

OHAKUNE: *O Bar and Restaurant* $$$
72 Clyde St. **Road map** E3. **(** *(06) 385 8268.* **FAX** *(06) 385 8262.*
Two open fires warm this recently renovated restaurant that features a
wooden horseshoe-shaped bar. Wood-fired pizza is a speciality. **🕭 ⊞ ⅄**
AE DC MC V

OTOROHANGA: *BeGuinness* $$
91 Maniapoto St. **Road map** E3. **(** *(07) 873 8010.* **FAX** *(07) 873 1613.*
Traditional country food with steak a speciality. Guinness available on
tap. The restaurant showcases landscape paintings. **●** *Mon.* **▤ 🕭 ⅄**
AE DC MC V

RAGLAN: *Marlin Café and Grill* $$
Raglan Wharf, 43 Rose St. **Road map** E2. **(** *(07) 825 0010.* **FAX** *(07) 825 0014.*
Seafood is a speciality here. Enjoy sea views and cook your own steak or
fish on the grill if you wish. **🕭 ⊞ ⅄**
MC V

RAGLAN: *Vinnies* $$
7 Wainui Rd. **Road map** E2. **(** *(07) 825 7273.* **FAX** *(07) 825 7262.*
Smoothie and juice bar and 120 international dishes to choose from. Built
around a 117-year-old kauri cottage. **●** *25 Dec, Mon (Jun–Aug).* **🕭 ⊞**
AE DC MC V

ROTORUA: *Sirocco* $$
1280 Eruera St. **Road map** E3. **(** *(07) 347 3388.* **FAX** *(07) 347 3389.*
The Mediterranean lunch is popular at Sirocco, where music (jazz, blues)
is integral to the dining experience. **●** *25 Dec.* **🕭 ⊞ ⅄ ♫**
AE DC MC V

ROTORUA: *Zanellis* $$
1243 Amohia St. **Road map** E3. **(** *(07) 348 4908.* **FAX** *(07) 349 0935.*
Italian cuisine with pasta and *gelato* (Italian ice-cream) specialities. Daily
specials using seasonal ingredients. Dinner only. **●** *Sun & Mon.*
AE DC MC V

ROTORUA: *Poppy's Villa* $$$
4 Marguerita St. **Road map** E3. **(** & **FAX** *(07) 347 1700.*
Go to Poppy's to sample New Zealand dishes. Rack of lamb is a
speciality. Recipient of Quality Cuisine Awards for meat dishes. **▤ 🕭 ⅄**
AE DC JCB MC V

ROTORUA: *Zambique* $$$
1111 Tutanekai St. **Road map** E3. **(** & **FAX** *(07) 349 2140.*
Zambique terms its modern Asian-Pacific fare "Urban Jungle Cuisine".
Exotic dishes. Great pride is taken in its coffee. **🕭 ⊞ ⅄**
AE DC MC V

TAUPO: *Mole and Chicken* $$
40 Taharepe Rd. **Road map** E3. **(** & **FAX** *(07) 378 7843.*
Good-sized portions are served at this relaxed English-style pub in
surburban Taupo. **●** *25 Dec.* **🕭 ⊞ ⅄**
DC MC V

TAUPO: *Prawn Works Bar and Grill* $$
Wairakei Tourist Park, Huka Falls Rd. **Road map** E3. **(** *(07) 374 8474.* **FAX** *(07) 374 8204.* Hand-feed prawns raised on the farm, then sit down and eat
some at the scenic restaurant. **●** *25 Dec.* **🕭 ⊞ ⅄**
AE DC MC V

TAUPO: *Finch's Brasserie and Bar* $$$
64 Tuwharetoa St. **Road map** E3. **(** *(07) 377 2425.* **FAX** *(07) 377 2426.*
Award winner of beef and lamb cuisine competition. Will cook your
freshly caught trout from Lake Taupo for you. **🕭 ⊞ ⅄**
AE DC MC V

For key to symbols see back flap

Price categories are for a three-course meal for one, not including drinks, inclusive of Goods and Service Tax (GST) charges of 12.5%.
[$] under NZ $25
[$][$] NZ$25–NZ$35
[$][$][$] NZ$35–NZ$50
[$][$][$][$] NZ$50–NZ$70
[$][$][$][$][$] over NZ$70

Credit Cards
AE American Express; *BC* Bankcard; *DC* Diners Club; *JCB* Japanese Credit Bureau; *MC* Master Card/Access; *V* Visa.
Children's Facilities
Small portions and/or high chairs available.
Vegetarian
Vegetarian selections are available on the menu.
Bring Your Own
A BYO listing allows diners to bring their own wine or beer to the restaurant, a cheaper option than purchasing them on the premises. A small fee may be charged for corkage.

Restaurant	Credit Cards	Children's Facilities	Reservation Recommended	Vegetarian	BYO
Taupo: *Walnut Keep* [$][$][$] 77 Spa Rd. **Road map** E3. ☎ & [FAX] *(07) 378 0777.* An award-winning restaurant specializing in South Pacific Rim cuisine. Walnut trees near the restaurant inspired its name. ● *25 & 26 Dec.* ♿ 🍸	AE MC V	●	■	●	■
Taupo: *Huka Lodge* [$][$][$][$][$] Huka Falls Rd. **Road map** E3. ☎ *(07) 378 5791.* [FAX] *(07) 378 0427.* The five-course set menu at this luxury resort changes daily and focuses on using fresh products. Pacific Rim flavours with Asian influences. Cocktail hour from 7pm, dinner at 8pm. ♿ ⛱ 🍸	AE DC MC V	●	■	●	
Tauranga: *Shiraz Café* [$][$] 12 Wharf St. **Road map** E3. ☎ & [FAX] *(07) 577 0059.* Middle Eastern and Mediterranean fare served in authentically decorated indoor and courtyard settings. ● *Sun.* ♿ ⛱ 🍸	AE DC MC V	●		●	
Tauranga: *Spinnaker's Restaurant and Brassierie* [$][$][$] 101 Tauranga Bridge Marina. **Road map** E3. ☎ *(07) 574 4147.* [FAX] *(07) 574 7774.* Alongside a marina with panoramic views of yachts and the harbour. One of Tauranga's premier seafood restaurants. ♿ ⛱ 🍸	AE DC MC V	●	■	●	
Thames: *The Gold Bar* [$][$] 404 Pollen St. **Road map** E2. ☎ *(07) 868 5548.* [FAX] *(07) 868 5125.* Décor reminiscent of the gold-mining era. An emphasis on seafood in pastas, chowders and fritters. Prime fillet stuffed with seafood is a speciality. Live entertainment occasionally. ● *Mon & Tues.* ☰ ♿ 🍸	AE DC MC V		■	●	
Thames: *Sealey Café* [$][$][$] 109 Sealey St. **Road map** E2. ☎ & [FAX] *(07) 868 8641.* Lamb and fish meals are done exceptionally well at this café with outdoor patio dining. Separate lunch menu and jazz music. ♿ ⛱ 🍸 ♫	AF DC MC V	●	■	●	■
Tongariro National Park: *The Grand Chateau* [$][$] Whakapapa Village. **Road map** E3. ☎ *(07) 892 3809.* [FAX] *(07) 892 3524.* Lamb and venison specialities are served in the Ruapehu Room at this famous hotel. Asian cuisine is available at the Pihanga Café. ♿ 🍸	AE DC MC V	●	■	●	
Waitomo: *Waitomo Caves Tavern* [$] Lemon Point Rd. **Road map** E3. ☎ & [FAX] *(07) 878 8448.* Good, cheap food in a fun atmosphere. A favourite of the locals. The hot chips are legendary. ● *Public hols.* ⛱ 🍸	AE MC V	●		●	
Whakatane: *The Chambers* [$][$][$] 40 The Strand. **Road map** F3. ☎ *(07) 307 0107.* [FAX] *(07) 307 0407.* Fine dining in a formal setting for evening meals, relaxed café-style setting for lunches. English beers on tap. Located in the former Whakatane District Council building. ♿ ⛱ 🍸	AE DC MC V	●	■	●	■
Whangamata: *Café 101* [$][$][$] 101 Casement Rd. **Road map** E2. ☎ *(06) 385 8758.* Seafood, spinach crêpes and vegetable strudel are specialities. Live piano music is featured. ● *Mon–Wed (1 Feb–25 Dec).* ♿ ⛱ 🍸 ♫	MC V	●	■	●	
Whitianga: *The Beach Café* [$][$] 5 Albert St. **Road map** E2. ☎ *(07) 866 5127.* Look through the restaurateur's personal fishing album while you wait for your meal. Seasonal seafood, pasta and steak dishes. Will cook fish caught by diners if time permits. ● *Sun & Mon (Jun–Aug).* ♿ ⛱ 🍸	MC V	●	■	●	■
Whitianga: *On The Rocks Bar and Restaurant* [$][$][$] 20 The Esplanade. **Road map** E2. ☎ *(07) 866 4833.* [FAX] *(07) 866 4888.* Built from recycled timber in a nautical theme, this award-winning restaurant takes great pride in its New Zealand cuisine. ☰ ♿ ⛱ 🍸	AE DC MC V	●	■	●	

WELLINGTON AND THE SOUTH

LEVIN: *Café Nua* $\$\$
7 Bath St. **Road map** E4. ((06) 368 0777.
Up-market café in a small town setting with good coffee, excellent cakes
and an interesting menu. Plenty of space to sit and meet the locals.
● Mon.
AE MC V

MASTERTON: *Bloomfields Restaurant* $\$\$\$
Ist Floor, Cnr Chapel St and Lincoln Rd. **Road map** E4. ((06) 377 4305.
Chilli squid with sundried tomatoes and char grilled beef with scallops
are two items on the New Zealand-inspired menu. ● Sun.
AE DC MC V

NEW PLYMOUTH: *Gareth's Restaurant* $\$\$
182 Devon St. **Road map** D3. ((06) 758 5104.
Venison and seafood are some of the specialities of this up-market
restaurant. Fixed-price menus offer good value. ● Public hols.
AE DC MC V

NEW PLYMOUTH: *Steps Restaurant* $\$\$
37 Gover St. **Road map** D3. ((06) 758 3393.
Beef and lamb dishes are the specialities of this well-patronized
restaurant that makes a point of presenting its food with flair. Steps to the
restaurant make disabled access limited. ● Sun & Mon.
AE DC MC V

OTAKI: *Brown Sugar* $\$
State Hwy 1. **Road map** E4. ((06) 364 6359.
Charming roadside restaurant built around a leafy courtyard. Fresh, café-
style food, good coffee and pleasant service. ● 25 Dec.
MC V

PAEKAKARIKI: *The Fisherman's Table* $\$
State Hwy 1. **Road map** E4. ((04) 292 8125.
Large family-orientated, budget-priced restaurant. An all-you-can-eat salad
bar is featured on the fixed-price menu.
AE BC DC MC V

PALMERSTON NORTH: *The Stage Door Café* $\$
90 King St. **Road map** E4. ((06) 359 2233.
Good-sized servings of grilled lamb salad or fresh mussels are highlights
of this inexpensive, casual, central café. ● 25 Dec.
AE DC MC V

PALMERSTON NORTH: *Ambrosia Café* $\$\$
149 Rangitikei St. **Road map** E4. ((06) 357 5777.
Busy but relaxed café just off The Square in Palmerston North's centre.
Interesting, regularly changed menu, highly recommended by locals for
its attention to fresh ingredients and presentation. ● Sun.
AE DC MC V

PALMERSTON NORTH: *Vavasseur* $\$\$\$
201 Broadway Ave. **Road map** E4. (06) 359 3167.
Cosy but lively atmosphere with excellent service. The menu includes
New Zealand lamb dishes. ● Sun & Mon.
AE DC MC V

WANGANUI: *Amadeus Riverbank Café* $\$
69 Taupo Quay. **Road map** E4. ((06) 345 1538.
Superb chicken and mango croissants are drawcards at lunch in this
popular café. More formal dining in the evening. ● 25 Dec.
MC V

WANGANUI: *Redeye Café* $\$
96 Guyton St. **Road map** E4. ((06) 345 5646.
Wanganui's student population frequent this mid-town café offering
large-sized servings at good prices. Cash only. ● Public hols.

WELLINGTON: *Kopi* $\$
103 Willis St. **Road map** E5. (& FAX (04) 499 5570.
Frequently voted Wellington's best Asian restaurant, Kopi offers
outstanding Malaysian food in a casual setting.
AE DC MC V

WELLINGTON: *Roti Chenai* $\$
120 Victoria St. **Road map** E5. (& FAX (04) 382 9807.
Malaysian and Indian food. Extremely popular, with quick and courteous
service. The lamb curry and *naan* bread are very good.
AE DC MC V

WELLINGTON: *The Green Parrot* $\$
16 Taranaki St. **Road map** E5. ((04) 384 6080.
One of the longest established cafés in Wellington. A late-night hang-out
serving the best mixed grill in town.
AE DC MC V

Price categories are for a three-course meal for one, not including drinks, inclusive of Goods and Service Tax (GST) charges of 12.5%. **$** under NZ \$25 **$$** NZ\$25–NZ\$35 **$$$** NZ\$35–NZ\$50 **$$$$** NZ\$50–NZ\$70 **$$$$$** over NZ\$70	**CREDIT CARDS** *AE* American Express; *BC* Bankcard; *DC* Diners Club; *JCB* Japanese Credit Bureau; *MC* Master Card/Access; *V* Visa. **CHILDREN'S FACILITIES** Small portions and/or high chairs available. **VEGETARIAN** Vegetarian selections are available on the menu. **BRING YOUR OWN** A BYO listing allows diners to bring their own wine or beer to the restaurant, a cheaper option than purchasing them on the premises. A small fee may be charged for corkage.	**CREDIT CARDS**	**CHILDREN'S FACILITIES**	**RESERVATION RECOMMENDED**	**VEGETARIAN**	**BYO**

WELLINGTON: *Logan Brown* **$$** 192 Cuba St. **Road map** E5. **(** *(04) 801 5114.* **FAX** *(04) 801 9776.* Housed in a former bank building, Logan Brown has fine dining in an informal setting. Pre-theatre and set menus are a speciality. **& Y**.	AE DC MC V	●	■	●	
WELLINGTON: *Sakura* **$$** Cnr Featherstone & Whitmore sts. **Road map** E5. **(** *(04) 499 6912.* Authentic Japanese food served either in the main restaurant or a traditional *tatami* matting room. Set menus during lunch and dinner offer excellent value for money. **&**	AE DC MC V	●	■	●	
WELLINGTON: *Boulcott Street Bistro* **$$$$** 99 Boulcott St. **Road map** E5. **(** & **FAX** *(04) 499 4199.* Located in a quaint, two-storeyed, former colonial family home just behind Wellington's main shopping precinct, this modern bistro is constantly rated among Wellington's best eating houses. **●** *Sun.* **& Y**	AE DC MC V		■	●	
WELLINGTON: *Brasserie Flipp* **$$$$** 103 Gluznee St. **Road map** E5. **(** *(04) 385 9493.* An innovative menu continues to make this appealing restaurant a winner with locals. **●** *Sun.* **& Y**	AE DC MC V	●	■	●	
WELLINGTON: *Icon Restaurant* **$$$$** Museum of New Zealand Te Papa Tongarewa, Cable St. **Road map** E5. **(** *(04) 801 5300.* Specialities of the restaurant are Pacific Rim and French cuisine. Superb views of Wellington Harbour are a bonus. **目 & 🔲 Y**	AE DC MC V	●	■	●	
WELLINGTON: *The White House* **$$$$** 232 Oriental Parade. **Road map** E5. **(** *(04) 385 8555.* The White House overlooks the water at Oriental Bay. Try New Zealand eel or duck with *kumara* (sweet potato). **●** *Sun.* **目 🔲 Y**	AE DC MC V		■	●	

MARLBOROUGH AND NELSON

BLENHEIM: *Gillan Estate Vineyard Restaurant* **$** 190 Rapaura Rd. **Road map** D5. **(** *(03) 572 9979.* **FAX** *(03) 572 9980.* Mediterranean food is served for lunch in the champagne cellar or outdoors. **●** *D, Jun–Oct.* **& 🔲 Y**	AE DC MC V	●	■	●	
BLENHEIM: *Bacchus* **$$** 3 Main St. **Road map** D5. **(** & **FAX** *(03) 578 8099.* Value for money in a stylish, warm atmosphere. The menu features fresh local produce and there is an extensive wine list. **●** *25 Dec.* **目 & 🔲 Y**	AE MC V	●	■	●	
BLENHEIM: *Bellafico Caffè and Wine Bar* **$$$** 17 Maxwell Rd. **Road map** D5. **(** *(03) 577 6072.* **FAX** *(03) 577 6076.* Flavoursome food and delicious desserts. The staff are very knowledgeable on food, wine and service. **●** *Sun (Jun–Sep).* **目 & 🔲 Y 🎵**	MC V	●	■	●	
COLLINGWOOD: *Courthouse Café* **$$** Cnr Gibbs Rd and Elizabeth St. **Road map** D4. **(** *(03) 524 8572.* **FAX** *(03) 524 8566.* Casual dining outdoors or inside Collingwood's former courthouse. Emphasis on fresh local produce and game meats. **●** *25 Dec.* **🔲 Y**	AE DC MC V	●	■	●	
HAVELOCK: *Mussel Boys* **$$** 73 Main Rd. **Road map** D4. **(** *(03) 574 2824.* **FAX** *(03) 574 2878.* Lively, casual eatery showcasing local green-lipped mussels. A range of fine Marlborough wines available. **●** *25 Dec.* **& 🔲 Y**	AE DC MC V	●	■	●	
KAIKOURA: *The Olive Branch Wine Bar/Café* **$$** 54 West End. **Road map** D5. **(** *(03) 319 6992.* **FAX** *(03) 319 6801.* The restaurant occupies a 1930s building and has a wide-ranging menu featuring local seafood. **●** *Tue (Jun–Aug).* **& 🔲 Y**	AE DC MC V	●	■	●	

Kaikoura: *Finz of South Bay* $$$ 103 South Bay Parade. **Road map** D5. ☎ *(03) 319 6688.* FAX *(03) 319 6687.* The menu emphasizes local seafood but has other choices. Superb setting with beach and mountain views. ● *Mon & Tue (May–Sep).* ♿ ⛱ 🍸	AE DC MC V	●	■	●	■
Nelson: *Broccoli Row Café* $$ 5 Buxton Square. **Road map** D4. ☎ *(03) 548 9621.* FAX *(03) 545 7424.* Mediterranean-style vegetarian and seafood are specialities of this central city café. Cosy interior and a courtyard. ● *Sun & public hols.* ♿ ⛱	AE DC MC V		■	●	■
Nelson: *Harbour Light Store Restaurant* $$$ 341 Wakefield Quay. **Road map** D4. ☎ *(03) 546 6685.* FAX *(03) 546 6335.* Views of Nelson harbour are a highlight of this restaurant with an eclectic range of food. Indian food evenings are a feature. ● *25 Dec.* ♿ 🍸	AE DC MC V	●	■	●	■
Nelson: *Lambrettas* $$$ 204 Hardy St. **Road map** D4. ☎ *(03) 545 8555.* FAX *(03) 545 8543.* Casual café with 1950s décor. Healthy menu features gourmet pizza, pasta and seafood. Children's playground. ● *Sun L (Jun–Aug).* ♿ 🍸	AE DC MC V	●	■	●	
Nelson: *The Boat Shed Café* $$$ 350 Wakefield Quay. **Road map** D4. ☎ *(03) 546 9783.* FAX *(03) 548 4650.* Asian and Mediterranean flavours combined with local seafood. Great harbourside setting with a diverse wine list. ● *25 Dec & 1 Jan.* ♿ ⛱ 🍸	AE DC MC V	●	■	●	■
Picton: *The Marlborough Terranean* $$$ 31 High St. **Road map** D4. ☎ *(03) 573 7122.* FAX *(03) 573 8881.* Fresh local seafood, lamb and beef are the specialities of this restaurant that offers courtyard and alfresco areas in addition to its beautifully decorated interior. Not suitable for children. 📋 ♿ ⛱	AE DC MC V		■	●	
Richmond: *Seifried's Vineyard Restaurant* $$$ Cnr Redwood Rd and State Hwy 60, Appleby. **Road map** D4. ☎ *(03) 544 1555.* FAX *(03) 544 1700.* Affordable dining in a vineyard setting with a children's play area. Fresh local produce. ● *Good Fri, 25 & 26 Dec.* ♿ ⛱ 🍸	AE DC MC V	●	■	●	
Takaka: *The Wholemeal Café* $$ 60 Commercial St. **Road map** D4. ☎ *(03) 525 9426.* FAX *(03) 525 9471.* This popular café has a varied and interesting menu with many vegetarian and seafood choices. It also has a gallery. ♿ ⛱	MC V	●	■	●	■

Canterbury and the West Coast

Akaroa: *French Farm Winery and Restaurant* $$$ French Farm Valley Rd. **Road map** C6. ☎ *(03) 304 5784.* FAX *(03) 304 5785.* Vineyards and sweeping lawns surround this delightful restaurant. Specialities include the Akaroa salmon tasting plate. ● *25 Dec.* ♿ ⛱ 🍸	AE DC MC V	●	■	●	
Arthur's Pass: *Chalet Restaurant* $$ State Hwy 73. **Road map** C5. ☎ *(03) 318 9236.* FAX *(03) 318 9200.* Nestled in the tiny village of Arthur's Pass, the Chalet offers both cheap bistro meals and more up-market dining in a rustic atmosphere. Venison and salmon are specialities. ♿ ⛱ 🍸	AE JCB MC V	●	■	●	
Arthur's Pass: *Oscar's Haus Alpine Café and Crafts* $$$ State Hwy 73. **Road map** C5. ☎ *(03) 318 9234.* FAX *(03) 318 9231.* A busy café well known for its vegetarian lasagne. Has a gallery adjacent featuring art and crafts from around the South Island. ● *Jun.* ♿ ⛱	AE BC DC MC V	●		●	■
Christchurch: *Annie's Wine Bar and Restaurant* $$$ The Arts Centre, Worcester Boulevard. **Road map** C6. ☎ *(03) 365 0566.* FAX *(03) 365 9821.* This popular restaurant has a wonderful location in the Arts Centre quadrangle, providing good food in a casual but chic environment. Good selection on the wine list. ● *25 Dec–2 Jan.* ♿ ⛱ 🍸	AE DC MC V	●	■	●	
Christchurch: *Le Bon Bolli* $$$$ Cnr Montreal St and Worcester Boulevard. **Road map** C6. ☎ *(03) 374 9444.* FAX *(03) 374 9442.* Winner of many awards, this French-style restaurant is very popular. The adventurous diner can sample bull testicles. ♿ ⛱ 🍸	AE DC MC V		■	●	
Christchurch: *Sign of the Takahe* $$$$$ 200 Hackthorne Rd, Cashmere. **Road map** C6. ☎ *(03) 332 4052.* FAX *(03) 337 2769.* Traditional fine dining complete with silver service. Specializes in high quality local produce. ● *25 Dec.* 🍸	AE DC MC V		■	●	

For key to symbols see back flap

Price categories are for a three-course meal for one, not including drinks, inclusive of Goods and Service Tax (GST) charges of 12.5%.
$ under NZ $25
$$ NZ$25–NZ$35
$$$ NZ$35–NZ$50
$$$$ NZ$50–NZ$70
$$$$$ over NZ$70

Credit Cards
AE American Express; *BC* Bankcard; *DC* Diners Club; *JCB* Japanese Credit Bureau; *MC* Master Card/Access; *V* Visa.
Children's Facilities
Small portions and/or high chairs available.
Vegetarian
Vegetarian selections are available on the menu.
Bring Your Own
A BYO listing allows diners to bring their own wine or beer to the restaurant, a cheaper option than purchasing them on the premises. A small fee may be charged for corkage.

	Credit Cards	Children's Facilities	Reservation Recommended	Vegetarian	BYO
Fairlie: *Old Library Café* $$ 6 Allandale Rd. **Road map** B6. ☎ & [FAX] *(03) 685 8999.* Built in 1914, the old Fairlie library has been tastefully renovated to create this pleasant restaurant. Lamb is a speciality. ⬤ *25 Dec.* 🍴 ♿ 🍸	*AE MC V*	●	■	●	
Fox Glacier: *Cook Saddle Café* $$ State Hwy 6. **Road map** B6. ☎ *(03) 751 0700.* [FAX] *(03) 751 0809.* A large stone open fireplace makes this pleasant restaurant inviting even on the wettest West Coast day. ⬤ *25 Dec.* 🍴 ♿ 🍸 ♫	*MC V*	●		●	
Fox Glacier: *Café Névé* $$$ State Hwy 6. **Road map** B6. ☎ *(03) 751 0110.* [FAX] *(03) 751 0020.* Great coffee and a wide range of home-cooked muffins and cakes. Other specialities include whitebait, venison and seafood. ⬤ *Jun.* ♿ 🍴	*MC V*	●		●	
Franz Josef: *Beeches* $$$ State Hwy 6. **Road map** B6. ☎ & [FAX] *(03) 752 0721.* Open all day, this extensive restaurant offers a range of specialities, including venison, whitebait and salmon. ⬤ *23–25 Dec.* ≣ ♿ 🍴 🍸	*AE DC MC V*	●		●	■
Greymouth: *Jones's Licensed Café and Bar* $$ 37 Tainui St. **Road map** C5. ☎ *(03) 768 6468.* Hearty portions are served in this casual restaurant that offers inexpensive, good value daily specials such as roast lamb. ⬤ *25 Dec.* 🍸	*AE DC MC V*	●		●	
Hokitika: *Café de Paris* $$$ 19–21 Tancred St. **Road map** C5. ☎ *(03) 755 8933.* [FAX] *(03) 755 5035.* This well-known, award-winning restaurant offers a taste of France in Hokitika. The menu features wild game from the West Coast. ♿ 🍴 🍸	*AE DC MC V*	●	■	●	■
Karamea: *Karamea Bight Restaurant* $$ Cnr Waverley St and Wharf Rd. **Road map** C4. ☎ & [FAX] *(03) 782 6800.* The friendly proprietors offer a wide range of cheap bar meals as well as full dining-room meals in the old-fashioned pub setting of the Karamea Village Hotel. Offers whitebait all year round. ♿ 🍴 🍸 ♫	*MC V*	●		●	
Karamea: *The Last Resort* $$ 71 Waverley St. **Road map** C4. ☎ *(03) 782 6617.* [FAX] *(03) 782 6820.* This restaurant is part of the major hotel complex in Karamea. Daily changing menu, with local delicacies such as whitebait and scallops offered in season. ♿ 🍴 🍸 ♫	*AE DC MC V*	●	■	●	■
Mount Cook Village: *Alpine Restaurant* $$$ The Hermitage. **Road map** B6. ☎ *(03) 435 1809.* [FAX] *(03) 435 1879.* The main restaurant at Mount Cook. Open year round, offering meals at cheaper prices than its sister restaurant, the Panorama. 🍸	*AE DC JCB MC V*	●	■	●	
Mount Cook Village: *Panorama Restaurant* $$$$ The Hermitage. **Road map** B6. ☎ *(03) 435 1809.* [FAX] *(03) 435 1879.* Watch the sun set on Mount Cook, Mount Sefton and the Footstool while dining in this up-market restaurant on venison and other New Zealand game meats. ⬤ *Apr–Sep.* 🍸	*AE DC JCB MC V*		■	●	
Timaru: *Zanzibar Restaurant and Bar* $$ 56 The Bay Hill. **Road map** C6. ☎ *(03) 688 4367.* [FAX] *(03) 688 5821.* Airy restaurant overlooking Caroline Bay. Seafood is a speciality, with fresh blue cod each day. ⬤ *25 Dec.* ♿ 🍴 🍸	*AE DC MC V*	●		●	
Westport: *The Bay House Café and Art Gallery* $$$ Tauranga Bay. **Road map** C5. ☎ & [FAX] *(03) 789 7133.* With a superb setting among coastal flaxes and sweeping views across Tauranga Bay, the Bay House is a great place for lunch, dinner or just coffee. Seafood is a speciality. ⬤ *Sun D, Mon & Tues (Apr–Oct).* ♿ 🍴	*AE MC V*	●	■	●	

OTAGO AND SOUTHLAND

BLUFF: *Lands End* $$
10 Ward Parade. **Road map** A7. & FAX *(03) 212 7575.*
A superb location at Stirling Point overlooking Stewart Island. Known for local blue cod, salmon and Bluff oysters (in season).

| | BC MC V | ● | ■ | ● | |

DUNEDIN: *Etrusco at the Savoy* $
8a Moray Place. **Road map** B7. *(03) 477 3737.*
Authentic Italian cuisine. Excellent location in a grand old restaurant with wood panelling and leadlight windows. ● *25 & 26 Dec.*

| | AE DC MC V | ● | ■ | ● | ■ |

DUNEDIN: *A Cow Called Berta* $$$
199 Stuart St. **Road map** B7. *(03) 477 2993.*
Lamb, venison, scallops, salmon and blue cod are some of the local produce cooked by the Swiss chef in this stylish restaurant. Located in a fine old Victorian terrace house. ● *Sun, 25 Dec–1 Jan.*

| | AE DC MC V | | ■ | ● | |

DUNEDIN: *Bell Pepper Blues* $$$
474 Princes St. **Road map** B7. & FAX *(03) 474 0973.*
A leading restaurant using New Zealand flavours and cooking styles. Housed in a 19th-century hotel building. ● *Sun & public hols.*

| | AE DC MC V | | ■ | ● | ■ |

GORE: *Gazebo Restaurant and Bar* $$$
Queenstown Hwy. **Road map** A7. *(03) 208 9029.* FAX *(03) 208 9252.*
Strong emphasis on Southland produce, including oysters and scallops, complemented by a wine list featuring many gold medallists.

| | AE DC MC V | ● | ■ | ● | |

OAMARU: *The Last Post Pub and Restaurant* $$$
12 Thames St. **Road map** B7. & FAX *(03) 434 8080.*
There is a choice of bar meals or à la carte dining with an extensive wine list at this restaurant housed in an old post office. ● *25 Dec.*

| | AE DC MC V | ● | ■ | ● | |

QUEENSTOWN: *The Cow* $
Cow Lane. **Road map** A6. *(03) 442 8588.*
The Cow offers delicious pizza and pasta in the rustic surroundings of a 140-year-old stone milking shed decorated with colonial brass and copper ware. ● *25 Dec.*

| | AE DC JCB MC V | | | ● | ■ |

QUEENSTOWN: *McNeill's Cottage Brewery* $$
14 Church St. **Road map** A6. *(03) 442 9688.* FAX *(03) 442 7480.*
A charming stone pub and restaurant featuring New Zealand meat, game, poultry and seafood. Enjoy local wines or one of the unique beers from the boutique brewery. ● *25 Dec.*

| | AE DC MC V | ● | ■ | ● | |

QUEENSTOWN: *Boardwalk* $$$$
Steamer Wharf. **Road map** A6. *(03) 442 5630.* FAX *(03) 442 9042.*
Mainly seafood but has also won lamb and beef awards. Excellent lake views from most tables.

| | AE DC JCB MC V | ● | ■ | ● | ■ |

TE ANAU: *The Olive Tree Café* $
52 Town Centre. **Road map** A7. *(03) 249 8496.*
Pleasant, laid-back café serving good, wholesome food. Huge salads, delicious home-made *foccacia*, cakes and desserts. ● *Jun–Oct.*

| | MC V | | ■ | ● | |

TE ANAU: *Bluestone Restaurant* $$$
20 Lakefront Drive. **Road map** A7. *(03) 249 7421.* FAX *(03) 249 8037.*
This restaurant is highly recommended by the locals. Specialities include venison, lobster and other local produce. Lake views.

| | AE DC MC V | ● | ■ | ● | |

WAIANAKARUA: *The Mill House* $$
State Hwy 1, Waianakarua (near Oamaru). **Road map** B7. & FAX *(03) 439 5515.*
This converted mill house has thick stone walls and exposed beams and features brasserie-style dining. ● *Mon–Wed.*

| | AE DC MC V | ● | ■ | ● | |

WANAKA: *Relishes Café* $$
99 Ardmore St. **Road map** B6. *(03) 443 9018.* FAX *(03) 443 7538.*
Timber décor and an open fire add atmosphere to this popular café. Venison and lamb specialities and local wines. ● *25 & 26 Dec.*

| | AE MC V | ● | ■ | ● | ■ |

WANAKA: *Cardrona Hotel* $$$
Cardrona Valley. **Road map** B6. *(03) 443 8153.*
A genuine gold-rush period pub. Lots of charm and good food. Also has a rustic courtyard area for outdoor dining.

| | AE MC V | ● | ■ | ● | |

For key to symbols see back flap

SHOPPING IN NEW ZEALAND

NEW ZEALAND has a lot to offer the visiting shopper, including goods not available in most other countries. Such items range from traditional Maori bone and greenstone carvings to sheepskin rugs and handmade wool sweaters. Many small towns in popular tourist areas have galleries where local crafts people sell their goods, and Auckland, Wellington and

Craft shop sign in Auckland

Out of New Zealand

Christchurch have major markets where artisans sell unique products. Because New Zealand is one of the most open economies in the world, with few tariffs and no import licensing, goods such as cameras and hi-fi equipment are very reasonably priced. New Zealand's wines *(see pp314–15)*, meats, seafoods, dairy products and fruits are also well worth sampling.

Kircaldie and Stains, Wellington's leading department store

SHOPPING HOURS

MOST SHOPS in New Zealand are open from 9am to 5pm or 5:30pm, Monday to Friday. Many stores are also open on Saturdays and Sundays. Late night shopping is usually available on Thursdays or Fridays, when stores stay open until 9pm.

Supermarkets and shopping malls in urban areas are open seven days a week, and many supermarkets stay open until 8pm or 9pm several nights a week. In small towns and rural areas, dairies often stay open long hours.

HOW TO PAY

CREDIT CARDS are accepted by most stores, usually with a minimum purchase limit. If your credit card is encoded with a PIN number, you can withdraw cash from one of the many automatic teller machines at banks and shopping centres. Identification, such as a passport or

driver's licence, is required when presenting traveller's cheques. Personal cheques may also be accepted, but shops prefer credit cards. New Zealand shopkeepers are not accustomed to bargaining and many also prefer cash transactions.

All goods sold in New Zealand are levied a Goods and Service Tax (GST) of 12.5 per cent, which is included in the purchase price. GST is not refunded when you leave New Zealand.

RIGHTS AND REFUNDS

THE CONSUMERS' INSTITUTE ((04) 384 7963) can provide detailed information about your rights as a buyer. If the goods purchased are defective, you are entitled to a refund. If you decide you do not like an item, many shops will allow you to return or exchange it for something else. If you want to return or exchange an item, you will need to present the receipt.

DEPARTMENT STORES

EACH OF THE four main cities has a major department store selling high quality goods. In Auckland, it is **Smith and Caughey**; in Wellington, **Kircaldie and Stains**; in Dunedin, **Arthur Barnett**, and in Christchurch, **Ballantynes**.

Deka, Farmers, Kmart and the Warehouse sell a wide range of lower priced goods, and have numerous branches throughout the country.

SHOPPING MALLS

LARGE INDOOR shopping malls are a feature of cities and larger towns. Most are located in the suburbs rather then central city areas, and usually include at least one supermarket plus a range of shops selling items such as clothing, sports equipment, household appliances and books. Many also have food halls selling a variety of inexpensive meals.

Shop assistant arranging a display of Zambesi fashion clothes

DAIRIES

DAIRIES ARE small convenience stores that can be found in towns and cities throughout New Zealand. Hours of opening vary, but most are open seven days a week from about 7am until late evening. They sell basic food supplies, snacks, drinks, newspapers and cigarettes.

ROADSIDE STALLS

ROADSIDE STALLS selling fruit and vegetables are common in major horticultural areas such as the Bay of Plenty, Marlborough and Central Otago. Many orchards encourage people to "pick their own", and sell the produce at a reduced price. Strawberries can be found everywhere in spring and summer; cherries in Marlborough at Christmas; apricots, nectarines and peaches in Otago around January–February, and kiwifruit in the Bay of Plenty from April to September. Visitors should also look out for the many cheese factories in Waikato, Taranaki, Marlborough and Canterbury which sell locally made dairy products.

Roadside stall sign

MARKETS

MOST NEW ZEALAND markets specialize in crafts rather than foods, although the Otara Market in South Auckland (see p89) is a notable exception. Here, a range of Pacific food specialities are sold. Auckland, Wellington and Christchurch have markets where crafts people sell from individual stalls. Opening times vary: in Auckland, the Victoria Park Market (see p89) is open daily; Wellington's Wakefield Market is open on Friday, weekends and public holidays, while Christchurch's Arts Centre market (see p222) is open at the weekend.

New Zealand-made crafts and souvenirs for sale in Blenheim

HANDICRAFTS

A WIDE VARIETY of shops selling locally made crafts and souvenirs can be found in New Zealand's main cities, tourist towns and resorts. In areas where the local craft industry is particularly strong, such as Coromandel (see p125) and Nelson (see p211), small galleries maintained by individual artists and crafts people are dotted along the roadsides. Museum shops, such as at the Museum of New Zealand Te Papa Tongarewa, Wellington (see p164–5), and Auckland War Memorial Museum (see p76), also sell top-of-the-range handcrafted products.

The variety and quality of New Zealand handicrafts is continually improving. Products worth buying are traditional Maori flax baskets, bone and greenstone jewellery and ornaments, *paua* (abalone) shell jewellery, ceramics, hand-blown glassware, wood products made from New Zealand's native timbers, and sheepskin and wool items (see pp330–31).

Colourful crafts for sale at Nelson's weekend market (see p208)

DESIGNER LABELS

NEW ZEALAND has a number of internationally successful fashion designers, whose clothing can be bought in boutiques in the main cities. Labels to look for are Trelise Cooper, Karen Walker, World, Zambesi and NomD. Top quality casual wool clothing is available under several labels, including Untouched World.

Quality outdoor clothing and equipment is available under the Canterbury, Heritage and Macpac brands (see p331). Arthur Ellis manufactures high quality Fairydown equipment, as well as the less pricey Great Outdoors brand.

What to Buy in New Zealand

NEW ZEALAND offers a wide range of unique goods. Some, such as bone and greenstone carvings and jewellery, and plaited flax items, are reflective of the country's Maori heritage, while others, such as sheepskin rugs and wool garments, reflect its strong agricultural base. Other good buys are wood products made from New Zealand's native timbers, ceramics, outdoor equipment, and food and wine. Hundreds of gift and craft shops, as well as department stores and museum shops, make it easy to find New Zealand-made products to suit every budget.

Plaited flax basket

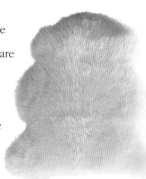

Sheepskin floor rug with thick, combed wool

Hand-knitted sweater

Sheepskin slippers

Wool and sheepskin products from New Zealand are major shopping attractions. Although most New Zealand wool is exported for use in carpets, merino wool is used locally for fine knitwear and suiting fabrics. Hand-knitted sweaters made from hand-spun, hand-dyed wool are widely available in department stores and souvenir shops, as are sheepskin rugs, car seat covers, jackets, boots, slippers, gloves, and souvenir items.

Lamb's wool muff

Woollen gloves

Bowl made from the trunk of a tree

Woodcrafts fashioned from native timbers are well known for their attractive grains and fine workmanship. The most commonly used woods are rimu, kauri, matai and beech. Many crafts people also use recycled timber as well as exotic species such as macrocarpa.

Wooden coasters with *paua* shell inlay

Kauri timber trinket box

Carved Maori figure with *paua* shell eyes

Finely carved traditional Maori club

Pendant with perforated spiral design

Greenstone (or jade) is New Zealand's most precious stone. Artisans craft it into a wide range of jewellery and ornaments using both traditional Maori and contemporary designs (see p235).

Bone, originally used by Maoris to fashion fish-hooks, is now used mainly for decorative items. Stylized fish-hook pendants, embellished with delicate tracery, are popular purchases.

Paua *(abalone) is a shellfish found around the New Zealand coastline, but it is treasured more for its iridescent inner shell than for its meat. It is used primarily to make pendants and earrings, and for inlays in wood-crafts and traditional Maori carvings.*

Paua shell and silver pendants and necklace

Box with inset *paua* shell

Wine goblet

Red glass vase

Hand-painted dish

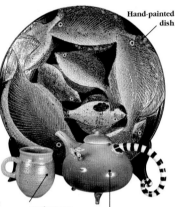

Perfume bottle

Ceramics and glassware *are the most widely available craft items in New Zealand. Ceramics range from rustic earthenware pieces to delicate ornamental works and top quality tableware. Hand-blown glassware is of high quality, and many artisans are happy to allow visitors to watch them at their work (see p 211).*

Earthenware coffee mug

Cat-shaped coffee pot

Outdoor equipment *made in New Zealand is among the best in the world. The leading brand is Macpac, which regularly tests its own equipment in the mountains of the South Island. The best places to buy such goods are special-ist outdoor equip-ment shops in the main cities.*

Tent in bag

Windbreaker

Backpack

Food and drink*, products of New Zealand's extensive farmlands, include excellent meats, fruit, dairy produce and wines. As well as lamb and beef, speciality meats such as ostrich and venison are available. Cheeses made by small boutique factories are worth trying, as is New Zealand's delicious ice cream and its honey from native plants. New Zealand wines have also gained a strong international reputation (see pp34 –5, 314 –15).*

Selection of Kapiti cheeses

Sauvignon Blanc from Marlborough

Kiwifruit flavoured chocolates

Jars of local honey

ENTERTAINMENT IN NEW ZEALAND

FROM PROFESSIONAL theatre, opera and ballet to Maori and Pacific Island culture, music and dance and "Down Under" rock music, New Zealand has a diverse entertainment scene. The liveliest places are the main cities, but even small provincial towns boast their own local bands and amateur performance societies.

Entertainer at Auckland market

New Zealand is on the itinerary of many international performers, although some of these venture no further than Auckland and Wellington. Maori culture is an important theme in the New Zealand arts, and is showcased at festivals and specialist venues, such as the New Zealand Maori Arts and Crafts Institute in Rotorua.

INFORMATION SOURCES

TOURISM NEW ZEALAND posts a yearly calendar of events around the country on its website *(see p333)*. Daily newspapers and magazines such as *North and South*, *The Listener* and *Metro* also provide details about current and upcoming performances.

The Edge, Auckland's main entertainment complex

MAJOR VENUES

THE MAJOR entertainment venues for the performing arts are located in the four main cities. These include Auckland's **The Edge**, which comprises the Aotea Centre, Town Hall and Civic Theatre; Wellington's **Festival and Convention Centre**; Christchurch's **Town Hall** and **WestpacTrust Centre**, and Dunedin's **Town Hall**.

BOOKING TICKETS

IT IS WISE to book in advance for most live performances. The easiest way to book is through the nationwide **Ticketek** system, either via the Internet or by telephone through its many agencies

around the country. In many cases, tickets can also be purchased at the venue.

THEATRE

PROFESSIONAL THEATRE companies are restricted to the main cities, while the smaller provincial towns are served by amateur troupes. Wellington has the most vibrant theatre scene, with three professional theatre companies *(see pp154–5)*: **Downstage**, a semi-national theatre; **Circa**, a co-operative established in the 1970s, known for its consistently excellent plays; and **Bats**, best known for experimental theatre performances. New Zealand's only national Maori theatre company, **Taki Rua**, specializes in indigenous ethnic drama and is based in Wellington, but also tours the country regularly with new productions.

Other professional theatre groups are the **Auckland Theatre Company**, which performs at the Maidment, Herald and Sky City theatres; the **Court Theatre** in Christchurch's historic Arts Centre; and the **Fortune Theatre**, located in Dunedin in an historic inner-city church.

CLASSICAL MUSIC, OPERA AND DANCE

THE **New Zealand Symphony Orchestra** is based in Wellington *(see pp154–5)* but tours the country regularly, covering about 50,000 km (31,000 miles) a year, making it one of the most travelled orchestras in the world. They sometimes perform outdoor city concerts in summer.

New Zealand's regional professional orchestra companies are of a high standard and

New Zealand Symphony Orchestra at the Town Hall, Wellington

Saxcess, New Zealand's premier saxophone quartet

perform regularly. The principal opera company is the **National Business Review New Zealand Opera**, which performs mainly at the Aotea Centre in Auckland. Canterbury and Hawke's Bay also have their own professional opera companies.

The **Royal New Zealand Ballet** is the oldest professional dance company in Australasia. It tours the country frequently with a wide range of work *(see pp154–5)*. The **Footnote Dance Company**, New Zealand's only national contemporary dance troupe, also tours the country regularly, presenting productions created by New Zealand's own choreographers and composers.

ROCK, JAZZ AND COUNTRY

KIWI ROCK MUSIC has a quirky charm that attracts fans from around the globe. The Muttonbirds, Dave Dobbyn and Neil Finn are among New Zealand's most internationally successful rock performers, occasionally performing in the country. Many local bands perform in pubs and popular venues such as Auckland's **Power Station**.

Events such as Wellington's International Festival of the Arts attract both local and international jazz performers *(see pp154–5)*, as do regional festivals such as the Bay of Islands Jazz and Blues Festival each August.

Entertainment posters

Country and Western has a strong following in New Zealand and there are a number of excellent singers and bands. Lovers of traditional country music should make their way to Gore in Southland during May and June to watch the Gold Guitar Awards.

MAORI MUSIC AND DANCE

TRADITIONAL MAORI performing arts are showcased at a number of venues, including the **New Zealand Maori Arts and Crafts Institute** at Rotorua *(see pp136–7)*, and at the **Auckland War Memorial Museum** *(see pp76–7)*, both staging daily concerts. The biennial three-day Aotearoa Traditional Maori Performing Arts Festival, held at different locations, features Maori culture, music and dance from around New Zealand. Tourist operators specializing in Maori heritage include music and dance as part of their programmes *(see p339)*.

Maori cultural performance at an arts festival in Wellington

DIRECTORY

INFORMATION SOURCES

Ticketek
[(09) 307 5000.

Tourism New Zealand
[(04) 917 5400.

MAJOR VENUES

Power Station
[(09) 377 3488.

Town Hall, Christchurch
[(03) 366 8899.

Town Hall, Dunedin
[(03) 477 4477.

The Edge
[(09) 309 2677.

Wellington Festival and Convention Centre
[(04) 801 4242.

WestpacTrust Centre, Christchurch
[(03) 366 8899.

THEATRE

Auckland Theatre Company
[(09) 309 3395.

Bats Theatre
[(04) 802 4175.

Circa Theatre
[(04) 801 772.

Court Theatre
[(03) 366 6992.

Downstage Theatre
[(04) 801 6946.

Fortune Theatre
[(03) 477 8323.

Taki Rua
[(04) 472 7377.

CLASSICAL MUSIC, OPERA AND DANCE

Footnote Dance Company
[(04) 384 7285.

National Business Review New Zealand Opera
[(09) 379 4020.

New Zealand Symphony Orchestra
[(04) 801 3890.

Royal New Zealand Ballet
[(04) 381 9000.

MAORI MUSIC AND DANCE

Auckland War Memorial Museum
[(09) 309 0443.

New Zealand Maori Arts and Crafts Institute, Rotorua
[(07) 348 9047.

SPECIALIST HOLIDAYS AND ACTIVITIES

DOC logo

LOVERS OF THE outdoors will find New Zealand an ideal place to pursue their interests, or to experience something they have never tried before. From quick thrills, such as bungy jumping, jet-boating and helicopter rides to mountain climbing, abseiling, white-water rafting and skiing, New Zealand offers a huge range of activities for outdoor enthusiasts. The best places to find out what is available are Tourism New Zealand, Department of Conservation (DOC) offices, visitor information centres and travel agents.

TRAMPING AND WALKING

WITH ITS 13 national parks, as well as many forest parks and protected natural areas, New Zealand offers immense opportunities for walking and tramping at all levels; tramping is the term New Zealanders use for trekking or hiking. A national network of walkways, ranging from short, well-graded paths to rudimentary alpine routes, thread their way throughout New Zealand, and every location boasts tracks and trails that allow visitors to experience the finest aspects of the local environment.

The best tramping routes are in the national parks, which are serviced by basic but comfortable huts costing between NZ$4 and NZ$14 per night. Several of these tracks – world famous for their beauty – have been designated "Great Walks".

Tramping can be done with a guide or independently. In the latter case, trampers are required to be self-sufficient in food, clothing and sleeping gear. Tramping huts vary in size and facilities, and it is wise to check with the DOC before setting off. It is also vital to check track and weather conditions with the DOC. Always sign in at the local DOC office or in intentions books provided at the beginning of major tracks. Although New Zealand has a sophisticated search and rescue system, it cannot operate if trampers do not leave a record of their whereabouts and expected date of return. On popular routes, such as the Abel Tasman Coastal Track and the Routeburn and Milford tracks, advance booking is essential.

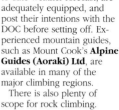

Walkway signpost

MOUNTAINEERING AND ROCK CLIMBING

WITH 30 PEAKS at heights over 3,000 m (9,840 ft), the South Island's Southern Alps provide climbers many opportunities for technically demanding mountain climbing. The principal climbing regions are the Mount Cook, Westland, Mount Aspiring, Arthur's Pass and Fiordland national parks, while in the North Island the Central Plateau offers the best climbing. The main season is from November to March. Weather in the mountains can change extremely rapidly, and it is important that climbers get an up-to-date weather forecast, are adequately equipped, and post their intentions with the DOC before setting off. Experienced mountain guides, such as Mount Cook's **Alpine Guides (Aoraki) Ltd**, are available in many of the major climbing regions.

There is also plenty of scope for rock climbing. Among the best locations are the volcanic rock outcrops of Christchurch's Port Hills *(p228)* and the limestone formations of Castle Hill in Canterbury *(see p240)*.

CAVING AND ABSEILING

NEW ZEALAND has extensive cave systems, among the most notable being the Waitomo Caves in the central North Island *(see pp118–19)* and the Takaka region in

Guided walk on Franz Josef Glacier *(see pp236–7)*

Abseiling in the Mangapu Cave system, Waitomo *(see pp118–19)*

northwest Nelson *(see p214)*. Some caves are very easily accessed, while others are more suited to experienced cavers. Black-water rafting, in which participants float in rubber tubes through extensive cave systems illuminated by glowworms, is a popular way of experiencing New Zealand's cave formations. Two of the best locations for this activity are Waitomo *(see p118–19)* and Westport *(see p232)*, where rafting operators run tours.

Both the North and South islands offer exhilarating abseiling. In the Waitomo area, tourists can descend down a 100-m (330-ft) hole into the "Lost World" *(see p119)* Mangapu Cave system with **Waitomo Adventures**.

CYCLING

CYCLE TOURING on New Zealand's highways and back roads is a popular way of seeing the country. Among the many scenic roads that are well suited to cycling are the Queen Charlotte Drive in the Marlborough Sounds *(see p200)* and State Highway 6 on the West Coast.

Mountain biking in Rangataua Forest *(see p140)*

An extensive network of off-road tracks is also available for mountain bikers. Hanmer Springs *(see p231)* and Victoria Forest Park *(see p231)* are among New Zealand's best mountain biking destinations.

SKIING

NEW ZEALAND has 26 ski fields, ranging from highly commercialized fields with sophisticated lifts and services to small fields owned by local ski clubs where visitors are welcome. Major fields are **Whakapapa Ski Area** and **Turoa Ski Resort** on the slopes of the North Island's Mount Ruapehu *(see pp140–1)*, the **Mount Hutt Ski Area** in Canterbury *(see p244)*, and **Coronet Peak**, the **Remarkables Ski Area**, **Cardrona Alpine Resort** and **Treble Cone** in Central Otago *(see pp192–3)*.

The ski season generally runs from mid-June to September. In the South Island, heli-skiing operators take skiers to untouched powder snow. Ski touring and cross-country skiing are possible in many locations, including the **Waiorau Snow Farm** near Wanaka *(see pp192–3)*.

Surfing at Whale Bay, Raglan
(see pp114–15)

WATER SPORTS

WITH A COASTLINE 18,200 km (11,300 miles) long and an abundance of lakes and rivers, New Zealand offers plenty of opportunities for visitors to participate in water sports. From Auckland's Hauraki Gulf northwards is a yachting paradise where experienced sailors can hire boats for "bareboat" cruising *(see pp86–7)*. Skippered sailing is more common, however, as the country's gusty winds can test even the most capable "boaties".

Surfing is popular, especially in the North Island at beaches like Piha *(see p84)*, Raglan *(see pp114–15)* and in the Bay of Plenty *(see pp124, 126)*. The calm waters of the country's harbours and lakes are suitable for windsurfing, and boards can be hired at many waterfront locations.

The Bay of Islands, Auckland's Hauraki Gulf, Nelson, the Marlborough Sounds, Fiordland and Stewart Island are prime venues for sea kayaking. Tours can take as long as a week. Kayaks can also be hired for a few hours' paddling around the harbours of Auckland, Wellington and other coastal cities.

New Zealand's fast-flowing rivers are excellent for white-water rafting and kayaking. Among the most challenging rivers are the Motu *(see p130)*, Rangitikei and Tongariro in the North Island, while the South Island has dozens of rivers, from the Buller on the West Coast to the Clarence in Canterbury. Among the rivers suitable for the inexperienced is the Whanganui River, the North Island's second longest river, which winds through the historic Whanganui National Park *(see p177)*.

There are many good dive spots, including the network of marine reserves around the New Zealand coastline *(see pp24–5)*. Near Whangarei, the dramatic underwater caves of the Poor Knights Islands are rated as one of the world's top diving destinations *(see p97)*. Further north, the Greenpeace boat, the *Rainbow Warrior*, is a well-known underwater wreck. In Fiordland, a unique marine ecosystem, tempered by huge quantities of freshwater run-off, attracts species nearer to the surface than in other areas.

HUNTING

BECAUSE MANY of the animals introduced into New Zealand by Europeans have no natural predators, they have become pests, and therefore hunting of big game is encouraged by the authorities. No licence is required, there is no restriction on the numbers killed and the season is generally open all year round.

Professional guiding companies operate throughout the country, many with access to extensive tracts of private land. Seven species of deer, wild pigs and goats are common in forests, while chamois and thar can be found in mountain areas of the South Island. The duck shooting season starts at the beginning of May and lasts eight weeks.

FISHING

NEW ZEALAND is justly renowned for the quality of its sea and freshwater fishing. Lake Taupo and the rivers surrounding it (especially the famed Tongariro) are internationally regarded as the Mecca of trout fishing *(see p139)*, although there are good rivers throughout the country. The trout fishing season runs from October to May. The main salmon rivers are on the east coast of the South Island. A licence is compulsory in order to fish for trout and salmon, and tackle is readily available.

The Bay of Islands is the centre of deep-sea marlin fishing *(see pp100–101)*. The

Kayaking over rapids on the Tongariro River

Fishing in the Waikato River near Huka Lodge *(see p293)*

best deep-sea angling is found on the North Island's east coast, northwards from the Bay of Plenty. The best fishing months are from January to May and licences are not necessary.

ECOTOURS

A LONG TRADITION of environmental activism in New Zealand has led to numerous ecotourism developments. There are many specialist nature tour operators to choose from, and guides working in the adventure tourism area, such as blackwater rafting *(see p118)*, often have a good knowledge of local flora and fauna.

There are numerous opportunities for bird watching *(see pp190–91)*, including at the Royal Albatross colony on Otago Peninsula, ocean birds at Kaikoura *(see p207)*, the white heron colony at Okarito and the immense birdlife of Farewell Spit *(see p215)*.

Kaikoura is synonomous with whale watching *(see p207)*. During winter there is nearly a 100 per cent chance of seeing sperm whales. Dolphin watching tours operate from many areas, including Banks Peninsula, the Bay of Islands and Southland.

Whale Watch® tour at Kaikoura *(see p207)*

Tandem skydiving over Hawke's Bay

AERIAL ADVENTURES

HOT-AIR BALLOONING, tandem parapenting (paragliding) and tandem skydiving are more adventurous ways of taking to the air than flying *(see p193)*. Commercial operators offering all three types of aerial thrill exist in the main cities and major resorts *(see p339)*. A hot-air balloon ride is a spectacular way to view the extensive Southern Alps and Canterbury Plains, while parapenting from Te Mata Peak in Hawke's Bay *(see p14 /)* and the Remarkables near Queenstown is a unique experience *(see pp192–3)*. Check with local visitor centres or travel agents for details of available services.

Aerial sightseeing is also popular throughout the country, either in small planes, helicopters or float planes. Highlights in the North Island include flights over the volcanically active White Island *(see p128)* and volcanic Tongariro National Park *(pp140–41)*. In the South Island, flights over Mount Cook, the Fox and Franz Josef glaciers *(see*

Flightseeing over Fiordland National Park *(pp278–81)*

pp250–51) and Fiordland *(see pp278–9)* are popular and readily available. Many flights touch down in spectacular locations, such as White Island and the glaciers of the Southern Alps.

Bungy jumping from the Kawarau Bridge, Queenstown *(see p274)*

BUNGY JUMPING

EVER SINCE A J Hackett used an historic bridge over the Kawarau River in Queenstown *(see pp192–3)* to launch the bungy jumping phenomenon, tourism operators have set up bungy jump sites in picturesque locations, usually on bridges above river gorges, in both the North and South islands.

Safety is a key issue in bungy jumping. Jumpers are weighed so that the correct length of bungy cord can be calculated for their jump. The cord is securely attached to their ankles before the jump from a bridge or platform.

JET-BOATING

BILL HAMILTON, a local engineer and farmer, perfected the design of the jet-boat so it is no coincidence that these highly manoeuvrable craft are so popular on the nation's waterways. In locations such as Waikato *(see p138)* and Queenstown *(see pp192–3)*, jet-boat operators take tourists through narrow canyons, across the shallowest of water and whirl 360 degrees "on a sixpence". Some operators offer jet-boat safaris, taking visitors on longer trips into the scenic back country. Mandatory life jackets are supplied.

GOLF

THERE ARE MORE than 400 golf courses in New Zealand, more per head of population than virtually any other country. Green fees can be as low as NZ$5 for a club in rural areas. Even the more exclusive city courses charge no more than NZ$50. Weekends are often reserved for members, although a number of clubs have reciprocal membership with overseas clubs, allowing visitors to play at any time. Major clubs have carts and clubs for hire.

FOUR-WHEEL DRIVE TOURING

IN THE HIGH country and rural areas of New Zealand are hundreds of rough tracks, many of which were created to provide access to farms, timber mills, gold mines and mining settlements. A four-wheel drive vehicle is a physically undemanding way to explore these locations. Numerous tour operators exist throughout the country, offering both day trips and longer safaris through varied terrain.

HORSE TREKKING

THE WIDE OPEN spaces of the country encourage horse riding and there are many operators who offer horse trekking through forests, high country trails or along one of the many beaches. Options

Horse trekking at Hanmer, North Canterbury

range from half-day or all-day treks to multi-day camping safaris. Some operations are conveniently located close to cities. Most operators cater for a range of riding abilities and provide all equipment.

SPECTATOR SPORTS

NEW ZEALANDERS are passionate about rugby. It is worth visiting a match during the rugby season from March to October *(see pp36–7)*. The Super 12 and National Provincial Championship are the major competitions. Matches generally attract large crowds, as do one-day cricket test matches. Highly entertaining, the atmosphere is best at the day–night matches which begin in the afternoon and are played through the evening under lights.

Horse racing is a national passion, and a number of big race meetings are held between November and April *(see pp36–7)*. Netball also has a large following, with the most exciting games often involving the national team, the Silver Ferns.

Tickets for sports events can be obtained from Ticketek *(see p333)*.

MAORI HERITAGE TOURS

TOUR COMPANIES offering genuine encounters with Maori heritage operate in a number of locations. Tours may include a visit to a *marae*, where participants share a *hangi* (a traditional feast) and learn about Maori protocol, myths and legends, dance and art. One such operator, **Te Urewera Adventures**, offers horse trekking and a stay on a *marae* in the Urewera country, spiritual home to the Tuhoe people.

Waikato supporters at a provincial rugby match

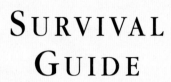

SURVIVAL
GUIDE

PRACTICAL INFORMATION

Tourism is one of New Zealand's most important industries, attracting over 1.6 million overseas visitors a year. As the industry has grown, services and facilities have improved to keep pace with demand. Visitors are well served by a wide range of accommodation and restaurants *(see pp292–309, 316–27).* There is easy access to good quality information through the many visitor centres and Department of Conservation offices. Many of the best attractions in New Zealand are free – particularly the national parks, beaches, lakes and rivers. New Zealanders are friendly people who are willing to offer assistance, although it is highly advisable for visitors to have at least a basic grasp of English as relatively few New Zealanders are fluent in other languages.

**Tourism
New Zealand
logo**

Visitor information centre, Viaduct Basin, Auckland *(see p70)*

WHEN TO GO

Spring, summer and Autumn (from September to April) are the most popular seasons for travellers, although the ski season is a major attraction during the winter months.

One word sums up the New Zealand climate: changeable. The north of the North Island is subtropical, while the remainder of the country is temperate. However, all regions are subject to sudden changes in the weather. In the South Island, it is not unusual for a hot summer day of 30 °C (86 °F) to be followed by temperatures as low as 15 to 20 °C (60 to 68 °F). Average summer temperatures range between 20 and 30 °C (68 and 86 °F), and winter between 10 and 15 °C (50 and 60 °F). The greatest climatic extremes are experienced in the inland Central Otago region, where summer temperatures often soar above 30 °C (86 °F) and in winter often fall to below 0 °C (32 °F). New Zealand has a pronounced west–east climate variation: the west coasts of both main islands are in the path of westerly winds, which sweep rain in from the Tasman Sea. Although the east is much drier and sunnier, the wet, humid climate of the west sustains dense and varied rainforests.

Spring is generally unsettled throughout the country, with more rain and wind than in other seasons. People crowd the coastlines, lakes and rivers during summer when water temperatures are pleasant for swimming in most regions. From February to late April, the weather tends to be warm and settled. Snow in winter falls mainly in the mountains, although the inland and coastal parts of the southern South Island occasionally experience heavy falls. Winter is not as cold nor as long in New Zealand as in the northern hemisphere.

TIME DIFFERENCES

New Zealand is 12 hours ahead of Greenwich Mean Time and two hours ahead of Sydney. Clocks are put forward one hour each October for daylight saving, which lasts until March.

PASSPORTS AND VISAS

Visitors to New Zealand must have a passport valid for at least three months longer than the intended period of stay. Visas are not required for Australian citizens or holders of a current Australian resident return visa, nor for visits of up to three months by residents of any of the 50 countries with which New Zealand has a visa waiver agreement. For a list of those countries, visit the website of the New Zealand immigration service at www.immigration.govt.nz. British citizens who have

Newmans tour coach on the Milford Road in autumn

◁ **Trampers at Green Lake, Fiordland National Park *(see p279)***

Department of Conservation information centre, Totaranui *(see p213)*

permanent UK residency also do not need a visa and are issued with a six-month visitor permit on arrival. Visas for tourists from other countries can be obtained through the nearest New Zealand embassy. When entering the country or when applying for a visa, visitors must give proof of a return air ticket and show they have sufficient funds for the duration of their stay – about NZ$1,000 per person per month.

To obtain a work permit for New Zealand, applicants must show they have an offer of employment. However, reciprocal working holiday schemes are maintained between New Zealand and a number of other countries. These allow visitors aged between 18 and 30 to work temporarily without first obtaining an offer of employment.

Vaccinations are not required for visitors entering New Zealand.

DEPARTURE FEE

An airport user fee is levied on passengers aged 12 and above departing from New Zealand's international airports. From Auckland, it is NZ$20, and from Wellington and Christchurch, NZ$25.

AGRICULTURAL RESTRICTIONS AND CUSTOMS ALLOWANCES

New Zealand relies heavily on its agricultural industries, and great effort is made to keep the country free of introduced pests and diseases

that could jeopardize the productivity of its farms and orchards. All fruit, meat, plant material and animals must be declared on arrival. Failure to declare quarantine items can lead to a fine of NZ$100,000 or five years in jail. If in doubt about the status of an item, declare it to the Ministry of Agriculture and Fisheries inspectors on arrival and they will advise you whether it is permitted. In many cases, items will be inspected,

Resort signboard

treated if necessary, and then returned to you.

Class A drugs are prohibited, as are firearms and weapons unless a permit is obtained from the New Zealand Police on arrival.

New Zealand is also party to an international convention designed to prevent trade in endangered species, and animal products such as ivory, turtle shell, whalebone, and rhinoceros and tiger derivatives are banned.

Visitors can buy duty-free goods on arrival, departure and at duty-free stores in cities *(see p88)*. For travellers over 17 years old, the following customs allowances

are applicable: 200 cigarettes, 250 grams of tobacco or 50 cigars, or a mixture of all three weighing no more than 250 grams; 4.5 litres of beer or wine and one 1,125 ml (40 oz) bottle of spirits or other beverages.

TOURIST INFORMATION

The central tourism body is **Tourism New Zealand** but the information service most tourists have contact with is the Visitor Information Network. Independently owned but coordinated by Tourism New Zealand, there are 100 of these information centres scattered throughout New Zealand, sporting a distinctive green logo. Open daily, they provide abundant information on local attractions and activities, sell maps and guidebooks, and arrange bookings for accommodation, tours, travel and activities. Some also sell souvenirs.

Department of Conservation visitor centres in the national parks are the best source of detailed information on activities and attractions in the parks, and many have excellent displays, audiovisual programmes and lectures on the natural history of the area. They also provide up-to-date weather forecasts and information about the condition of roads, rivers and tracks.

Tourist Information FM radio (88.2 FM) carries information on areas that tourists are travelling through, with commentary on the history and culture and availability of local services. It broadcasts 24 hours a day. Broadcasts in German are on 100.4 FM and in Japanese on 100.8 FM.

Enjoying the sun at Scorching Bay, Wellington *(see p167)*

Entry is free to the Te Papa Museum *(see pp164–5)*

OPENING HOURS AND ADMISSION PRICES

AT THE HEIGHT of the season, most major tourist sites are open seven days a week, but it is best to check in advance. Admission prices to attractions vary: in some cases, entry is free, while many galleries and museums request a donation or modest entry charge. Entry into the national parks is free, although access to certain areas is possible only with an approved guiding company. Private companies run New Zealand's many adventure tourism ventures, and charges vary according to the activity.

For opening hours of retail outlets, see p328.

ETIQUETTE

LIKE AUSTRALIA, New Zealand is a relatively informal society. On the whole, the people are relaxed and open, enjoy sharing their country

with overseas visitors, and are happy to assist tourists needing information or help. Dress standards vary depending on the venue, but most restaurants and cafés are happy with tidy casual wear.

Smoking is banned in offices, shops, airplanes, public transport and taxis. In restaurants, it is restricted to designated areas. It is not acceptable to smoke in private homes without first asking the permission of the host. If invited to a New Zealander's home for a meal, it is appropriate to take a bottle of wine or an item of food to share, but most New Zealanders will be uncomfortable with ostentatious gifts.

Tipping in restaurants and hotels is not obligatory, although it has become more widespread with the increase in overseas tourists. Many New Zealanders do not approve of tipping, but it is not inappropriate to reward particularly good service in a restaurant, (about ten per cent of the bill), or to tip a taxi driver, bartender or porter a few dollars.

Maori/English toilet sign

DISABLED TRAVELLERS

DISABLED TRAVELLERS are well catered for in New Zealand. Every new or substantially renovated building is required by law to have adequate access for people with disabilities. As a result, most hotels, restaurants, tourist sites, cinemas, airports and shopping centres have wheelchair facilities, and

guide dogs for the blind are always welcome.

Airports provide ground staff to assist with boarding and disembarking disabled passengers, although trains and buses are often inaccessible without assistance. Avis has cars available with hand controls, but 14 days' notice must be given *(see p361)*. All major cities and towns have taxis which carry wheelchairs.

Some tourism adventure activities may be difficult to access for the disabled, although operators are usually keen to assist provided sufficient notice is given.

TRAVELLING WITH CHILDREN

NEW ZEALAND, with its wide, open spaces, lack of dangerous animals and low crime statistics is a safe place to take children for a holiday. Children are well catered for in most types of accommodation, but motels are particularly suitable for families, with family rooms and self-catering facilities. Restaurants often have children's menus or small portions, and many have high chairs. Major international fast food chains are represented in New Zealand, along with a wide selection of local takeaway services. Large department stores and shopping malls have nappy changing facilities and feeding rooms.

Many of New Zealand's top attractions appeal equally to children as to adults, such as the Museum of New Zealand Te Papa Tongarewa *(see pp164–5)*, the International Antarctic Centre *(see p225)*, and the national parks.

Air, coach, train and boat operators offer a range of discounted prices for children, which makes holidaying with families affordable. Children under five are required by law to be restrained in an infant car seat. Car hire firms will rent these out for a small fee, but they should be given advance notice if possible.

Spectators dressed casually at a cricket match in Wellington

STUDENT TRAVELLERS

STUDENTS WITH a valid ISIC (International Students Identity Card) can obtain substantial discounts on travel, especially on internal flights. Students are also entitled to reduced charges in cinemas, theatres, art galleries and museums. To find out what special deals are available, students should contact their local student travel office in their country of origin. The card can be purchased only by students who are studying courses at a school, university or a polytechnic.

NEWSPAPERS, MAGAZINES, RADIO AND TELEVISION

EACH OF THE main cities has its own morning newspaper, while provincial cities and towns have afternoon newspapers. *The New Zealand Herald*, the country's largest, is published in Auckland. Wellington is the only centre with both morning and afternoon daily papers, *The Dominion* and *The Evening Post*. The Christchurch *Press* is the South Island's largest newspaper. The *Otago Daily Times* is published in Dunedin and the *Southland Times* in Invercargill. The best current affairs magazines are

A selection of daily newspapers

The Listener and *North and South*, and for specialized business news *The National Business Review* and *Independent Business Weekly*. A wide range of overseas magazines and newspapers, such as *Time* and *The Economist*, are readily available in book stores and newsstands.

The state-owned, non-commercial National Radio is renowned for the quality of its broadcasting, offering extensive news and current affairs programmes, plays and music. The main free-to-air television channels are TV1, TV2 and TV3. TV1 and TV3 screen mostly local programmes whereas TV2 relies heavily on US programmes. Pay channel Sky offers specialist channels, such as CNN and National Geographic.

CONVERSION CHART

Imperial to metric
1 inch = 2.54 centimetres
1 foot = 30 centimetres
1 mile = 1.6 kilometres
1 ounce = 28 grams
1 pound = 454 grams
1 pint = 0.6 litres
1 gallon = 4.6 litres

Metric to Imperial
1 centimetre = 0.4 inches
1 metre = 3 feet, 3 inches
1 kilometre = 0.6 miles
1 gram = 0.04 ounces
1 kilogram = 2.2 pounds
1 litre = 1.8 pints

ELECTRICAL SUPPLY

NEW ZEALAND'S electrical current is 230/240 volts 50 hertz, although most hotels and motels provide 110 volt AC sockets for electric razors. For all other equipment, an adaptor is necessary, as power outlets accept only flat, two- or three-pin plugs, as illustrated.

Standard New Zealand three-pin electrical plug

DIRECTORY

EMBASSIES AND CONSULATES

Australia
72–78 Hobson St, Wellington.
(*(04) 473 6411.*

Canada
61 Molesworth St, Wellington.
(*(04) 473 9577.*

United Kindgom
44 Hill St, Wellington.
(*(04) 495 0889*

USA
29 Fitzherbert Terrace, Wellington.
(*(04) 472 2068.*

TOURISM ORGANIZATIONS

Christchurch and Canterbury Marketing
Cnr Oxford Terrace and Worcester Boulevard.
(*(03) 379 9629.*
w *www. christchurchtourism.co.nz*

Hawkes Bay Tourism
2nd Floor Civic Court, Napier.
(*(06) 834 1918.*
w *www. hawkesbaytourism.co.nz*

Maori Tourism Development Board

2/270 Jervois Rd, Herne Bay, Auckland.
(*(09) 376 6509.*
@ *oormsby@ unitec.ac.nz*

Totally Wellington
33 Gilmer Terrace, Wellington.
(*(04) 916 1205.*
w *www.wellington.net.nz*

Tourism Auckland
287 Queen St, Auckland.
(*(09) 307 7999.*
w *www. aucklandnz.com*

Tourism Dunedin
50 The Octagon, Dunedin.
(*(03) 474 3801.*
@ *tourism.dunedin@ dcc.govt.nz*

Tourism Nelson
Cnr Trafalgar and Halifax sts.
(*(03) 546 6228.*
w *http://nelson.net.nz*

Tourism New Zealand
89 The Terrace, Wellington.
(*(04) 917 5400.*
w *www.purenz.com*

Tourism Rotorua
1106 Arawa St, Rotorua.
(*(07) 348 4133.*
@ *marketing@ tourism.rdc.govt.nz*

DISABLED TRAVELLERS

Disability Information Centre
(*0800 17 1981.*

Personal Security and Health

NEW ZEALAND is one of the safest countries in the world to visit. New Zealanders have a reputation for being friendly and law-abiding, and the political and economic climate is stable. Violent crimes occur in New Zealand as in any other society, and visitors need to take sensible precautions to protect themselves and their property. The greatest risks, however, are environmental; many tourists have been caught out in the mountains or bush with inadequate food and clothing, having underestimated the terrain and the speed with which New Zealand's weather can change.

Outdoor Safety
Mountain Safety Council logo

Police car

Fire engine

Ambulance

PERSONAL SAFETY

THERE ARE few areas in New Zealand that are not suitable for tourists to visit. However, unlike large European and Asian cities, the streets are often deserted after dark and it is not advisable, particularly for women, to walk alone at night. Use common sense by avoiding parks and poorly lit, secluded places, especially in urban areas after dark. Even in the main cities there is little public transport late at night, although taxis are readily available and are safe to board.

Many tourists hitchhike, and although trouble-free in most instances, it is not recommended as a safe form of getting around the country, especially if travelling alone. Women, in particular, should never hitchhike alone.

Road accidents are a major public health issue in New Zealand, and tourists intending to drive should make themselves aware of the road rules *(see p359)*. The speed limit is 100 km/h (60 mph) on the open road and 50 km/h (30 mph) in urban areas. While most of the road network is sealed, many back roads are gravel and require extra care *(see p360)*. It is compulsory to wear seat belts in cars.

PERSONAL PROPERTY

TRAVELLERS NEED to take sensible precautions with their property in New Zealand. Petty crime such as theft from cars can occur, and is best avoided by making sure vehicles are locked and by keeping valuable items such as passports, credit cards and traveller's cheques in a money belt or in a hotel safe deposit box. A comprehensive travel insurance policy that covers personal property loss or theft is advisable.

LOST PROPERTY

STOLEN PROPERTY should be reported to the police, although the chances of recovering the goods will depend on the circumstances.

Policewoman   **Fire officer**

The police will issue a report, which can be used to support an insurance claim, if necessary. Most shopping malls, hotels, airports, train and bus stations operate a lost property service.

MEDICAL TREATMENT AND INSURANCE

NEW ZEALAND has excellent medical services. The telephone numbers of all general practitioners and hospitals in each area are listed near the front of each regional telephone book.

Under New Zealand's accident compensation scheme, visitors are covered for personal injury by accident, entitling them to coverage for medical and hospital expenses but not for loss of earnings outside New Zealand. However, non-accident medical treatment is not free. Even though medical attention is reasonably priced, visitors are advised to make arrangements for adequate medical and dental cover before leaving home.

A doctor's prescription is necessary to obtain most forms of medication in New Zealand. Visitors bringing in a large quantity of medication should have a doctor's certificate to avoid difficulties with Customs. No vaccinations are needed to enter New Zealand.

PHARMACIES

NEW ZEALAND has an extensive network of pharmacies (more commonly called chemists) which offer everything from cosmetics to prescription drugs. Qualified chemists can be relied on to provide free advice but prescriptions must be written out by a doctor. Major towns have urgent pharmacies, which are open until late at night. Their telephone numbers and addresses are available in the front section of the local telephone directory.

ENVIRONMENTAL HAZARDS

WITH NO dangerous animals including any species of snakes, and few contagious diseases, New Zealand poses a low risk to the visitor. Its changeable climate is probably the greatest threat, especially to people who venture into the wilderness unprepared. Hypothermia can set in quickly and be fatal, and it is vital to take warm clothing, food and drink even when going for a day's walk in the bush or mountains. Many tramps involve river crossings, and water levels can rise extremely rapidly after heavy rain. It is often necessary to take shelter and wait until rivers drop to a safe level.

New Zealand's clean air, coupled with a thinner ozone cover, means that sunburn

Pharmacy in Auckland

can occur quickly. A good hat and sun block with a rating of at least SPF 15+ are essential items in summer.

Lifeguards patrol popular beaches, and red and yellow flags indicate areas where it is safe to swim. However, the New Zealand coastline is extensive, and in areas where there are no lifeguards, there may be dangerous rips. Rivers also claim many lives, sometimes those of trampers who are too impatient to wait for flood waters to subside.

Giardia, a waterborne parasite that causes diarrhoea, stomach cramps and nausea, is present in many waterways. It is best to avoid drinking from lakes, ponds or rivers without boiling or treating water first. The water supply in most towns and cities is generally excellent and usually safe to drink.

The tiny, black, bloodsucking sandfly is the greatest environmental irritant, biting exposed skin and causing an annoying itch. They are particularly bad on the west coast of the South Island, but can usually be kept at bay with a good insect repellent.

Sunburn warning sign

Surf rescue boat at Mount Maunganui *(see p126)*

Banking and Local Currency

A LARGE NUMBER of banking institutions operate in New Zealand, almost all of them foreign owned. Major banking chains include the Bank of New Zealand, WestpacTrust, National Bank and ANZ. Branches of all the leading chains can be found in the central business districts of the major cities, while suburban shopping centres generally have branches of one or two banking institutions. Foreign currency can be readily exchanged at banks and private moneychangers. There is no restriction on the amount of foreign currency that can be brought in or taken out of New Zealand, although people carrying more than NZ$10,000 in cash must make a declaration to Customs.

Bank logos

BANKING

T HE NEW ZEALAND banking system is modern and efficient. However, electronic banking has led to a decline in the number of bank branches, and some small rural towns no longer have a local banking service. If travelling to a remote area, it is advisable to check in advance what facilities for exchanging or accessing money are available. Banks are open from 9:30am to 4:30pm Monday to Friday, and banks at international airports open to coincide with incoming and outgoing flights. International exchange rates are displayed in most major banks.

TRAVELLER'S CHEQUES

T RAVELLER'S CHEQUES are still the safest way to carry large sums of money. Thomas Cook and American Express traveller's cheques are widely accepted in New Zealand. Foreign currency cheques can be cashed for New Zealand dollars at banks, American Express and Thomas Cook branches, and private money-changers, some of which display bureaux de change signs. Major hotels will accept traveller's cheques as payment for accommodation. Some souvenir shops in major cities and resort areas are also willing to accept traveller's cheques, but it is best to ask before making a purchase.

CREDIT CARDS

A LL MAJOR credit cards are used in New Zealand. Visa, Mastercard, Diners Club, and American Express are the most widely accepted, and can be used to book and pay for hotels, rental cars and airline tickets, as well as to pay for entry to major tourist facilities and for purchases from shops. In small shops and cafés, however, credit cards may not always be accepted, so it is wise to always carry some cash. The logos of the credit cards accepted are usually clearly displayed in shops.

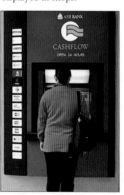

Withdrawing cash from an ATM in Auckland

AUTOMATIC TELLER MACHINES AND ELECTRONIC TRANSFER

A TMS (Automatic Teller Machines) are widely available in New Zealand and can be found in shopping centres and outside banks in all towns and cities. Travellers should check with their own bank before leaving home whether they can use their debit card to access cash through ATMs in New Zealand; this will differ from bank to bank depending on what international banking networks they belong to. It is possible to withdraw cash from an ATM using a credit card with an encoded PIN number: the "Plus" logo on an ATM indicates this service is available to VISA card holders, while the equivalent symbol for Mastercard holders is "Maestro".

Sign displayed by a private moneychanger

MONEYCHANGERS

M ONEYCHANGERS can be found in downtown locations in the major cities and resort areas. They are generally open from 8am to 7:30 or 8pm on weekdays, and from 10am until early evening on weekends, offering an alternative after banks have closed for the day. However, their commissions and fees are higher than banks.

DIRECTORY

LOST CARDS AND TRAVELLER'S CHEQUES

American Express
℡ 0800 441 068.

Diners Club
℡ 0800 346 377.

Mastercard
℡ 0800 449 140.

Visa
℡ 0800 445 594.

LOCAL CURRENCY

THE UNIT of currency in New Zealand is the New Zealand dollar (NZ$), divided into 100 cents (c). One and two cent coins have now been taken out of circulation and prices for cash purchases are rounded up or down to the nearest five cents. Although New Zealand converted to decimal currency in 1966, a few of the old-style coins are still in circulation, especially the sixpence, shilling and two shilling (equivalent and legal tender for 5 cents, 10 cents and 20 cents respectively). Small shops, cafés and taxis may find it difficult to provide change for $50 or $100 notes, and it is best to carry cash in $10 and $20 notes. To make it more difficult for counterfeiters and to ensure notes last longer, plasticized bank notes are gradually replacing the traditional paper notes.

Bank Notes

New Zealand's bank notes are issued in denominations of $5, $10, $20, $50 and $100. Sir Edmund Hillary, the first man to climb Mount Everest (see pp19, 50) features on the $5 note, and 19th-century women's suffrage campaigner Kate Sheppard is on the $10 note.

NZ$100 note

NZ$20 note

NZ$50 note

NZ$5 note

NZ$10 note

5 cents (5c)   10 cents (10c)

20 cents (20c)   50 cents (50c)

Coins

Coins currently in use in New Zealand are 5c, 10c, 20c, 50c, $1 and $2. The 5c piece shows the tuatara (a spiny-backed reptile), while the 10c piece features a traditional Maori carving. The 20c and $1 coins carry the national icon, the flightless kiwi.

1 dollar (NZ$1)

2 dollars (NZ$2)

Using New Zealand's Telephones

NEW ZEALAND HAS A MODERN, sophisticated telephone system. Public payphones are operated by the major telecommunications company, Telecom, and are widely distributed on streets in towns and cities, as well as in public buildings, airports and shopping centres. Hotels charge a premium for calls from hotel rooms, so it is best to use public payphones instead. There is also an extensive mobile telephone network for those wanting the convenience of their own telephone.

Public Telephones

MOST NEW ZEALAND public payphones accept only prepaid phonecards and credit cards. Telephones located in well-supervised areas, such as shopping malls, may accept coins. Signs on the outside of phone boxes indicate what mode of payment is acceptable for the particular payphone. Phonecards can be purchased at supermarkets, newsagents and dairies as well as Post Shops.

Public telephone booths

Public telephone boxes have a receiver, a 12-button key pad, a set of instructions, a list of useful numbers and both white and yellow page telephone directories. A free information service number (123) enables callers to find out the likely cost of an overseas call or the cost of reversing the charges prior to making the call. There is no charge for making emergency 111 calls from a public payphone. Toll-free 0800 numbers are also free.

Mobile Telephones

MOBILE TELEPHONES can be used throughout most of New Zealand, apart from remote and mountainous areas, such as some sections of the west coast of the South Island. Visitors can rent mobile phones on a short-term basis although this is an expensive option. For tourists wanting the convenience of a mobile phone, a cheaper alternative is to buy a phone that uses prepaid cards. These phones can be purchased for under NZ$100 and prepaid cards are readily available at bookshops and dairies.

Home Country Direct

VISITORS FROM about 50 selected countries can use the Home Country Direct service to make calls through a telephone company in their country of origin. The calls are billed to the caller by his/her home telephone company. Check the White Pages of the Telephone Directory for the numbers to dial.

If using a payphone to make an international call, it is cheaper to use one of the discounted Telecom prepaid cards than a credit card or phonecard. These are available at Telecom outlets, dairies and service stations.

Advertisement for E-mail and Internet services at a café

Fax and E-Mail Services

POST SHOPS, photocopying shops and many hotels, motels and even hostels will send and receive faxes on your behalf. There is a fixed charge per page.

Cybercafés operate throughout New Zealand, providing E-mail and Internet services to travellers. Cafés will set a visitor up with an E-mail address, if necessary, but it is best to obtain an address with one of the major Internet servers before leaving home.

Using a Coin/Phonecard Operated Phone

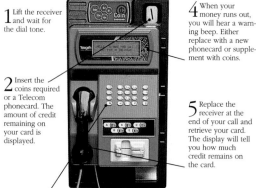

1 Lift the receiver and wait for the dial tone.

2 Insert the coins required or a Telecom phonecard. The amount of credit remaining on your card is displayed.

3 Dial the number and wait until you are connected.

4 When your money runs out, you will hear a warning beep. Either replace with a new phonecard or supplement with coins.

5 Replace the receiver at the end of your call and retrieve your card. The display will tell you how much credit remains on the card.

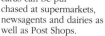

Phonecards
These are available in $5, $10, $15, $20 and $50 denominations.

Visitors can also send and receive E-mails at many hotels. The Yellow Pages of the telephone directory carries the names of places offering fax and E-mail and Internet services.

TELEPHONE DIRECTORIES

EACH REGION in New Zealand has a separate telephone directory. Each directory contains white pages, which list residential and commercial telephone numbers in alphabetical order as well as emergency and government department numbers, and yellow pages, which list business numbers according to industry groupings. In the larger regions, such as Auckland, Wellington and Christchurch, white and yellow pages are contained in separate volumes.

REACHING THE RIGHT NUMBER

• For long distance within New Zealand (STD calls), dial the correct area code, then the number.
• For an international number (IDD call), dial 00 followed by the correct country code, then the area code and number.
• For local and national directory enquiries, dial **018** (50c per enquiry).
• For international directory enquiries, dial **0172** ($1.50 per enquiry).
• For all internal operator-assisted calls, dial **010**.
• For all international operator-assisted calls (credit card collect calls), dial **0170**.
• For price-defined international calls, dial **0160** instead of 00 at the beginning of the call ($2.80). If you call the international operator on **0170**, the charge is $4.50.
• The prefixes **021**, **025** and **029** are mobile telephone numbers and **0800** numbers are toll free.
• See also Emergency Numbers, *p347*.

Postal Services

NEW ZEALAND'S postal service is run by New Zealand Post. Letters and parcels can be sent through Post Shops, which are either owned by or are agencies of New Zealand Post. Many Post Shops are located in bookshops. Hours of opening vary between Post Shops, but most are open at least from 9am to 5pm.

DOMESTIC AND INTERNATIONAL MAIL

THERE ARE two main classes of domestic mail: FastPost, which arrives the day after posting, and standard post, which takes two to three days. A standard post letter within New Zealand costs 40c, and FastPost costs 80c.

International airmail takes a minimum of one week to reach most countries. Letters and parcels sent via the cheaper International

New Zealand postwoman

Economy mail system take three weeks. Non-urgent parcels should be sent through EconomyPost, while urgent documents and parcels will reach their destination within a few days via International Express.

A number of private courier companies also offer competitive rates for sending letters and parcels overseas.

STAMPS

STAMPS CAN be bought at supermarkets, dairies, newsagents and Post Shop branches. New Zealand Post's Stamp Business Unit produces 12 commemorative issues a year and one to three definitive stamps.

Stamps with New Zealand outdoor themes

POSTBOXES

NEW ZEALAND uses standard and FastPost postboxes. These can be found on street corners or outside Post Shops. In busy areas they will be cleared twice daily, once at noon and once at 5pm.

Standard and FastPost boxes

POSTE RESTANTE

THE MAIN post office in each town serves as a poste restante. Have mail addressed clearly: c/- (care of) "Poste Restante, Central Post Office", followed by the name of the appropriate town. Poste restante mail will be held for three months. A passport or some other form of identification is needed to claim Poste Restante mail.

TRAVEL INFORMATION

THE VAST majority of visitors arrive in New Zealand by air. Auckland is the busiest port of entry, followed by Christchurch. Once in New Zealand, tourists generally use the domestic air network to get around, particularly to travel from resorts in the North Island to the South Island. The coach network covers most major

**Air New Zealand's
koru (fern) logo**

routes in the country. The rail network is limited, but some of the major routes travel through spectacular scenery. For visitors wanting to explore New Zealand away from the main transport routes and resorts, a car is the best way to travel. The roads are in good condition, although extra care is needed on alpine routes and back country roads.

Ansett Australia flight en route to New Zealand

ARRIVING BY AIR

AROUND 15 international airlines fly into New Zealand, and others, such as **British Airways**, serve the country only on a codeshare basis (using a local airline to serve their routes). The national airline, **Air New Zealand**, has an extensive international network, with either direct or codeshare links with 130 countries worldwide. It is particularly active in the Australian and Southern Pacific sectors.

Air New Zealand, **United Airlines** and **Qantas** fly into the United States, mostly to cities on the west coast, while **Cathay Pacific**, **Singapore Airlines**, **Malaysia Airlines**, **Japan Airlines** and **Korean Air** depart from the major Asian airports for New Zealand. **Aerolineas Argentina** flies direct from Auckland to Buenos Aires.

INTERNATIONAL FLIGHTS

NEW ZEALAND is a three and a half hour flight from eastern Australia, 10 hours from Pacific Rim cities such as Singapore, Hong Kong and Tokyo, and about 24 hours

from Europe. Taking account of delays and transfers, a flight from Europe can be extremely taxing and it is a good idea to arrange a stopover either in Asia, the United States or one of the Pacific Islands.

New Zealand has three principal international terminals. Auckland is the major gateway, followed by Christchurch and Wellington. Auckland airport has the most direct international connections, including links to Argentina, Canada, Chile, China, Germany, Indonesia and Japan. Christchurch and Wellington airports have fewer direct international links and

primarily service trans Tasman flights, although both have direct flights to Fiji and Western Samoa. Christchurch also has direct links to Singapore. It is also possible to fly direct from Australia to Hamilton, Palmerston North, Dunedin and Queenstown. By international standards, none of the airports are congested and they are rarely affected by bad weather.

AIR FARES

BECAUSE NEW ZEALAND is a relatively remote country, air fares can be expensive,

**International
signpost at
Christchurch**

particularly during the peak season from December to February when airlines charge premium rates. However, a wide variety of discounted fares are available during the low season. These can provide significant savings of up to 50 per cent off full economy fares, although they may lack flexibility and carry cancellation penalties. It is a good idea to get prices from a number of travel

AIRPORT	INFORMATION	DISTANCE FROM CITY
Auckland	(09) 275 0789	21 km (13 mile
Wellington	(04) 385 5123	8 km (5 miles)
Christchurch	(03) 358 5029	11 km (7 miles
Dunedin	(03) 486 2879	30 km (18 mile

The "City of Sails" design of Auckland International Airport

agents or direct from airlines before making a booking. Ask about special promotional fares, such as two-for-one tickets, advance purchase excursion fares, student discounts, special deals for senior citizens and rates for stand-by flights. Also compare the rates for "open return" tickets with fixed date return tickets. Check the limitations and penalties before buying a special rate ticket.

ON ARRIVAL

DURING FLIGHTS to New Zealand visitors are given customs declaration documents to complete. These are to be handed in on arrival, along with passports. Fresh food or plant material must be placed in bins provided before the immigration area. Heavy fines are imposed on people who fail to declare quarantine items into the country *(see pp342–3)*.

Auckland, Wellington and Christchurch airports have a wide range of shops and postal and telecommunication services. Car hire firms operate from the airports, and banking facilities are open to coincide with international flight arrivals *(see p348)*. Transfer from the airports to the city centres is straightforward: taxis and shuttles (vans with trailers for carrying luggage) are available for door-to-door service, and buses run regular services to the city centres. Bookings can be made at the airports for further domestic air travel.

Airport bus

Door-to-door shuttle

Airport taxi

DIRECTORY

AIRLINE CARRIERS

Aerolineas Argentina
((09) 379 3076.
W www.aerolineas.co.nz

Air New Zealand
((09) 336 2400.
W www.airnz.co.nz

British Airways
((09) 366 3211.
W www.british-airways.com

Cathay Pacific
((09) 379 0833.
W www.cathaypacific.com

Japan Airlines
((09) 379 3202.
W www.jal.co.jp/english/.
index_e.html

Korean Air
((09) 303 0166.
W www.koreanair.com

Malaysia Airlines
((09) 373 2741.
W www.malaysiaairlines.com.my

Qantas New Zealand
((09) 357 8700.
W www.qantasnz.co.nz

Singapore Airlines
((09) 379 3209.
W www.singaporeair.com

United Airlines
(0800 508 648.
W www.unitedairlines.co.nz

Auckland's domestic and international terminals are in separate buildings about 1 km (0.6 mile) apart, but a free shuttle service operates between the two buildings from 6am to 10:30pm daily. At Christchurch and Wellington, the international and domestic services are located in the same building.

TAXI FARE TO CITY	BUS TRANSFER TO CITY	SHUTTLE FARE TO CITY	TRANSFER TIME TO CITY
NZ$40	NZ$12	NZ$15	45 mins
NZ$15	NZ$5	NZ$8	20 mins
NZ$20	NZ$2.70	NZ$10	20 mins
NZ$45	Not available	NZ$15	30 mins

Domestic Air Travel

NEW ZEALAND has an extensive domestic air transport
network, linking all of the major and provincial
cities as well as many smaller towns. Although it is a
small country, New Zealand's long, thin shape means
land travel between major centres such as Auckland,
Wellington and Christchurch is time consuming. As a
result, air services play a crucial transport role. The two
main domestic carriers are **Air New Zealand** and
Qantas New Zealand. Air New Zealand also owns
airline companies operating feeder services to provincial centres. Fares can be expensive, but a wide
range of heavily discounted fares are available,
particularly if travellers are prepared to be flexible and
to book well in advance.

**Air New Zealand domestic flight
arriving at Wellington airport**

AIR ROUTES AND AIRLINES

AIR NEW ZEALAND and Qantas
New Zealand both
operate national networks
connecting the main cities
and provincial centres,
including the major tourist
resorts of Rotorua and
Queenstown. Some 26 towns
and cities are serviced by
regular scheduled flights.
Feeder services to provincial
centres are operated under
the Air New Zealand Link
banner, which comprises
Air Nelson, **Mount Cook
Line** and **Eagle Air**. Flights
to many provincial centres
involve flying first to a major
airport, such as Auckland or
Christchurch, then transferring
to another flight. It is also
possible to fly from Invercargill to Stewart Island, from
Auckland to Great Barrier
Island, and from Wellington
to Blenheim, as an alternative

to travelling between these
destinations by ferry.
　Origin Pacific Airways
operates flights between
Auckland, Hamilton, New
Plymouth, Tauranga, Napier,
Palmerston North, Wellington
and Nelson. Flights from
Dunedin to Christchurch,
Nelson and Wellington operate
if there is enough demand.
They also offer charter flights
that can include scenic tours
en route if required.

DISCOUNTS FOR OVERSEAS VISITORS

AIRLINES OFFER discounted
domestic air fares as part
of an international package,
so it is advisable to check
with a travel agent before
departure. Various air passes
can be bought which allow
visitors to make a number of
single domestic flights for a
set price. Air New Zealand's
"Explore New Zealand" air
pass is a coupon-based
system. Visitors can buy a
minimum of three and a
maximum of eight coupons
(approximately NZ$500 for
three and NZ$1,300
for eight), and each
coupon can be used
for one flight sector.
For instance, a direct
flight from Auckland
to Christchurch will
cost one coupon.
The pass is only
available to overseas
visitors and can be
bought in their home
country in con-
junction with an
international air

ticket or, in New Zealand, on
presentation of an inter-
national ticket. However,
passes purchased in New
Zealand are subject to 12.5
per cent GST.
　Qantas New Zealand offers
a "Scenic Standby" air pass
system for overseas tourists.
Travellers can buy coupons
(about NZ$500 for three
coupons), a 10-day unlimited
travel pass (about NZ$600), or
a one-month unlimited travel
pass (about NZ$1,000). These
passes can be bought in New
Zealand on presentation of a
passport. The disadvantage of
this system is that seats are
allocated on a stand-by basis.

FLY–DRIVE DEALS

A CONVENIENT WAY to travel
in New Zealand is to fly
to a destination and then
continue by car. Arrange-
ments can be made for
different drop-off and pick-up
points for hire vehicles; for
example, it is possible to fly
from Auckland to Queens-
town, then drive from
Queenstown to Christchurch.
Air New Zealand and Qantas
New Zealand have links with
the major car hire firms,
which offer discounts to
passengers travelling on those
airlines *(see p358)*.
　A wide range of fly–drive
packages operate from
Auckland to the South Island
during the ski season, including deals combining
flights, campervan or car
rental, and ski lift passes at
very competitive rates. Travel
agents and airlines offer a
variety of special promotions,
and it is best to shop around
for the most suitable and
economical package.

**Mount Cook Line ski-planes in snowy
conditions at the Mount Cook Airfield**

Passengers checking in at Christchurch International Airport

AIR FARES

S TANDARD DOMESTIC FARES can be expensive, but airlines allocate a variety of fares to each flight, and even people making bookings at short notice can sometimes get a good deal. Air New Zealand, for instance, offers "Gotta Go" fares which are permanently discounted at 65 per cent.

Advance purchase fares offer the best deals on scheduled flights within New Zealand, but carry conditions: they have to be paid for either 7, 14 or 21 days in advance of the flight and may require a minimum stay of one Saturday night and a maximum of 30 days. Usually no refunds are offered.

Children below two fly for free on an adult's lap, and children aged 3 to 12 pay 50 per cent of the adult fare.

CHECKING IN

O N DOMESTIC FLIGHTS, air lines require passengers to check in 30 minutes before the flight departs. It is not necessary to confirm flights, but it is a good idea to make sure they are on time.

BAGGAGE RESTRICTIONS

A LL PASSENGERS, including children, travelling economy class on domestic flights have a baggage allowance of 32 kg (70 lb).

DIRECTORY

DOMESTIC AIRLINES

Air New Zealand (including Mount Cook Line, Eagle Air and Air Nelson)
Domestic Reservations.
[0800 737 000.

Qantas New Zealand
Domestic Reservations.
[0800 800 146.

Origin Pacific Airways
Domestic Reservations.
[0800 302 302.

The maximum weight for cabin baggage is 5 kg (11 lb) and must be storable under the seat in front or in an overhead locker. Personal articles, such as an overcoat, handbag or camera, may be carried into the aircraft.

PRINCIPAL DOMESTIC AIR ROUTES

Domestic flights operating between major cities, complemented by a host of connecting flights between smaller towns and tourist resorts, cover the country quite comprehensively. Flying is ideal for those with limited time to spend in the country.

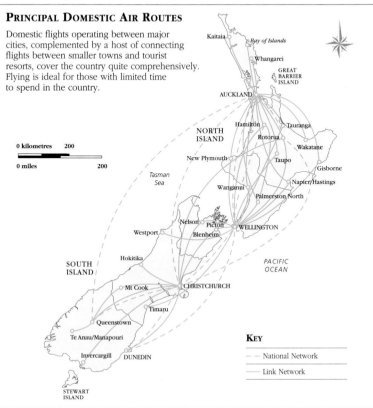

0 kilometres 200

0 miles 200

Kaitaia
Bay of Islands
Whangarei
GREAT BARRIER ISLAND
AUCKLAND
NORTH ISLAND
Hamilton
Tauranga
Rotorua
Wakatane
New Plymouth
Taupo
Gisborne
Tasman Sea
Wanganui
Napier/Hastings
Palmerston North
Nelson
Picton
WELLINGTON
Westport
Blenheim
Hokitika
PACIFIC OCEAN
SOUTH ISLAND
Mt Cook
CHRISTCHURCH
Timaru
Queenstown
Te Anau/Manapouri
Invercargill
DUNEDIN
STEWART ISLAND

KEY

- - National Network

— Link Network

Travelling by Train, Coach and Inter-Island Ferry

Tranz Rail travel pass

Aᴌᴛʜᴏᴜɢʜ ɴᴇᴡ ᴢᴇᴀʟᴀɴᴅ does not have an extensive rail network, trains connect all the main cities and passenger journeys are outstanding for their breathtaking scenery, some not visible from the road. The mountainous terrain has forced railway engineers to build spectacular viaducts and long tunnels. Coaches connect most points throughout the country and cater for independent travellers as well as those who prefer guided tours. The North and South islands are connected by two ferry companies, with several sailings each day.

TranzAlpine Express crossing Kowai Bridge near Springfield

Tʜᴇ Nᴇᴡ Zᴇᴀʟᴀɴᴅ Rᴀɪʟ Nᴇᴛᴡᴏʀᴋ

Tʜᴇ ʀᴀɪʟ ɴᴇᴛᴡᴏʀᴋ is operated by a private company, **Tranz Rail Ltd**, which also owns the Interislander and Lynx ferry services. Passenger rail services connect the major cities as well as a number of provincial centres, including Tauranga, Rotorua, Napier, Palmerston North, Picton, Timaru, Invercargill and Greymouth.

Sᴘᴇᴄɪᴀʟɪᴛʏ Tʀɪᴘs

Aʟʟ ᴛʜᴇ ᴋᴇʏ rail routes travel through areas of scenic interest. Justifiably popular is the TranzAlpine journey from Christchurch to Greymouth, which crosses the Canterbury Plains before cutting dramatically through the Southern Alps via the Otira Tunnel *(see pp240–41)*, and on through the rainforests of the West Coast. Many visitors return to Christchurch on the same day, while others buy a one-way ticket and proceed by road from Greymouth to other attractions on the West

Coast. The TranzCoastal, which runs between Picton and Christchurch, is also popular for the splendid scenery of the Kaikoura coast.

In Otago, there are two excursion trains – the Taieri Gorge Railway *(see p262)* and the Kingston Flyer *(see p277)*.

Cᴏᴀᴄʜ Tᴏᴜʀs

Cᴏᴀᴄʜ ᴛʀᴀᴠᴇʟ is a safe, efficient and popular means of transport for tourists in New Zealand. The main operators are **InterCity Coachlines** and **Newmans Coach Lines**. Coach travellers have the option of joining

InterCity coach on State Highway 6, West Coast

a guided tour, taking regular scheduled services, or using one of the travel pass options available to independent travellers. Most New Zealand cities and towns are linked by InterCity, which has both scheduled services and three-month travel passes. Discounts of 30 per cent and 50 per cent are sometimes available on scheduled services, although these are subject to cancellation penalties.

The **Magic Bus** is another service that offers a travel pass system targetted at backpackers. Travellers buy a national coach pass, which they can use at any time within six months of purchase. Other coach companies also service specific routes in the various regions.

Tɪᴄᴋᴇᴛs ᴀɴᴅ Bᴏᴏᴋɪɴɢs

Bᴏᴏᴋɪɴɢs ꜰᴏʀ rail travel can be made through travel agents, or by calling Tranz Rail Reservations seven days a week from 7am to 9pm.

New Zealand trains do not have separate sections for different classes. However, there is a multi-tier fare structure for both rail and ferry travel, and discounts of up to 50 per cent on standard fares are often available, especially during off-peak periods. Always ask for the best possible price when making a booking.

Tʀᴀᴠᴇʟ Pᴀssᴇs

Aɴ ᴇᴄᴏɴᴏᴍɪᴄᴀʟ and independent way to travel is by using a Tranz Rail "Best of New Zealand Pass", which combines rail, ferry and coach. A pass is credited with a number of points, and is debited for each leg of travel undertaken. For example, a 1,000 point pass will allow you to go from Northland to Dunedin via various resorts and attractions, using a combination of train, coach and ferry. Travel on a pass is 30 per cent cheaper than standard fares. Passes must be used within six months of purchase and each leg of the journey must be booked 24 hours in advance.

The Top Cat catamaran entering Wellington Harbour

INTER-ISLAND FERRY SERVICES

T HE MAIN inter-island ferry service between Wellington and Picton is provided by the **Interislander** fleet, which carries passengers, cars and freight. Although fares on the three Interislander ships are not cheap, they operate five return trips a day, taking about three hours each way. They have restaurants, bars, cafés, movie theatres, children's rooms, observation decks and "quiet rooms" for business people. Travellers can book for other Tranz Rail services on board. In summer, the ferries are augmented by two high-speed catamarans, the **Lynx** and the **Top Cat**, which make the trip from Wellington to Picton in 1 hour 45 minutes. A relaxing way to travel, the ferries are also an excellent way to see the Marlborough Sounds.

It is advisable to book in advance for the ferries, particularly during school holidays and especially if you are taking a car across the strait.

PRINCIPAL RAIL, COACH AND FERRY ROUTES

In New Zealand, travel by the national coach network, the scenic rail network and the inter-island ferry services enables visitors to cover the entire country, except for the most inaccessible parts of the South Island. Local bus companies service smaller towns.

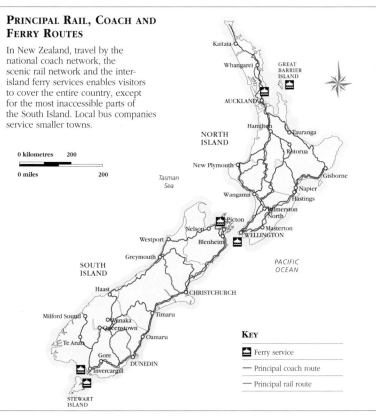

0 kilometres 200

0 miles 200

Kaitaia

Whangarei

GREAT BARRIER ISLAND

AUCKLAND

Hamilton

Tauranga

NORTH ISLAND

Rotorua

New Plymouth

Gisborne

Tasman Sea

Wanganui

Napier

Hastings

Palmerston North

Nelson

Picton

Masterton

WELLINGTON

Westport

Blenheim

Greymouth

SOUTH ISLAND

PACIFIC OCEAN

Haast

CHRISTCHURCH

Milford Sound

Wanaka

Timaru

Queenstown

Oamaru

Te Anau

Gore

DUNEDIN

Invercargill

STEWART ISLAND

KEY

⛴ Ferry service

— Principal coach route

— Principal rail route

Travelling by Car

Motorway signboard in Auckland

Avis rental booth at Auckland International Airport

Aₗₜₕₒᵤgₕ the public transport system offers plenty of options for travelling between towns and cities, a car allows you to thoroughly explore New Zealand's scenic rural areas, and gives you the flexibility to stop at small country cafés, wineries and other points of interest, or simply pause to admire a view. Outside the main cities the roads are relatively uncongested, and in some areas virtually empty. Roads are generally in good condition, although even the major highways have many winding, hilly sections. Multi-lane motorways with lane dividers exist only on the approaches to the main cities.

DRIVING LICENCES

Pʀₒᵥᵢᵈₑᵈ ʏₒᵤ have a legal domestic or International Driving Permit, you can drive on New Zealand roads. If your licence is not in English, bring an English translation or get an International Driving Permit. All drivers, including overseas visitors, must carry their licence with them when driving around New Zealand.

CAR RENTAL

Rₑₙₜₐₗ ₒₐʀₛ are readily available throughout the country with a large range of rental companies to choose from. Companies such as **Avis**, **Budget** and **Hertz** have nationwide networks.

Rates vary enormously depending on the size of car,

season and length of rental period. Off-season rates for a small car can be as low as NZ$30 a day, while a four-wheel drive vehicle at peak season rates can cost NZ$140. Rates are cheaper in the main cities than in the more remote towns, where rental companies have fewer cars available.

Some car hire firms offer fixed kilometre/mileage rentals, which are suitable for sightseeing around one of the major cities for two or three days. For longer rental periods and open road travel, it is better to choose a deal allowing you to travel an unlimited number of kilometres/miles. Fuel is not included in the rental price.

Rental companies frequently offer special promotions, such as combining car rental with

ski packages. When renting a car, discuss your travel plans with the company so that they can advise you on the most appropriate deal.

Smaller companies appear to charge less than the established ones, but they do not always include in their quotations features such as insurance. Some companies may also charge extra if you want to return the car to a depot other than the one you rented it from.

Sometimes car rental companies charge low rates for people to drive from one location to another where cars are needed, for example, from Wellington to Auckland. This is an economical way to travel, but sightseeing time may be limited as cars usually need to be delivered urgently.

Most rental companies will not hire to anyone under the age of 21. Companies prefer to be paid by credit card, and even if payment is by cash or traveller's cheque they are likely to ask for a credit card imprint as security against loss or damage.

State Highway 1 parallelling the railway line along the Kaikoura coast

OTHER VEHICLES

A POPULAR FORM of transport with visitors to New Zealand is a campervan or motorhome. The largest companies, such as **Maui Rentals** and **Kea Campers**, have depots in Auckland, Christchurch and Queenstown. Campervans are available in a range of sizes, from two-berth to six-berth. All are equipped with a refrigerator and gas cooker, and some of the more luxurious have their own shower, toilet and microwave. Prices vary greatly throughout the year. In summer, a two-berth van will cost about NZ$140 a day

Maui Rentals campervan parked near Auckland waterfront

and a six-berth van about NZ$240 a day, while from May to September the same vehicles will cost about NZ$55 and NZ$120.

New Zealand is an ideal place for travelling by campervan, as camping grounds can be found in virtually every town, often in beautiful locations *(see p295)*.

INSURANCE

C AR AND campervan rental rates usually include insurance cover for collision damage and theft from the vehicle. However, insurance policies often carry a very high excess payment, in some cases around NZ$1,500 for a car and NZ$5,000 for a campervan. Many companies offer "excess waiver" options, allowing payment of a daily rate of around NZ$10 to NZ$20 to reduce the excess to under NZ$200. Personal accident plans are available, but this risk should be covered by comprehensive travel insurance. Insurance for drivers under 25 is more expensive.

Service station selling both petrol and diesel

FUEL

T HE MAJORITY of New Zealand cars run on petrol, while most four-wheel drive vehicles and campervans use diesel. Petrol is reasonably priced (about half the price of petrol in Europe). It is dispensed by the litre and is available in regular unleaded and premium unleaded grades. Diesel is also reasonably priced and easily obtained.

Fuel is bought from gas stations, commonly known as "service stations". Many city stations are open until late at night and some remain open 24 hours. Even the very small settlements have a service station or shop with a petrol pump, but these are often closed in the evening and on weekends, so fill up in town to avoid running short of fuel when travelling long distances. Most service stations also sell a range of basic grocery items as well as newspapers and magazines.

Speed limit sign

ROAD RULES AND SIGNS

N EW ZEALANDERS drive on the left-hand side of the road. All signposting follows standard international symbols, and all distances are in kilometres. The speed limit is 100 km/h (60 mph) on the open road and 50 km/h (30 mph) in urban areas. Excessive speed is a major hazard on New Zealand roads, and speed cameras are scattered throughout the country, both on the open road and on city streets. Cameras record the details of vehicles exceeding the speed

limit and drivers are fined on a graduated scale depending on the speed. Travelling 50 km/h (30 mph) in excess of the speed limit may result in a 28-day licence suspension. Because of New Zealand's many winding roads, signs warning motorists to slow down to a recommended speed are very common.

A broken or solid yellow line down the centre of the road means it is illegal to overtake another vehicle because of poor visibility. Main highways have passing lanes at regular intervals. When turning, drivers must give way to traffic not turning and to all traffic crossing or approaching from the right.

Drink-driving laws are strictly enforced in New Zealand. A driver may be required to give a breath screening test at any time. The legal blood alcohol level is 80 milligrams of alcohol per 100 millilitres of blood (30 milligrams for a driver under 20). Police in the countryside are every bit as vigilant as in the cities and often conduct random breath testing.

Traffic accidents involving injury must be reported to the police within 24 hours. When an accident involves another vehicle, drivers should exchange insurance company details. It is best not to accept responsibility for an accident but rather inform the police of what happened and let them decide.

It is compulsory for both drivers and passengers to wear seat belts, and babies and children under five must be put in an infant's car seat.

Drivers moving slowly past sheep on a state highway

ROAD CONDITIONS

CONSIDERING THE small population and the size of the country, the quality of New Zealand's roads is excellent. However, visitors used to travelling long distances on two- or three-lane freeways with no opposing traffic need to take care. Median barriers exist only on motorways in the major cities, and on other roads the only thing separating drivers from opposing traffic is a painted centre line. Because of New Zealand's hilly terrain, stretches of winding road are common even on the major state highways. Another potential hazard are railway lines that cross main roads. Flashing lights and railway barriers are usually activated to indicate an approaching train, but these may be absent in remote areas, and it is wise to reduce speed at all railway crossing signs.

Many back roads leading to scenic areas or points of interest are unsealed, for example the road leading to the Oparara Basin north of Karamea *(see p232)*. These roads require extreme care as they are often narrow and it is easy to lose control on the gravel surface or on verges. Winter driving is generally trouble-free, but ice and snow in the mountainous and inland areas of the South Island can cause problems.

SIGNS ALONG COUNTRY ROADS

Different road signs offer warnings and instructions for drivers. Speed limits vary depending on the conditions of the road and the amount of traffic. Notably hazardous are railway crossings, gravel roads, and one-lane bridges, where traffic moving in the direction of the large white arrow has priority. Drivers should be wary of stock or wildlife straying onto roads.

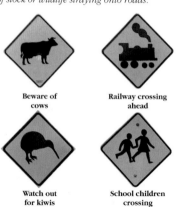

Beware of cows

Railway crossing ahead

Watch out for kiwis

School children crossing

Be careful of penguins

Slippery gravel road

Be aware of pukekos on the road

One-lane bridge ahead

AA breakdown service truck

Grit is regularly scattered on these roads to prevent cars from skidding, but it is advisable to check on road conditions with the DOC or Automobile Association before travelling over alpine routes such as Arthur's Pass *(see pp240–41)* and Haast Pass *(see p271)*.

One-lane bridges are common on minor highways and back roads, particularly on the west coast of the South Island. A red arrow means you must give way to opposing traffic. Occasionally, drivers will come across combination rail-and-road bridges and it is important to heed flashing lights indicating that a train is approaching.

Rail-and-road bridge near Kumara Junction

Wandering farm stock are sometimes a problem, although generally only on minor roads. It is relatively common to be delayed by farmers shifting mobs of sheep along country roads. Drivers need to be patient and drive extremely slowly while the animals move past. Possums and other nocturnal animals often venture on to the roads at night and drivers should drive carefully in order to avoid hitting them.

ROADSIDE ASSISTANCE

CAR HIRE companies deal with breakdowns involving their own vehicles, and will arrange to provide replacements, if necessary. The **Automobile Association** (AA) is a nationwide motoring organization providing breakdown services and information on road conditions. Other services offered include provision of detailed maps covering every area of New Zealand, guides covering all types of accommodation, from camping grounds to luxury hotels, technical advice and touring information. The AA has offices in almost every large town. Members of most overseas motoring organizations have reciprocal rights with the New Zealand AA. To get the benefit of AA services while in New Zealand, take your home motoring organization card into an AA office in New Zealand where you will be issued with a temporary membership.

AA membership entitles you to six free breakdown callouts a year, as well as discounted rates at some hotels and motels and on car rental.

INNER-CITY DRIVING

IF DRIVING in New Zealand cities, an up-to-date street map is essential, especially for spotting one-way streets. If possible, avoid the peak traffic hours of 7:30am to 9am and 4:30pm to 6pm, especially in Auckland and Wellington. Traffic reports are broadcast on local radio stations *(see p345)*.

Parking is readily available in downtown areas, in metered parks (operated by coins), parking buildings and shopping mall car parks. Local councils administer parking, and parking wardens

issue fines to vehicles that are parked illegally or that have expired meters.

Most cities have clearway zones and during certain times vehicles parked in these areas may be towed away. If this occurs, call the local traffic authority or police to find out where your car has been impounded. Retrieving the car involves paying an on-the-spot fine.

Typical coin-operated parking meter in a downtown car park

General Index

Acknowledgments

DORLING KINDERSLEY would like to thank the following people whose contributions and assistance have made the preparation of this book possible.

CONTRIBUTORS

HELEN CORRIGAN is a Wellington-based freelance writer, editor researcher and publicist. She has a background in journalism and radio and since 1995 has been involved in public relations for galleries and government departments.

ROEF HOPMAN is a public relations consultant and freelance writer in Auckland. Formerly Chief Editor of *Design Trends*, he organizes public relations projects for Pacific Rim countries and contributes to various publications.

GERARD HUTCHING is a freelance journalist who specializes in natural history and the environment. He has written several books, including *The Natural World of New Zealand* which won the 1999 Montana Book of the Year (environment).

REBECCA MACFIE is an award-winning Christchurch-based journalist. She specializes in business and current affairs feature writing, and contributes to a range of New Zealand newspapers and magazines.

GEOFF MERCER lives in Hastings. He has written for daily newspapers in Wellington and Hawke's Bay. He now compiles oral histories, writes and publishes biographies, and contributes articles to various publications.

SIMON NOBLE lives in Nelson and has a long involvement in the region's natural, historic and scenic areas. He is the author of *The Treasured Pathway*, a guide to a heritage highway through northern Nelson and Marlborough.

PETER SMITH is an Auckland artist, educator, writer and yachtsman, and former principal of Auckland College of Education. Much of his writing is in the areas of education and arts curriculum and yachting.

MICHAEL WARD is a chef who has worked in the food industry for some twenty years. Michael has a keen interest in promoting New Zealand food and wine.

MARK WRIGHT is a Dunedin-based freelance writer whose work ranges from articles on travel, technology and health to classic cars. He has a background in radio and writes scripts for television and video.

FOR DORLING KINDERSLEY
SENIOR PUBLISHING MANAGER Louise Bostock Lang
PUBLISHING MANAGER Kate Poole
CARTOGRAPHIC EDITORS Casper Morris, David Pugh
PRODUCTION Michelle Thomas
PUBLISHING DIRECTOR Gillian Allan

INDEXER
Kay Lyons

ADDITIONAL PHOTOGRAPHY
Louise Goossens

SPECIAL ASSISTANCE
Debbie Ameriks and Amelia Manson, Office of Treaty Settlements, Wellington; Tim Amos, Department of Conservation, Wellington; Lane Ayr, Bay of Islands Swordfish Club; Kate Banbury, Waitomo Glow Worm Caves New Zealand, Otorohanga; Jennifer Beatson, Latitude Nelson; Black's Point Museum, Reefton; Hughie Blues and Amanda Turner, Waikokopu Café, Waitangi; Julia Bradshaw, Lakes District Museum, Arrowtown; Linda Burgess, Wellington; Dennis Buurman, Ocean Wings; Elizabeth Caldwell, Arts Council of New Zealand; Cathedral Church of St Paul, Wellington; Alan Cooper, Geology Department, University of Otago, Dunedin; C.P. Group, Auckland; Croyden Aircraft Company, Gore;

Jo Darby, Tourism Industry Association New Zealand; Carol Davidson, New Zealand Festival 2000; Department of Conservation Visitor Centres; Jenny Dey, Photosource New Zealand Ltd; Richard Doyle and Lisa Hoffman, Christchurch City Council; Far North Regional Museum, Kaitia; Tammy Fromont and Nineke Metz, Destination Northland Limited; Dianne Gallagher, New Zealand Mountain Safety Council Inc.; Jane Gilbert, Film New Zealand; Gillooly family, Farewell Spit Safari, Collingwood; Donna Gray, Abel Tasman National Park Enterprises; Lesley Grey and Sharon Pasco, Stewart Island Promotion Association; Frank Habicht, Paihia; Haoni Waititi Marae, Auckland; Lee Harris, Fiordland Travel Limited, Queenstown; Tania Harris, Waitangi National Trust; Christine Harvey, Whale Watch®, Kaikoura; Cameron Hill, Air New Zealand, Auckland; Hillary Commission; Barbara Hinkley and Suzanne Knight, Museum of New Zealand Te Papa Tongarewa; InterCity Coachlines; Anne Irving, City Gallery, Wellington; Peter Jackson, Blenheim; Jean Johnston, Wellington City Council; Kapiti Cheese; Kelly Tarlton's Underwater World and Antarctic Encounter, Auckland; Michael Liao, Kiwifruit Country, Te Puke; Fay Looney, New Plymouth; Peter McCleavey Gallery, Wellington; Ruth McGirr, Robert McDougall Art Gallery and Annex, Christchurch; Bill and Joan MacGregor, Lake Hawea; Robert McGregor, Art Deco Trust, Napier; Annabelle MacKenzie and Cathy Muker, New Zealand High Commission, Kuala Lumpur; Cathy Maslin, Key-Light Image Library; Heather Mathie and Betty Moss, Alexander Turnbull Library; Darryl May, Oamaru; Montana Marlborough Winery; Anita Moreira, Air New Zealand, Kuala Lumpur; Morven Hills Station, Oamaru; Museum of Caves, Waitomo; Newmans Coach Lines; New Zealand Fighter Pilots Museum, Wanaka; Okarito Nature Tours, Westland; Old Mandeville Airport, Gore; Otago Early Settlers Museum, Dunedin; security staff, Parliament House, Wellington; Libby Passau and Nick Turzynski, Hodder Moa Beckett Publishers Ltd; Jacky Payne; Penguin Place, Otago Peninsula; Meng-Chong Phang, New Zealand Tourism Board, Singapore; Clive Ralph, Napier; Rewa's Village, Kerikeri; Chris and Phil Rose, Wairau River Wines; Royal Albatross Centre, Taiaroa Head; Russell Museum; Mary Sharrock, Ansett Airways, Australia; Jenny Shipley, MP, Wellington; Stone Store, Kerikeri; Annalese Taylor, New Zealand Tourism Board, Auckland; Judith Tizard, MP, Tourism Auckland Office; Tourism Industry Association New Zealand; Tranz Rail Ltd; Tom Van der Kwast, Picton; Andrew and Jeannie Van der Putten; Visitor Information Centres; Tim Warren, Visual Impact Pictures Ltd; concert staff, Whakarewarewa Thermal Village, Rotorua; Whangarei Museum of Fishes; Dr Rodney Wilson, Auckland War Memorial Museum; Jane Wynyard, The Royal New Zealand Ballet.

PHOTOGRAPHY PERMISSIONS
The publisher would like to thank the following for their assistance and kind permission to photograph at their establishments.

Graham Abbott, Hanmer Springs Thermal Reserve; Art and Gourd Gallery, Golden Bay; Ashford Craft Village, Ashburton; Auckland International Airport; Auckland Zoological Gardens; Avis, Auckland International Airport; Babich Winery, Auckland; Grant Barron, Olveston House, Dunedin; Café de Paris, Hokitika; Canterbury House Vineyards, Waipara; Christ Church Cathedral, Christchurch; Dr Fiona Ciaran, Aigantighe Art Gallery, Timaru; Clapham Clock Museum, Whangarei; Coal Town Museum, Westport; Dargaville Maritime Museum; DFS Galleria, Auckland; Driving Creek Railway and Potteries, Coromandel; Dunedin Public Art Gallery; Dunedin Railway Station; The Edwin Fox, Picton; Ana Foreman, Weta Shop, Coromandel; Gibbston Valley Winery, Queenstown; Lindsay Hazley, Southland Museum and Art Gallery, Invercargill; Helen and Ross Ivey, Glentanner Station; Kevin Judd, Cloudy Bay; Steve Jones, Science Centre, Manawatu

Kingdom, Kaitaia; Stuart Landsborough's Puzzling World, Wanaka; Left Bank Art Gallery, Greymouth; Le Brun family, Blenheim; Malcolm McLaughlan and Peter Thornley, Icon Restaurant, Wellington; Maori Arts and Crafts Institute, Rotorua; Royce McGlashen, Nelson; Matakohe Kauri Museum, Dargaville; Mountain Jade Greenstone Factory, Hokitika; Mt Bruce Wildlife Centre, Wairarapa; Mountford Vineyard, Canterbury; Museum of Transport and Technology, Auckland; Museum of Wellington City and Sea; New Zealand Automobile Association; New Zealand Rugby Museum, Palmerston North; North Otago Museum, Oamaru; Nigel and Teresa Ogle, Tawhiti Museum, Hawera; Outdoor Heritage, Newmarket; Out of New Zealand, Auckland; Parnell Fire Service; Parnell Police Station; Pegasus Bay, Canterbury; Provincial Council Buildings, Christchurch; Queenstown Rafting; Rainbow's End Adventure Park, Auckland; Rippon Vineyards, Wanaka; St John's Ambulance; St Paul's Cathedral, Dunedin; Shantytown, Greymouth; Sheraton Auckland Hotel; Shotover Jet, Queenstown; Southward Car Museum, Paraparaumu; Stockton Mine, Westport; Thames School of Mines and Mineralogical Museum; Tramway Museum, Paekakariki; Waiau Waterworks, Coromandel; Waipara Springs, Canterbury; Whakarewarewa Thermal Village, Rotorua; Whale Watch®, Kaikoura; Whanganui Riverboat Centre; Zambesi, Wellington.

PICTURE CREDITS

t = top; tl = top left; tlc = top left centre; tc = top centre; trc = top right centre; tr = top right; cla = centre left above; ca = centre above; cra = centre right above; cl = centre left; c = centre; cr = centre right; clb = centre left below; crb = centre right below; cb = centre below; bl = bottom left; br = bottom right; b = bottom; bc = bottom centre; bcl = bottom centre left; bcr = bottom centre right.

The publisher would like to thank the following individuals, companies and picture libraries for permission to reproduce their photographs:

AGL AERIAL IMAGERY: 37br; AIR NEW ZEALAND: 352tc; ANSETT AUSTRALIA: 352cla; ART DECO TRUST: 144bl.

BAY OF ISLANDS SWORDFISH CLUB: 101tc, 101cla; PETER BUSH: 18t, 31cr, 36tc, 36cr, 36bl, 69tr, 117clb, 155bl, 333cr, 344bl.

CHRISTCHURCH CITY COUNCIL: 216; CITY GALLERY, WELLINGTON: 162tr; CORBANS WINES: 34tl.

DEPARTMENT OF CONSERVATION, WELLINGTON: 189tr, 217b, 236tr, 334tc; DESTINATION NORTHLAND LIMITED: 94cl, 101cra, 106bc, 107tl.

GARETH EYRES, EXPOSURE: 36clb, 37tl, 39bc, 40cr, 56–57, 97br, 106c, 119cra, 142–143, 184–185, 202–203c, 213tl, 237cr, 269br, 281tr, 335tl, 336tl, 336b, 337t.

FIORDLAND TRAVEL LIMITED: 278tr, 282tr, 282cla, 282clb, 282bl, 283tl, 283cl, 283cr.

HODDER MOA BECKETT PUBLISHERS LTD: 31bl.

INTERCITY COACHLINES: 356bc.

KEY-LIGHT IMAGE LIBRARY: Warren Jacobs 20–21; Brian Enting Photography 21tl; Warren Jacobs 24tr; Andy Radka 24cl; Nick Servian 28br, 28–29c; Michael Pole 32tr; James White 32clb; Graham Meadows 32bc; Nick Servian 32br; Gary Bowering 35bc; Graham Radcliffe 40bl; Brian Enting Photography 45bl; Andy Belcher 62tl; Geoff Mason 62tr; Brian Enting Photography 62br; Warren Jacobs 98–99; Richard Cory-Wright 117br; Brian Enting Photography 140clb; Andy Belcher 141cr; Michael Hall 150; Nick Servian 163tr; Graham Radcliffe 171br; Peter Laurenson 181crb; Warren Jacobs 181br; Brian Chudleigh 192tr; Geoff Mason

193br; Caroline Hobbs 237tr; Nic Bishop 242bl; Geoff Mason 245cl; Tim Hawkins 250bc; Warren Jacobs 270cl; Nic Bishop 271ca; Peter Reese 288cl; Geoff Mason 334bl; Ron Redfern 335c; Warren Jacobs 339tl; Geoff Mason 354br; Graham Radcliffe 356cl; KIWIFRUIT COUNTRY: 127tr.

LAKES DISTRICT MUSEUM: 277c; HOLGER LEUE: 20br, 24cr, 25bl, 32cla, 32–33c, 47bc, 63cr, 63br, 66cl, 71cl, 72tl, 73bl, 75tr, 76br, 81bc, 87t, 90bl, 91tl, 101br, 111b, 118cl, 120br, 121tc, 125br, 128tr, 129crb, 136tl, 141tr, 188tr, 188cla, 190tl, 192–193c, 225br, 230tl, 236tl, 242br, 250tr, 250cl, 251tl, 252, 265c, 270br, 274tl, 275c, 276tr, 278br, 280tr, 280cr, 280bl, 281cl, 281b, 284tl, 286cl, 286bc, 287br, 295cl, 360cla, 360cra, 360bl, 361cl; ROB LUCAS: 22bl, 22bc, 22br, 23tlc, 23bl, 23crb, 130tl, 242tl, 250tl, 270tl, 281cr.

ROBERT MCDOUGALL ART GALLERY AND ANNEX: 30bl; DARRYL MAY: 266tl, 266cla, 266cl, 267ca, 267ca; ROD MORRIS: 1 (inset), 15tc, 22tl, 22clb, 22cb, 22crb, 23tl, 23tr, 23cla, 23cra, 24tl, 45cr, 87cl, 190tr, 190cl, 190bl, 190br, 243cr, 249cl, 264cr, 270bl, 287cr, 289tl; MUSEUM OF NEW ZEALAND TE PAPA TONGA-REWA: 27bl, 28tl, 28bl, 29tl, 29cr, 31tl, 44tr, 44bc, 45trc, 49ca, 55bl, 164tl, 164tr, 164cla, 164clb, 165tl, 165cr, 165clb, 344tl.

NATIONAL PARTY OFFICE: 51bc; NEWMANS COACH LINES: 342br; NEW ZEALAND FESTIVAL 2000: 38tc, 154clb, 154–155c, 333tl; THE NEW ZEALAND HERALD: 16b, 51tr, 115bl, 155tc; NEW ZEALAND MOUNTAIN SAFETY COUNCIL INC.: 346tl.

OFFICE OF TREATY SETTLEMENTS: 43ca, 51cl; OLVESTON HOUSE: 263tl.

LLOYD PARK: 21br, 33bl, 33bc, 188–189c, 189br, 238–239, 245tc, 245cra, 245cr; PHOTOSOURCE NEW ZEALAND LTD: 2–3, 8–9, 33cl, 33cr, 33clb, 37tr, 37clb, 37bl, 38bl, 41c, 41b, 52–53, 60cl, 107cra, 117bl, 119bl, 148tl, 159cl, 174–175, 180tr, 180bl, 191tr, 192tl, 192br, 193tl, 211bc, 236cl, 243tl, 251cra, 279cr, 338tl, 339cr.

THE ROYAL NEW ZEALAND BALLET: 90cr, 155br.

SCIENCE CENTRE AND MANAWATU MUSEUM: 173tr, 173br, 173bl; SKY CITY AUCKLAND LIMITED, 72tl; STEWART ISLAND PROMOTION ASSOCIATION: 286tl; SUPERSHUTTLE: 353c.

TOURISM NEW ZEALAND: 54bl, 55br, 58tl, 93b, 95tl, 293cl, 295t, 338bl, 342tc, 359cl; ALEXANDER TURNBULL LIBRARY: 9 (inset), 16c, 28tr, 29tr, 29b, 30tl, 31br, 34cl, 42, 43bl, 44tl, 44cl, 44bl, 44cla, 45tc, 45br, 46tl, 46c, 46bl, 46br, 47br, 48tr, 48clb, 48bl, 49c, 49bc, 49br, 50tl, 50clb, 50cb, 53 (inset), 57 (inset), 60tl, 60bl, 60–61c, 61tl, 61cr, 83br, 135br, 169br, 185 (inset), 224cr, 233cl, 291 (inset), 341 (inset).

VISUAL IMPACT PICTURES LTD: 14, 24bl, 25cr, 25br, 26tr, 33cra, 33crb, 33cla, 37cra, 38cr, 76tr, 78–79, 101bl, 107crb, 110, 115cl, 121bl, 126bl, 140tr, 180tl, 188clb, 189tl, 193bl, 212tr, 244tl, 272–273, 289cr, 290–291, 294br, 340–341.

WAITANGI NATIONAL TRUST: 39cr, 94br, 102cl, 102bl, 103tl, 103bl; WAITOMO GLOW WORM CAVES NEW ZEALAND: 118tl; WELLINGTON CITY COUNCIL: 85br, 154br; DR KIM WESTERSKOV: 84cr, 101crb, 147br, 191tl, 191cra, 191cb, 264tl, 278tl; WHALE WATCH®: 207cla.

Front Endpaper: All special photography except CHRISTCHURCH CITY COUNCIL: bc; HOLGER LEUE: br; VISUAL IMPACT PICTURES LTD: cl.

Front Cover: All special photography except: AGL AERIAL IMAGERY: crb; DK PICTURE LIBRARY: cla; WORLD PICTURES: Nick Holt t.

Back Cover: All special photography except HOLGER LEUE: tl, bcr; ROD MORRIS: cr.

Spine: ROD MORRIS: b.

Further Reading

ART AND CULTURE

Contemporary Painting in New Zealand Dunn, M., Craftsman House, Auckland 1996.

Dream Collectors: 100 Years of Art in New Zealand Wedde, I., Walsh, J. and Johnson, A., Te Papa Press, Wellington 1998.

A History of New Zealand Architecture Shaw, P., Hodder Moa Beckett, Auckland 1998.

Looking for the Local: Architecture and the New Zealand Modern Clark, J. and Walker, P., Victoria University Press, Wellington 2000.

Maori Art and Culture Starzecka, D.C. (ed.), David Bateman, Auckland 1996.

New Zealand Pottery: Commercial and Collectable Henry, G., Reed Publishing, Auckland 2000.

Old New Zealand Houses 1800–1940 Salmond, J., Reed Publishing, Auckland 1998.

100 New Zealand Craft Artists Schamroth, H., Godwit, Auckland 1998.

100 New Zealand Paintings Brown, W., Godwit, Auckland 1997.

FICTION

Believers to the Bright Coast O'Sullivan, V., Penguin, Auckland 1998.

The Best of Katherine Mansfield's Short Stories Mansfield K., Random House, Auckland 1998.

The Best of Owen Marshall Marshall, O., Random House, Auckland 1997.

The Bone People Hulme, K., Picador, Auckland 1986.

Land of the Long White Cloud: Maori Myths, Tales and Legends Kanawa, K.T. and Foreman, M., Penguin, Auckland 1997.

Live Bodies Gee, M., Penguin, Auckland 1997.

The Matriarch Ihimaera, W., Reed Publishing, Auckland 1996.

Once Were Warriors Duff, A., Tandem Press, Auckland 1990.

100 New Zealand Poems Manhire, B. (ed.), Godwit, Auckland 1994.

Owls Do Cry Frame, J., Random House, Auckland 1999.

Plumb Gee, M., Penguin, Auckland 1981.

Potiki Grace, P., Penguin, Auckland 1986.

Reconnaissance Kassabova, K., Penguin, Auckland 1999.

Season of the Jew Shadbolt, M., David Ling Publishing, Auckland 1988.

Skylark Lounge Cox, N., Victoria University Press, Wellington 2000.

GEOGRAPHY AND GEOLOGY

Aotearoa and New Zealand: A Historical Geography Grey, A., Canterbury University Press, Christchurch 1995.

Awesome Forces: The Natural Hazards That Threaten New Zealand Campbell, H. and Hicks, G., Te Papa Press, Wellington 1998.

Contemporary Atlas of New Zealand Kirkpatrick, R., David Bateman, Auckland 1999.

Historical New Zealand Atlas Malcolm McKinnon et al (eds.), David Bateman, Auckland 1997.

HISTORY AND POLITICS

A Concise Encyclopaedia of Maori Myth and Legend Orbell, M., Canterbury University Press, Christchurch 1998.

The Discovery of Aotearoa Evans, J., Reed Publishing, Auckland 1998.

Historical Dictionary of New Zealand Jackson, K. and McRobie, A., Addison, Wesley, Longman, Auckland 1996.

Making Peoples: A History of New Zealanders from Polynesian Settlement to the End of the 19th Century Belich, J., Penguin, Auckland 1996.

New Zealand, the Story So Far: A Short History Bohan, E., Harper Collins, Auckland 1997.

The Oxford History of New Zealand Oliver W.H. (ed.), Oxford University Press, Wellington 1981.

Politics in New Zealand Mulgan, R., Auckland University Press, Auckland 1997.

The Treaty of Waitangi Orange, C., Bridget Williams Books, Wellington 1991.

NATURAL HISTORY

A Field Guide to the Alpine Plants of New Zealand Salmon, J., Godwit, Auckland 1999.

Field Guide to the Birds of New Zealand Heather, B. and Robertson, H., Viking, Auckland 1996.

Game Animals of New Zealand Roberts, G., Shoal Bay Press, Blenheim 1998.

Kiwi: New Zealand's Remarkable Bird Peat, N., Godwit, Auckland 1999.

Native Trees of New Zealand Salmon J., Reed Publishing, Auckland 1996.

Natural History of New Zealand Bishop, N., Hodder and Stoughton, Auckland 1992.

The Natural World of New Zealand Hutching, G., Viking, Auckland 1998.

Te Wahi Pounamu: Southwest New Zealand World Heritage Area Apse, A., Craig Potton Publishing, Nelson 1997.

OUTDOOR ACTIVITIES

Classic New Zealand Mountain Bike Rides Kennett, P., Kennett, S. and Kennett, J., Reed Publishing, Auckland 1998.

Classic Tramping in New Zealand Barnett, S. and Brown, R., Craig Potton Publishing, Nelson 1999.

Classic Walks of New Zealand Potton C., Craig Potton Publishing, Nelson 1997.

New Zealand: Pure Adventure McLennan, C., David Bateman, Auckland 1999.

A Tramper's Guide to New Zealand's National Parks Burton, R. and Atkinson, M., Reed Publishing, Auckland 1998.

Glossary

CULTURE

Aotearoa: Maori name for New Zealand, literally "Land of the Long White Cloud", coined by the explorer Kupe's wife *(see p15)*

haka: war dance and song performed by males *(see p28)*

hangi: style of cooking food in an earth oven where the heat is provided by special stones or embers *(see p135)*

hongi: greeting by pressing noses together. When people *hongi*, their *hau* or life essence intermingles

iwi: tribe, people. A *hapu* is a subtribe and *whanau* an extended family

kai: food. Any word with *kai* in it relates to food, for example *kai moana* (seafood) *(see p107)*

kete: woven basket made from the fibre of flax, kiekie or pingao plants *(see p29)*

mana: authority, prestige, psychic power

maori: ordinary or usual, used by indigenous New Zealanders from the 19th century to distinguish themselves from *pakeha* (stranger or different)

Maoritanga: Maori culture

marae: gathering place, open courtyard in front of a village meeting house where important meetings, funerals and entertainment take place *(see p114)*

mere: flat greenstone war club, most highly valued of weapons *(see p198)*

moko: tattoos incised on the faces, buttocks and thighs of men and the lips and chins of women *(see p28)*

pa: fortified village or stockade *(see p48)*

pakeha: stranger, person of European descent

poi: ball made of leaves attached to a piece of string and used by women in graceful dances *(see p28–9)*

tane: man, male

tangi: funeral

taonga: treasures, cultural items such as carvings or woven cloaks passed down through the generations

tapu: holy, sacred, forbidden; taboo in English

tiki: from *heitiki*; prized greenstone figure worn around the neck. Debate continues over the origins and religious significance of this ornament *(see p28)*

wahine: woman, female

waiata: songs. There are many types, for example *waiata tangi* (laments) and *waiata aroha* (love songs)

waka: canoe. The masterpieces were elaborately carved 30-metre *waka taua* or war canoes *(see p45)*

whare: house. There are a number of different houses: *whare runanga* (meeting house) *(see p26)*; *whare whakairo* (carved house); *whare puni* (family sleeping house)

GEOGRAPHY AND NATURE

kauri: huge forest tree growing in northern New Zealand *(see p22)*

kea: uncommon but inquisitive alpine parrot whose name is derived from its call *(see p23)*

kiwi: flightless, nocturnal indigenous bird which uses its long beak to probe in the earth for worms *(see p1)*

koru: the spiral, the principal motif used in Maori carving, inspired by the unfurling fern frond or *koru*; it signifies "awakening, the process of growth, joy" *(see p22)*

kumara: sweet potato, transported from Polynesia to New Zealand where it became a staple food *(see p43)*

manuka: shrubby plant popularly known as the tea tree with proven anti-bacterial qualities, source of honey and oils *(see p22)*

paua: black coloured shellfish known elsewhere as abalone, prized for its beautiful shell which is worked into jewellery *(see p331)*

pohutukawa: large spreading coastal tree covered in scarlet flowers during early summer, hence described as the "Christmas tree" *(see p23)*

ponga: tree fern

pounamu: greenstone or jade, the most precious stone used in jewellery and weapons, found in the South Island and traded with North Island tribes *(see p 235)*

Te Ika a Maui: the fish of Maui, the North Island

Te Wai Pounamu: South Island

EVERYDAY WORDS AND PHRASES

Haere mai: Welcome

Haere ra: Goodbye (from the person staying to the one going)

E noho ra: Goodbye (from the person going to the one staying)

Ka pai: Thank you

Kia ora: Thank you, good luck, good health

Tena koe: Hello (to one person)

Tena koutou: Hello (to more than three people)

Kei te pehea koe: How are you?

Kei te pai: Very well, thank you

WORDS COMMONLY FORMING PLACE NAMES

ao: cloud

atua: spirit or gods

awa: river or valley

hau: wind

ika: fish

iti: small

kai: food

kainga: village

kare: rippling

manga: stream, tributary

manu: bird

maunga: mountain

moana: sea or lake

motu: island

nui: big

one: beach, sand or mud

papa: flat, broad slab

po: night

puke: hill

puna: water spring

rangi: sky, heavens

roa: long

roto: lake

rua: two, hole

te: the

wai: water

wero: challenge

whanga: bay or inlet

whenua: land or country

EYEWITNESS *Travel Guides*

COUNTRY GUIDES

Australia • Canada • France • Great Britain
Greece: Athens & the Mainland • The Greek Islands
Ireland • Italy • Japan • Mexico
Portugal • Scotland • Singapore
South Africa • Spain • Thailand
Great Places to Stay in Europe
Taste of Scotland

REGIONAL GUIDES

Barcelona & Catalonia • California
Florence & Tuscany • Florida • Hawaii
Jerusalem & the Holy Land • Loire Valley
Milan & the Lakes • Naples with Pompeii & the
Amalfi Coast • Provence & the Cote d'Azur • Sardinia
Seville & Andalusia • Sicily • Venice & the Veneto

CITY GUIDES

Amsterdam • Berlin • Brussels • Budapest
Cracow • Delhi, Agra & Jaipur • Dublin
Istanbul • Lisbon • London • Madrid
Moscow • New York • Paris • Prague • Rome
San Francisco • Stockholm • St Petersburg
Sydney • Vienna • Warsaw • Washington, DC

NEW FOR SPRING 2001

Bali & Lombok • Boston • Chicago
Cruise Guide to Europe and the Mediterranean
Germany • New England • New Zealand

For updates to our guides, and information on
DK Travel Maps & Phrasebooks

VISIT US AT
eyewitnesstravel.dk.com

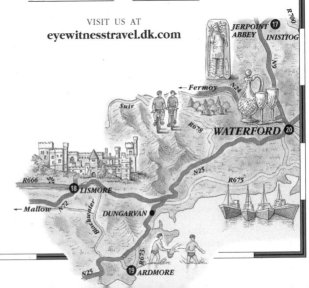

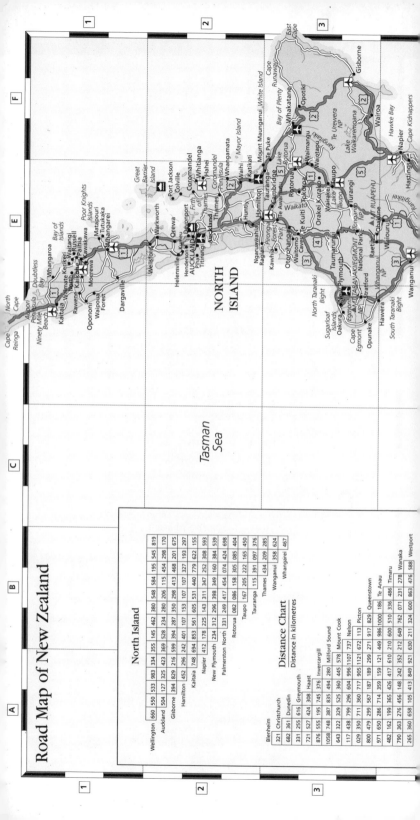

Road Map of New Zealand

North Island